Chichester Excavations III

Miss K. M. E. Murray, F. S. A.

Chichester Excavations III

by

Alec Down

with specialist contributions by
Justine Bayley, M.Sc.   Sarnia A. Butcher, B.A., F.S.A.   R. A. G. Carson, F.S.A.
Dorothy Charlesworth, M.A., F.S.A.   Prof. Barry Cunliffe, M.A., Ph.D., F.S.A.
G. Dannell, F.S.A.   M. G. Fulford, B.A., Ph.D., F.S.A.
B. R. Hartley, M.A., F.S.A.   Brenda Dickinson, B.A.   Mark Hassall, F.S.A.
Martin Henig, D.Phil., M.A., F.S.A.   Richard Hodges, B.A.
Frank Jenkins, F.S.A. Roger Lintott   Alison McCann, B.A.   D. Mackreth, B.A.
R. R. Morgan Sheila Morgan   Valery Rigby, B.A.   C. J. Young, M.A.

Published for
Chichester Civic Society
Excavations Committee
by

Phillimore

Acknowledgements

The Committee wish to record their thanks to the undermentioned bodies whose generous donations have made this publication possible:

H.M. Department of the Environment
West Sussex County Council
Chichester District Council
Chichester City Council
Chichester Museum Society
Chichester Civic Society
Sussex Archaeological Society
Anglia and General Development Ltd.
The Chichester Society

ISBN 0 85033 272 9

Published by
PHILLIMORE & CO. LTD.,
Shopwyke Hall, Chichester, Sussex.

Printed by
UNWIN BROTHERS LTD.,
The Gresham Press,
Old Woking, Surrey.

*An "open letter" to Miss K. M. Elisabeth Murray, M.A., B.Litt., F.S.A.
from Francis Steer.*

Chichester
December 1977

DEAR BETTY,

I trust that you will please forgive me for writing what amounts to an "open letter", but it would be inappropriate if I copied your entry in *Who's Who* and still more unfortunate if I had been asked to contribute an obituary notice to *The Times*, so I am trying to sail between Charybdis and Scylla.

You and I have known each other for a good many years – years which I have enjoyed and of which I treasure the memories. Your kindness and friendship have meant much to me and to many other people; neither can I adequately express my astonishment when I was asked – out of the blue as the saying goes – to write a foreword to this book.

What a lot you have crammed into your life. You were educated at Oxford; you have held important offices in the Universities of Cambridge and Manchester; you were a Research Fellow at Oxford; you have been a Fellow of the Society of Antiquaries for 31 years. For 22 years you were the Principal of Bishop Otter College where you guided numerous young people in formulating their careers. You were the ever-patient, wise, and good-humoured Chairman of the Sussex Archaeological Society from 1964 to 1977 and now you are the President of that Society which was established in 1846. These are only a few of your many achievements.

But I must also mention among these good works your physical activities (and how fortunate you are) of which only one is walking the length of the Sussex Downs every Easter. You have also been a stalwart fighter for the preservation of those Downs – one of the most beautiful tracts in England; you battle as a Councillor against those whose knowledge is not as great and whose aesthetic sense is not so acute as your own; you protect the amenities of your beloved Heyshott and, in fact, many other areas of West Sussex. How you find time to serve on so many Committees defeats me and yet to all of them you contribute so much clear thinking. You doubtless inherit this ability from your distinguished grandfather, Sir James Murray, the creator of the Oxford English Dictionary, and from your father whose great book on board games could only have been compiled by someone possessing outstanding powers of concentration and analysis.

I have seen you as a practical archaeologist patiently scraping in trenches or heaving heavy buckets of soil to the spoil heap. But you have also been the Chairman of the Chichester Excavations Committee and largely responsible for the policies which have been followed with such admirable results. You have written the reports of excavations with which you have been closely concerned, and you have devoted much time to the affairs of the great palace at Fishbourne where your sound advice has been invaluable as in so many other directions.

Although Sussex has been your home for many years, Kent has also benefitted from your scholarship. *The Constitutional History of the Cinque Ports* which was published in 1935 is still the standard work on the subject and a monument to your industrious and meticulous research. All your writings, whether as books, or papers in learned journals, testify to your skill in grasping essentials and presenting the evidence in the clearest possible language. The recently published biography of your grandfather, so appropriately entitled *Caught in the Web of Words*, was an act of devotion on your part to his memory, and has put you in the top rank of authors.

You are also a very successful gardener and one who, as Kipling said, realises that "gardens are not made by singing 'Oh, how beautiful!' and sitting in the shade". From Heyshott to Africa, Mexico or the United States of America is a long way, and yet you have been to those and other countries where I am sure you have tramped through jungles, studied the relics of past civilisations, and marvelled at the immensity and colour of the Grand Canyon. But you have an equal delight in the beauty of England, Scotland and Wales – each has a charm of its own and although the scenery may not be so grand there are, for example, little churches, stately homes, and the countryside which give you pleasure. Yes, you have had a full life and, thank God, you can still pursue your many interests with vigour and obvious enjoyment.

Now comes the final paragraph which is really why this letter is being written. I want to say, on behalf of all your friends and on behalf of all the organisations to which you have given such devoted service, how much we are all in your debt. You have constantly been giving and now the time has come when something – if only a token – must be given to you. This third volume of reports on excavations in Chichester is dedicated to you with gratitude, admiration and affection; may it give you pleasure and remind you of happy hours of digging up the past. I feel sure that you, and all of us who interest ourselves in history of all periods, will realise what we owe to Alec Down who directs the excavations in Chichester with such zeal, authority, and amazing results; he is the main author of this book and, like you, seems to be endowed with the gift of perennial youth.

May every blessing be yours in the years which lie ahead.

Yours ever,
FRANCIS

Author's Note

This volume records the results of a seven-year programme of rescue excavation in the North-West Quadrant of the City, coupled with *ad hoc* rescue digs at various points within and without the walls. From the excavated material now at our disposal it has been possible to considerably extend our knowledge of the Roman pottery of the 1st century A.D., and both fine and coarse wares are widely published. Volume 4 (already in course of preparation) will take a stage further the study of the late Roman fine wares begun in this volume.

The late Saxon, medieval and post-medieval pottery is also fully treated in the following pages and current research into the post-medieval pottery in the Graffham area, coupled with excavations within the town, should enhance our knowledge of the ceramics of the 16th to 18th centuries.

The intensive documentary research work carried out by Mr. Morgan and his group has enabled us to publish a Gazetteer of post-medieval sites within the city and this will be followed in Volume 4 by a survey of all standing structures dating from the medieval period up to the 18th century.

Towards the end of the period reviewed in this book there was a radical change in the concept of rescue excavation in Chichester. The Excavations Committee in conjunction with the Department of the Environment appointed a full-time Director to co-ordinate work within the city and its environs, with temporary staff being engaged from time to time for specific projects. The main emphasis however is still on the elite force of trained excavators, entirely unpaid, and supplemented as necessary by students and local volunteers. But for their devoted efforts the cost of rescue excavation in Chichester would be impossibly high and many opportunities would be lost by default.

I would like to thank the West Sussex County Council, particularly the County Archivist and her staff, the staff of the County Library, the County Surveyor and his staff; the Chichester City Council; the officers of the new District Council, the Diocesan Board of Education and the Estates Department of the Department of the Environment at Portsmouth, all of whom gave us help and encouragement in a number of different ways. We owe a debt of gratitude to Norman Cook, F.S.A., and Ralph Merrifield, F.S.A., Director and Deputy Director respectively of the former Guildhall Museum of London, who kindly assisted us in the early days of the project on problems of conservation and identification. The generous and continuing help given to us by the Post Office is deeply appreciated and details of this are to be found in the introduction to the main section. We are grateful to our friends the Architects, Roth and Partners, and to a number of contractors, notably Keith Andrews Ltd., John Snelling Ltd., H. Geall Ltd. and Frank J. Privett Ltd. who co-operated with us at various stages of the enterprise, and special mention must be made of the developers for the Adcock's site, Anglia and General Developments Ltd. who consulted us well in advance of demolition and building construction, to our mutual advantage. It is hoped that this type of liaison between developers and archaeologists may set a pattern for others to follow.

One of the most pleasant aspects of producing a volume of this nature is that it enables me to pay a tribute to the people who have helped, not only with the excavations, but with the backroom work as well. This Report is the work of many hands. The specialist contributors, whose names are on the title page and the supervisors, draughtsmen, photographers and laboratory workers who have regularly devoted their spare time to assist in the many chores associated with the reduction into a coherent form of a vast mass of excavated material. The North-West Quadrant excavations were supervised by Keith Lintott (Area 1), Brian Boddy, M. A. B. Lyne, Janet Hinde (Mrs. Janet Upton), Roger Hammond and Ronald Maskelyne (Areas 2, 3, 4, 5 and 6), and their assistants J. Eschbaecher, W. Shannon, Jane Powell, Jeffery Collins and E. Crosland. Area 7 (Tower Street) was supervised by Louise Miller assisted at various times by E. Barsley, D. Dethlefs (U.S.A.), M. Mathewman (U.S.A.), J. Fisher and R. Loverance. The photography was carried out by Geoffrey Claridge, R.I.B.A., Janet Hinde and John Adams, with Jerome O'Hea being responsible for the aerial photography. Conservation has been the responsibility of Ronald Maskelyne for most of the period under review, and Joyce and Jane Maskelyne and latterly Ruth Palmer and Dorothy Mellor have been concerned with the pottery processing. Susan Eeles, Frank Greenaway, David S. Neal, John Piper, Lesley Smith and Max Wholey produced the pottery and finds drawings, while the plans and sections were executed by the writer. Pauline Castle capably dealt with the various MSS and typed the whole volume.

Finally, I owe a special debt to Susan Eeles, Jenny Hotston, Irene Cooper, Jane Russell, Helen Porter, Geoff Busbridge, John Piper, Roger Lintott, Jim Shields and James Ayling without whose continuing help the volume could not have been completed in time.

This long list of acknowledgements could well have been longer. All of the people and organisations mentioned above, and many more besides, have made a significant contribution towards the history and archaeology of this famous and lovely city. They deserve the regard of Cicestrians everywhere.

ALEC DOWN

February, 1977

Specialist Reports not in the main volume

It has not been possible, for reasons of cost, to publish all the specialist reports in this volume, and those unpublished are available as archival material to students who may wish to consult them. They can be seen in the Chichester District Museum, Little London, Chichester, by arrangement with the Curator, and copies may be had for a small fee. A duplicate set is lodged with the West Sussex Record Office.

J. E. Pratt	– Reports on charcoal samples from various sites in the North-west Quadrant.
Dr. R. F. Tylecote	– Report on the bronze slag from Tower Street.
J. Pilmer, M.A.	– Patterned flue tiles from Chichester.
	– The opus sectile stones from Tower Street.
Dr. Helena Barnes	– The human skeletal remains from North gate.
Valery Rigby	– Detailed report on the early Roman fine wares from the North-west Quadrant (includes material not in main report).
Alan Outen	– Report on selected animal bones from Area 7.
Dr. Peter Ovenden	– The bell mould samples from Chichester.

viii

Contents

List of Plates

ACKNOWLEDGMENTS TO PLATES

John Adams: Frontispiece, plates 11–14; Geoffrey Claridge: plates 2–6, 8–9, 16, 17; Alec Down, plate 15; J. Hinde, plates 7, 10; J. J. O'Hea, plate 1; Institute of Archaeology, London, plates 18, 19.

Bibliography

AISLINGEN 1959 — Die römischen Donau – Kastelle Aislingen und Burghöfe, *Limesforschungen 1*, 1959.

ARTHUR, forthcoming — Arthur, P., "The Roman Lead Glazed Pottery", in Crouch, K., Excavations at Staines, *LAMAS Transactions 27*, forthcoming.

ATKINSON 1941 — Atkinson, R. J. C., "A Romano-British Potter's Field at Cowley, Oxon", *Oxoniensia VI*, 1941.

BIANCHI 1969 — Bianchi, R., *Rome, The centre of Power*, Thames and Hudson, 1969.

BIDDLE and BARCLAY 1974 — Biddle, M., and Barclay, K., "Winchester Ware", in *Medieval pottery from excavations*, ed. V. Evison, H. Hodges and J. G. Hurst, 1974.

BÓMS 1942 — Bóms, E., "Die Kaiserzeitliche Keramik von Pannonien", 1, Die Materialem der Fruhen Kaiserzeit, 1942.

BOON 1966 — Boon, G. C., "Roman window glass from Wales", in *Journal of Glass Studies*, VIII, 1966.

BOON 1972 — Boon, G. C., in *Monmouthshire Antiquary* III, pt. ii, 1972–3.

B.M. 1926 — British Museum: *Catalogue of the Engraved Gems and Cameos*, No. 3111, London, 1926.

B.M. 1929 — British Museum: *Guide to Greek and Roman life*, 1929.

B.M. 1951 — British Museum: *Guide to the Antiquities of Roman Britain*, 1951.

CALVI 1963 — Calvi, M. C., *I. Vetri Romani del Museo di Aquileia*, 1963.

CAMULODUNUM — Hawkes, C. F. C., and Hull, M. R., *Camulodunum, First Report on the Excavations at Colchester, 1930–1939*, Society of Antiquaries Research Report, No. XIV.

CHARLESWORTH 1959 — Charlesworth, D., in "The Roman Bath-House at Red House", *Archaeologia Aeliania XXXVII*, 1959, by Daniels, C. M.

CHARLESWORTH 1972 — Charlesworth, D., in *Verulamium Excavations I*, by Frere, S. S., 1972.

CHENET 1941 — Chenet, G., *Lá Ceramique Gallo-Romaine D'argonne due IVe Siècle et la Terre Sigillée décorée à la molette*, Mâcon, 1941.

CHICHESTER 1 — Down, A., and Rule, M., *Chichester Excavations 1*, 1971.

CHICHESTER 2 — Down, A., *Chichester Excavations 2*, 1974.

CHIESA 1966   Chiesa, G., Sena., *Gemme del Museo Nazionale di Aquileia*, Aquileia, 1966.

CONWAY 1906   Conway, R. S., *Melandra Castle*, Manchester, 1906.

CORSTOPITUM   Forster, R. H., and Knowles, W. H., *Corstopitum: Report on the Excavations in 1910, 1911*.

COYSH   Coysh, A. W., *Blue and White Transfer Ware*.

CLAUSENTUM 1958   Cotton, M. A., and Gathercole, P. W., *Excavations at Clausentum, Southampton, 1951–54*, London, 1958.

CLIFFORD 1961   Clifford, E. M., *Bagendon, A Belgic Oppidum*, A record of the Excavations of 1954–56, Cambridge 1961.

CUNLIFFE 1970   Cunliffe, B. W., *The Saxon culture sequence of Porchester Castle*, Ant. J. 1, 1970.

CUNLIFFE 1971   Cunliffe, B. W., *Excavations at Fishbourne Volume 2: The Finds*, Leeds, 1971.

CUNLIFFE 1973   Cunliffe, B. W., "Manor Farm, Chalton, Hants", in *Post-Medieval Archaeology*, Vol. 7, 1973.

CUNLIFFE 1974   Cunliffe, B. W., "Some late Saxon Stamped pottery from Southern England", in *Medieval Pottery from Excavations*, ed. Evison, V. I., Hodges, H., and Hurst, J. G., 1974.

CUNLIFFE 1975   Cunliffe, B. W., Excavations at *Porchester Castle, 1*, London, 1975.

DANGSTETTEN   *Bericht des römische Germanischen Kommission, 51–52*, 1970–71.

DELORT 1953   Delort, E., *Vases ornés de la Moselle*, Nancy, 1953.

DOWN 1967   Down, A., "Excavations in Chapel Street, Chichester 1967", *S.A.C. 106 (1968)*.

DOWN, forthcoming   Down, A., "*Excavations at Chilgrove and Upmarden*".

DUDLEY 1949   Dudley, H. E., *Early Days in North-West Lincolnshire, A Regional Archaeology*, Scunthorpe, 1949.

DUNNETT 1966   Dunnett, R. B. K., "Excavations on North Hill, Colchester", in *Arch. J.*, No. 123, 1966.

DUNNING 1959   Dunning, C. G., "The Earlier vessel from Ipswich", Anglo-Saxon Pottery; a symposium, in *Medieval Archaeology*, No. 3, 1959.

DURA-EUROPOS   *Excavations at Dura – Europos, Final Report.* Vol. IV, part iv, Fasicule 1.

EVANS 1974   Evans, K. J., "Excavations on a Romano-British site, Wiggonholt, 1964", in *S.A.C. CXII*, 1974.

EVETTS 1948   Evetts, L. C., "The lettering of Romano-British Inscribed stones", in *Arch. Ael.* 4th Series, XXVI, 1948.

EXNER 1939   Exner, K., Die Provinzialromischen Emailfibeln de Rheinlande, in *Bericht der Römische-Germainischen Kommission*, 29, 1939.

FREMERSDORF 1959   Fremersdorf, F., *Römische Gläser mit Fadenanflage in Kölne*, 1959.

FROMOLS 1939   Fromols, J., "L'atelier ceramique de Sept-Saulx (Marne) de couvert et fouille par M. Bry", in *Bull. Soc. Arch. Champ.*, 1939, pt II, 31–37.

FULFORD and BIRD 1976   Fulford, M., and Bird, J., "Imported pottery from Germany in late Roman Britain", *Britannia 6*, 1975.

FULFORD 1975   Fulford, M., "The pottery", in Cunliffe, B. W., *Excavations at Porchester Castle*, I, 1975.

FULFORD 1975   Fulford, M., "New Forest Roman pottery", *B.A.R. 17*, Oxford, 1975.

FURTWANGLER 1896   Furtwangler, A., *Beschreibung der Geschnittenen Steine im Antiquarium*, Berlin, 1896.

GENISHEIM–BOBINGEN 1969   Genisheim–Bobingen, *Mitteilungen des Historischen Vereins der Pfalz*, 67, 1969.

GERRA 1956   Gerra, C., Arca . . . Gemnis quae compta coruscat, in *studi Calderini e Paribeni*, *iii*, Milan, 1956.

GILLAM 1970   Gillam, J. P., *Types of Roman coarse pottery vessels in northern Britain*, third edition, Newcastle upon Tyne, 1970.

G.M.P. 1954–55   Guildhall Museum Publications: "*Small Finds from Walbrook*".

GRIFFITHS, forthcoming   Griffiths, M., *Excavations at Exeter*.

HAEVERNICK 1967   Haevernick, T. E., Die Verbreitung des Zarten Rippenschalen, *Jahrbuch des Romisch-Germanischen Zentral Museum Mainz*, 1967.

HANWORTH 1968   Hanworth, R., "The Roman Villa at Rapsley, Ewhurst", in *Surrey Archaeological Collections LXV*, 1968.

HARDEN 1939   Harden, D. B., *Roman window glass from Jerash and later parallels*, Iraq, vi, 1939.

HARDEN 1959   Harden, D. B., "New light on Roman and early medieval window glass", in *Glastenische Berichte 32K*, Heft VIII, 1959.

HARDEN 1974   Harden, D. B., "Window glass from the Romano-British bath house at Garden Hill, Hartfield, Sussex", in *Ant. J.*, Vol. LIV, Pt. II, 1974.

HARTLEY 1973   Hartley, K. F., *Current Research in Romano-British Coarse Pottery*, C.B.A., Research Report No. 10, London, 1973.

HEIGHWAY, forthcoming   Heighway, C. M., *Excavations at Gloucester*.

HENIG 1972   Henig, M., "The origin of some Ancient British Coin Types", in *Britannia*, III, 1972.

HENIG 1974 — Henig, M., *A Corpus of Roman Engraved Gemstones from British Sites*, B.A.R. 8, 1974.

HENKEL 1913 — Henkel, F., *Die Romischen Fingerringe der Rheinlande*, Berlin, 1913.

HERMET 1934 — Hermet, F., *La Graufesenque*, Paris, 1934.

HODGES 1977 — Hodges, R. A., "The Local and Imported Pottery from Melbourne Street, Southampton", in Hinton, D. A., ed., *Excavations in Melbourne Street, Southampton*, C.B.A., 1977.

HODGES 1976 — Hodges, R. A., "Some early Medieval French Wares in the British Isles: an Archaeological assessment of the early French Wine Trade with Britain", in Peacock, D. P. S., *Pottery and Economic Archaeology*, Seminar Press, London, 1976.

HOD HILL i — Brailsford, J. W., *Antiquities from Hod Hill in the Durden Collection*, London, 1962.

HOFHEIM 1913 — Ritterling, E., "Das Frührömische Lager bei Hofheim im Taunas", *Annalen des Vereins fur Nassauische*, 1913.

HOLDEN 1963 — Holden, E. W., "Excavations at Hangleton", in *S.A.C. 101 (1963)*.

HOLLING 1971 — "A preliminary note on the pottery industry of the Hampshire-Surrey borders", in *Surrey Archaeological Collections, LXVIII*.

HOLWERDA 1941 — Holwerda, J., "*De Belgische Waar in Nijmegen*", 1941.

HUGHES 1961 — Hughes, B., *English and Scottish Earthenware*, 1961.

HULL 1958 — Hull, M. R., *Roman Colchester*, Report of the Research Committee of the Society of Antiquaries of London, XX, Oxford, 1958.

HULL 1963 — Hull, M. R., *The Roman Potter's Kilns at Colchester*, Oxford, 1963.

HULTSCHE 1882 — Hultsche, F., *Griechische und Romische Metrologie*, edition 2, Berlin, 1882.

INSTINSKY 1962 — Instinsky, H. U., *Die Siegal des Kaisers Augustas*, Baden-Baden, 1962.

JACOBS 1912 — Jacobs, J., Sigillatafunde aus einem Romische Keller zu Bregenz, *Jahrbuch fur Altertumskunde*, VI, Vienna, 1912.

JAHRESHEFT 26, 1930 — *Jahresheft des Österreichischen Archäologischen Instituts 26*, 1930.

KAJANTO — Kajanto, I., *The Latin Cognomina*.

KARNITSCHE 1955 — Karnitsche, P., "Die Verzierte Sigillata von Lauriacum", *Forschungen in Lauriacum*, Band 3, Linz, 1955.

KIBALTCHITCH 1910 — Kibaltchitch, T. de, *Gemmes de la Russie Méridionale*, Berlin, 1910.

KINGSHOLM 1958   Kingsholm, Glos., *Guide to the Antiquities of Roman Britain*, London, 1958.

KINGSTON   Kingston upon Hull Museums. *Hull Pottery Bulletin, No. 5.*

KLOIBER 1962   Kloiber, E., "Die Graberfelder von Lauriacum", *Das espel Mayrfeld*, 1962.

KOETHE 1938   H. Koethe 1938, "Zur gestempelten belgischen keramit, Aus Trier"; *Festschrift für August Oxe*".

KNORR 1912   Knorr, R., *Sudgallische Terra-Sigillata = Gefässe von Rottweil*, Stuttgart, 1912.

KNORR 1919   Knorr, R., *Topfer und Fabriken verzierter Terra-Sigillata des ersten Jahrhunderts*, Stuttgart, 1919.

LETHBRIDGE 1953   Lethbridge, T. C., "Burial of an Iron Age Warrior", *Proc. Camb. Ant. Soc.* XLVII (1953), 25–37.

LOESCHKE 1909   "Keramische Funde in Haltern", *Mitteilungen der Altertums Kommission fur Westfalen, 5*, S. Loeschke, 1909.

LONGTHORPE 1974   Frere, S. S., and St. Joseph, J. K., "The Roman Fortress at Longthorpe", *Britannia V, 1974.*

LUTZ 1970   Lutz, M., L'Atelier de Saturninus et de Satto à Mittelbronn (Moselle), *XXIIe, Supplèment À Gallia*, Paris, 1970.

MACDONALD and CURLE 1928–9   Macdonald, G., and Curle, A. O., "The Roman Fort at Mumrills near Falkirk", *Proceedings of the Society of Antiquaries of Scotland*, LXIII, 1928–9.

MACK 1964   Mack, R. P., *The Coinage of Ancient Britain*; second edition, London, 1964.

MATTINGLY and SYDENHAM 1923   Mattingly, H., and Sydenham, E., *The Roman Imperial Coinage 1*, London, 1923.

MAY 1969   May, T., "*The Roman Pottery found at Silchester*", Reading, 1916.

MAY 1930   May, T., "*Catalogue of the Roman Pottery in the Colchester and Essex Museum*", Cambridge, 1930.

NAMUR 1969   *Annales de la Societé Archáeologique de Namur, 55*, 1969.

NAPOLITANO 1950   Napolitano, A. M., "Gemme del Museo di Udine probable provenienza Aquileiese", *Aquileia Nostra XXI*, 1950.

NEWSTEAD   Curle, J., "*A Roman Frontier post and its people; the Fort of Newstead in the Parish of Melrose*", Glasgow, 1911.

NIESSEN 1911   Niessen, C. A., *Beschreibung Romischer Altertuner*, Sammling Niessen, Cologne, 1911.

OSWALD 1920   Oswald, F., and Davies Pryce, T., "*An introduction to the study of Terra Sigillata*", London, 1920.

OVENDEN   Ovenden, P., "*Examination of a fragment of bell mould from Chichester*", in archive; copies available from Chichester District Museum.

PARTRIDGE, forthcoming

Partridge, C., "Excavations at Skeleton Green, Puckeridge, Herts.", forthcoming.

PEACOCK 1971

Peacock, D. P. S., "The petrology of the coarse pottery", in Cunliffe, B. W., *"Excavations at Fishbourne"*, Leeds, 1971.

PFEFFER and HAEVERNICK 1958

Pfeffer, W. Von., and Haevernick, T. E., Zarte Rippenschale, *Saalburg Jahrbuch* XVII, 1958.

PITT-RIVERS 1887

Pitt-Rivers, *"Woodcuts"*, Lieut.-Gen. A. Pitt-Rivers. "Excavations in Cranbourne Chase", i (1887).

RAIMBAULT 1973

Raimbault, M., *Gallia* 31, 1973.

RAMM 1971

Ramm, H. G., in Butler (ed.), *"Soldier and Civilian in Roman Yorkshire"* (Leicester U.P., 1971).

REUSCH 1943

Reusch, N., "Metz Als Herstellungsort belgischen Keramik", Germania, *XXVII* (1943).

RHEINGÖNHEIM 1969

Ulbert, G., *Das Frühromische Kastell Rheingönheim*. Die Funde aus den Jahren 1912 and 1913. Romische-Germanische Kommission des Deutschen Archaologischen Institute, *Limesforschungen* Bands 3 + 9, Berlin, 1969.

RICHBOROUGH II

Society of Antiquaries Research Report No. VII, Second Report on the Excavations of the Roman Fort at Richborough, Kent. Bushe-Fox, J.P., Oxford, 1928.

RICHBOROUGH III

Society of Antiquaries Research Report. Third Report on the excavations of the Roman Fort at Richborough, Kent, Bushe-Fox, J.P., Oxford, 1932.

RICHBOROUGH IV

Society of Antiquaries Research Report No. XVI, Fourth Report on the Excavations of the Roman Fort at Richborough, Kent, Bushe-Fox, J.P., Oxford, 1949.

RICHBOROUGH V

Society of Antiquaries Research Report, Fifth Report on the Excavation of the Roman Fort at Richborough, Kent, Cunliffe, B. W., London, 1968.

RICHTER 1956

Richter, G. M. A., *Metropolitan Museum, New York, Catalogue of engraved gems*, Rome, 1956.

RICKEN and FISCHER 1963

Ricken, H., and Fischer, C., *"Die Bilderschüsseln der Romischen Töpfer von Rheinzabern"*, Bonn, 1963.

RICKEN and LUDOWICI 1948

Der Römischen Töpfer von Rheinzabern. Katalog VI. Speyer, 1948.

RIGBY 1973

Rigby, V., "Potters stamps on Terra Nigra and Terra Rubra found in Britain", *C.B.A. Research Report* 10, ed. A. Detsicas, 1973.

RISSTISSEN 1970

Ulbert, G., "Das Römische Donau-Katsell Risstissen, Teil I *"Urkunden zur ver-und Frühgeschichte aus Südwurtemburg-Hohensollern, Heft 4"*, Stuttgart, 1970.

RITTERLING 1912   Ritterling, E., "Das frurömische Lager bei Hofheim im Taunus", Annalen des Vereins für Nassauische, *Altertumskunde und Geshichtshorschung*, 40, 1912.

ROBINSON 1975   Robinson, Russell H., *The Armour of Imperial Rome*, 1975.

ROUVIER-JEANLIN 1972   Rouvier-Jeanlin, M., "Les Figurines Gallo-Romaines en terre cuite au Musée des Antiquités Nationales", *XXIVe supplement à Gallia*, Paris, 1972.

ROGERS 1974   Rogers, G. B., "Poteries Sigillees de la Gaule Centrale, Vol. 1, Les motifs non Figurés", *XXVIIIe supplément à Gallia*, Paris, 1974.

SAALBURG 1972   *Saalburg Jahrbuch*, Bericht des Saalburg Museums, XXIX, 1972.

SELLYE 1939   Sellye, I., "Les Bronzes Émaillés de la Pannonie Romaine", *Dissertationes Pannonicae*, Ser. 2, fasc. 8, Budapest, 1939.

STEAD, forthcoming   Stead, I. M., *Excavations at Old Wintringham, Humberside*, forthcoming.

STEER 1965–66   Steer, F., in *Report of the Society of the Friends of St. George and the descendants of the Knights of the Garter*, Vol. 4, No. 7, 1965/66.

SUTHERLAND 1970   Sutherland, C. H. V., *The Cistophori of Augustus*, Royal Numismatic Society, 1970.

SWARLING 1925   *Society of Antiquaries Research Report No. V*, "Excavation of the Late Celtic Urnfield at Swarling, Kent", Bushe-Fox, J.P., Oxford, 1925.

TERRISSE 1968   Terrisse, J.-R., "Les Ceramiques Sigillees Gallo-Romaines des Martres-de-Veyre (Puy-de-Dôme)", *XIXe supplement á Gallia*, Paris, 1968.

THEOPHILUS   Theophilus, "*On divers arts*", ed. J. G. Hawthorne and C. S. Smith, Chicago, 1963.

TOYNBEE 1964   Toynbee, J. M. C., *Art in Britain under the Romans*, Oxford, 1964.

TOYNBEE 1965   Toynbee, J. M. C., *The Art of the Romans*, 1965.

TYLECOTE   Tylecote, R. F., "*Examination of material from Chichester bell-casting pits*", in archive; copies available from Chichester District Museum.

VERULAMIUM 1936   *Society of Antiquaries Research Report No. XI*, "Verulamium; A Belgic and two Roman cities", Wheeler, R. E. M., and Wheeler, T. V., Oxford, 1936.

VERULAMIUM 1   *Society of Antiquaries Research Report No. XXVIII*, Verulamium Excavations, Vol. 1, Frere, S. S., Oxford, 1972.

WACHER 1969   Wacher, J. S., "Excavations at Brough-on-Humber, 1958–1961", *Report of the Research*

	Committee of the Society of Antiquaries of London, XXV, Leeds, 1969.
WATERMAN 1957	Waterman, D. M., "A group of Claudian pottery from Clausentum", 1939, *Hants. Field Club*, XIX (1955–57).
WEBSTER 1973	Webster, G., and Dudley, D. R., *The Roman Conquest of Britain*, London, 1976.
WEDLAKE 1958	Wedlake, W. J., *Excavations at Camerton, Somerset*, 1958.
WHITER	Whiter, L., *Spode . . .*
WROXETER 1942	*Birmingham Archaeological Society*, "Report on Excavations at Wroxeter (The Roman City of Virconicum), in the County of Salop", 1923–27, Atkinson, D., Oxford, 1942.
YOUNG 1972	Young, C. J., "Excavations at the Churchill Hospital 1971", interim report, *Oxoniensia* XXXVII, 1972.

Abbreviations

ANT. J.	*Antiquaries Journal.*
ANT. SCOT.	*Proceedings of the Society of Antiquaries of Scotland.*
ARCH. CANT.	*Archaeologia Cantiana.*
ARCH. AEL.	*Archaeologia Aeliana.*
ARCHAEOL. JOURN.	*Archaeological Journal.*
B.A.R.	*British Archaeological Reports.*
E.C.C.T.	*English Ceramic Circle Transactions, Vol. 9.*
F.T.J., 1964	*Foundry Trades Journal, Oct. 8th. 1964.*
J.R.S.	*Journal of Roman Studies.*
M.Z., 1917–18	*Mainzer Zeitschrift, 1917–18.*
O.1937	Oswald, F., *Index of Figure-Types on Terra Sigillata* ("Samian ware"), Supplement to the Annals of Archaeology and Anthropology, Vol. XXIV, Nos. 1–2, University Press of Liverpool, 1937.
P.P.S.	*Proceedings of the Prehistoric Society.*
S.A.C.	*Sussex Archaeological Collections.*
S.N.Q.	*Sussex Notes and Queries.*
S. & S., 1958	Stanfield, J. A., and Simpson, G., *Central Gaullish Potters*, University Press of Durham, London, 1958.
T.B.W.A.S.	*Transactions of the Birmingham and Warwickshire Archaeological Society.*
T.B.A.S.	*Transactions of the Birmingham Archaeological Society.*
T.L.	*Transactions of the Lichfield and South Staffordshire Archaeological and Historical Society.*

PART I

The Gazetteers

The Excavations

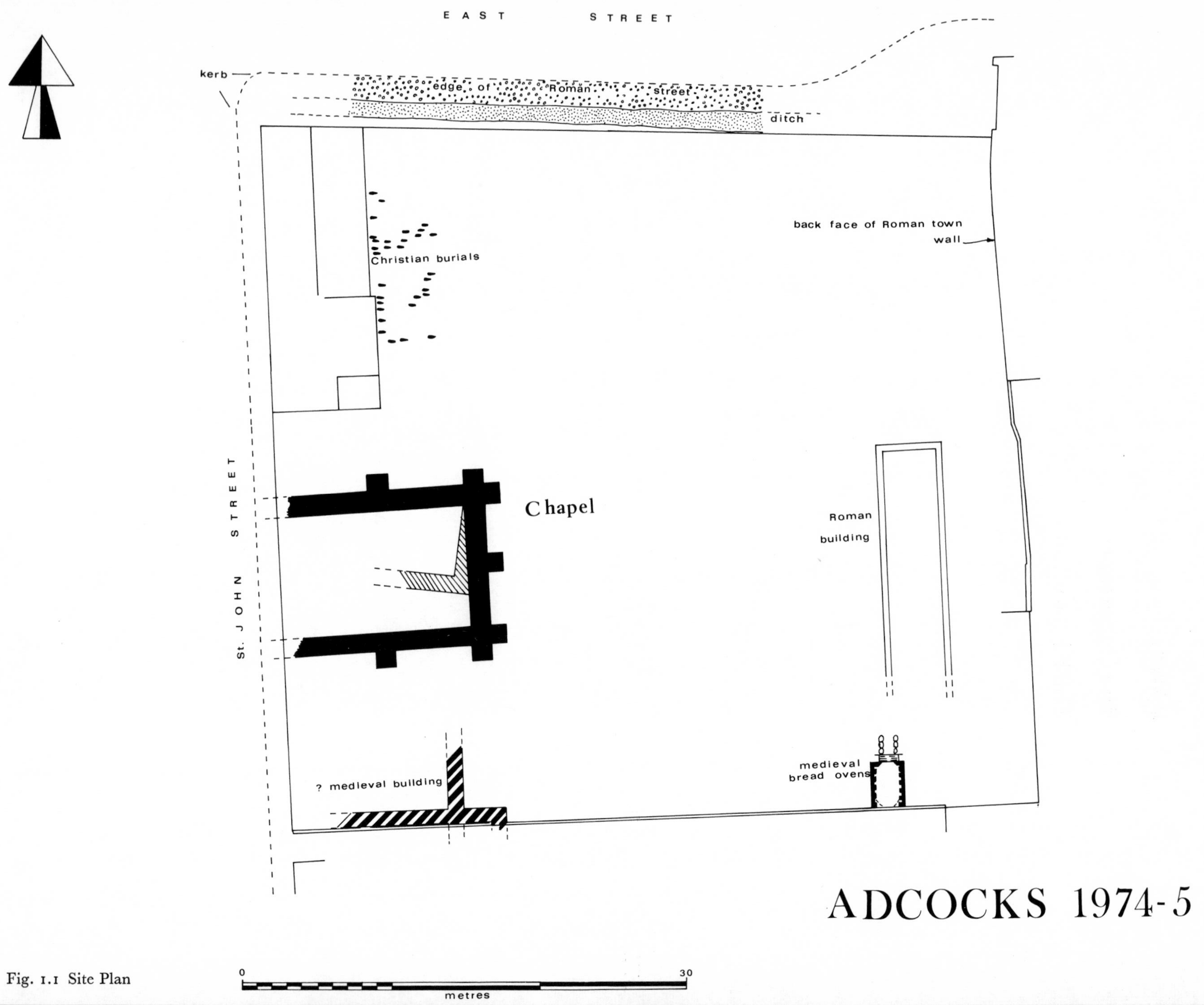

ADCOCKS 1974-5

EAST STREET

kerb

edge of Roman street

ditch

back face of Roman town wall

Christian burials

Chapel

Roman building

medieval bread ovens

? medieval building

St. JOHN STREET

0   30
metres

Fig. 1.1 Site Plan

1

Adcock's Site, Eastgate, 1974–75

In 1973 we were approached by the Architects Roth and Partners on behalf of their clients, the Anglia and General Development Company who had acquired the site of Adcock's Garage at Eastgate for development. Some concern was felt about the possibility of delays due to the presence of Christian burials, as part of the cemetery of the Blackfriars had been found when the site to the west of St. John's Street had been developed in 1966 and a long delay in the building programme resulted.

As none of the existing buildings on the Adcock's site were to be demolished until the start of the contract, the best that could be arranged was that we should dig trial holes at the south end of the site in part of the garage in the winter of 1973 and observe the groundwork when it commenced in 1974. Four trial holes were dug; these showed a wall foundation running east–west on the boundary of the site and turning north and south. The wall footing was 1 metre wide, 1 metre deep and constructed of small flints in a hard white mortar. It was dug into earlier pits containing medieval wares and is unlikely to be earlier than *c.* 15th century in date. At the east end of the small area excavated, traces of a flue were found with a number of pottery wasters (see Fig. 1.3 and below), but the feature was so badly mutilated by pits that it was impossible to establish with certainty that it was a kiln, although there appears to have been one in the vicinity. No traces of burials were found during the trial excavations.

Observations on contractors ground work in Autumn 1974–75 (Fig. 1.1)

Roman:

(a)   *The Roman street*
    At the northern boundary of the site, preliminary foundation and service trenches cut the south edge of a layer of compacted gravel. This had a silted up ditch running east–west along the southern limits and there is no doubt that this represented the south edge of Roman East Street. It extended *c.* 1.65 metres south of the kerb and the width of the ditch was approximately 1.35 metres. Several periods of re-metalling were noted, with the later ones overlying the silt in the ditch.

(b)   *The Building*
    Underpinning work against the back face of the Roman town wall necessitated excavation of a wide trench parallel to the wall and on the west side of it. During these operations a flint wall running north to south was located. It was bonded with Roman tile and cut through an earlier occupation layer containing early 2nd-century samian. A small excavation was mounted to examine this feature in more detail and it was seen that the wall was sealed by a layer of clay which may represent the "tail" of the bank behind the wall. The building was 9.6 metres west of the Town wall, near enough to the defences to ensure that it would be demolished and the ground levelled when the wall was constructed at some time towards the end of the 2nd century A.D. The full dimensions of this structure could not be established due to later pits which cut it on the south side, but it was at least 4.3 metres wide and in excess of 10.5 metres long.

1

Medieval:

(a) *The Christian Burials* (Fig. 1.1)

A total of 36 inhumations were raised during foundation digging and underpinning operations. All were supine and aligned east–west and most were badly disturbed by earlier foundations and pits. Previous contractors work west of St. John's Street[1] had established that the cemetery of the Black-friars extended up to the south boundary of East Street and that later burials of local Catholics were inserted after the Dissolution of the monasteries in the reign of Henry VIII. Later burials of women and children were also noted at Adcocks, but it is not known for how long after the Dissolution the land remained in use as a cemetery.

The burials petered out a short distance from the western boundary of the site and although no trace of a boundary wall was found there could well have been one. In the 13th century there were tenements along the south side of East Street but the exact site of these has not been located and it cannot be said whether they were present when the cemetery was established, or whether the land was acquired in 1337 and the tenements demolished to allow the friars to enlarge their burial ground and cloister.

(b) *The Chapel*

A large building was found aligned east to west, south of the burials. The walls were constructed of flints and greensand in a hard white mortar and were in excess of 1.5 metres in width. It was buttressed at the corners and at intervals along the walls, and in the one area where it was possible to carry out a hasty excavation it was seen that the wall footings were 1.2 metres deep and built partly on to the natural gravel and partly over an earlier deep feature which was filled with loose rubble which had subsided, leaving large voids below the east wall of the building. Traces of the foundations of an earlier building on a slightly different alignment were noted.

The width of the building (excluding the buttresses) was 9.6 metres but the length could not be established as it runs below St. John's Street.

The excavators had six hours to complete examination of the eastern end of the building before site works commenced, and at a later date a weekend's work was possible on the western part. This was badly damaged by later buildings which had been cut through and in some cases built on to, the chapel.

No evidence of date was found.

Discussion

There is little doubt that the design and alignment of the building shows that it is ecclesiastical. The burials ended slightly north of it which in turn suggests that it may have been a mortuary chapel serving the burial ground. It *is* possible that it might have been the church of the friars, but the position of the tower as shown on the Norden Map of 1595 seems to indicate that this was much further south, probably near the site of the existing St. John's Church.

(c) *The Bread Ovens* (Fig. 1.2 and Pl. 16 and 17)

Two bread ovens were found during underpinning operations along the south boundary. These were located one above the other and are described in order of their appearance.

Oven 1. This was rectangular in shape, but only just under half survived the first impact of the machine, and so the width can only be conjectured. It was

2

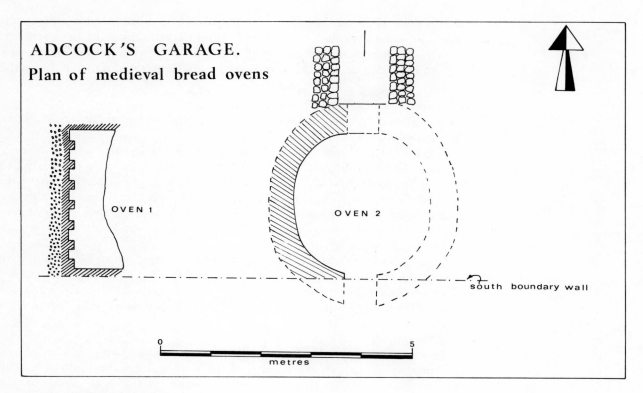

Fig. 1.2 Medieval bread oven

constructed of medieval roof tiles set in clay baked hard by successive firings of the oven. The superstructure, also of clay and tile, had collapsed inwards when the oven was abandoned, and a reconstruction is not possible, nor could the flue be located. It did not exist on the north side above the flue of Oven 2 (see below) and it may have been fired from the east side, which was destroyed by the mechanical excavator.

Oven 2. Below the floor of Oven 1 was a mass of baked clay and tile, and when this was removed it was seen that there was an elliptical oven below. This was aligned north–south and was very well constructed of medieval roof tiles set in mortar with an arched flue at both ends. It was 3 metres long and 2.75 metres wide. This seems much too large for a domestic bread oven and both ovens probably served the requirements of the Blackfriars community. The design is unusual, most bread ovens have only one flue, but perhaps the size of Oven 2 made it necessary to load and unload it at both ends at the same time.

The roof tiles were typical 13th-century peg tiles heavily grogged with flint, and most with a patchy green glaze. In addition, part of a 13th/14th century glazed jug of local manufacture was found in the collapsed debris from Oven 1. A date of *c.* mid 13th to mid 14th century for these ovens is therefore postulated.

In the Spring of 1976, a new sewer pipe was laid along St. John's Street from south to north. This terminated at a point just short of the alignment of the chapel discussed above. Observations on the pipe trench showed that there was considerable disturbance to a depth of 2 metres, with large amounts of building rubble being present. Sections across several wall footings were observed, and the results of the

3

observations show that considerable robbing of one or more buildings must have taken place at some time before St. John's Street was laid out in the early 19th century. No burials were found during this first phase of re-sewering, which bears out the point made above, namely that the cemetery terminated north of the chapel.

Site History (information from Mr. R. R. Morgan)

The area covered by Adcocks was part of the land occupied by the Blackfriars from the 12th century.

In 1228 Edmund Earl of Cornwall founded a house of Dominican or Blackfriars in Chichester. The founding of the Priory was after 1253. Initially the friars lived in temporary buildings, first laying out a churchyard for the burial of the dead. On 11th April 1254 Edmund quit – claimed the whole of their plot, with all the services, giving them leave also to acquire other sites around, so that they might have a suitable place to enclose the whole with a hedge, and to build their oratory and other cloistral offices.

In July 1285 King Edward I was in Chichester with Queen Eleanor and the Queen bought a plot of land from ? John Blel, 104 feet by 44 feet (which was held of the Earl of Cornwall) and gave it to the friars. Shortly afterwards she bought another area from Sir John the Chaplain, "and for her soul's sake" gave it, on 30th April 1286, to the friars.

In 1297 there were in excess of 34 friars.

When laying out their land it became necessary to enclose two public ways – one from St. Andrews Church in the Pallant to the City wall on the south side of the friars plot; the other from Southgate to Eastgate under the City wall (Poukes Lane). A new road was required by Royal Writ southwards from St. Andrews to the City wall.

In 1337 the friars lacked enough space for a church, churchyard and cloister and were given leave to acquire five plots of land 400 feet by 300 feet, contiguous to homestead so that they could enlarge their burial ground and cloister and build a church and houses.

At the time of the Dissolution there were 7 brethren in great poverty. On 8th October 1538 the House was taken into the Kings hands. It stood empty for a year and was subsequently purchased by Edward Mylett ("site and house, with church, belfry and churchyard and all buildings, garden and lands within and without precincts of same").

By 1550 nearly all the buildings had been pulled down.

Sources
V.C.H. (Sussex), Vol. 2, p. 94.
V.C.H. (Sussex), Vol. 3, p. 77.
Poland, "*The Friars in Sussex*".
S.A.C. 89.
S.A.C. 29.
West Sx Record Office Add. MSS. 2920–39; 999 and 6155.

Fig. 1.3   **The Medieval Pottery from Adcocks Kiln**

1. Neck of a jug; fabric hard fired, oxidised reddish buff, with a little sand tempering.
2. Neck of a jug with crudely made handle. One of three found of which one was probably a waster. Additionally, two other handles found which *were* wasters. Fabric is partially reduced but is basically the same as No. 1 with the exception of a few small flint grits. The ware is reminiscent of the coarse wares from the early Roman kiln in Chapel Street (p. 205) and is probably Reading clay also.

   A fourth jug rim was made in a much finer levigated material, with some sand and a few small grits.

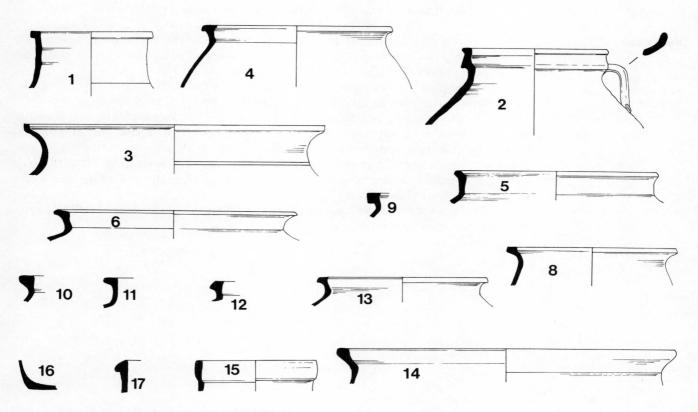

Fig. 1.3 Medieval pottery from the Adcock's Kiln (¼)

3. Neck of a wide mouthed vessel in similar oxidised fabric to No. 1 but grogged with selected small translucent grits.
4 and 5.   Cooking pots in similar ware to No. 3.
6. Cooking pot, patchily reduced, fabric as No. 2.
7. Cooking pot with club rim, grey core, oxidised reddish buff. *Not illustrated.*

8. Rim of cooking pot in similar fabric to No. 2.
9. Square rimmed vessel; sandy oxidised fabric.
10. Similar rim to No. 9; reduced dark grey.
11. Cooking pot, reduced grey; chalk and flint grogging.
12. Cooking pot, grogged as No. 11, but oxidised.
13. Cooking pot; similar ware to No. 2.
14. Cooking pot; fabric as No. 2.
15. Rim of large ? jug; fabric as No. 2.
16. Base of cooking pot, oxidised fabric heavily grogged with selected flint grits. There is probably a slight angle to the base, but not enough survives to be absolutely certain.
17. Rim of vessel in a coarse fabric heavily grogged with small grits and reduced grey.
18. *Not illustrated*. Fragment of a floor or hearth tile (see Fig. 11.8, No. 55, for example). One of several found, all heavily burnt and reduced. These may have been production rejects which were built into the kiln fabric.

Discussion

The large concentration of pottery collapsed across the remains of a twin flue taken with the fact that some of the wares are wasters, points strongly to a kiln or kilns operating on that part of the Blackfriars site.

In general, from what can be seen, the standard of competence appears to be below that of the kilns in Southgate and Orchard Street. The forms suggest a date of *c.* 13th/14th century, but the absence of any sizeable fragments of jug and cooking pot bases makes a comparison with other production centres difficult. It appears that some glazing was undertaken, as a few of the miscellaneous body sherds have glaze splashes on them, but none of the jugs with their crude strap handles, showed any signs of glazing and it may be that what glaze splashes there were derived from the production of glazed floor tiles.

It is likely, in view of the location, that the kiln was operated by the Blackfriars for their own domestic requirements.

Fig. 2.1

Northgate 1973–74

In 1973 the West Sussex County Council commenced the construction of the Northgate circulatory road system. This involved excavation for a dual carriageway through the southern end of Oaklands Car Park and tennis courts. Observation on the site works was maintained by the staff of the City Museum and the Writer. Removal of the top soil to a depth of 1 metre by machines made observation difficult, and the discovery of a complete Roman pot by a workman in addition to other finds of pottery made by the observers, made a controlled excavation imperative.

With the co-operation of the County Surveyor and his staff, who kindly placed a machine at our disposal, a small part of the area was mechanically trenched and then deepened by hand digging. Several pits containing only Roman pottery were found, and cut into a shallow grave in the gravel below the top soil was the lower part of a skeleton aligned north–south. The upper part above the pelvis had been destroyed by a modern surface water drain. No grave goods were present.

Observation and fieldwork during subsequent operations by the County Council Works Unit clearly showed that there had been at least two periods of activity on the site during Roman times.

Period 1, *c.* mid to late 1st century – onwards (Fig. 2.1)

A number of truncated pits were found on the line of the road. These contained pottery dating from the Conquest to the 2nd century and included a rim sherd from a lead glazed vessel identical in form and decoration to a complete vessel found in the St. Pancras Roman cemetery (*Chichester* 1, p. 77, Fig. 5.12 and Pl. 14). It was not possible under the prevailing conditions to do more than excavate and survey some of the pits.

Period 2, *c.* late 2nd to late 4th century

At some time later and probably at the turn of the second century, burials were placed on the site. In addition to the inhumation found during the controlled excavation, elements of sixteen others were noted during road works, and of these, five were inhumations, making a total of six inhumations out of seventeen burials.

One of the cremations had grave goods which included a silver ring incorporating a denarius of Caracella dating to A.D. 200, but nothing was found with the other burials. The inhumations had suffered badly from the acid soil and this made it difficult to detect them during the machining operations. Many were undoubtedly missed under these conditions and the total of seventeen recorded does no more than indicate the presence of a cemetery on the east side of the road issuing from Northgate and to suggest that the larger part of this burial ground extends northwards below the remainder of the car park and tennis courts.

Discussion

The pottery recovered from the two pits excavated on the line of the road suggests a date bracket of *c.* mid 1st to early 2nd century. Butt beaker and other Gallo-Belgic types were represented as were coarse ware types which could fit into a 2nd-century context. There is ample evidence from other areas of the town, e.g. outside the west, south and east gates, to show that up to the time when the town

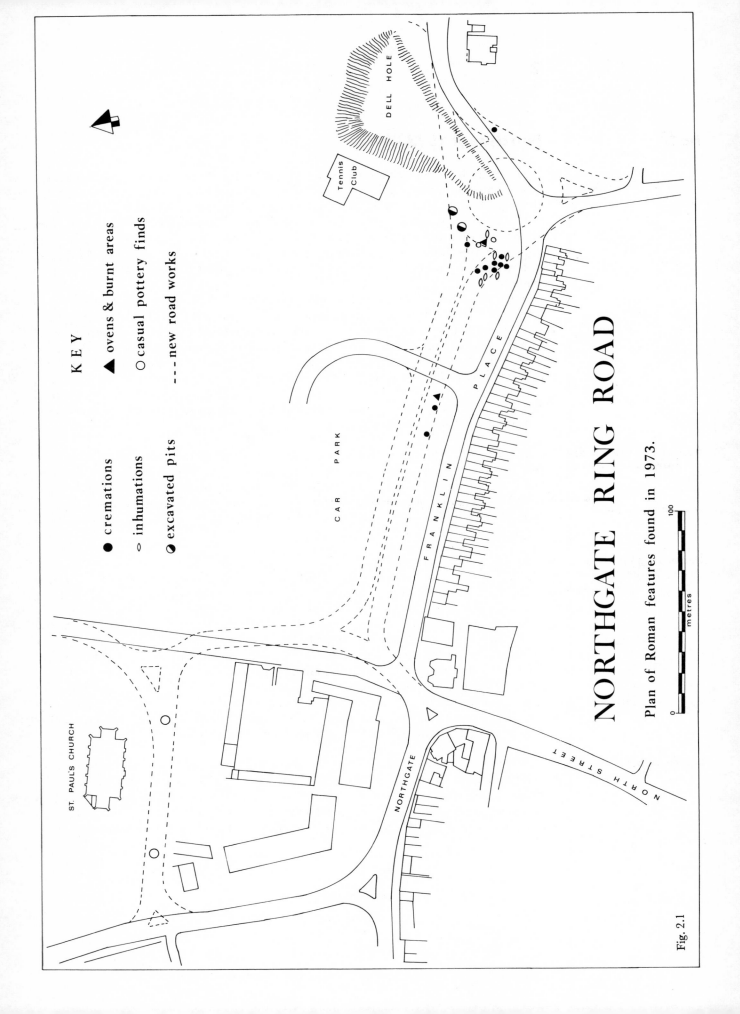

KEY

▲ ovens & burnt areas
○ casual pottery finds
--- new road works

● cremations
◐ inhumations
◑ excavated pits

NORTHGATE RING ROAD

Plan of Roman features found in 1973.

ST. PAUL'S CHURCH

DELL HOLE

Tennis Club

CAR PARK

FRANKLIN PLACE

NORTHGATE

NORTH STREET

0   100
metres

Fig. 2.1

walls were constructed in the late 2nd century, Roman Chichester was either an open town or was enclosed by a larger defensive perimeter which has yet to be discovered. It is quite likely that the earlier town extended northwards beyond the line of the later defences and that the pits belong to that period in the towns' development.

The cemetery came later; an estimate of the date must wait upon a careful examination of a larger sample of burials than the one available, but there are indications of an early to mid 3rd century date for the burials so far discovered. The signet ring in Burial 3 cannot have been deposited before early 3rd century and the relatively high proportion of inhumations in the sample is a further indication of a late date. The much larger sample of 326 burials from the St. Pancras cemetery outside Eastgate showed that only 3.5% were inhumations and that most of these were likely to be 3rd to late 4th century in date, as by the 3rd century, inhumation was replacing cremation as the burial custom in Britain. It could well be that the Northgate cemetery developed at this time, when land for burial in the earlier cemetery at Eastgate was becoming scarce.

Of the burials, only No. 1, the inhumation found in the trial trench was archaeologically excavated. The remainder were seen and plotted as they were exposed (and in most cases destroyed), by the mechanical digger, and the remains, with the exception of Burial 3 were only fragmentary. The pottery and other finds are stored in the Chichester District Museum.

Fig. 10.48

The Grave Goods from Burial 3

The cremated bones were in a large grey ware vessel, the top of which had been completely destroyed by the machine. It was possibly a variant of cemetery type 24A (*Chichester* 1, Fig. 5.20) and luckily the grave goods were lying on the top of the cremated bones and escaped damage.

1. Bronze enamelled disc brooch. See p. 288 and Fig. 10.48.
2. Silver signet ring with a denarius of Caracella and Severvs, *c.* A.D. 200 as the bezel. Only half of the ring was present and this may be another instance of the "slighting" of the object before deposition in the grave.
3. Two fragments of either a large diameter silver finger ring, or, more likely, an ear-ring. Incomplete and very worn; diameter approximately 25 mm.
4. A pair of very corroded bronze rings, probably ear rings.
5. Amber bead.

Fig. 3.1

The Medieval Kiln at Southgate

In 1974, work started on the construction of the new Magistrates Courthouse. The site is located north of the old Courthouse (see plan), and a watching brief was arranged by permission of the West Sussex County Council and through the kind offices of the Architects, Roth and Partners. Thanks are due to them and also to the builders, John Snelling Ltd., who gave us every facility for observation.

Work in 1970, at the rear of Nos. 41 and 42 Southgate (*Chichester* 2, Fig. 3.1 and p. 21), showed that medieval wasters and part of a kiln bar were present in pits at the rear of the garden, indicating the presence of medieval kilns nearby. The observations of the 1974 work stemmed from this find.

Traces of three kilns were found and one was excavated (see Fig. 3.2). Excavation of the deep hole for the cell block was carried out at a very fast rate and it was only possible to locate, survey and excavate part of Kiln 3. Kilns 1 and 2 were seen in section in the foundation trenches and their position was plotted and a large waster tip, of which only a small area was within the site, was located at the north-west end only a few hours before it was sealed off.

The Kiln

This was a small kiln of the updraught type, fired from the east end. There was a small clay dome in the centre of the firing chamber which would have supported the kiln bars, and the kiln was dug into natural clay. Traces of the base of the kiln wall remained, in the presence of a few flints set into the clay around the south-west end of the kiln, the remainder having been destroyed by the mechanical digger. The kiln was filled with clay and waster fragments, and leaning against the wall at the west end were two roof tiles of unusual shape (see below).

Dug into the clay against the west end of the firing chamber were two complete pots, a cooking pot and a tripod pitcher, with part of a third vessel, a spouted pitcher, alongside. This latter vessel had been cut away by the machine, but the impression in the soil against the tripod pitcher showed that it had been in position alongside the others. The two surviving pots were inverted and empty and were wasters, and their presence against the west wall of the kiln is a matter which cannot be satisfactorily explained.

The kiln was of different construction to the one excavated in Orchard Street (*Chichester* 1, pp. 153–65). The Southgate kiln was dug into the natural clay, was capable of being fired from one end only, and had no interior kiln walls like the Orchard Street example. It was also less than half the size, being slightly under 1.5 metres in length overall as against 3.2 metres for the Orchard Street kiln.

The Wares
Figs. 3.3–3.4

Only a small amount of material was recovered during building operations; this is not surprising in view of the speed with which the foundations were dug by machine. A large mass of spoil was taken out when the cell block foundations were dug and it is certain that a lot of kiln material was lost. At the west end, the waster tip referred to above had large amounts of glazed roof and ridge tiles and it was possible to salvage some of these before the area was covered with concrete. Due to

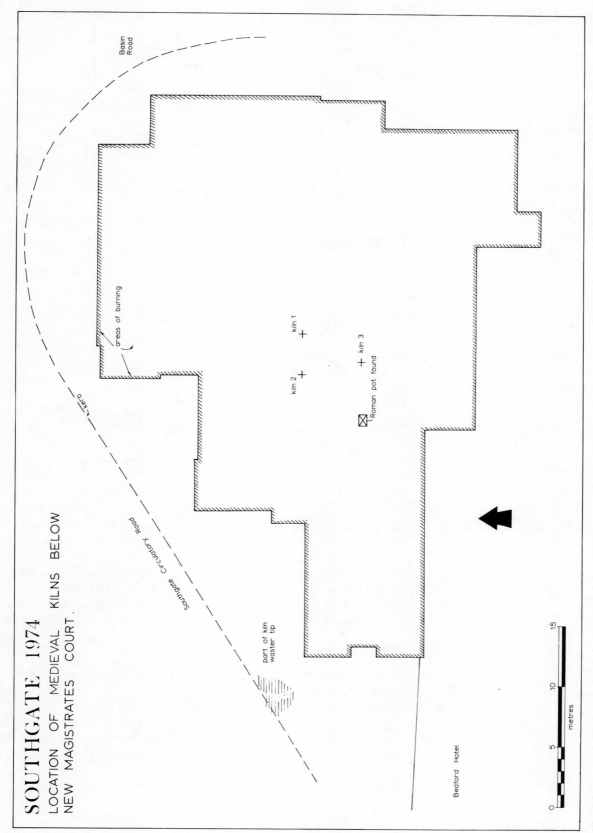

SOUTHGATE 1974
LOCATION OF MEDIEVAL KILNS BELOW
NEW MAGISTRATES COURT.

Basin Road

Kerb

Southgate Crematory Road

areas of burning

kiln 1

kiln 2

kiln 3

Roman pot found

part of kiln
waster tip

Bedford Hotel

metres
0   5   10   15

Fig. 3.1

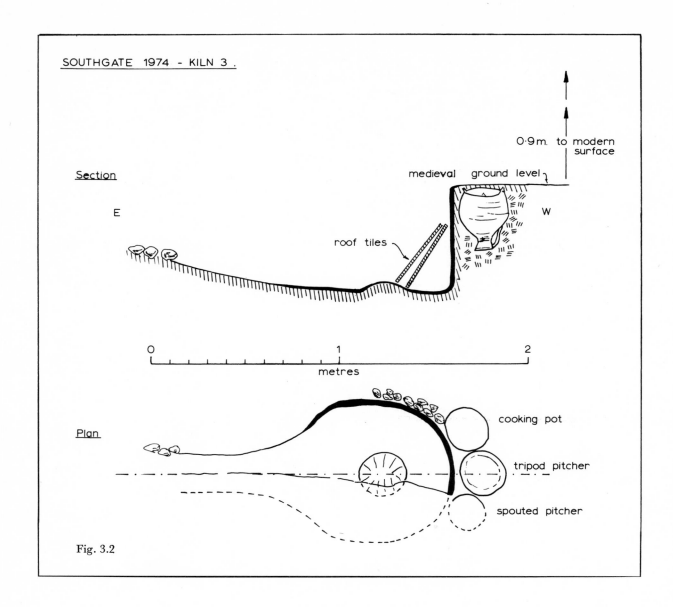

SOUTHGATE 1974 - KILN 3.

0·9m. to modern surface

Section

medieval ground level

E

W

roof tiles

0   1   2

metres

Plan

cooking pot

tripod pitcher

spouted pitcher

Fig. 3.2

these conditions the following list of wares is probably incomplete and not enough samples of the various types were found to be able to come to any firm conclusions, particularly about the roof furniture. Nevertheless, these examples are a welcome addition to the growing amount of medieval kiln products found in Chichester.

The Jugs

One complete jug or tripod pitcher was found inverted and buried alongside the wall of the kiln, and the rims of several others were found as wasters. They are slightly different from the Orchard Street variety (*op. cit.* Fig. 7.12, 43, 45), the neck and upper body being grooved instead of rilled, and there were no signs of embossing on the body. The greatest difference seems to be in the handles, which are in the form of a simple strap (Fig. 3.3, Nos. 1 and 2), with central slashing. A few fragments of tripod feet were found, but no thumbed bases. Only two thumbed-base sherds were found at Orchard Street, and it seems likely that tripod pitchers were the main "jug" line in both kilns.

1. Jug handle in a sandy buff fabric, external green glaze on top surface, two longitudinal slashes.
2. Jug handle; sandy grey fabric with some flint grits; brown glaze on top surface, three longitudinal slashes. One other example, heavily overfired, not illustrated but generally as No. 1.
3. Rim of pitcher; fine sandy fabric with some flints, oxidised reddish-buff with irregular grooving around the neck and faint traces of a patchy brown glaze.
4. Complete tripod pitcher in a sand tempered fabric oxidised pale buff; horizontal grooving on neck and body, and the grooves on the neck are deep enough to justify the description "rilled". The glaze is pale to dark brownish green.
5. Part of a spouted pitcher in a grey gritty fabric oxidised to buff outside and with a green glaze inside. This vessel was also buried alongside the kiln, the remainder having been destroyed by the contractor's machine. It must, therefore, be strictly contemporary with No. 4.

Cooking pots

6. Complete large cooking pot in a grey fabric, flint grogged, oxidised reddish buff, but with partially reduced patches. This vessel was inverted and empty alongside No. 4, outside the kiln wall.
7 to 10.   Vessels in similar fabric to No. 6.
11.   Grey fabric, flint gritted, but oxidised red.

Not illustrated

12.   Similar form and fabric to No. 9 but oxidised red.
13 and 14.   Similar form to No. 12, but reduced to a dirty grey.

Pans

Sherds from two shallow pans were found:
15 and 16.   In a flint grogged fabric oxidised reddish-buff, with internal green/brown glaze extending over the rim in the case of No. 15.

Roof furniture

(a) *Peg tiles*. Two types of fabric were noted on the examples found:

Fabric A: Fine grey; sand tempered with a few flint grits. Oxidised to a pale red; tile thickness 10 mm; width of tile 170 mm.

Fabric B: Pale grey: well grogged with small crushed flints of a fairly uniform size. Oxidised to a pale buff; tile thickness 15 mm; width, 192 mm.

No lengths could be postulated for either type, but by analogy with the shouldered tiles discussed below they are likely to be c. 265 to 310 mm if it is assumed that a normal tile might terminate just above the "shoulder".

No glaze was noted on the four examples in Type A fabric, but this is not conclusive as in all cases, half or less than half of the tile was recovered. Glaze was noted on all the Type B fabric tiles and this generally extended from c. 150–155 mm up

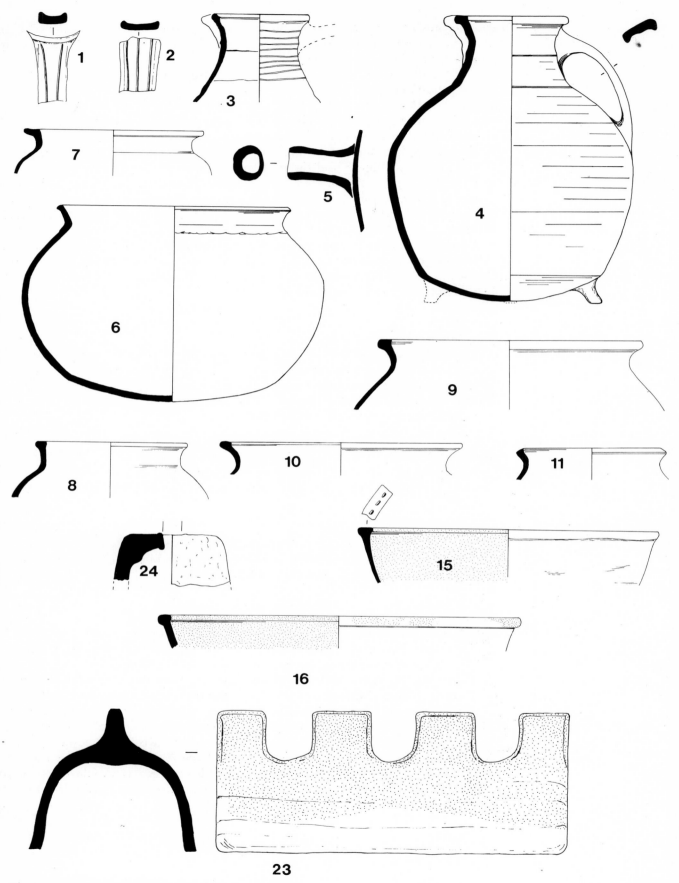

Fig. 3.3 Southgate: Wares from the Medieval kiln ($\frac{1}{4}$)

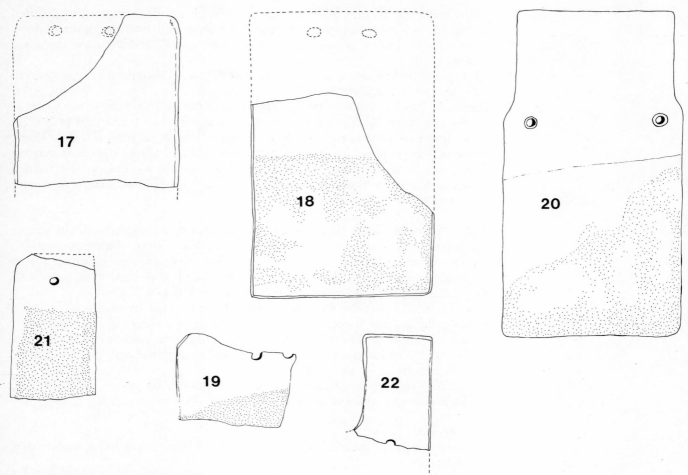

Fig. 3.4 Southgate: Tiles from the medieval kiln (¼)

from the bottom of the tile, although in one instance (No. 19) it came within 60 mm of the top. The colour varied from dark green to light brown. Some of the tiles, notably the two shouldered ones, showed a sharp line of demarcation where the glaze ended, and the coating was noticeably thicker at the bottom, indicating that the tiles were dipped in the glaze, and finally stacked vertically in the kiln.

17.   Roof tile in Type A fabric.
18 and 19.   Roof tiles in Type B fabric.

(b)   *Shouldered peg tiles*. Two tiles were found stacked on their bases inside the kiln when it was excavated, having presumably been left there after the last firing. Both were underfired wasters and both were complete. The fabric was heavily gritted and there was a thin wash of glaze across the lower half. The outstanding feature of these tiles is that they have a projection at the top end which gives them a "shouldered" appearance. No other tiles resembling them have been found in Chichester as far as this writer is aware, nor can parallels from elsewhere be cited. They were made in a mould, and the glazing of the lower part indicates that they were intended to overlap one another.

15

20. Shouldered tile, 60 mm thick, heavily gritted fabric; glaze originally extended *c.* 190 mm up from the base, but has been fired well into the porous fabric. Two other fragments of non-standard tile were found, and these are discussed below.

21. Part of a "lug" from a tile; it is 87 mm wide and is chamfered across the top left-hand corner, Fabric B.

22. Lug in Fabric B, 70 mm wide. The position of the hole and the shape where it has broken, suggests that it might perhaps be the female counterpart of No. 20.

No firm explanation can be offered for these tiles at present, but their shape suggests that perhaps they may be facing tiles instead of roof tiles, and may, in fact, have been a special "one off" production job, as if they had been a standard line it is likely that they would have been noted before in earlier excavations.

(c) *Ridge tiles.* A few ridge tiles were recovered from a section through the waster tip before it was concreted by the builders. None were complete, and the number of crenellations and the length of the tiles can only be conjectured. By analogy with the 16th-century roof tiles found at All Saints (*Chichester* 2, Fig. 7.12, 43, 45), the length could be between 350 and 370 mm.

The end crenellations were well bonded to the ridge by means of an overlapping flange which was doubled back under the ridge, giving additional reinforcement to the ends. The intermediate ones were just applied to the crest of the ridge and luted on to it. Adhesion was correspondingly poor and must have been a frequent cause of wasters.

23. Ridge tile, reconstructed from a number of waster fragments, in Fabric A, oxidised pale red with green to brown patchy glaze.

(d) *Chimney vents*

24. Only one fragment found; in soft gritty oxidised fabric, very much under-fired and a waster.

Discussion

There are very great similarities and some differences between the products of this group of kilns and the one from Orchard Street. Both localities made roof tiles, but the Orchard Street kiln did not produce evidence of ridge tile manufacture, whereas the Southgate kilns did. However, only one of the Orchard Street kilns has been excavated, and this line of products could have been made in a neighbouring kiln.

Both sites produced a range of cooking pots, pans, chimney vents and fine tripod pitchers, with the pitchers from Orchard Street being of a finer quality than the Southgate ones, having especially elaborate handles. No glazed pans were seen at Orchard Street, but this line was made at Southgate, as were internally glazed spouted pitchers. These are relatively minor differences and are not likely to indicate a big difference in date. It is likely that the Southgate kilns were roughly contemporary with the one in Orchard Street, and Barton's suggested date of *c.* 13th century for this kiln could fit the Southgate industry as well (*Chichester* 1, pp. 163–4).

4

(Fig. 4.1)

Addendum to Roman Gazetteer

Fig. 4.1 (see *Chichester* 1, pp. 7–17 and Figs. 4.1 and 4.2, and *Chichester* 2, pp. 33–37 and Figs. 4.1 and 4.2). The numbers run on from *Chichester* 2.

North East Quadrant

89. *Northgate* (outside the walls). This volume p. 7.

Trial excavation and observation on road works in 1974 showed the following features:
  (a) Roman pits belonging to occupation pre-dating 2nd-century town defences.
  (b) Roman burials (cremation and inhumation) indicating a late cemetery *c.* 3rd–4th century A.D.

90. *North Street (rear of No. 59).*

Builders trench in garden at rear (against south wall) struck part of a Roman wall constructed of flints in mortar at a depth of 2.15 metres. This was almost under the garden wall and was aligned east–west.

91. *North Street (surface water drainage trench in November 1976):*
  (i) *Temple of Neptune and Minerva.*
    A tile-bonded wall was found; it was constructed of flints in creamy mortar and was *c.* 0.8 metre wide. It was aligned north–south and was in alignment with the Roman street. A wall, 0.45 metre wide, joined it at right angles on the east side. This feature was noted in front (west) of No. 71 North Street and must be the same wall as that observed in 1967 in a service trench opposite No. 70. (See *Chichester Excavations* 1, p. 9, No. 9, and pp. 51–52, also Fig. 4.2, this volume, p. 19.) The wall is very close to the point where the Cogidubnus inscription was found in 1723 and is very likely to be part of the temple of Neptune and Minerva.
  (ii) At a point 9 metres south of the temple wall was a substantial wall foundation running southwards for a distance of 23 metres. It was 1.5 metres below ground level and *c.* 0.77 metre wide. One course of ashlar masonry survived above the foundations in some places. This may be part of a large public building south of the temple and a substantial part must lie below the Assembly Rooms to the east.
  (iii) Eleven metres south of the south boundary of St. Olaves Church, part of a destroyed Roman hypocaust sealed by a layer of black earth which in turn was sealed by a paved area which may be part of the medieval market place. The most southerly point viewed was opposite the Market Hall.

92. *Rear of Jay's Marine in St. Martin's Lane.*

A Roman mortar floor was found when a new wall foundation for a barn was dug. This was 1.75 metres below modern ground level and sealed an earlier pit.

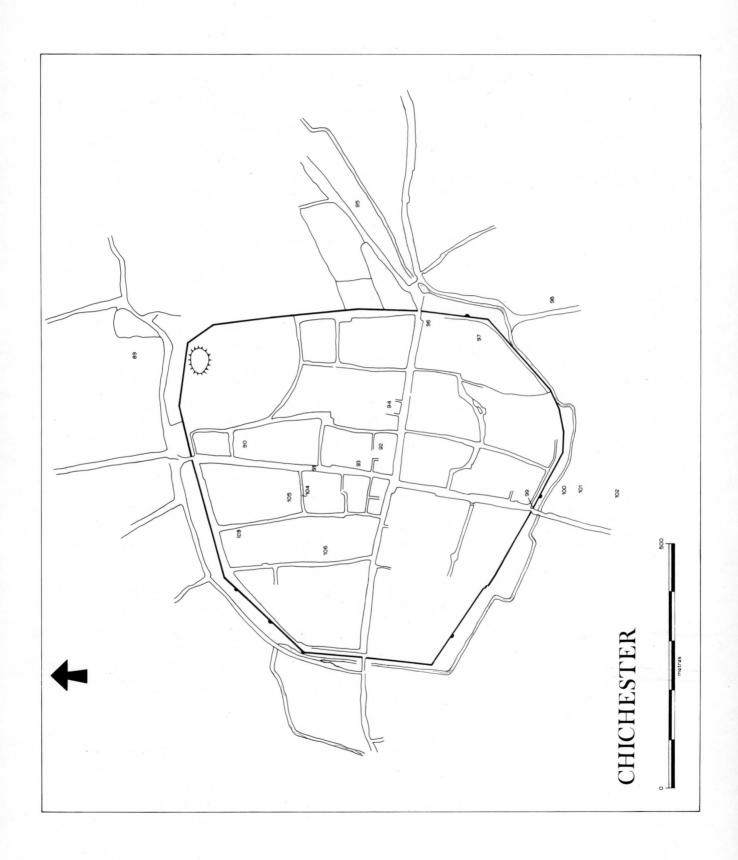

CHICHESTER

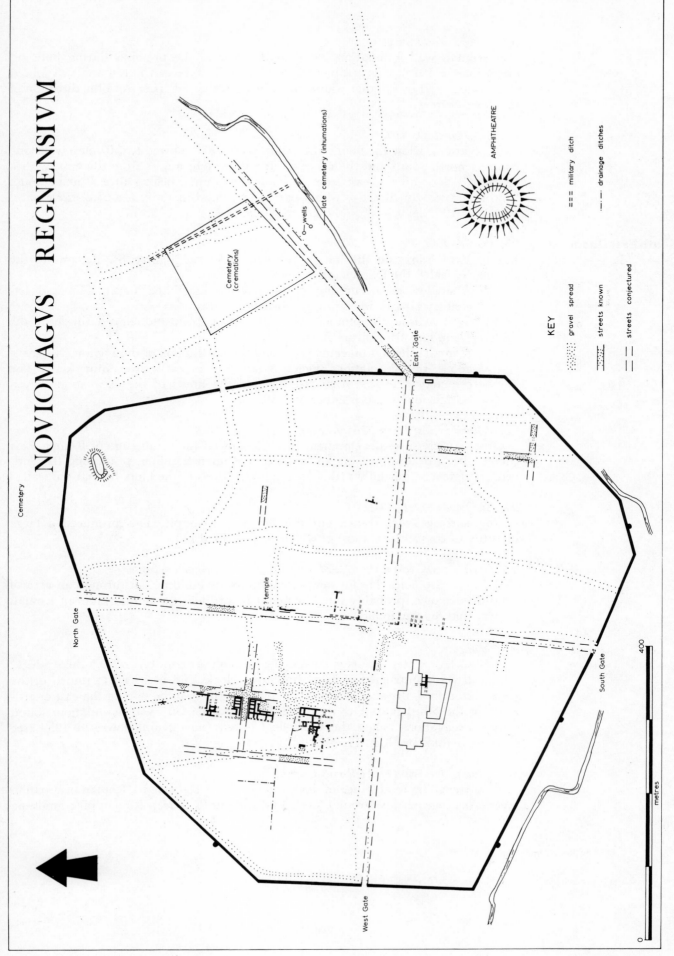

NOVIOMAGVS REGNENSIVM

Cemetery

North Gate

West Gate

South Gate

? temple

East Gate

Cemetery (cremations)

wells

late cemetery (inhumations)

AMPHITHEATRE

KEY

gravel spread

streets known

streets conjectured

═══ military ditch

—·— drainage ditches

metres

0   400

Fig. 4.2

93. *No. 82 North Street.*

A Roman wall foundation found at the rear of the premises during building operations in 1975. This ran northwards below St. Olaves Church and was joined at the south end by another wall coming in from the west (i.e. from the direction of the North Street).

94. *St. Andrew Oxmarket.*

Excavations below the floor of St. Andrews in 1976 showed two Roman walls one running north–south and the other joining it at right angles from the east, with a tessellated floor on the east side. These features must belong to a Roman house fronting on to East Street of which parts were found in 1959. See *Chichester Excavations* 1, p. 10, Nos. 13–15, and *Chichester Excavations* 2, p. 113.

South East Quadrant

95. *Outside Eastgate*

Rescue excavations on the line of the new link road joining St. Pancras to the Hornet, revealed the following features:

(a) A shallow ditch running east–west alongside Stane Street. This had 1st-century pottery including Gallo-Belgic wares.

(b) Two wells and a number of cesspits with pottery and coins dating from the 1st to late 4th century A.D.

(c) A small inhumation cemetery along the north bank of the Lavant. No grave goods, but associations suggest a late 4th- or early 5th-century date. The cemetery extended eastwards beyond the limits of the excavation. Seven burials found and fragments of others.

96. *Adcock's, East Street* (this volume p. 1).

Observations on re-development in 1975 showed the south edge of Roman East Street with a drain alongside and part of a Roman building, pre-dating the 2nd-century defences, partially sealed by the lower levels of the bank behind the wall.

97. *St. John's Street, 1976.*

New surface water trench cut through a Roman pit. This produced a large quantity of coarse ware, most of which was oxidised red.

98. *Outside south–east walls: Caledonian Road (ex Caledonian depository).*

Column base holes dug for new extension inside building cut through an area of deep disturbance, probably pits but might be a ditch. Large quantities of Roman pottery and tegulae found.

99. *Southgate.*

New surface water drainage trench cut through a masonry wall 0.5 metre thick. The wall was constructed of faced limestone blocks and was seen to return in the west section for a distance of 2.5 metres. This is likely to be part of the east guard-room of the Southgate. The wall is in line with the City wall foundations found during excavations below the Catholic Church (now Rumbelows) in 1959 (see *Chichester Excavations* 1, p. 11, No. 26).

100. *Southgate: South of Methodist Church.*

Trial trenching in advance of development in 1976 showed a Roman occupation layer *c.* 0.4 metre below ground level. This was cut by a deep Roman pit containing large amounts of iron slag, probably forge slag, and may indicate the presence of a Roman smithy outside the Southgate.

101. *Outside Southgate, Magistrates Court site.*
Complete Roman ovoid beaker found 2.1 metres deep during excavation for the new cell block in 1974.

102. *Outside Southgate; Old Gas Works site.*
Excavations during 1975–76 south of the railway line have revealed the following features:
- (i) A ditch, *c.* 4.6 metres wide and 1.5 metres deep, draining south,west towards the harbour. No dating evidence recovered from it.
- (ii) Roman timber buildings alongside silted up ditch and pits cutting it. Two of these had burnt daub and 3rd–4th-century pottery and coins. This site will be fully reported in Volume 4.

North West Quadrant

103. *Chapel Street.*
- (i) New surface water drainage trench cut through several walls belonging to a Roman house on the west side of the Roman north-south street, part of which is below Chapel Street. See this volume p. 79 and *Chichester Excavations* 1, p. 15, Nos. 65 and 67. The same excavation unearthed part of a human cranium and several long bones at a depth of approximately 1.5 metres on the east side of the Roman street.
- (ii) Further south and just north of the junction of Chapel Street with Crane Street, the pipe trench sectioned the north edge of the Roman east-west street (Street 3), just east of where it joins the north-south street below the old Central Girls School (see also this volume p. 66 and fig. 7.14).

104. *Crane Street.*
Surface water drain trench cut through part of a Roman tile bonded wall aligned east–west at a depth of 1 metre. This is south of Street 3.

105. *Chapel Street–Crane Street area (Area 6)* (this volume p. 138).
- (a) Roman metalling, north of Street 3 and sealing earlier pits. A line of post-holes on east side.
- (b) Purchases Garden: Roman timber buildings and clay-pits found.

106. *Tower Street* (this volume pp. 139–157).
- (i) A number of pre-Flavian timber buildings, the earliest probably military storehouses.
- (ii) The northern part of the Thermae, including a deep stone built water cistern. At least four phases of alteration and re-building noted.
- (iii) A large drainage ditch running east–west, similar in profile to that found below County Hall (*Chichester 2*, pp. 39–58).
- (iv) Contractors roadworks during the excavation showed that the Thermae extended westwards below the houses on the west side of Tower Street, and a massive wall, 1.8 metres wide, running east–west at the junction of Tower Street with West Street. Probable extent of Thermae complex is thought to be *c.* 5,500 square metres.

5

Addendum to Saxon and Medieval Gazetteer

Fig. 5.1 (see *Chichester 2*, pp. 7–13, and Fig. 2.1. The numbers run on from *Chichester 2*.

North East Quadrant

55. *North Street 1976.*

Surface water drainage trench showed a layer of pitched flints, chalk and mortar at a depth of between 0.3 and 0.5 metre. This extended in front of Market Hall and sealed the destruction levels of a Roman house. It may be part of the medieval market place.

South East Quadrant

56. *Adcocks, East Street* (this volume p. 2).

Observations during development in 1974–75 showed that the Blackfriars cemetery extended across the northern part of the site. Thirty-six inhumations were raised in advance of building operations. South of these was a chapel which may be the Chapel of Rest for the cemetery; this extends below St. John's Street.

Two medieval bread ovens, probably belonging to the conventual buildings were found at the south end on the boundary with Moore & Tillyer. They were constructed of medieval roof tiles, were three metres long and one above the other.

Trial excavations in 1973 at the south end revealed part of a ? kiln, with pottery wasters, of medieval date. See also *Chichester Excavations* 2, p. 10, No. 16 and 17.

57. *Outside Eastgate.*

Rescue excavations along line of new road linking St. Pancras to the Hornet in 1976 showed the following features:
1. Postholes and slots belonging to medieval houses fronting on to the south side of St. Pancras, with medieval pits at the rear of the properties. The pottery gives a date range of *c*. 13th to 15th centuries.
2. A timber-lined drainage ditch running southwards and draining into the Lavant.

58. *Southgate: New Magistrates Court site 1974* (this volume p. 10).

At least three medieval kilns noted and one excavated during building operations. Wares similar to those from Orchard Street (see *Chichester Excavations* 1, pp. 153–64), and dated to 13th century.

59. *Outside Southgate: Old Gasworks site, west of Basin Road.*

Excavations in advance of development showed a shallow ditch which ran southwards along the west side of Basin Road and turned westwards. No later artifacts than medieval roof tiles and pottery found.

South West Quadrant

60. *No. 50 West Street.*

Part of a medieval oven observed at the rear of the premises during building operations in 1975.

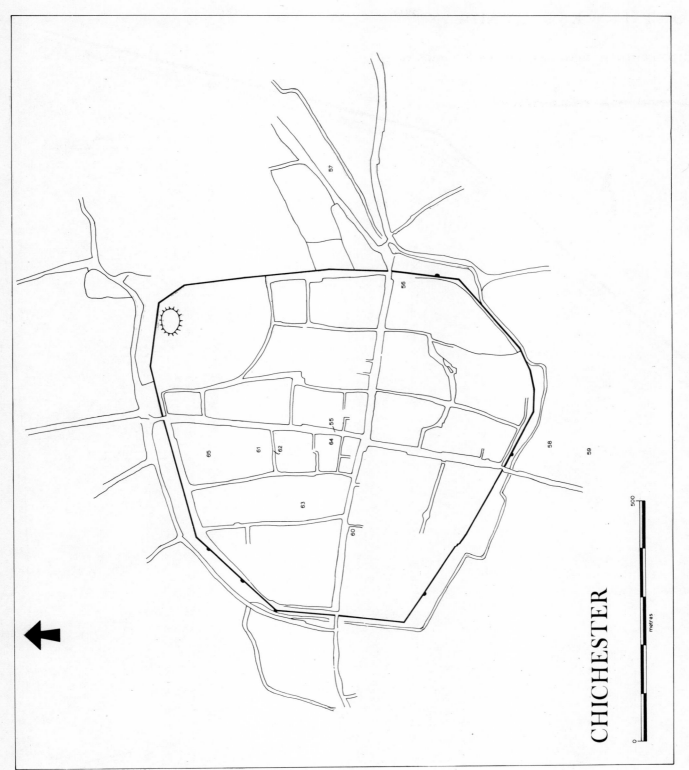

CHICHESTER

Fig. 5.1

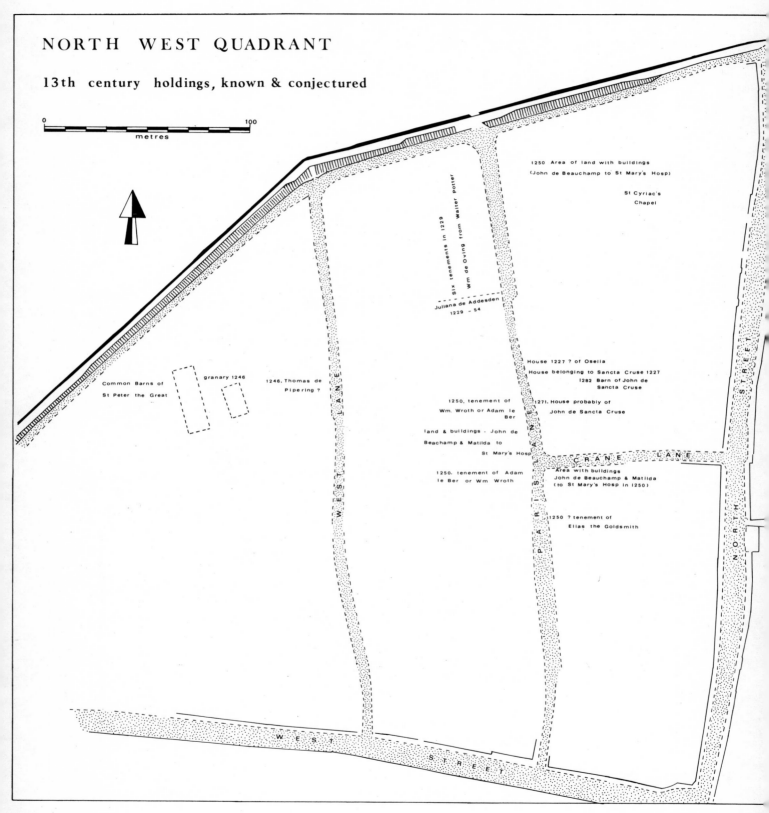

NORTH WEST QUADRANT

13th century holdings, known & conjectured

0 ──────────────── 100
metres

1250 Area of land with buildings
(John de Beauchamp to St Mary's Hosp)

St Cyriac's
Chapel

Six tenements in 1229
Wm de Oving from Walter potter

Juliana de Addesden
1229 - 54

House 1227 ? of Osella

House belonging to Sancta Cruse 1227

1282 Barn of John de
Sancta Cruse

1271. House probably of
John de Sancta Cruse

Common Barns of
St Peter the Great

granary 1246

1246. Thomas de
Pipering ?

1250, tenement of
Wm. Wroth or Adam le
Ber

land & buildings - John de
Beachamp & Matilda to
St Mary's Hosp

1250. tenement of Adam
le Ber or Wm Wroth

CRANE   LANE

Area with buildings
John de Beauchamp & Matilda
(to St Mary's Hosp in 1250)

1250 ? tenement of
Elias the Goldsmith

WEST   LANE

PARIS   LANE

NORTH   STREET

NORTH

WEST   STREET

Fig. 5.2

61. *Chapel Street–Crane Street area* (*Area 6*) (this volume pp. 130–132).
Purchases Garden.
    (a)   Middle to late Saxon pits found.
    (b)   Part of a cultivated area, with medieval plough scars cutting into Roman levels. Probable date from 13th–15th century. This may be part of a holding given by John de St. Cross to St. Mary's Hospital in 13th century. Traces of timber buildings on east side.
Crane Street.
    Oval well found on north side of Crane Street. Pottery suggests date of 14th century.

62. *Crane Street, 1976.*
    Surface water drainage trench exposed old road surface, probably the medieval street.

63. *Tower Street* (this volume pp. 158–170).
    (a)   Slots of a ? Saxon building aligned north–south alongside Tower Street. Many Saxon pits from *c.* 9th to 11th century found.
    (b)   Medieval bell founding pits, probably 14th century, together with part of a bell mould in position over a flue.
    (c)   Two houses, one dating from *c.* 14th century of timber construction; the second of masonry construction at the south end of the site, partly under No. 51 Tower Street, dated *c.* 15th century.

64. *Shirley's, North Street, 1974.*
    Part of a medieval wall foundation found at the rear of the property during re-building. This ran north–south and had the remains of an oven built against the west side of the wall.

65. *St. Cyriacs Chapel* (see also *Chichester Excavations* 2, p. 13, and note below).
    Trial excavations in 1973 on the supposed site of the chapel, proved negative, due to the presence of a large Victorian greenhouse which had destroyed earlier features. Medieval pottery and a coin found, and traces of earlier, ? medieval, building material.

A Note on the Chapel of St. Cyriac, Chichester
by Alison McCann

    The Chapel of St. Cyriac was founded by Earl Roger de Montgomery at some time between the conquest of England in 1066 and his death in 1094. It was probably founded as a chantry chapel to house a single priest to pray for the soul of Earl Roger and his ancestors. It was given by Earl Roger to the Abbey of St. Martin at Troarn in France, and was among the possessions confirmed to the Abbey by Henry II in 1155.

However, in another confirmation dated to *c.* 1155–58, the chapel is not mentioned among the Abbey's possessions in Chichester. It seems, therefore, that either the chapel had passed from the monastery's possession, or else its value was so small that it was not worth mentioning. Certainly by 1247 the chapel had declined to being the habitation of a recluse. By his will made in that year, Geoffrey de Glovernia, Dean of Chichester, among other bequests, ordained that 1 penny should be paid annually on the anniversary of his death to "the recluse of St. Cyriac".

The unnamed recluse did not apparently continue to receive his annual penny for very long. In 1269 Henry III came to Chichester, and someone drew his attention to the chapel, which by then was so impoverished that its revenues could not support a priest to celebrate there. The King immediately granted 50 marks to endow the chapel, and 5 marks a year to be paid for the support of a Chaplain. Stephen de Midhurst was appointed Chaplain, with the duty of celebrating in the chapel daily, presumably for the spiritual benefit of Henry III and his family.

The stipend was not very large, but even so it seems to have been constantly in arrears in the years immediately following Stephen de Midhurst's appointment as Chaplain. The Liberate Rolls for 1270–72 contain frequent references to the arrears of the stipend of "Stephen the Kings Chaplain in St. Cyriac's chapel, Chichester". After 1272 there are no more references in the Liberate Rolls to the payment of the stipend. Either it was being paid regularly, or else as seems more likely, Stephen had died and no successor had been appointed. After 1272 there is no reference to the chapel for over a century. By 1405 when it next appears in the records, it no longer housed a chantry priest, but had declined again into a hermitage. In 1405 Robert Rede, Bishop of Chichester, granted an indulgence to anyone who would assign "any of the goods conferred on them by God as charitable supplies towards the support of Richard Petevine, hermit of the chapel of St. Cyriac founded in the city of Chichester, and to the repairs of the same chapel".

There is only one more reference to the chapel as a religious establishment. In 1486 one Thomas Trybe was presented to the court of the peculiar of the Dean of Chichester for going around the countryside collecting money towards the repair of the chapel of St. Cyriac. There is no indication of what right Trybe had to do this, and the outcome of the case is not known. It is evident however that at this date the chapel was still regarded as a religious building.

It is not known whether the chapel was still in use at the time of the Reformation. It was listed among the Chantry lands, and by 1579 was secularised and let to a tenant, presumably for use as a barn or store. The chapel and the land around it eventually became the property of the Hospital of St. Mary in Chichester. The chapel still existed in 1820 when it is said to be in a ruinous condition. The derelict building probably finally disappeared when the land around it was divided up and part of it taken into the garden of the fine new house recently purchased by Richard Murray, now No. 40 North Street.

The title deeds of the piece of land around the chapel, are preserved among the records of the Hospital of St. Mary in the Diocesan Record Office. From these it is possible to locate the approximate site of the chapel. It lay along the lane called St. Cyriac's Lane or Street, which ran down the north side of the property which is now No. 40 North Street, originally running right through to Chapel Street. The Gardner map of Chichester of 1769 shows the surviving eastern end of the lane terminating in a building which is very probably St. Cyriac's chapel.

Note: A fuller version of this article appears in *S.A.C.* 113, pp. 197–9.

Gazetteer of Post Medieval Sites and Buildings 1450–1750 by R. R. Morgan

The Roman, Saxon and Medieval Gazetteers (see *Chichester Excavations* 1 and 2), depended mainly on archaeological and documentary sources to record buildings largely no longer extant. This Gazetteer has to recognise different criteria; firstly, properties from the previous period which survived during the post-medieval period (marked †, for provenance see *Chichester* 2); secondly, the significant increase in development over the period, which changed the face of the City. Any development which has survived largely in its original form is marked *

Another significant fact which has emerged is the concentration, by 1750, of ownership into a few hands. This is exemplified in Fig. 6.3. The form in which each of the four quadrants and the suburbs have developed is shown in Fig. 6.2.

The general condition of the City
There is no surviving description of the city in 1450. In the early part of Queen Elizabeth 1's reign the streets were described as "very mierie, full of watrie and dirtie places, both lothsome and noysome". A local act of 1575 reinforced the old obligation to pave. The four main streets were already paved and owners had now to maintain them (*S.A.C.* 90). The streets again fell into decay in the early and middle 18th century. Eventually the Paving Commissioners started new paving in 1792, and soon the four main streets and St. Martins Lane, Friary Lane, Little London and Shambles Alley were completed. For the end of the period we are indebted to James Spershott who recorded his memories of the early years of the 18th century; "the city had a very mean appearance in comparison with what it has since arrived at (i.e. in 1783). The buildings were in general very low, very old and their fronts framed with timber which lay bare to the weather . . . there were very few houses, even in the main streets, that had solid brick fronts . . . there were many blank places in the main streets of dead walls, gateways, etc., that are now since filled up with buildings . . . the backlanes had a very mean appearance but few houses a bad one." (For a collection of descriptions 1586–1948 see *Restricted Grandeur*, compiled by T. J. McCann, *W.S.R.O.*)

There is a useful detailed description of some properties (owned by D. & C. and Vicars Choral) in the Parliamentary Survey of 1649 (*W.S.R.O.* Cap. 1/30). In 1604 there were 7 inn-holders, 34 alehouse keepers and 2 vintners (Ballard). The population in 1524 was about 2,000, and in 1740, 3,712 (May). Buildings, etc., for which there is documentary or archaeological evidence are described below.

List of Abbreviations

A.C.	*Ancient Charters (W.S.R.O. Cap. 1/17).*
B.C.	*Boxgrove Chartulary (S.R.S. 59).*
C.C.	*Cathedral Chartulary (S.R.S. 46).*
Ch.C.	*Chantry Certificate.*
Ch.	*Chapter Acts (S.R.S. 52).*
C.P.	*Chichester Papers.*

C.W.	*Chichester Wills (in W.S.R.O.).*
City N.18	*Quarter Sessions Rolls (in W.S.R.O.).*
C.L.	*City Council Leases.*
City A.Y.	*City Rentals (in W.S.R.O.).*
Cutten	*Cutten Papers (W.S.R.O.).*
D. & C.	*Dean and Chapter.*
D.C.L.	*Dean and Chapter Leases (W.S.R.O. Cap. 1/27).*
Dobell	*Dobell Deeds (S.R.S. 29).*
G.	*Goodwood Records (W.S.R.O.).*
H.T.	*Hearth Tax (S.A.C. 24).*
Harris MSS.	*Harris Family MSS (in W.S.R.O.).*
P.M.	*Post Mortem Inquisitions.*
P.S.	*Parliamentary Survey (W.S.R.O. Cap. 1/30).*
R. (with date)	*=earliest documentary records seen in W.S.R.O.*
Rp.	*Raper MSS (W.S.R.O.).*
S.A.C.	*Sussex Archaeological Collections.*
S.M.L.	*St. Mary's Hospital Leases (W.S.R.O. Cap. IV/5).*
S.R.S.	*Sussex Record Society.*
V.C.H.	*Victoria County History, Sussex.*
V.C.L.	*Vicars Choral Leases (W.S.R.O. Cap. III/5A).*
V.P.	*View of Frankpledge (W.S.R.O. K1-7).*
W.D.	*West Dean Catalogue.*
W.S.R.O.	*West Sussex Record Office Document reference.*

Acknowledgements

The card index of documentary sources, from which this gazetteer has been prepared, has been laboriously compiled over the last eight years by the Chichester Documentary Research Group. I am greatly indebted to Sheila Morgan, Brian Bird and Jeanne Corah who have done a great deal of hard work, and very particularly to the County Archivist and her staff (especially Alison and Tim McCann and Peter Wilkinson) for their constant support and guidance.

North East Quadrant

This quadrant continued to be the major business and market area, with most of the small churches and the civic buildings.

North Street (east side).
* *1. Guildhall Street to Greyfriars (No. 61); *W.S.R.O.* Add. MSS. 12519/27 and 2886/7; *H.T.*; *A.C.*; *C.L.* 140; *W.D.* 101. Tenements, malthouses, gardens, R. 1670.
* †2. St. Peters, North Street ("The Less").
     Demolished 1957.
* †3. Old Guidhall.
* †4. Property to south; *A.C.* 73.
* *5. "Old Cross" site; *P.S.*; *H.T.*; *V.C.L.*
     Previously "Green Dragon". 12 hearths in 1670.
* 6. No. 70 and adjoining properties; *D.C.L.*; *P.S.*; *H.T.*
     70 known as "Collins" (*D. & C.* No. 113), R. 1577.
* *7. Assembly Rooms and Council House; *C.L.*; *V.C.H.* Vol. 3, p. 78.
* *8. St. Olav's Church.

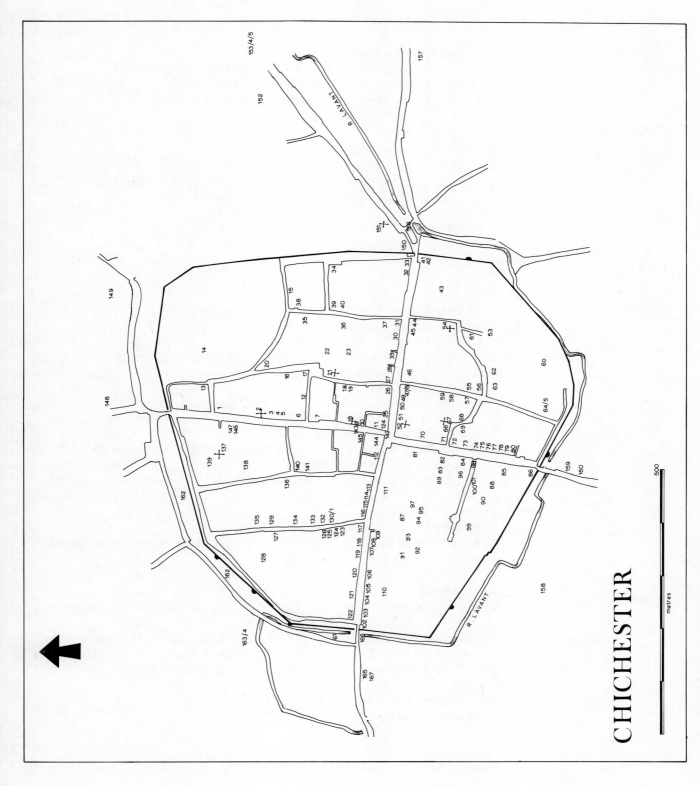

CHICHESTER

metres

500

Fig. 6.1 Plan of post-medieval sites 1450–1750

†9. St. Olav's Rectory.
10. Market House site; *C.L.*, *H.T.*
    Previously "Crown" Inn, then tenements.
11. No. 84; *W.S.R.O.* Add. MSS. 10927; *C.P.* 46.
    "Little Anchor" Inn.

Lion Street (Custom House Lane).
12. Slaughterhouse on north side 1581; *G.* (E3938).
†* *Shamble Alley* (Crooked S Lane; Trumpet Lane); *C.P.* 24; *S.A.C.* Vol. 50.
    For foot passengers only. Contained butchers' stalls.

Priory Lane.
†13. St Peter-near-the-Guildhall.
*†14. Grayfriars (Priory Park); *C.P.* 2; *V.C.H.* Vol. 3, p. 80.
    Chancel used by City as Guildhall from 1541 to 1731 and for Assizes until
    1768; grounds leased and house built thereon.
*15. Quakers' Meeting House; *V.C.H.* Vol. 3, p. 164.
    18th century.

St. Martins Lane.
41 dwellings by 1780.
*16. Tiled Barn; *S.M.L.*
    "Lately built" 1608.
*17. No. 3 St. Martin's Square; *V.C.H.* Vol. 3, p. 78; *C.P.* 24.
    Custom House in 18th century.
18. North Corner Crooked S Lane; *Ch.C.*; *W.S.R.O.* Add. MSS. 2585; *C.L.*;
    C.P. 46. Owned by Brotherhood of St. George, then City; tenements and
    stable; Trumpet Inn.
19. Tenement south of Crooked S Lane; *W.S.R.O.* Add. MSS. 1479 and 12525;
    H.T. Called "St. George's Row".
20. North end to Hospital; *S.M.L.*
    Orchard and barns of St. Mary's Farm, with mansion house in northern
    apex, burnt down by 1678. By 1750 the Street frontage had been developed
    with tenements, stable and carthouses leaving orchard still in the centre.
†21. St. Martin's Church. Demolished 1906.
†*22. St. Mary's Hospital.
†23. Great Garden of St. Mary's Hospital; *S.M.L.*
    Area south of Hospital continued as garden, with barns, street frontages
    only being developed.

East Street (north side).
24. Corner of North Street; *S.M.L.*; *Willis* (Spershott); *H.T.*; Shop, etc.,
    R. 1669.
25. Westminster Bank site; *Ch.*; *W.S.R.O.* Add. MSS. 10592; *C.P.* 46.
    Known before 1527 as "Swan", later "Royal Swan". "Low timber built
    house" 1718. Rebuilt early 18th century. 12 hearths 1670. Burnt down 1897
    (then a shop).
26. West corner of St. Martin's Lane; *C.L.*
    Messuage known as "White Oven".

CHICHESTER

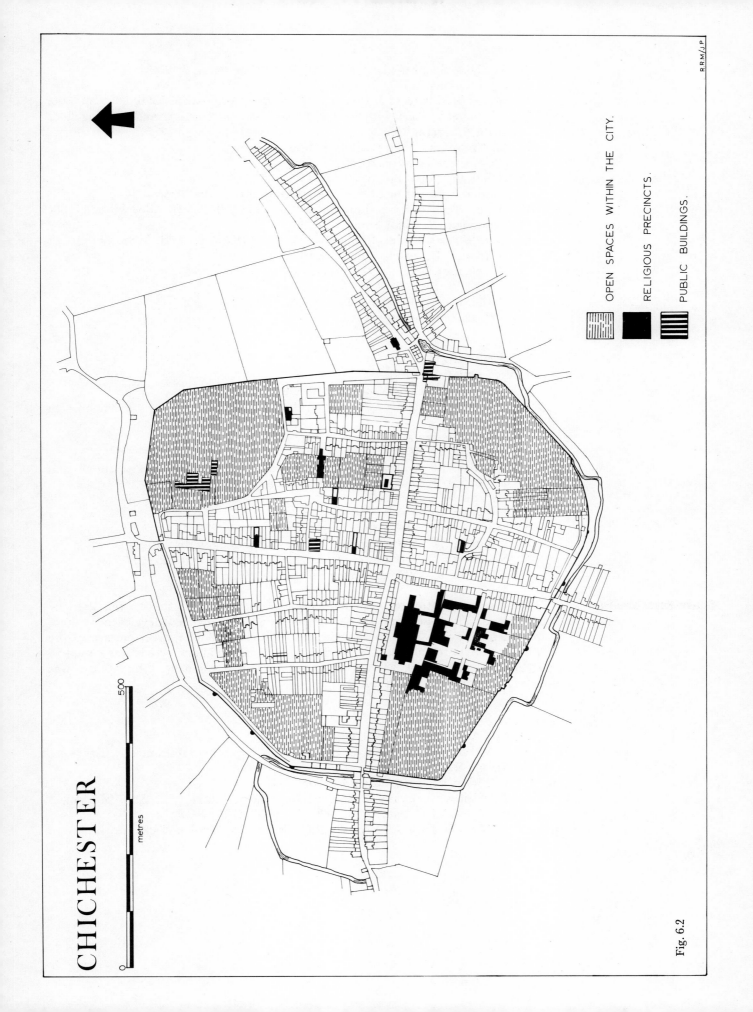

metres 500

OPEN SPACES WITHIN THE CITY.

RELIGIOUS PRECINCTS.

PUBLIC BUILDINGS.

Fig. 6.2

RRM/JP

27. Marks & Spencer Site; *W.S.R.O.* Add. MSS. 2846; *H.T.*
     2 messuages 1737.
28. No. 21 East Street; *D.C.L.*; *P.S.*; *W.S.R.O.* Add. MSS. 5996, etc.; *Rp.* 608.
     Tenement 1556 with way to Church on east: cellars and malting floor
     1649; 9 hearths 1670.
*†29. St. Andrew's Church and Cemetery; *V.P.*
     Cemetery mentioned 1491.
†30. Cow Lane (Vico Bovum); *V.P.*
     Encroachment in 1491. Through route from East Street.
31. West Corner of Little London; *D.C.L.*; *P.S.*; *W.S.R.O.* Add. MSS. 11188;
     Tenements *R.* 1583; Shop in 1649.
32. No. 48/9 East Street (Shippams); *S.M.L.*; *W.S.R.O.* Add. MSS. 11190.
     Robert Hitchcock, pinmaker 1663.
33. No. 50 East Street; *S.M.L.* (abut); *C.L.*
     Land *R.* 1663.
34. Corner of East Row and East Walls (south) *C.L.*
     Croft and Buildings 1456.

Little London (Savory Lane).
33 dwelling houses by 1780.
35. From Hospital north to Priory Road; *S.M.L.*
     Known as "Bowling Green". On orchard of St. Mary's Farm in 17th
     century.
36. Tenements (west side); *S.M.L.*; *R.* 1683.
37. Malthouse; *S.M.L.*
     Malthouse in 1695, previously a Meeting House, later a stable and
     granary; then part of King of Prussia Inn.
38. Cockpit House; *H.T.*
     4 hearths in 1670.
39. Museum; *C.L.*; *W.S.R.O.* Add. MSS. 5632, etc.; *H.T.*
     Garden *R.* 1529; messuage, malthouse and stable by 1750.
40. Nos. 31 and 32; *W.S.R.O.* Add. MSS. 5632, etc., and 2254; *H.T.*
     Garden *R.* 1598; tenements in 1641.

South East Quadrant

The quadrant continued to be dominated by the Blackfriars Land, even after the
Dissolution, as it passed into single ownership which restricted development there
until the New Town area building in the 19th century. The street pattern of the
4 Pallant Streets remained. The road east from East Pallant which was closed in
1289 (*Chichester* 2; p. 10, 18) was partly reconstituted when St. John's Street was
constructed in the 19th century.

East Street (south side).
†41. City Gaol; *S.A.C.* 89; *S.A.C.* 79.
     At Eastgate. Built by proceeds of Sale of Workhouse Lands by City.
†42. Forge; *S.A.C.* 89.
     Within Eastgate, adjoining Gaol 1473.
†43. Blackfriars (including Corn Exchange Site); *V.C.H.* Vol. 2, p. 94; Vol. 3
     p. 77; *W.S.R.O.* Add. MSS. 999, 2920–39, 6155; *P.M.*
     After the Dissolution of the Blackfriars (8th October 1538) nearly all the

buildings were pulled down. In 1610 only turret of Church, gatehouse and outbuildings remained, but there was a messuage called "Blackfriars" about 1600. Passed through several families. Eventually mansion house built on East Street frontage by Page family.

44. No. 57; *D.C.L.*; *P.S.*
    Stable and little house in 1581; shop in 1649.

45. No. 58/9 (Bell Inn); *C.L.*; *R.* 1629; *C.P.* 46; *G.* (E. 1827); *W.S.R.O.* Add. MSS. 10617.
    Also known as "Coach", "Fleece", "Golden Fleece", "Coach and Horses", "Coach and Bell".

46. No. 76/7; *D.C.L.*; *P.S.*; *H.T.*
    House and abuttals *R.* 1573. Known as "Millwards". 5 hearths 1670.

47. No. 80; *C.P.* 46.
    George Inn, recorded 1623.

48. Nos. 81/2; *C.P.* 46; *V.C.H.* Vol. 3, pp. 92–3.
    Hall of Guild of St. George.

49. No. 83; *D.C.L.*; *P.S.*; *A.C.*
    Granted to *D. & C.* 1492–3; recorded as houses or shops thereafter, with gateroom leading to N. Pallant at rear of No. 80; in 1649 had malting floor and loft at rear.

50. No. 84; *D.C.L.*
    R. 1492–3 (tenement) as abuttal of No. 83.

51. No. 87/9; *D.C.L.*; *H.T.*; *P.S.*
    New built tenement in 1536–7. Described as "Star" in 1574 and shop in 1588–9.

*52. No. 90/92; *S.M.L.*; *H.T.*; *C.P.* 46; *V.C.H.* Vol. 3, p. 75.
    No. 91 was previously Parsonage House of St. Mary-in-Foro. No. 92 "Royal Arms" commonly known as "Old Punch House". Present house built in 1595.

53. *Friary Lane* (George Street); *B.C.*; *D.C.L.*; *Chichester* 2, p. 10.
    Was moved eastwards to present position in 1763.

Baffins Lane (Meeting House Lane).

*54. Baffins Hall (Meeting House); *V.C.H.* Vol. 3, p. 164; *W.S.R.O.* Add. MSS. 5667.
    Unitarian Church (Presbyterian or Dissenters).

North Pallant.

55. No. 8; *W.S.R.O.* Add. MSS. 1479; *H.T.*
    Capital messuage with malthouses 1635; 10 hearths 1670.

*56. Pallant House; *V.C.H.* Vol. 3, p. 76; *C.P.* 4; *H.T.*
    5 hearths in 1670; "Plough" 1684; Henry Peckham built present house about 1712.

57. No. 11; *A.C.*; *D.C.L.*; *P.S.*; *C.P.* 46.
    Tenements *R.* 1464: "Globe" in 1683, with orchard.

58. No. 12; *A.C.*; *D.C.L.*; *P.S.*; *H.T.*
    "Trentmarks" *R.* 1435 (tenement and garden and free access to All Saints); 8 hearths in 1670. House of Thomas Miller (Mayor, M.P., Bt.).

59. No. 13 (City Club); *A.C.*; Harris MSS.; *D.C.L.*; *P.S.*
    Tenement 1435; "Spread Eagle" in 1604.

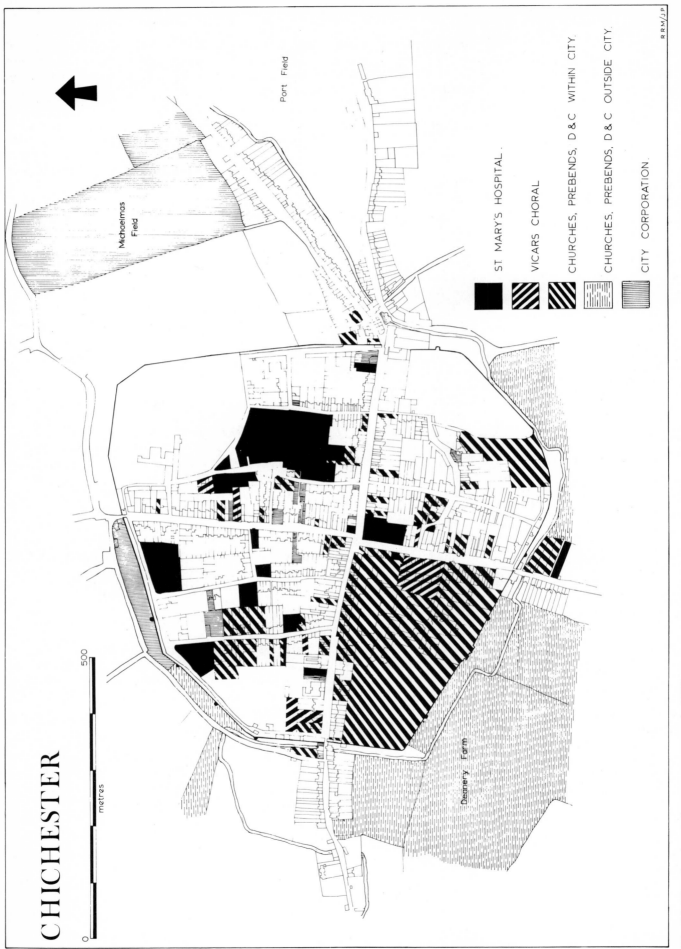

CHICHESTER

Port Field

Michaelmas Field

Deanery Farm

metres

0   500

ST MARY'S HOSPITAL.

VICARS CHORAL

CHURCHES, PREBENDS, D & C WITHIN CITY.

CHURCHES, PREBENDS, D & C OUTSIDE CITY.

CITY CORPORATION.

R RM/JP

Fig. 6.3 Map showing main property owners in 1750

East Pallant.
    60. "Sickleases"; *D.C.L.*; *P.S.*
          1½ acres, divided much of time into 4 gardens, orchards and cottages.
    61. Culverhouse Close; *S.M.L.*; *W.S.R.O.* Add. MSS. 12543.
          Croft of land; workhouse 1737, previously barn *R.* 1695.
    62. Nos. 3–6; *C.L.*; *D.C.L.*
          Messuage and garden; *D. & C.*; *R.* 1562.
    63. Tenement and garden (south side); *D.C.L.*; *R.* 1555.

South Pallant (Plough Lane).
    64. East side; *W.S.R.O.* Add. MSS. 2596.
          Messuage newly built in 1599 with 2 acres adjoining and cottage to north.
 *65. No. 5; *C.P.* 4.
          1689 on house.

West Pallant.
 †66. Parsonage House; *C.P.* 5; *S.M.L.*; All Saints Terrier.
*†67. All Saints Church.
    68. Tenements to east of Church; *D.C.L.*; *H.T.*; *P.S.*; *R.* 1539.
    69. Opposite Church; *S.M.L.*; Dobell Deeds.
          Tenement and shop used as a stable in 1676–7.

South Street (east side).
    70. Nos. 62–75; *S.M.L.*
          Continuous recording of properties (see *Chichester* 2, p. 11), throughout this period.
    71. "White Horse" Inn; *V.C.L.*; *P.S.*; *Rp.*; *C.P.* 46; *V.C.H.* Vol. 3, p. 77.
    72. No. 60; *W.S.R.O.* Add. MSS. 12516/22.
          2 messuages in 1684.
    73. No. 55 (Supermarket); *V.C.H.* Vol. 3, p. 76; *S.R.S.* 29 (No. 692); *W.S.R.O.* Add. MSS. 1674 and 11188; *Willis* (Spershott) p. 67.
          Farrington's house in 1609: "large house" in 1718.
    74. No. 54; *D.C.L.*
          Formerly 2 stables, then tenement.
    75. No. 51; *D.C.L.*; *P.S.*
          R. 1562 (tenement); "new built" 1649 (hall, wainscotted parlour, 5 chambers over, woodyard).
    76. "King's Head" Inn; *D.C.L.*; *P.S.*
          R. 1562 (tenement); 1649; "7 low rooms, 5 over, stable, woodyard".
          Landlords named from 1740.
    77. No. 46; *D.C.L.*
          R. 1562 (tenement).
    78. No. 43; *D.C.L.*
          R. 1562 (tenement).
    79. Regnum Club (No. 45); *Rp.*
          House of Thomas Miller 1687, then Sir John Miller.
    80. Old Theatre; *C.P.* 9; *Rp.*
          1669 "Great messuage", subsequently malthouse and granary, adapted as theatre in 1764. Present building erected 1791 by tontine subscription.

This quadrant continued under Cathedral domination.

South Street (west side).

81. Cross to Vicar's Hall; *D.C.L.*; *S.M.L.*; *P.S.*
    The whole row was in the ownership of the *D. & C.* and St. Mary's during the period; mainly shops.

*†82. Undercroft (White Horse Cellar).

*†83. Vicars' Hall.

84. Vicars' Hall to Canongate; *V.C.L.*; *P.S.*
    Vicars' Choral properties (see 96 below).

85. Canongate to No. 33; *D.C.L.*; *P.S.*
    All in ownership of *D. & C.*; *R.* 1569, of tenements with gardens.

86. Within Southgate; *C.L.*; *W.S.R.O.* Add. MSS. 237 and 8779; *G.* (E 4253).
    Messuage and stable, *R.* 1436.

Close.

*†87. Cathedral.

88. Chantry and Choristers Garden; *D.C.L.*

*†89. Chapel of St. Faith.

*†90. Deanery; *P.S.*; *S.R.S.* 52.
    Present building 1725. Original building adjoined south wall; was damaged in Civil War Siege and by 1649 was "much dilapidated".

*†91. Bishop's Palace and Chapel.

*†92. Gatehouse; *S.R.S.* 46.
    Built about 1327.

*†93. Treasurer's House; *P.S.*
    Earlier building on site of present one (1834).

*†94. House of Wiccamical Prebends; *V.C.H.* Vol. 3, p. 154; *P.S.*

*†95. House of Royal Chantry Priests; *V.C.H.* Vol. 3, p. 153.

*†96. Vicars' Close Properties; *C.P.* 14; *V.C.L.*
    Enclosed square until 1825 when houses backing to South Street were fronted thereto.

*†97. Paradise; *P.S.*; *D.C.L.*
    Burial ground.

*†98. Canongate; *V.C.H.* Vol. 3, p. 158–9.

*†99. Residentiary; *V.C.H.* Vol. 3, pp. 155–6.

*†100. Chantry; *V.C.H.* Vol. 3, p. 156.

101. House south side of Canon Lane (front of Chantry); *D.C.L.*; *P.S.*; *R.* 1595; stable by 1649.

West Street (south side).

*†102. Toll House.
    Described as "Porter's Lodge" in 16th and 17th centuries.

*†103. Castle Inn; *D.C.L.*; *H.T.*; *C.P.* 46.
    2 little tenements in 1569; described as "ruined and decayed" in 1649. "Three Kings" in 1754; lately "Duke of Richmonds Arms". Present name by 1792.

104. Nos. 39–40; *W.S.R.O.* Add. MSS. 6373 and 12510; *G.* (E. 3453). *R.* 1611 (tenements and garden).

105. No. 44; *C.P.* 46.
  "Coopers Arms" to 1880 then "Red Lion".
106. Nos. 47–51; *D.C.L.*; *H.T.*
  R. 1566 of tenements, shops and gardens.
*†107. Prebendal School.
108. No. 53; *S.R.S.* 52.
  Was "Subdean's Place".
109. No. 54; *D.C.L.*; *H.T.*
  R. 1562 (tenement and garden).
110. Chancellor's Garden; *D.C.L.*
  Behind all above properties, to boundary of Bishop's Garden. Surrounded by stone wall.
111. From Bell Tower to West Street; *D.C.L.*; *C.P.* 46; *P.S.*; *H.T.*; *C.C.*; *V.C.H.* Vol. 3, p. 73.
  Row of tenements, inns and shops with Churchyard or Sun Gate at West end, Middle Gate in centre of row and Cross Gate at East end. Further row of tenements, yards and stables behind and adjoining Churchyard wall. The inns were "Coach and Horses" ("Sun"), by Bell Tower, "Royal Oak" ("Star"), "Crown" ("Crown and Sceptre"). All the properties were demolished in 1848/52.

North West Quadrant

This quadrant continued to have a low density of population throughout the period although the two main streets attracted ribbon development at an early stage. Tower Street, Chapel Street, Crane Street and North Walls Walk had only isolated properties until the end of the 16th century.

There were still no churches right through to 1750; the first ever in the quadrant was St. Peter the Great (19th century). The internal street pattern was, however, established by 1450 and continued throughout the period. The quadrant was the last in Chichester to develop with intensive building and the medieval pattern of gardens and pastures continued into the 17th century, indeed the County Hall main site was still pasture up to the present century.

West Street (north side).
*112. Dolphin and Anchor; *C.P.* 23; *W.S.R.O.* Add. MSS. 5233–4; *H.T.*
  Earliest reference (Dolphin) in 1649; 23 hearths in 1670. Originally two inns with shop between.
113. No. 11; *D.C.L.* (Abuttals).
  Tenement, *R.* 1554.
114. No. 12 (Morants); *D.C.L.*; *H.T.*
  R. 1554 "newly erected" 1611; 13 hearths 1670; "Royal Oak".
115. No. 13 (Morants); *D.C.L.*; *S.R.S.* 58; *C.W.*; Dobell; *P.S.*; *H.T.*
  "The Boot"; Tenement and gardens *R.* 1554; 7 hearths 1670.
*116. Oliver Whitby School (Morants); *V.C.H.* Vol. 3, p. 74.
  Founded 1702.
*117. St. Peters (Subdeanery).
  Previously Custom House.
118. Nos. 19–21; *D.C.L.*
  4 tenements and gardens *R.* 1539.

119. Nos. 23–4; *S.M.L.*; *H.T.*
    Tenements from 1670.
*120. "John Edes House"; *C.P.* 52; *W.S.R.O.* Add. MSS. 6457–9; *V.C.H.* Vol. 3, p. 73.
    Present house completed 1696. Also known as "Westgate" House.
121. Nos. 29–30; *W.S.R.O.* Add. MSS. 11414–9; *V.C.L.*
    Dwellinghouse 1739.
122. Nos. 34–5; *A.C.*; *D.C.L.*; Cutten; *P.S.*; *H.T.*
    "Brinkhurst", 2 tenements and gardens *R.* 1477.

Tower Street (Lower West Lane).
13 dwelling houses (1–4 tenements) by 1780.
123. Nos. 3/4; *V.C.L.*; *P.S.*
    Tenements *R.* 1603.
124. Nos. 5/6; *G.* (E. 1780/1); *H.T.*
    Tenement in 1602.
125. Nos. 7/8; *V.C.L.*; *P.S.*
    R. 1609.
126. Library (No. 9) St. Richards House; *D.C.L.*; *C.W.*; *P.S.*
    Tenement *R.* 1521.
127. No. 21; *D.C.L.*
    Garden 1601; tenement 1618.
128. Common Barns and Long Croft; *D.C.L.*; *P.S.*; *W.S.R.O.* Add. MSS. 6392/6 and 6421/2 and 8493; *C.W.*; *City N.* 18.
    With tenement called Blackhurst and Rectory of St. Peter the Great. Corn, hay and pulses grown in 1613. Barns, cottages and stable in 1649. Scene of disastrous fire in 1654.
129. No. 30; *D.C.L.*; *W.S.R.O.* Add. MSS. 1901–26.
    Gardens up to early 17th century then up to 8 tenements.
130. No. 46; *D.C.L.*; *P.S.*
    Church Storehouse in 1562; 9-roomed house in 1649.
131. Nos. 43–5; *S.M.L.*
    Garden prior to 1678; subsequently tenement and Poor House for parish of St. Peter the Great.
132. No. 44; *S.R.S.* 52; *W.S.R.O.* Add. MSS. 6156.
    "Culverhouse Garden" 1527.
133. Lancastrian Grange Site; *D.C.L.*
    Gardens in 1527; tenements in 1713.
134. St. Peter's Vicarage; *D.C.L.*; *P.S.*; *H.T.*
    Gardens in 1580; tenements in 1649.
135. Gardens of Bishop Arundel's Chantry; *S.A.C.* 92.
    Valuation of 1535.

Chapel Street (Upper West Lane).
Contained 20 dwellings (1–4 tenements) by 1780.
136. Central Girls' School Site (demolished 1975); *S.M.L.*
    Tenements and gardens recorded from 1625; 4 cottages on site by 1726. To north of the site a garden and barn in 1580.
†137. St. Cyriac's Chapel (see p. 25).

138. Gardens of North Street houses.
   The north-east part of Chapel Street had little separate existence, being the gardens of the properties on the west side of North Street.
139. Cherry Garden; *S.M.L.*
   Croft of land *R.* 1588.
140. No. 19 (Corner of Crane Street); *S.M.L.*; *W.S.R.O.* Add MSS. 2458; *H.T.*
   Variously stable and garden, tenements, storehouse, malthouse with vaulted cellar before becoming Independent Chapel in 1796.
141. Rear of Perrings; *S.M.L.*
   "Three Tuns", previously tenements.

North Street (west side).
*142. Cross; *C.P.* 1; *V.C.H.* Vol. 3, p. 73; *City AY* 105.
   Erected about 1500.
143. Old Corn Market House; Ballard; *Willis* (Spershott).
   Stood on posts close to channel in middle of street.
144. Nos. 1–6; *D.C.L.*; *P.S.*; *H.T.*
   Shops and tenements *R.* 1556.
145. Nos. 7–8; *D.C.L.*
146. Fernleigh site; *W.S.R.O.* Add. MSS. 6146–7; *P.S.*; *D.C.L.*; *A.C.*
   Previously a brewhouse and banquetting house (2 buildings, one behind the other).
147. Nos. 41–2; *A.C.*
   Tenements 1520.

Outside the Walls

Outside Northgate.
Mainly 19th- and 20th-century development. During the study period there was very little domestic development and throughout this was mainly farmland belonging to the City and St. Mary's Hospital Farm and included Broyle Farm, Penny Acre, Horsedown, Sloe Fair Field and Spittalfield.
*148. Cawley Almshouses; *V.C.H.* Vol. 3, p. 81.
   Founded as almshouses in 1625/6; converted by City into workhouse 1681. United Poorhouse 1753, with extensions added subsequently.
149. Pesthouse; *V.C.H.* Vol. 3, p. 82.
   Erected 1665. Demolished 1920.

Outside Eastgate.
The Chichester needle manufacturing industry probably started in the 16th century and was soon concentrated, but not exclusively, in St. Pancras, and until the Civil War, Chichester had much of the English manufacturing trade. Much of the parish was destroyed in the Civil War Siege, both by attackers and defenders. The rebuilding of the houses was slow (14th-century references to, e.g. Richard de Nedler may refer to needle vendors).
150. Eastgate (north) outside wall; *S.R.S.* 58; *D.C.L.*
   Forge and blacksmith's tenement *R.* 1574; subsequently a timber yard.
*†151. St. Pancras Church; *V.C.H.* Vol. 3, p. 166.
   Destroyed in siege (1642); rebuilt 1750.
152. Michaelmas Fair Field; *C.L.*; *W.S.R.O.* Add. MSS. 10617.
153. Joy's Croft; *C.L.*

*154. Hospital of St. James and St. Mary Magdalen.
155. St. James' post; *V.C.H.* Vol. 3, p. 82. Stone obelisk dated 1714 (former N–E boundary of City).
*156. Eastgate Chapel (formerly Baptist, then Unitarian); *V.C.H.* Vol. 3, pp. 82 and 164; *S.A.C.* 29, p. 221; *W.S.R.O.* Baptist Records.
Completed 1728; previous building 1673.
157. Portfield, Guildenfield; *C.L.*; *D.C.L.*

Outside Southgate.
Mainly 18th-century development. Tenements demolished while Chichester was a garrison town and during Civil War period.
158. Deanery Farm and Hop Gardens; *P.S.*; *D.C.L.*; *W.S.R.O.* Cap. II/4/1; *Harris MSS.*
Contained Mansion House, houses, barns, stables. Demolished in Civil War. Continued as farming unit throughout period.
159. East side Southgate; *D.C.L.* and *S.M.L.*
R. 1607.
160. Richmond Terrace; *W.S.C.C.* deeds.
Previous tenement and garden 1687.

Outside Westgate.
Mainly 18th-century development.
161. No. 8 Orchard Street; *W.S.R.O.* Cap. II/4/12.
Previous house burnt down in Civil War Siege; since barn.
162. South side Orchard Street; *C.L.*; *G.* (E. 1796–1824); *W.S.R.O.* Add. MSS. 10600–3.
"Realls" and "Campis" Meadow and barn, nursery.
163. Potters' Field; *W.S.R.O.* Add. MSS. 6145.
Name referred to in Tithe Award Map 1847; of earlier origin.
164. Scuttery Field; *D.C.L.*; *C.L.*
R. 1479. Arable land, cottage.
*†165. St. Bartholomew's Church; *V.C.H.* Vol. 3, p. 161.
Previous Church destroyed 1642.
166. White Horse Inn, Westgate; *D.C.L.* and *P.S.* (Abuttals); *C.P.* 46.
167. Tannery; *W.S.R.O.* Add. MSS. 10812.

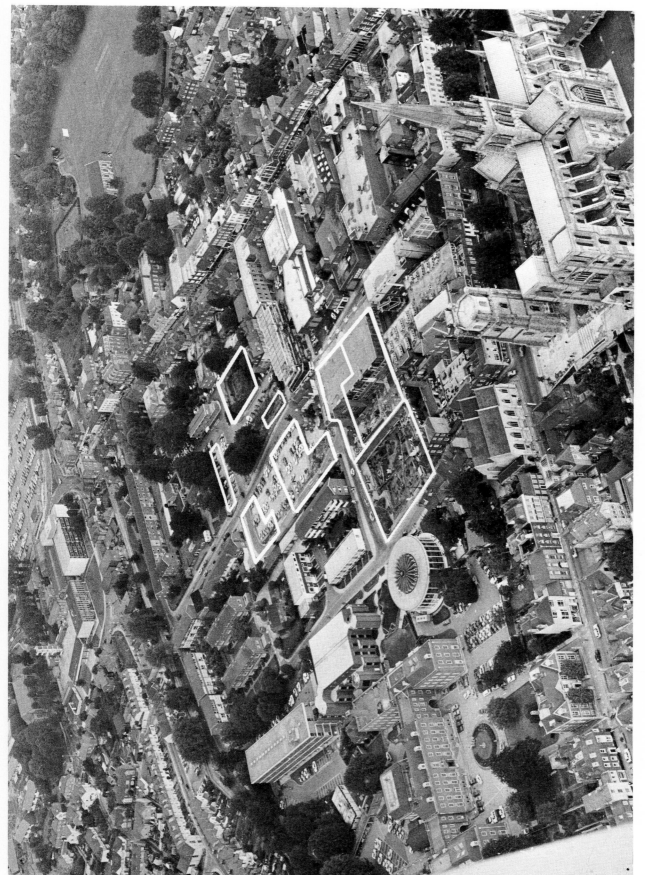

1. North-west Quadrant, looking north-east. Aerial view of excavation sites. (Photo: Jerome O'Hea)

2. Area 2, Trench G, looking south. A: Kiln 1, B: Kiln 2, C: partly robbed wall of House 2.
(Photo: G. Claridge RIBA)

3. Area 2, Trench G. Roman street 2 with partially robbed wall of House 2 on right and postholes of Saxon building cutting street. (Photo: G. Claridge RIBA)

7

Excavations in the North-West Quadrant, 1968–75

**Introduction
(Fig. 7.1 and Pl. 1)**

In 1967, trial excavations by the present writer on land at the rear of Smurthwaite's shop in North Street (*Down* 1967), located a north–south Roman street with timber buildings on the east side and late Saxon pits cutting the street. The point was made in the report that any further opportunities to excavate in the area should be followed up, as it was of outstanding archaeological importance.

Less than two years later the City Council offered to allow excavations on a piecemeal basis on the temporary car park which replaced Smurthwaite's garden, and the offer was accepted. The area initially excavated comprised a long strip alongside the 1967 trial trenches (Area 1), so as to follow up the features noted there. From this small acorn grew a very large oak: seven years and seven sites later a total of over 4,000 square metres had been dug in the vicinity and a wealth of information about all periods of the City's history extracted.

Before Area 1 had been completed, the Diocesan Board of Education, who owned the Central Girls School on the west side of Chapel Street (Area 2), gave us permission to excavate in the playground on the west side of the school in advance of their sale of the property to the Post Office Corporation for development. The site changed hands soon afterwards, but by then the results coming in from the excavation enabled us to make out a convincing case to the Post Office, who readily agreed to allow the work to continue unchecked and also arranged for demolition of other properties owned by them in the vicinity so that the investigation could proceed unhampered, well in advance of their own plans. This was co-operation on the grand scale and was of tremendous value to the excavators as it meant that much of the work could be carried out at a relatively slow pace. In addition to the school site we were offered, and accepted, the Wool Store (Area 3), Clemens Yard (Area 4), and Gospel Hall site (Area 5). We also held a watching brief over the groundwork for Post Office Building No. 1, when 16,000 cubic yards of spoil were excavated by machine.

This enabled us to plan part of the Roman Thermae and submit a case for excavating the adjacent car park in Tower Street in advance of development. The Chichester City Council were no less generous in making available Purchase's Garden and the area north of Crane Street (Area 6), and finally, in 1974, the Tower Street car park and the builders site to the south (Area 7), were handed over for total excavation in advance of the proposed multi-storey car park project, which would destroy all the archaeological layers on the site.

The result of the chain reaction sparked off by the initial trial excavation and report has been to provide, for the first time in Chichester, a properly stratified sequence for the Roman occupation over a wide area, and a significant advance in our knowledge of the late Saxon, medieval and post-medieval periods. Without the goodwill of the organisations mentioned above, this could not have been achieved; without the skill, devotion and hard work of the standing army of volunteer excavators, the task could not have been attempted.

During the seven years in which the North-West Quadrant sites were being dug, work went on in other areas both inside and outside the town, and most of these

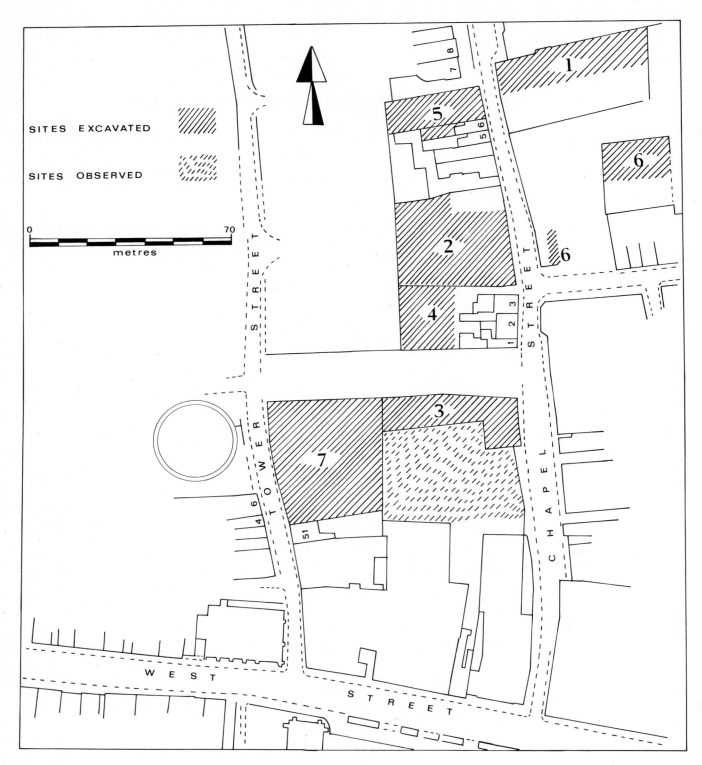

Fig. 7.1

have been published in Volumes 1 and 2. From the North-West Quadrant alone came over 2,400 small finds and more than 8 tonnes of pottery; over 54,000 hours of volunteer labour went into the excavation in addition to countless unrecorded hours of behind-the-scenes work in the laboratory and pottery store.

It is impossible, for reasons of space to mention by name everyone who took part in this marathon effort, although grateful acknowledgements to the supervisors and specialist assistants is given elsewhere. The best monument to the work of the volunteers is this report, which records as faithfully as may be, their achievements.

Summary

Pre-Roman occupation

The evidence for a pre-Conquest settlement on the site of Chichester has now accumulated to the point where it merits serious consideration. The North-West Quadrant excavations yielded a total of fourteen Early Iron Age coins; an amphorae stamp which could date from 1st century B.C. to A.D. 10 at the latest; a number of Arretine sherds, some of which are of Augustan date and a group of Gallo-Belgic imports, seen both at Fishbourne and Chichester, which appear to be too early to be classified as "invasion" wares. Against this is the absence (so far), of structures which can be attributed to a pre-Roman occupation, or groups of pre-Conquest Atrebatic coarse wares which an Early Iron Age settlement should have. There is a hint of an ancient turf line in Area 2 below the earliest military timber buildings, and elsewhere, in Areas 3 and 7 there were occupation layers below the earliest features, but insufficient evidence is available to show that they were pre-invasion levels. If the dating of the fine wares is reliable, then it is possible, if not highly probable, that the North-West Quadrant sites are peripheral to an earlier Atrebatic settlement.

Roman

The military occupation

A number of timber buildings were found along the west side of Chapel Street (Areas 2, 3, 4 and 5), of which at least one phase, and probably two others, was military. The regularity of the plan suggests that they were barrack buildings. Many fragments of 1st-century legionary equipment were found, and there is no doubt that the area was part of the Second Legion's base camp and that this occupation dates from late A.D. 43. The original base camp may have lasted for perhaps two years at the most, but there remains a possibility that some form of military depot may have been present for a longer period of time.

The timber buildings seen in Areas 3 and 7 (Figs. 7.24–7.52) were probably store buildings, and they appear to have remained standing for some time before being demolished, with the site remaining undeveloped and possibly waterlogged until the late Flavian period.

Industrial activity

Two pottery kilns producing high class imitation Gallo-Belgic butt beakers and other fine wares were found in Area 2. The kiln products are not common in Chichester and the possibility that these kilns were either served by legionary potters or were owned by contractors making pots for the legion, cannot be discounted. This phase of activity post-dates the Period 1 timber buildings in Area 2 and may again perhaps point to a depot activity. Roughly contemporary with the potteries

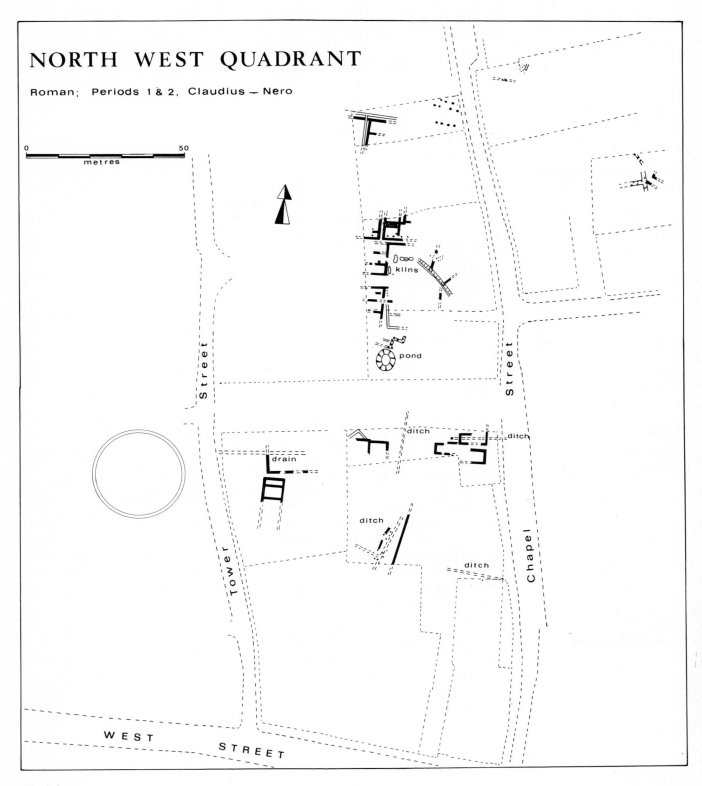

NORTH WEST QUADRANT

Roman; Periods 1 & 2, Claudius — Nero

0 ____ 50
metres

kilns

pond

Street

Street

ditch

ditch

drain

ditch

ditch

Tower

Chapel

WEST STREET

Fig. 7.2

was the enamelling of small objects, probably of jewellery. Many small crucibles were found with a vitreous glaze on the rim showing that they had been used for this purpose and this type of work may have continued for some decades.

The development of the native town

During the early Flavian period (Period 3), a range of more substantial buildings replaced the timber structures alongside Chapel Street. They show evidence of regular planning and may represent the earliest buildings erected in the native town of King Cogidubnus.

Towards the end of the 1st century, the streets were laid out and it is likely that the construction of the Thermae (Area 7) and other important public buildings were commenced slightly earlier, during the lifetime of the old King. It seems that the town's development may have slowed down after his death, when the client kingdom of the Regni would have passed fully under Roman control, and there is now conclusive evidence to show that the landscaping of the central area of the town, which was covered by a vast spread of gravel, was not completed until well on into the 2nd century.

The Thermae

Excavations in Areas 3 and 7, linked with earlier work and observations on service trenches have shown that the Thermae complex is approximately 5,500 square metres in area, with most of it lying below Morants and the houses north of the church of St. Peter the Great. A number of phases of alteration were noted. The water was supplied from a cistern located in the working area north of the baths, the waste being drained back into one of the main sewers which ran along the northern boundary.

Antonine to early 4th century

A series of timber buildings existed alongside the Roman street in the Chapel Street sites. These were replaced in the late 3rd to early 4th centuries by substantial masonry built houses on the north-west and south-west corners of the cross roads (Houses 1 and 2).

4th to 5th century

By the late 4th century the houses were partly in decay and the streets unrepaired. There is evidence of a sub-division of some of the rooms and corridors in House 1, with wattle partitions being erected and hearths built upon the tessellated pavements. Layers of rubbish and silt accumulated on the streets, and the town drains (repaired in the earlier part of the century), were silted up and the timber revetment collapsed. The general impression is one of neglect and slow decay. The coin series appears to end in the last quarter of the 4th century, but although no new money was reaching the town, a money economy may have continued in use until well on into the 5th century.

Late Saxon

There was considerable occupation of the areas along both sides of Chapel Street and on the east side of Tower Street in the late Saxon period. In the 8th to 10th centuries, pottery and coins constitute the only evidence, but slight remains of timber structures were located in Areas 2 and 5 which probably date to 11th to early 12th century. This appeared, from a study of the pits, to have been the peak period of Anglo-Saxon occupation, and the picture which emerges is of small peasant holdings, sometimes on and sometimes alongside the old Roman streets.

45

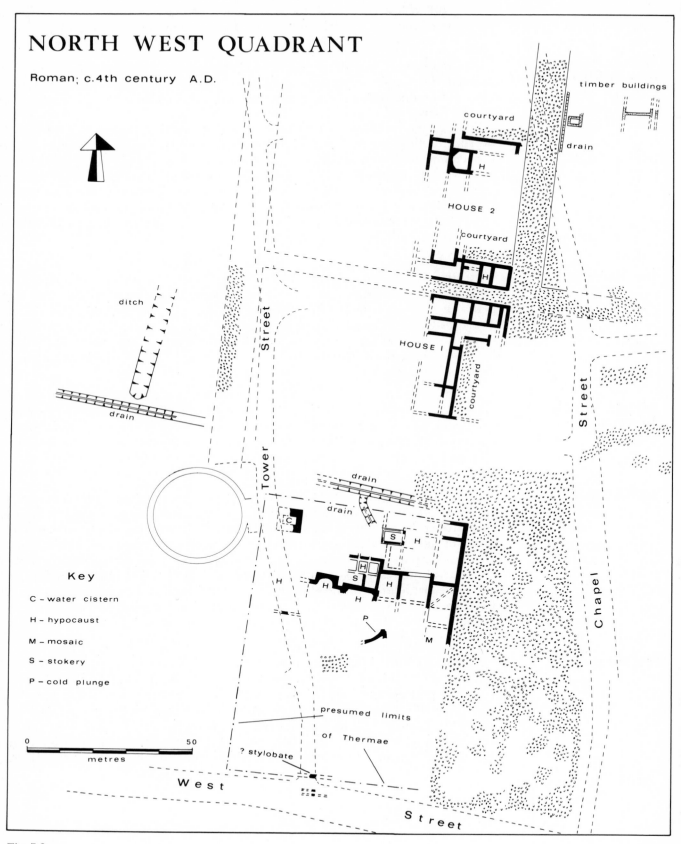

NORTH WEST QUADRANT

Roman; c.4th century A.D.

timber buildings

courtyard

drain

HOUSE 2

courtyard

H

ditch

Street

HOUSE 1

courtyard

drain

Street

drain

Tower

drain

C

S

H

H

S

H

H

H

Chapel

Key

C – water cistern

H – hypocaust

M – mosaic

S – stokery

P – cold plunge

P

M

presumed limits

of Thermae

0   50

metres

? stylobate

West   Street

Fig. 7.3

Medieval

From the early 12th to the 16th century, domestic occupation in the Chapel Street area appears to have been sparse, with most of the holdings being farmland or garden. In Area 6 (Purchase's Garden), evidence for medieval cultivation is clearly seen, and this may be linked with the documentary evidence for a holding of John de Sancta Cruce in the 13th century.

In Tower Street, the picture is quite different. A succession of medieval timber houses dating from *c.* 13th century, and fronting on to Tower Street were recognised, with part of a later, 15th-century masonry house at the south end.

Part of the site was used by itinerant bell founders in the 14th century, to cast bells for the cathedral.

Post-Medieval

Documentary sources show that most of the land in Area 7 was owned by the Dean and Chapter and St. Mary's Hospital until fairly recent times. They show evidence for a succession of tenements and a storebuilding from the 13th century up to the time when the National and Lancastrian Schools were built on either side of the Fighting Cocks Public House, in the 19th century.

Area 1. Chapel Street, Trenches A.1, A.2, A.3 and A.4 (Figs. 7.4–7.5)

The trial excavations of 1967 had shown the eastern edge of a Roman street with timber buildings alongside it and with late Saxon pits cutting the Roman levels. The street sealed earlier Roman layers which could only be briefly examined at that time. Our return to the site in 1968 at the invitation of the City Council was conditioned by the need to preserve at least two-thirds of the temporary car park at a time. This policy entirely ruled out a large area strip excavation and it was thought best under the circumstances to cut a long trench along the north side of the site alongside and to the north of the 1967 trial trenches. Trenches A.1 and A.2 were cut first, with A.3 and A.4 being an extension eastwards, but these last two trenches were utterly featureless, all stratification having been destroyed by centuries of cesspit digging. They are therefore excluded from the discussion.

Roman: Period 1; Phase 1, pre-Flavian

The earliest level on the site was A.1.26, which was a gingery clay adjudged to be natural, but with some occupation tread upon it and cut by a number of small postholes and shallow pits. The pits produced only small featureless scraps of Roman grey ware, but trodden into the layer were two sherds of South Gaulish samian dated Claudius–Nero. The only other feature noted was part of a building of post-trench construction (A.27), and two scraps of Gallo-Belgic white ware were recovered from the slot. It is not certain whether there is more than one phase of activity represented here. The features, with the exception of the slot, were sealed by layers of clay, A.14 and 23, which were barren of pottery, and these in turn were sealed by the gravel layers making up the street.

Further east in A.2, was a pit, A.42, which was sealed by a layer of clay and which contained no coarse pottery likely to be later than Flavian, together with three sherds of samian classified "1st century", and this pit is assigned to Period 1 on that evidence together with that of the stratification.

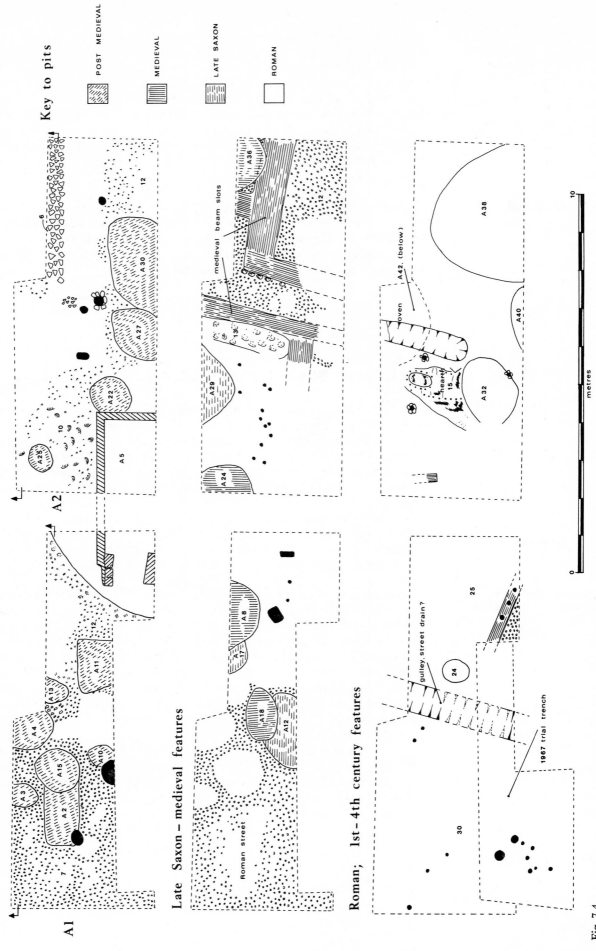

AREA 1, TRENCH A

Post medieval, c. 16th – 19th centuries

Late Saxon – medieval features

Roman; 1st – 4th century features

Key to pits

POST MEDIEVAL

MEDIEVAL

LATE SAXON

ROMAN

medieval beam slots

Roman street

gulley, street drain?

1967 trial trench

oven

hearth

metres

Fig. 7.4

Period 2; Phase 1,
c. **late 1st–early**
2nd century

At some time in the late 1st century (see below, Area 2), the Roman street was laid down. This is classified as Street 1 in all later discussions and is the Roman ancestor of the late Saxon street which ultimately became Chapel Street. It runs from north to south and crosses Chapel Street at an oblique angle (Fig. 7.3). Only the eastern part of the street was sectioned, and this was badly cut about by later pits. There were at least four loads of gravel dumped, spread and compacted, with three layers of bonding material used between. This usually consisted of dirty gritty soil, but in some areas (see Areas 2 and 3) clay and chalk, and sometimes sand, was used as a bonding agent. The layers noted above may have represented an initial metalling followed by three phases of re-metalling, but they were clean and featureless except for the top layer (A.1.7) which had a sticky tread upon it and medieval pottery trodden into it. It is more likely that the bottom two layers at least were laid as part of one operation. No dating evidence was recovered from the metalling.

A small U-shaped gulley (Gulley 1) ran alongside the street on the east side and may have served as a drain although this could not be established with certainty. It contained mid-1st-century coarse ware types including imitation T.N. platters, but as it was truncated and not related directly to the street there is a possibility that it might be an earlier, Period 1, feature. Just east of the street in A.1 was a layer of occupation material (A.1.9) with many oyster shells, containing Flavian and 1st-century samian together with residual Gallo-Belgic wares. Further east, in A.2 and probably contemporary was a layer of brown clay (A.2.14), badly cut away by pits. This contained 1st-century wares and a samian sherd of Trajanic date.

Contemporary with this layer were two hearths, one superimposed upon the other, both surrounded by a number of small stakeholes, and immediately adjacent on the east side, a rectangular oven which was filled with compacted Roman wall plaster after it went out of use. Three stone packed postholes which form a right-angle may be associated with this period as may be the short length of slot for a timber beam. The hearths were partly destroyed by Pit A.32 which had nothing later than Trajanic samian in it. The disabilities inherent in narrow trench excavations were nowhere more apparent than here, but it can still be seen that the occupation at this point on the east side of the Roman street at the turn of the 1st century was of modest proportions and consisted of small domestic timber buildings with associated hearth and pits. This reinforced the impressions gained from the earlier trial excavations.

Period 2; Phase 2,
Antonine

Only one feature can be placed in phase 2, this is Pit A.38, which contained no later material than Antonine samian.

Period 3; late Roman,
c. **4th century**

The period 2 hearths were sealed by a layer of brown clay through which were cut a number of stakeholes relating to a later structure which may have been medieval. The clay contained two late colour-coated wares from the New Forest, dating to the 4th century.

Large numbers of 4th-century pottery sherds were found in A.3 and A.4 in the heavily churned-up layers resulting from the cesspit digging of later centuries, but as in 1967, no structures were found which could be related. It may well be that the substantial late Roman occupation which is attested by these wares, would have fronted on to the Roman North Street.

Period 4; late Saxon
c. **10th–11th century**

Only three pits and no structures can be assigned to this period. One pit (A.12) was cut through the Roman street and produced large quantities of late Saxon and

AREA 1

Trench A 2, North Section

Trench A 1, North Section

grey sticky earth

gravel & brown earth

compacted gravel

clay & flints

clay & oyster shells

silty clay

yellow clay

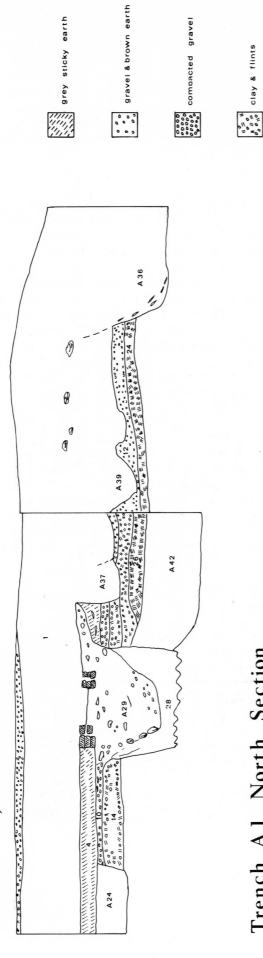

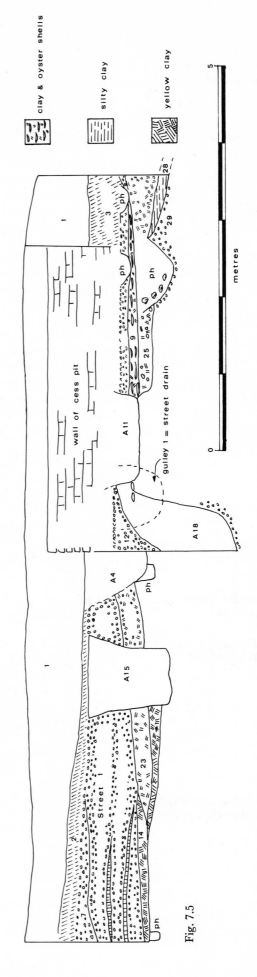

Fig. 7.5

0   5

metres

Saxo-Norman wares, a selection of which are published below (p. 345 and Fig. 11.2). They comprised Porchester type rilled wares, numbers of shallow pans with crimped and straight rims and several complete cooking pots. The other two pits (A.17 and A.29) had similar wares.

A discussion on the evidence for middle to late Saxon occupation in the area is presented with the section of the report dealing with Areas 2 and 7 and will not be anticipated here.

Period 5; Medieval, c. 12th–13th century

(a) *Structures*

Attenuated elements of four structures can perhaps be deduced from the features shown on the plan (Fig. 7.4).

At the east end of the trench A.2 were shallow slots relating to two timber-framed buildings. These were cut into a layer of gravel, A.2.12, which contained nothing later than medieval roof tiles and unglazed coarse wares of *c.* 12th–13th century, and a residual sherd of middle Saxon ware, *c.* 7th–8th century. West of the slots was a pattern of stakeholes which suggests part of a wattle construction. The stakeholes cut the late Roman clay layer which may itself be demolished daub from a Roman building and the stakeholes are obviously later. They are tentatively assigned to Period 5 but could quite as easily belong to Period 4.

Further west in A.1 were four postholes, two large and two small, which appear to be part of a series. One posthole had three coarse-ware medieval sherds in it; the remainder were barren, but the level from which they were dug indicates a Period 5 date.

(b) *Pits*

Four pits, A.8, A.18, A.24 and A.36, are assessed as Period 4 on the evidence of their contents, which were medieval coarse wares and residual Saxon-Norman fabrics. No glazed wares were found, and the pits are likely to be 12th–13th century rather than later.

Period 6; Post medieval, late 15th–17th centuries

The Roman and medieval layers were cut by a number of post-medieval pits and a few postholes which cannot be assigned to any one phase. The pits are grouped according to what evidence is available, and are briefly discussed below.

Phase 1, c. 15th century
Pits A.2 and A.30. The latest dated artifacts in these pits were painted wares of the middle 15th to early 16th centuries. These were present in significant quantities and were mainly unabraded. The 19th century pit A.4 also had a number of painted ware sherds and roof tiles of contemporary date.

Phase 2, 16th–17th centuries
Pit A.13. Period 7; 19th century.
Pits A.4 and A.11, contained Victorian and earlier wares.

Discussion

This admittedly small sample shows some interesting gaps. No glazed wares of the 13th–14th centuries were noted in the pits of the medieval period, and there seems to be a gap from the coarse wares of the early medieval period until the post-medieval painted wares make their appearance. This might indicate a lack of building development on this side of Parislane (Chapel Street) in the medieval period, and it could be because the land on the east side of the street belonged in many instances to holdings extending through from North Street and that the tenements and associated cesspits are further east. The presence of painted-ware types and roof tiles of the same period points to a 15th-century tenement nearby, probably fronting on to Parislane.

Areas 2 and 4—Central Girls School and Clemens Yard (Figs. 7.6–7.22)

These two sites are adjacent and it is convenient to deal with them together. Area 2, the Central Girls School site was excavated from 1969 to 1972, and Area 4, Clemens Yard, which abuts it to the south, was completed during 1973.

Area 2 comprised Trenches E, F, G, H, K, J and L; Trench K was a trial trench cut along the front (east) of the School while it was still standing, in order to test the extent of the gravel metalling eastwards from the Roman cross roads (see below). The results were duplicated when the school building was demolished and Trench K is, therefore, excluded from this discussion. Area 4 consisted of one trench (M), which was cut immediately south of Trench E in Area 2.

Period 0; A.D. 43 at the latest

This could only be identified with any certainty in part of Trench G and is represented by a thin spread of dark organic clay (G.200) resting directly on to natural clay, and may be the remains of an ancient turf line. Several small sherds of undateable grey ware and a few scraps of food bones were found trodden into it and it is possible that these may derive from a pre-Roman source. Part of this layer showed some disturbance (G.188) and this area yielded a small fragment of Arretine ware.

Period 1; c. A.D. 43 plus

This phase is defined as the first recognisable layer resting upon natural clay and producing evidence of Roman occupation:

Trench G/H

Occupation spread (G.190) above (G.200) turf line. Provincial Arretine wares, Tiberio-Claudian samian and Gallo-Belgic fine wares, together with early 1st-century coarse ware types including bead rimmed jars.

Trench J

J.98 was a layer of brown silty clay resting upon natural gravel. Two sherds of Tiberian provincial Arretine were found in it, together with Gallo Belgic fine wares and contemporary coarse wares. A pit, partly in the south section (Pit J.36) may also belong to this phase. It was truncated by a later timber slot and the fill indicates an early date. Two fragments of Tiberian provincial Arretine were found in the fill, together with rusticated and white painted wares.

Trench E

Layer E.182 and E.154 rested upon E.210 (natural). The samian is Claudian with one piece of Tiberian Arretine.

52

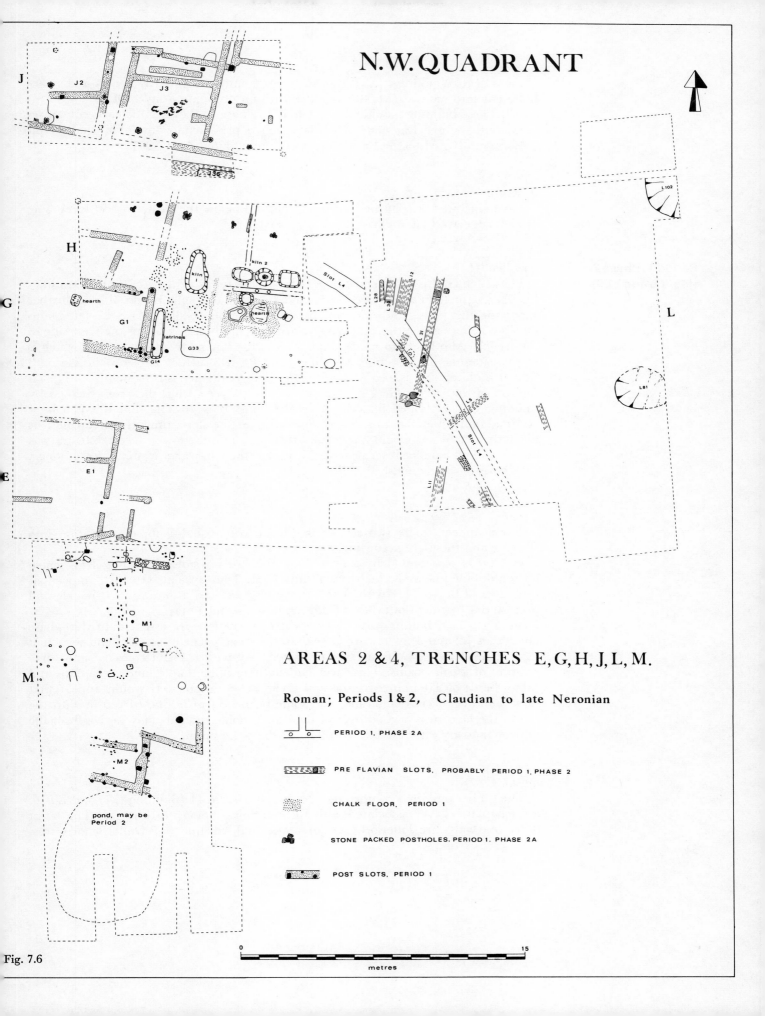

N.W. QUADRANT

AREAS 2 & 4, TRENCHES E, G, H, J, L, M.

Roman; Periods 1 & 2,   Claudian to late Neronian

PERIOD 1. PHASE 2A

PRE FLAVIAN SLOTS, PROBABLY PERIOD 1. PHASE 2

CHALK FLOOR. PERIOD 1

STONE PACKED POSTHOLES. PERIOD 1. PHASE 2A

POST SLOTS, PERIOD 1

Fig. 7.6

0   15

metres

Trench M

Parts of two buildings (M.1 and M.2) represented by patterns of post and stake-holes cut into natural (M.68), together with an occupation layer M.71, and a pit M.82. These buildings could in fact belong to Phase 2; they are the earliest features in M and the one fragment of samian gives a pre-Flavian date. The shallow pit (M.82), cutting M.68, had a fragment of samian dated A.D. 30–45.

Trench L

Layer 115 was the churned up top of natural below the earliest street level. The samian suggests a Claudian date.

**Period 1; Phase 2
(Fig. 7.6 and Pl. 6)**

Trench G/H

Phase 2 in G/H is represented by a series of slots for two ranges of timber buildings together with their associated floors and hearths. It might be possible to further subdivide this phase into (a) and (b), with the slots (G.35) below the later kilns possibly being earlier than the slots relating to the building along the west side of the trench. Also likely to be contemporary is the latrine trench Slot G.14 which is just outside one of the timber buildings, and Pit G.33 which is below the Period 3 timber building and is also a cesspit. The dating evidence is consistently early, but the top of the latrine G.14 and the occupation layer within the area enclosed by Building G.1 contained material from the kilns. It is possible that this is a later accumulation; had the kilns been functioning at the same time as the latrine it is likely that the wares would have found their way into the lowest levels, but this was not so, and on balance it seems more likely that the kiln wares accumulated amongst the debris of the demolished buildings.

Trench J

There appear to be two sets of buildings which qualify for classification into Phase 2 and these are accordingly listed as 2(a) and (b).
Phase 2(a) is represented by a set of stone packed postholes (Building J.1), which form a double line and which extend into G/H. They are cut into J.93, an occupation layer of brown clay with charcoal, which produced a military belt buckle and plate and a fragment of armour from the lorica segmentata.
Phase 2(b). Two buildings of post trench construction are assigned to this phase (Buildings J.2 and 3). They are later than the stone-packed postholes and were first seen at the level of G.86, a layer of brown clay with a lot of charcoal and some residues of burnt beams. This layer had nothing later than Claudian samian and three sherds of Tiberian Arretine and Gallo-Belgic imports. It would appear that these buildings were demolished and some beams burnt *in situ*. Mixed in with the top of the layer was a good deal of sand and chalk, and this may derive from the pottery industry later established a few yards to the south.

Trench E

The timber buildings comprising slots 5, 7, 8, 10 and 11 (Building E.1) and E.216, an occupation layer associated with the buildings, belong to Phase 2. The latest dated fine wares are Tiberio/Claudian samian and Arretine, plus Gallo-Belgic wares.

Trench M

No features can be assigned to Phase 2 unless, as suggested above, the three fragments of buildings tentatively placed in Phase 1 belong here.

Trench L

A series of slots were cut into the natural below the area covered by the later Roman cross roads. They were all disassociated lengths, some of them on the same alignment as the Phase 2 timber buildings in G/H, J and E, and it is likely that these may belong to the same phase. Only in one slot (L.12) was any dating evidence found. This had a chip of first century samian with a sherd of provincial Arretine of Tiberian date. All these slots appear to pre-date the curved slot L.4, which is also likely to be pre-Flavian (see below).

Two pits on the east side of Trench L are pre-Flavian and are assigned to Phase 2. Both are latrines; Pit L.81 has early samian, none later than Claudian, together with crucible fragments and Pit L.102 was constructed as a *pissoir* with the sides being lined with amphorae sherds. The make-up layers which subsided into the pit had Flavian samian, but the lower levels of fill had nothing later than Claudian together with many lumps of vitrified clay, probably from a demolished oven or kiln.

AREA 2, KILN 1

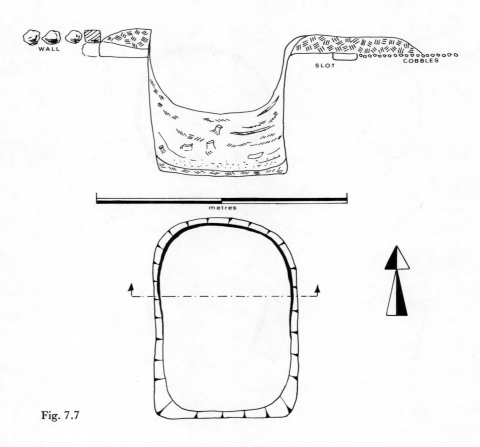

Fig. 7.7

Trench G/H: The Kilns

Two kilns were found, dug through the Period 1 layers.

Kiln 1 was a small updraught kiln aligned north–south and fired from the south end. It was first identified as Pit G.40, and two large greensand slabs, postbases for the Period 3 building, had partially slumped into the fill. The kiln cut away the west side of the Period 1 chalk floor, and also part of one of the Period 1, Phase 2 slots (see Fig. 7.7).

The firing chamber was small and traces of burning on the clay were noticeable only at the base, probably because the kiln was fitted with a clay brick lining (see below). It was apparent that the kiln had been dismantled and then backfilled, and the backfilled material included many pottery wasters and some waste Reading clay.

Kiln 2. This was 1.25 metres east of Kiln 1 and aligned east–west. There was a stoking chamber at each end, with a small step cut in at the rear, presumably as a seat for the stoker. The kiln was abandoned in working condition with the firing chamber still lined with clay bricks and the central plinth to support the radial kiln bars still in position. The fill was similar to that of Kiln 1. The firing chamber was built in the shape of an inverted cone. It was lined with small, slightly curved clay bricks which were rectangular in section, and these were keyed in so as to give a

AREA 2, KILN 2.

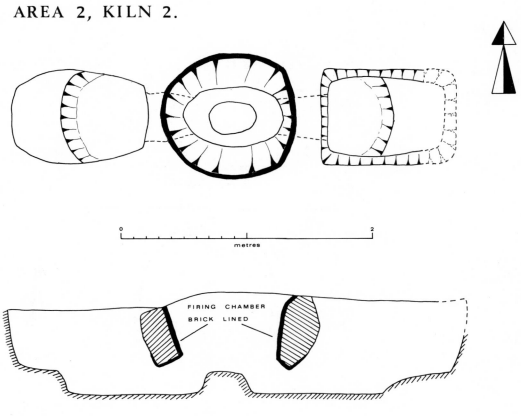

Fig. 7.8

"basket weave" effect. The wall of the firing chamber behind the bricks was baked red, and it is likely that at least one firing was carried out to thoroughly dry out the clay before the bricks were put in. There were probably built in "green", i.e. unfired, and baked in the first firing. The life of the kilns cannot be estimated; it would have been possible to replace the brick lining in both kilns on a number of occasions and it cannot be established whether both kilns functioned at the same time. It is quite possible that they did, although not simultaneously. The alignment of the two kilns would give a choice of three wind directions, with kiln 1 being used when a strong south or south-west wind was blowing. Kiln 2 may have been fired from both ends at once or from one end at a time. Experiments in re-firing this (see below) using both ends at once were successful.

The discovery of Kiln 2 coincided with the conclusion of some pottery firing experiments carried out at the Chilgrove Roman villa sites using kilns constructed for the purpose and pottery in imitation Romano-British forms made in a variety of clays from the locality. Sufficient pots were left over from these experiments to enable one firing of Kiln 2 to be attempted, giving a load of approximately three-quarters of the total capacity. Bringing this kiln back into production after a lay-off of over nineteen centuries was a qualified success, with over 85% of the wares properly fired at a temperature varying between 850–900 degrees Fah.

The wares

The wasters indicate that a wide range of pottery was manufactured, from the very fine butt beakers, carinated bowls and rusticated jars, to the coarser wares, including bead rimmed jars, lids, platters, bowls and cooking pots. These are fully discussed below (pp. 204–211 and Figs. 10.3–10.5) and only a brief outline is needed here. Technically the fine wares are of a high standard of excellence, and yet until these kilns were found, very few sherds of these wares had been recognised in Chichester, and where they have been noted it has always been assumed that they were imported from Gaul in the invasion period or just after. The question as to whether the potters operating these kilns were working for the military is a valid one and must be considered on its merits and this is discussed more fully elsewhere in this volume (p. 210).

Other industrial processes

Directly associated with the kilns were two pits (Fig. 7.6). One was a small pit on the south side of Kiln 2. It was filled with waste Reading clay and pottery wasters and was partly cut away by a timber beam partition belonging to the later Period 3 building. The second pit (H.17) was lined with Reading clay and was probably a puddling pit. It contained a fragment of a crucible used in enamelling (see below, p. 254), and together with the fragment found in the pond in Area 4 is the earliest stratified example of this type of industrial activity that we have, and the indications are that it was earlier or at least contemporary with the kilns.

Whether this enamelling was associated with bronze working is not clear, but it seems certain that the items enamelled were small, having regard to the size of the crucibles. Brooches, studs and loop fasteners are likely products and it seems logical to suppose that the enamelling would be an end process in the manufacturing chain, and that the articles were also made nearby. There is a hint that the glass frit may also have been produced (p. 255). Two small hearths in Trench E (E.189 and 206) may have been part of this process. Both had crucibles and E.189 had a piece of glass frit. There is some doubt about their date; they may have operated in the pre-Flavian periods and were sealed by layers containing late 1st century samian.

The majority of the several hundred crucible fragments come from later layers, and while some of them are undoubtedly residual in these contexts it may be safest to assume that some are not, and that this metal working and enamelling phase went on for some time, probably being moved from one locality to another. The earliest possible date is now seen to be Period 2, at a time when other forms of industrial activity were present or had just vacated the site. The terminal date can only be guessed at, but there is no reason why the industry could not have functioned at least up to the end of the 1st century.

Period 2; Phase 2
Fig. 7.6

Trench M

At the south end of Trench M was a large depression filled with silty clay with alternate bands of charcoal which appeared to have been deposited by flotation. In the bottom of the silt was part of a small crucible (see above) and a silver minim of Epaticcvs. The Flavian timber building (M.4) extended southwards over the fill, and while the top layers of clay and charcoal (M.74 and 77) had Flavian pottery, the earlier clayey silt (M.83) had nothing later than Neronian samian. The feature itself may have originally been dug for clay, but there seems no doubt that it functioned as a pond for some considerable time afterwards and that during this period a large amount of charcoal was deposited in it at intervals, resulting in the flotation layers described above (see also Fig. 7.9). It seems on what evidence is available that the pond must fall somewhere between Period 1 and Period 3 and it is therefore assigned to Period 2, Phase 2.

Trench L

Above the slots classified as Period 1, Phase 2, was a wide slot (Slot L.4). This had originally been dug to a width of 1.75 metres and then it appears that some form of shallow revetment was inserted, reducing the width to 1.3 metres, with gravel packing being laid behind the insert.

The slot was shallow, slightly stepped along the west side and had a thin layer of sandy silt in the bottom. Above this, the later street metalling had pressed down into it. It was noted that the slot curved slightly but definitely off to the northwest, to the point where it was completely destroyed by the deep foundations of the 4th-century House 2.

The function is uncertain, but it may have been a shallow, timber-lined drain. The fine silt in the bottom contained a pre-Flavian samian stamp and a few chips classified "1st century" and a bronze zoomorphic loop fastener (Fig. 10.35, No. 72) which was probably military in origin although in design it may have Iron Age affinities.

Period 3; *c.* Flavian to early 2nd century

Phase 1

Trench G/H

At some time after the Period 2 kilns went out of use and were backfilled, a building (G.2) was constructed on the site on a north–south alignment. It comprised substantial flint and greensand footings 0.5 metre wide which probably supported a timber framing. It had two buttresses or pad bases on the west and south sides and was 5 metres wide and at least 5.5 metres long on the north–south axis. The full extent of the building northwards could not be established with certainty as the

58

Section R–R

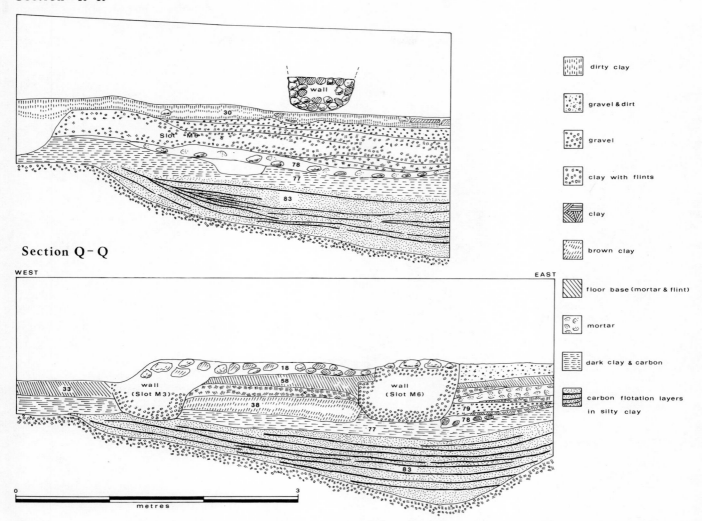

Section Q–Q

Fig. 7.9

4th-century house foundations and hypocaust destroyed it. There is a slight hint of a wall in the presence of a few flints below the hypocaust floor but this line cannot be proved. The building was sub-divided by a slot (G.22) for a timber beam which cuts away one of the puddling pits belonging to the earlier kilns. One hearth (G.179) set against the south wall, can definitely be assigned to this building. Two postholes (G.178 and 179) were inserted into the floor separated only by a large flint, and a third posthole (G.117), which cuts a kiln puddling pit, is probably contemporary.

A spread of dirty occupation material (G.130) inside the building produced many bronze studs and three fragments of kiln beakers in addition to food debris. No close dating evidence was recovered from the occupation layer within the building, but it clearly postdates the kilns and is sealed by a layer of clay (G.124) containing Flavian samian which may derive from the demolished clay walls of the building. It is accordingly assigned a Flavian date although there is a possibility that it might be earlier. It is unlikely to have had a long life (see below, Phase 3).

59

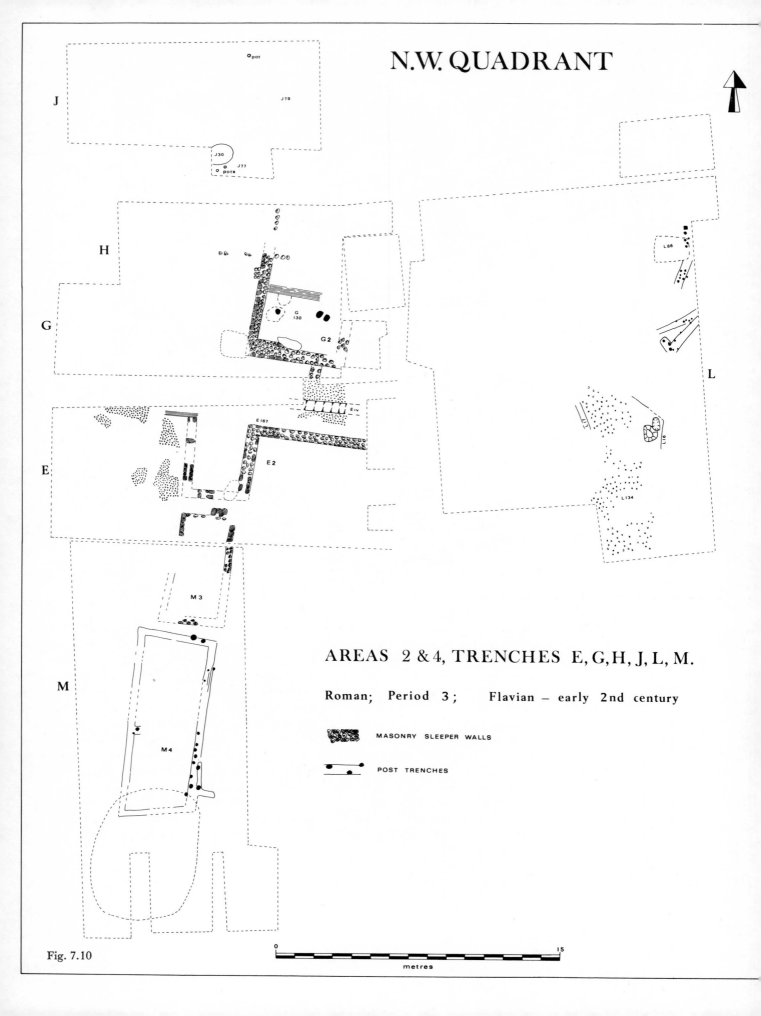

N.W. QUADRANT

AREAS 2 & 4, TRENCHES E, G, H, J, L, M.

Roman; Period 3; Flavian — early 2nd century

MASONRY SLEEPER WALLS

POST TRENCHES

Fig. 7.10

0   15

metres

4. Kiln 2 after re-firing. The clay brick lining of the firing chamber can be seen just above the makeshift kiln bars.

5. Area 2, Trench J. Late or sub-Roman hearth laid against wall of House 2, later robbed.
(Photo: G. Claridge RIBA)

6. Area 2, Trench G. Latrine, Slot G.14. (Photo: G. Claridge RIBA)

Phase 2

Trench E

Part of a building (E.2) of similar construction to Building G.2 was found. This is on the same alignment, but full details of the ground plan could not be ascertained. The east–west wall (see Fig. 7.10) which turned south and then petered out was well constructed on a flint base of which up to three courses survived in places, with the top course being finished off with squared greensand blocks. The other fragments which make up the walls are of a single course of greensand only, set in clay. The fragmentary nature of these remains make the interpretation shown in Fig. 7.10 open to some doubt and all that can be said of them is that the small sections shown were laid to make a straight line.

There was a dearth of dating evidence from inside the building as the contemporary occupation layers had been destroyed by later intrusions, but E.167, the occupation layer on the outside of the walls had Trajanic samian as the latest dated artifacts, plus one fragment of crucible.

Probably contemporary with Building E.2 was a small timber revetted drain (slot E.iv) which ran east–west, north of the north wall of the building and parallel with it. This contained large amounts of crucible fragments which may suggest that enamelling was still going on at the turn of the 1st century.

Trench M

Elements of two buildings can be seen aligned north–south (Fig. 7.10). The most northerly one (M.3), extends southwards from Trench E and appears to have been of similar construction to Building E.2, i.e. dwarf walls of flint and greensand to support a timber frame. A layer of greensand chippings (M.39) which spread over part of the foundations and is probably the collapsed upper courses of the wall, had Trajanic samian, which implies a construction date of *c*. late 1st to early 2nd century.

The second building (M.4) was of post trench construction, and the south end was built over the filled in pond (see above, p. 58). It is likely to be late or post Flavian and is probably contemporary with Building M.3.

Discussion

Of the four buildings aligned north–south in Area 2 and 4, three are constructed with cill beams for timber framed buildings and this marks a significant change in construction techniques. The fourth building is of standard post-trench construction. They appear, from their alignment, to be part of a single phase of development, but when the sparse dating evidence is looked at it seems possible but not certain, that Building G.2 might be earlier than the others, and may have had a shorter life. We may in fact be looking at a replacement of Building G.2 by E.2, M.3 and M.4, and this could be because G.2 was replaced by a slight timber building (Fig. 7.12) which in turn was demolished when Street 2 was laid out. This would help to explain the absence in G of accumulated occupation layers containing later pottery outside the building, as appears to have occurred outside Building E.2. Some support for the suggestion of an earlier demolition of Building G.2 comes from the stratification (Fig. 7.13). Slot G.22 (part of Building G.2) was sealed by two layers of clay, G.124 and G.64. The bottom layer had no samian later than Flavian, while G.64, which was immediately below the street, and into which Building G.3 was dug, had a sherd of late 1st to early 2nd-century samian.

Alternatively, these four buildings could have been constructed at the same time, with G.2 being demolished in advance of the others, but this is felt to be less likely in view of the pottery evidence. Building G.2 is accordingly assigned to Phase 1, while Buildings E.2, M.3 and M.4 are placed in Phase 2.

61

AREA 2, TRENCH E
South Section, A–A

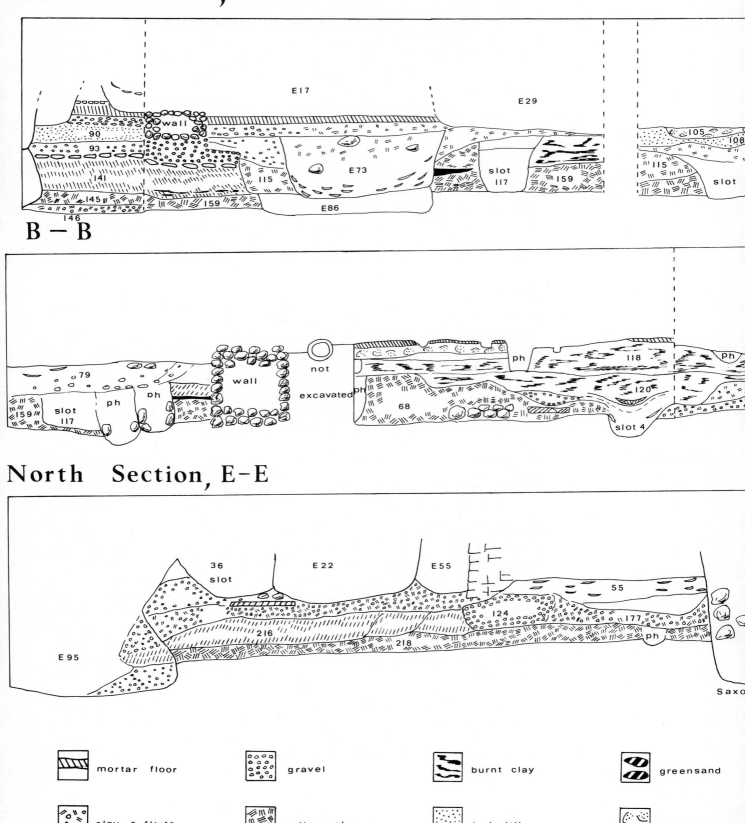

Fig. 7.11

Legend:
- mortar floor
- clay & flints
- gravel
- yellow clay
- burnt clay
- dark fill
- greensand
- mortar

0 ___ metres ___ 5

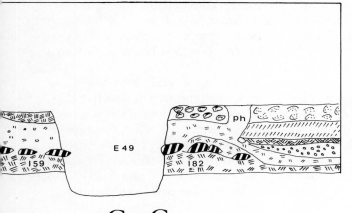

E 49

159

182

ph

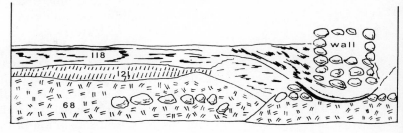

D-D

118

121

68

wall

C-C

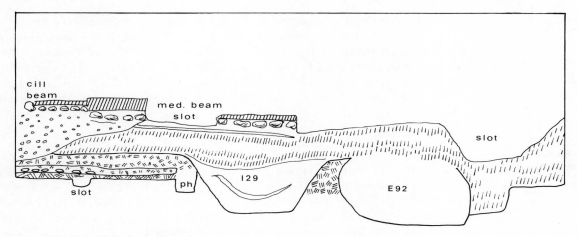

cill
beam

med. beam

slot

slot

ph

129

E 92

slot

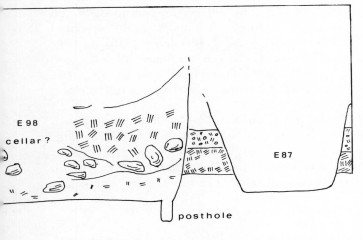

E 98
cellar?

E 87

posthole

brown clay

dirty clay

Trench L

Below the line of the later Street 1 and above L.115, was a thin layer of gravel metalling L.134/148. This was covered by a layer of greenish silt containing pottery and food debris. The gravel had a sherd of Flavian samian in it. It was discontinuous owing to many later pits cutting it, but was not thick enough to warrant consideration as a street and is more likely to have been part of a courtyard or metalled area outside a building or buildings.

A number of features may be contemporary, including several short lengths of slot (slots L.6, L.16 and L.17) and a number of random alignments of post trenches, none with any close dating evidence, but all sealed below later layers of street gravel. Slightly earlier than these, but probably within Period 3 is Pit L.88, a rectangular pit sealed by a layer of clay L.135. It is evident that more than one phase exists in the confused arrangement of slots and burnt beams on the west side of Trench L but the only firm indication of date comes from two layers, L.126 and L.147, into which one of the slots is cut. Both layers have Flavian samian and nothing later.

Trench J

No structures can be assigned to Period 3, but the contemporary ground surface is represented by the following features: J.77, a layer of dirty brown clay; J.79/80, a shallow depression in J.77 which contained many flecks of Reading clay and a large amount of residual Period 1 wares; Pit J.30, a shallow pit at the south end of the trench; J.74, a layer of soft brown clay, this had three complete but empty vessels dug into it; J.74, 77 and 79/80 all had Flavian samian as the latest dated wares.

Period 3; Phase 3, late 1st century (Fig. 7.12)

Trench G/H

At some time in the Flavian period, Building G.2 was demolished, the ground levelled up and eventually a slight timber structure (Building G.3) was erected. The date for this structure rests on the contents of two layers; G.64, a layer of clay which was above G.124 which in turn sealed Building G.2, and G.65, a thin layer of gravel which was laid down over part of G.64. Building G.3 was cut into these layers. G.64 had three Flavian samian sherds and one classified as "late 1st to early 2nd century", and G.65 had one South Gaulish samian sherd. Enough could be seen of the structure to show that it had a slight timber framing and had a plank on edge inserted inside the hut along the south wall. There are a number of stake and postholes, most of which make no coherent pattern, but which belong to this phase.

West of the building there was a good deal of burnt clay and charcoal, some of it derived from two hearths, G.70 and G.81.

On the north side of Building G.3, and partly cut away by the foundation trench for the 4th-century house was a sharply defined layer of clay with flints (G.71). This had nothing later than Vespasianic and "1st century" samian. A row of stakeholes placed close together were set along the layer in an east–west alignment, exactly on the line of the later street, and it was cut away at the east end by the drain alongside the earliest street.

Discussion

The phase of activity represented by these ephemeral structures did not last very long. The absence of any large quantities of domestic refuse suggest that perhaps the site was part of an industrial complex. The "fence" implies that at this stage the area

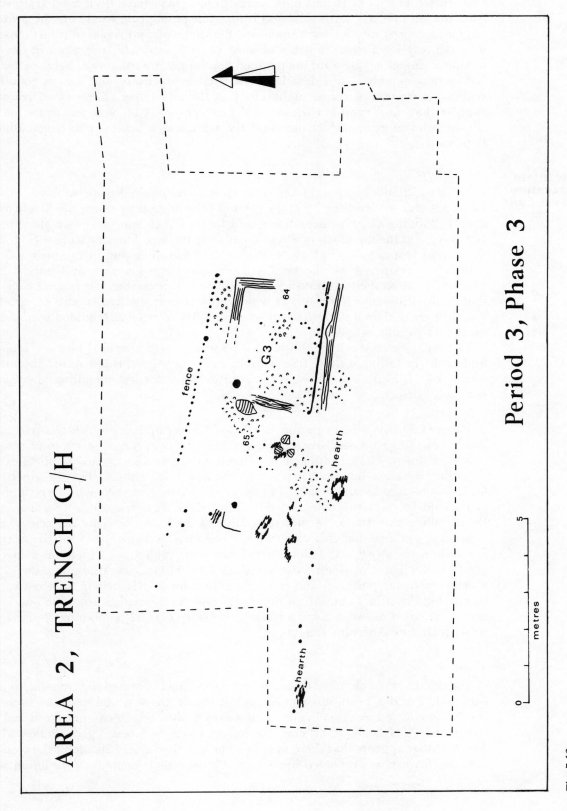

AREA 2, TRENCH G/H

Period 3, Phase 3

fence

G3

64

65

hearth

hearth

0   metres   5

Fig. 7.12

covered by Trench G/H and southwards from it may have been a separate entity from the land on the north side, and it may not perhaps be stretching the evidence too far to suggest that having demolished Building G.2 and replaced it further south to make way for a street, a delay of some years ensued which resulted in the area having a temporary use until the planned development went ahead. Such a situation is common enough in this decade of the twentieth century and can be paralleled within the context of rescue archaeology in the city today. There is no reason to suppose that the Regnii at the turn of the 1st century A.D. were any less subject to the vagaries of economic chance and the whims of a central planning authority than we are.

Period 4; early to late 2nd–early 3rd century (Fig. 7.14 and Pls. 2 and 7)
Phase 1

Trench G/H

Streets 1, 2 and 3 were laid out. This must have required the demolition of some buildings and the levelling up of the ground prior to putting down the first layers of gravel. Building G.3 was demolished and layers G.124 and G.64 (see above) were put down and the metalling of Street 2 laid over the top. The east section (Fig. 7.13) shows part of a slot alongside the lower levels of metalling and this in turn is almost completely destroyed by the later 4th-century house footings, and only a short distance away to the west no trace of it remained due to the later house being on a marginally different alignment. It would appear that the first spread of metalling was little more than a thin spread of gravel (G.61) which was bounded by the drain on the north side (see above).

The latest dated sherd for this layer is a samian sherd classified Flavian-Trajanic, and as the metalling is quite thin it could easily have been trodden into the surface afterwards. Nevertheless, an early 2nd-century date for this metalling operation is probably correct.

Phase 2

Layer G.35 (not seen in section) was a local make up layer which was part of the next re-metalling process, when a much thicker layer of dirty re-used gravel (G.32) was laid down. G.35 contained one sherd of Antonine samian, so the next re-metalling may not have taken place before mid 2nd century. The metalled layer G.32 was re-used local "hoggin" (a mixture of gravel and clay) with large amounts of tile and brick, many nails and domestic debris. The practice of re-using gravel for metalling the streets was noted in most of the many sections cut across them, suggesting perhaps that this material was collected and stockpiled for the purpose.

South of the street was a slot aligned east–west (gulley 2), which cut a layer of gravel G.85. This slot yielded two sherds of Central Gaulish Antonine samian, and together with the postholes and part of another slot (G.21) belong to a sequence of timber buildings in Trench E to the south, and is discussed below. The only other feature assigned to Phase 2 was a rectangular cesspit (G.32) containing 2nd-century wares including Antonine samian.

Phase 1

Trench L

Trench L conveniently straddled the cross roads formed by the junction of Streets 1, 2 and 3, with only small areas in the north–west and south–west corners not being covered by gravel. The earliest gravel layer which can be considered as a street surface is L.111/120, being the lowest levels of Street 1 (see section M–M, Fig. 7.16). It appears that there may have been a tiled side-walk along the west side and this feature was repeated higher up. The abraded remnants were found when

AREA 2, TRENCH G/H, SECTION G–G

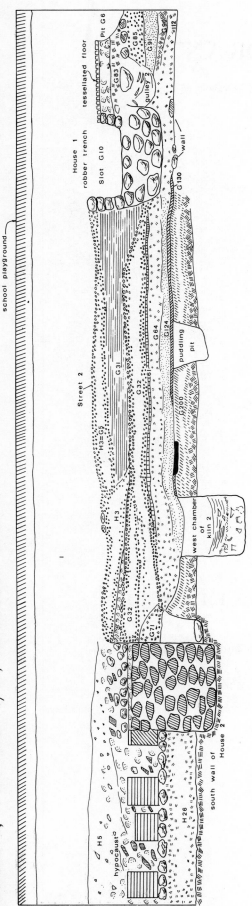

Pit G 6
tessellated floor
G85
G83
G91
House 1
robber trench
Slot G10
gulley
G96
G112
wall
G130
Street 2
G124
G64
G31
G32
G3=G5
puddling pit
H3
G200
west chamber of kiln 2
G71
G32
G32
south wall of House 2
H5
hypocaust
H26
G64

SECTION F–F

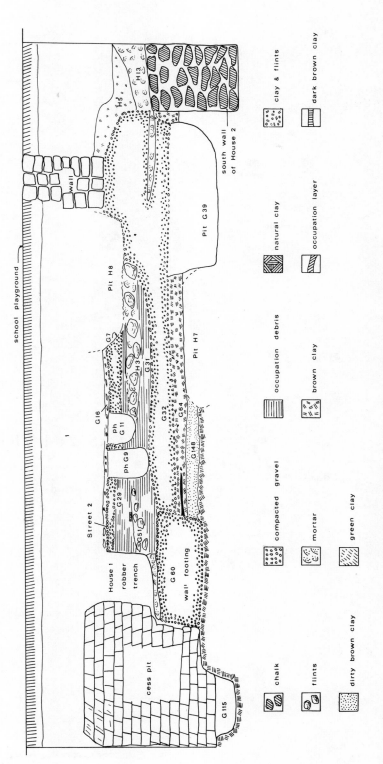

school playground
H13
H5
Pit H8
Pit G 39
south wall of House 2
wall
G7
H3
G31
Pit H7
G16
G32
G64
ph G11
G148
ph G9
Street 2
G29
G51
House 1
robber trench
G60
wall footing
cess pit
G115

chalk

flints

dirty brown clay

compacted gravel

mortar

green clay

occupation debris

brown clay

natural clay

occupation layer

clay & flints

dark brown clay

metres

Fig. 7.13

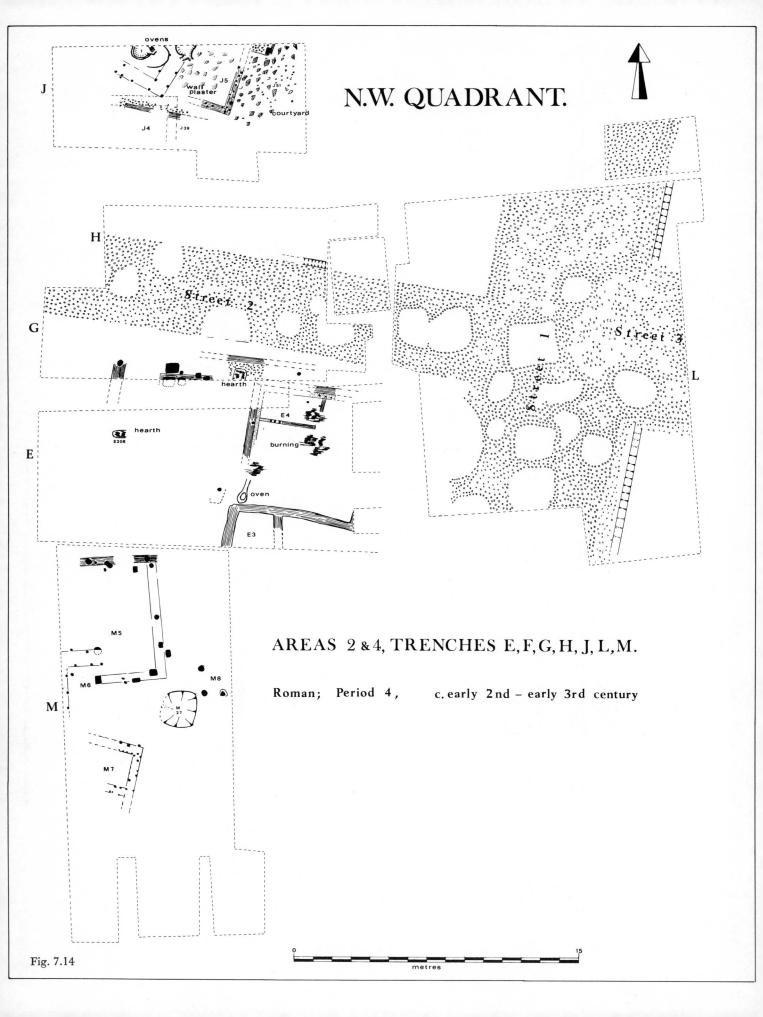

N.W. QUADRANT.

J

ovens

wall
plaster

J5

J51

courtyard

J4   J39

H

G

Street 2

Street 1   Street 3

hearth

E4

E

hearth

E206

burning

L

oven

E3

M5

M8

M6

M
27

M

M7

AREAS 2 & 4, TRENCHES E, F, G, H, J, L, M.

Roman; Period 4,   c. early 2nd – early 3rd century

Fig. 7.14

0   15

metres

AREA 2, TRENCH L, NORTH SECTION K–K

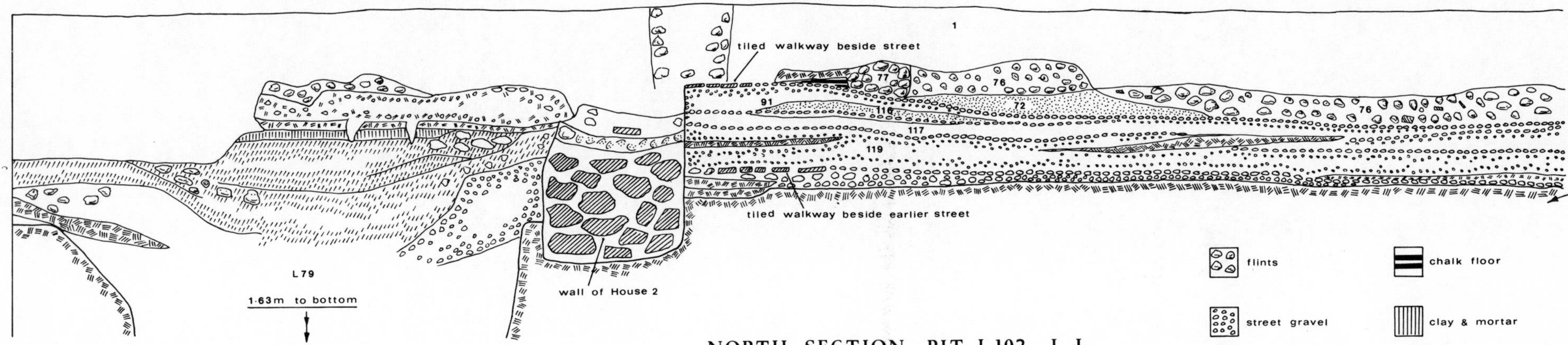
1
tiled walkway beside street
77
76
72
76
91
116
117
119
tiled walkway beside earlier street
L79
1·63m to bottom
wall of House 2

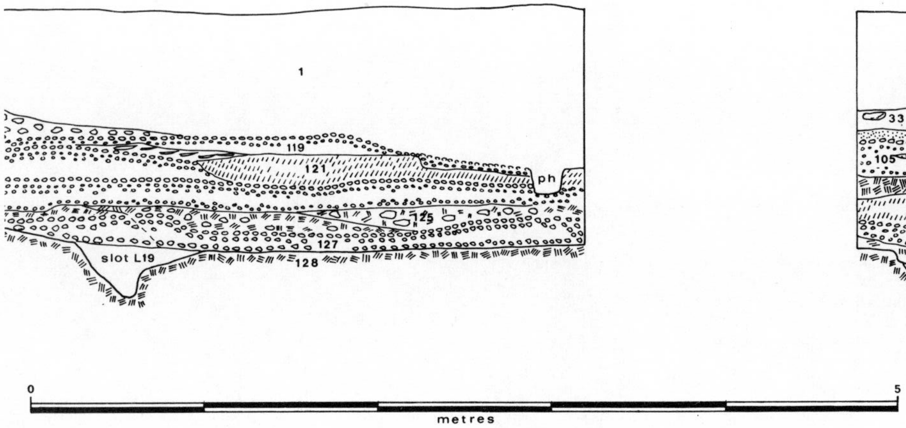
1
119
121
ph
125
127
128
slot L19
0
5
metres

NORTH SECTION PIT L102 L–L

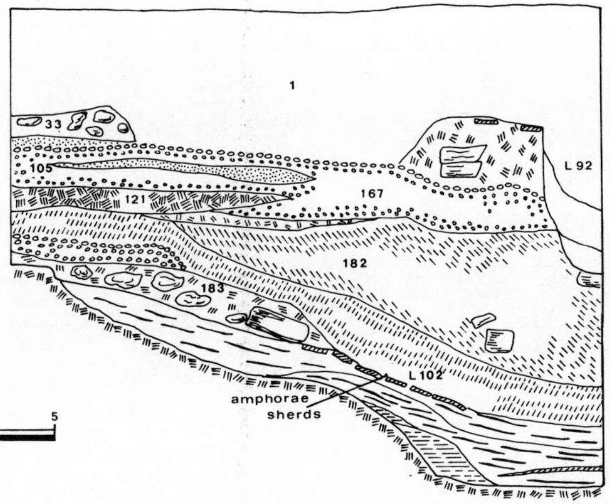
1
33
105
121
167
L92
182
183
L102
amphorae
sherds

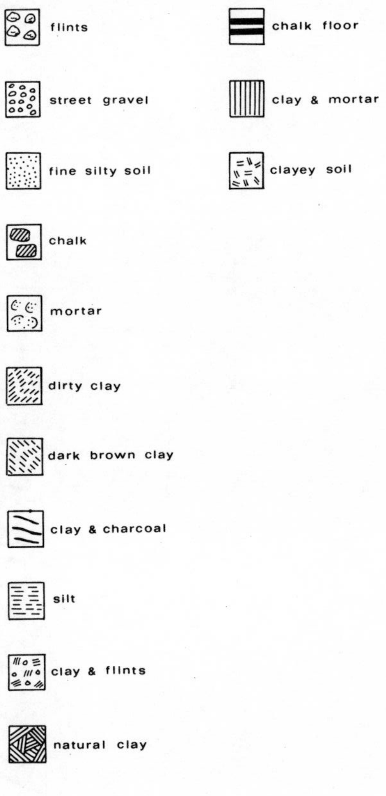
flints
street gravel
fine silty soil
chalk
mortar
dirty clay
dark brown clay
clay & charcoal
silt
clay & flints
natural clay
chalk floor
clay & mortar
clayey soil

Fig. 7.15

N.W. QUADRANT, AREA 2, TRENCH L.

SOUTH SECTION, (PART)   N–N

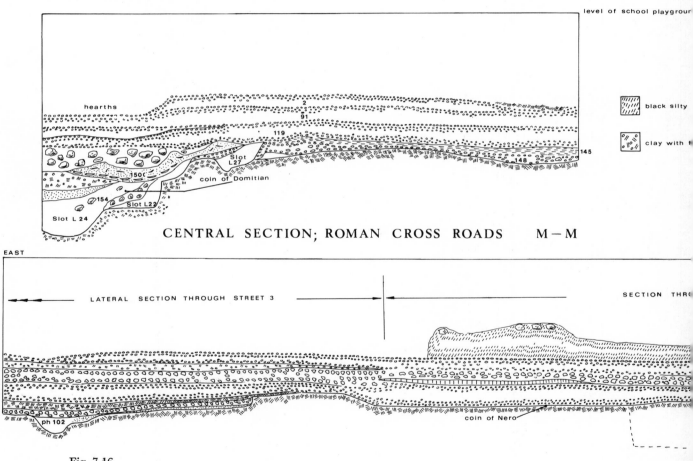

CENTRAL SECTION; ROMAN CROSS ROADS   M – M

Fig. 7.16

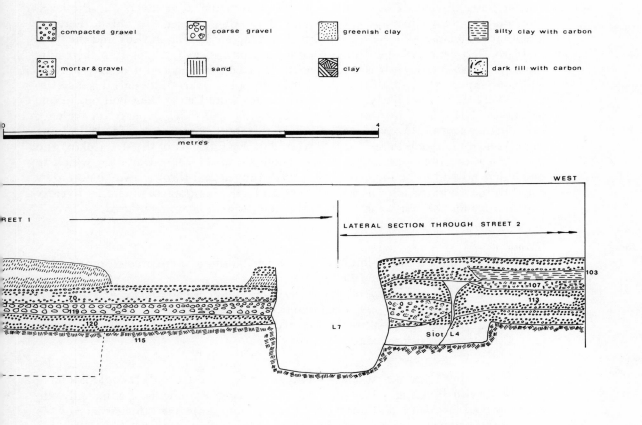

compacted gravel

coarse gravel

greenish clay

silty clay with carbon

mortar & gravel

sand

clay

dark fill with carbon

0   4

metres

WEST

STREET 1

LATERAL SECTION THROUGH STREET 2

103

107

113

70

119

120

115

L 7

Slot L 4

the street was first discovered. It drained to the east, and slots L.19, L.22, L.24 and L.27 are probably successive drains which appear to have been obliterated by later layers of gravel which "crept" forward and filled them in. They were probably timber revetted, but the gradual raising of the street level by successive metallings would make it necessary to replace them. The earlier street surface L.111/120 had nothing later than Flavian and "1st century" samian, together with a coin of Nero A.D. 63–64. The drain contemporary with the earliest Phase 1 street is Slot L.19 at the north end and slot L.24 at the south end. There seems to be a hiatus in the centre where Street 3 could be expected to branch off to the east.

No closely dateable material comes from Slot L.19, but the silt in Slot L.24 (L.154) had an unworn sestertius of Domitian dating to A.D. 86.

Phase 2

The second phase of metalling represented by layer L.119 had early 2nd-century samian. The layer was orange clay with flints, rather cleaner than the Phase 2 make-up of Street 2. There is no reason to suppose that they were anything but contemporary as it would be necessary to keep the street levels at least approximately the same.

Discussion

It may be possible to put forward a case for the earliest level of Street 1 to pre-date the earliest layer of Street 2 and there is no stratigraphical evidence to refute this. On the basis of what dating evidence we have from the street layers and the levels immediately below them, it appears that the earliest Street 1 could be Flavian, albeit late Flavian and if the sherd of Flavian-Trajanic samian in G.61 and the "late 1st–early 2nd century" sherd in G.64 are both pushed as far back into their date bracket as possible, then it is quite feasible that both streets could be late Flavian and contemporary, or that Street 1 is earlier by a few years, although this is felt to be unlikely. It is more likely that the cross roads would have been laid out in one operation. The exact date is open to some question, and much depends on evidence from further south in Area 3 (see below). In this writer's view it would be straining the evidence too much to opt for a Flavian date for this part of the street plan, and by implication, the re-planning of the whole town. The fine wares on which so much depend had to be imported, sold, used, broken and thrown away before they could be incorporated into the street layers, and a new assessment of late 1st to early 2nd century for the commencement of the new Roman layout is offered.

Phase 1, *c.* early 2nd century

Trench J

During Period 4 a succession of slight timber buildings were erected on the site, of which only fragments could be isolated.

Layers J.39/41 were layers of clay containing 2nd-century samian, and J.40 was a thin occupation layer on J.39. The latest samian was Central Gaulish Hadrianic.

Building J.4 was of post trench construction, dug into J.39. Only the angle formed by two walls survived.

Phase 2

After Building J.4 went out of use, Building J.5 was constructed. It could not have co-existed with Building J.4 in view of the differing alignments. Again, only the angle formed by two walls survived, but it is noticeable that this structure was aligned with the street, and a courtyard or hardstanding of gravel (J.51), topped off with amphorae sherds was laid on the east side. This gravelled area was built up

72

AREA 2, TRENCH J

North section, H–H

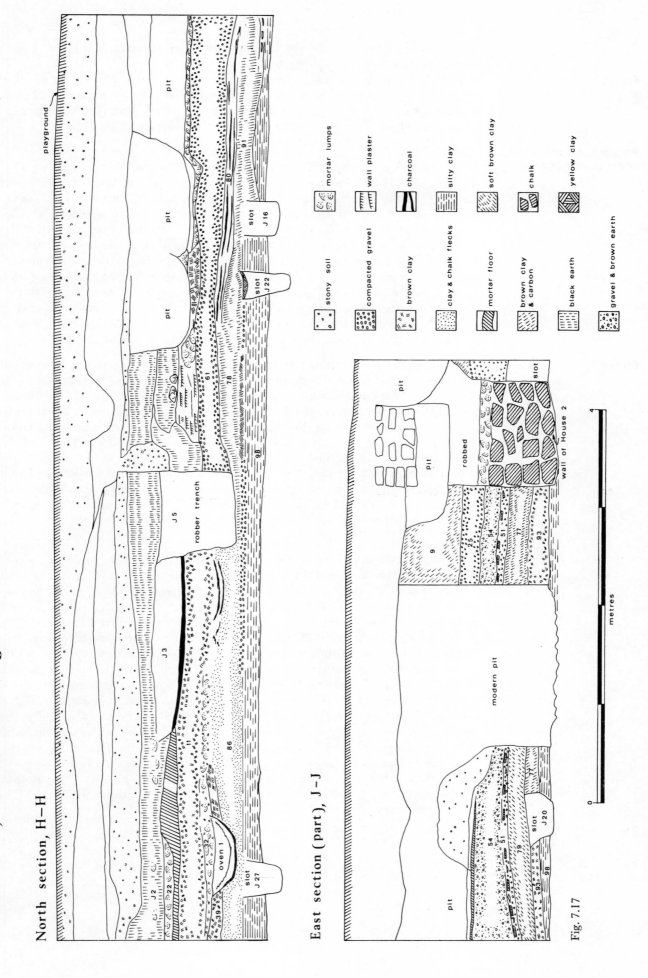

East section (part), J–J

Fig. 7.17

during the 2nd century and the latest pottery from the make-up layers J.54, 55, 53 and 25 is Antonine.

Phase 3

During Phase 3 a series of ovens were constructed on the west side of Building J.5, which by that time must have passed out of use. An arrangement of stakeholes around the south and east side of the oven shown on the plan (Oven 1) may indicate some form of windbreak or perhaps a slight building.

Phase 1, _c._ early 2nd century – Antonine

Trench E

At some time in the 2nd century, Building E.3 was constructed. By that time Building E.2 had been demolished and the slots for the later structure were cut through part of the rubble. Only the northern part of Building E.3, which must have been of timber framed construction, with the sleeper beams set in clay, was excavated. It runs southwards outside the limits of the excavation and the fill of the slots suggests an Antonine date. On the north side were a number of hearths, E.206, E.140, E.160 and a banjo-shaped oven, which appear to be contemporary. The presence of a number of crucible fragments relating to bronze enamelling on hearth E.206 and the presence of quantities of nails, brackets and iron slag over the rake-back areas suggests that the occupation was still "industrial" rather than domestic, although the presence of amounts of domestic refuse indicated that some of the people using the site may have been living on or near the job.

Phase 2

Building E.4 was a timber framed building with, in one room, mortar cills laid against the beam on the inside so as to house the wattle inserts designed to hold the clay walls. This construction detail has not been noted before in Chichester. Only part of the building survived but it can be seen from the plan that part of one room was partitioned off, with a doorway in the south-east corner. The floors were made up with layers of clay that had been baked red and which appeared to have accumulated from some hot process (possibly from the superstructures of demolished ovens), over a long period. The limits of the building on the north and east sides can be set by the streets, but its extent southwards could not be established. It could have existed with Building E.4 but is more likely to have replaced it, especially in view of the fact that it partly overlays some of the Phase 1 hearths.

Trench M

Postholes and slots representing fragments of possibly five buildings were found cut into a horizon dated to the second century. The layers making up the level were a layer of dirty occupation, M29/43, M.53, M.54 and M.38/55. With the exception of M.55 which was a local spread of gravel, the other layers were derived from demolished clay daub mixed in with some occupation debris to make the contemporary ground surface. M.29/43 contained quantities of combed plaster from the exterior of the previous generation of buildings, as did a contemporary pit (M.27), which had large quantities of building debris including plaster. Relatively few tegulae were found, which may indicate either a robbing and re-using of the tiles or possibly the use of thatch or wooden shingles as roofing material. The dating evidence from these layers is early 2nd century samian, and no specifically Antonine pieces are present. Three small hearth areas lay on the horizon, east of Building M.7.

Of the five groups of postholes and slots representing buildings, M.5 is the most coherent and probably pre-dates the slight wattle structure M.6. Building M.7 has two walls which make an angle and part of an internal partition, but nothing else survives. All three buildings were dug into M.53 and Buildings M.6 and M.7 might be contemporary.

AREA 4, CLEMEN'S YARD, TRENCH M; North Section   O–O

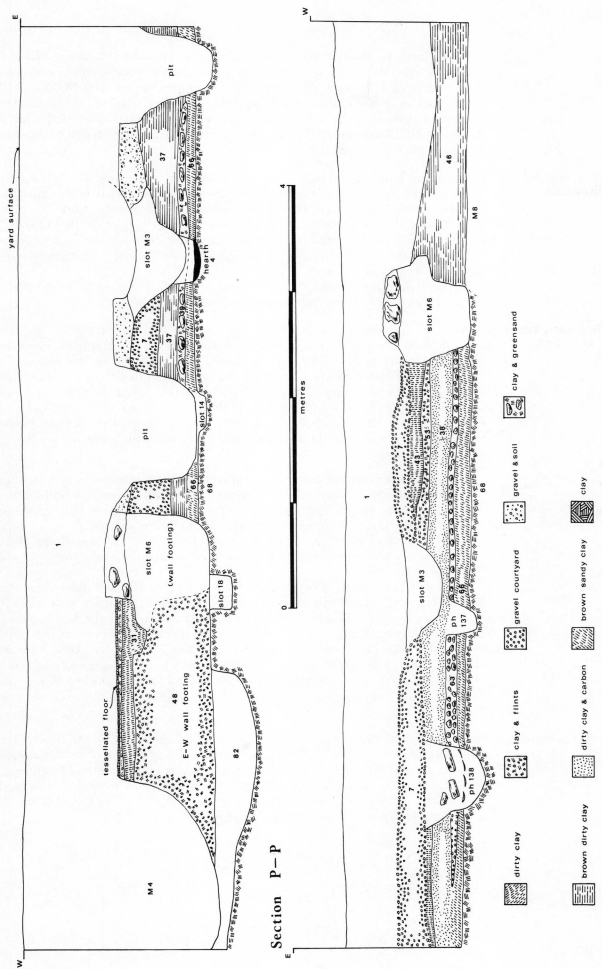

Section P–P

key:
- dirty clay
- clay & flints
- brown dirty clay
- dirty clay & carbon
- gravel courtyard
- gravel & soil
- clay & greensand
- brown sandy clay
- clay

metres

Fig. 7.18

Three large postholes make up part of another structure (Building M.8). These were dug into M.29 and the size of the posts suggest a more substantial building than M.6 or M.7. It is possible that it may be contemporary with Building M.5.

All that can be said of these structures is that they cut early 2nd-century destruction levels and there is nothing later than 2nd-century material associated with them. A mid to late 2nd-century date is offered but there is no evidence to show which buildings were constructed first.

Period 5; c. mid 3rd to early 4th century

The latter half of the third century seems to have been a period when activity on the site was at a low ebb. It is not known how long the Period 4 structures in J, E and M lasted, but no later periods of building are detectable until the masonry built houses are constructed in the fourth century. It is possible (see below), that Building E.5 may have been incorporated into later development for a time.

This period of inactivity may be contrasted with the rapid changes which took place in the previous periods.

Street 2 does not appear to have been re-metalled during this time although considerable erosion of the top surface had taken place.

Period 6; c. early 4th to late 4th century Fig. 7.20

At some time possibly in the early 4th century, two masonry built houses were erected along the west side of Street 1. House 1 on the south side of Street 2, and House 2 on the north. They are numbered and discussed in the order of their appearance. House 1 covers Trenches E, M and the south part of G, while House 2 has its southern boundary in the north part of G/H, covers Trench J and extends northwards into Area 5 and beyond. Both houses extend westwards below Lancastrian Grange and it is possible that the western boundaries of both properties rest upon the east side of the Roman street which is partly below Tower Street.

Phase 1

House 1

The foundations were constructed of gravel (hoggin) and it may well be that the north wall slightly encroached on to Street 2 when the house was built. The west section across the street (Fig. 7.13) shows the gravel footings cut through the street with the later layer of dumped rubbish (G.31) being carried forward over the external offset and piled up against the base of the wall. The situation is different in the east section, but this records a later addition to the building and will be discussed under Phase 2.

No closely dated pottery comes from the foundation slots and indeed the absence of 3rd century colour coated wares might indicate an earlier date than early 4th century for this building. In Phase 1 the house appears to have had a rectangular courtyard surrounded by an ambulatory, with a range of rooms on the west and north sides (the south end is uncertain), and the west side is below Lancastrian Grange. The plan of the north-east corner, which is ambiguous, could not be clarified due to the presence of large and deep school foundations and heavy robbing of the Roman footings, and the Phase 2 alterations have also obscured the original plan.

Description of Rooms:

Room 1. Internal dimensions were 5.2 metres by 5.6 metres; only one small fragment of tessellated floor remained. The walls were completely robbed down to the footings.
Room 2. East of Room 1 and measuring 3.1 metres by 5.6 metres; fragments of a tessellated floor remained. The arrangement of these two rooms suggests perhaps that they were originally one, with the centre wall (now robbed out) being placed across at a later time. This is incapable of proof.

7. Area 2, Trench L. Section across Roman street 1, looking north. (Photo: J. Hinde)

8. Area 3, Trench W. Period 2 Roman timber buildings. (Photo: G. Claridge RIBA)

9. Area 2, Trench W. Building W.5. A — infant burial in tiled cyst. (Photo: G. Claridge RIBA)

Room 3. South of Room 1. Exact dimensions uncertain but likely to have measured 5.6 metres by 4.1 metres internally. The north and east walls were robbed down to their hoggin footings but the south wall had a mortared cill to take a substantial sleeper beam and had a line of tiles set along the inner edge. The floor was of yellow/buff mortar with a good deal of crushed brick and small flints and was smoothly rendered on the top. It was 15 cms thick.

Room 4A and 4B. These formed part of a corridor, although later modified. In Trench E (Fig. 7.20), the east–west wall at the north end of the corridor joins another wall of similar construction aligned north–south. A possible explanation is that the corridor on the east side of the courtyard (Room 4B) was accessible from the remainder of the ambulatory (Room 4A), by a door at the north end, and it is likely that this arrangement was repeated at the south end also.

Room 5. South of Room 3; no dimensions can be given for this room due to almost total destruction by large pits. No south wall partition could be established, but if Room 6 and Room 5 were of equal size north–south then a dimension of 7 metres is suggested. One fragment of tessellated floor remained at the north end.

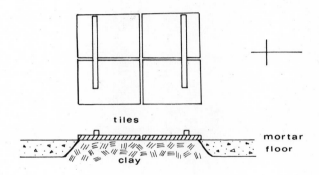

AREA 4; TRENCH M.
Plan & section of Period 6, phase 1 hearth

Fig. 7.19

Room 6. Only the east end of this room was within the excavation. In Phase 1 it had a floor of similar construction to that in Room 3. Incorporated into the floor when it was laid was the base of a tiled hearth with two brick bars mortared across the top (see Fig. 7.19). The hearth base was prepared first, from a thick layer of rammed yellow clay and the mortar floor screeded up to it. Presumably this was to insulate as far as possible the hearth from the floor, so as to prevent heat cracking of the latter. The "hearth" may in fact have supported a charcoal brazier as it was set up against the east wall and there was no sign of a flue or excessive heat on the wall.

Room 7. South of Room 6; only the north–east corner of the room was within the excavation but the position of the south wall makes it *c.* 7.4 metres north–south. No traces of a floor remained.

Phase 2   No date can be offered for this phase of alteration to House 1, but it is clear that the arrangements at the north–east corner were modified.

77

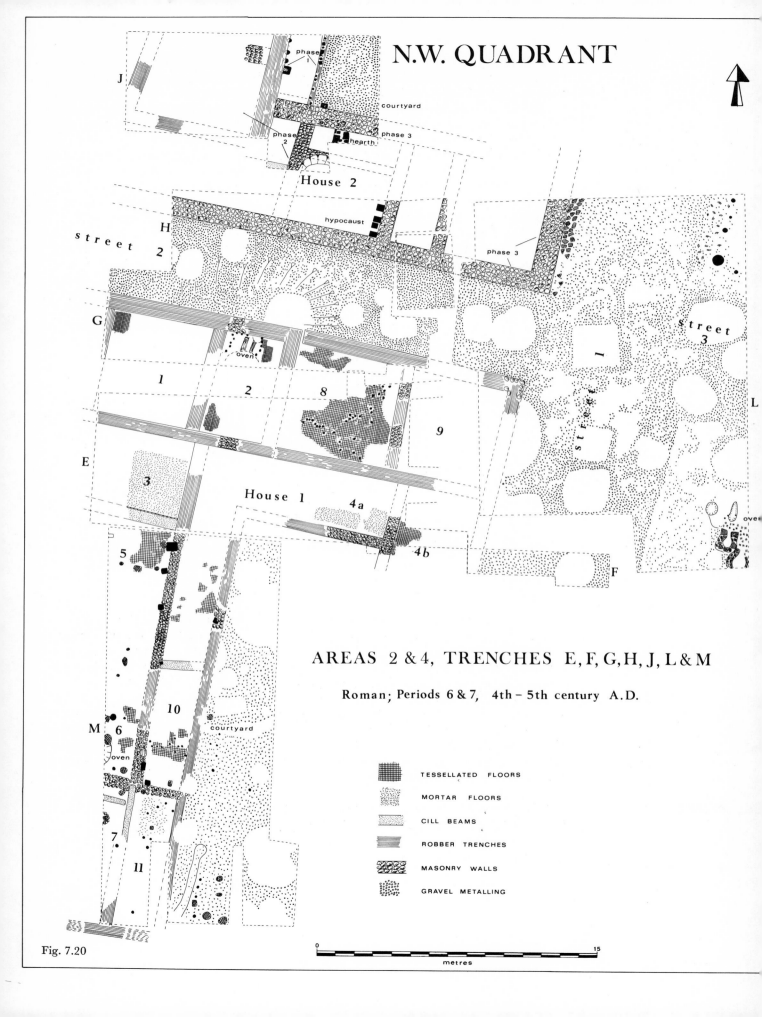

N.W. QUADRANT

AREAS 2 & 4, TRENCHES E, F, G, H, J, L & M

Roman; Periods 6 & 7, 4th – 5th century A.D.

▨	TESSELLATED FLOORS
▦	MORTAR FLOORS
▨	CILL BEAMS
▤	ROBBER TRENCHES
▨	MASONRY WALLS
▨	GRAVEL METALLING

Fig. 7.20

0   15

metres

Room 8. Measuring 5.8 by 5.8 metres, was built on to the east side of Room 2, with the north wall foundations stopping just short of the north–east corner of Room 2. Whereas the earlier footings were of hoggin, both the north and the east walls of Room 8 were of flint (see Fig. 7.20) and if there were any earlier foundations present these must have been removed when Rooms 8 and 9 were built. It is likely, when the depths of the Phase 1 and 2 foundations are compared, that the Phase 2 footings replaced timber cills and it is just possible that the Phase 1 masonry structure may have initially incorporated the Period 4, Phase 2, Building E.5, the remains of which fit quite well into the area covered by Room 8.

The tessellated floor was laid directly on to the baked clay of Building E.5 with no more than a thin screed of dirty mortar in between.

Room 9. c. 5 metres by 5.5 metres; only a short length of robber trench along the south and north sides and part of the almost totally robbed north–east corner, was seen, but this was enough to establish the position.

Room 6. The mortar floor and oven were overlaid by a tessellated floor. This is ascribed to Phase 2 but could have taken place at any time during the life of the building.

The Courtyard

A gravel spread (M.7) extended along the east side of Rooms 10 and 11, and was bounded on the north side by Room 4A. Its eastern boundary was outside the excavated area but was probably contained within the projected range of the corridor (Room 4B). It was *c.* 0.20 metre thick and constructed of gravel with some reddish creamy mortar and a fair inclusion of soil. It was well compacted and the material was obviously re-used from elsewhere.

Although badly mutilated by later pits, certain areas remained where it was possible to identify the debris from the destroyed house lying upon it. This comprised a certain amount of dirty yellow clay which was probably collapsed daub, painted wall plaster, tegulae and Horsham stone tiles from the roof, and greensand, flint and chalk from the walls. Part of a pottery water pipe found in the top of the layer may indicate a piped water supply from an adjacent well.

Apart from the small area sealed by debris from the house, the gravel was covered by fine black earth (M.30) containing medieval and post medieval wares. Pottery from within the layer contained only residual samian and coarse wares which do not permit of close dating. The absence of third and fourth century colour coated wares may again be significant and point to an earlier date than early 4th century for the house, but on the other hand, the latest dated sherd within the gravel may reflect only the date when it was removed from its last location. It could have been stockpiled for some time before being re-laid as a courtyard.

House 2

The house was built on the north-west corner of the cross roads. The west side extends below Lancastrian Grange while the northern boundary lies somewhere north of Area 5 (Gospel Hall), below the houses on the west side of Chapel Street. Fragments of walling and part of a pink mortar floor were noted by the writer when a new surface water drain was laid in November 1976 and it is reported that Carlyon Britton saw Roman walling in a gas main trench in front of the Chapel further north in 1937. This may also belong to the same house and would make it a very large one. Evidence from Area 5 (see pp. 119–121) indicates that the house was not built in its final form until after the turn of the 3rd century, when it was extended eastwards towards Street 1. The later house foundations were extremely well constructed, being at least 1 metre wide and up to 1.1 metres deep and built of large chalk blocks in clay. This had an advantage in that subsequent stone robbing operations left the chalk untouched and the later footings are therefore easily identifiable. The width and depth of the foundations suggest perhaps that this building, or parts of it, might have been of two-storey construction.

A number of phases of development and decline are perceptible; the development phases are discussed below, while the house in decline is considered under Period 7.

Phase 1

At this stage it is possible to see part of a building, aligned with the street, which was probably constructed of timber and clay, with painted wall plaster on the clay walls. Slot J.5 was a narrow slot containing postholes cut through a gravel courtyard, with a number of postholes on the same alignment, west of the slot and 1.7 metres from it. This is probably part of a corridor. There was the hint of a slot at the south end, running east–west, and badly cut about by a later robber trench. Evidence for the type of construction comes from a layer of collapsed wall plaster on the west side of the robber trench for the later building, and cut by it and the original construction trench. This showed how large sections of clay wall had slumped across, with most of the wall plaster being upside down except where it had "jack-knifed" as it came down.

This phase may well equate with Phase 1 in Area 5 (see below). It cannot be recognised further south in G/H, where the deep excavation for the later hypocaust destroyed most of the earlier layers, but it is likely that the Phase 1 building stood back from the street corner.

Phase 2

At this stage it appears that a stone built house replaced the timber one. On the west side of the earlier corridor a room was built, the plan of which survives in part in three sections of robber trench. This appears to have had a flint buttress (J.31) built on the inside of the east wall and as the walls have been completely robbed it is a fair assumption that all the foundations were of flint. Also possibly part of this phase is a mortar wall base (J.34) on the same alignment and west of it. This cut through the collapsed wall plaster from Phase 1, and was cut away on the north side by the robber trench for the Phase 3 wall. It is in line with the earlier Slot J.5 and may be a corridor wall. It turns to the east and could scarcely have co-existed with the Phase 3 wall or an earlier wall on the same alignment unless another corridor running eastwards is postulated. There was a layer of mortar with a straight edge on the north side, coming off the west side of this wall a little further south and this cannot be reconciled with any of the other features unless perhaps a later cill beam base is suggested. Even so, the area enclosed would be too small for a room.

Phase 3

At some time in the 4th century, the third phase of building was carried out. This was a major reconstruction and involved the building of solid, well constructed walls with chalk footings and the extension eastwards of the house complex and possibly southwards as well. The alterations to the house in Area 5 will be discussed in that section.

At the south end, where the house abuts on to Street 2, a small hypocaust was constructed, and the deep excavation for this cut away all but the earliest layers.

80

Stratigraphically, it is possible to determine the point at which this took place, as two sections across Street 2 show the layer of mortar representing builders tread, spreading a little way across the street from the wall footings (Fig. 7.13).

In Trench L, the south-east corner of the house where it abutted on to the cross roads enclosed a series of pits, some containing crucibles, and with a metal-working flue above. All of these features must have been below the floor of the later house and it seems likely, if not certain that they were outside the house complex in the earlier phases.

In Trench J, a wall was constructed which abutted on to the earlier Phase 2 wall on the east side. This was of typical Phase 3 construction, i.e. the footings were of chalk and its relationship to the earlier wall is clearly seen. Whether this wall was a replacement for an earlier one on the same alignment is impossible to say, but it could have been.

The Streets

During Period 6 it is likely that the streets were made up at least once. Street 2 (Fig. 7.13) shows a layer of gravel which is indistinguishable from G.32 above the layer of builders tread discussed above, while on Street 1 (Fig. 7.15) the contemporary street surface is probably L.91, with a tiled footway set along the west side by the wall of House 2. The date when these layers were put down cannot be established with any certainty. No dating evidence later than late Antonine samian is present and there is an absence of the later Roman fine wares, e.g. New Forest and Oxford types. Too much emphasis need not be laid upon this point, however, in view of the probable time lag involved in the stockpiling and re-use of the street gravel, but it might be reasonable to assume a late 3rd to early 4th century date for the final phase of housebuilding of Houses 1 and 2, followed immediately by a re-metalling of the streets, sealing the construction tread from House 2 in the process.

There was no construction tread in the street metalling from House 1. This could be explained by the layer of dirty gravel and rubbish (G.31) dumped against the foundations of House 1 in a hollow which had formed against the side of the house (Fig. 7.13).

The section implies that the street was originally intended to drain southwards after the second re-metalling (the earliest street appears to have drained northwards into the small drain). There was no sign of a drain on the south side, and the foundations of House 1 must have been subject to a considerable amount of water during wet weather, particularly after House 2, Phase 3 was built, when run-off from the roof would be discharged directly on to the street unless there was a surface drain. A possible explanation for excavation of the street gravel to expose the foundations was that serious structural defects became apparent in the north wall of House 1 which necessitated a partial re-building. Whatever the reason, the considerable hollow resulting from the removal of the gravel was filled with dumped rubbish (G.31) which consisted of dirty gravel and large amounts of domestic rubbish and debris from demolished buildings. The latest dated artifacts were colour coated wares from the New Forest and Oxford kilns, and the deposit is dated *c.* mid 4th century on the basis of the evidence.

Period 7, late 4th to 5th century

The excavation of the top layers of late or sub-Roman occupation on the site was carried out with special care to try to establish the terminal period of the life of the buildings. The familiar problems of the absence of very late 4th and early 5th century coin types and of any dateable pottery reassert themselves, and it is only possible to record what appears to be the latest activity on the sites which can be associated with the buildings and, by implication, a late or sub Roman occupation.

House 1 (Fig. 7.20)

At some time towards the end of the life of the building, part of the corridor along the west side of the courtyard was divided up into rooms by laying cill beams across (Rooms 10 and 11). There is also evidence for a re-building of Room 7 where the earlier partition wall is replaced by a beam slot a little further to the south, and where beam slots have been inserted into the dwarf walls which supported the superstructure. Additionally, a number of shallow post sockets were inserted into the wall base or, in some instances, near to it. Their position implies a re-build of an existing structure, with roof supports being inserted and then incorporated into a mortared wall. These features imply an *ad hoc* repair of a structure already partly in decay, but the subdivision of the rooms may suggest a change of use, from that of a town house, the residence of a wealthy family, to a partly derelict building being lived in by a number of separate family units. The impression is strengthened by the numbers of post and stakeholes driven or dug into the floors in Rooms 5, 6, 8.10 and 11, and an oven dug through the floor of Room 6. At the north end of Room 2 were two flues of an oven set against the wall, partly destroyed by a later pit, with stakeholes belonging to a wattle wind-break around it. They were sealed by a layer of burnt clay (G.35) (possibly the oven superstructure) and this in turn had a tiled hearth set on it. Layer G.25 had two mid 4th century coins and New Forest wares and was covered with occupation debris.

Pl. 5

House 2

Here the only evidence comes from Trench J, where a tiled hearth was found built up against one of the walls and laid on the base of a mortar floor (J.21) which had a sherd of New Forest red ware on it, together with a coin of Valens. A late 4th-century coin of Valens or Valentinian 1 from Pit J.13, and an unstratified coin of Gratian may be further indications that the house was still in occupation in the late 4th century.

The streets

The postholes of a timber structure or possibly a fence were driven in along the east side of Street 1 and one post at right angles indicated that the structure or fence was turning eastwards along the line of Street 3. As the postholes were dug through the top layer of metalling they must be fairly late in date but as they appear to relate to the street it seems sensible to consider them as within the period when the street was operating and they are therefore assigned to Period 7.

Two small ovens and two tiled ovens, one slightly higher than the other, formed a group in the south-east corner of Trench L, just off the line of the road. They were covered with a layer of gravel and clay (L.8) which may well have been the upcast from pit digging through the streets. The only dating evidence consisted of Roman pottery and the two larger ovens were built of Roman tegulae. They may have been operating at a time when the streets were still being used, as they are off the line of Street 1. A thick layer of green silt (L.72) lay above the metalling in areas undisturbed by later pits. This may represent the final abandonment of the street as such. It contained New Forest purple wares and a coin of Gratian as the latest dated artifacts. Layers of accumulated dirt *above* the street including upcast spread from later pit digging had coins of Gratian and Valens.

Street 2

The layer of dumped rubbish (G.31) (see Period 6) was covered with a thin layer of metalling G.5/7 and H.3. This must represent the last metalling of the street before the breakdown of urban amenities, and comprised dirty re-used gravel from elsewhere. The latest dateable sherds were New Forest fine wares, all very abraded and worn, and a coin of mid-4th century date.

Discussion

Areas 2 and 4 together covered parts of two Roman town houses and a cross roads in what must have been, in the early to mid-4th century, a prosperous area of the town. By the later 4th century the slow decline had set in, the houses become semi-derelict and sub-divided, with hearths and ovens cut into floors. Layers of silt and rubbish had accumulated in worn hollows in the streets and a general picture of decay and neglect is apparent. Late 4th-century coins of Gratian, Valens and Valentinian 1 lying on the floors and hearths in the houses and in the silt above Street 1 give some hint of the date when the transition from prosperous town houses to semi-derelict slums was complete, but offers no information as to the length of time the life of the city remained at this low ebb. No coins occur in the north-west quadrant sites after Valens, and the picture is repeated in the two Chilgrove villas (*Down*, forthcoming), where the coin series end at Magnentius and Valentinian 1 respectively, and yet there is clear evidence that life contained in both farms after disastrous fires; the land continued to be worked and the inhabitants were making their own iron tools and drying corn, using the shells of the buildings, with make-shift lean-to shelters built inside them. Although there is no evidence for destruction by fire in Chapel Street the comparison is otherwise valid.

Although the north-west quadrant coin series is slightly later than Chilgrove, the breakpoint is still short of the end of the 4th century (Fig. 10.57). This seems a clear indication that no new issues were reaching Chichester in the late 4th century but it must still be a matter for conjecture when coin usage was finally abandoned; it may not have been until the early 5th century.

The Romano-British temple on Bow Hill excavated by Carlyon Britton in 1931 (*V.C.H.* 3, p. 51), was reputed to have coins of Theodosivs (A.D. 395) although none are known from the villas a short distance away. The Porchester series (*Cunliffe* 1975, pp. 194–7) goes on until A.D. 402 which is later again than the north-west quadrant. In neither place need it indicate the abandonment of the site, but merely the moment in time when a money economy ceased to be a facet of a society that was reverting to a more primitive life-style.

Period 8, Saxon:
***c.* 8th to early 12th century**

Phase 1
***c.* 8th–10th century**

The first indication of Saxon occupation is seen in the hand-made wares of the 8th to 10th centuries which, in Areas 2 and 4, are noted only as residual material in later pits. For a description of the wares see p. 341. One imported Hamwih-type pitcher from the region of Paris was found in Pit L.8 along with several baked clay loom weights. The pitcher dated to *c.* 9th–10th century and probably got here by way of the French wine trade and the same is true of a later vessel from Beauvais (see p. 352) found in Pit L.17.

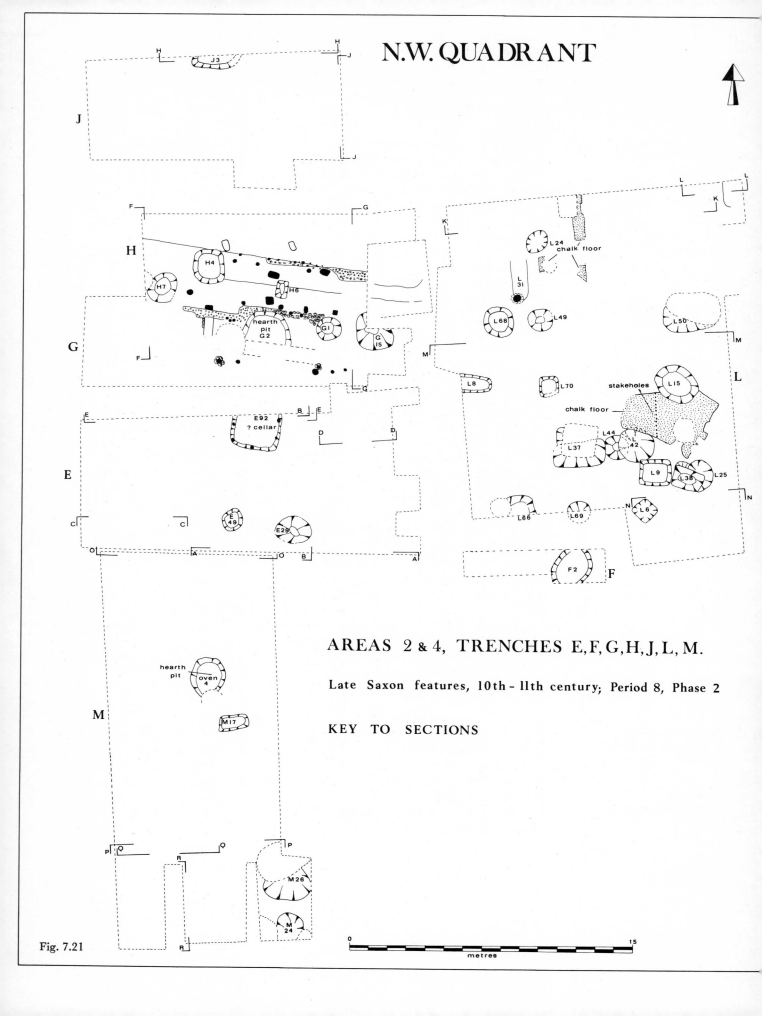

N.W. QUADRANT

AREAS 2 & 4, TRENCHES E, F, G, H, J, L, M.

Late Saxon features, 10th–11th century; Period 8, Phase 2

KEY TO SECTIONS

Fig. 7.21

0   15
metres

A silver half penny of Eadgar (A.D. 959–75), from the Chichester Mint was found in Pit L.37 and a silver penny of Aethelred (A.D. 978–1016) from posthole L.24, and these two coins, taken with the pottery, constitute the only evidence for Phase 1.

Phase 2, early 11th to early 12th century

Fig. 7.21

At some time during this phase, some development appears to have taken place on the surface of the old Roman streets. This need not mean a deliberate selection of the street surfaces for building and it is probably true to say that the traces have survived only where they are recognised as being cut through a definite horizon. Elsewhere in Areas 2 and 4, severe robbing for building stone probably before and certainly after Phase 2 had almost completely destroyed any traces of structures.

Trench J

The only feature to be assigned to Phase 2 is Pit J.3 a shallow scoop with late Saxon coarse wares, and a number of goat horn cores. The base of the pit was clay lined and burnt red. It may have been a hearth pit (see below in G and M).

Trench G/H

A line of postholes, some square cut and shallow, some round and deep were cut into the Roman street surface just north of a shallow hearth Pit G.2. The postholes bordered a layer of yellow clay which may be the base of a clay wall. Parallel with these postholes and 2.5 metres to the south was another line of postholes cut through the tessellated floors of House 1 and on the west side was part of a beam slot aligned north–south which might be part of the same structure. A third line of postholes to the north, on the same alignment and 2.5 metres away from the centre line may also belong to the building, and there is another layer of clay and a number of stakeholes belonging to a wattle construction. The postholes were cut from the same horizon and appear to make up a rectangular building, although no ends can be postulated. If this is a correct interpretation then the old Roman wall of House 1 must have been previously robbed. An examination of the fill from the robber trench shows that there are no later sherds than the coarse unglazed wares of the late Saxon period and, therefore, an earlier robbing could be quite feasible. This might have taken place when the town was being refortified in the late 10th to early 11th century as a strongpoint against the Danes, when building stone would have been needed to repair the walls.

The hearth Pit G.2 was contained within the area of the structure and, like Pit J.3 was little more than a scoop with burnt clay around the sides and large amounts of soot and coarse late Saxon pottery. Possibly contemporary was a small rectangular pit, containing a goat skull which was cut into the old street just north of the hearth pit.

Four deep cesspits appear to postdate the building; these are G.1, G.15, H.4 and H.7, all of which contained groups of stamped and rilled Saxo-Norman wares. A selection of those from Pit H.4 are published (see p. 347). All four pits are 11th century on the basis of the wares, which may push the date of the building back to the earlier part of Phase 2.

Trench E

Possibly part of the same building is Pit E.92 which may have been a small cellar, as five postholes were located around the edges (Fig. 7.21) and dug into the trampled clay floor was a complete late Saxon pot (Fig. 11.3) with its rim level with the floor. The fill of the pit or cellar had nothing later than unglazed Saxo-Norman fabrics.

Trench M

Three pits, M.17, M.24 and M.26 are classified as Saxo-Norman on the basis of their wares, and a third hearth pit (Oven 4) was found. It was of similar depth and shape to J.3 and G.2 and had a number of broken Saxo-Norman cooking pots in the fill. No structure could be associated with it due to very great disturbance by later pits.

Trenches L and F

The whole area of the Roman cross roads was honeycombed with pits of all later periods (Fig. 7.21) and only those pits which are free from contamination by later disturbance are considered.

Fragments of two floors of rammed chalk, one with a row of stakeholes across it, survived. Both floors were no more than a few centimetres thick and were laid directly on to the Roman street gravel. One fragment of floor postdates Pits L.42 and L.44, the latter being a late Saxon cesspit with large amounts of pottery including complete vessels (pp. 345–348). The wares in this pit are dated late Saxon – Saxo-Norman – and are at the early end of Phase 2. The floor is cut by Pit L.15, another cesspit with nothing later than middle-late Saxon pottery. No postholes forming any kind of structures can be assigned to the floors.

The trial Trench F, south of L (Fig. 7.21), had one large pit (F.2) cut through the Roman street. This had a clay seal and contained a closed group of Saxo-Norman wares.

Discussion

The evidence of the pottery shows that there was occupation on the site from at least the 8th century and possibly as far back as the 7th. The local wares from this period are handmade and underfired and rarely survive in a recognisable form in a highly disturbed urban context, and due to this disturbance factor and the friability of the pottery, associated structures have so far been impossible to identify.

It is clear that as time went on, activity on the site increased as the numbers of cesspits producing closed groups of late Saxon wares testify. For some reason, most of the pits were dug through the Roman street levels, with relatively little disturbance of the areas covered by the late Roman houses.

During the excavation of Areas 2 and 4, a careful examination was made of every sherd of post-Roman pottery to try to establish whether any earlier, pre-7th-century Saxon pottery was present. None of the sherds isolated for special consideration could be said to be earlier than 8th century, with 7th century as the earliest possible date.

Period 9; medieval, c. 12th to 15th century

Phase 1; early medieval, c. mid to late 12th century

Activity on the site during the mid to late 12th century seems to have been minimal, judging by the number of pits which can be said to be 12th century on the basis of the wares or the stratification.

Trench J

Fig. 7.22

Pit J.4 partly cut the earlier Period 8 hearth pit and yet pre-dates the robbing of the Roman foundations, which are cut in turn by the 13th–14th-century Pit J.19. The relationship of these features puts Pit J.4 between the events and it is assigned to Phase 1. The fill had only abraded Saxo-Norman wares.

No structures can be identified for this phase and only the following pits can be assessed as possibly or probably 12th century on the basis of their stratification and contents. All had late Saxon wares, mostly abraded and featureless body sherds of Saxo-Norman to early medieval unglazed wares which are impossible to date closely:

> *Trench G/H:* Pits G.16 and G.26.
> *Trench L:* Pits L.20, L.28 and L.34.
> *Trench E:* Pit E.47.
> *Trench M:* Pits M.8 and M.28.

Phase 2;
13th to 14th century

During this phase, most of the sections of the Roman wall foundations not previously robbed, appear to have been quarried for flints and there is some evidence for slightly increased activity on the sites.

Trench J

Six pits can be classified within Phase 2. Of these, Pit J.8 is probably the latest as it contained a rod handle from a 14th-century jug together with glazed sherds. Two other pits, J.19 and 21 had glazed wares and medieval peg tiles, the first clear indications of buildings in the vicinity. Possibly also within Phase 2 is the line of postholes cutting the robbed out Roman wall. The robber trench had only unglazed Saxo-Norman wares and the postholes had nothing later. They must relate to a structure south of the trench and just outside the excavation limits but they are probably earlier in time than the pits mentioned above, which may have destroyed part of the structure.

Trench G/H

Pit G.19 possibly belongs to Phase 2 as it is cut from the medieval horizon although it has nothing but residual Roman wares in it.

Trench E

Several short lengths of beam slot of different dates; a number of pits and scores of postholes and stakeholes make up a confused pattern. Pits E.34, 55 and 95 had one or more glazed sherds of Phase 2 date. The remainder had unglazed medieval sherds and peg tile fragments. No coherent structure could be worked out, but one arrangement of stakeholes must derive from the positioning and re-positioning of hurdles rather than wattle huts.

Trench M

Pits 9, 14 and 21 are probably Phase 2 on the basis of their contents and stratigraphical relationship, and Pit M.25 may belong to the same phase. All save Pit. M.25 had 13th century glazed sherds as the latest artifacts.

Trench L

Pit L.3, L.18, L.39 and L.41 were all probably early 14th century and had a proportion of glazed wares. No structures could be identified.

Phase 3;
c. 14th–15th century

Phase 3 can only be seen in the pits; no structures being recognised. These are presented in chronological order of their contents.
Pit J.16 – A deep cesspit cutting Pit J.8. 14th-century glazed roof tiles.

87

Pits G.3 and G.4 – Late medieval glazed fabrics and contemporary coarse wares.
Pit M.5 – Glazed wares and one sherd of brown glazed ware probably 15th century.
Pit M.13 – Paint under glaze sherds of 15th century date.
Pit L.2 – Paint under glaze wares.
Pit L.4 – 14th-century wares, but probably later.
Pit L.11 – Painted wares (unglazed) of mid-15th-century to early 16th-century date.

Discussion

A study of the various phases of pit digging through the site during the 250-year span of Period 9, highlights how little activity there was at any one time. It is clear that there were no substantial buildings on the site, although the presence of roof tiles in the pits in Trench J suggest that perhaps there was a building nearby. The more ephemeral type of timber structure would not survive the intensive pit digging activities of the later periods, but no trace at all remains of domestic or other occupation. Very little glazed wares were found in the pits of the period and this may be compared with Area 1 on the opposite side of the road, where no glazed fabrics were found, although from a much smaller sample. Even allowing for the destruction of some of the Period 9 pits by later ones there is still no significant amount of residual medieval glazed wares in the later pits as would be expected if occupation was intensive during Period 9.

There was an increase in activity during Phase 2, and a little is known of the situation in the mid-13th century from documentary sources. Three holdings are known on the west side of Parislane (Chapel Street), which probably spanned the sites (Fig. 5.2). From north to south these were:

Tenement of Wm. Wroth (or Adam le Ber).

Land and buildings – owned by John de Beauchamp and Matilda and given to St. Mary's Hospital.

Tenement of Adam le Ber (or Wm. Wroth) (see above, ownership is uncertain).

It is possible that some or all of the buildings implied in the documentary sources may have been further west and outside the limits of the excavation and that for the most part they may have been barns or storebuildings. On the basis of what can be seen of the physical evidence it appears that domestic occupation throughout the period was sparse, and it may well be that the area was largely or partly farmland or gardens throughout the medieval period and later (see below).

**Period 10;
c. 16th to 18th century**

**Phase 1,
c. 16th century**

During Phase 1 very little activity is discernable. Only three pits, Pit G.14, L.72 and M.10 can be recognised as having 16th-century wares as the latest artifacts although some are present as residual material in later pits. The Norden Map of Chichester dated 1595 (*Chichester* 2, Pl. 1), shows the north-west quadrant as virtually empty of houses and it is likely that a similar situation existed at the beginning of the century.

**Phase 2,
c. 17th century**

In Trench L an arrangement of postholes is seen which can be interpreted as part of a timber structure, possibly a small barn. One of the postholes cuts Pit L.59 which had no dateable finds and is of uncertain date, but otherwise the relationship of the postholes to earlier pits seems to imply a 17th-century date. There is a reference in a lease of 1625 to a "tenement and garden plot" on the site (information from the Documentary Research Group) and the remains of the structure seen in Fig. 7.22 may belong to the tenement.

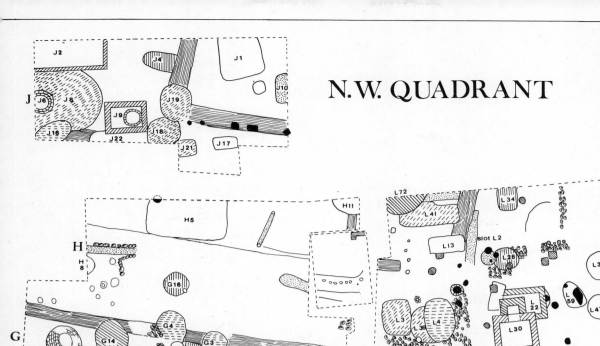

N.W. QUADRANT

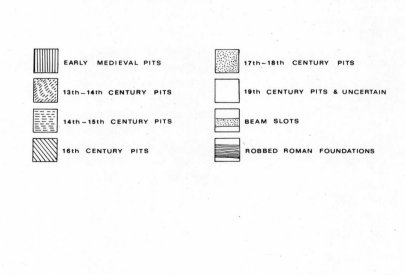

AREAS 2 & 4, TRENCHES E,G,H,J,L,M.

Post Saxon features; medieval – 19th century, Periods 9, 10 & 11

▦ EARLY MEDIEVAL PITS		░ 17th–18th CENTURY PITS
▨ 13th–14th CENTURY PITS		☐ 19th CENTURY PITS & UNCERTAIN
▤ 14th–15th CENTURY PITS		░ BEAM SLOTS
▧ 16th CENTURY PITS		▤ ROBBED ROMAN FOUNDATIONS

0   15

metres

Fig. 7.22

The Gardner Map of 1769 shows five houses on the site and the land tax records of 1786 confirm this. Mrs. Sheila Morgan has analysed the pottery from one of the cesspits relating to these cottages when they were towards the end of their life (see p. 371). The remains of the foundations of the cottages can be seen on the plan as fragments of rubble walling cut by the footings of the 19th-century school. The two wells, L.55 and L.78, belong to these houses.

**Period 11,
19th century**

In the 19th century, Trench J was at the rear of a wheelwrights shop which was later incorporated into the Girls' School. The cesspits are at the rear of the premises and are represented by Pits J.1, J.2 and J.9. The school was built in 1882 on the areas previously occupied by the five cottages, and some of the cesspits in E and G/H relate to the earlier years of the life of the building, before main drainage was installed.

(Fig. 7.23)

Area 3 – the Wool Store Site

The Area excavated as Area 3 comprised the eastern half of the former Prior's Wool Store (Trenches W, Y and Z). This was the only part of the site later to be occupied by Post Office Building No. 1 which could be dug in advance of building works. The remainder of the land to the south was already occupied by Post Office buildings and plant which were not to be demolished before construction work began. Observations had been carried out in 1962 (*Holmes* 1965) when the new cable chamber extension was put in. The recording was in the hands of the present writer, so some continuity of experience existed. After completion of the Wool Store excavation, observation was maintained on the deep excavation for the new building and a trial trench (Trench A) was dug at the south end of the site, just north of the back wall of Morants. It was realised that features belonging to the Roman Thermae, first noted during alterations to Morants in 1959 and 60 (*Holmes* 1965, p. 10), would run through into the Post Office site.

Period 0; A.D. 43 at the latest (see Areas 2 and 4.p.52)

Trench W, Y and Z
A layer of brown clay (W.32) lay above the natural clay with flints. This was barren of finds, but was not natural, having carbon flecks in it. There was no sign of an ancient turf line, but this layer could well be contemporary with G.200 in Area 2. It equates with Y.41 in Trench Y; which had a small fragment of Roman glass in it, and Layers Z.56 and 66 in Trench Z, which may also be contemporary. Z.66 had a small bronze stud, possibly from a belt.

Period 1; Claudian, A.D. 43 plus

Trench W
A number of post and stakeholes were cut into W.32 (Building W.1). These appear to represent a building of post trench construction of which parts of two walls at right angles survived. The stakeholes were mainly confined within the area of the post trenches, which were very difficult to establish owing to the very dry weather. The larger postholes may belong to a different structure (Building W.2). They were oval in shape, suggesting perhaps that they had been rocked out when the building was demolished. Along the north side of the trench ran a shallow ditch (Slot W.4). This ran eastwards from Trench Y, where it was identified as Slot Y.12. One sherd of pre-Flavian samian was found in it and a silver minim of Tasciovanus was recovered from the silt in the bottom.

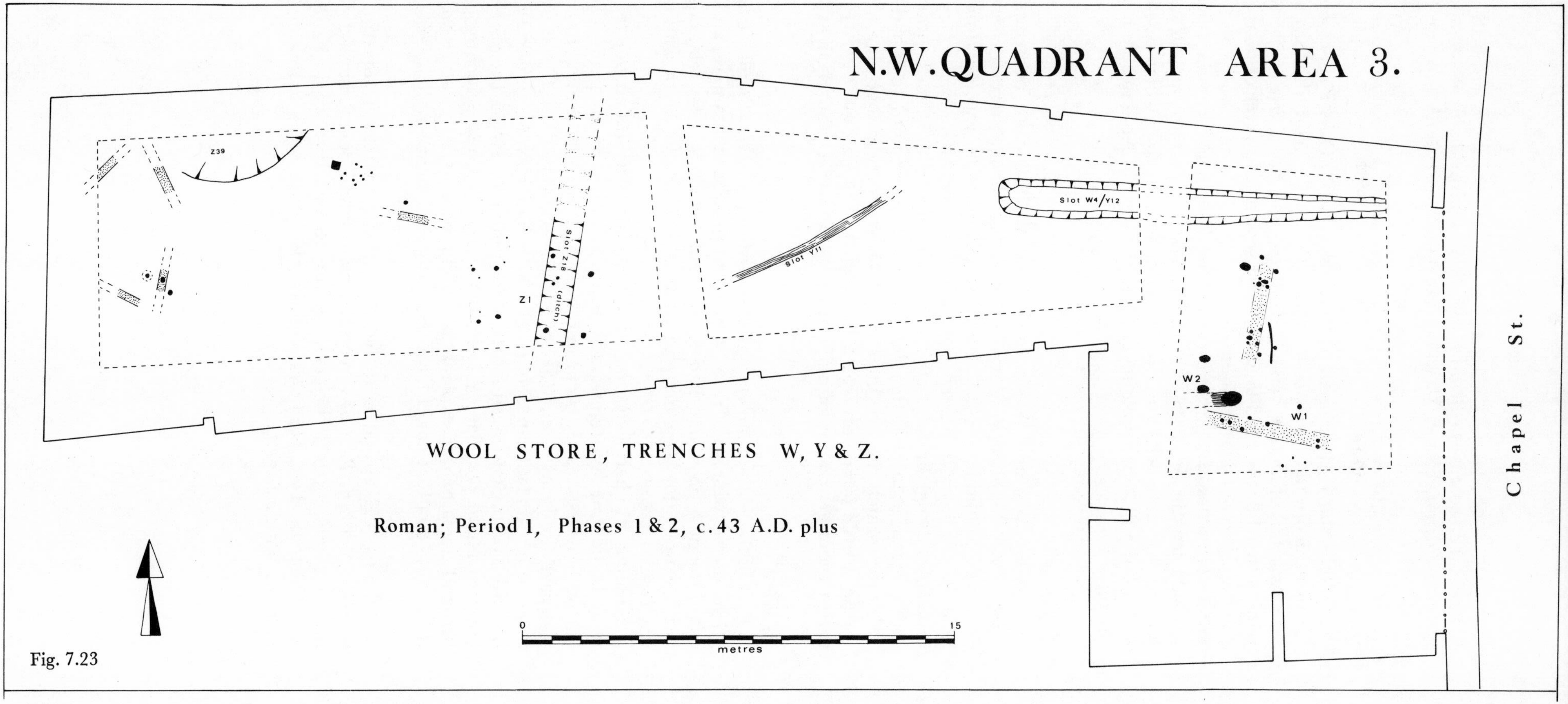

N.W. QUADRANT AREA 3.

Chapel St.

WOOL STORE, TRENCHES W, Y & Z.

Roman; Period 1, Phases 1 & 2, c. 43 A.D. plus

Slot W4/Y12

Slot Y11

Slot Z18 (ditch)

Z1

Z39

W1

W2

0   metres   15

Fig. 7.23

Trench Y

Slot Y.12 ran eastwards into Trench W and probably contemporary with it was a narrow drain, Slot Y.11 which ran north–east. Both of these features were cut into Y.41.

Phase 1

Trench Z

A ditch, Slot Z.18 drained from south to north. Only a short length survived and it was no more than a shallow drain which had partly silted up before being filled in. It was full of animal bones, mainly ox, and had a few coarse ware sherds and a samian sherd dated pre-Flavian. It was sealed by a layer of flints (Z.65) which had one fragment of Claudian samian.

Phase 2

The postholes of a structure (Building Z.1) which cut the filled in ditch and a few odd lengths of beam slot which make no pattern, are all cut from the same horizon and may belong to this phase, as does Pit Z.39 which is sealed by layer Z.39 and has the Period 2 building cut into the top fill. No dateable material came from the pit.

Period 2; Claudio-Neronian (Pl. 8)

Trench W

Buildings W.3 and W.4 cut into layer W.29 and are contemporary, W.3 being built above the filled in Slot W.4. Both were of post trench construction with tie-beams at ground level (one charred section of beam was found in position with the holes in the beam lining up exactly with the postholes in the clay below). Lines of stakeholes along the sides of the wall slots may either be for wattle hurdles or for shuttering pegs to hold the clay walls in position until they had dried out. Layer W.29 into which the buildings were dug was dirty orange clay with many voids in it from wattle fragments which had rotted. The clay must derive from the walls of the previous generation of buildings (W.1 and W.2). No artifacts were found.

Phase 1

Trench Y

Part of the plan of a rectangular structure (Y.1) was found. It had a thin layer of gravel on the west side (Y.35) which had pre-Flavian samian, and the building was cut through Y.34 which had no dateable artifacts. The relationship between the north wall of this structure and what is possibly the south wall of Building Y.2 is unclear.

Phase 2

Building Y.2 had only one wall that can be identified but the plan shows that there is the hint of a right-angle turn northwards at the point where it abuts, or is cut by Building Y.3. It is cut into Y.41 and the only artifact to come from the slot was part of a bead-rimmed jar of early 1st-century date. It was overlaid by a thick layer of burnt daub and charcoal which had Flavian samian in the top and this may well be the destroyed fabric of the building. This is the only evidence that the building might post-date Y.1. Both Y.2 and Y.3 had evidently been destroyed by fire and a reasonable explanation might be that Y.1 was already demolished by then, but equally it could have been a replacement for the others.

Phase 3

Building Y.3 appeared to be of normal post trench construction but had the exterior planked. Part of three sides were found and these had clear traces of the bottom plank, set into the clay, against which a layer of dark organic rubbish had accumulated. Two postholes slightly off centre were found inside the building, together with a hearth.

92

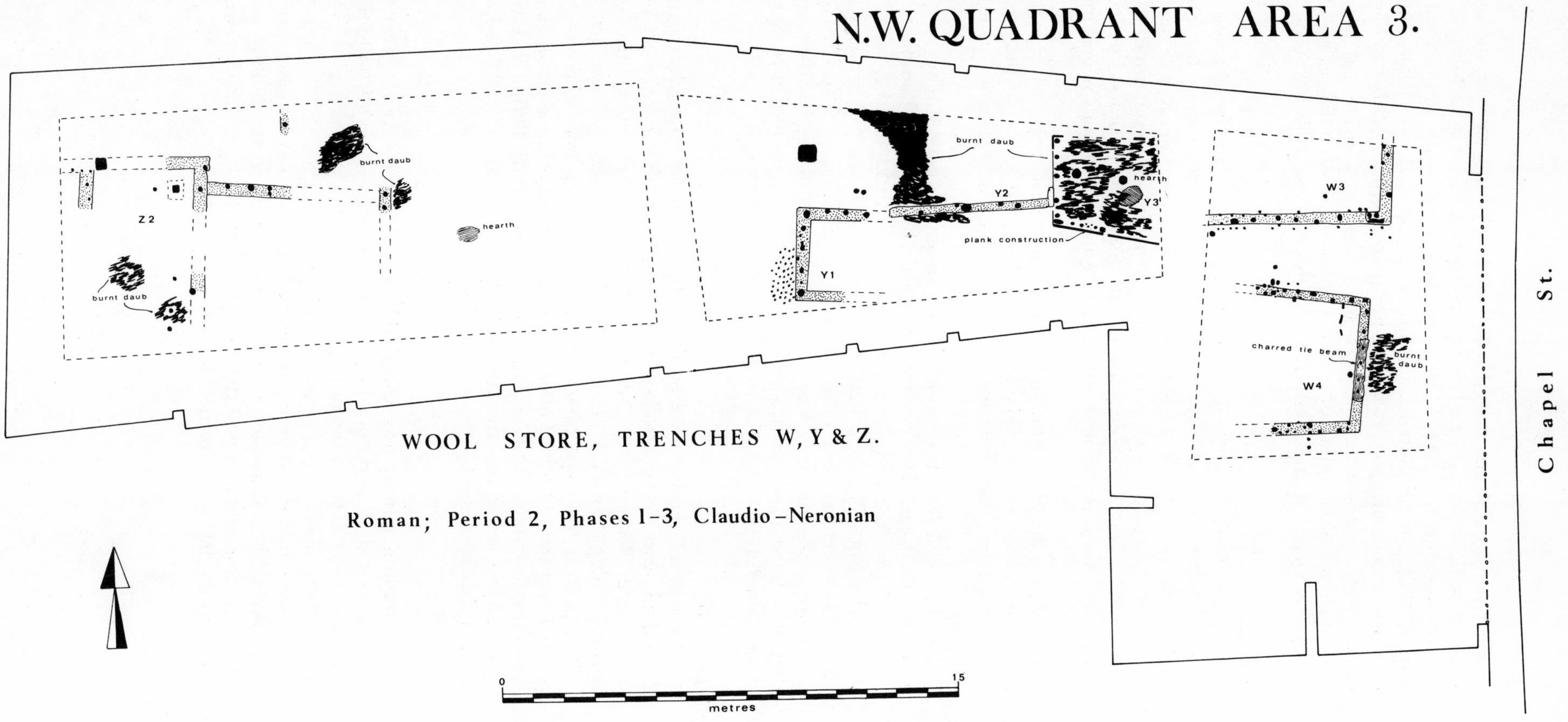

N.W. QUADRANT AREA 3.

Chapel St.

W3

W4

burnt daub

Charred tie beam

hearth

Y3

burnt daub

Y2

plank construction

Y1

hearth

burnt daub

Z2

burnt daub

WOOL STORE, TRENCHES W, Y & Z.

Roman; Period 2, Phases 1–3, Claudio–Neronian

0   metres   15

Fig. 7.24

The building did not extend into Trench W, and viewing the plan as a whole it seems that it might well be later than the rest of the structures. The original floor was represented by Y.48, a layer of dirty tread with many food bones and one fragment of samian dated 1st century. Layer Y.45 was laid upon it and must represent a second floor. It was of hard trodden clay with two sherds of Claudian samian in the surface. A third floor level, Y.43 was laid above this. It also had two samian sherds of Claudian date and a lot of occupation debris, and this was covered in turn by charcoal and daub from the demolished walls and roof.

Phase 2

Trench Z

Only one feature can be assigned to Period 2. This is part of a timber building (Z.2), aligned east–west. It was of similar construction to the Phase 2 Buildings further east and appears to have suffered the same fate, as several patches of burnt daub and charcoal survive between the later pits. The contemporary ground surface may be Z.38 and Z.30 – clay layers with a good deal of food debris, several sherds of Claudio-Neronian samian and one fragment of samian which might be Flavian.

Discussion – Periods 0 to 2

Period 0 is highly tentative, being no more than disturbed natural into which later features are cut, and the fragment of glass in Y.41 and the bronze stud in Z.66 could either have survived from the pre-Conquest period or have been trodden in later on.

The Period 1 features consist of two small drainage ditches, a gulley and traces of slight buildings. The evidence is scarce but gives a Claudian date. It may be compared with the Period 1 features in Areas 2 and 4.

It is not until Period 2 that any considerable activity is noted. By then, wattle and daub structures have been erected and at least two phases are seen. Some of the buildings appear to have remained standing until the early Flavian period when they were burnt down, either accidentally or as part of a deliberate policy of clearing rather squalid huts to make way for other development.

Period 3; Flavian to early 2nd century

Phase 1; c. early Flavian

Trench W

At this stage the Period 2 buildings had been demolished and the residual daub from the houses spread and layers of clay (W.18, 22 and 23) were put down to level up the site. Three pits (W.18, W.19 and W.21) were dug into layer W.18 and a shallow gulley (Slot W.3) drained into Pit W.21 which was evidently a small sump.

The pottery from W.22 had one Flavian samian sherd and one probably Flavian as the latest dated finds. There was a quantity of occupation material in this layer, including food bones and coarse and fine wares from Period 2. Layer W.23, which was dumped across the area above Building W.1 and Slot W.4, had three Flavian samian sherds in the fill.

Trench Y

No building activity was discernable in Phase 1. A layer of green silty clay (Y.36) accumulated or was dumped above the burnt residues of buildings Y.2 and Y.3. This had early Flavian samian.

Elsewhere a layer of greensand chippings in clay (Y.32) and clay layers Y.31 and 34 were laid down above the Period 2 horizon. Y.32 also had Flavian samian.

It may well be that the green silt accumulated in the hollows on the site over a period of time when it was derelict and that the layers of clay were put down to make up the levels for further development.

94

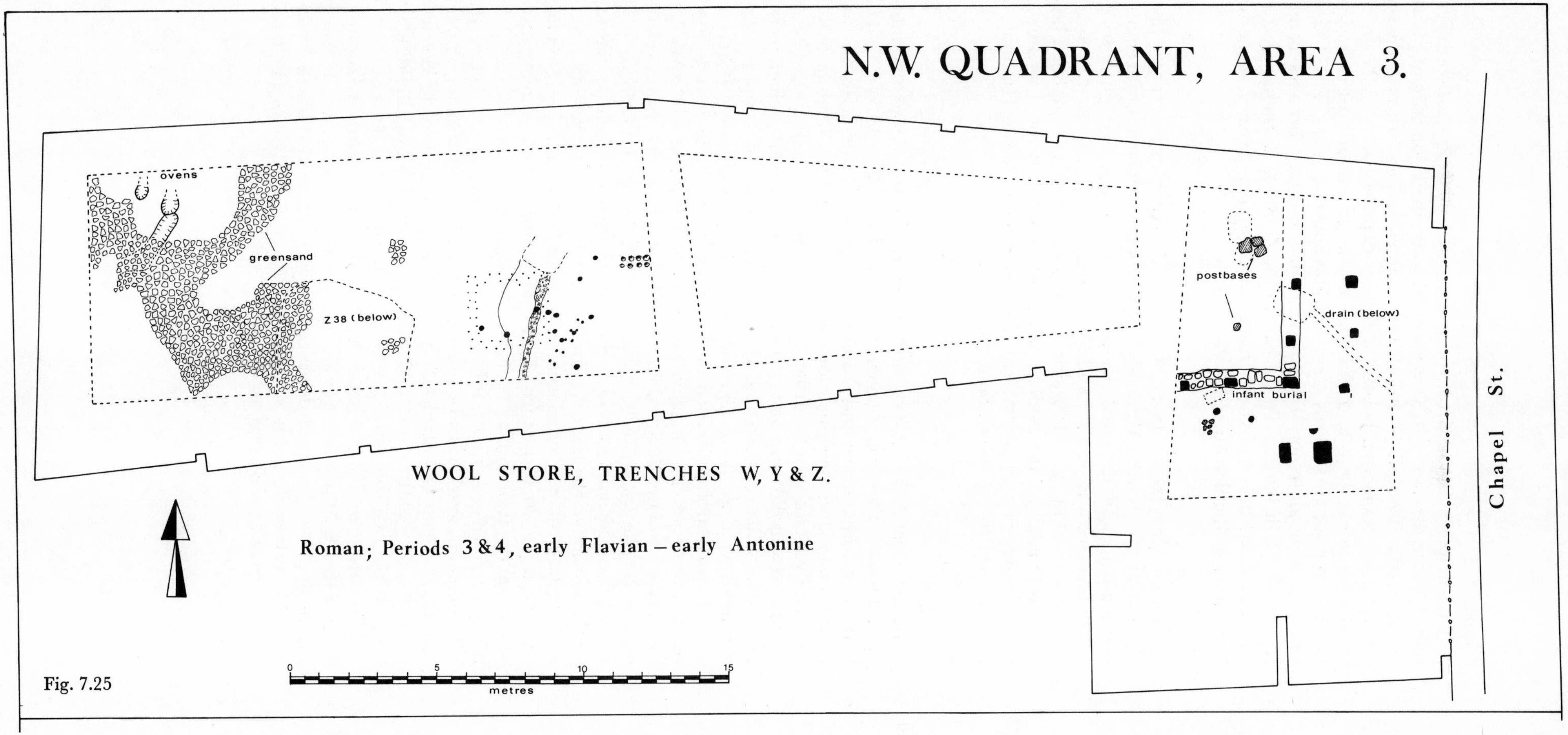

N.W. QUADRANT, AREA 3.

Chapel St.

drain (below)

infant burial

postbases

ovens

greensand

Z 38 (below)

WOOL STORE, TRENCHES W, Y & Z.

Roman; Periods 3 & 4, early Flavian – early Antonine

0 5 10 15

metres

Fig. 7.25

Trench Z

The early Flavian horizon was represented by Z.38 – a layer of dirty brown clay with Flavian samian in it. It was cut by four small domestic ovens at the north-west corner and a deep pit (Z.38) on the south side. This ran into the section and could not be safely excavated beyond a certain depth (see Fig. 7.29, section B–B). It was filled with burnt daub and charcoal and large amounts of pottery and food bones. Of the samian, two sherds were pre-Flavian, one was *c.* A.D. 55–70 and one was Flavian. Several items of badly corroded military bronzes came from this pit, including a belt buckle. To the east of Pit Z.38 was a confused pattern of stakeholes cut into Z.38. Some of these made a rectangular pattern suggesting an enclosure formed by a double row of hurdles.

Phase 2

At some time later a layer of greensand chippings in yellow clay (Z.39) was put down over the trench. Although badly eroded, sufficient of it remained to show that it extended across the whole trench and it is seen in the centre section in Trench Y to the east (see above, Y.32 and Fig. 7.25). A similar layer was noted further west in Area 7 (see below, p. 144) and it can be seen as part of a planned layout. The dating is again Flavian on the evidence of the samian but it could well be late Flavian and was probably contemporary with the construction of the Thermae, of which it must have formed the northern boundary.

Period 4; early 2nd century to Antonine (Pl. 9)

Trench W

By the early 2nd century a dirty layer of clay with large amounts of charcoal had been dumped above the Flavian levels (W.18, W.22 and W.23). This layer (W.15), had early 2nd century and Antonine samian in it and it seems that the area may have remained undeveloped for some time after the Claudian buildings had ceased to exist. Part of a substantial building (W.5) was found. The footings were of greensand and flint and had post sockets set in the walls, which were 0.6 metre wide. Only two walls survived and the full size cannot be conjectured. Postholes for a verandah were set along two sides and there was an infant burial against the south wall. It was carefully buried in a cyst made of tegulae with a complete tile across the top to seal it. Two massive postholes were found cut into W.15 just south of the south-east corner of W.5 and it cannot be certain whether they relate to this building or not. No life span can be conjectured for the building W.5; it could be slightly earlier than the samian evidence for W.15 might suggest, as this layer existed only on the outside of the building. Inside the walls was a layer of brown clay which had nothing later than Flavian samian in it and it is quite feasible that the house may have been put up at the turn of the 1st century and be contemporary with the latest of the buildings of similar construction in Area 2 (see Area 2, Period 3). It could have remained standing until the early Antonine period before the next phase of development caused it to be demolished, and gravel laid across the top. If, prior to the large spread of gravel being laid out in the centre of the town, the original Roman north–south street had extended further south, Building W.5 would have been on the east side of it. No Period 4 features were seen in Trenches Y and Z.

The dating evidence within the Period is consistently Claudio-Neronian except for two sherds of possible Flavian samian in the top of the destruction levels above two of the huts. A similar destruction level was noted in Area 7 (see below, p. 140) and this almost certainly spreads below the County Library on the west side of Tower Street (*Down* 1965, p. 47).

Comparison of the pottery from Area 3 with that from Areas 2 and 4 further north throws up two interesting facts. The first is that the volume of finds of all kinds is very much less from Area 3, even allowing for the difference in size of the area excavated. The second point is that only two sherds of pre-Claudian samian are known from Area 3, as compared with the very much larger sample of Arretine and provincial Arretine from Areas 2 and 4.

The answer may be that Area 3 was peripheral to the military zone during the first few years of the Conquest and that the area was not redeveloped until much later on. The Period 2 structures could possibly have been ancilliary buildings connected with the original military occupation which were later adapted to civilian use, being eventually destroyed when the land was required for another use.

Certainly, the total of eleven finds of military equipment (mainly from Trench Z) is an indication that the earliest occupation was military, but none of the finds are stratified in the earliest layers. Apart from those found in later pits only two might possibly be stratified in a pre-Flavian layer. These come from the layer above the top fill of the ditch (Z.18).

Period 5; Antonine to ? late 3rd century

Trenches W, Y and Z

At some time, probably early in the Antonine period, a layer of gravel was laid down across the whole of the site. By this time Building W.5 had been demolished. The gravel layers were badly eroded in Trenches Y and Z and the most complete sections through it are seen in Trench W (Fig. 7.32). The earliest gravel layer, which sealed W.15, averaged 0.20 metre in thickness and was well compacted. No significant dating evidence was found from the Period 5 metalling in any of the trenches, but it cannot be earlier than Antonine on the basis of the samian evidence from W.15 (see above, Period 4). The Period 5 metalling is represented by W.14, Y.29, Y.30 and Z.33.

Discussion

The gravel spread recorded above is part of a large area laid down in the centre of the town, the boundaries of which are not yet fully defined. It extends from the east side of the Thermae (see Fig. 7.3), and as far north as Area 3, probably up to the south boundary of House 1 in Area 4. It has been located as far south as Nos. 1 and 2 South Street (*Chichester* 2, pp. 1–5 and Fig. 1.2), and as far east as North Street (observation on contractors trenches by the writer). It was recorded when the Post Office was built (*Cottrill* 1934, pp. 159–65 and Fig. 1) and again by J. Holmes and the writer in 1962 (*Holmes* 1965, p. 8 and Fig. 4). In 1934 and 1962 it was thought that this gravel might represent the Forum, but it is now seen to be much too large, although it is fairly certain that the Forum must have been located somewhere near to it, possibly below the complex of buildings which make up the Dolphin and Anchor.

The date it was laid down is now clearly seen to be well on into the 2nd century, and not, as hitherto thought, in the last quarter of the 1st. It represented a considerable landscaping operation but it may be fallacious to assume that it was one large open space. The buildings on the west and north-west corner have been identified and the projected line of Roman North Street is likely to provide the eastern boundary, as recent road works have shown a number of buildings along the east side of the projected line (Fig. 4.2). It is possible that the gravel covered more than one insula and it would be unwise to assume that no buildings existed upon it. Holmes (*op. cit.* p. 10) noted part of a wall in one of the column base holes in 1962

97

which he thought was 4th century, and only further large scale excavation in the critical areas will resolve the problem.

Confirmation of an Antonine date for this part of the town replanning came in November 1976 when observation by the writer on a surface water drainage trench in West Street immediately south of the Dolphin and Anchor, showed the same layer of gravel sealing a layer of flints, greensand and mortar which appeared to be the spread rubble from a destroyed building. Below the rubble was dirty brown clay with charcoal, painted wall plaster and other building debris and the writer recovered part of a rim of a Dr. 33 from it which Mr. Dannell dates as Antonine.

The next question which arises is whether the central metalling is contemporary with the re-planning of the town as a whole which has hitherto been assumed to be late Flavian. It is possible that it came slightly later. Over 700 cubic metres of street metalling were removed from Area 2 when the cross roads was excavated, and the samian evidence gives a probable early 2nd century date for the earliest street. There was no later samian sealed below the gravel as there was in Area 3 and West Street and it may well be that the streets came first in what now appears to be an extensive and protracted planning operation, involving the digging and transportation of thousands of tons of gravel from outside the city.

The transition from military base via native town to *civitas* seems to have taken a century or more, from A.D. 43 to at least the middle of the 2nd century, and in the secondary phase, the familiar problems of availability of resources would no doubt have played a part in slowing down the process. It is a matter for speculation as to whether it was complete before the town became constricted within its defences at the end of the 2nd century.

Period 6; ? 4th century

Evidence of a second layer of metalling is seen in all three trenches, but most clearly in W. A bonding layer of sand was laid down on top of the earlier level and the next layer of gravel (W.3, Y.5 and Z.2), was compacted on top. In Z, the sand layer was absent, but a layer of sticky black soil (Z.32) replaced it. The gravel in Z was destroyed on the west side by Pit Z.12 and is not seen in the section further west (Fig. 7.30). It is replaced by dirty clay and charcoal (Z.40) which was sealed by a layer of clay (Z.10) and a coin of Trajan dated A.D. 98–99 was recovered from it. Z.10 was in turn overlaid by a spread of mortar, probably from a destroyed building in the neighbourhood. A glance at the levels shows that the gravel metalling never existed at that point and it must have terminated where Pit Z.12 cuts the section. It did not exist in plan within the trench, but the layer of greensand below it did, and it is possible that Trench Z just clipped the corner of a destroyed building.

Only in Trench W is any clue to the date found. Layer W.3 had New Forest purple slipped ware in it, and it could have been laid down at any time after the late 3rd century, but a 4th-century date is probably more likely on historical grounds. The dirty tread immediately overlaying W.3 had five mid-4th-century coins in it.

Period 7; late 4th to early 5th century

No evidence existed for any activity during this Period.

Period 8; Saxon, *c.* 8th to early 12th century

No structures or pits belonging to the late Saxon period could be isolated. A number of postholes were found cutting the gravel but these appear on the basis of their fill or relationship to be later. A number of pits had residual late Saxon and Saxo-Norman pottery, and fragments of two loomweights of baked clay were found which could be Saxon, but no sherds were present which could be dated earlier than the 10th century.

Period 9; Medieval, *c.* **late 12th to 15th century**

Trench W

Two pits, W.8 and W.13 were dug through the Roman gravel. Pit W.8 may be slightly earlier on the basis of the pottery, but both fall within Phase 1.

Phase 1; mid to late 12th–13th century

Trench Y

A number of postholes cut through the gravel on the north side of the trench and it is possible to make out part of a structure from the pattern. Several of the related postholes have coarse wares of 12th–13th-century date and the building may be of this Phase or later.

Trench Z

Four pits, Z.10, Z.13, Z.20 and Z.23 are classified as Phase 1 on the basis of their contents and stratification, and several large postholes may also be contemporary on the basis of their fill. The whole area is so badly disturbed by pits and the later vats belonging to the Wool Staplers that no coherent pattern can be worked out.

Phase 2; *c.* **14th century**

This is only perceptible in Trench Z, where three pits, Z.1, Z.2 and Z.8, have 14th-century material as the latest artifacts.

Phase 3; *c.* **late 14th to 15th century**

Trench W

Pit W.6 may belong to this phase. It postdates Pits W.8 and W.13 and has no later material.

Trench Y

Fragments of three slots, Y.4, Y.5 and Y.10 are probably Phase 3 and the first two make up the corner of a structure. The area enclosed by these slots (Y.33) had part of a glazed strap handle, while the layer above (Y.15) which may be part of the destruction level of the building had many roof tiles, some glazed, and paint under glaze wares of the 15th century. Pits Y.3 and Y.11 are assigned to Phase 3, the latest dated material from Pit Y.3 being 14th–15th-century glazed wares and from Pit Y.11 numbers of peg tiles, the latest of which may postdate the 14th century.

Trench Z

Four pits, Z.4, Z.5, Z.12 and Z.21 may be assigned to Phase 3, but the dating is strictly on the contents and it is by no means certain that the pits are not later.

Period 10; *c.* **16th to 18th century**

Phase 1; *c.* **16th century**

Pit W.14 was a deep rectangular pit sealed below a layer of burnt clay. The contents were late medieval glazed wares, painted wares of 15th-century date and roof tiles which might be later. The pit fill suggests an early 16th-century date at the latest.

Trench Y

Two deep rectangular slots (Y.1 and Y.2) were dug through the Roman gravel, and this was later backfilled. They could have been cesspits as they were *c.* 1.25 metres deep. The fill suggests a late 16th-century date. A well (Pit Y.2) was probably contemporary. This was not fully excavated, as it was partly in the north section, but the contents suggests an early to mid-16th-century date.

99

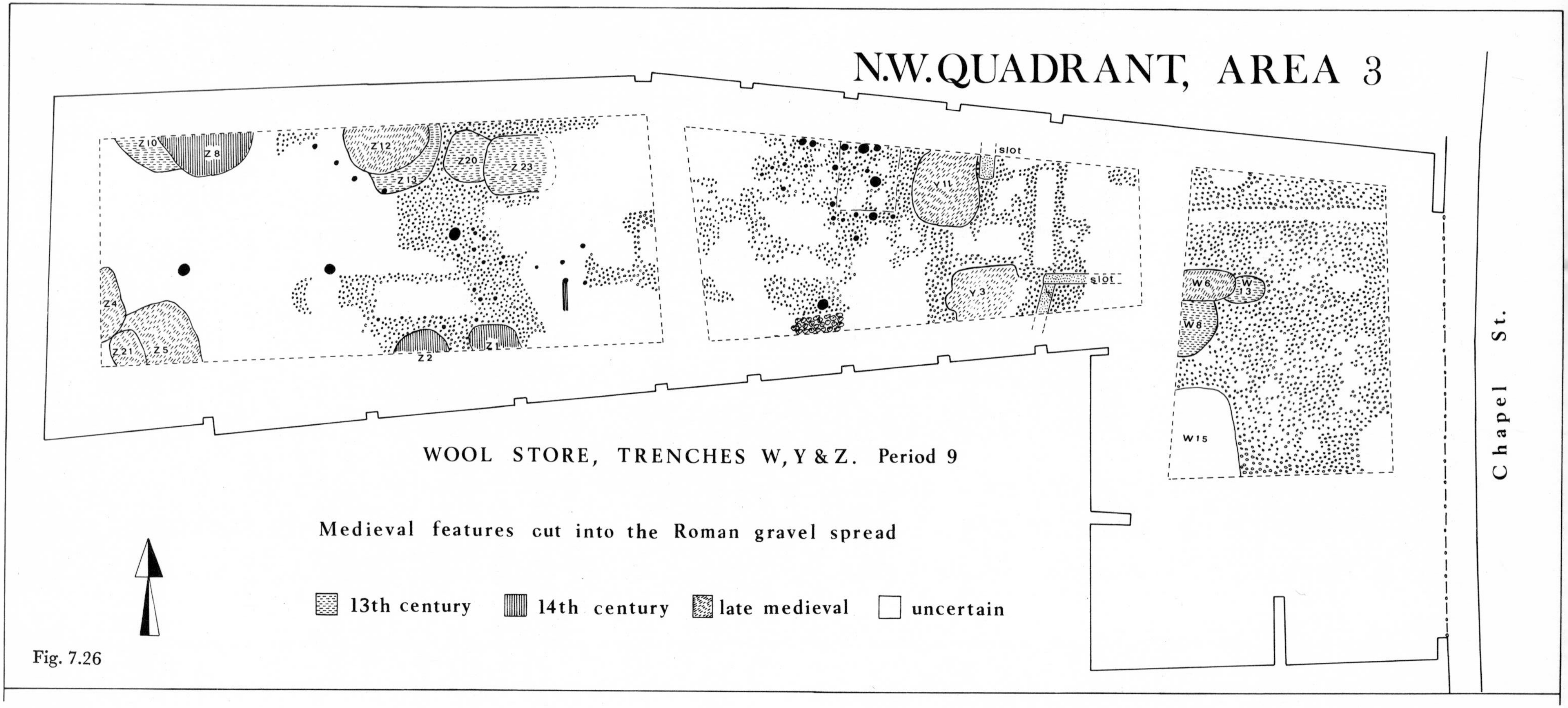

N.W. QUADRANT, AREA 3

Chapel St.

W 9
W 10
W 8
W 15

101S
101S

Y 11
Y 3

Z 23
Z 20
Z 19
Z 12
Z 21
Z 2

Z 18
Z 10
Z 9
Z 11
Z 5
Z 4

WOOL STORE, TRENCHES W, Y & Z. Period 9

Medieval features cut into the Roman gravel spread

☒ 13th century ▥ 14th century ▧ late medieval ☐ uncertain

Fig. 7.26

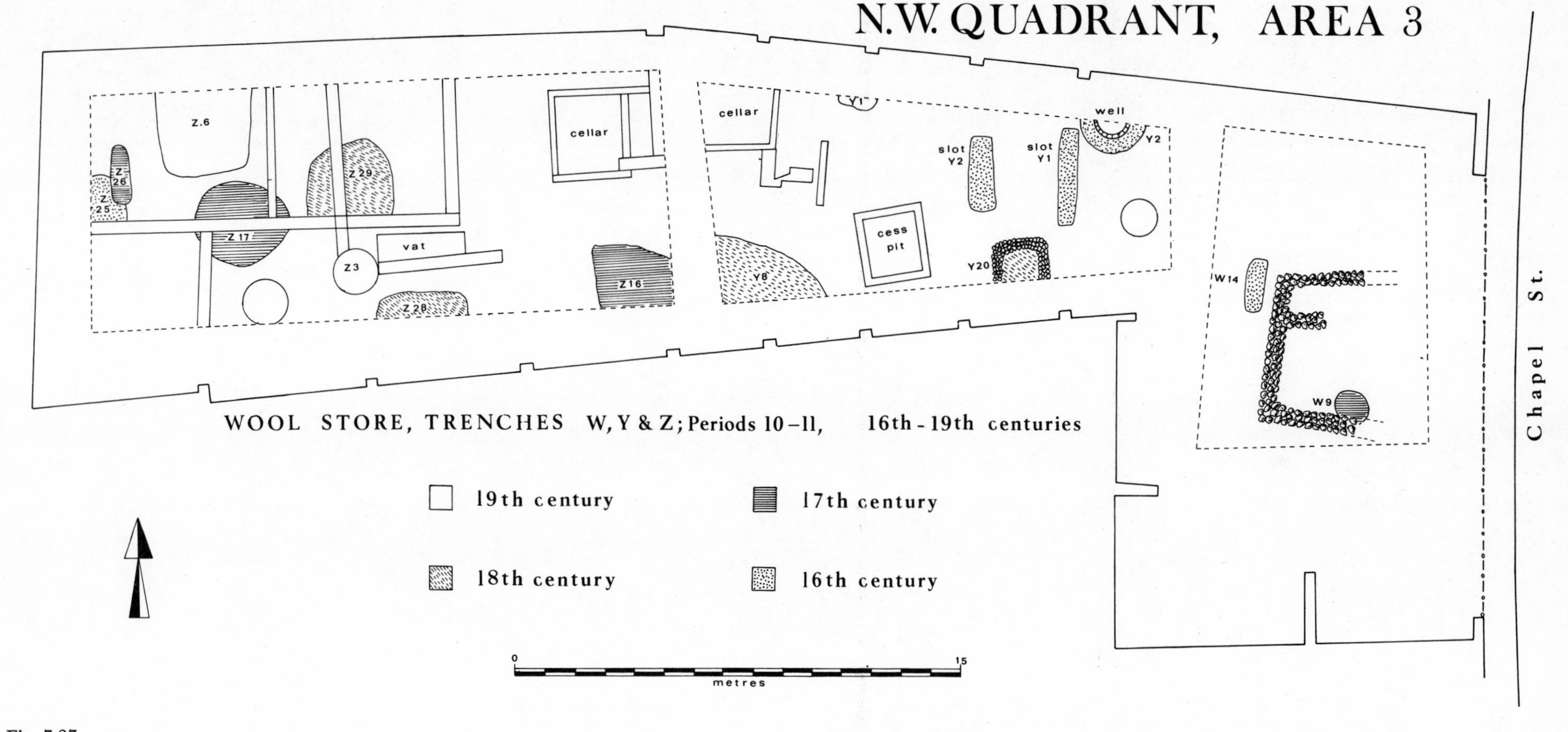

N.W. QUADRANT, AREA 3

Chapel St.

WOOL STORE, TRENCHES W, Y & Z; Periods 10–11,   16th–19th centuries

19th century

18th century

17th century

16th century

metres

0   15

Fig. 7.27

W 9

W 14

well

Y 2

slot
Y 1

slot
Y 2

Y 11

cess
pit

cellar

Y 20

Y 6

cellar

Z 16

cellar

Z 6

Z 22

vat

Z 3

Z 28

Z 17

Z 26

Z 25

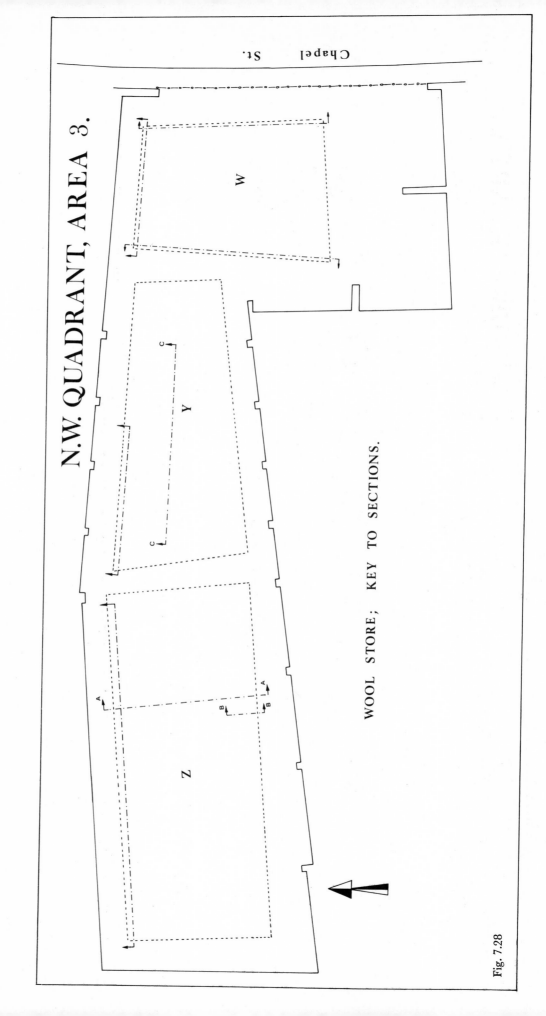

N.W. QUADRANT, AREA 3.

Chapel St.

WOOL STORE; KEY TO SECTIONS.

W

Y

Z

Fig. 7.28

AREA 3, WOOL STORE, TRENCH Z.

Section A—A

Pit Z 38, East face, B-B

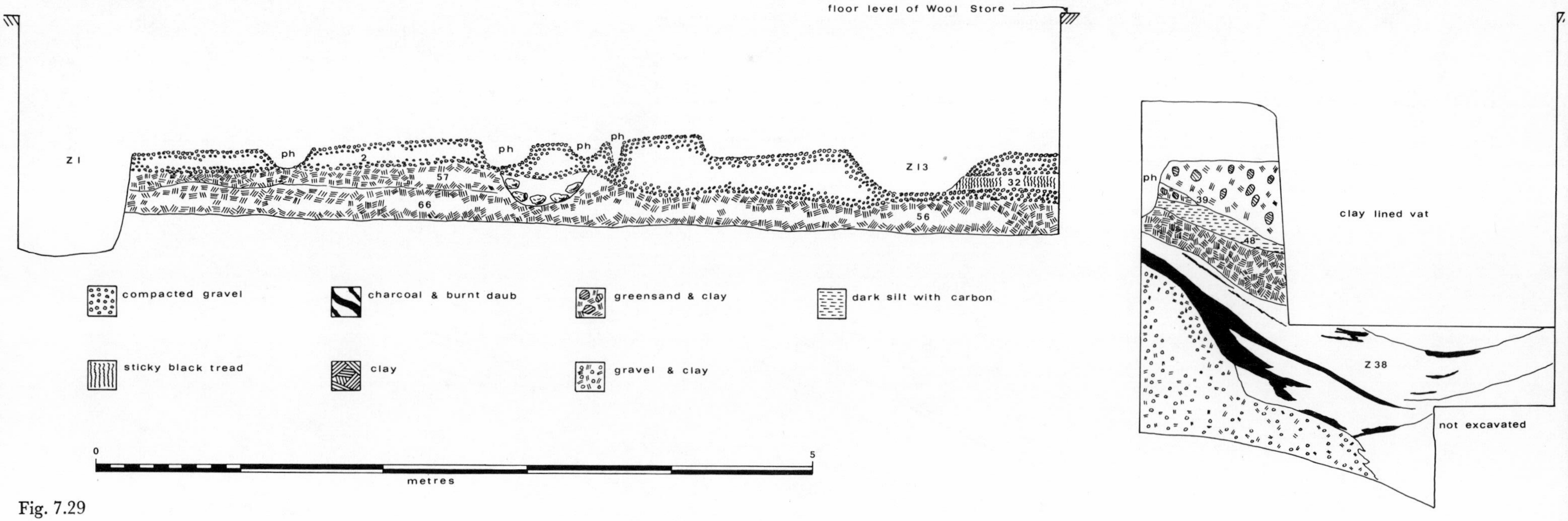

floor level of Wool Store

clay lined vat

not excavated

z I

z 38

ph

ph

ph

ph

ph

ph

ph

z 113

z 113

66

57

56

32

31

18

compacted gravel

sticky black tread

charcoal & burnt daub

clay

greensand & clay

gravel & clay

dark silt with carbon

metres

0

5

Fig. 7.29

AREA 3, WOOL STORE, TRENCH Z, NORTH SECTION

0·m to 7·3 m

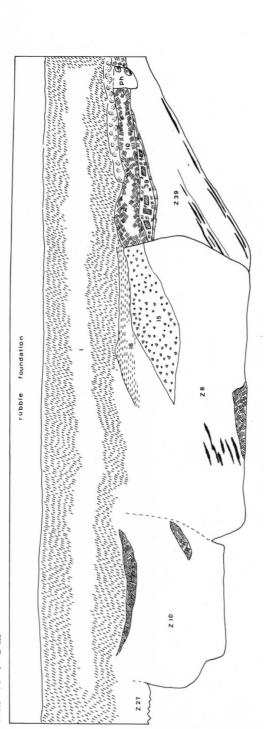

7.7 m to 18·4 m

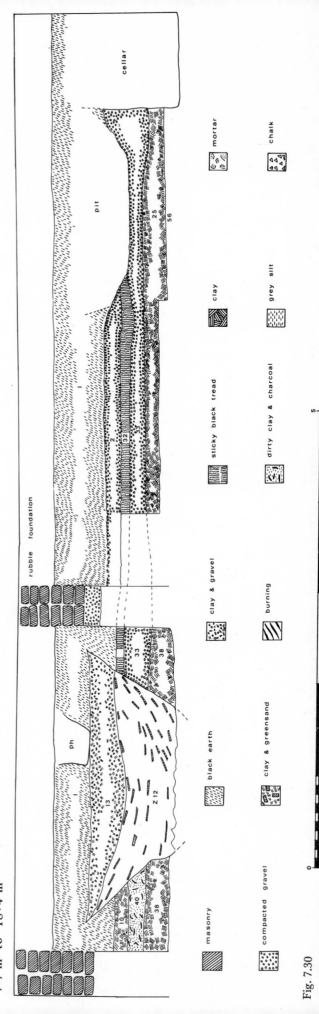

masonry	black earth	sticky black tread	mortar
compacted gravel	clay & greensand	clay & gravel	dirty clay & charcoal	clay	chalk
		burning	grey silt

Fig. 7.30

AREA 3, WOOL STORE, TRENCH W, WEST SECTION.

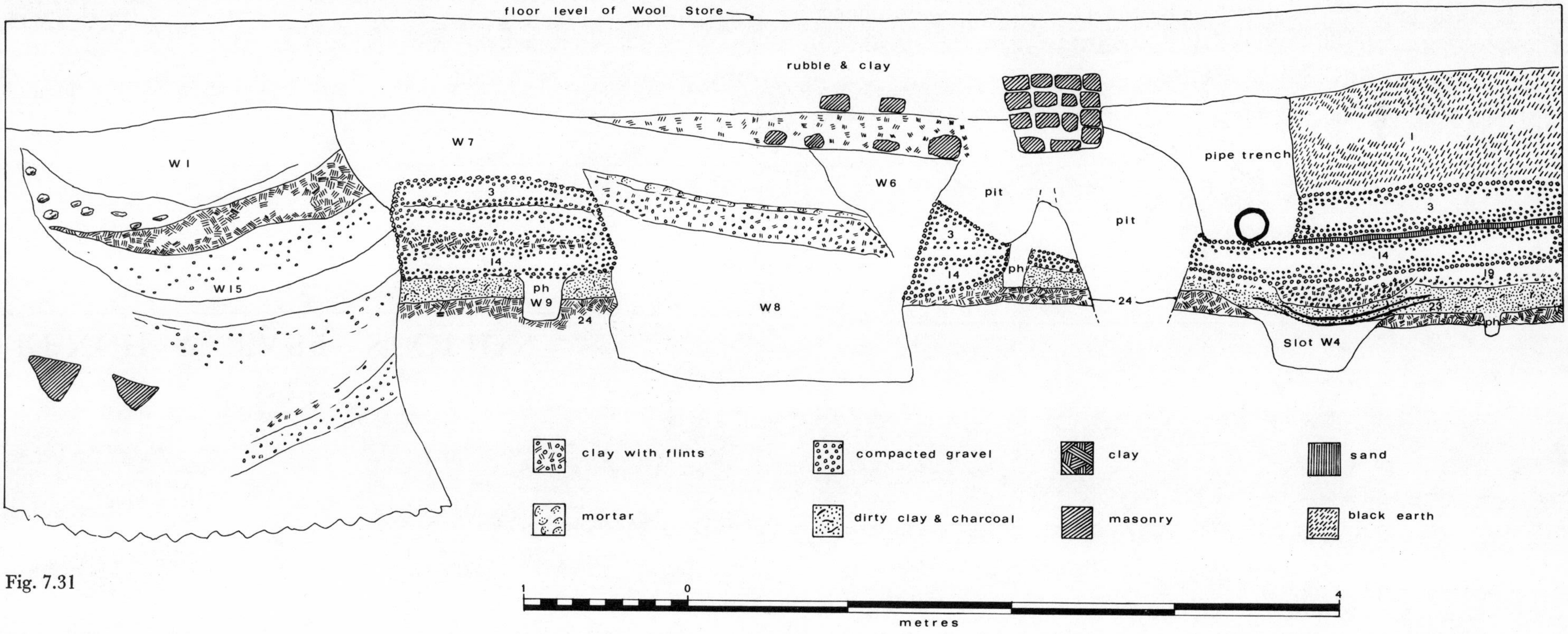

floor level of Wool Store

rubble & clay

pipe trench

Slot W4

pit

pit

W6

W7

W8

W9 ph

W1

W15

ph

24

24

3

14

19

3

14

3

14

Fig. 7.31

clay with flints	compacted gravel	sand	black earth
mortar	dirty clay & charcoal	clay	masonry

metres

0   4

AREA 3, WOOL STORE, TRENCH W, NORTH SECTION.

rubble & clay

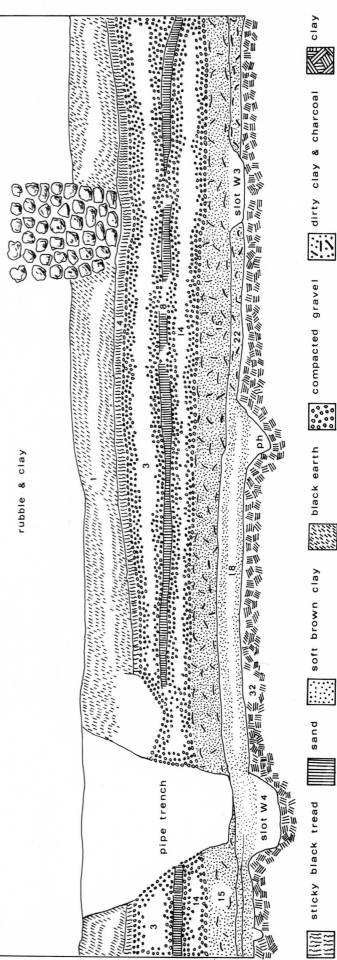

TRENCH W, EAST SECTION.

rubble & clay

clay

dirty clay & charcoal

compacted gravel

black earth

soft brown clay

sand

sticky black tread

AREA 3, WOOL STORE, NORTH SECTION, TRENCH Y

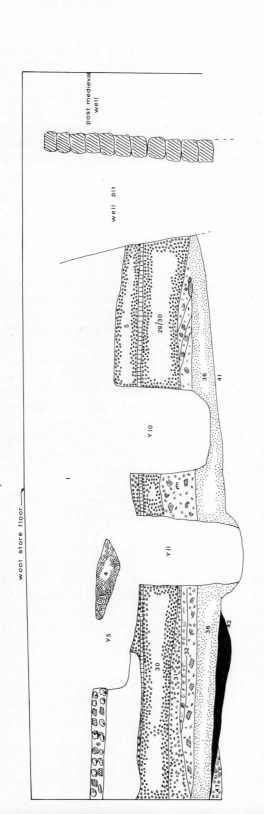

TRENCH Y, CENTRAL SECTION C–C

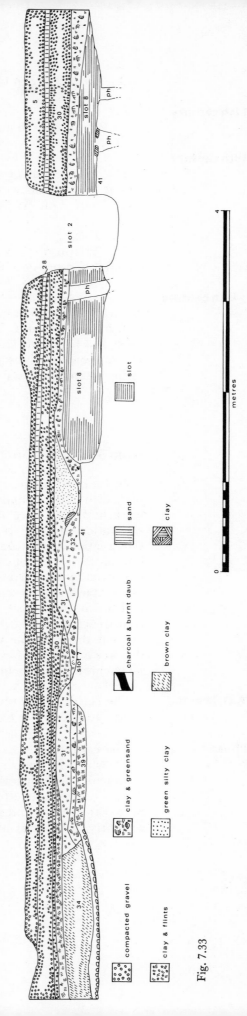

compacted gravel

clay & flints

clay & greensand

green silty clay

charcoal & burnt daub

brown clay

sand

clay

slot

Fig. 7.33

Trench Z

One pit (Z.25) can be assigned to Phase 1 on the basis of the pottery.

Phase 2; 17th century

Trench W and Z

Pit W.9, Z.6, Z.16 and Z.17 are dated as Phase 2.

Phase 3; 18th century

Trench W

The foundations of a small rectangular building were found below the black topsoil (W.1). This was built directly on the Roman gravel and partly overlaid a small Phase 2 pit (W.9) and this provides the only evidence of date.

Trench Y and Z

Two pits in Y (Y.8 and Y.20) and two in Z (Z.28 and 29) had 18th-century material and pre-date the Wool Staplers and are accordingly classified as Phase 3.

Period 11; 19th century

The whole of Area 3 was covered by buildings in the 19th century and the surviving foundations of some of these are seen in Trench Z. They had a connection with the wool industry as can be seen from several clay lined vats and the fact that the drains below the later Wool Store floor had numbers of wooden bale pegs in the silt. At some time later the Wool Store was built and a concrete floor laid across the earlier foundations and cellars.

(Fig. 7.34)

Area 3 – Trial Trench A

In June 1973, a trial trench (Trial Trench A) was opened up on Post Office land just north of the boundary wall of Morants (see Fig. 7.34). By this time the ground-work for Post Office Building No. 1 had commenced and this involved a deep excavation and the removal of over 16,000 cubic metres of soil from the site. Observation on the contractors operations was combined with a hasty rescue dig to link up the results of earlier observations in Morants in 1960 with what was being destroyed by the current work. The top metre of soil was taken off with a machine, as the object of the exercise was to locate and record the Roman Thermae building, and if time permitted, to go below it for dating evidence. The dimensions of the trial trench were just under 100 square metres and it was positioned where it was thought the Thermae would be if it extended northwards into the site. Although this was a high pressure rescue dig, the evidence is presented where possible in the same chronological sequence as the remainder of the sites.

Period 0; A.D. 43 at the latest

The earliest layer observed was A.21, a layer of orange clay with flints resting upon natural. It was barren of finds, but had charcoal flecks in it.

Period 1; Phase 1, c. A.D. 43 plus

The earliest features were Slot A.2, A.26 and Slot A.6. Slot A.2 was a narrow drain which ran northwards and was traced for a distance of nine metres in the contractors hole. It was 0.30 metre deep, 0.45 metre wide and had probably been timber revetted. The fill contained one sherd of Tiberio-Claudian samian. Layer A.26 was a shallow pit which had been partially destroyed by a later ditch. The fill was dirty clay and it had fragments of white slip coated butt beaker, Gallo-Belgic

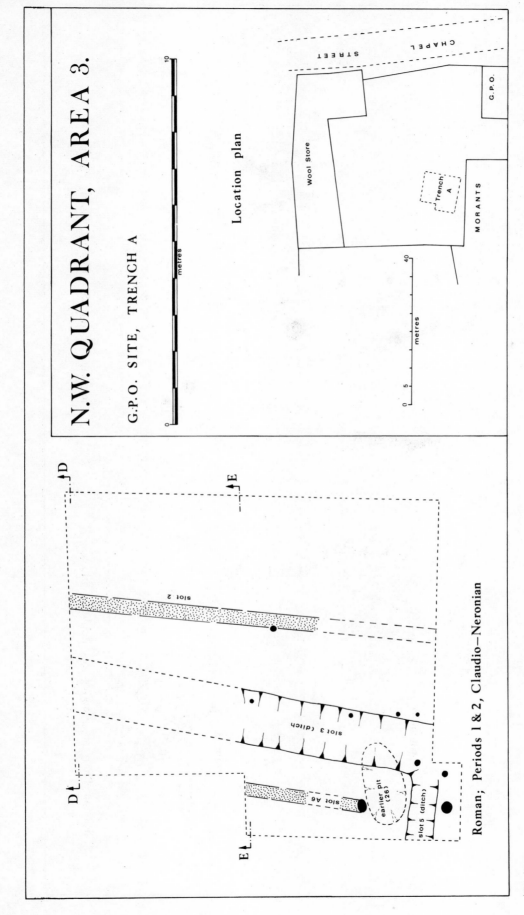

N.W. QUADRANT, AREA 3.

G.P.O. SITE, TRENCH A

Location plan

Wool Store

Trench A

MORANTS

G.P.O.

CHAPEL

STREET

metres

slot 2

slot 3 (ditch)

slot A6

earlier pit (26)

slot 5 (ditch)

D

D

E

E

Roman; Periods 1 & 2, Claudio–Neronian

Fig. 7.34

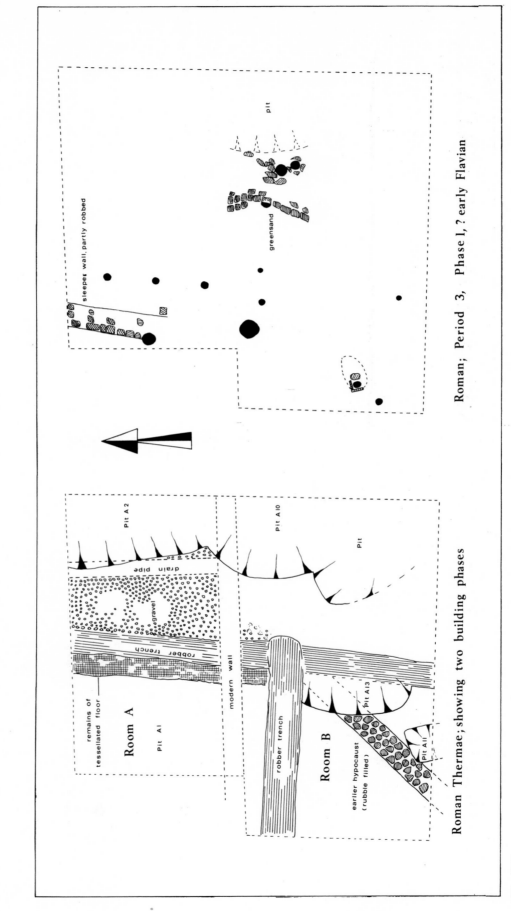

Roman; Period 3, Phase 1, ? early Flavian

sleeper wall, partly robbed

greensand

pit

Room A

remains of
tessellated floor

Pit A1

drain pipe

gravel

robber trench

modern wall

Pit A 2

Pit A10

Pit

Room B

robber trench

earlier hypocaust
(rubble filled)

Pit A13

Pit A11

Roman Thermae; showing two building phases

Fig. 7.35

white ware and some iron slag. A slot (A.6) was aligned north–south and terminated in a posthole at the south end just short of the pit (A.26). It may be contemporary with Slot A.2 as it is on the same alignment and both slots were cut into A.21. No dating evidence was recovered.

Period 2;
c. Claudius-Nero

Slot A.3 was a shallow drainage ditch running north–south. It was joined at right-angles by Slot A.5, another narrower drain coming in from the west side. The fill of both ditches contained large amounts of food bones and oyster shells and one sherd of Claudian samian. The ditch postdated the Pit A.26 which is partially truncated, and continued southwards below Morants.

Period 3; ? early
Flavian

Phase 1

Layer 11 was a layer of dark brown clay with a lot of organic material in it. It sealed the Period 2 layers and had the postholes of a timber building cut through it and part of a sleeper wall of greensand blocks survived on the surface. No closely dateable sherds were found and this Period is thought to be c. early Flavian by comparison with Period 3 elsewhere.

Phase 2

The Phase 1 building was demolished and a layer of brown clay (A.10) was put down. It had two sherds of samian of which the latest was Nero-Vespasianic in date. It could well have been a levelling up layer as it appears on both sides of the robber trench for the Thermae wall in Section E–E (see Fig. 7.36).

The Thermae

The relationship between the Thermae wall and Layer A.10 is not clear due to the robbing, as the robber trench has destroyed the evidence at a crucial point where the layers of make-up and metalling outside (east) of the wall, abut the footings. There may have been an earlier wall of slighter proportions, but this is incapable of proof. All that can be said is that there were parts of two rooms in the area covered by the trial trench, which for convenience will be classified as Rooms A and B, with Room A being the most northerly.

Room A. This had a tessellated floor of which only a strip 0.5 metre wide survived along the west side of the robbed wall. The rest was destroyed by a large medieval pit (A.1). The floor was constructed of white tesserae cut from hard chalk and these were laid on a foundation of pinky white mortar which had a sherd from a purple-slipped New Forest beaker in it, suggesting a date of late 3rd to 4th century from the laying of the floor, if not for the construction of this part of the Thermae. A date of early 4th century for the floor is preferred.

Room B. This was south of Room A, the dividing wall having been robbed out.

Phase 1

At this stage the room was heated by a cross flue hypocaust and was probably part of a tepidarium as no signs of excessive heat were noted.

Phase 2

At some time later the room, and probably the associated range of rooms (see below, Area 7) was replanned and converted into a cold room. The flue was filled with rubble, mainly greensand, and this had a sherd of Claudio-Neronian samian in it which is probably residual. A pink mortar floor was constructed above and a white tessellated pavement laid on it. On the east side of the wall the ground level was made up by dumping layers of clay and greensand (A.17). This was barren, but a thin spread of bronze slag in it suggests that the building of the Thermae

111

AREA 3, G.P.O. SITE, SECTIONS D–D & E–E

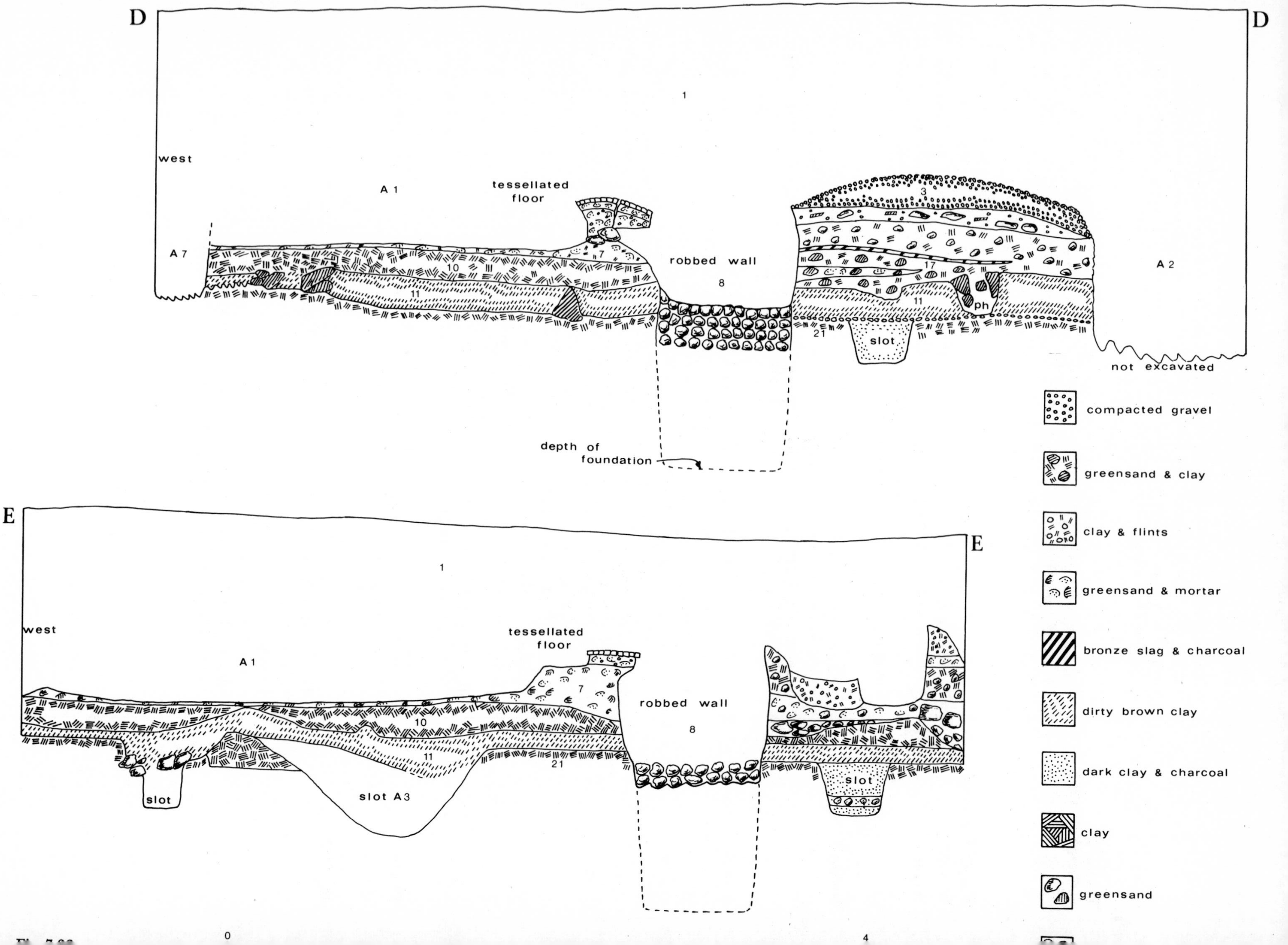

compacted gravel

greensand & clay

clay & flints

greensand & mortar

bronze slag & charcoal

dirty brown clay

dark clay & charcoal

clay

greensand

D

west

A 7

tessellated floor

A 1

10

11

7

robbed wall

8

depth of foundation

slot

21

11

ph

17

3

A 2

not excavated

E

west

tessellated floor

A 1

10

11

slot A 3

slot

7

robbed wall

8

21

slot

destroyed an earlier bronze working process. The layer of gravel above the make-up layers was well compacted and had medieval and Saxo-Norman sherds in the top. Observations on the large excavation by the contractor a few feet away to the north showed that the east wall of the Thermae extended northwards for a further 15 metres before it was seen to turn westwards. Only the bottom few centimetres of the foundations could be traced as the large machines used by the contractors were sited in the hole and taking vertical "bites" out of the section but luckily not quite deep enough to destroy the whole of the foundations in one go. At a point 9 metres from the north boundary of the trial trench there was a change. The foundations terminated and then began again about 0.30 metre further on, the footings at this point being deeper. This added another 6.2 metres to the north end of the building, and allowing for the thickness of the walls, gave a room 4.2 metres by 7.2 metres east–west.

The foundations of the east wall of the Thermae as levelled and projected on to the section drawing (Fig. 7.36) were 1.5 metres deep from floor level, and the unrobbed portion was too solidly mortared for us to excavate it in the available time.

As a result of the trial excavation and observation it has been possible to trace the east wing of the Thermae for a distance of 27 metres, and if this is related to the observations in 1960 (*Holmes* 1965) then a total of 57 metres can be postulated (see Fig. 7.3). During observations and limited excavation in 1960, it was noted that there were filled in cross-flue hypocausts below the floor(s) seen in the column base holes. This was confirmed again in 1973, and it can be seen that part of the east wing which originally started life as a series of heated rooms was subject to a change of function later on. This may have been between the late 3rd to early 4th century if the evidence of the New Forest sherd is accepted. Later in the summer of 1973 the contractors cut an access ramp down the west side of the Post Office site and this sectioned a whole series of rooms belonging to the Thermae. At the north end of the site, near the top of the ramp, we carried out a hasty excavation lasting 48 hours to clean and record the features present. In doing so, we discovered and sectioned a deep drain or sewer, similar to the one found below County Hall (*Chichester* 2, pp. 39–58 and Pl. 3). As this feature was later excavated a few metres away on the west side of the ramp in Area 7 (see below), the excavation is dealt with in that section.

Later Periods

The speed with which this excavation had to be carried out precluded any detailed examination of later periods. It was noted however that the robber trenches contained only unglazed Saxo-Norman and early medieval wares, as the latest finds.

Area 5 – Gospel Hall Site

In 1973 the Post Office arranged for demolition of the recently acquired Gospel Hall (see Fig. 7.1) sufficiently in advance of the new road (The Providence) to allow us to occupy the site for a year. The site had to be dug in two parts owing to the problems of soil dumping and the need to leave it backfilled. Accordingly, two trenches were dug, Trench O at the east end of the site with a view to further examining the frontage of House 2 with the Roman street and Trench P was dug immediately west of it, and in the final stages it was extended southwards into the garden of No. 6 Chapel Street to trace part of House 2.

Period 0

Natural Soil was clay with flints, (0.65 and P. 94)

The former was barren but P.94 had six small fragments of Roman grey ware in the top. No trace of the old turf line was found.

Period 1;
c. A.D. 43 plus

Most of the area covered by Trench O was garden from the mid 2nd century onwards, consequently the earlier features were badly eroded by cultivation. Nevertheless, a thin layer of pale yellow clay (0.67) with some charcoal in it overlaid natural (0.65) at the east end, and this had postholes cut through it. It was barren of finds, but a layer of brown clay in Trench P (P.89) which may equate with it, had three small fragments of undateable grey ware.

Period 2;
Claudius–Nero

Fig. 7.37

Trench O

Cut into natural and through 0.67 where it survived were postholes and slots belonging to a building (Building 0.1). The postholes and slots were very badly truncated by later cultivation and pit digging but three lines of postholes, some in post pits, could be clearly seen and a few lengths of beam slots were present (see Fig. 7.37). Two slots produced dating evidence – part of a butt beaker and a fragment of pre-Flavian samian. It is just possible that two buildings were present as the most southerly line of postholes diverge slightly, but it is most likely that they are all part of the same building and that it is part of a store or granary.

Trench P

At the west end of the site three phases of activity were noted:

Phase 1

A number of small postholes were cut into P.79 and while some of these make a sequence in alignment with the timber buildings, another group do not and may relate to an earlier phase of activity.

Phase 2

The slots of a rectangular structure (Building P.1) were found. The slots cut P.79 and the building was in alignment with those found further south in Area 2 (Fig. 7.6), and may well be contemporary. One sherd of Claudian samian came from the slots.

Phase 3

Building P.1 was demolished and Building P.2 of similar construction was erected. It had Tiberian Arretine and Claudian samian in the slots and was cut through P.79 and the slots of the earlier building. Also probably contemporary are two sets of slots further east. The buildings to which they relate had been almost completely destroyed by the 4th century house but the small fragments remaining were sealed by layer P.60, an occupation layer with nothing but pre-Flavian material in it, including provincial Arretine, Gallo-Belgic white wares and early 1st century coarse wares.

114

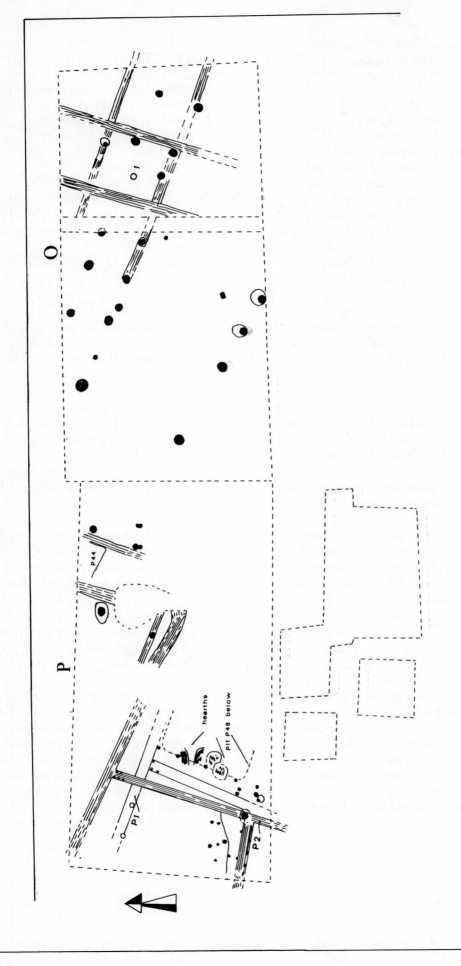

No 7 CHAPEL STREET

P44

hearths

Pit P48 below

P1

P2

AREA 5, GOSPEL HALL, TRENCHES O & P

Roman; Period 2, Claudius–Nero; Period 3, Flavian – Trajan

0

metres

15

Fig. 7.37

**Period 3;
Flavian–Trajan**

No building activity seems to have taken place during this period. In Trench O the Period 2 building was sealed in part by layers 0.62/63, 0.64 and 0.66. Layer 0.64 was a make-up layer of brown clay which had an infant burial in it (probably inserted from higher up when the land was garden) and containing much debris from an earlier building, e.g. tesserae and tegulae, as well as domestic pottery. The latest dated artifact was a samian sherd dated Nero-Vespasian. Layers 0.62/63 were clay layers, 0.63 having some blue gault clay, and they were apparently make-up layers. Elsewhere on the same horizon, but disassociated by reason of intervening pits, was a layer of green silty clay (0.66), which had Trajanic samian.

In Trench P two phases of occupation were noted:

Phase 1

A pit (P.48) was dug through the Period 2 levels. Only a small part of this feature survived, the fill was loose gravel and it had no artifacts. It was sealed by Layer P.74, yellow clay with mortar flecks which was probably demolished daub. The latest dated pottery was a sherd of ? Flavian South Gaulish samian.

Phase 2

A series of small hearths were constructed on top of P.74; these could not be related to any structure.

**Period 4;
c. early 2nd to early 3rd century**

Trench O

At this stage the east end of the site had become a cultivated plot, probably a garden, and remained so for a long time. The clay make-up layers 0.62/63 were riddled with signs of root activity and probably indicate a shrubbery on that part of the site.

Fig. 7.38

Phase 1 (undated)

Trench P

A layer of dark brown clay was laid down above P.74, sealing the earlier hearths, but later hearths were laid upon it, suggesting that this was just the renewal of a floor. No boundaries to the implied room could be found.

Phase 2

P.46 sealed Layer 71. This was brown clay with flints and mortar and may have been intended as a floor. It had a small hearth on it.

Phase 3

A shallow wall footing of flints (P.64) cut Layer 46. This was directly below a later clay partition wall but on a slightly different alignment and it had a gap in it (see Fig. 7.38) which suggests a doorway. Only two small sections survived; it is likely that it was a dwarf wall for a timber-framed structure (Building P.3), and that only the western end was within the excavation.

**Period 5;
c. 3rd to c. early 4th century
(Pl. 10)**

Building P.3 wall footings were covered by a layer of dirty clay (P.61) and this was sealed in turn by an occupation layer P.41 which had a late Antonine samian sherd in it. As viewed in section they appear to be make-up layers for another building (House 2, Phase 1, see above.)

A thin mortar floor (P.7) was laid upon the make-up layers P.61 and 41 and on the west side of a later masonry wall which may not be Roman, or, if so, post dates all other features. This had a flat pilae tile set in it and may have been a corridor along the east side of the building. Bounding it on the west side was the clay partition wall, which was 0.28 metre wide and plastered and painted on both exterior surfaces. Two similar clay wall partitions joined it at right angles, giving the elements of four small rooms. Two of the floors were tessellated, the other two being mortar. Little remained of the rooms, which were largely destroyed by the wall foundations

116

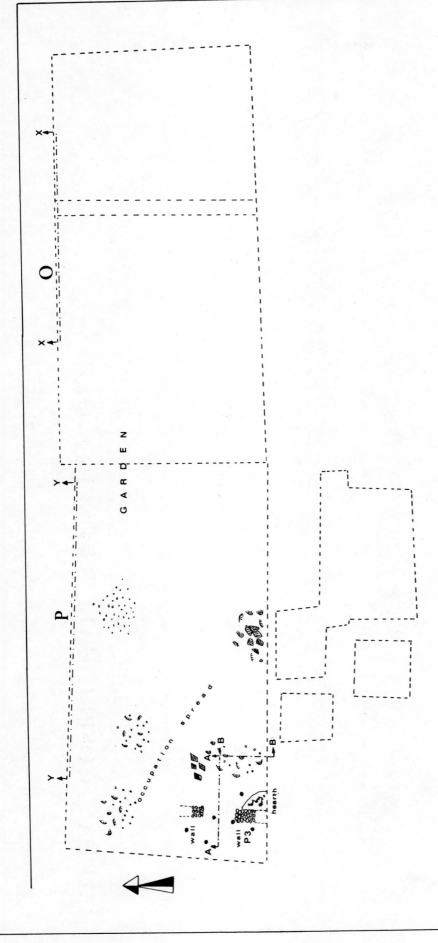

No.7 CHAPEL STREET

G A R D E N

occupation spread

wall

wall
P3

hearth

AREA 5, GOSPEL HALL, TRENCHES O&P

Roman; Period 4, c. early 2nd – early 3rd century

0   metres   15

Fig. 7.38

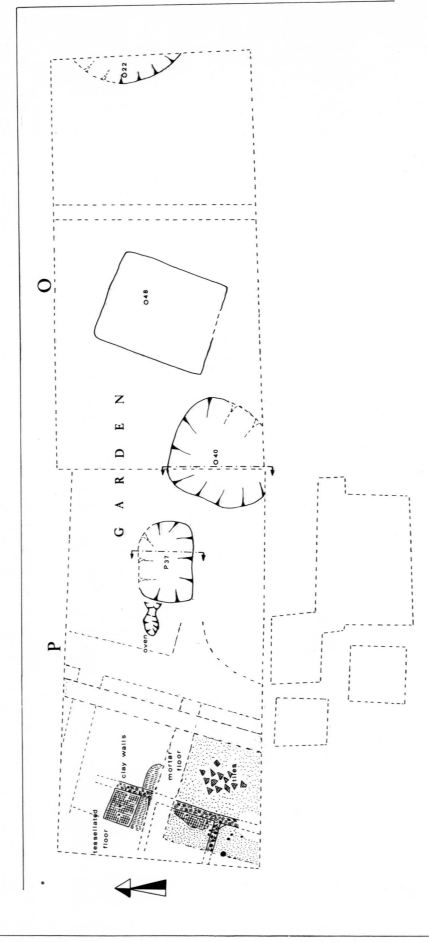

No.7 CHAPEL STREET

AREA 5, GOSPEL HALL, TRENCHES O&P

Roman; 3rd—early 4th century, Period 5, House 2, phase 1

Fig. 7.39

of the second phase of building. The floor foundations were thin and consisted of no more than a few centimetres of dirty mortar into which the tesserae were set. A number of small postholes were driven into the floors in two of the rooms (Fig. 7.39) while the building was still functioning as they were sealed by the collapsed daub from the walls when this part of the building went out of use. The layer of daub had a number of broken tegulae on it and the destruction levels were cut away by the robber trenches for the Phase 2 foundations.

Phase 1 cannot be any earlier than late Antonine on the evidence of the samian sherd from P.41, the make-up layer sealed by the mortar floor, and an early 3rd-century date for the Phase 1, House 2, is likely. It is impossible to trace any re-building phases in the small area excavated unless the postholes cut through the floors represent temporary roof supports, and the length of Phase 1 must remain conjectural as must its eastern boundary. Four pits were excavated in the garden to the east of the house. Three of these, Pits P.37, O.40 and O.48 pre-dated the Phase 2 house and must be roughly contemporary with Phase 1. Pit P.37 cut an earlier oven which is also probably Phase 1. All the pits appear to be 3rd century on the basis of their fill, but Pit O.48/49 may be the earliest as it has no New Forest wares or other colour coated wares in it. It was sealed by layer O.61, which had a fragment of Pevensey ware.

The other three pits had New Forest, Colchester and Lezoux wares and Pits O.40 and P.37 were particularly rich in finds of fine colour coated wares and glass as well as painted wall plaster and building debris from a destroyed building or buildings. The fill from these two pits indicates the presence of a prosperous town house nearby of which the fragments seen in Areas 2 and 5 may represent only a small part. No Oxford wares were present in the pits (see below, p. 262) and Dr. Fulford's suggestion of the end of the 3rd century for the New Forest wares present is perhaps a good pointer to the date when they were closed. It is by no means certain that the Phase 2 re-building of House 2 took place immediately after the turn of the century and there are good reasons for supposing that it may not have been until well on into the first quarter of the 4th century before this happened.

Period 6; *c.* early 4th to late 4th century

Fig. 7.40

At some time after the backfilling of Pits O.40 and P.37 in the garden on the east side of House 2 (Phase 1), the house was reconstructed. The full extent of the building may never be known, but it extended as far south as Street 2; eastwards to abut Street 1, but the western boundary is unknown. The house extends northwards below No. 7 Chapel Street, so it is at least 60 metres north–south and recent observations on street works (November 1976) confirmed that the walls of a Roman house lay below the road as far north as the Chapel. This would give House 2 a north–south dimension of approximately 105 metres, which would make it very large indeed. The Phase 2 rebuilding took in part of the area used as garden in the 3rd century, and the rest may have been a courtyard with a mortar floor. This courtyard was bounded on the south and west sides by a corridor (Room 6). To the south was an apsidal room (Room 9), possibly a tepidarium, with Room 10 to the east of it. A range of rooms existed west of the apse, of which two, Rooms 7 and 8 were partly within the excavation.

With the exception of some parts of the corridor wall the walls had been robbed down to the chalk foundations. No floors survived other than that of Room 6,

119

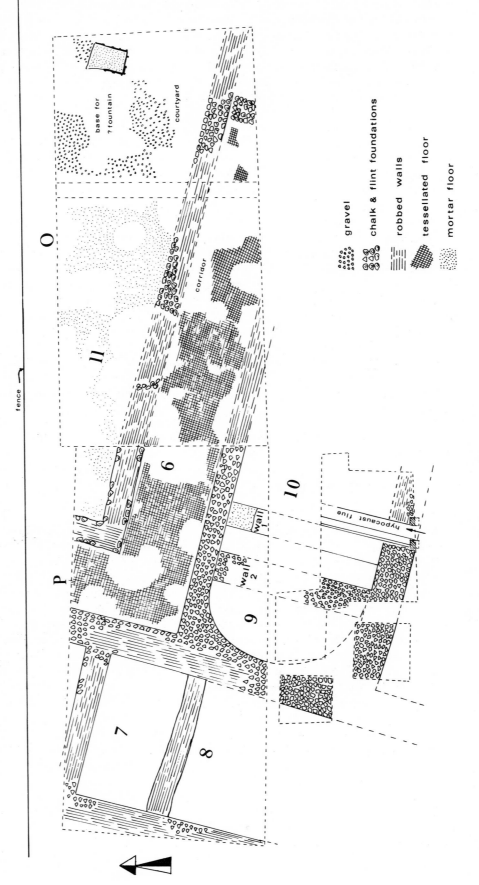

No 7 Chapel Street

fence

base for
? fountain

courtyard

corridor

O

11

6

P

7

8

9

wall 2

wall 1

10

hypocaust flue

gravel

chalk & flint foundations

robbed walls

tessellated floor

mortar floor

AREA 5, GOSPEL HALL, TRENCHES O & P

Roman; part of House 2, Period 6; 4th century

0   15

metres

Fig. 7.40

although there were traces of a mortar floor base in the area of Rooms 9 and 10 and many fragments of a very fine polychrome mosaic were found in later pits and one piece in the robbed out hypocaust in Room 10.

Room 6. The tessellated floor of the corridor was constructed on a matrix of pink mortar (O.8). The corridor was 2.8 metres wide and turned northwards under No. 7 Chapel Street. At the east end it terminated at a north–south flint wall of which only a small section survived where it butted up against the north wall of the corridor. The relationship of the house to the Roman street could not be determined at this point, but it is unlikely that the courtyard would have been open to the street and another north–south wall is postulated further east and adjoining the street.

Layer P.33, a layer of black soil just below the mortar matrix for the corridor had New Forest red slipped wares, while two late 3rd century coins came from the floor base and make-up below it.

Room 7 (5.4 metres east–west and 3 metres north–south) *and Room 8* (5.4 metres east–west) were divided by a robbed out wall footing. No trace of a floor remained in either room and the collapsed daub and roof tiles which lay upon the floors of the Phase 1 house appeared unconsolidated, with the wall plaster still in large fragments, nor had the debris been levelled off as would be expected if another floor was to be laid on top. It is a possibility that these two rooms may have had plank floors, but no traces of joists were seen.

Rooms 9 and 10. Two phases of building are detectable here.

Phase 1

The base of a mortar wall (wall 1), of which only a small fragment survived, was found aligned north–south and cut by the robber trench for the north wall of Rooms 9 and 10. A faint trace of it was seen in the extension dug in the garden of No. 6 Chapel Street. It may pre-date the apsidal room; there is no evidence either way.

Phase 2

At this stage a wall (wall 2), was built across the apse. It was keyed into the main wall and was of the same construction, e.g. chalk blocks set in clay. Only the bottom two courses remained unrobbed. A mortar floor (Layer P.8) was laid on either side of the wall and this may have been the base for a polychrome mosaic, of which a number of fragments were found re-deposited in the robbing fill above the floor; in the hypocaust and trodden into the base of the floor. East of the wall was a hypocaust of which one flue was found aligned north–south. This was constructed of pilae tiles set in mortar; most of these had been robbed but the impressions were left on the west side of the flue. An examination of the south wall of Room 10 where the flue entered suggests that the hypocaust construction was contemporary with the building of the room and that it must have been fired from further south. The severe robbing makes it impossible to say for certain that the very fine mosaic fragments belonged to Phase 2 or that they came from Rooms 9 and 10, but it is very likely that they did, as they were all concentrated in that area.

Room 11. This may have been a courtyard with a pink mortar floor (O.15/35). The earlier garden (O.29) was levelled up by layers of clay and gravel (O.20 and O.23) and the pink mortar laid on top. This was eroded at the east end of the site, so that the gravel layer was exposed, and cut through it was a mortar base, probably for a small foundation or statue (see Fig. 7.40 and *Cunliffe* 1971, p. 126 and Fig. 36). A recent surface water drainage trench cut through Chapel Street (November 1976) sectioned part of the pink mortar floor outside No. 7 Chapel Street.

121

Period 7; late 4th to early 5th century

There are no features which can be identified as belonging to a later period of alteration and development after Period 6 in this part of House 2. The house in decline was seen only in a few areas where the tessellated floors had been patched with tiles and where layers of daub, wall plaster and domestic rubbish had accumulated upon the floors when the building was derelict. The latest coins from the layers above the floors and from pits dug through them are two of Valens or Valentinian (A.D. 364–378) and a barbarous minim of mid to late 4th century.

See also the discussion under Areas 2 and 4 (p. 83).

Period 8; late Saxon, c. 8th to 12th century

(Fig. 7.41)

No late Saxon features other than pits can be postulated and these are classified in two groups:

Group 1: Late Saxon c. 8th–10th century
Late Saxon wares of *c.* 9th to early 10th century were found in Pit O.34 which is later than the Group 2 Saxon Pit O.8 which it cuts. The wares were probably derived from Pit O.8 where they were residual (see also p. 348 and Fig. 11.4).

Group 2: Saxo-Norman, c. early 11th to early 12th century
Nine pits are classified as Saxo-Norman (see Fig. 7.41).

Period 9; medieval, c. 12th to 13th century

(Fig. 7.41)

No structures can be attributed to the medieval period and the only hint of any features other than pits are a small group of postholes to the south of Pit P.27 which may represent part of a small windbreak around the pit, and a few isolated postholes and a short length of slot. The pits are grouped into two phases classified as "early" and "later". Few glazed wares were present, and no definitely 14th century wares could be identified. Many of the pits were dug to win building material from the Roman foundations which may account for the scarcity of domestic wares in the backfill.

Period 10; c. 16th to 18th century

(Fig. 7.42)

No 16th-century features or wares could be distinguished and only two pits containing 17th-century wares were found. Occupation seems to have been slight until well on into the 18th century when at least six pits were found with 18th–19th-century pottery in them.

Period 11; 19th century onwards

Elements of two buildings can be seen on the plan.

Phase 1

A series of postholes, some square cut, which make no regular plan. Two of these are sealed by the later Phase 2 wall.

Phase 2

Part of a rectangular building of which the shallow footings of two walls were found. It was cut away on the west side by the bath of the Baptist Chapel (Gospel Hall).

Discussion

As in Areas 2 and 4 further south, occupation on the site after the mid-late Saxon period seems to have been slight. The Norden Map of 1695 shows the area to be open ground, but buildings and a garden are shown on the Gardner May of 1769. In 1786 and 1789 a Malthouse is recorded in the Land Tax returns.

122

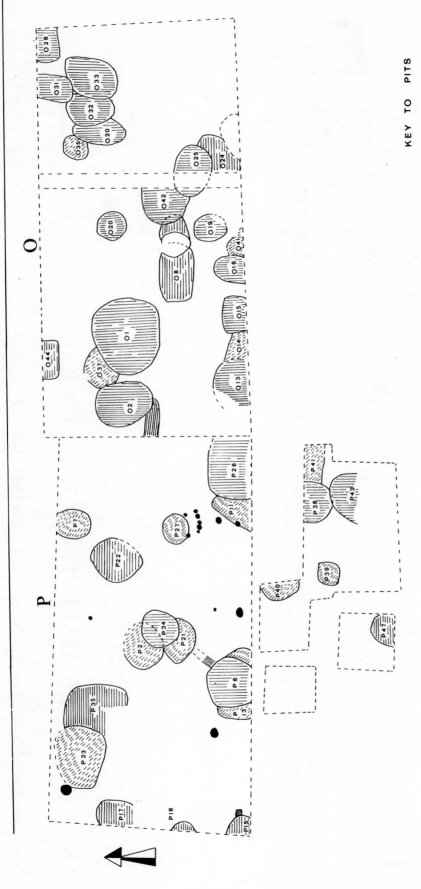

No 7 CHAPEL STREET

KEY TO PITS

Late Saxon

Early medieval

Later medieval

AREA 5, GOSPEL HALL, TRENCHES O & P

Late Saxon & Medieval features, Periods 8 & 9

0   15

metres

Fig. 7.41

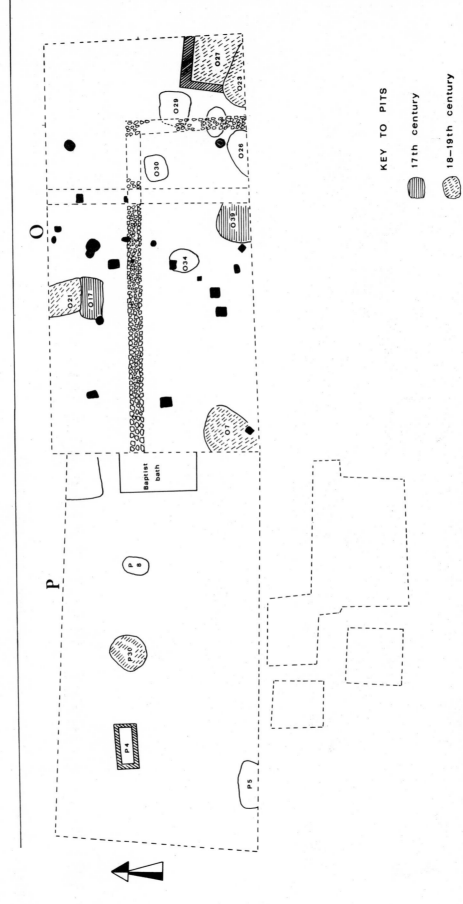

No 7 CHAPEL STREET

P

O

KEY TO PITS

17th century

18-19th century

uncertain

AREA 5, GOSPEL HALL, TRENCHES O & P

Post medieval: 17th – 20th century, Periods 10 – 11

0   15

metres

Fig. 7.42

AREA 5, O&P, NORTH SECTION

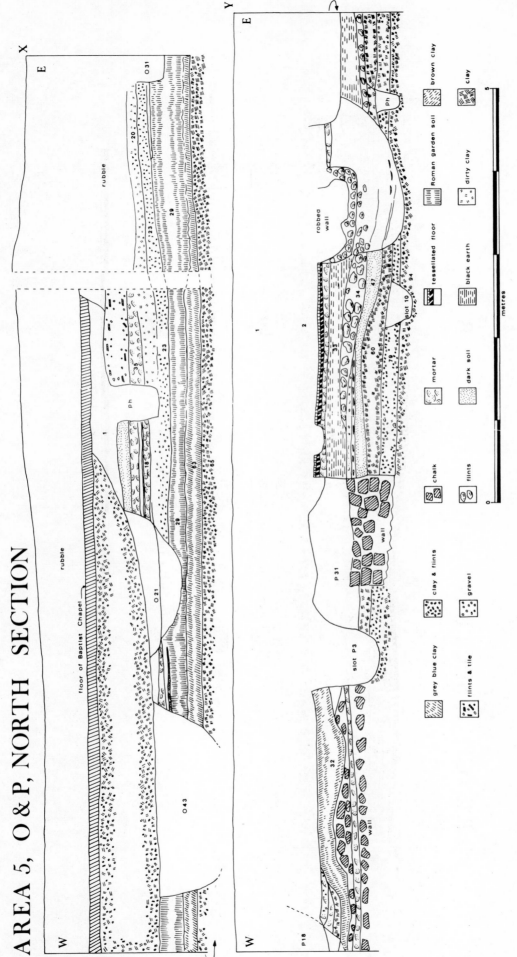

Fig. 7.43

TRENCH P, SECTION A–A

B–B

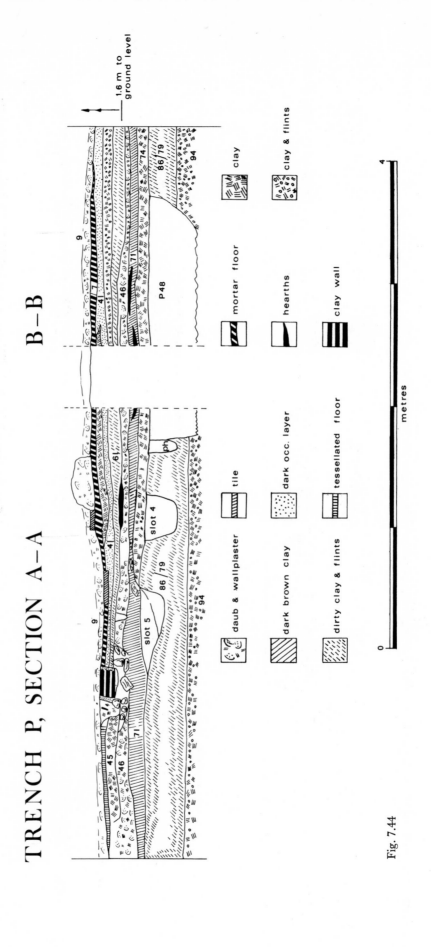

1.6 m to ground level

daub & wallplaster	tile	clay
dark brown clay	dark occ. layer	clay & flints
dirty clay & flints	tessellated floor	
mortar floor		
hearths		
clay wall		

0   metres   4

Fig. 7.44

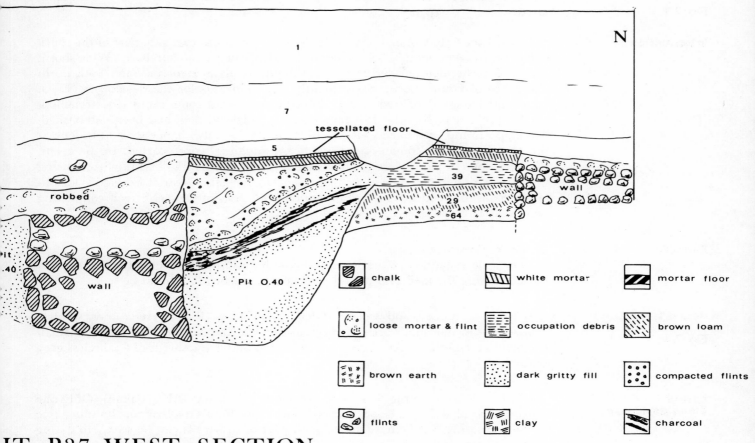

N

		chalk			white mortar			mortar floor
		loose mortar & flint			occupation debris			brown loam
		brown earth			dark gritty fill			compacted flints
		flints			clay			charcoal

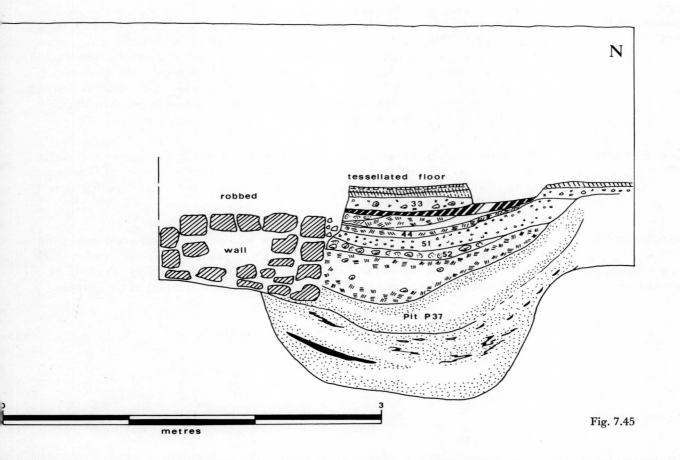

N

metres

Fig. 7.45

Fig. 7.1

Area 6 – Purchase's Garden and land at the rear of Nos. 16–18 Chapel Street

Introduction

In 1973 the City Council offered us the opportunity to excavate part of the south end of a garden previously belonging to No. 31 North Street (Purchase's Wine shop). This was to be incorporated into re-development plans involving land both north and south of Crane Street. Subsequently, the architects for the developers (E. G. Nash and Partners) offered us the chance to carry out some rapid trial trenching on the east side of Nos. 16–18 Chapel Street, which by then had been demolished. The opportunity was taken as it was likely to be the only chance we had to look at the east side of the Roman crossroads before building works started. In the event, the development plans were abandoned; only the area south of Crane Street being built upon, and at the time of writing the new Chichester District Council is formulating plans for residential development on both sides of Chapel Street, comprising our Areas 1, 2 and 6.

Period 0

Trench R, Purchase's Garden
Very little remained of the Roman levels due to intensive cultivation of most of the site during the medieval period, and no ancient turf line could be seen.

Period 1; c. A.D. 43

Fig. 7.46

A layer of stained and worm ridden yellow clay (R.31) rested upon natural yellow clay in one small area at the south end of the trench. This had one small fragment of Tiberian ? Arretine ware in the top and a few sherds of featureless grey pottery.

Period 2; Claudius–Nero?

Cut into R.31 were the slots of two structures (R.1 and R.2, see plan). Only one short length of R.1 can be seen as it is cut away by a later Roman building (see below). Building R.2 is in alignment and part of two walls can be seen. No dating evidence came from the slots.

Period 3; c. Flavian to 2nd century

Part of a building (R.3) was found, also cut into R.31. It was seen as two sections of what appeared to be a wide and shallow slot and it may well have been cut from a higher level. Along both sides of the slots, which were 1 metre wide, was a series of small postholes, and the area contained within the lines of postholes was a well compacted yellow clay (R.30) which made a straight edge with the surrounding R.31. It is most likely to have been the base of a very wide clay wall. No dating evidence came from R.30 or any of the postholes, but it is seen to postdate Building R.1 and is tentatively assigned to Period 3.

Period 4; 2nd to early 3rd century

No features can be recognised for this Period although there is abundant ceramic evidence for occupation during that time. There was a large amount of Hadrianic and Antonine samian in association with wall plaster and other building debris residual in later pits (see below).

Period 5; 3rd to 4th century

Phase 1, c. late 3rd to early 4th century

Layer R.23 was brown-yellow clay with some mortar at the north-east end of the trench. It was cut away by a series of shallow pits (see below), and contained a sherd of red slipped ware which Dr. Fulford has classified as probably local. It also contained the base of a grey ware pot with blue pigment residues in the bottom.

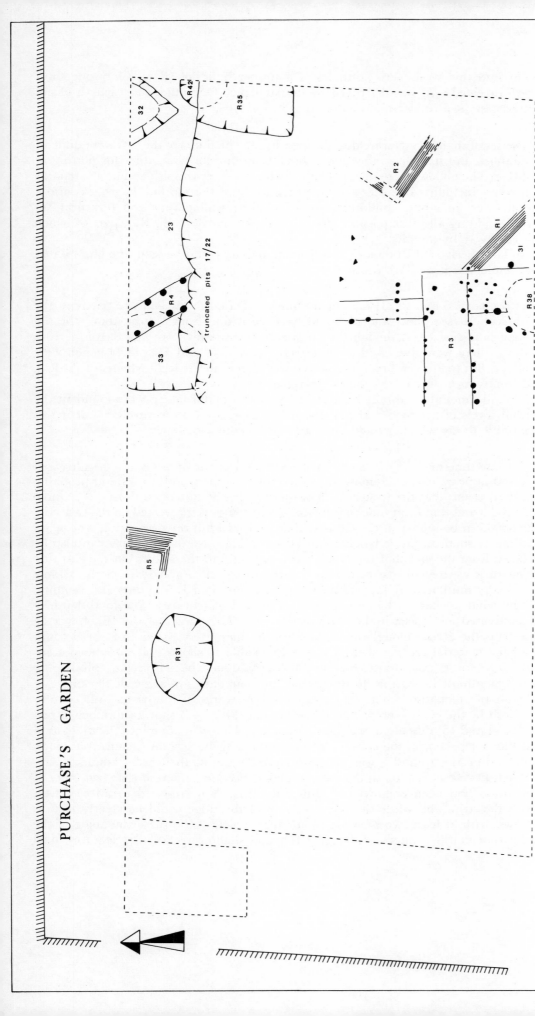

PURCHASE'S GARDEN

R42
R35
32
R2
23
R1
R4
31
truncated pits 17/22
33
R38
R3
R5
R31

AREA 6, TRENCH R

Periods 1-5, Roman features

0   5
metres

Fig. 7.46

Cut into this layer were postholes of a timber building (R.4). Only one short length survived as it was destroyed by the later pits. One other short length of slot further east (R.5) may be contemporary.

Phase 2, 4th century

A series of shallow pits were dug through R.23. The limits of the pits were difficult to establish and it appears they could have been dug for clay either for potting or building. The hollows were then backfilled with domestic rubbish and large amounts of pottery, including one sherd of Oxford ware from the top fill. There was also a considerable amount of building debris including wall plaster and tiles from an earlier building and it is possible that it derived from Building R.4, part of which was cut away by the pits.

No later periods of Roman or sub-Roman activity could be seen, the latest dated coin found was *c.* mid-4th century.

Period 8; late Saxon, *c.* 10th–11th century

Two pits (R.9 and R.23) may be assigned to Period 8. Pit R.9 was partly in the south section (see plan) and seems to have been dug from or just above the old Roman land surface. Although the latest wares in the pit were late Saxon, *c.* 10th century, there were five hand-made vessels (see p. 341 and Fig. 11.1) which were earlier, *c.* 8th to 9th century. Three more were found in Pit R.23 which cut Pit R.9, and from which they were probably derived.

A small amount of abraded wares in "Saxo-Norman" fabric were found in the bottom levels of the medieval ploughsoil but these were so featureless that it was impossible to say whether they were early 12th century or later.

Period 9; *c.* late 12th to 14th century

At some time in the early medieval period most of the area became a cultivated plot and appears to have remained as such for at least two centuries and probably longer. It seems that the western half of the trench was cultivated during the whole of Period 9 and that from time to time timber buildings were erected on the east side. The northern boundary of the cultivated area was within the excavation, and what is in fact a small negative lynchet can be seen. The eastern boundary can also be deduced from the fact that the lynchet curves round to the south. On the east side of the strip were elements of perhaps two buildings (R.5 and R.6). Both of these were badly mutilated by later forms of activity, Building R.5 by pits and Building R.6 by what appears to be an extension of the cultivated area. The total depth of the cultivated soil is seen in the south section (Fig. 7.50, Layers 7 and 16). Layer 16 represents the earlier ploughsoil. An analysis of the pottery based on a sherd count of all the material recovered from Layer 16 (Table 1) shows that no later pottery than 15th century got into this level and these could have been from later pit digging as it was almost impossible to determine the boundaries of some of the pits dug through the ploughsoil. Some paint-under-glaze wares of the early 15th century may well be the latest sherds. The Period 9 plan (Fig. 7.47) shows a number of pits (R.12, 14 and 15) dug along the south boundary. They were dug into the ploughsoil and did not penetrate the subsoil. Their position in the section is shown although as viewed on the ground it was not possible to determine their exact boundaries.

When first seen as scars in the natural clay it became apparent that two types of cultivation had been employed at different times. A narrow ridge ran east–west across the strip, and while the furrows south of the ridge could be clearly seen as furrows, with at least two separate ploughings, north of the ridge the angle of the cultivation marks changed (see Fig. 7.47), and shallow rectangular features filled

PURCHASE'S GARDEN

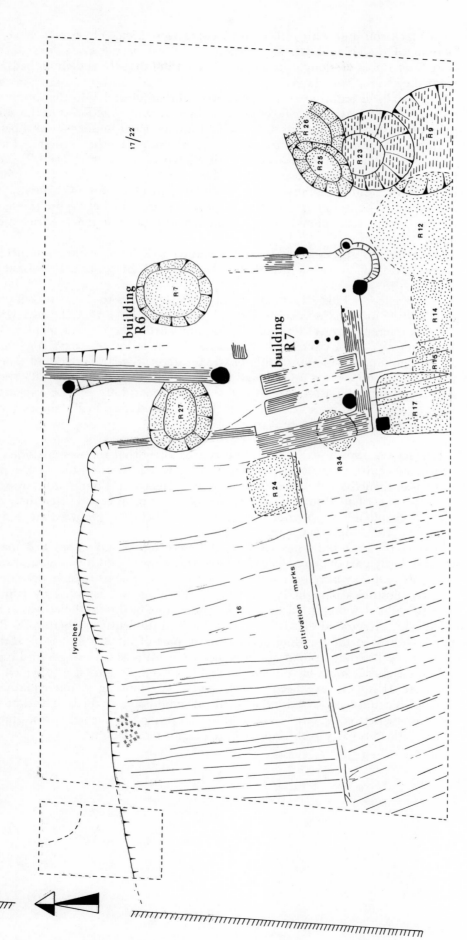

late Saxon

medieval

AREA 6, TRENCH R

Late Saxon to medieval, c. 10th–14th centuries, Periods 8–9

Fig. 7.47

with black soil and with well defined edges were seen. These may have been the bottom of mulching beds. Excavation of several of the slots showed that there were faint traces of plough scars below, indicating that the mulching beds, if that is what they were, came later.

The total soil build-up as measured from the natural clay to the top of R.16 was between 30–35 cms and 55–60 cms if measured to the top of R.7 and this soil growth must point to regular make-up, probably from adjacent middens over a period from *c.* 16th century at the latest to possibly 13th century at the earliest if Layer R.16 is included. The cultivated area did not extend as far west as Trial Trench S (see below), as the uneroded Roman levels there were 0.57 metre above the plough scars in Trench R, and since the southern boundary must have been Crane Street (known since the 13th century), it follows that the plot must have been quite small, certainly not big enough for a plough team using oxen. It is possible that a breast plough was used.

There are references in the late 13th century to a John de Sancta Cruce (or John de St. Cross) who held land in Crane Lane, North Street and East Lane (Chapel Street).

A reference in 1282 (*S.A.C.* 89, p. 118, AY 4), refers to the rent of a plot at the gate leading to his barn in Crane Lane. Earlier, in 1277 (*W.S.R.O., Add. MSS.* 2594), there is reference to the lease of a house and curtilage . . . and mention of a yard belonging to Sancta Cruce in Crane Lane. The mention of a barn suggests possibly a small-holding on the north side of Crane Street. Sancta Cruce had tenements in North Street opposite the Guildhall (*S.A.C.* 89, p. 118, AY 4) in 1283 and in 1277 had tenements in East Lane (*W.S.R.O., Add. MSS.* 2594), so he appears to have been a person of some substance, and the cultivated strip in Purchases garden may have been his in the 13th century.

Period 10;
***c.* 15th to 16th century**
Fig. 7.48

During the 15th to early 16th century it is likely that the western side of the site continued under cultivation, and Layer R.7, which overlaid the earlier ploughsoil R.16 was then the cultivated topsoil. It was clearly distinguishable from R.16 by the fact that it had a good deal of yellow clay lumps in it and since these could not have been ploughed up from the natural clay below it follows that it must have been imported from elsewhere.

Traces of three buildings (R.8 to 10) were found. Of these, R.8 may be the earliest. Only part of one slot survived and this showed that it was a fairly substantial structure and may have been a barn. The west side appears to have been demolished and the postholes ploughed or dug away. Building R.9 is dated by two pits, R.4 and R.5. Pit R.5 pre-dated the building since one of the postholes was cut into the edge. The latest dated sherds from the pit were 14th century, whereas Pit R.4 which partly destroyed the building and cut away part of Pit R.5 had 15th–16th-century wares in it. Building 10 had nothing later than 14th-century wares in the postholes, and these sherds must have been derived from the ploughsoil into which the posts were set. It might have been a replacement for Building 8, but equally all three structures could have co-existed as a line of small barns or sheds. The date should in any case lie between *c.* late 14th and 15th century, giving the narrowest time bracket, but a 15th to *c.* early 16th-century date cannot be ruled out.

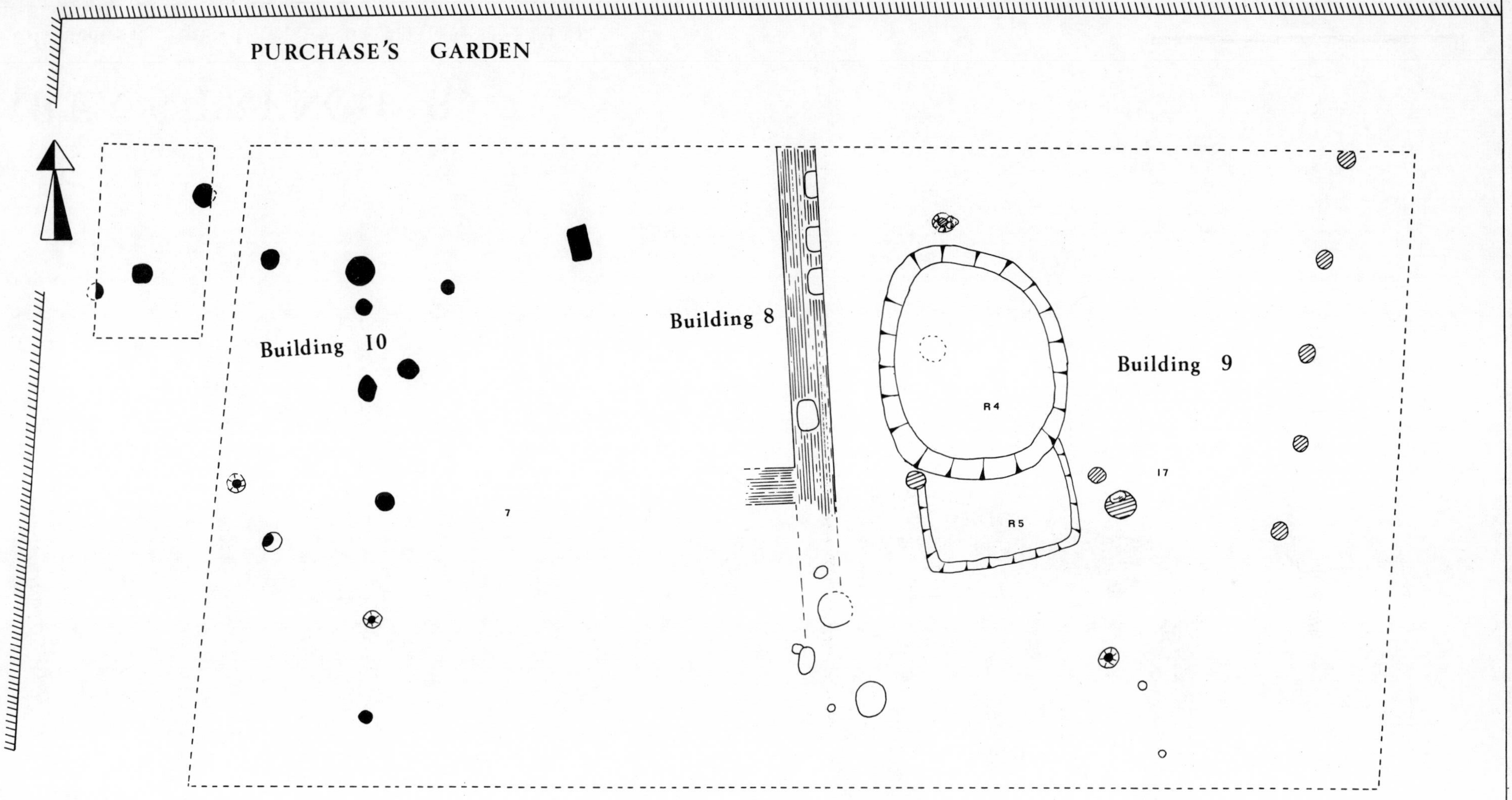

PURCHASE'S GARDEN

Building 9

17

Building 8

R4

R5

Building 10

Building 9

7

metres

0   5

AREA 6, TRENCH R.

Late medieval timber buildings, c. 15th – 16th centuries, Period 10

Fig. 7.48

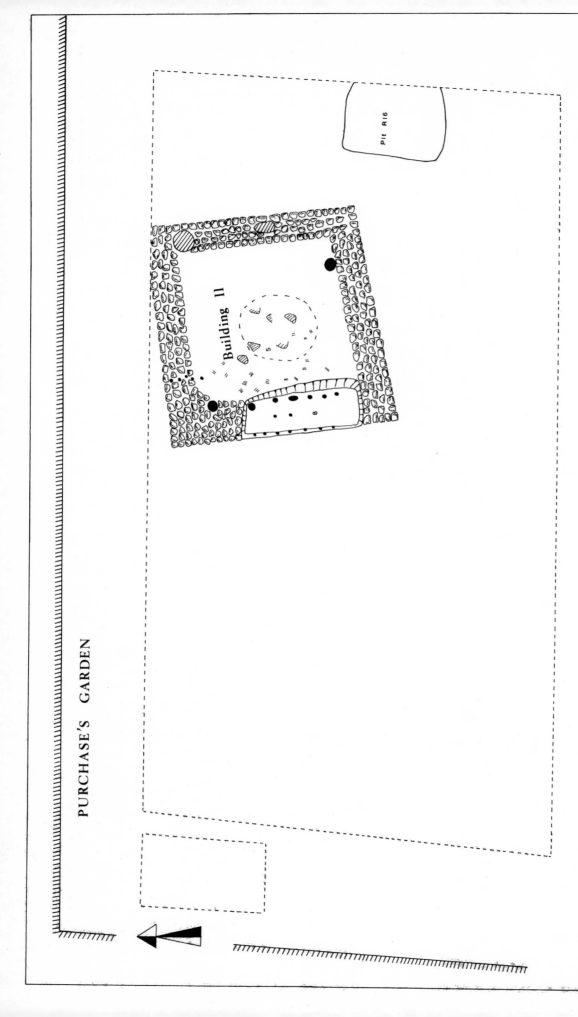

PURCHASE'S GARDEN

Pit R16

Building 11

0 metres 5

AREA 6, TRENCH R.

Post-medieval; 16th–17th century features, Period 11

Fig. 7.49

TABLE 1

AREA 6, TRENCH R, PURCHASE'S GARDEN
Analysis of finds from the Lower Ploughsoil (R.16)

Pottery		Saxo-Norman	Medieval, 12th–13th century	Medieval, c. 14th century	15th century	16th century	Post Medieval 17th century
Unglazed	..	39	83	10	3	Nil	Nil
Glazed	..	—	50	35	2	Nil	Nil
Tile ..	..	—	11 ?	12 ?	7	Nil	Nil
Slate ..	..	—	?	7	?	—	—
Totals	..	39	144	64	12	Nil	Nil

Period 11;
c. 17th century
Fig. 7.49

At a depth of 0.57 metre from the modern ground level was a rectangular wall footing (Building R.11). It was constructed of flints in creamy mortar; the walls were 0.75 metre wide and the building was approximately 3.75 metres square inside. Two shallow post sockets were found in the east wall, which may be contemporary with it and there may have been others lost when the footings were robbed. The building was set over a complex of pits of which the latest (Pit R.4) had 15th–16th-century material and the width of the foundations suggests that it was necessary to provide a wide raft to avoid subsidence. Even so, it is unlikely that the structure was of solid masonry construction and it is more likely to have been a timber-framed building resting upon extra wide dwarf walls. Inside, the floor was Layer R.5, brown clay with a lot of pottery and roof tile. The tiles were post-medieval, 16th–17th century and much of the pottery was painted wares of the mid-15th to early 16th century. The latest dated sherd from the wall footing was a fragment of Bellarmine which could be 17th century. Part of the west wall of the building was later cut away by a pit dug exactly along the line of the foundations. This was one metre deep and had a line of small postholes along the east side and a corresponding line of stakeholes along the west. There were also two holes along the centre. The impression is of a narrow pit lined with hurdles on each side. The fill contained mortar and flints from the demolished wall and had nothing later than early 16th century painted wares.

It is not known how long this building survived. The foundations were covered with just over half a metre of black garden soil and no traces of robbing or demolition could be seen. In the 19th century there was an ornamental garden, with shrubbery and paths laid out and these are shown on the Ordnance Survey Map of 1875. The foundations for the path were dug to the same depth as the wall footings, indicating that by the late 19th century there had been a further soil growth of 0.50 metre from the early 17th century horizon.

AREA 6, TRENCH R, PURCHASE'S GARDEN, SOUTH SECTION

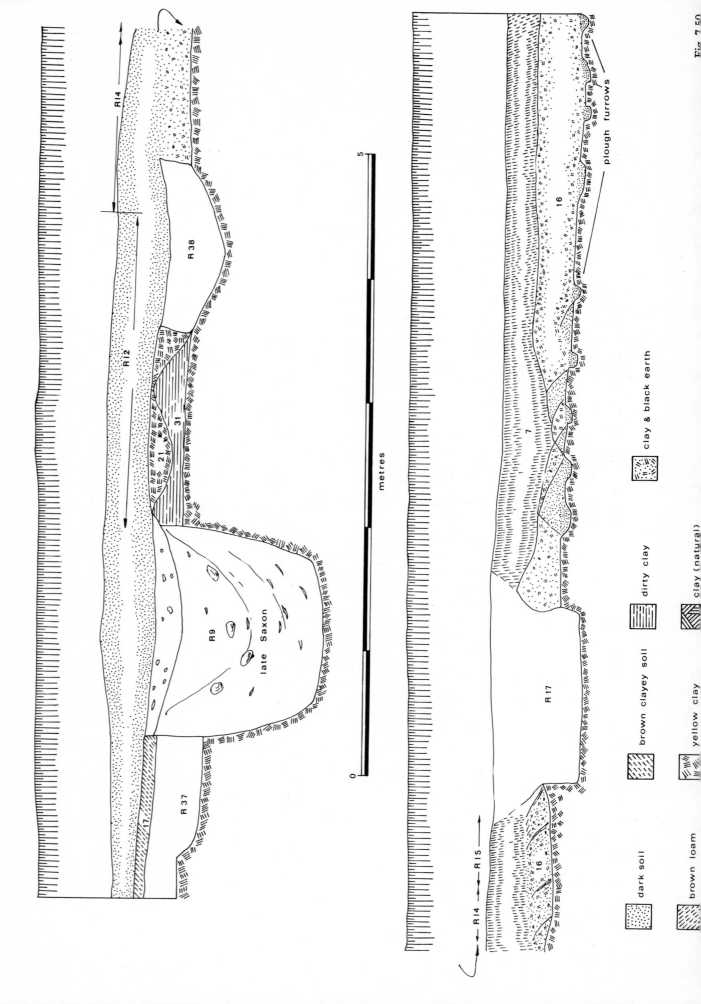

R14

R12

R 38

R 31

21

R 9

late Saxon

17

R 37

R14 → ← R15

R14 →

16

7

7

16

R 17

16

plough furrows

metres

5

0

dark soil

brown clayey soil

dirty clay

clay & black earth

brown loam

yellow clay

clay (natural)

Fig. 7.50

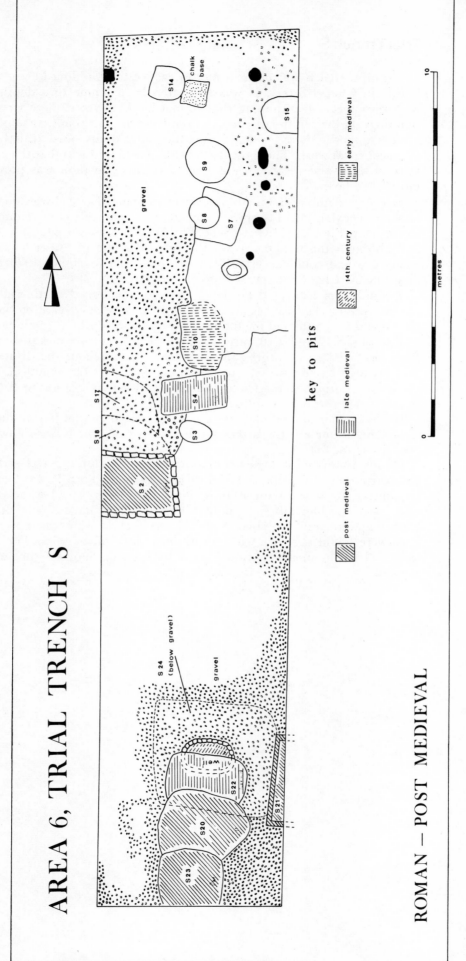

AREA 6, TRIAL TRENCH S

S 24
(below gravel)

gravel

well

S 23

S 20

S 22

S 21

S 2

S 18

S 17

S 3

S 4

S 10

gravel

S 8

S 7

S 9

chalk
base

S 14

S 15

key to pits

post medieval	late medieval	early medieval
	14th century	

ROMAN — POST MEDIEVAL

0   metres   10

Fig. 7.51

Fig. 7.51

Trial Trench S

The trial trench was cut *c*. 8 metres east of the building line of the demolished houses in Chapel Street. It was excavated by machine to a depth of 0.75 metre with the object of examining the Roman levels to see if there were any masonry buildings on the south-east corner of the Roman cross roads corresponding to those on the opposite (west) side. Very little opportunity was available for detailed archaeological work. The most that could be achieved was that the exposed features were cleaned and recorded and some limited excavation was possible below the gravel (see below).

Roman. At a depth of 0.8 metre a layer of compacted gravel was found which could only be the extension of the gravel spread on the east side of the Roman north–south street below the Central Girls' School in Area 2. This was patchy and badly eroded and although the trench was on the projected line of Street 3 (see Fig. 7.3) no conclusive line could be established although in November 1976 an "edge" was found below Chapel Street (see this Volume, p. 21).

A number of truncated postholes were found aligned north–south. These were cut into yellow clay which may at one time have been covered by the gravel but no date could be postulated for the postholes, they could be Roman or later.

Two pits, S.17 and S.18 were sealed by the gravel layer and these were sectioned. Both produced 2nd century samian, Pit S.17 having four sherds of Antonine ware and Pit S.18 having two sherds of similar date, one East Gaulish. This reinforces the evidence from Area 3 (p. 97) and West Street (p. 98) for an Antonine date for much of the town landscaping.

It was evident that no masonry buildings existed on that part of the site, but some indication of one a little further south and east of Area 6 was found during recent roadworks (p. 21).

Medieval. A number of medieval pits were cut through the gravel and it was possible to excavate some of them. A 14th-century oval well (Pit S.1) was found at the south end of the site. It was built of flints and re-used Roman ashlar and the construction and design was basically so weak that it collapsed on the south side and was partially robbed and filled in. Numbers of glazed and unglazed domestic pots of the 14th century were found together with glazed jugs with rod handles. The well may have belonged to one of the tenements held by John de Sancta Cruce or his heirs (see above).

Area 7 – Tower Street Car Park

Introduction
Fig. 7.1

Observation on contractor's work in 1960 at the rear of Morants and observation and excavation in 1972 when Post Office Building No. 1 was built (see Area 3, p. 113) showed that part at least of the Roman Thermae was below the car park occupying the land on the east side of Tower Street opposite the County Library. The site was scheduled to become a multi-storey car park which would result in the complete destruction of all the archaeological layers, and after work on the Post Office access ramp next door (see above, p. 113) had shown a complete section through a number of heated rooms, strong representation was made to the City Council by the Committee and its parent body the Civic Society, to allow total excavation in advance of the car park project. In return, we undertook to leave a basement, 2.5 metres deep, which would allow for the provision of an extra sub-basement level for the car park.

It was greatly to the credit of the City Council that they readily agreed to the excavation. The Post Office, to whom we were already deeply indebted, co-operated once again by making alternative car parking space available to the City Council on land in Chapel Street already excavated by us. By the time work commenced in April 1974, local government reorganisation had taken place and the new Chichester District Council replaced the old City Council on the day we moved on to the site. It is pleasant to record that we received the same help and encouragement from the new authority as we had enjoyed from the old.

The excavation finally totalled approximately 1,300 square metres, all open at the same time, and went on for 440 days non-stop. To facilitate recording, the site was divided into six areas, A to F (see Fig. 7.53, plan and key to sections).

Period 0; A.D. 43 at the latest

Evidence for pre-Conquest occupation in the vicinity was attested in the form of a few abraded sherds of the pre-Roman Iron Age (p. 187), probably dating from the 2nd to 1st century B.C. Two coins, one of Cunobelin and one of the Durotriges (p. 330 and Pl. 18) were found in post-Roman layers, and a number of sherds of Arretine and provincial Arretine ware were found in the Period 1 and 2 levels and also as residual material. Neither the coins nor the Arretine can be conclusively tied in with a pre-Conquest presence in Chichester, but as with the other "early" material, they are present and cannot be ignored. No trace of an early turf line above natural could be identified.

Period 1; A.D. 43 plus

The earliest occupation levels noted were in D and E. In D, a layer of yellow clay with flints and charcoal flecks (D.47) rested upon natural. It had a few Roman grey ware sherds in the top. The same layer further south (E.76) had a bone counter, food bones and grey ware sherds, all small but unabraded, trodden into the top.

Cut into D.47 was a shallow drainage gulley (Ditch 3). It marked a change of level, as the ground on the north side had been scarped away (see Fig. 7.52). The ditch drained westwards and had a fall of 1 in 28. It was filled with dumped burnt daub and charcoal from a destroyed building (see below), and there was a good deal of Reading clay in the top fill which had probably been used as daub in hut walls. A samian stamp of Claudian date was found in the Ditch fill.

It is possible that three short lengths of slots, E.17, B.11 and B.12 might be contemporary. They were cut into natural, but as they survived only as fragments between later pits they could not be clearly associated with any Period. They do not appear to relate to the Period 2 buildings and might well be earlier.

139

A thick layer of charcoal and burnt daub (D.40) lay upon D.47 and this partially filled Ditch 3 and spread across to the north of it. It might well be the same layer found in the trial trench across the County Library site on the opposite side of Tower Street in 1965 (*Down* 1966). No building could be associated with this destruction layer, although the postholes of a later structure were cut into it (see Fig. 7.53).

The destruction layer contained Tiberian Arretine, Claudian samian and three sherds of residual Iron Age ware.

Contemporary with Period 2 were two shallow sumps; the fill (D.36) had food debris, iron slag and pre-Flavian samian as the only dateable artifacts.

Building A. East of D.40 was part of a timber-framed building cut into a layer of green clay (D.44). Only a few small sections of slot could be traced and the very dry weather made interpretation extremely difficult, but the most westerly slot quite clearly cut the fill of Ditch 3 and appeared to join a short length of slot with the remains of a burnt beam in it, running east–west (Fig. 7.52).

Building B. Immediately south of Building A was a second structure aligned north–south of which rather more survived. Here, the slots had housed cill beams which had been charred before insertion into the ground. They had rotted in position and their outline could be clearly seen. The vertical timbers had been cut off, leaving a short end protruding from the beam, and where this had occurred, a layer of iron pan had formed around the timbers, making them an easy matter to locate when excavating. The slots produced two large fibulae, a fragment of armour from the *lorica segmentata*, Claudian samian and a sherd of residual Early Iron Age ware. The building was cut away on the south side by the deep construction trench for the thermae apse. It was 6.8 metres wide and was traced over a distance of 8.6 metres. Traces of two cross beams were seen (see plan). Both buildings are in alignment with the series of Period 1 buildings in Areas 2, 4 and 5 and are almost certainly contemporary. Possibly also of the same date is a short length of slot (B.10) east of Building A and in line with the south wall. It must belong to a different structure as it is narrower. It was sealed by a layer of clay containing Hadrianic samian (see below).

Parts of three structures at the north-east end of the site might also be contemporary.

A layer of Reading clay (A.32) was found near the north-east corner; this appeared to have been laid as an underfloor and there were a number of joist impressions in the clay, aligned east–west. Part of a line of square cut postholes on the west side may represent the south wall of this structure (Building C) as it is roughly square with the run of the joists, but due to local disturbances there was no direct relationship.

Cut into A.32 (natural), was a slot (A.31) aligned north–south. There was the outline of a beam in it, with two small postholes at the north end. It had Reading clay flecks in the fill, and this and the different alignment suggests that it is another, perhaps slightly later phase of building.

Discussion

The regular alignment of Buildings A, B and C, taken together with the finds of early pottery and military equipment indicate that while they were not the first phase of activity on the site they were probably military and, seen in conjunction with those in Area 3, they could well be storebuildings.

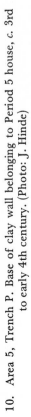

11. Area 7, Tower Street. Slots of Period 2 Roman timber storebuildings, looking north. (Photo: John Adams)

10. Area 5, Trench P. Base of clay wall belonging to Period 5 house, *c.* 3rd to early 4th century. (Photo: J. Hinde)

12. Area 7, Tower Street. Roman Thermae — Apse of Room 1, looking east. (Photo: John Adams)

AREA 7, TOWER STREET.

PERIODS 1-2. A.D. 43 – NERO

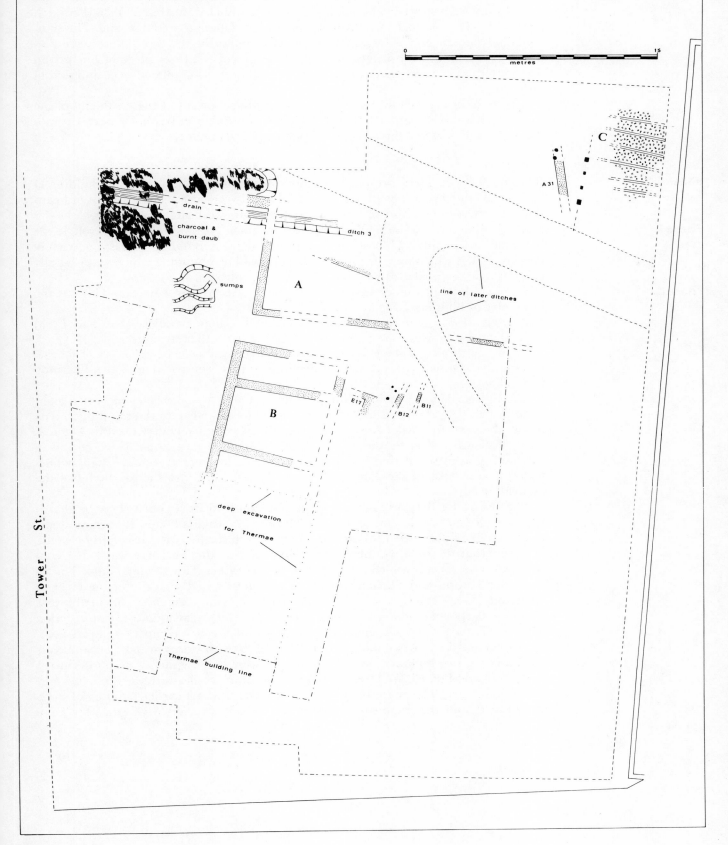

0   15
metres

C

A 31

drain

charcoal &
burnt daub

ditch 3

sumps

A

line of later ditches

B

E 17

B 12

B 11

Tower St.

deep excavation

for Thermae

Thermae building line

Fig. 7.52

After the Period 2 buildings had been demolished, the north part of the site at least appears to have lain derelict and open to the elements. A layer of greenish silt (E.73/D.36) covered buildings A and B and the iron pan formation around the stumps of the timbers protruding from the cill beams may indicate that the site was periodically waterlogged. This silt layer can be paralleled in Area 3 (Y.36, Period 3, see p. 94). It contained seventeen fragments of Tiberian Arretine and Tiberian/Claudian samian and a fragment of Flavian samian in the top. There were also many food bones, Gallo-Belgic butt beaker fragments and one piece of Early Iron Age pottery. The contents of the layer suggest that it accumulated over a period of some years.

A layer of brown-yellow clay was deposited above the silt at the north end of the site, where it was designated D.30/D.33/E.78. A number of postholes were cut into this layer and possibly three phases of buildings are present:

Phase 1

Buildings D and E. These comprise two short lengths of slot, cut into D.30. Building D had the south-west corner present, but Building E was just a single length of beam slot 3.7 metres long with two large postholes on the west side.

Phase 2

Buildings F and G. Building F was an arrangement of postholes cut through the layers of burnt daub (D.30) at the west side of the site. Building G was a pattern of large postholes which may be part of the south wall of a building which was partially cut away by the medieval well pit. This was cut through D.33.

Phase 3

Building H. A small timber structure measuring 3 metres by 3 metres. This cut the beam slot of Building E.

Unclassified. Two other short lengths of beam slot, both parallel (D.13 and E.13) were aligned east–west but cannot be related to any other structures.

At the south end of the site the green silt layer was sealed by a layer of mortar but this is discussed with the section dealing with the construction of the Thermae (see below).

Sealing the Period 2 storebuilding (Building C) in A was a layer of brown-loam (A.29). This had Flavian and 2nd century samian and cut into the top fill was part of a timber structure (Slot A.5), which was almost completely destroyed by Ditch 2.

At the south end of the site was a large rectangular excavation which cut away the south end of the Period 2 Building B and the layer of green silt (E.73) which sealed it. The apse of the Thermae (Room 1) was built into the south end of the excavation.

The reason for digging such a large excavation is obscure, but it may be that it was intended to fire the hot room through the apse originally and that there was a later change of plan, with the stokery being moved further east. It is fairly certain, however, that the hole was dug at the same time as the Thermae was being constructed in the form in which it is seen in Fig. 7.54 rather than at a later date. The fill of the excavation had Flavian samian as the latest dated wares, and the layer of green silt (E.73) cut by the excavation, had a Flavian samian stamp in the top. This is a fairly conclusive date for a Flavian or later excavation and construction of the north part of the Thermae. The fill of the hole, which comprised Layers F.44, 46, 49, 50 and 51 in descending order, had the Flavian wares in most of the layers including the two bottom ones. Also in the fill were two fragments of an inscription (see p. 275 and Fig. 10.25), fragments of marble, opus sectile, patterned flue tiles and domestic pottery. This material must have derived from an earlier building of some importance, and the fragment of inscription, which was very well cut, may have

142

AREA 7, TOWER STREET.

PERIOD 3, FLAVIAN TIMBER STRUCTURES

KEY TO EXCAVATION & SECTIONS

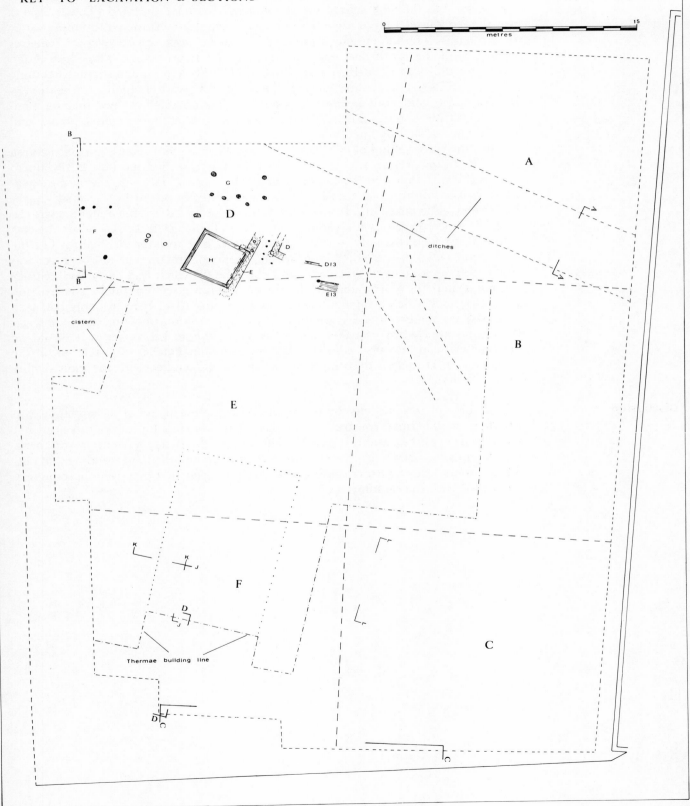

Fig. 7.53

been part of an Imperial dedication. It is possible that they are from an earlier Thermae, destroyed when the baths were re-built or modified in the late 1st century, but this is at present incapable of proof.

After the hole was backfilled, layers of clay were used to bring up the level, and it was noted that there was a good deal of pink mortar from the building operations mixed up with, and trodden into, the top of the clay.

The cistern. On the west side of the site and partly under the road (Tower Street) was the remains of a large stone built cistern which was constructed to supply water to the baths. The dimensions, assuming it to have been square, were 7.2 metres square, with the north and south walls being 2.4 metres wide. The construction trench for the cistern (Pit E.94 and E.70) had five Flavian samian sherds, including a stamp, and two first century pieces; 1 sherd dated Flavian-Trajanic in Martre-des-Veyres fabric, and nothing later. It would appear on this evidence that the construction of the cistern and the Thermae apse were likely to be contemporary and late Flavian or slightly later.

After the construction of the cistern and the Thermae hot rooms, part of the area north of the hot rooms was covered by a layer of screeded mortar (E.37), up to 11 cms thick. It appeared to peter out where it had a boundary with the deep excavation discussed above, but elsewhere it was laid directly on to the green silty layer and sealed a Flavian stamp. It was not seen on the north side, at the boundary with D, where it was replaced by a layer of greensand and clay (D.29/E.48) and on the east side it was recognised only in small patches in B, due to later pit digging and the robbing of Ditch 2. D.29/E.48 had Flavian/Trajanic samian. The mortar layer was topped off by a layer of greensand and clay (E.60) which had early 2nd century samian. Where the mortar abutted the cistern wall it was seen to seal the construction pit (E.94) into which it later subsided when the pit settled. It is probably best seen as a base for the greensand chippings, and as the area north of the hot rooms was a working area where the fuel had to be brought into the stokeries it would be convenient to have a well constructed hard-standing. Patches of gravel above the greensand in D suggest that the final surface was remetalled with the most readily available material.

Discussion

The three phases of slight timber structures at the north end of the site appear to pre-date the Thermae construction or reconstruction, but the time span need not have been very great, and it is possible that some of them may have been workmens' huts later demolished when the building was finished and the hard standing laid out. They did not extend further south and this may suggest that they were in some way connected with the building work.

144

It is now possible, as a result of the excavations of 1974–75, coupled with the work in Area 3 in the previous year and the information gained in 1960, to visualise the probable extent of the Thermae, even if most of the construction details are absent. The total surface area, assuming that the southern boundary rested on West Street, was of the order of 5,500 square metres including the hardstanding and cistern north of the range of heated rooms. The northern boundary is assumed to be that of the east range of rooms, the footings of which were traced during observation on the construction works in Area 3 (p. 113). The eastern limits were firmly fixed by the gravel metalling and the only boundary which is not fairly certain is the western one.

When the County Library was built in 1965, no trace of the Thermae was found when the site was trial trenched by the present writer, but a Post Office service trench dug down the centre of Tower Street in 1975 and carefully watched by us, cut through part of a hypocaust and wall foundations opposite Nos. 4 and 5 Tower Street, just west of Room 1 (see Figs. 7.3 and 7.54). The indications are that the western limits of the Thermae complex fall somewhere between this point and the Library building, which means that a substantial area of the public baths must lie below St. Peters Church and the houses north of it.

At the south end of Tower Street the contractors trench struck a massive wall constructed of fine grained limestone blocks and greensand. It was 0.30 metre below the road surface and measured 1.8 metres wide. It was aligned east–west and may have been a stylobate. South of this wall was a layer of mortar 6 cms thick, and further south again (see Fig. 7.3) was a wall also aligned east–west. This did not appear to cross the pipe trench and was only seen in the west section. Further south, 0.60 metre from the second wall was a third, on the same alignment. This wall did cross the trench. Both walls were 0.30 metre wide and there was no trace of Roman street gravel from the point where the pipe trench left Tower Street to where it terminated at a manhole on the south side of West Street, so it may well be that the Thermae area extends beyond the ? stylobate to the third wall. In 1960, observations on the column bases dug for the extension of Morants showed that below the tessellated floor to the north of the mosaic fragment, there was a filled in cross flue hypocaust and this was noted again in Trench A in Area 3 in 1973. The massive apse identified by Holmes (*Holmes* 1965) as part of the cold plunge bath cannot be satisfactorily related yet to the features found in the 1974–75 excavations, but here again, two periods of construction were noted.

Just south and east of the apse, a layer of gravel above creamy mortar was sectioned during the building operations in 1960. This might conceivably be part of the palaestra.

The position becomes a little clearer when the recent excavations are considered, although almost total robbing for building stone during the Norman and medieval periods has made interpretation difficult and in some cases impossible. As far as can be seen there were three main periods of construction and alteration, with some evidence, as we have already noted (p. 144) for perhaps an earlier structure on part of the site, which might be an earlier bath house. To avoid confusion with the chronological sequence imposed on the sites, the Thermae building periods are classified as A to C and are summarised below.

**Period A; probably
period 3 (Flavian)**

This comprised a range of hot rooms (Rooms 1 and 2) which were fired from the north end, while another room on the west of Room 1 and now below Tower Street may have been fired from the west side. Further east, below Morants, the situation is less clear, but it seems likely on the evidence of the filled in cross flue hypocausts

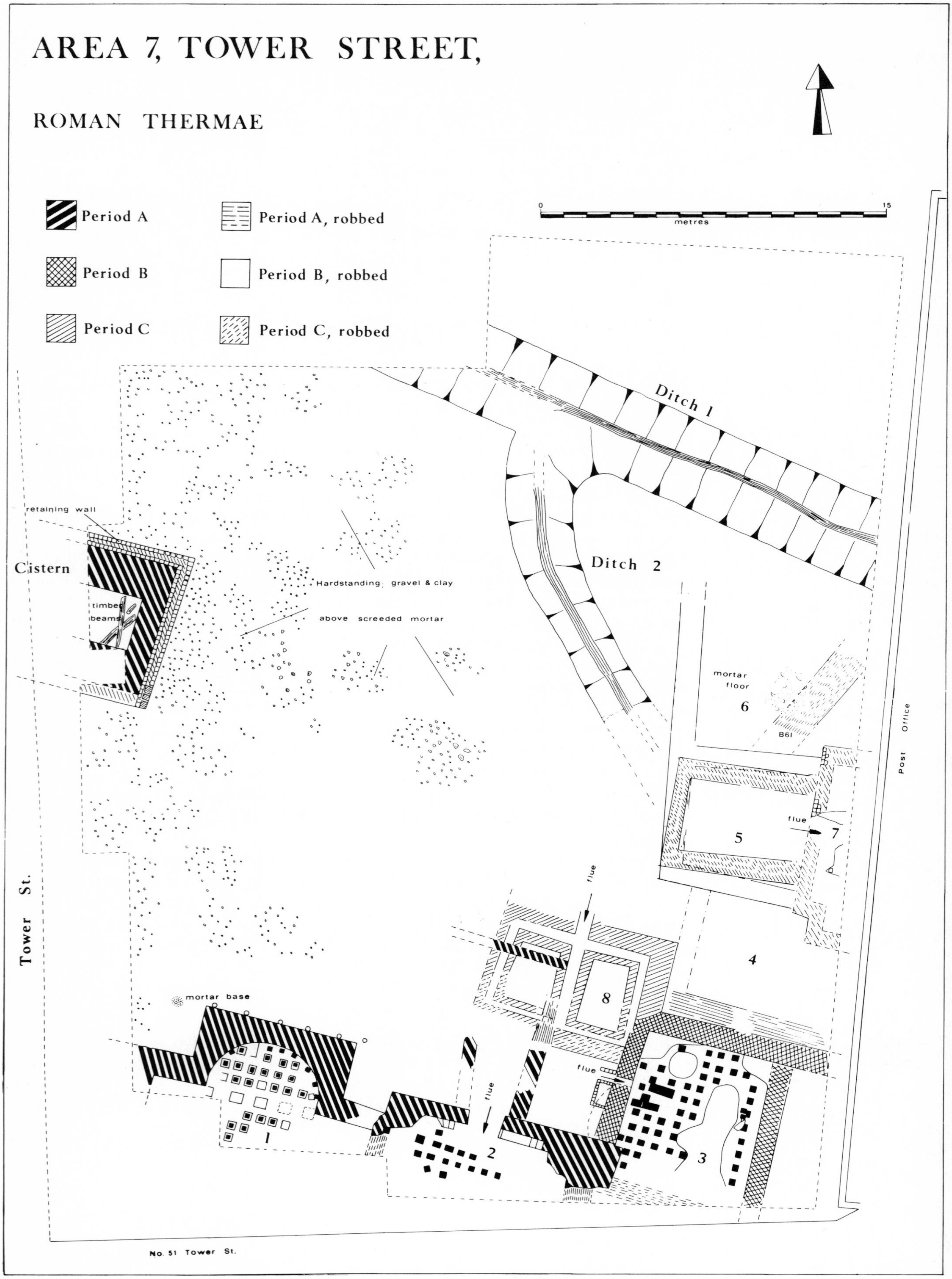

AREA 7, TOWER STREET,

ROMAN THERMAE

Period A

Period A, robbed

Period B

Period B, robbed

Period C

Period C, robbed

0   metres   15

Ditch 1

Ditch 2

retaining wall

Cistern

timber beams

Hardstanding, gravel & clay

above screeded mortar

Tower St.

mortar base

mortar floor

6

B61

5

flue

7

4

flue

8

flue

flue

1

2

3

No. 51 Tower St.

Post Office

Fig. 7.54

which showed no sign of any great heat, that the rooms along the south-east side were tepid in Period A and those further north in the same wing were unheated. Rooms 7 and 5 (see plan), may not have existed in Period A and the waste water from part of the baths must have been piped out through the area later occupied by Room 5, to discharge into the drain (Ditch 2), which in turn ran into the main east–west sewer (Ditch 1). Little can be said about Room 4; all that survived the robbing was a raft of roof tiles in the centre which had been part of the original floor make-up, and the south wall, which had been robbed, but which could be seen to pre-date the north wall of Room 3 which was built against it. Possibly contemporary with Period A hot rooms was a short length of robber trench (B.61) which ran diagonally to the main alignment. It is possible that it might be part of the earlier building hinted at in the fill of the Thermae apse excavation (see above), or that it belonged to Period A and was the start of a large apse running eastwards into Area 3. The fill contained 1 fragment of Hadrianic samian, tessarae from a mosaic, glass, marble and painted wall plaster from a building. The robber trench of the north wall of the Period B Room 5 which cut it, had similar derived material but there was a fragment of Antonine samian in it. This suggests that the Period B alterations involving the destruction of part of the Period A building took place at some time after the mid to late 2nd century.

Period B; *c.* mid to late 2nd century

At this time, a number of alterations and additions appear to have taken place. The tepid rooms along the south-east end of the east wing may have been converted to cold rooms at the same time; the hypocausts filled in and a mosaic and tessellated floors were laid on substantial foundations. Room 3 (see plan) may have been added to the main structure and this was fired from the west side. Rooms 5, 6 and 7 seem to date from this period and appear to have been unheated. Room 6 survived only as part of a mortar floor laid partly above the filled in robber trench B.61 and in one section of robber trench along the west side. The corner where it should have turned westwards was destroyed by later pits. The boundaries of the original Room 5 were seen only in the robber trenches, which in turn were cut by the robbed out walls of the later stokery.

Period C

A channelled hypocaust (Room 8) was added on to the north side of Room 2 and this took in the northern part of the stokery. There was so much disturbance from the medieval bell founding pits in the area that it could not be clearly established where the room was fired from, but slight traces of what might have been a flue were found at the north end. The stokery for Room 3, if it was still functioning, must have been severely restricted, and the same can be said for Room 2, where there is some evidence that the flue may have been blocked by that time, which indicates that Room 2 must have received its heat from the west side, through Room 1. On the other hand, the restriction of the stoking areas may indicate an increased use of charcoal as a fuel and this would require less space for rake back and fuel storage.

The stokery for Room 2 was largely destroyed by the garderobe pit belonging to the 15th-century house above, but a section across the accumulated charcoal and rubbish in the adjacent Room 3 stokery (Fig. 7.55) shows that this steadily built up to 0.70 metre thick and appeared to have been periodically "floored" with loose mortar. There were quantities of domestic rubbish and window glass and other

147

AREA 7, EAST SECTION ACROSS PART OF ROOM 8 L—L

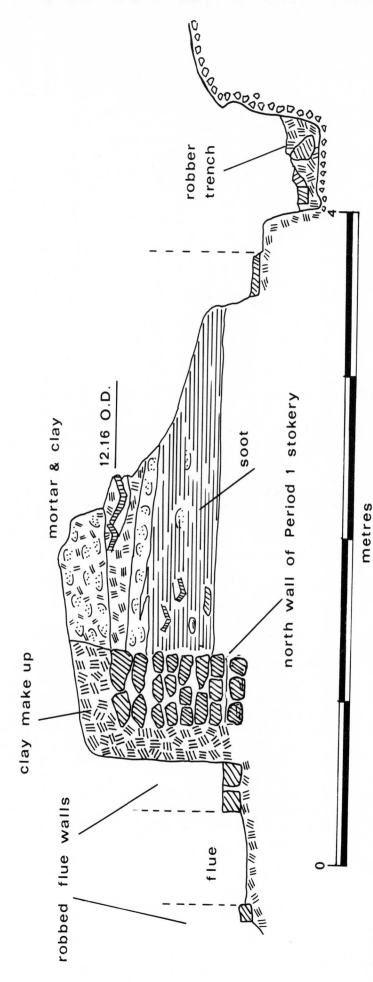

robber trench

12.16 O.D.

mortar & clay

soot

north wall of Period 1 stokery

clay make up

robbed flue walls

flue

0   1   2   3   4   metres

Fig. 7.55

building material thrown down and trodden in, and two infant burials (probably twins since they were placed together) were inserted into the fill and covered by a layer of charcoal. There was an absence of late Roman colour coated wares, which may be significant, and none of the domestic pottery present was closely dateable. It is obvious that the material raked back from the flues to ensure a good draught was initially dumped into the stoking area until the build-up forced the operators to excavate the charcoal and dump it away from the Thermae. This would cease to be necessary if a changeover to a fuel producing little or no residues, or the abandonment of the stokery due to re-planning, supervened. Whichever of the alternatives is correct, the absence of late Roman colour coated wares, which are plentiful enough elsewhere on the site, may indicate that the changeover, and by implication, the construction of Room 8, took place well before the 4th century. It must be stressed that the evidence is negative and there may be other reasons why no later dated material was present in the stokery, but Room 5 (see below), which may have become a stokery in Period C, had quantities of New Forest wares in with the charcoal, and this may be another indication that Room 3 had ceased to be fired from the west side before that time. It is possible that the final alterations to Rooms 5 and 7 also fall within Period C. Room 7 appears to have been converted to a hot room and was fired from Room 5 which became the stokery. The earlier Room 5 walls had been robbed and backfilled by that time but there was no conclusive dating evidence in the fill. At this stage it seems likely that waste water ceased to be discharged into the ditch via Room 5 and this may have become derelict although not robbed for masonry until the medieval period. The silt in the bottom of the slot of the drain had New Forest and Oxford sherds in it, and is perhaps a pointer to the time when the alterations took place.

It may be that these modifications indicate changes of function. A municipal bath house of this type would probably have facilities for "Turkish" and "sauna" types of bathing and the premises would no doubt be altered from time to time not only to effect necessary repairs to the structure but also to cater for the prevailing fashion in bathing.

Fig. 7.57

The water supply

The cistern at the north end of the hardstanding seems to have been the main, if not the only, source of water for the baths. It was massively constructed of large squared greensand blocks and the bottom was *c.* 3.2 metres from the contemporary ground level, and just over 5 metres from modern ground surface. It had a tile bonded retaining wall 0.5 metre wide around the sides and the foundations must have supported a cistern at a height sufficient to ensure an adequate head of pressure to the baths. The water would have been pumped up into the tank manually and although no traces of the actual cistern remained it is likely that it was of masonry, rendered inside with waterproof *opus signinum*, as large amounts of pink mortar were found in the robbed filling. There were no traces of pottery water pipes on site at all, and if they were used it would be surprising if no fragments remained after robbing. Lead pipes seem to be most likely in view of the absence of other evidence; these would have had a high re-use potential and would be certain to be preferentially robbed when the building began to decay. The pipes would need to be supported for a short distance of 15 metres from the cistern to the nearest point of Room 1 and thereafter would be supported by the building itself. No traces of iron collars which might suggest wooden pipes were found.

149

AREA 7. SECTIONS ACROSS ROMAN SEWER

Section A—A, East.

Post Office site, West section.

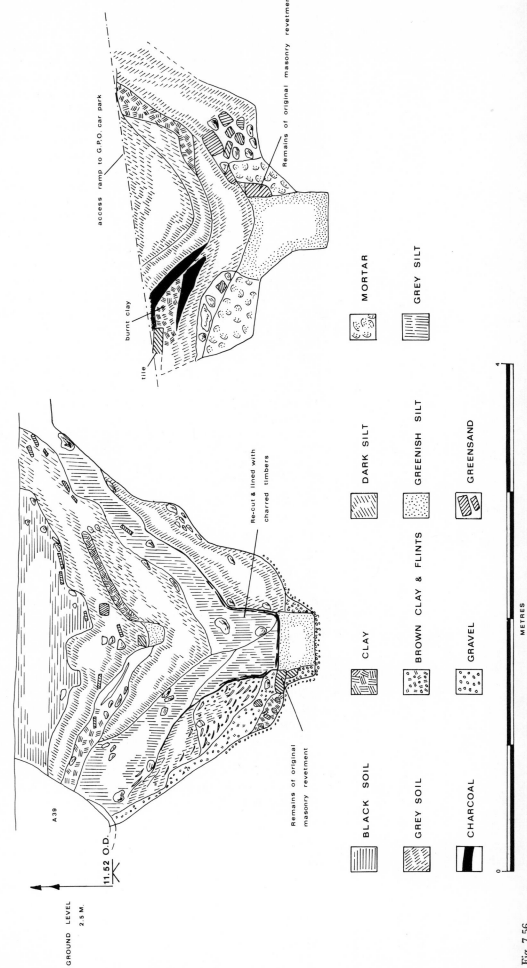

Fig. 7.56

Two oak beams were recovered from the bottom of the cistern. There may have been others, but due to restrictions imposed upon us by the need to avoid undermining Tower Street, and the requirements of safety, it was only possible to excavate a small part of the cistern. The beams measured 2.25 by 0.19 by 0.19 metres and 2 by 0.29 by 0.39 metres respectively.

Pumping during Roman times had caused considerable cavitation in the gravel around the cistern base, which caused the walls to settle inwards and eventually the east side collapsed dramatically when the coffer dam constructed for the excavation, was withdrawn.

The beams showed some signs of external worm attack but were otherwise sound. They may have been part of the superstructure of the pumping equipment.

Fig. 7.56

The drains

Ditch 2 drained from the direction of Room 7 into Ditch 1 (see below). It had been completely robbed out, with only the narrow channel in the bottom remaining, but it is likely that it was originally of masonry construction, and as there was no trace of it below Room 5 it must be concluded that drains from various parts of the Thermae discharged into it at that point. It does not seem possible for it to have functioned when Room 5 became a stokery and it may have become redundant and an alternative drain provided elsewhere. There must have been other drains from the baths; the biggest single source of waste water would have been the large cold plunge bath and this would have had to drain northwards below or alongside a series of hot rooms for a distance of at least 25 metres. This would be feasible, but it has not been possible to check the levels at the plunge bath end to establish what fall would be possible. An alternative path for some of the waste water would be possible if there was a north–south sewer into which it could drain on the west side. A glance at Fig. 7.3 shows that there might well be one. The sewer found below County Hall in 1960 and excavated again by us in 1972 (*Chichester* 2, pp. 40, 42) is not in direct alignment with Ditch 1 (see below), although they are parallel and obviously part of the same system. A logical explanation is that they may both discharge into a central north–south sewer which has still to be located, but which might run along the west side of the Thermae complex. It would be necessary for the subsidiary sewers to discharge into the main at different points to avoid "backing-up".

Ditch 1

This was certainly constructed at the same time as the street systems and the main public buildings. It ran east–west across the north of the site and was sectioned below the Post Office access ramp in Area 3 (p. 113) and a 19-metre length was excavated in Area 7, giving a very large sample of the fill. In the first phase it was a masonry built drain approximately 0.45 metre wide and possibly up to 1.5 metres deep. This would have been capped off with stone and would have had access points along its length for cleaning. Although almost certainly contemporary with the County Hall ditch, there was no evidence that the latter had ever been masonry revetted and the sections show no sign of a cut back on either side of the drain to accommodate a wall (see *Chichester* 2, Fig. 5.4, Section A–A and Fig. 7.56, this volume).

151

Some years later the masonry appears to have collapsed, probably due to lack of maintenance, and a good deal of silt washed down into the drain bottom. This may have occurred at a time when the municipal life was at a low ebb, when public works and amenities would have become (as always) an early casualty. A likely period might have been during the disturbances of the late 3rd century.

When the drain was cleared out, most of the collapsed masonry was taken away and the watercourse was re-cut into the silt at a higher level and lined with charred timbers including a plank at the bottom to facilitate cleaning. The practice of charring timbers has been noted before; presumably it was to slow down bacteriological attack on timbers buried in soil, but this belief may have been erroneous, as the Overton Down experiments indicate (*P.P.S.* 1966, XXCII, p. 332, Table XI).

No attempt was made to recut the ditch on the correct alignment and it can be seen to be wandering off line in the plan (Fig. 7.54). The evidence suggests a free standing box drain with a planked bottom, probably braced back against the sides of the ditch, which was then backfilled. A great deal of contemporary surface rubbish went in with the backfilling and this included quantities of late Roman colour coated wares (Oxford and New Forest), some of which were lodged vertically against the outside face of the timber revetment. The Oxford red wares in particular are not likely to have reached Chichester much before the end of the 3rd century and it is likely that the re-establishment of the drain may be placed at early on in the 4th century. This, as we have seen elsewhere (Areas 2 and 5), was a period of re-building and expansion in Chichester.

Finally, the timber revetment collapsed and the drain silted up, with no more than a sinuous trickle of water running along it. The subsequent settlement left a V-shaped depression which became a dump for domestic refuse and building material, and while no date can be given for this period it is likely that it paralleled the slow decay of urban amenities seen in Houses 1 and 2 (see above, p. 83) and probably the decline set in towards the end of the 4th century. The latest coin below the medieval layers in the top of the ditch was lost at some time after A.D. 373.

The Thermae in decay

There is no direct evidence for the date at which the baths ceased to function. The coin series ends in the last quarter of the 4th century and the thorough and systematic robbing of the building in the post Roman periods effectively destroyed all floor levels. The run-down may have been slow, in keeping with the slow decline in town life seen elsewhere. In Room 5 there appears to have been a late phase, where timber beams were laid outside the walls which by then must have been demolished but not robbed out, and part of a wall constructed of greensand and flint and laid down on the accumulated layers of charcoal in the stokery. This may be a very late or sub-Roman phase unrelated to the functioning of the Thermae. In Room 3, a thick layer of clayey silt had washed down amongst the pilae supporting the floor, indicating that part of the floor had been broken down and that the building was roofless for some time; this could have occurred after robbing had commenced.

Most of this seems to have taken place in the Saxon-Norman period as nearly all the post-Roman material in the robber trenches was unglazed late Saxon wares. The major robbing is most likely to have been carried out when building stone was needed for the construction of the Norman Cathedral a few yards away in the late 11th and early 12th century.

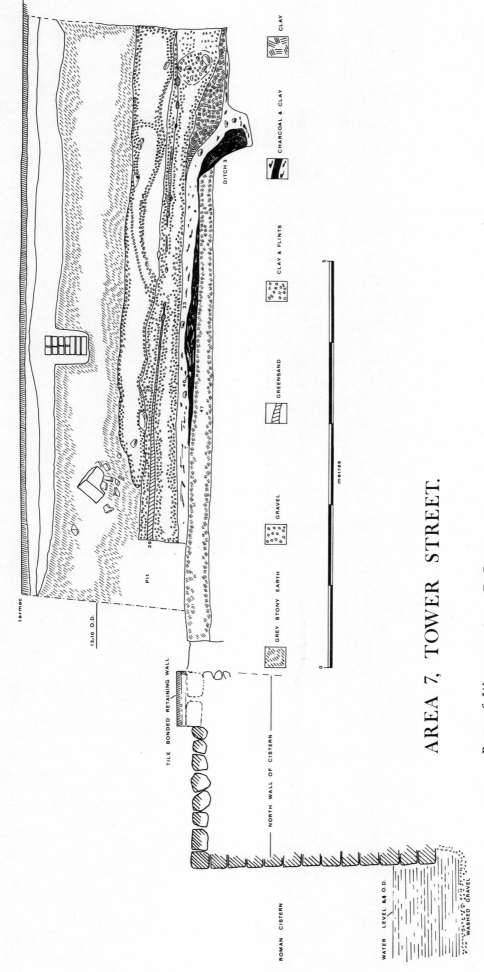

AREA 7, TOWER STREET.

Part of West section B–B

Fig. 7.57

AREA 7, TOWER STREET.

Part of South section through robbed Thermae C—C

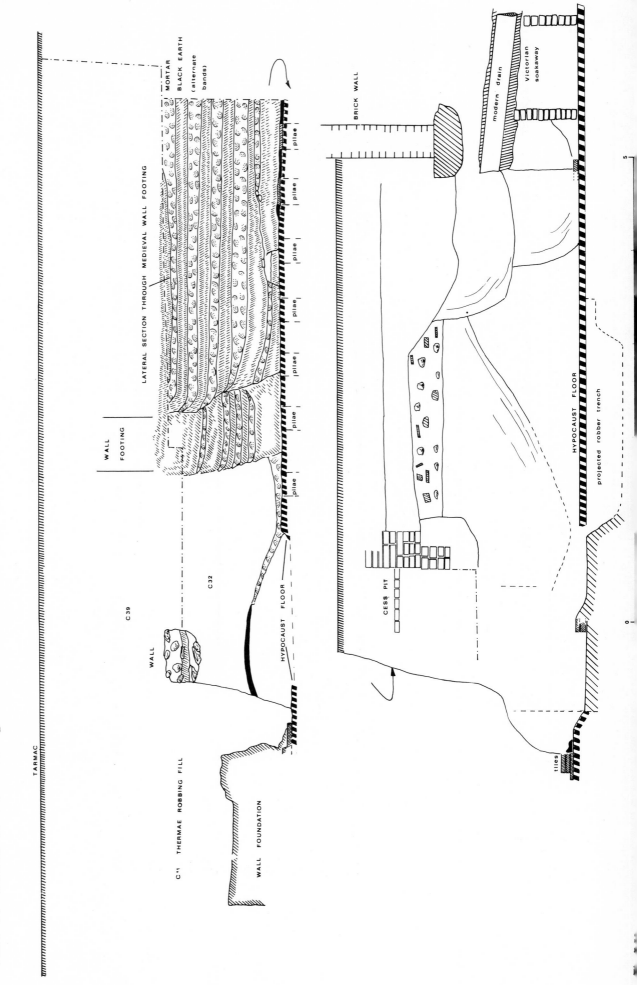

TARMAC

MORTAR

BLACK EARTH
(alternate bands)

LATERAL SECTION THROUGH MEDIEVAL WALL FOOTING

WALL FOOTING

C 39

C 32

WALL

C 1 THERMAE ROBBING FILL

WALL FOUNDATION

HYPOCAUST FLOOR

pilae

BRICK WALL

modern drain

Victorian soakaway

HYPOCAUST FLOOR

projected robber trench

CESS PIT

tiles

0

5

AREA 7, TOWER STREET.

West section across apse of hypocaust, Room 1.   D–D

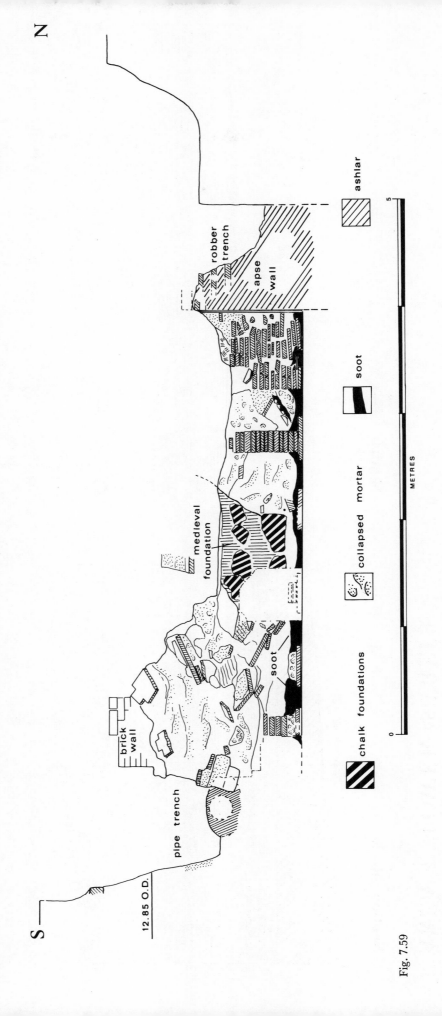

Fig. 7.59

AREA 7, TOWER STREET.

Section K–K

Section J–J

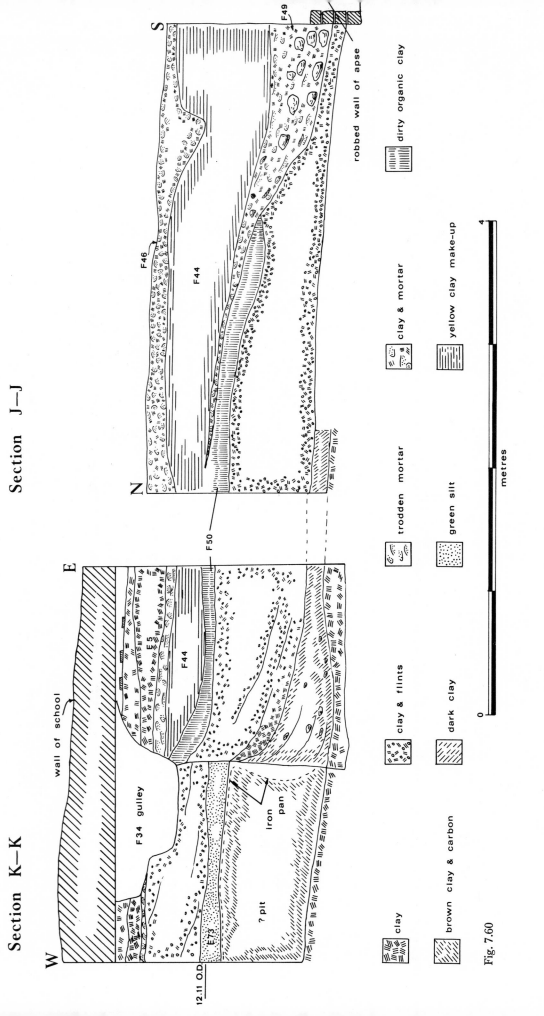

Fig. 7.60

Legend:

dirty organic clay

clay & mortar

yellow clay make-up

trodden mortar

green silt

clay & flints

dark clay

clay

brown clay & carbon

metres 0 ... 4

13. Area 7, Tower Street, looking east. D: Roman sewer (Ditch 1), E: Garderobe pit and postholes of medieval house M.2.

14.   Area 7, Tower Street. Part of medieval House M.6. A: garderobe pit; B: hearth, C: oven. (Photo: John Adams)

Building Materials

Fine grained limestone, Upper Greensand and flints are the local building materials and all were present in what remained of the fabric of the building. The floors, where these survived, were of hard pink *opus signinum* reinforced with tiles in the heated rooms. Elsewhere, the tessellated floors were seen to be cut from hard chalk or limestone. Only one mosaic is known; the fragment found in 1960 (*Holmes* 1965), but it is likely that there were others, some perhaps still awaiting discovery. From the number of *opus sectile* stones found (*Pilmer, J.*, in archive), it is estimated that at least one part of the Thermae or its environs was paved in this fashion. Some of the stones were cut from chalk and limestone; others were in Purbeck or Sussex marble and had been masons rejects before being re-used as paving.

It was noted that Reading clay had been applied around the base of the hypocaust pilae in the hot rooms and also around the piers of the flues to insulate them against excessive heat. It must have only been partially successful as many of the pilae were badly flaked and friable and it could be seen where local repairs to the floor had become necessary from time to time and groups of pilae badly out of line with the rest, had been inserted. The practice of using Reading clay in this fashion has been noted at Upmarden Roman Villa (*Down*, forthcoming).

The fragments of interior fittings found exhibit a similar fine degree of workmanship to those found at Fishbourne. Marble wall veneer and flooring sections were found, some imported from Greece and Italy and cut and worked on site. These and the many fragments of Purbeck or Sussex marble frame mouldings point to a high degree of sophistication and elegance for a small cantonal capital, but may perhaps be more clearly understood in relation to the Flavian palace at Fishbourne. It may well be that the palace of Cogidubnus was closely followed by the construction of the Thermae in the growing native town which was his capital, and that the same masons and workmen were employed. The scope of the Thermae, some 5,500 square metres, shows the same facility for planning on the grand scale that can be so clearly seen at Fishbourne and against this background, the Temple of Neptune and Minerva with its famous inscription, may perhaps fall into place as yet another monument to an energetic and wealthy client King determined to outshine all his contemporaries in the splendour and importance of his capital and palace.

Events seem to show that the initial impetus was lost after Cogdubnus died and the Regni came directly under Roman rule, and that what began in the grand manner in the late 1st century limped on in a partially developed state until the late 2nd century (see p. 98).

Not enough of the Thermae has been available for excavation so far to clearly chart the vicissitudes of the building from its construction to eventual decay in the 5th century, but the work carried out from 1973 to 1975 in Areas 3 and 7 should provide a framework to which all future discoveries in the area of the baths can be related. This framework will inevitably be modified as more information comes to light.

Considerable activity during the period was attested by numbers of pits, most with the distinctive late Saxon and Saxo-Norman fabrics (see pp. 341–50), and some with earlier wares. These have been grouped into two phases, largely on the evidence of the pottery.

Phase 1, *c.* late 9th to 10th century

Pit D.38 was a small round pit (Fig. 7.61) dug through the Roman gravel and it had a large amount of hand-made gritty wares (p. 343 and Fig. 11.1). This was a closed group, being sealed by the later Saxon building S.1 (see below). Some of the wares might possibly be earlier, but the date bracket of *c.* 9th to early 10th century is likely to be correct.

South of Pit D.38 was Pit E.51. This was fairly shallow and had cut an earlier, probably Roman, pit. There was a thick layer of charcoal and baked clay in the bottom and the fill contained many late Saxon pottery wasters. Pit E.49 to the east, and several pits dug through it also had late Saxon pottery wasters, and many fragments of baked clay daub with clear impressions of wood varying between 10–15 mm in diameter were also present. It is likely that Pit E.51 functioned as a pottery clamp and that the daub derived from the superstructure. Two other features also showed evidence of pottery manufacture; Pit E.38 was probably a cesspit but had been backfilled with the material from a clamp or kiln, including baked clay, wasters and several large blocks of charred oak (Fig. 7.62 for section: information on timber from Mr. J. Pratt). Layer C4/16 was a deposit of charcoal, pottery wasters and baked daub similar to that found in Pit E.51. Here, all the material had been backfilled into a vast hole left when the Thermae was robbed for building stone, and is again evidence for a destroyed clamp.

Discussion

It cannot be established whether the wasters indicate the beginnings of commercial pottery manufacture or whether they relate to the firing of domestic wares by individual family units. Some of the vessels are wheel turned, and others might have been hand made and finished on a slow wheel. The fact that some trouble was apparently taken to construct a wattle and daub superstructure for the firings may indicate something more ambitious than normal domestic production for immediate family needs. Our own experiments in that direction (Chilgrove 1971), showed that wares technically equal to the Phase 1 pottery could be fired quite well on a bonfire with very little trouble.

The clamp/kiln in C.4/16 was probably destroyed when the Thermae was robbed for building stone. The absence of any glazed wares and the presence of large amounts of Saxo-Norman fabrics in the robbing fill suggests that the robbing took place in the late 11th to early 12th century and this may be equated to the need for building stone when the Cathedral was being built. There is no indication of the time lag between the abandonment of the clamp/kiln and the destruction by robbing, but it could well have been a century later if the date for the pottery is right.

Phase 2, *c.* early 11th to early 12th century

Occupation in the second phase seems to have increased, to judge by the number of Phase 2 pits, and this parallels development alongside Chapel Street (Area 2, pp. 83–86). The pits seem to follow the line of the street, with one series going off to the east at right-angles, suggesting, perhaps, that the buildings associated with the pits were north and south of this line. Traces of two sets of slots which may relate to two different buildings were located.

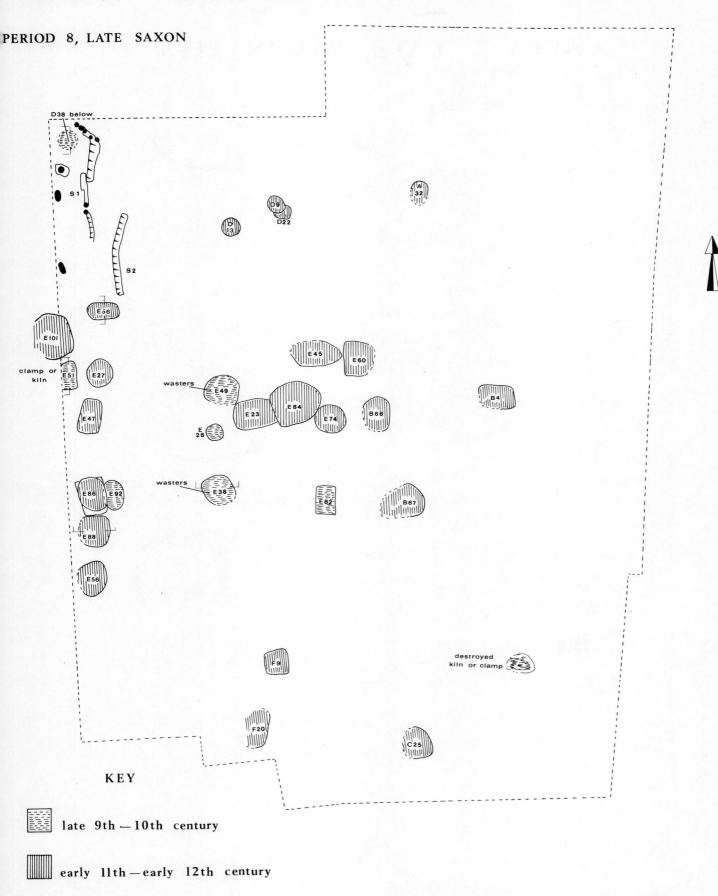

AREA 7, TOWER STREET.

PERIOD 8, LATE SAXON

D38 below

S 1

S 2

E 56

E 101

clamp or kiln
E 51   E 27

E 47

wasters   E 49

E 23   E 84   E 74   B 66

E 28

wasters   E 38

E 86   E 92

E 82   B 67

E 88

E 56

D 9
D 22

D 3

A 32

E 45   E 60

B 4

F 9

destroyed
kiln or clamp

F 20

C 25

KEY

late 9th — 10th century

early 11th — early 12th century

Fig. 7.61

0   15
metres

AREA 7, LATE SAXON PITS

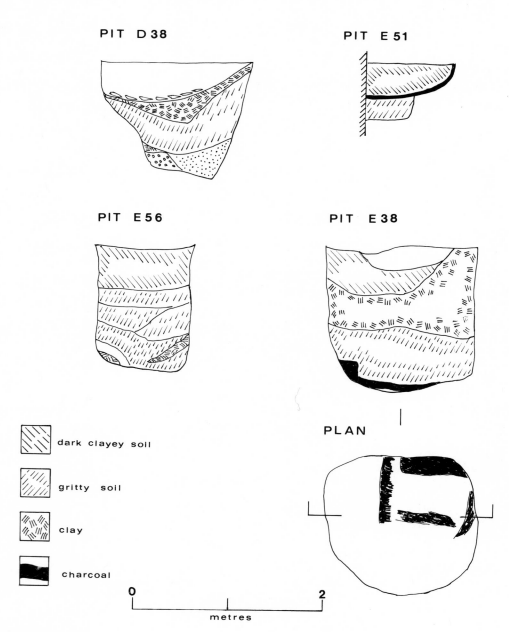

PIT D 38

PIT E 51

PIT E 56

PIT E 38

PLAN

dark clayey soil

gritty soil

clay

charcoal

0   2

metres

Fig. 7.62

Building S.1

This consisted of three sections of discontinuous slot with some postholes set in them. The slots were triangular in section as was the one belonging to the second building (see below). The structure was cut away at the south end by a pit but seemed to curve round at the north end, with a number of postholes set very close together. Three large postholes may have marked the centre line of the building, in which case it would have been a narrow structure three metres wide. It enclosed Pit D.38 which is assumed to be earlier. Pottery from the slot and some of the postholes was all coarse late Saxon ware and included stamped fragments and part of a spouted pitcher. These features were seen to be below the medieval house, which partly destroyed them.

Building S.2

This was a short length of slot of similar section and with similar pottery in it, on the east side of Building S.1 and far enough away to be sure that it was not part of the same structure. No other traces were found, but the impression is that it belonged to a building roughly contemporary with S.1 and that it was part of the west side.

A total of 20 pits were classified as Saxo-Norman on the basis of their contents and relationship. There were undoubtedly others, wholly or partly destroyed by later pit and well digging to judge by the amount of residual Saxo-Norman material present in later deposits. All of the pits seen in Fig. 7.61 had large numbers of unabraded coarse wares and appeared to be primary deposits. In addition to the coarse wares the common denominators were food bones, including sheep, ox and goat, and often winkle shells. One pit produced a large number of cherry stones. It has been noted many times before when excavating late Saxon pits in Chichester that goat horn cores and winkle shells are distinctive features. They are much less common in later pits (and where found could easily be re-deposited), and wholly absent from Roman pits.

The goats may be an indication of a semi-pastoral situation, away from the main streets in late Saxon Chichester, with perhaps numbers of small holdings each supporting a family and their domestic animals, of which the goat might well have been the most useful, being able to subsist on minimum grazing; a source of milk, meat and clothing, with the inedible residues finishing up in the cesspit.

Period 9; *c.* late 12th to 15th century

Fig. 7.63

The site during Period 9 showed continuing signs of occupation; at some time after the establishment of the See at Chichester the land, or most of it, appears to have passed into the ownership of the Dean and Chapter. This may have occurred in the 13th century or possibly earlier, and parts were still in ownership in the 18th (see below).

Phase 1, *c.* 12th to 13th century

It is almost impossible to distinguish between the pits of the late 12th century and those of the Saxo-Norman period (Period 8, Phase 2), in terms of the pottery, nor can the emergence of glazed wares in the pits help very much. So far, no late Saxon glazed wares similar to those found at Winchester (*Biddle and Barclay*, 1974, pp. 137–65) have been identified here and while it is fairly certain that some of the sherds found with a patchy green glaze are late 12th century, there has so far been no external dating evidence to assist in identification. Some of the coarse wares are beginning to change at this time, being generally finer and harder fired, and more sand is being used as grog, but the point at which these wares merge into the most

161

AREA 7, TOWER STREET

Period 9, Medieval; 12th – 15th century

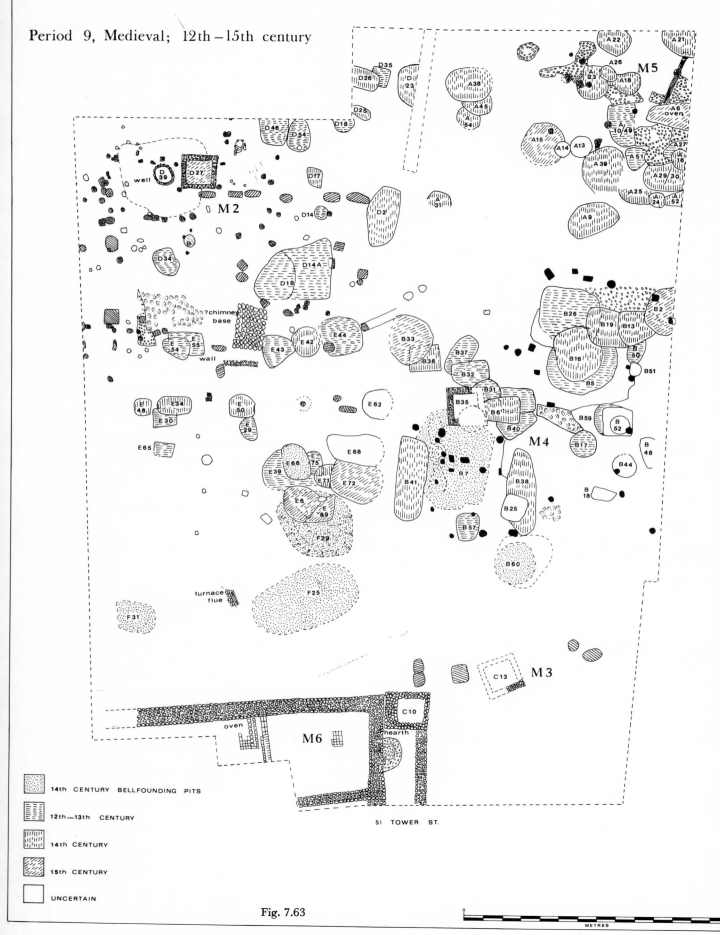

14th CENTURY BELLFOUNDING PITS

12th – 13th CENTURY

14th CENTURY

15th CENTURY

UNCERTAIN

Fig. 7.63

51 TOWER ST.

METRES

easily recognisable wares of the 13th century cannot be located. Lacking precise dating criteria, it is only possible to say that certain wares are likely to be "early medieval", *c.* 12th century, as opposed to "Saxo-Norman", on the basis of the relationship of one pit or layer to another.

Within the limitations imposed by the pottery it has been possible to arrive at a rough grouping of pits which should fall within the phase late 12th to early 13th century. Reference to the plan (Fig. 7.63) shows that these all appear to be in the northern part of the site, with the area of deep robbing in the hot end of the Roman Thermae being completely free from Phase 1 activity. This might conceivably be because stone robbing was still in progress during the late 12th century and the area may have been heavily cratered and unfit for settlement.

No structures can definitely be assigned to Phase 1 but it is likely that some of the unassigned postholes in the area of the Phase 2 house, M.2, may belong to a Phase 1 house. A well (D.39) was constructed with a large well pit 4.2 metres in diameter; this had probably been dug to eliminate a number of earlier cesspits and to prevent seepage from later ones. It had been backfilled after the well was built, with clay and flints, well consolidated. The fill of the well pit (D.34) had only one sherd of glazed ware, the remainder being Saxo-Norman and early medieval coarse wares, suggesting an early medieval date. The well was very poorly built, it was of dry-stone construction, with flints and re-used Roman tiles. It collapsed on the south side and may have been abandoned at some time in the 13th–14th century. Orchard Street type strap handles (*Chichester* 1, Fig. 9.5) were found in the top fill of the well. Later-dated painted wares of the 15th century were found right in the top but these derived from a later pit (D.40) which cut part of the well top away. The dating evidence for the construction is best seen in the material from the well pit, which was surface debris at the time of the construction, and a date of *c.* late 12th to early 13th century is proposed for it, and, by implication, to the house it served (House M.1).

At some time after the well was backfilled, and it may have been part of the same process, a number of the Saxon and early medieval pits in the north-west area of the site (Pits D.9, D.18, D.14A, E.27, E.26, E.41, E.30, E.43 and 44) were consolidated with a thick layer of stiff green clay, probably dug from the harbour. Considerable trouble had been taken about this and in some instances the pits had been completely or partly excavated and the clay put in and tamped down. There seems little doubt that it was felt necessary to consolidate an area which by then must have been heavily riddled with cesspits, in order to build another house.

Phase 2, *c.* late 13th to mid 14th century (Pl. 13)

House M.2 (see Fig. 7.63)

This was of timber construction and the walls may well have been of "cob" as there was enough dirty clay in the layers above the postholes to account for part at least of the destroyed superstructure. The two focal points from which to attempt a reconstruction in plan are the stone built garderobe pit (D.27) which was dug partly into the earlier well pit and was adjacent to the well, and a raft of flints and tiles set in stiff green clay which may have been the base for a chimney. The postholes which appear to be contemporary and make up the plan of the house are hatched diagonally on the plan. As far as can be seen, it appears that the house extended just south of the ? chimney base. The northern limits are outside the excavation, as there appears to be an outshut around the garderobe pit which extends northwards.

163

The latest dated pottery from the garderobe Pit D.27 was late 14th century paint-under-glaze wares. These were just below the clay seal which topped off the pit, and must represent the latest pottery to be discarded before the pit (and possibly the house) went out of use. Pits of this type, built into the house structure, must have been regularly cleaned out and the contents dumped into a pit dug away from the house, and the paint-under-glaze wares suggest a *terminus post quem* for the house of *c.* late 14th to early 15th century, but the construction date could have been half a cer   ry earlier or more.

House M.3

At the south end of the site, and largely destroyed by post medieval cesspit digging and the foundations of House M.6, was part of a stone built garderobe pit (C.13) of similar construction to D.27, and a line of large postholes cut deep into the robbed fill of the Thermae. This might well be the forerunner of House M.6, but there is no conclusive dating evidence from the pit except a few glazed ridge tiles which could be 13th–14th century in date, and nothing from the postholes, which need not be contemporary with the pit but which probably are. All that can be said is that some of the basic elements of a house are present and that it pre-dates House M.6.

The Bell Founding

Below the accumulated layers of post-medieval debris at the south end of B was an area of dark soil with much charcoal, medieval roof tiles, roofing slate and bronze slag (B.7). This layer extended westwards across to Tower Street and it was obvious that considerable activity relating to metal working had taken place. Some initial confusion resulted from the fact that the hot end of the Roman Thermae occupied part of the same area and redeposited charcoal and burnt clay from the Roman stoking processes were also present. Examination of B.7 showed that it was the top of a large irregular pit, the sides of which appeared to have been broken down in places and which had been backfilled in a haphazard fashion. Great difficulty was experienced in working out the boundaries of this feature as the tip lines appeared to follow no normal pattern. There was, however, a logical explanation (see below).

In the bottom of the pit was the remains of a flue (Fig. 7.65 and Pl. 15) and resting upon it was the base of what was later found to be a bell mould. This was 0.86 metre in diameter and had been partly destroyed by a pit cut through the west side, but enough remained of the soundbow profile to enable Mr. George Elphick[1] to make a correct identification. Further confirmation came from Dr. R. F. Tylecote whose analysis of two fragments of bronze metal found in one of the pits (*Tylecote*, in archive) showed this to be bell metal, a tin bronze with a tin content of 24%, the normal specification for medieval bell metal. Slag samples examined by Dr. Tylecote were seen to be from a crucible or ladle, and samples of mould fragments examined showed that these were mainly clay, bonded with organic material such as straw or dung.

The method of casting medieval bells is described by *Theophilus*, writing in the 12th century, and can be briefly re-stated here.

1.   *The preparation of the cope*

An oak arbor, constructed from dry oak, was mounted horizontally so that it functioned as a pole lathe. It was turned by operating a cranked handle attached to one end, and the arbor was tapered so as to facilitate its eventual withdrawal

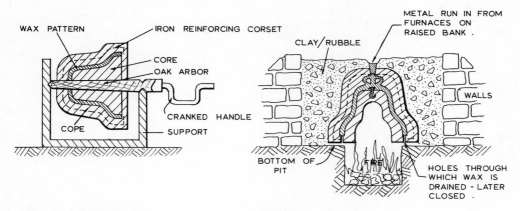

Fig. 7.64 Possible reconstruction of medieval bell-founding process

from the mould. A number of layers of wet clay were applied evenly around the arbor, each one being allowed to dry thoroughly before the next was applied, until the inside shape of the bell had been achieved. The clay core was then finished off by smoothing with abrasive stones while the arbor was being turned. After this operation, sheets of wax were carefully prepared and applied to the outside of the core until the required thickness of the bell had been reached. Any inscription that was to be placed on the bell was incised into the wax at this stage. Following the application of the wax, successive layers of clay were applied to the outside to form the "cope", and when the required thickness had been achieved, reinforcing bands were placed around the cope, followed by more layers of clay. The arbor was then withdrawn and part of the inside of the core was taken out to lighten the assemblage and to permit some contraction of the metal during cooling. Wax patterns for the cannons were luted to the top end of the bell mould and an iron hook was inserted through the hole in the top to serve as a suspension for the bell clapper.

2. *Founding*

The bell mould was then placed with the bottom downwards over a trench dug to form a flue, and some form of retaining wall was built around the mould to support it. The fire, when it was lighted, melted the wax which ran out from holes in the base of the mould, and at the same time baked the core and the cope. The holes were then sealed and the molten bell metal was applied from the top, usually by ladle if small bells or other vessels were being cast, but in the event of a large bell the metal would be heated in a furnace built as close as possible to the mould, so as to minimise heat loss, and the molten metal run down a trough.

3. *De-coring and lifting the bell*

As soon as possible after the casting, the core would be broken out so as to prevent the bell cracking. The retaining wall around the cope would be demolished and the bell raised by alternately levering up first one side and then the other and packing earth underneath. It is easy to understand the reason for the shapeless appearance of Pit B.7 when the laborious nature of the operation required to get the bell out of the pit without it cracking or warping, is understood.

165

4. *Finishing and tuning*

Theophilus describes how to finish the bell by putting it back on a pole lathe and polishing it with abrasive stones, and how the various semi-tones for a peal can be achieved by varying the thickness of the soundbow.

AREA 7, BELLFOUNDING PIT

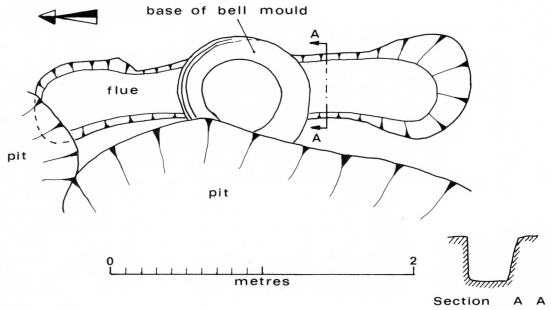

Fig. 7.65

The pits

A number of pits produced material from the founding process and a selection are illustrated (Fig. 7.66), but only Pits B.7, B.60, E.66, F.25, F.29 and F.31, can be said to have been probably or definitely associated with the process. Of these, B.7 had a trench for a large bell and F.29 (Fig. 7.67) was undoubtedly one of the furnace pits for heating the metal. Only the lower part of this pit survived, the remainder having been cut away by Pits E.6, E.69 and a large post-medieval cesspit F.3. It had large amounts of bronze slag and the central area was full of charcoal. It is likely that the furnace occupying this pit was used for heating fairly small amounts of metal at a time, using refractory crucibles which would probably have had an iron frame with a thick clay lining on the inside (see Fig. 7.66, No. 8). Small hand bells and domestic vessels such as skillets and cauldrons would have been cast by this means.

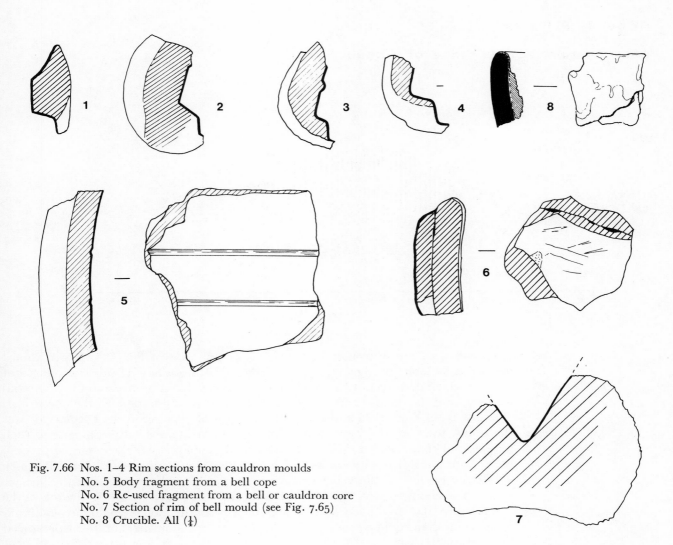

Fig. 7.66 Nos. 1–4 Rim sections from cauldron moulds
         No. 5 Body fragment from a bell cope
         No. 6 Re-used fragment from a bell or cauldron core
         No. 7 Section of rim of bell mould (see Fig. 7.65)
         No. 8 Crucible. All ($\frac{1}{4}$)

This pit also produced the most reliable dating evidence for the process. Trapped between the slag at the bottom and the side of the pit were several large fragments from a Horsham type 14th-century glazed jug. A complete specimen (Fig. 11.6, No. 12) was found in an adjacent pit (E.66), which was also full of charcoal, slag and mould fragments. Just over half of a third jug was recovered from another bell founding pit, F.25.

AREA 7: PIT F29

East section across base of furnace pit

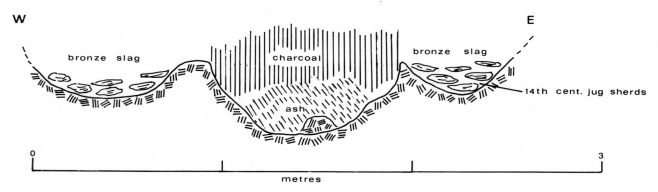

Fig. 7.67

Part of a second flue (Fig. 7.63) was found just west of Pit F.25. It was almost destroyed by later pit digging, only one short length of the west side surviving, but the pits which destroyed it had large quantities of residual bronze founding material in them, and it is almost certain that this flue is contemporary with the one in B.7. The pits B.60, E.66, F.25 and F.31, had no signs of burning in the bottom nor was there any trace of any other flues. All the pits contained large amounts of bell moulds and charcoal and they may have been dug for clay for the founding process, being later backfilled with the mould fragments. There appears to be no pit which is sufficiently close to the bell founding trench in B.7 to have served as the furnace from which the molten metal would have been run down a trough to the top of the bell mould. A bell of the size indicated by the base of the mould would have required more metal than could be supplied quickly by crucible pouring, and this would need to be immediately adjacent to the mould. The absence of any trace of an adjacent furnace was noted at Winchester (*F.T.J.*, 1964, pp. 460–2) also, and it may be that the furnace was erected above ground on a bank in order to get sufficient height for the pouring.

Following upon examination of the slag by Dr. Tylecote, Dr. Peter Ovenden of Southampton University examined a sample cut from the base of the bell mould found in B.7. His examination led him to conclude that the construction of the mould base was consistent with the lost wax process of founding (*Ovenden, P.*, in archive). Traces of a waxy substance (spermaceti) were found on a core fragment

168

and the clay for the cope and core seems to have been used in conjunction with either straw or dung as a binder. The inside surfaces of the core and cope (those in contact with the metal), were well finished and reduced to a dense black, with small flecks of bronze showing in the surface. In section, the cope fragments, whether from small bells or large cauldrons is not certain, varied from brick red to yellow/buff near the exterior surfaces.

The Chichester Cathedral bells

The bell founding pits were situated on land formerly belonging to the Dean and Chapter, less than 100 metres from the Cathedral. There is no surviving documentary record as far as we know, of any accounts for the making or repair of bells, but it is certain that this was the main purpose of the activity. Only one bell mould has positively been identified but more than one bell could have been cast over the same trench as the succeeding operation would tend to destroy all traces of the previous one. Mr. R. R. Morgan writes:

"The earliest mention of bells comes from the Cathedral Chartulary. Bell ringers are mentioned in 1188, 1245, 1256 and 'great bells' in 1320. The Cathedral had two belfries (the central tower and the Great Belfry) before the separate bell tower was begun in the late 14th century. The bells in the modern tower include three by Phelps (1729) and one by Taylor (1877). Bell founding was recorded in the St. Pancras area *c.* 1594 to 1605 (Thomas Giles and Anthony Wakefield).

It is very likely that any bell founding in the 13th or 14th centuries in Tower Street was carried out by itinerant founders employed by the Cathedral to carry out specific work. The site is on land which was owned by the Dean and Chapter and it was probably the nearest vacant space to the Cathedral at the time, which implies that the land to the south, between the site and West Street had been built upon."

The relationship between the founding activities and House M.2 are not clear, but it is quite possible that the house was there at the time the bell founders moved in (assuming that they were itinerants). The casting of the bells and domestic vessels which were an important sideline need not have been a lengthy business and it may well be that the founders came and went within the space of a year.

A possible reconstruction of the methods used in medieval times is shown in Fig. 7.64.

Phase 3 A; *c.* late 14th to early 15th century

After the bell founding was completed and the pits filled in, a building (House M.4) was erected, partly over B.7 and extending east and northwards across an area honeycombed by 13th- and 14th-century pits. The remains of a stone-built garderobe pit (B.35) was found cut partly into B.7. What remained of the final filling was indeterminate, being mainly 14th century pottery and roof tiles, but perhaps the best hint of the date comes from a posthole which cut Pit B.2, where the latest pottery was an internally glazed sherd which could be 14th century but which is likely to be later (see Fig. 7.63, the postholes adjudged to belong to this building are shown in solid black). House M.2 could still have been functioning at this time and it appears from the plan that House 4 was built on part of the same holding, and if not a replacement for the earlier house may perhaps be considered as an extension of the same family's living quarters.

Traces of another structure (House M.5) were visible in the north-east corner of the site, where a series of postholes and a short length of slot were cut into pits containing 14th-century pottery. These postholes make no coherent pattern and the structure or structures cannot have been of much substance. The slot was partly destroyed by a late medieval oven (A.6) on the south side and it is considered that the date for this building or buildings must fall between *c*. mid to late 15th century.

At the south end of the site, part of a large masonry built house was found (House M.6). The walls were well constructed of flints and chalk and at the west end the foundations went very deep into the robbed fill of the Thermae. Alternate layers of mortar and earth were laid as a foundation for all except the main external north wall (Fig. 7.58) and the settlement over the years was not much more than 15–20 cms, suggesting perhaps that the load was not very great.

A large chalk built garderobe pit (C.10) was built onto the north-east corner and this was reached by a narrow passage 1.5 metres wide. A small hearth built of tiles placed on edge in clay was situated against the east wall of the main building, in the passage and adjacent to the garderobe pit. Both the pit and the outside passage wall were built onto the main structure and might have been added afterwards.

West of the passage and hearth was a room measuring 4.5 by 5.5 metres, which had the remains of a tiled floor. The tiles were green glazed and many were present in later cesspits cutting the building. Further west was a narrow wall built of medieval roof tiles mortared together. This could not be fully investigated as the area immediately south of it was denied to us by the presence of a manhole and foul sewer connection belonging to No. 51 Tower Street. It seemed to be the east wall of an oven, possibly a bread oven, which had been built up against the north wall of the room. It had a tiled floor consisting of discoloured green-glazed tiles and these had a layer of charcoal on them. The rest of this feature had been destroyed by the wall of the National School, but it is very likely that the room was part of the kitchen area.

Discussion

The house was solidly built and was probably at least two stories high at the west end where it fronted on to Tower Street. No conclusive evidence came from below the remains of the floor but the latest dated artifact in the garderobe pit was a glazed jug handle which postdates the 14th century (Fig. 11.7, No. 26) and which is probably 15th century. Apart from this, the fill contained large amounts of roof tiles and slate in all the layers, which suggests that the backfill material was debris either from an earlier building or resulting from a re-roofing programme. The even distribution through the layers may indicate that the material was stockpiled ready for backfilling as required. Again, it is assumed that the pit was regularly cleaned out up to the time of the final filling, which need not have been until late on in the 15th century. Even then, the abandonment of the pit need not indicate a *terminus post quem* for the house. Another garderobe, put in a more convenient place, might have been substituted for Pit C.10, but lacking the complete plan this can only be conjectured. However, the possibility that this house was still standing in the 16th century should not be ignored.

Site History (information from Mr. R. R. Morgan)

The southern part of Area 7 was owned by the Dean and Chapter at least from the 13th century up to the 18th, and the area occupied by House M.6 was the site of a tenement granted by the Dean and Chapter to Thomas de Pipering (a mason) in 1246. John Hallestede held property on the site in the 14th century and it is possible that House M.3 could have been his.

Other 13th-century and later tenements probably fronted onto Tower Street, but these have yet to be identified although their remains can be seen on the ground.

More documentation is available for the post-medieval periods in Area 7, and the Documentary Research Group have produced a series of maps enlarged from the Ordnance Survey of 1875 (Figs. 7.68 to 7.71), showing some of the property holdings. These can in some instances be related to features on the ground.

The site history is presented in narrative form prepared by Mr. R. R. Morgan and this is followed by a brief discussion of the archaeological features. The marginal references on Figs. 7.68 to 7.71 are the research groups' unique site reference numbers. The southern limit of the site is the north boundary fence of No. 51 Tower Street which is shown on all maps and the eastern limit of the plots shown in the documentary research maps is the line of the north–south wall dividing the site from the Post Office land. This is a property boundary line of some antiquity, being shown on the Gardner Map of 1769 and probably "fossilised" for many centuries previously.

Site History

(The site is divided into three plots for convenience; from north to south – *T.69/72* Woolstore; *T.73* National Schools (north); *T.74/75* National Schools (south).)
T.69/72. This plot has been in the ownership of St. Mary's Hospital until recently. Frontage to Tower Street 94 feet 6 inches; depth 134 feet. The earliest possible reference is in 1239 (*Cathedral Chartulary S.R.S.* 46/489), where the Dean and Chapter grants a plot to St. Mary's "wherein shall be built a building". There is only one other site of St. Mary's property in Tower Street (north end, west side) and the description does not fit. If this site is the one referred to in *S.R.S.* 46 it can be seen as a further indication of the inertia affecting property ownership where the Church was concerned.

In 1562 there was a garden with a tenement occupied by John Wylde. Throughout the 17th century it is described as a garden but a tenement is mentioned in 1678 (Richard Blatchford). It was a tenement until 1752 when it is described as a tenement used as the Poor House for the Parish of St. Peter the Great. In 1766 Wm. Humphrey the brewer had it, and brewers and publicans are recorded thereafter for the southern half until about 1885. From about 1808 it is referred to as "Fighting Cocks", and tradition has it that it had a sign painted by George Morland (1763–1804). The rent paid to St. Mary's was one shilling per year or one fat hen. The sale price in 1885 was £450. The "Fighting Cocks" fronted on to Tower Street but also had a property (tenement) at the rear of the next property to the south.

Meanwhile the northern half of this plot became the Royal Lancastrian School in 1811. It was built for the Royal British Institute for the Education of the Poor, on the plan of Joseph Lancaster (1778–1838), and was for boys (the equivalent girls' school was near Little London). A body of local citizens (28 in number) raised £600 to build it. It took 167 boys, mainly C. of E., and was known at one time as the British School. The City Council bought it in 1907 and it was sold to Priors in 1911, who used it as a Wool Store. The Post Office bought it in 1967.
T.73. This plot had long been in the ownership of the Dean and Chapter. Frontage 31 feet 9 inches; depth 134 feet. Earliest reference is again 1239, and if this is accurate it was the house of Richard Smethe. In 1562 it was a tenement, stable, garden and backroom known as Churches Storehouse, and is soon after described as a tenement and remains so until the 19th century.

In 1649 the existing tenement is described . . . "3 lower rooms and a cellar and 3 chambers over . . . and 3 garrett lofts over the said chambers and a backyard with a pump of water in it and garden plots (now turned into tenements)". The lessee fourteen years before (in 1635), was William Porter. It is likely that a number of

171

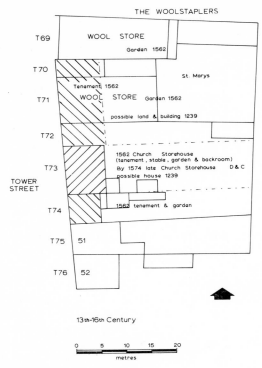

Fig. 7.68

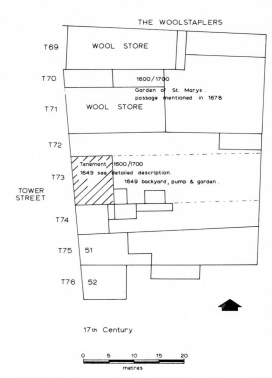

Fig. 7.69

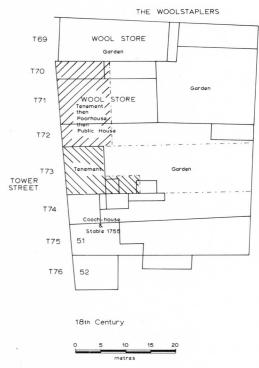

Fig. 7.70

172

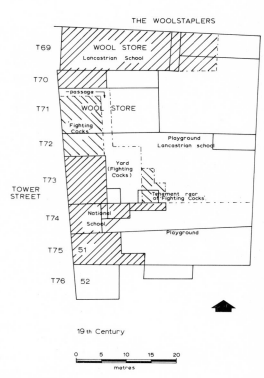

Fig. 7.71

tenements succeeded one another on the site. By the 19th century the house fronting Tower Street had the yard of the "Fighting Cocks" at the back of it and in 1870 the house was replaced by the National School.

T.74/75. The plot was described as a stable in the 17th century and two tenements in 1810. It became part of the National School in 1870. Frontage was about 40 feet originally.

The Features on the Ground

Period 10; Phase 1, *c.* 16th century

Very few features can be assigned to this period. Within the plot T.69/72 were two pits (B.27 and D.20), which are probably of this date. The tenement occupied by John Wylde in 1562 was not located, but it seems from the description (see above) that part of the area was garden and the tenement could be further north and just outside the excavation.

Further south, in F, was a shallow pit which appeared to have been intended as a well. It was circular in shape and had been built to one side of an oval pit. The construction was poor, being flint and greensand in clay and it was only 2 metres deep – not enough to have functioned efficiently as a well, even in the wettest weather. The greenish organic deposit in the bottom suggests that whatever the original intention may have been, it was used as a cesspit. Most of the dateable artifacts were 14th century or earlier, but there was a small group of painted wares in with it which may bring the date when it was finally backfilled into the early 16th century. Its position brings it just within the boundary of Plot T.74, which in 1562 was a tenement and garden (Fig. 7.72).

Below the brick floor of the basement below the National School were a series of brick lined postholes (shown dotted in Fig. 7.72) which may relate to the Churches Storehouse on the site in 1562.

Phase 2, *c.* 17th to 18th century (Fig. 7.71 and 7.72)

Plot T.69/71. Three pits only are recorded of this date (D.10, E.18 and E.24). The area is recorded as a garden belonging to St. Mary's Hospital during the whole of Phase 2 and this is reflected in the sparse evidence of occupation.

Plot T.73. The western end was destroyed by the basement for the School, but east of it was a rectangular well pit (E.76) with a wall (E.41), built of chalk and brick. This well remained open and was only sealed by a stone slab, and had some 18th- to 19th-century pottery in the top. The fill of the well pit, which is a better guide to the construction date, had one fragment of stoneware which is likely to date to the 17th century and the stone slab sealing the well was one metre below the modern ground level. Of this, 0.5 metre was made up for the school playground and the later car park and it is clear that the contemporary ground level for the well was at the level of the slab.

In 1649, Plot T.72 had a tenement, backyard, pump and garden (see above). A pump implies a well, and it is likely that E.41 supplied the water to this and possibly later establishments.

Plot T.74/75. Only one feature can be identified as possibly late 17th century and this is Pit F.4 (Fig. 7.72) which contained an interesting group of late 17th- to early 18th-century wares (see p. 365 and Fig. 11.12).

The plot is recorded as having a stable in the 17th century and a coach house and stable in 1755, and yet the fill of the pit contained high quality wares including a number of wine bottles, one bearing the seal of the "proud" Duke, Charles Seymour, sixth Duke of Somerset, who lived at Petworth House. One may legitimately speculate as to how a wine bottle of this proud and overbearing man, of

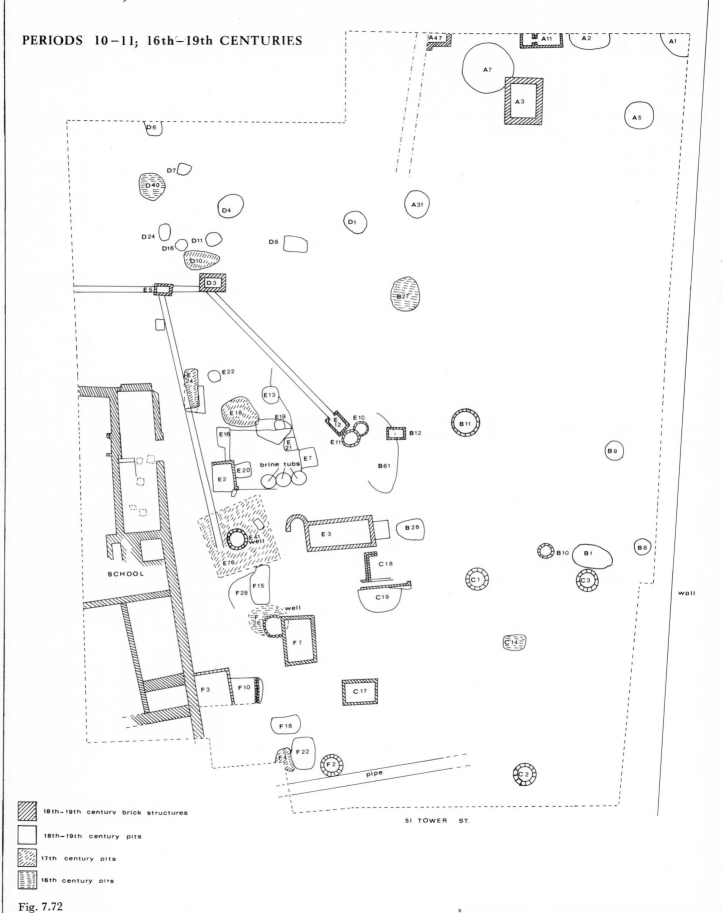

AREA 7, TOWER STREET

PERIODS 10–11; 16th–19th CENTURIES

A47 A11 A2 A1

A7

A3

A5

D6

D7

D40

D4 A31

D24 D11 D1

D16 D8

D10

D3 E5

B27

E22 E24

E13

E18 E19 E10

E16 E12

E E11 B12 B11

E21

E7 B61 B9

brine tubs

E2 E20

E41 well B28

E76 E3 B10 B1 B8

SCHOOL F28 F15 C18 C1 C3

well C19

F26

C14

F7

C17

F3 F10

F18

F22 C2

F2 pipe

□ 18th–19th century brick structures

□ 18th–19th century pits

▨ 17th century pits

▦ 16th century pits

51 TOWER ST.

wall

Fig. 7.72

METRES

whom Macauley wrote "that with him, pride of birth and position amounted almost to a disease", came to be in a cesspit behind a coach house and stable in Tower Street. There is no evidence that the Duke owned the property, and the pit was backfilled early on in the 18th century at the latest. A possible explanation might be that the coach house and stables were owned or run by a former retainer of the Duke, who kept up his links with Petworth House. While 17th- to 18th-century sack bottles are common enough in Chichester, those bearing the Somerset crest and the motto of the Garter are not, and both the bottle and the rest of the contents of the pit suggest a better-class connection than that implied by the property description.

Period 11; *c.* 19th to early 20th centuries

By the early 19th century the frontage along Tower Street had assumed the form it had until recent years. At the north end of the site the Lancastrian School was built in 1811, and some of the cesspits below the school can be seen in Fig. 7.72. These yielded large amounts of scholars' slates, some with the names carefully scratched or written on in copper-plate. With the help of the local press, the relatives of some of the schoolboys who were there in the late 19th and early 20th century were located. One scholar, Alfred Heath, now 71, was traced by an enterprising journalist and given back the slate he had handed in to the school when he left the infants school in 1915.

Plot T.71/73. The "Fighting Cocks" Inn (previously a Poor House) covered most of the area. It had a passage behind it which led to a yard, and this was located, with the bases of three brine tubs still in position on the north side. Two of these yielded coins of 1803 and 1805 respectively. The well (E.41) was probably still in use at this time. An inventory of 1873 shows that the public house was of modest proportions with only twelve chairs and three tables and a small number of glasses.

Plots T.73/74. These plots were occupied by the National School which replaced the Storehouses owned by the Cathedral. The School was finally demolished in 1974 and 1975, the last section being pulled down by the excavators. The area east of the school building was playground, with a number of 19th-century cesspits below. At the moment of writing (January 1977) the site is a sunken car park, pending development, with all the archaeological levels having been removed to a depth of 2.5 metres.

Footnotes

[1] I am indebted to Mr. George Elphick the authority on medieval bell founding, who paid several visits to the site at my invitation and made the original identification of the bell mould.

[2] Drawing reproduced by kind permission of the *Foundry Trades Journal*, to whom thanks are due.

NOVIOMAGVS REGENSIVM

DISTRIBUTION OF PRE-INVASION FINDS

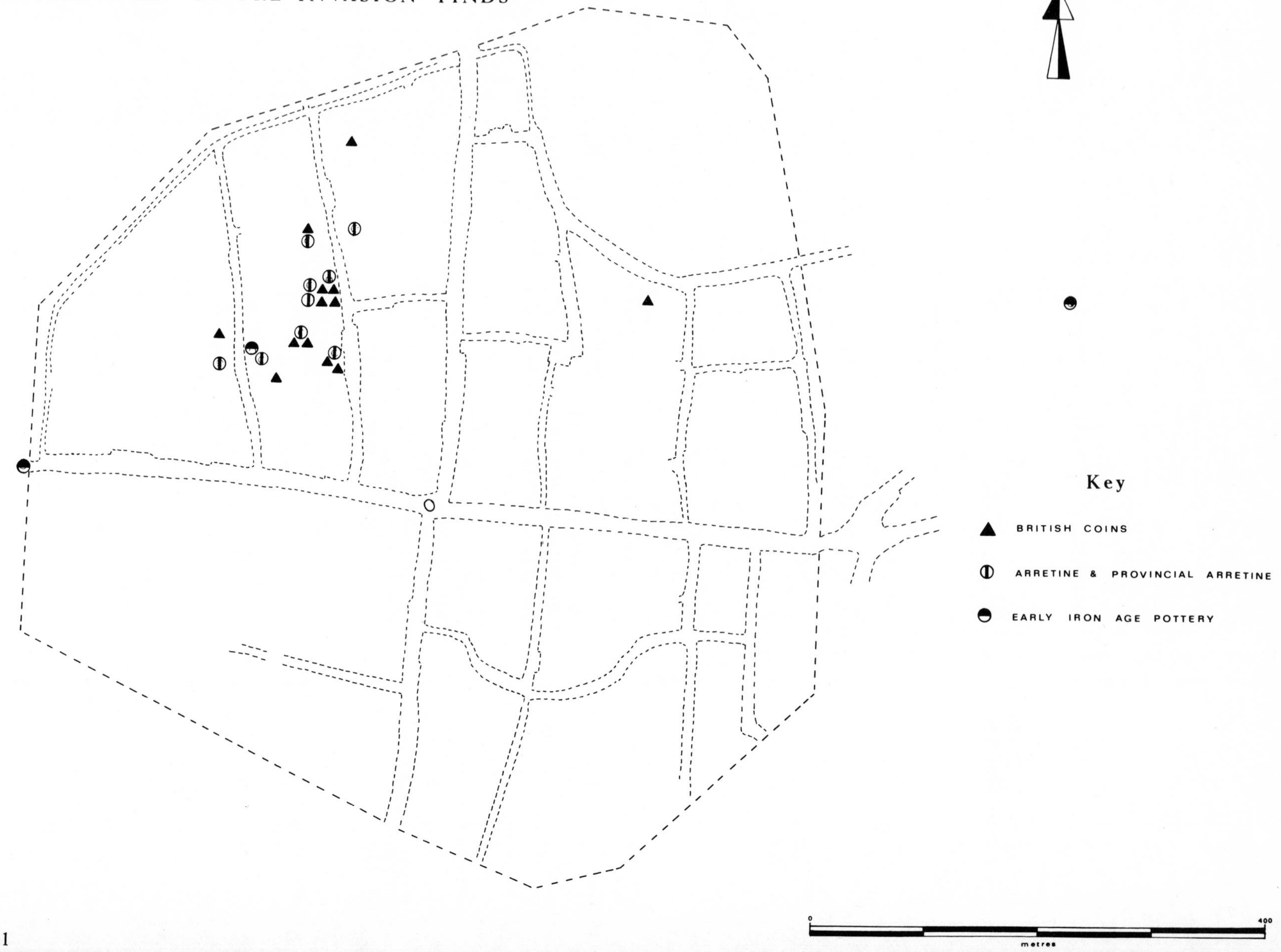

Key

▲ BRITISH COINS

◐ ARRETINE & PROVINCIAL ARRETINE

◑ EARLY IRON AGE POTTERY

Fig. 8.1

8

Chichester: The First Hundred Years

by Barry Cunliffe

The examination of the large Roman settlement at Fishbourne between 1961 and 1968 presented a picture of the early years of Romanisation in the Chichester region which, though internally consistent, was severely limited in value by the virtual absence of a suitable body of relevant information from the urban centre of Chichester, which lay only a mile away to the east. Now, after 8 years of intensive excavation (1968–75) in the north-west quarter of the walled town, a sufficiently large area has been thoroughly examined to provide both the basis and the occasion for a reconsideration of the Chichester-Fishbourne region in the first hundred years of Roman occupation.

Something must be said at the outset about the nature of the archaeological evidence. Most of the area excavated had been densely occupied, dug into and turned over during the last two thousand years. One has only to look at the plans showing Saxon and medieval pits to appreciate how much of the Roman levels has been disturbed. For this reason the ground plans of early Roman features are in places tantalizingly incomplete and it is frequently impossible to relate one piece of structural evidence to another. A second point deserving emphasis is that the pre-Flavian levels are for the most part very thin, the entire period often being represented by no more than 20 cms of soil accumulation. The intensive activity during this period, the transient nature of the structures, and the fact that the soil has been churned up, mean that much old rubbish has been incorporated in later layers. This can lead to confusion and misunderstanding. The discovery of a piece of military bronze equipment in a late pre-Flavian level clearly cannot be taken to imply the presence of the army at that date. Having made these points, however, it should be said that the surviving evidence in archaeological terms is of a high quality and, with care, can be used to reconstruct a sequence of development for this part of the city, which will allow certain tentative historical interpretations to be offered.

Summary of the early Roman development in the north-west quarter

In the detailed reports above, Alec Down has divided the early development of the city into five major periods, which may be briefly summarised as follows:

Period 0: possible pre-Roman occupation.
Period 1: earliest timber buildings – Claudian.
Period 2: industrial activity – Claudio-Neronian.
Period 3: timber buildings on stone cills and an early bath building – early Flavian.
Period 4: the rebuilding of the baths and the laying out of the street grid – late Flavian to Trajanic.

These periods, which are broadly applicable to each of the excavated areas, can be sub-divided into phases. Detailed descriptions of the individual structures and of the dating evidence are given in the relevant sections of the main report. Here we will be concerned to comment briefly on each in terms of the overall development of the city before finally offering some speculations about the potential historical implications.

177

Period 0: ? Pre-Roman

Period 0 poses difficult problems. In stratigraphical terms it is represented by nothing more than the ground level immediately pre-dating the earliest Roman layers, and at best consists of a thin layer of soil totally devoid of structures. On this evidence alone one would conclude that the excavated area presents no evidence of pre-Roman occupation, yet when the finds from subsequent layers are considered there appears to be a consistent group of pre-Roman material. The coarse wares (pp. 187–188) are unimpressive, consisting only of a small collection of sherds which could be pre-Roman, although of course it is possible that some of the "Roman" coarse ware will eventually prove to pre-date the conquest. The excavation has, however, produced twelve Iron Age coins, to which two from other excavations in the city should be added. The finds from the recently excavated site include four of the Atrebates (two of Tincommius, two of Verica), five of Cunobelin, three of Epaticcus, one of Amminus and one of the Durotriges, all representing small change minted in the 1st century A.D. While such a collection would be consistent with the finds one would expect on a late pre-Roman Iron Age market site, they could equally as well have been brought to the site early in the post-conquest period to augment low-denomination Roman bronze coinage which remained in short supply for some years.

In addition to this native pre-Roman material, there is a not-insubstantial collection of imported pottery, comprising Terra Rubra and Terra Nigra vessels (pp. 190–205), Arretine and Early South Gaulish samian (pp. 225–227) and a few fragments of amphorae (pp. 243–244), for all of which a late Augustan–early Tiberian date of manufacture seems probable. In other words, a group of pottery made before *c.* A.D. 20 was in use in Chichester, and sherds of it were found in layers of Claudian to Flavian date.

While it could be argued that the current dating of these pre-Claudian fine wares is in need of serious revision, this view finds little support in current writing. If, then, we accept the specialists' dating, two alternative explanations present themselves: either the pre-Roman material represents an *in situ* pre-Claudian occupation or old stocks of pottery were in use in Chichester during the pre-Flavian period. On balance the latter explanation seems to be the more probable for three reasons: no stratigraphical evidence was found to suggest an Iron Age occupation; no consistent body of pre-Roman coarse ware could be identified; and, as Valery Rigby points out (p. 201) the collection of pre-Claudian imported wares from Chichester-Fishbourne does not contain the full range of contemporary types, but only selected forms, which could imply that consignments of old stock were being off-loaded on the Chichester consumers. Individually, these points are not particularly significant, but together they are sufficiently persuasive to suggest that the earliest occupation on the excavated site (and at Fishbourne) was no earlier than the Claudian period.

We must, however, examine the alternative hypothesis. It could be that a centre of pre-Roman occupation lay outside the area excavated in the north-west quarter, and that when the Claudian occupation began, valuables, including small change and fine pottery, which had been in the possession of the locals, found their way into the Roman settlement. There would be nothing unreasonable in supposing that pottery imported in the 20's was still in use in the 40's, and the native coins would still have been useful in the early years of occupation as small change. The only observation to weigh against this hypothesis is that it would have to be extended to explain the similar range of early imported pottery found at Fishbourne, a mile away. While this is by no means impossible, especially if it is supposed that the pre-Roman centre lay between the two, it might be felt that the coincidence is too great.

The problems posed by Period 0 have been exposed in some detail here, if only to make the point that there can be no certain solution as yet. In the present state of knowledge, we must avoid the temptations of emphasising one view at the expense of the others simply because of personal preference and preconceptions. The only advances that are likely to be of immediate value will come from the examination of further areas of the original ground surface in and around Chichester in an attempt to discover undisputed structures or levels of pre-Roman date.

Period 1: Claudian

The earliest structural evidence recognisable in the north-west quarter (designated here as Period 1) consists of fragments of timber buildings, best represented in Areas 2 and 4, constructed of upright timbers placed in shallow foundation trenches, some of which may well have taken horizontal cill-beams. Evidence of this kind of structure, though fragmentary, extends over the entire excavated area, and is invariably associated with pottery of no later than the Claudian period. Several bronzes of Roman military type were found in contemporary levels (on Site 2/4: Trench J) and a number of others have come to light in later layers. There can therefore be little reasonable doubt that the buildings were of Claudian date and were in use at a time when military equipment was present in the Chichester region.

Although the plans of the buildings cannot be recovered in any detail, one striking fact to emerge is that they were for the most part all aligned in the same direction, slightly off line with the later street grid. There is nothing inherently difficult in supposing that they represent military buildings belonging to the first Roman garrison in the area. The style of building and the ordered layout is suggestive of military planning, and, as the evidence from the forts at Longthorpe and Waddon Hill will show, there is no longer any need to believe that individual military buildings were precisely and regularly designed in the pre-Flavian period.

The quantity of military material in the immediate vicinity would go some way to support this view. An alternative must however be considered, that the excavation lay within the civilian vicus of a fort, the exact location of which has yet to be discovered. If this were so, we would have to assume that the army had a hand in the layout of the settlement, but such a suggestion is consistent with evidence from other sites, e.g. Verulamium.

There is little to choose between the two alternatives; both are equally possible and until more evidence is available it is unwise to speculate further.

Period 2: Claudio-Neronian

Period 1 appears to have been short-lived. In Areas 2/4 the early levels were superseded by extensive remains of industrial activity. Two pottery kilns were built, producing a range of fine-ware forms, including butt-beakers and girth beakers, together with jars, bowls and dishes, while nearby there was evidence of other industrial processes, including bronze-working and enamelling. A large pond, quite possibly connected with these activities, was found in Area 4. Nearby, in Areas 3 and 5, a series of building-levels was recorded, representing successive phases in the rebuilding of timber-framed structures, while in Area 7 substantial timber buildings were seen, together with layers of burning and some iron slag. Associated finds consistently suggest a pre-Flavian date for this period.

The industrial activity implies beyond reasonable doubt that in this period the excavated area did not lie within a fort. While such evidence would not be inconsistent with the area being a vicus, it could equally well be that the Period 2

179

occupation represents the first civilian phase in the development of the town. The fine pottery and the enamelled bronzes which the craftsmen in Areas 2/4 were producing would have been entirely appropriate to a developing civilian market in a highly Romanised area. The presence of military bronzes in layers of Period 2 date need be no more significant than the sherds of Augustan and Tiberian pottery found with them, all of which presumably represent rubbish survival from the earlier phases.

Period 3: Flavian-Trajanic

Early in the Flavian period there would appear to have been a major change of policy with regard to this part of the settlement, represented by a period of demolition and levelling. In the northern part of the site (Areas 2/4) a new series of timber buildings were erected on ground cills constructed of greensand blocks and flints. In the southern part of the site, however (Areas 3 and 7), it would seem that large areas were left open and unencumbered by buildings. There is some suggestion that beyond the southern limit of Area 7 an early bath suite may now have been built. The evidence for this is admittedly indirect and consists of a mass of building rubble, including patterned flue tiles, marble, *opus sectile* elements and fragments of an inscription, found filling a deep excavation associated with the construction phase of the later baths, the northern part of which extended into the excavated area.

Dating evidence for these early stages is sparse, but it seems probable that Period 3 began in the late Neronian or early Flavian period.

In the northern region occupation continued, possibly accompanied by a continuation of industrial activity, at least until the end of the 1st century. To the south, work began on the construction of the new baths (or an extension of the old) at some time during the Flavian period. The new suite, which can hardly be other than the public baths of the city, probably extended as far south as the main east–west street, occupying in all an area of 5,500 square metres. The reconstruction, in grand style, of this major public building, may well have been part of a programme of urban expansion. On present showing, however, the street grid, in Areas 2/4, seems to have been laid out a little later, at the end of the 1st or early in the 2nd century, providing a parallel with the situation in Silchester.

Period 4: Hadrianic-Antonine

With the establishment of the street grid and the construction of at least some of the major public buildings, the first stage in the development of the city came to an end. Thereafter it was largely a matter of rebuilding and infilling within an existing structure. This is true of the north-west quarter with one exception, the great spread of gravel metalling which was laid down in the centre of the town some time in the Antonine period. There can be no doubt that this was associated in some way with the construction, or reconstruction, of the forum and basilica which most likely occupied the prime site at the junction of the main north–south and east–west streets. The story of this building must, however, await the results of future excavations.

Chichester and Fishbourne in the 1st century

Having now summarised the main phases in the development of the north-west corner of the town, it remains to consider the evidence derived from the excavations of 1968–75 in a broader context and in particular in relation to what is known of Fishbourne. Perhaps the most surprising thing to emerge from the comparison is the very close similarity between the main stages in the evolution of both sites, not only

180

in historical terms but also in relation to the styles of building involved and the social implications which follow from them.

Sufficient has been said about the problem of the late pre-Roman Iron Age occupation in the area. There can be little reasonable doubt that the great series of dykes, the Chichester Entrenchments, which lie to the north of the city, defined the limits of the territory of a pre-Roman oppidum, the centre of which probably lay at one time either to the south of Selsey in a region long since eroded by the sea or in some other area so far unexplored. The possibility that other settlement areas may have existed within the enclosed territory should not be overlooked. There is no need to suppose that all the functions of a late Iron Age oppidum were centralised in one place. Having said this, however, it must be stressed that there is no firm evidence for pre-Roman occupation at Chichester or Fishbourne. All that can safely be said is that there may have been occupation in the region, but not in the areas which have been examined by excavation.

The earliest definable structures at both Fishbourne and Chichester are timber buildings of Claudian date associated with Roman military metalwork. Two of the Fishbourne structures are similar to military granaries, while the Chichester buildings are not unlike those found in forts of the Claudian period. One plausible explanation would therefore be to see Chichester as the site of a military base, with Fishbourne providing harbour and storage facilities for it. The exact nature and extent of these two elements is difficult to define, nor can we be sure that the Chichester buildings lay within the defences of a fort. One of the most important questions to be posed by the new evidence from Chichester is the exact size and location of the fort. Roman military material has been found over a considerable area, and a ditch of pre-Flavian date and defensive proportions was found beneath the Roman cremation cemetery to the east of the walled area, but there is no certainty that it was military in origin, and if it was it can hardly have been a defensive enclosure for the buildings found in the north-west quarter. The problem is made even more difficult by the rapidity with which certain early forts seem to have been rebuilt and resited within a particular location. In other words, while a military presence on the site of Chichester seems established, there is little more that can safely be said of its location and development.

A reasonable historical context for the presence of the army is suggested by the campaign of Vespasian and the Second Legion in A.D. 43–44, when they are known to have marched westwards to conquer the tribes of Dorset and neighbouring areas. A military base with good harbour facilities in friendly territory would have been essential. Once the resistance of the western tribes had been overcome, forts established in their territory and a frontier zone constructed along and in advance of the Fosse Line, the significance of a rearward establishment such as Chichester-Fishbourne would have been considerably diminished. So great would have been the demand on manpower at this time that it would seem probable that the Chichester base was abandoned or the establishment cut to a skeleton detachment, especially as it lay within a client kingdom.

It has been suggested that the military buildings went out of use at Fishbourne within a few years of the invasion. The military-style buildings in Chichester were also soon superseded by an industrial phase, which can be dated to the 50's. If the Period 1 buildings were military then either the garrison had departed by this time or was resited elsewhere in the immediate locality. The evidence cannot be pushed any further. It is however quite wrong to suppose that the appearance of military bronzes in subsequent layers *proves* a later military presence.

The industrial activity at Chichester in the Claudio-Neronian period (Period 2) is particularly interesting, for it implies a sophisticated market able to afford and appreciate fine pottery in Roman style. Significantly this is broadly contemporary with Period 1B at Fishbourne, where the inhabitants were adorning the walls of their well-built timber houses with painted plaster, nor should it be forgotten that it was during the Neronian period that a statue of the emperor was erected in the town. The impression given by these scattered observations is that Romanisation developed fast in the region in the first two decades following the invasion.

Period 3 was represented at Chichester by a phase of levelling and rebuilding. Timber houses were built on dry-stone cills, while a (presumed) early bath house, fitted with stamped box-tiles and adorned with marble and *opus sectile* work was built somewhere towards the centre of the town. It was in precisely this period (Neronian to early Flavian) that the "proto-palace" was built at Fishbourne, with a bath-house provided with decorative fittings closely comparable to those of the early baths at Chichester. Even the stone cill construction for timber buildings is represented at Fishbourne at about this time. The coincidence is remarkable and can reasonably be explained only by assuming that the same architects and builders were responsible for both buildings. They may well, also, have been employed to build the bath house at the neighbouring villa of Angmering. Three elaborate building-projects at this early date within the space of a few miles must clearly demonstrate a considerable concentration of wealth within the area.

Some time during the Flavian period (Period 3) the Chichester baths were wholly or partially rebuilt. What little survives of the new structure shows it to have been constructed of well-cut and well-coursed ashlar masonry and to have been adorned with mosaics as well as imported and local marbles. The similarity in style and quality to the Flavian palace at Fishbourne is impressive. We may fairly assume that the same building gangs were working at both. Once more it would seem that the two sites were developing in parallel.

It has been suggested that the Fishbourne palace was the official residence for the local client king, Tiberius Claudius Cogidubnus. If so it is tempting to see his hand in the contemporary development at Chichester, which must have included not only the baths but also the temple to Neptune and Minerva, where the famous inscription mentioning his name was set up. What other buildings were erected at this time it is impossible to say, but in all probability the other necessities of civilised urban life, the forums, basilica and theatre, would not have come into existence until after Cogidubnus' death. When future work exposes more of the Flavian town it will be interesting to see whether the authorities were attempting to follow a Gallic plan or were allowing their town to develop along provincial British lines.

Cogidubnus cannot have lived much after 80. This date is therefore likely to mark a turning point in the development of Chichester and Fishbourne, for on his death his kingdom would have been fully integrated into the provincial administrative system, and his town would have been redesignated as a *civitas peregrina* requiring a forum and basilica in which to enact its civil business. Fishbourne, we know, soon lost its standing and was divided, modified and partly demolished. At Chichester the changes are less easy to detect but at least part of the street grid does not appear to have been laid out until this time and then followed a massive programme of replanning, represented by the Antonine gravel spread. Whether these changes were a deliberate act on behalf of central government to make Chichester conform to the provincial norm, or were merely the normal developments one would expect in an expanding town in the second century, it is impossible yet to say. Once more we must await the results of future excavation.

The excavations of 1968–75 in the north-west quarter of the town have enormously increased our understanding of the origins and early development of Chichester, but many questions remain to whet our appetite. We can only hope that the happy combination of enlightened District and County Councils, responsible developers and a skilful excavation team will continue to allow this wealth of fascinating detail to be released from beneath the modern city.

PART II

**The Finds
from the
North-West Quadrant**

9

Early Iron Age

Early Iron Age, Pre-Conquest and "Overlap" Pottery.

Fig. 9.1

Type A

Three types of coarse ware have been isolated; these are distinguishable on the basis of form and/or fabric, and all are residual in Roman and later layers.

Early Iron Age: c. 2nd to 1st century B.C.
1. *Area 3. W.23*
   Heavily gritted sherd oxidised a pale buff. Could be briquetage. *Not illustrated.*
2. *Area 7. D.30*
   Heavily gritted sherd reduced dark grey. *Not illustrated.*
3. *Area 7. E. 73*
   Softy gritty featureless sherd; from the silt layer above the early timber buildings north of the Thermae. *Not illustrated.*
4. *Area 7. Slot E.11*
   Sherd in similar fabric to No. 3. *Not illustrated.*
5. *Area 2. G.106*
   Rim sherd of a heavily gritted vessel oxidised to a pale buff. Fabric very soft and crumbly. *Not illustrated.*

Type B

Pre-Conquest: 1st century A.D.
6. *Area 5. Pit O.29*
   Rim of vessel in a hard gritty fabric reduced to dark grey, wheel turned.
7. *Area 3. W.15*
   Body sherd of a jar in a coarse grey ware, heavily gritted and handmade but probably finished on a slow wheel. *Not illustrated.*
8. *Area 2. Pit L.81 (F)*
   Bead rimmed, shell tempered vessel; grey fabric but reduced black on exterior.
9. *Area 2. Pit E.101*
   Shell tempered fabric reduced dark grey/brown. A good deal of organic material was used as additional tempering and this has burnt out. *Not illustrated.*
10. *Area 7. D.40*
    Rim of vessel, sandy ware grogged with flint and reduced black.

Type C

"Overlap" material. c. late Atrebatic continuing into the post-Conquest period.
11. *Area 4. M.77*
    Rim of shallow platter. Fabric is reduced grey with large voids due to organic matter having burnt out in the firing. No flint grogging.
12. *Area 4. M.77*
    Base sherd from a vessel in a black fabric, probably handmade, with a lumpy exterior burnished surface. *Not illustrated.*
13. *Area 2. G.117*
    Sherd in a light grey ware, flint gritted and hard fired. *Not illustrated.*
14. *Area 2. G.117*
    Sherd in a hard gritty fabric, reduced black on the outside. *Not illustrated.*
15. *Area 5. P.56*
    Sherd in a grey gritty ware reduced darker grey on the outside but oxidised to a reddish buff on the inside. It looks typically "medieval", but is not. *Not illustrated.*
16. *Area 5. O.29*
    Base of a vessel in sandy ware reduced grey.
17. *Area 5. O.29*
    Sherd in identical fabric to No. 14. *Not illustrated.*

18. *Area 2. Slot E.4*
    Base sherd in a gritty fabric, fairly fine. Oxidised reddish buff inside; exterior smoothed.
19. *Area 2. Slot E.4*
    Three sherds from one vessel. Heavily shell tempered fabric reduced dark grey. *Not illustrated.*
20. *Area 2. Slot E.4*
    Burnt sherd, some organic tempering, oxidised reddish buff outside. *Not illustrated.*
21. *Area 2. Kiln G.2*
    Rim of a small beaker; dark grey ware with small flint grits, oxidised greyish buff.
22. *Area 5. P.49*
    Body sherd of a large vessel in a grey porridgey fabric with some large flints. *Not illustrated.*
23. *Area 5. J.86*
    Sherd in a dark grey fabric, heavily flint gritted. *Not illustrated.*
24. *Area 2. Slot G.14*
    Base of a vessel in sandy ware with some flint inclusions, exterior reduced black.
25. *Area 2. Slot G.14*
    Sherd from the bottom of a tall jar. The fabric is well fired with a few selected flint grits and reduced grey. *Not illustrated.*
26. *Area 2. Slot G.14*
    Body sherd from a large storage jar, very coarse ware with large flints. *Not illustrated.*
27. *Area 2. Slot G.14*
    Three large body sherds from a thin walled storage jar in a sand tempered fabric with a few large flints and fully oxidised to a sandy buff colour. *Not illustrated.*
28. *Area 2. Pit G.36*
    Sherd from the shoulder of a large jar. The ware is sand tempered and hard and there are a few small grits. Reduced grey and with external burnishing.
29. *Area 2. Kiln G.2*
    Body sherd from a large vessel in a grey fabric, flint gritted. *Not illustrated.*
30. *Area 2, Kiln G.1*
    Similar fabric to No. 28 but more heavily flint grogged. *Not illustrated.*
31. *Area 2. Kiln G.1*
    Sherd in a sand tempered, heavily burnt fabric, reduced dark grey. *Not illustrated.*
32. *Area 2. Kiln G.2*
    Sherd in a sandy fabric with some flint grits, reduced dark grey. *Not illustrated.*
33. *Area 2. Kiln G.1*
    Similar fabric to No. 31. *Not illustrated.*

Discussion

The few sherds in the Type A fabric must derive from sporadic activity during the first two centuries B.C. and cannot yet be connected with any definite settlement within the area covered by the City. The same can be said of the Type B fabrics which could and probably did extend from the late 1st century B.C. up to a decade or so before the invasion. But it is the Type C wares which pose the greatest problems. Viewed in the same context as the Early Iron Age coins and the "Arretine" wares they might be equated with an Atrebatic presence on the ground in the years before A.D. 43, but at present the matter is incapable of proof. It is not possible to judge on the basis of fabric alone which, if any, of these sherds were made by native potters operating before the Conquest as the same fabrics persist well after A.D. 43. Nor do the forms, where they occur, help much, as they are repeated also. There is a complete absence of structures from the earliest levels of human activity excavated within the North-West Quadrant which could be confidently interpreted as belonging to a pre-Roman oppidum or nucleated settlement, and indeed, all we are left with is a small number of coins (fourteen), a growing amount of early Italianate Arretine pottery, other fine wares, and a number of coarse ware sherds which are of doubtful validity if an Atrebatic pre-Roman date is postulated.

In the circumstances only a strictly non-commital attitude to the problem is permissible, at least until the vexed question as to the viability of the present dating of the Arretine ware is settled. It may be that there *was* a pre-Roman settlement in the period immediately prior to A.D. 43 and that the present excavations are only on the fringe of it. In that case it is likely to lie to the north and west of Chapel Street. Such a settlement would have had trade links with Rome, if the pottery is to be explained. On the other hand, if the present accepted dates for Italianate Arretine ware are invalid, then it would be possible, as Dannell has suggested elsewhere (cf. *Fishbourne*) for these wares to be included amongst the quartermasters "issue" material to the Second Legion in the early days of the invasion. This would explain their presence in a primary context in the earliest "military" layers on the sites within the City. In almost every instance the Arretine wares are found with South Gaulish "provincial Arretine" and Claudian wares and this would be feasible if the Arretine was later than hitherto thought; it would be contemporary with the other wares and not residual from earlier occupation levels which cannot in any event be seen on the ground.

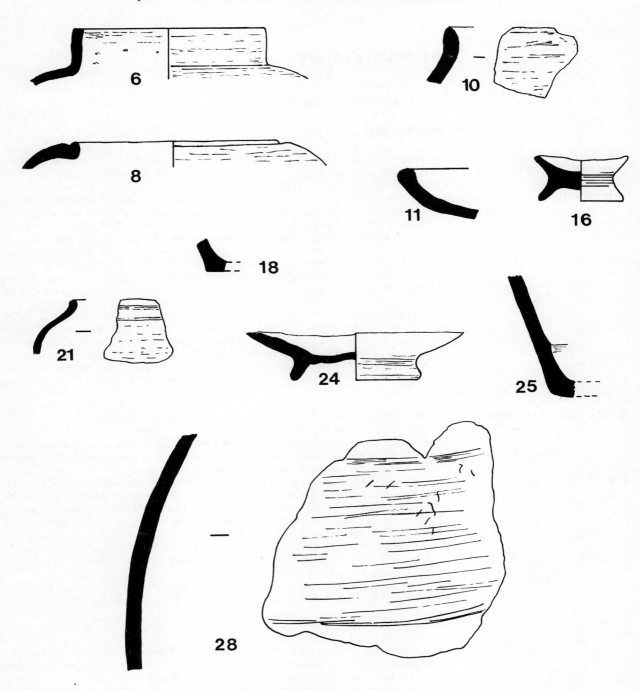

Fig. 9.1 N.W. Quadrant: Atrebatic and 'overlap' pottery ($\frac{1}{4}$)

10

Roman

The Roman Pottery

The Early Roman Fine Wares

by Valery Rigby

The Gallo-Belgic Imports

Introduction

The terra nigra (TN) and terra rubra (TR) has been divided into two groups, the material from the early stratified groups which is dealt with in detail and the residual and unstratified material which is briefly dealt with in the table showing the incidence of forms and fabrics (Table 1). The report is in three sections; the first is a list of potters stamps including all stamps found to date in Chichester; the second deals with the description and classification of the unstamped pieces which is incorporated into the main body of the pottery report, and the third section surveys all the finds to date in the area and their significance. Obviously when all the TN and TR is being appraised, the finds from Fishbourne must be included since both areas must be part of the same extensive settlement. Unfortunately not all the material from previous excavations nor all the chance finds in the museum collections could be located, so where possible, information deducted from published reports has been used to fill gaps in the range of forms or in the total numbers. Deduced information is indicated in the text.

The classification of the vessel-forms and fabrics is based upon those published in *Camulodunum* with the use of sub-types where necessary (*Camulodunum* 1946; p. 202). The range of platter forms is covered by Camulodunum Forms 1 to 16, the cup forms by Forms 56 and 58, pedestal beakers by Forms 74 to 79, and beakers by Forms 82, 84, 91, 112 and 120. Where necessary the classification has been supplemented by that produced for the Gallo-Belgic wares from Nijmegen (*Holwerda* 1941). The classification of both forms and fabrics has been discussed at greater length elsewhere (*Rigby* 1972; p. 8).

1. The potters stamps

Fig. 10.1

(a) *NAME STAMPS*

GB 1   [ΛN]DECO° (CH 11, CH/69/CS, 153)
Radial stamp; no evidence of decoration survives. Large platter, with a functional foot ring. TR 1(C) – pale orange fine-grained paste; coral slip on the interior, highly polished finish; light orange self coloured exterior, polished finish.

Andecos die 1A1. This is the most common die used by the potter *Andecos*, stamps have been identified at Camulodunum (3), Baldock (1) and the King Harry Lane Cemetery, St. Albans, Herts. (1). The TN cup, Cam. 56, occurred in a Claudio-Neronian grave group at St. Albans, while the TN platter sherd found during the 1970 excavations at Colchester was in a group with other imported G-B wares of late Tiberian or Claudian date. Stamps from other dies have been found at Camulodunum (2), Ipswich, Suffolk, and Bagendon, Glos. – all on TN. Examples are less common on the Continent and have been identified at Speyer, Worms, Kreuznach, none is closely dated.

Andecos' specialisation in platters of Cam. Form 8 and in TN suggests that he began work *c.* A.D. 25/30 and was still working in the Claudian period. The site of his pottery is not known.

GB 2   [ASS]INO (*S.A.C.* 94 (1956), Fig. 5, No. 2)
Radial stamp, with at least two bordered rouletted wreaths, one inside the stamp, the other over-stamped. Large platter, with a relatively thin base. TN – blue-grey fine-grained paste; darker lower and paler upper surfaces, with a polished finish.

Assinos die 1A1. Although stamps from this die are common on the Continent there is only one other from Britain, from Camulodunum, No. 23, found in a Period II–III context,

190

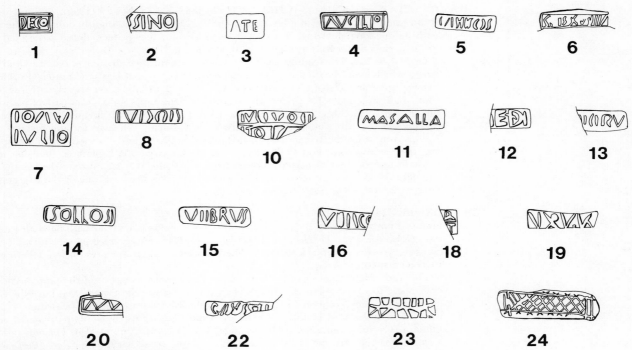

Fig. 10.1 Gallo-Belgic potters' stamps (⅓)

post-dating the Conquest but pre-dating the Boudiccan destruction. None of the Continental finds are closely dated which can definitely be attributed to Assin(n)os but there is a stamp on a TR platter, the reading of which is uncertain, from Haltern (*Loeschcke* 1909, taf. 30,9). Assin(n)os could have been one of the earliest known potters to manufacture TN in the late Augustan period, in which case it is unlikely that he worked after *c.* A.D. 30.

GB 3   ATE (CH 9, CH/62/DG2, 90)
Central stamp within an incised circle. Large cup, Cam. 56. TN – under-fired, fine grained paste with black ironstone (?) grits; dark blue-grey core, white cortex, dark blue-grey surfaces; no finish survives due to burning and lamination.

Aetius die 3G1. No other stamps from this die have been identified although there are several examples which include the same letters and are versions of the name Aetius or Ateius. At least two different potters must have been involved for versions occur in contexts from the late Augustan to the Neronian period. One potter, whose products reached Trier and the cemetery at Prunay, worked at Courmelois, Marne, another may have worked at La Prosne, Marne (*Koethe,* 1938, No. 3).

GB 4   ΛVCNI° (CH 6, CH/70/CS, 487)
Central stamp within three incised circles. Small platter, slightly domed at the centre. TN – dark blue-grey fine-grained paste; blue-black surfaces, badly flaked and laminated; trace of polished finish on interior; matt exterior.

Avelucnios die 2A2. The reading is uncertain. No other stamps from this die have been identified although the last five letters are the same and are in the same style as the die of the potter *Velucnio.* The style is so similar, the dies were probably made by the same die-cutter and possibly belong to the same potter, ? *Avelucnios.*

The only example of a Velucnio stamp in Britain is from *Camulodunum*, No. 153; the form, fabric, decoration and finish are almost identical to the Chichester piece, which supports a close connection. On the continent, stamps from the same die have been found at Trier and Hunenknepchen à Sampoint, Hachy (Luxembourg), they are on TR platters dated to the Tiberian or Tiberio-Claudian period. The remainder are on TN and are from Hedderheim, Bingen, Koln, Bavay. The site of the kilns is not known. Tiberio-Claudian.

191

GB 5   CASSICOS or CANICOS (CHM 2, CH 48, JSa 450), (*S.A.C.* 94 (1956), Fig. 5, No. 5)
Radial stamp within two double incised circles. Large platter, slightly domed at the centre, with a functional footring. TN – hard blueish-white fine-grained dense paste; light grey surfaces, smoothed exterior, highly polished interior.

    Cassicos die 2A1. The reading is not certain owing to the poor shaping of the third and fourth letters which could be double-S or a smudged N. There is at least one potter of each name known from previous finds, Cas(s)icos who worked at Metz, on the river Moselle, and Canicos, a large-scale TN potter who worked at Sept-Saulx for at least part of his working life (*Reusch*, 1943, Abb. 2, No. 1; *Fromols*, 1938, Pl. A, No. 19). The quality and style of the die suggest that the potter is most likely to be Cassicos. Whoever the die belongs to, the stamps from it are fairly common in Britain – Camulodunum (8), including 7 stamps from the 1970 excavations, and Baldock (1). All are on large TR 2 platters, four classified as Cam. 5; four of the Colchester finds are from pit groups which post-date the Conquest but pre-date the Boudiccan destruction. It appears that Cassicos was one of the few potters to concentrate on TR in the Claudio-Neronian period.

GB 6   EXOBINIIS
Stamped horizontally on the exterior, 5 mm above the base, on a jar with barbotine decoration, Holwerda Type 74 (*Holwerda* 1941; No. 636). Hard fine-grained paste, with a blue core, dark grey cortex and black surfaces. The decoration comprises rows of self-coloured matt spots on a matt ground.

    The impression is not clear so that the reading is uncertain, but of the potters known to have made this type of jar, the stamps of Exobinus are the right shape and have the correct number of letters. None of his stamps have otherwise been identified in Britain, but they were found in the pre-Claudian Cemeteries O and E at Nijmegen, on plain carinated beakers similar to Camulodunum Form 120 (*Holwerda* 1941; Pl. VII, 236 and 243). The only published material for the jar-type is an unstamped example from Bagendon, Glos. (*Clifford* 1967, Type 50).

    Potters stamps on small jars and beakers are not common in Britain, they are only a small fraction of the stamps on Gallo-Belgic imports and most belong to one potter, *Bellius* (see below, p. 00). Stamps have been found at Camulodunum, Cirencester, Gloucester, Wall, Margidunum, Richborough, Wroxeter and Southwark which suggests a strong military connection in the period between *c.* A.D. 50 and 80. Few of the stamps occur on sherds of sufficient size for the forms to be classified definitely, plain carinated jars occur at Richborough, Wroxeter and Southwark while the only jar with barbotine decoration is the one under discussion.

    One of the largest collections of beakers with potters stamps comes from the various Roman cemeteries at Nijmegen. It appears that at least 19 potters used name stamps and that between them they produced variants of four basic types, the two carinated beakers discussed above, the plain example, cf. Form 120 and the decorated beaker, Holwerda Type 74, as well as necked bowls, Holwerda Type 27A and globular jars with barbotine decoration, cf. Form 92. Only one name, *Benios*, appears on platters and cups in TN and TR and also on beakers, but different dies were used and it is possible that more than one potter is represented.

    A potter called Benios worked at Sept-Saulx, Marne, making TN platters and cups of Forms 8 and 56, for at least part of his working life, so that beakers may have been made there too. Despite this there seems to be little else to connect the TN and TR potters with those making stamped thin-walled closed forms. The fabrics are black or very dark grey and so literally have to be classified as TN, but they have a different quality of colour being more truly black than was ever achieved by potters making cups and platters, and they are also much darker in fracture and finer in texture, but they are not even reduced versions of TR 3. Most "TN" beakers are plain while those in TR 3 are always decorated and when they are decorated it is frequently with barbotine patterns, a method never used on beakers in TR 3. However, the areas of production did overlap and there was nothing to prevent unstamped vessels being made alongside stamped versions of both groups of vessel-types.

GB 7   IVLIO/AVOT (IS) (CH 5, CH/70/CS, 641)
Central stamp within a bordered rouletted wreath and a superimposed incised circle. Small platter slightly domed at the centre, with a moulded foot-ring. TN – white fine-grained paste with black flecks, ? ironstone; blue-grey surfaces, polished interior, matt exterior. Very hard fired and thin-based.

192

Julios die 1C1. A most unusual stamp which has to be read from two directions, no other stamps from this die have been identified although a similar one reading IVLIO/TOVA – Julio avot(is) retrograde – from one direction was found at Trier.

GB 8   IVLIOS (CH 4, CH/70/CS, 604)
Central stamp within a bordered rou'etted wreath. Small platter, domed at the centre. TN – hard blueish-white paste; variegated dark blue-grey surfaces, highly polished interior, facetted polished exterior.
Julio die 2G4. The die became clogged with clay when it was being used so that the impression is not complete. No other stamp can be definitely attributed to it; however, the stamp listed below, GB 9, published as IVOVOD, is almost certainly from this die. It was made by a die-cutter who made at least ten of Julios' dies. Stamps from these dies are fairly common in Britain, particularly at Camulodunum. The stratified examples were found in post-Conquest contexts.

GB 9   IVOVOD (*S.A.G.* 94 (1956), Fig. 5, No. 3)
Missing from Museum. Central stamp on a TN platter. The stamp is probably from the same die as GB 7 above. *Not examined*.

GB 10 IVLIVOLI/(S) ITOV(A) or IVLIVSOLI/(S) ITOV(A)
Central stamp. Small platter. TN – hard, pale blue-grey fine-grained sandy paste; blue-black surfaces; highly polished upper surface.
Julios die 601. No other stamps from this die have been identified. One name is Juliu – a version of Jul(l)io(s) – but the final three letters as they stand – OLI – have not been identified. They may represent a shortened form of *Solitus*, a rare TN potter who used a double-line die, a stamp from which was found during the 1970 excavations at Colchester.
Taking all the possible versions of the name, Julios is the most common one found in Britain and if they all belonged to one "firm", it was the most important supplier of the British market in the post-Conquest period but was much smaller in the earlier years of the 1st century A.D.
No production centres have been identified, although a potter Julios probably worked at Sept-Saulx, Marne. In the absence of kiln material the precise significance of the differences in size, spelling and style on the 21 dies is not known. More than one potter was concerned, for stamps have been found in contexts from the late Augustan to the Neronian period; in the early period on typologically early forms and a few on TR; in the late period on typologically late forms and only on TN. Whether or not the different potters were all part of the same "firm" remains to be established along with the precise number of production centres used. It is possible that a branch was set up in Britain, obviously at Camulodunum judging by the weight of finds there which include examples from dies not yet found on sites on the continent. However, there are no easily isolated style characteristics which are limited to British finds. The stamps of die-cutter "G" are more common here than elsewhere (see GB 7) so they are the most likely candidates. Others are the double-line stamps showing Julios associated with the slaves Solitus and Atesatis (see above GB 9; *Colchester* 1970, GB 43; *Verulamium*, unpublished, Verulamium museum), for to date, stamps from these dies have not yet been found on sites on the continent. Given the expanding market for TN in Britain following the conquest, the firm of Julios is just the type of producer to have moved part of his operations to that market.

GB 11 MASALA (CHM 1, *S.A.C.* 94 (1956), Fig. 5, No. 1)
Radial stamp adjoining a double incised circle. Large platter, with a functional footring. TN 1 (A) – hard blueish-white fine-grained dense paste; battleship grey slip on the interior surface, with a polished finish; mottled blue-grey self coloured lower surface with a smoothed matt finish.
Masalla Die 1A1. No other stamps from this die have been identified, though there is a stamp bearing the same name from an undated context at Compiègne. The die was well cut and the style suggests that the potter may have worked in the area of Rheims. The fabric is unusual, TN 1, that is, with a dark firing slip on the upper or interior surface only, is much more scarce than the equivalent in TR.

193

GB 12 MEDI (CH 3, CH/70/SC, 634)

Radial stamp with at least one incised circle. Large platter, possibly a variant of Cam. 5. TN – under-fired, fine-grained paste, with black ironstone (?) flecks; blue-grey core, off-white cortex; blue-black surfaces, matt facetted exterior, polished upper surface.

Med(d)illus die 1A2. Stamps from this die have been identified at Camulodunum, No. 116 (5) and Hacheston, Suffolk (1), none dated. Other stamps from closely related dies have been found at Camulodunum, Nos. 111–115 and Eccles, Kent; all are placed radially on TN platters. There seems little doubt that Medillus's products were imported through Camulodunum.

Medillus worked on a large scale, judging from the number and distribution of his stamps, specialising exclusively in large TN platters, Cam. 2 and 5. His workshop was at Rheims, in one of the most important areas for the production of G–B wares. Stamps have been found at Trier, Stahl, Dalheim, Epinay St. Beuvre, Bavay, Tournai, Agreau and Blicquy (3).

A stamp from a die used on a typical TN platter was found on the rim of an early mortarium in the collection of the Guildhall Museum, probably from London (information from Mrs. K. Hartley). This could indicate that at some time during his working life Medillus made mortaria. Stamped mortaria are not known before the Neronian period, so the production of stamped mortaria must have been towards the end of his production span. The use of the same die suggests that he was producing TN and mortaria in the same factory.

GB 13 SA]CIRV; CHM 3, *S.A.C.* 94 (1956), Fig. 5, No. 4

Central stamp within an incised circle. Cup, almost certainly Cam. 56. TN – buff fine-grained paste; very dark blue-black surfaces with a highly polished finish.

Sacirus die 1B1. There is a fragment from the same die on a TN platter from Period 1 at Fishbourne, but the name is uncertain (*Cunliffe* 1971, Fig. 80, No. 5). It is possibly Sacirus, like an unstratified stamp from Camulodunum, No. 127, which reads ƧΛCIRV, on a TN cup Cam. 56.

GB 14 SOLLOS, CH/70/CS, 516

Central stamp, small platter. TR 1C) – soft, orange-red fine-grained paste; self coloured surfaces in flaking condition. Finish originally polished.

Sollos die 1C1. The only stamp from this die to be identified is on a TR platter, Form 8, found at Trier in a grave group dated to mid 1st century A.D. (*Koethe* 1938; Abb. 2, No. 35). Several stamps from different dies have been found at Camulodunum, all are on TN and all the stratified examples are from post-Conquest contexts. In addition, there is a stamp reading – SOTTV – which probably is the work of the potter Sollus, from Winchester (information from Dr. J. Collis). A potter Sollus worked at Courmelois, Marne, but dies reading – SOLLUS – were not found there so possibly there were two potters of the name and more than one factory.

GB 15 VIIBRVS (CH, 2 CH/70/CS, 484)

Central stamp within at least three deeply incised circles. Medium sized platter slightly domed at the centre. TN – hard blueish-white paste with black flecks (? ironstone); dark blue-grey surfaces, polished finish but matt within the foot-ring.

Vebrus die 1A1. No other stamps from this die have been identified, but there is a very similar stamp from Camulodunum, No. 152. It is possible that one die was moulded from the other, for the Chichester stamp is identical except that it is proportionally smaller than the Camulodunum one. The kiln site has not been identified.

GB 16 VIIICO/ . – VINCO(S) or VILICO(S) (CH 10, CH/70/CS, 2166)

Radial stamp with at least two incised circles within the position of the stamps. Large platter with a functional footring. TN – the clay had been poorly prepared and shows mixing planes in the fractures. White fine-grained paste; blue-grey surfaces, matt exterior, polished interior.

Vilicos die 1A1. No other stamps from this die have been found so that the reading remains uncertain, possibly VINCOS or VILICOS. Claudio-Neronian.

GB 17 Λ [. . . . .] Radial stamp with at least one double incised groove outside the stamp. Large platter. TN 1 – pale blueish-white fine-grained sandy paste; patchy light and dark blue-grey exterior, facetted finish; grey slip on the upper surface with an even, smooth but dull finish. *Not illustrated.* The first letter is so without character that the die and the potter cannot be identified. It is probably A rather than M, and the stamp may belong to ANDECOS, see above, GB 1.

GB 18 . . . .RA/. . .IT ?[VOCA]RA/[FEC] IT? (CH 8, CH/70/CS 517, Kiln 1)
Central stamp within one incised circle. Small platter with a narrow footring, 2 mm wide. TN – blueish-white fine grained paste with black ? ironstone grits; blue-grey surfaces, highly polished interior, polished exterior.
Vocara die 2G1. The die and the potter has not been identified. The bottom line almost certainly reads FECIT, while the most likely name for the upper line is VOCARA. Vocara used at least four double line dies, all of which included fecit. The closest to the Chichester stamp is on three small platters Cam. 7B, found in Cemetery OH at Nijmegen (*Holwerda* 1941, No. 152B). The kiln site has not been identified. Claudio-Neronian.

(b) *MARKS*
GB 19 Mark (CH 7, CH/70/CS 625)
Radial stamp located between single incised circles. Large platter, slightly domed at the centre, with a functional footring. TN 1 – blueish-white paste, fine grained sandy, silver grey exterior, matt finish; light and dark silver grey slip on the upper surface; polished finish.
Die 1A1. A stamp from the same die has been found at Camulodunum on a TN platter, but no other dated examples have been identified. The use of illiterate "pattern" stamps or marks comprising a number of letters or motifs occurred in the late Augustan period but is more characteristic of the later period of the G–B industry, after A.D. 40. The kiln site has not been identified. *c.* A.D. 40–65.

GB 20 Mark (CHM 5, 389) (*S.A.C.* 94)
Central stamp within a double incised circle. Cup, probably Cam. 56. TN – pale grey fine-grained sandy paste, dark blue-grey surfaces; polished finish.
Die 1A1. Two TN cups bearing stamps from the same die have been found at Camulodunum (No. 218). One was found during the 1970 excavations in a Claudio-Neronian pit group. Similar stamps on TN cups have been found at *Hofheim* (*Ritterling*, 1911, Abb. 64, No. 14). Probably made *c.* A.D. 40–65. *Not illustrated.*

GB 21 Mark (*S.A.C.* 94, Fig. 5) not examined

(c) *UNASSIGNED FRAGMENTS*
GB 22 CH/71/CS, Slot J.27 and J.98
The edge of an impression, completely unreadable. Central stamp; small platter, Form 7B. TR 2 – orange fine-grained paste with red ? grog grits; patchy polished finish on the upper surface; smoothed less glossy lower surfaces. The foot-ring shows no sign of wear. *c.* AD. 25–60. *Not illustrated.*

FISHBOURNE – the potter's stamps on Terra Nigra and Terra Rubra (see *Cunliffe*, 1971, Fig. 80, Nos. 1–5).
1. ATTISSVS. The Haltern die – late Augustan, *c.* A.D. 20 for this die at the latest. Radial stamp on a platter in TR 1(C).
2. DANN[OMAROS]. A potter who supplied Haltern – late Augustan, *c.* A.D. 20 at the latest for this die. Radial stamp on a platter in TR 1(C).
3. VOVIIO, possibly a stamp of Novidos. Probably Claudian. Central stamp on a small platter in TN.
4. [BI]NIO, almost certainly the stamp of the potter Benios or Bentos. The stamp is from the same die as one found at Exeter so that the die may have been used after *c.* A.D. 50.
5. [SACI]RV or VR[ICAS] retro. Stamps from different dies occurred at Camulodunum (No. 127) and Chichester, see above GB 13.

6. PAPILOS (*S.A.C.* 76, p. 159)

A radial stamp on a TR platter. Not examined. No other stamps of this potter have been identified in Britain, but finds are fairly common on the continent, at Vertault and Rheims (possibly kiln sites), Trier – on a TR platter Form 8, Mainz and Weisenau. Probably Tiberio-Claudian.

TABLE 1

THE INCIDENCE OF FORMS USING THE CAMULODUNUM CLASSIFICATION

Forms		TR 1(A)	TR 1(C)	TR 2	All TR	TN	Total	TR 3
Platters	2	0	0	0	0	6	8.7%	
	3	0	2	0	2	2	5.8%	
	5	1	3	1	5	3	11.6%	
	7A	0	0	0	0	1	1.4%	
	7B	0	1	0	1	0	1.4%	
	8	0	1	2	3	4	10.1%	
	9	0	0	1	1	1	2.9%	
	13	—	—	—	—	4	5.8%	
	14	—	—	—	—	12	17.4%	
	16	—	—	—	—	12	17.4%	
Holwerda	81(i)	—	—	—	—	1	1.4%	
TOTAL		1	7	4	12	46	58	
Platter Sherds		1	4	5	7	40	47	
Cups	56	0	1	0	1	3	5.8%	
	58	0	0	2	2	1	4.3%	
TOTAL		0	1	2	3	4	7	
Bowls	50	—	—	—	—	4	5.8%	
Bowl Sherds		—	—	—	—	2	2	
Pedestal Beakers	76	4	0	0	4	—	4	
	74/79	3	0	0	3	—	3	
Body Sherds		8	0	0	8	—	8	
Girth Beakers	82							1
	84							2
Body Sherds								1
Butt Beakers	112							6
Globular Beakers	91							2
Body Sherds								7
Plain Sherds								5
Beaker Bases								4
TOTAL – TR 3 Beakers								28

Table 2

A COMPARISON OF THE GALLO-BELGIC IMPORTS FROM CHICHESTER AND FISHBOURNE

Forms		All finds from Chichester						Fishbourne						Chichester and Fishbourne					
		TR 1(A)	TR 1(C)	TR 2	All TR	TJN	% Total	TR 1(A)	TR 1(C)	TR 2	All TR	TJN	% Total	TR 1(A)	TR 1(C)	TR 2	All TR	TJN	% Total
Platters	1	1	—	—	—	0	0	—	—	—	—	1	1.5	—	—	—	—	1	0.5
	2	0	0	0	0	9	7.2	0	0	0	0	6	9.2	0	0	0	0	15	7.9
	3	0	2	0	2	3	4.0	0	3	0	3	1	6.2	0	5	0	5	4	4.7
	4	0	0	0	0	0	0	0	1*	0	1*	0	1.5	0	1*	0	1*	0	0.5
	5	1	7	3	11	10	16.8	3	1	0	4	1	7.7	4	8	3	15	11	13.7
	6	0	0	0	0	0	0	0	1	0	1	0	1.5	0	1	0	1	0	0.5
	7A	0	0	0	0	1	0.8	0	0	0	0	0	0	0	0	0	0	1	0.5
	7B	0	1	0	1	0	0.8	0	0	0	0	0	0	0	1	0	1	0	0.5
	8	0	1	2	3	7	8.0	0	0	0	0	5	7.7	0	1	2	3	12	7.9
	9	0	0	2	2	1	2.4	0	0	0	0	0	0	0	0	2	2	1	1.6
	13	—	—	—	—	8	6.4	—	—	—	—	5	7.7	—	—	—	—	13	6.8
	14	—	—	—	—	20	16.0	—	—	—	—	3*	4.6	—	—	—	—	23*	12.1
	16	—	—	—	—	28	22.4	—	—	—	—	20	30.8	—	—	—	—	48	25.3
Holwerda	81(i)	—	—	—	—	1	0.8	—	—	—	—	0	0	—	—	—	—	1	0.5
Cups	56	0	1	2	3	5	7.2	0	2	3	5	2	10.8	0	3	5	8	8	8.4
	58	0	0	2	2	3	4.0	0	0	0	0	7	10.8	0	0	2	2	10	5.3
Bowls	50	—	—	—	—	4	3.2	—	—	—	—	0	0	—	—	—	—	4	2.0
TOTAL		1	12	11	24	101	125	3	8	3	14	51	65	4	20	14	38	152	190
% TOTAL		0.8	9.7	8.9	19.4	80.6	—	4.6	12.3	4.6	21.5	78.5	—	2.1	10.6	7.4	20.1	79.9	—

2. The Incidence of Forms and Fabrics

Only one of the common platter forms in the collection found at Chichester is not represented in the early groups, this is the large platter Cam. Form 3. There are two examples each in TR 1(C) and TN, the former are pre-Claudian while the latter are Claudian at the latest. The beakers in TR 3 are less well represented in the early groups than the platters and cups, for the best examples of Cam. Forms 82, 84 and 112 occurred as residual material in groups of much later date. They are all standard products in form and fabric and so none have been drawn. In addition there are three examples of forms and variants, which are worth recording in detail despite their contexts.

Fig. 10.2

1. *Area 2. E.218*
   Rim sherd from a small platter, Cam. Form 7A – the variant with concave facets – in typical TN. Pale blue-grey fine-grained paste; dark blue-grey surfaces, polished upper surface, patchy polished lower surface. A relatively rare variant in Britain with finds confined to Camulodunum, Essex, Snailwell, Cambridgeshire, Baldock, St. Albans and Braughing, Puckeridge-Braughing, Hertfordshire, and Silchester, Hampshire. The complete examples from St. Albans and Snailwell were found in rich cremation burials, which are Claudian at the latest (*Lethbridge*, 1953, Fig. 3, No. 53.17). The form was made in both TN and TR, but examples in TR outnumber those in TN by five to one. It was in production by the late Augustan period, for although it was not identified at Oberaden, it occurred at Haltern. The few stamped examples suggest that it is essentially a pre-Claudian form although it may have continued in production into the early Claudian period *c.* A.D. 45.

2. *Area 2. Slot J.27 and 98*
   A small platter, Cam. Form 7B – the variant with straight facets and marked off-sets – in typical TR 2. Orange fine-grained paste, with red ? grog grits; self-coloured polished finish on the upper surface, smoothed less glossy exterior. In good condition,' the foot-ring shows no evidence of wear.
   This is the most common variant of Cam. Form 7 in Britain, it appears to have been made only in TR in the Tiberio-Claudian period.

3. *Area 2. E.103*
   A rim sherd from a small platter, Cam. Form 9A – the variant with an off-set – in typical TR 2. Dark red fine-grained paste; highly polished interior surface, less glossy smoothed exterior.
   A rare form on British sites which has been identified only at Camulodunum, Essex, and Old Winteringham, Humberside. It is more common on the Continent where it occurs in several cremation cemeteries in the area of the Lower Rhine – Nijmegen, Chantmelle, Fouches and Blicquy. The form was made in both TN and TR and was in production in the Claudian period.

Discussion

The collection of imports is fairly large and includes one stratified group which is sufficiently large and well dated to provide valuable information about the relative importance of the cup and platter forms current in the pre-Flavian period. The stamps list totals 13, one being too fragmentary for identification. As it stands, the list ranks near the top of the league-table for finds from British sites and along with the remaining unstamped pieces show that Chichester was an important market for G–B wares.

In detail the stamp list exhibits features typical of a British site, with Name stamps heavily outnumbering illiterate Marks, stamps on platters, those on cups and beakers, stamps on TN and those on TR, although the proportion of stamps on TR is above the usual maximum of just over one-fifth. There are four radial stamps which must be from large platters and which constitute over 30% of the list. It is a high proportion but it is reflected generally amongst the unstamped sherds, about 25% of which are also from large platters. The make-up of the stamp list reflects the collection as a whole.

Predictably the only name to be represented more than once is Julios, the most common and widely found name on G–B wares in Britain. Two names, Aucilios and Vilicos, have not been identified elsewhere possibly because of the mis-reading of their stamps. Masalla is known from continental finds but has not been previously identified in Britain. The remaining seven names have been identified at Camulodunum yet out of the total list only three Names and the Mark are from known dies, consequently more than half of the stamps are unique. A high proportion of unique stamps is typical of collections from British sites with the result that the average number of stamps

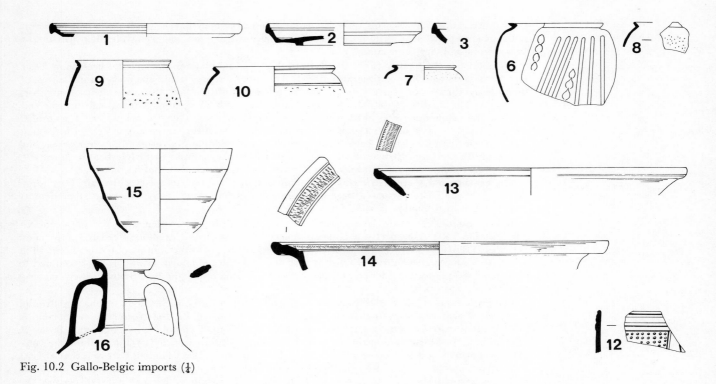

Fig. 10.2 Gallo-Belgic imports ($\frac{1}{4}$)

per potter is less than two stamps while the average number of stamps per die is just over 1.5 stamps. Neither can reflect the scale of output or methods of the G–B potters but they may reflect the method of distribution to Britain.

Clearly the potter(s) or "firm" of Jul(l)ios must have been the largest supplier(s) of TN to Britain (see GB 10). In addition, Andecos and Medillus, each represented by at least six stamps at Camulodunum and by finds on two other sites, were also important suppliers. The production centre of only Medillus is known, it was near Rheims at Sept-Saulx, Marne, while Sollos, a large supplier to Camulodunum at least, may have worked nearby at Courmelois. There is evidence from other sites of an important trading connection with the Rheims area and the finds from Chichester conform to the pattern. It appears that a group of large producers provided large consignments but could not satisfy the demand so that a much larger group of small producers each contributed a small amount. The range of forms is limited to the most common types found in Britain so that simple variants and those made only in TN predominate. Large platters of Forms 2, 3 and 5 make up about one quarter of the total but they are difficult to date if not stamped since they were standardised in the late Augustan period yet were still in use in the Claudian period and so form a significant element in post as well as pre-Conquest groups. Individually the most common types are the platter Forms 14 and 16 which are the most common and widely found platter types in Britain and neither of which was standardised much before the beginning of the Claudian period. The most notable gap is in the range of small moulded platters grouped together as Form 7, for only two out of a possible seven sub-types were found. All were standardised before the Conquest, some by the late Augustan period, but those represented here are the latest of the variants, one of which was still in production in the Claudian period.

The only cups represented are the commonest Forms 56 and 58. Variants of the former were being made by *c.* A.D. 10 and were still being produced in the Neronian period. The stamp evidence suggests that Form 56 made up a "set" with the platter Forms 7 and 8. Form 58 was standardised during the Tiberian period and production continued into the Flavian period. Although it was distributed over a wider area than Form 56 it has not been found in such numbers. Form 58 occurs alongside the platter Form 16 in the south-west peninsula, South Wales and in Flavian contexts in Yorkshire and together they too may have made up a "set". The fact that at Chichester Form 58 is almost as common as Form 56, while Form 16 is the most common type of all, suggests an important phase of import after *c.* A.D. 65.

A limited range of bowl-forms, all in TN only, were available so that the small group here conforms to the general pattern. In Britain they occur only in post-Conquest contexts while their distribution shows strong military connections.

In contrast to the quality of the sherds from the cups and platters, the pedestal beakers in TR 1 and the beakers with incised decoration in TR 3 are poorly represented. The finds mainly consist of small body sherds consequently their classification is difficult and the assessment of numbers uncertain. The quality of the fabrics is good and the classified examples are typical in form and fabric of finds from other sites in Britain. Their scarcity conforms to the general pattern, the number identified and the area of distribution are smaller than those of the cups and platters, with the best and greatest quantity of finds being concentrated at Camulodunum, Verulamium-Prae Wood and Braughing-Puckeridge. Predictably, there are more and better examples of the butt beaker, Form 112, for this was the most common beaker in TR 3 and had the widest distribution.

The beakers in TN are restricted to two examples, one of them stamped, of the same rare form, Holwerda Type 74, a carinated beaker decorated with barbotine spots. The only other definite example is from Bagendon (see GB 6).

Only a limited range of the possible varieties of TR are represented with the pre-Claudian TR 1(B) and TR 1(A) respectively absent and very scarce, while the most long-lived and commonest varieties, TR 1(C) and TR 2 are predominant. The presence of two examples of platter Form 13 in TN 1(A) is unexpected since this finish is rare and hitherto the known examples were confined to early moulded platter types found at Camulodunum, Verulamium (the King Harry Lane cemetery) and Braughing-Puckeridge.

The proportion of TR in the collection as a whole is just on the high side of normal for Britain. Continental evidence suggests that the higher the proportion of TR the greater the proportion of pre-Claudian material in the group. Here the total is made up from only four vessel-types, Forms 3, 5, 8, 56 and 58, which were available in both TN and TR. The varieties of TR used for the large platters, Forms 3 and 5, strongly suggest that all but one are of pre-Claudian date and that at least half, accounting for a quarter of the total for these forms, are probably late Augustan. There is no matching group of small platters and cups of an equally early date which makes it unlikely that the large platters were derived from occupation of the site in the late Augustan period.

When all the G–B imports from Chichester and Fishbourne are considered as a group from a single extensive settlement the importance of the area as a market for G–B wares is underlined. The stamp list is more than doubled to 28 stamps which makes it the fourth largest in Britain, equal to Silchester, and behind only Camulodunum, which in any case is way out on its own with 500 stamps, Verulamium-Prae Wood-St. Albans with 52, and Braughing-Puckeridge with 32. If only settlement material is considered, Chichester-Fishbourne rises to joint third place, for Verulamium can muster only a dozen stamps. The quantity of unstamped classified sherds is almost trebled to 189 (see Table 2) forming a collection which clearly ranks high behind Camulodunum and Braughing-Puckeridge.

The general balance of the extended stamp list is not radically altered, however, when the potters are examined in detail some important changes emerge. The importance of Jul(l)ios as a supplier of TN is maintained, while five potters, all common at Camulodunum and found on at least two other sites in Britain, are added – Assinos, Attissus, Dannomaros, Benios and Cassicos. The Cassicos stamp is from the same die as all his finds in Britain, suggesting that he concentrated on producing platters in TR 2 principally for the British market in the Claudio-Neronian period since identified examples from this die are absent from the Continent. Another potter at work in the Claudian period is Benios. His Binios stamp is from the same die as one from Exeter, suggesting that it was in use after c. A.D. 50. It is the remaining three potters which introduce a new trend of late Augustan products into the stamp list, a trend absent in the Chichester list although strongly represented in the unstamped sherds. Attissus and Dannomaros, definitely, and Assinos, probably, supplied Haltern with TR and so were at work before c. A.D. 16 if the latest date for the abandonment of Haltern is accepted, or before c. A.D. 9 if the earliest one is accepted. The Attissus stamp is from the same die as the Haltern stamp and so can scarcely post-date c. A.D. 20 at the latest; the Dannomaros stamp is not from the Haltern die but it must pre-date c. A.D. 25 at the latest. Excluding the doubtful Haltern suppliers – Assinos and also Julios and Aetius, late Augustan potters comprise 7.1% of the stamp list, a percentage which is remarkably close to that of the late Augustan platters.

Comparison of the two collections shows that they are somewhat different in detail, possibly as a result of chronological factors, but also possibly due to some chance quirk in the distribution of the finds, for the sample is fairly small. The most notable differences are that the proportion of TR at Fishbourne is less than at Chichester while by far the most important vessel-type is the platter

Form 16; together they suggest that Nero-Flavian material is more important at Fishbourne. There is a significant group of large platters of Forms 3 and 5 which are identical in form and date fabric to the Chichester examples and which together comprise 10% of the total. The Fishbourne material, however, also adds no small moulded platters or cups of equivalent date to the range of forms, although it does widen the range with single examples of the relatively rare large moulded platter Forms 4 and 6, both of which are in TR and could be pre-Claudian in date. For sites which appear to have no pre-Conquest occupation in their immediate vicinity, both Chichester and Fishbourne have produced a sizeable collection of late Augustan TR accounting for 44.7% of the TR alone though only 6.8% of the total collection.

Amongst the TN there are only two definitely pre-Claudian pieces, both platters, one in micaceous TN, Form 1, from Fishbourne, the other, Form 7A, from Chichester. The addition of the known early TN to the TR lifts the percentage overall to 9.4% at least. Given the amount of pre-Claudian TR there should be some early examples of Forms 2, 3 and 5 in TN, but lacking the stamps they cannot be identified definitely.

Just how and why the early material reached the area remains uncertain. There are no large groups of accompanying locally-made late pre-Roman Iron Age wares from either Chichester or Fishbourne to support the idea of a pre-Claudian settlement in the vicinity of the excavated areas. The imbalance of the group of early imports which is comprised almost entirely of large platters in TR also argues against pre-Claudian occupation. With the notable exception of the samian, none of the other imported and fine table wares are definitely pre-Claudian, although some of the large flagons in white "pipeclay" wares could be. The early material, therefore, seems to be confined to samian and a very limited range of imported TR with a trace of TN.

If the early material does not belong to a pre-Conquest settlement it could be out-of-date stock gathered together either on the Continent or even at Camulodunum, to fill gaps in the supplies to the invading armies. Alternatively it could have been off-loaded onto the native population in the years immediately following the Conquest when demand was overtaking supply and the chance of profits great. Both hypotheses are attractive since they can be extended to cover any apparently embarrassingly early material from any site, including Camulodunum. There are however pre-Claudian imports, possibly even late Augustan imports, following the debacle in Germany, from Braughing-Puckeridge, Herts. The collection includes examples of the earliest known G–B wares as well as stamps from the Haltern die of Attissus, on a platter of Form 3, in TR 1(C), identical to those from Fishbourne, Camulodunum, and Oare, Wilts. Despite the fact that the latter finds were found in post-Conquest contexts, they must have been made before c. A.D. 20 at the latest and the possibility remains that they could be pre-Claudian imports.

The greatest range of early stamps and forms is concentrated in the Essex-Hertfordshire area which suggests an entry point in the pre-Claudian period, if not at Camulodunum then somewhere upstream on the north bank of the Thames. In the immediate hinterland the widest range of forms and fabrics would be available and there could have been a minimal time lag between production, distribution and use. With increasing distance from the point of import, the range of forms would probably decrease and the time lag increase, with supplies being dependent on a surplus at the main markets in the east. The chances of out-of-date stock being introduced would also increase, and in this particular context Chichester-Fishbourne may well have been an outlying area receiving only a restricted range of the most easily available forms and fabrics at any time. If the settlement of Chichester-Fishbourne imported G–B wares via Camulodunum, or some other port to the east, an unbalanced group could have resulted so that the early TR platters may be derived from a pre-Claudian site somewhere in the immediate vicinity.

The collection from Chichester-Fishbourne shows that it was an important market for G–B wares and that its trading connections were the same as those of Camulodunum and, therefore, also south-eastern England. If there was a pre-Claudian settlement which imported G–B wares it probably did so via Camulodunum. The main import occurred after the Conquest, continued into the Flavian period, and was probably by a direct route into the area.

Other Imports, Fine Wares and Potter's Stamps

The colour-coated wares were examined and identified by Dr. K. T. Green.
"Pompeian" Red wares
4. Rim sherd from a platter Cam. Form 17 in a variety of Pompeian red ware. Creamy buff fine-grained sandy micaceous ware, with fine red grog tempering; mica-dusted orange slip with a matt finish on the exterior, partly overlaid at the lip by a thick coral-red slip covering the interior. Highly polished finish; very worn. Diameter 22 cm: pre-Flavian – early Flavian. *Not Illustrated. Area 5. Pit 0.40.*

201

5. Sherd, probably from the lid of a Cam. 17. The paste is like that of No. 4 with traces of a dark pink, highly micaceous slip. Pre-Flavian – early Flavian. *Not Illustrated. Area 2. G. 32.*

The basic platter and lid forms were made in a number of fabrics which vary in colour and texture of the paste and the finish of the outside but which all have a similar thick red highly polished slip on the inside. Presumably there were a number of production centres and there is no evidence to connect them with the main centres of the Gallo-Belgic industry. Many examples occur at Camulodunum, Gloucester and Fishbourne (Type 3), so that its scarcity at Chichester is surprising.

Colour-coated wares

(a) *Central Gaulish imports*
6. (Type 1 – high round shoulder, narrow everted rim), variant 1A – barbotine decoration. Several large sherds forming an almost complete upper body from a beaker with barbotine decoration below the slip. Brittle, cream dense paste; metallic brown slip, variegated in tone (Fabric 1), Central Gaulish, *c.* A.D. 70–100. *Area 4. Pit M.27.*

Sherds from similar beakers:
Pit M.34. – hairpin motif only.
M.53. – hairpin and scale motifs.

A fairly rare type of beaker from the Flavian period onwards. Examples have been identified at *Fishbourne* (Type 227), *Verulamium* 1, Fig. 111, 397; *Richborough IV*, Pl. LXXXIX, 396; *Silchester*, Pl. XLVII, 48; *Chichester* 1, Fig. 5.22, Group 89b.
7. Rim sherd from a small example with a flattened rim with very fine sand rough-casting. *Area 4. M.53.* Central Gaulish, *c.* A.D. 70–120 (Fabric 1).
8. Rim and sherds from a beaker with sparse fine sand rough-casting. Bright orange fine-grained paste; brick-red slightly glossy slip. Central Gaulish *c.* A.D. 70–120. *Area 2. J.77* (Fabric 3).

Sherds from similar beakers: *Area 2. J.80; Area 4. M.26; Cirencester 1961*, D. IV, 31 Basilica Period 1, *c.* 90–140 (*J. Wacher*, unpublished).
9. Sherds from a beaker with coarse grog rough-casting. Cream fine-grained sandy paste; thick metallic bronze slip. Probably an import from Central Gaul. There are body sherds from at least four others in similar fabric:
Area 1. Pit A.38. – shoulder sherd from a globular jar with marked girth groove. White paste, metallic brown slip.
Area 2. L.50. – Body sherd.

(b) *Lyons ware*
10. Rim and body sherds from a beaker with coarse sand rough-casting below a slight shoulder groove. Pale greenish paste; greenish bronze metallic slip. Burnt along the edge of the rim. Pre-Flavian. *Area 2. E.75.*

There are sherds from three similar beakers and a lamp with moulded decoration from the site in general:
Area 5. P.47; Area 2. Pit E.95; Area 2. G.124 and *Area 2. G.155* (lamp).

(c) *Other wares*
11. Rim and body sherd from a beaker with fine-sand rough-casting; orange fine-grained paste; brown exterior, red-brown interior slip. Possibly an import; probably Flavian. *Area 5. 0.54. Not illustrated.* Fishbourne Type 265; red ware with a chocolate slip. Sherds also from *Area 2.H.26; Area 2. E.104.*
12. Rim sherd from a small open bowl with relief decoration. Orange fine-grained sand-free paste; dark orange-buff patchy surfaces. The surviving decoration comprises part of a V-shaped zone in-filled with raised spots. No parallels known. Dr. K. T. Greene suggests that it is probably a copy of a moulded cup from South Gaul, possibly an import and pre-Flavian in date. There are sherds from a bowl in similar ware with moulded decoration in rather high relief which were found at Fishbourne. The decoration is in the form of a running scroll with sycamore leaves (*Cunliffe* 1971: Fig. 85, 22 – Period 1). Judging from the fabric, both pieces could be from the same source. *Area 2. Pit H.19.*

Self coloured wares
13. Rim sherds from a platter or shallow bowl with a band of rouletting inside. Creamy pink fine-grained ware with red grog grits; burnished surface with red streaks; two grooves define

the rouletting. The fabric closely resembles TR 1 without the red slip. Possibly an import; the form is not one of those known to be within the repertoire of the TR and TN potters of Gaul. The only parallel is a complete platter in burnished coral-red ware in Yorkshire Museum and thought to be from York. Probably 1st century A.D. *Area 6. R.7 and R.17.*

14. Sherds from a large shallow bowl with a grooved pie-dish rim decorated with a rouletted band. The fabric closely resembles TN but the fabric is not known to be within the repertoire of TR or TN potters in Gaul. Blueish white fine-grained sandy paste with dark ironstone grits, patchy blue-grey surfaces; highly burnished lip and interior, rilled matt finish below the rim. Rouletted band on the rim. The form and decoration is paralleled by bowls from London and Mildenhall, Wiltshire. The example from London is from the site of 38 Moorgate, and is in a version of "London ware" – dark grey-black micaceous ware with a highly burnished glossy finish (information from Mr. G. D. Marsh). The second bowl has a markedly domed base (Devizes Museum). Probably late 1st century A.D. *Area 2. E.104* and *Area 4. M.37* and *M.53.*

Copies of Gallo-Belgic imports

15. Several sherds from a facetted pedestal beaker in imitation TR 1(A); orange fine grained paste; red-brown micaceous slip with a highly burnished external finish. Possibly a local product; pre-Flavian.
Area 2. Pit H.18 and *19.* It is a high quality copy of a type of Gallo-Belgic pedestal beaker normally made in TR 1(A) which is found commonly in the region between Rheims, Epernay and Troyes and presumably made somewhere in that area. To date, no examples of the genuine imports have been identified in Britain but there is another similar copy from Richborough (*Richborough* IV, Pl. LXXXIX, 39A, unstratified).

There may be a local source, probably at Chichester, given the range of the types inspired by Gallo-Belgic imports made at the Chapel Street kilns. *Area 2. J.77.* Rim sherd from an identical beaker. *Not illustrated.*

Large flagons with two handles

16. Complete neck and two handles from a small version of Cam. Form 161, a single cordon on the neck and three-rib handles. In typical ware for the form, fine-grained with sparse red grog grits, self coloured slip on the exterior with a smoothed finish. An import; pre-Flavian. There is an identical flagon from a burial in the King Harry Lane cemetery, St. Albans, in a burial which is Claudian at the latest. (Excavations by Dr. I. M. Stead.) *Area 2. G.65.*

Potter's stamps on coarse wares (these are numbered through from Fig. 10.1)

20. *Mark. Area 3 (2176)*
Central stamp; small platter, slightly domed at the centre, no evidence of decoration or of the foot-ring survives. Dark grey fine-grained core; brown cortex; dark blue-grey micaceous surfaces, burnished finish. No other stamps from this die have been identified although it is a fairly common basic type of die used on coarse ware cups and platters. A few examples have been found on imports and these could have been the prototypes though it is such a simple yet effective motif that prototypes would scarcely have been essential. The basic motif was used at at least five production centres one of which was local to Sussex, for examples have been found at Wiggonholt and Fishbourne, Period 1 (*Evans* 1974, Fig. 9, 17; *Cunliffe* 1971, Fig. 80.11). Other centres were at Hacheston, Suffolk, *Camulodunum* (No. 225), and Southwark, in the second half of the 1st century A.D. and rather earlier at Rushden, Northants. *N.B.* – (unpublished Ipswich Museum; *Camulodunum* 1946; excavations by Mr. H. Sheldon, publication forthcoming; excavations by Mr. P. J. Woods, publication forthcoming).

21. *Mark (Chichester Museum 311)*
Central stamp within a combed circle. Platter, domed at the centre with an incised spiral on the underside. Same fabric as No. 20. The impression is distorted and worn so that the reading is uncertain. No other stamps from this die have been identified, but No. 23 is probably from the same die. A local product. *Not illustrated.*

22. *Mark (Area 2. E.161)*
Central stamp, no evidence of decoration on the upper surface but a burnished spiral on the underside. Platter; no evidence of foot-ring. Similar fabric to No. 20.

The stamp is incomplete and worn and identification is uncertain. It may be from the same die as No. 21. The similarities in fabric, form, decoration and stamps suggests that all three platters are from the same local production source.

23. *Mark. Area 3. W.28*
Central stamp on a platter; within a wreath of burnished chevrons bordered by concentric circles. Flat base, slightly domed upper surface. Very dark grey ware with fine sandy grits, burnished micaceous surfaces. No other stamps from this die have been identified. It is a copy of a double line Name stamp, such copies occur on imported cups and platters in TN in the later period of the G–B industry after *c.* A.D. 40, but were never plentiful judging by the number of recorded finds. The closest parallels to this platter are two stamps on TN platters Cam. 16; one found at Camulodunum (No. 242), the other found at Nijmegen, in Cemetery S, dated *c.* A.D. 37–70 (*Holwerda* 1941, No. 168). No similar stamps have been found on coarse ware vessels in Britain. A local product.

24. *A Mark with a border*
Central stamp; cup or bowl with a moulded foot-ring. White fine-grained sand free ware with a thin light orange slip on the exterior only. No other examples from this die are known. The piece is unusual in several ways. The stamp itself is unusual in having a border although it resembles many stamps names and marks used on mortaria. Only two others have been found with similar borders, one on a cup from Fishbourne, the other on a cup or bowl in similar white ware from Southwark (*Cunliffe* 1971, Fig. 80.9; excavations by H. Sheldon, publication forthcoming).

Stamps on vessels in white ware are uncommon and apart from the examples cited above, there are bowls with semi-literate name stamps from grave groups found at Winchester and Neatham, Hants. Probably Flavian. Fishbourne – the potters stamps and marks on platters and cups in coarse ware. (References refer to *Fishbourne*, Vol. II.)

Fig. 80.6, BELLVS F(ECIT). On the underside of a flat-based platter towards the edge of the base. Bellius occurs in a number of different versions and on a variety of different fabrics and forms including TR platters of Cam. 8, beakers in "TN" of Hofheim Form 85A and this platter in a sandy coarse ware. Two beakers, those from Aachen and Bavay are also stamped with the impression of an intaglio. (See *Richborough* IV, pp. 240–1.)

The dies and versions of the name are exclusive to particular fabrics so there could be more than one potter involved (see above No. 6). The beakers may have been made at Bavay, *c.* A.D. 50–80. An import. The remaining five Marks (Fig. 60.7–11) are almost certainly from a local source and taken with the four from Chichester, excluding the Mark on the white ware bowl, as well as those from Wiggonholt and Hardham Camp, attest to the vigour of a local pottery industry in Sussex which made stamped platters and cups of types which can be classified as imitation Gallo-Belgic. With the exception of Camulodunum, this is the most concentrated group of related Marks on locally made and distributed wares in any region of Britain. The pottery was obviously set up in the second half of the 1st century A.D. to supply the market of Chichester-Fishbourne and other Roman settlements nearby. Production on a ? (fairly) large scale occurred at Rowlands Castle and this could be the source for the stamped platters and cups.

The Pottery from the Early Roman Kilns in Area 2

The kilns produced a wide range of products from a graduated series of butt beakers, rusticated jars and carinated bowls, very finely executed, to large pear-shaped bead rimmed jars and cooking pots. Judged on the ratio of wasters only, it would seem that production of butt beakers, shallow bowls and bead rimmed jars were high compared with other types, but this may be misleading as the butt beakers especially, being thrown very thin, would be likely to have a higher proportion of rejects.

Large amounts of well-levigated Reading clay were found in puddling pits and in the kilns as well. It was a pale reddish pink, was extremely plastic and threw very well. Some of it was made into imitation butt beakers and fired in kiln 2 during the later *ad hoc* pottery experiments,[1] and one was fired in a modern kiln under oxidising conditions. The oxidised example, not surprisingly, was identical in fabric to the oxidised kiln wares, and there is little doubt that the source of clay for some at least of the kiln production was along the shores of Chichester harbour, where Reading clay outcrops in places.

An examination of pottery made from this clay shows that it varies in section from a reddish sandy buff to a darker red and that in the coarser wares there may be a fair proportion of sand. When reduced it varies from dark blue/grey to grey, possibly depending on the amount of sand present and also on the degree of firing, with the lighter grey wares being the hardest fired. Not all the wares attributed to the kilns show these characteristics; many appear to be standard grey wares, but these are the coarser fabrics and it may well be that the potters selected the Reading clay as being more suitable for the fine ware production by reason of the improved throwing characteristics, and used the London clay, which is found on the site, for the coarser wares.

Figs. 10.3–10.5

K.1 *Butt beakers*

Some examples with external zones of white slip decoration with intermediate narrow lines of burnishing, probably carried out using the bowl of a small bone spoon (one was found in Kiln 1 with the base of the bowl heavily polished). Zones of rouletting between an upper cordon and intermediate groove, and rouletting again below this. Burnished above cordon and over lip.

The fabric varies from red to pale pink/buff when oxidised and there is evidence of white to pale cream slip.

The size ranges from *c.* 13 to 27 cms in height.

K.2 *Rusticated beakers*

The typical form is high shouldered with a lightly burnished rim and shoulder and with a zone of rustication beneath the shoulder. The vessel illustrated has traces of a pinky white slip, which extends from the top of the rusticated zone probably down to the base. The fabric is fine and hard fired, reduced to grey. No examples occur with bases, but these are likely to be as K.1 (rusticated beakers).

The attractive two-tone rusticated beaker from Slot G.14 (No. 00, Fig. 0.0) is almost certainly a kiln product. The fabric is identical and here the production technique appears to have been to produce a fully oxidised vessel with a zone of off-white slip below the burnished shoulder.

K.3 *Girth beakers*

Very fine and thin ware, one example oxidised, the other reduced. Well-burnished exterior and over lip.

K.4 *Carinated bowls*

K.4.1 Hard grey reduced fabric, burnished exterior and over lip.

K.4.2 Reduced, sandy light grey fabric, burnished exterior over a black slip.

K.4.3 Fine sandy buff ware highly burnished on exterior and over rim. The oxidised versions are a dirty buff.

K.4.4 Sandy fabric reduced grey; unburnished. This is a much coarser product than the others.

The finish on the finer vessels, K.4.2 and K.4.3 varies from a lustrous black through to light grey on the reduced wares. The wall thickness of the finest examples is as little as 1.5 mm in places.

K.5 *Shallow dishes/lids*

This type appears to function equally well as a shallow dish *or* a lid. The footrings, where they survive, are well turned and neatly executed, but in most cases would have been difficult to grasp if the vessel was used as a lid.

K.5.1 Sandy reddish fabric, flat rim.

K.5.2 Similar fabric, but reduced grey; rounded rim.

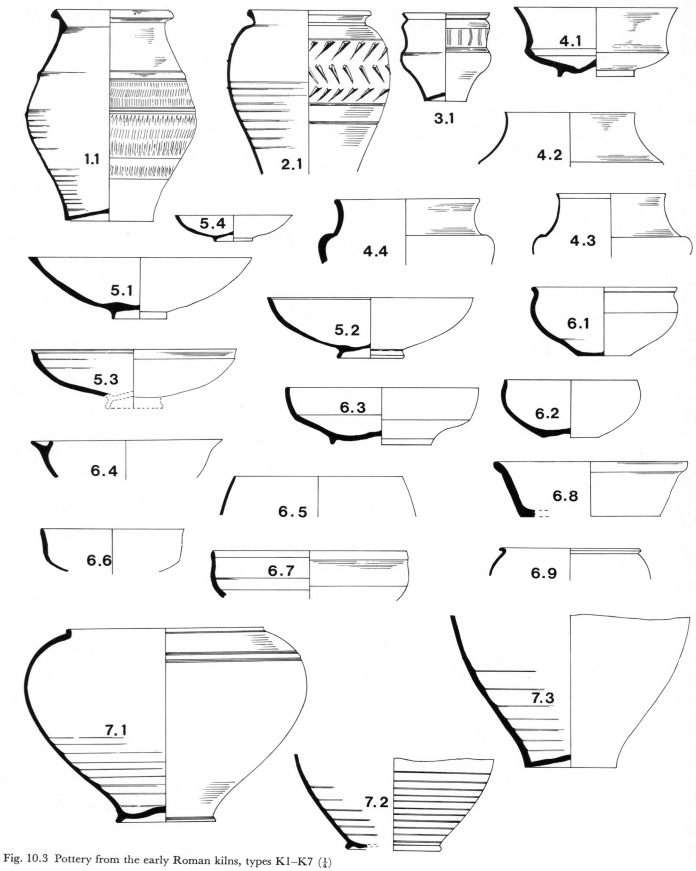

Fig. 10.3 Pottery from the early Roman kilns, types K1–K7 ($\frac{1}{4}$)

K.5.3   Similar fabric, reduced grey/black, recessed rim.
K.5.4   Possibly a small lid, similar fabric to 2 and 3.

K.6   *Bowls*
   K.6.1   Dirty buff/orange ware, flint and shell gritted.
   K.6.2   Pale pink oxidised fabric without grits.
   K.6.3   Partially oxidised dirty reddish buff ware.
   K.6.4   Bowl (possibly lid) with bifid rim, sandy fabric with a few small grits, oxidised dirty buff.
   K.6.5   Steep walled bowl in hard fine off white fabric. Might not be a kiln product.
   K.6.6   Carinated bowl in greyish white fabric reduced black. Burnished exterior and over rim.
   K.6.7   Steep walled bowl in fine grey ware, burnished exterior and over lip.
   K.6.8   Grey fabric, smoothed exterior.
   K.6.9   Fine grey reduced fabric.

K.7   *Pear shaped jars with bead rims*
   K.7.1   Large quantities found as wasters. Fabric is fine, dark grey when reduced and oxidises to reddish buff. All burnished on shoulder and lip.
            Some examples noted with vertical white painted stripes extending from shoulder groove to base.
   K.7.2   Lower half only, but footring and form suggest that it is the same shape as K.7.1. Exterior smoothed and has horizontal shallow tooled lines.
   K.7.3   Possibly a variant of K.7.1 although there is no footring.

K.8   *Jars*
   K.8.1   Reddish fabric, reduced to grey.
   K.8.2   Large jar in sandy grey ware with a band of burnishing below neck.
   K.8.3   Sandy buff oxidised fabric.
   K.8.4   Sandy pale grey ware.
   K.8.5   Sandy pale grey ware.
   K.8.6   Necked jar in hard fired grey ware; burnished exterior.
   K.8.7   Fine grey fabric, slightly micaceous, burnished rim and shoulder.
   K.8.8   Sandy light grey ware, burnished exterior.
   K.8.9   Dirty reddish fabric reduced dark grey. Burnished above shoulder groove.
   K.8.10 High necked jar in sandy grey ware oxidised to reddish buff.
   K.8.11 Sandy reddish fabric.
   K.8.12 Sandy ware, slightly reddish, reduced to black; burnished exterior.
   K.8.13 Sandy grey ware.
   K.8.14 Fine sandy grey ware.
   K.8.15 Fine reddish ware reduced to grey.
   K.8.16 Grey ware.
   K.8.17 Similar ware to K.8.15, reduced brown/grey; burnished on neck and lip.
   K.8.18 Similar ware to K.815, reduced black, burnished on neck and lip.
   K.8.19 Necked jar in fine off white fabric.
   K.8.20 Sandy light grey ware.
   K.8.21 Body sherd from a large vessel in fine grey ware, probably an ovoid shape. The sherd is from the shoulder.
   K.8.22 Necked jar; sandy light grey ware reduced black, exterior burnished.
   K.8.23 Fine grey sandy ware.
   K.8.24 Narrow mouthed jar in sandy reddish ware.
   K.8.25 Vessel in fine grey sandy ware, burnished on shoulder and rim.
   K.8.26 Narrow necked jar in fine grey ware which shows some lamination. Burnished exterior and over lip.

K.9   *Platters*
   K.9.1   Imitation TN platter (Cam. 4) in fine grey ware burnished inside and out.
   K.9.2   Dark grey fabric, slightly spongy in appearance, burnished exterior and over lip. May not be a kiln product.

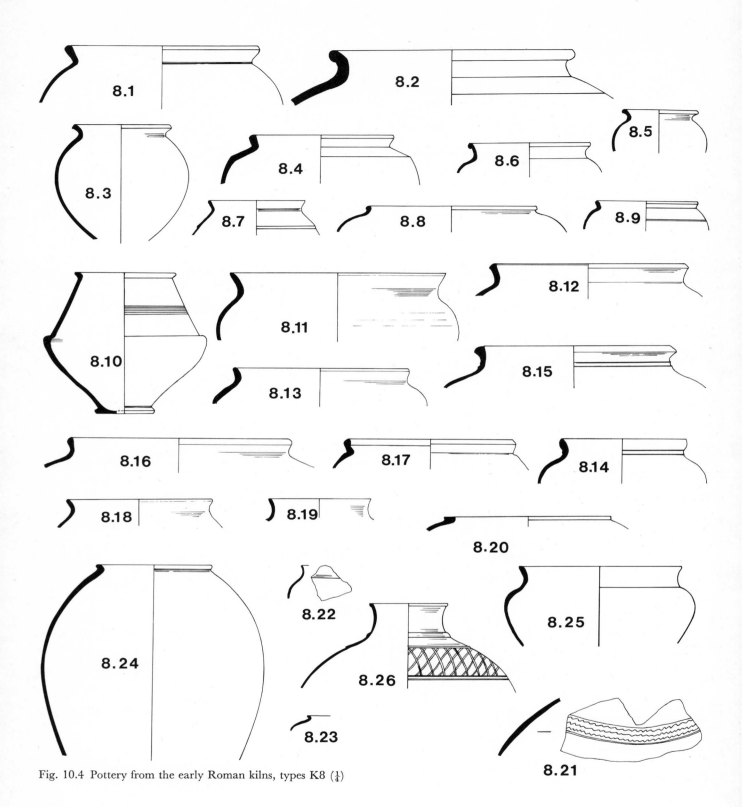

Fig. 10.4 Pottery from the early Roman kilns, types K8 ($\frac{1}{4}$)

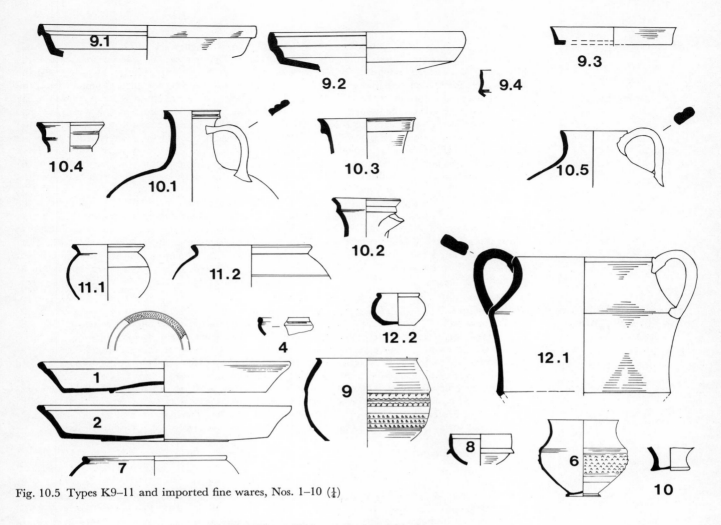

Fig. 10.5 Types K9–11 and imported fine wares, Nos. 1–10 (¼)

K.9.3   Dirty reddish ware reduced black.
K.9.4   Light grey/white sandy ware reduced black: burnished inside and out.

K.10 *Flagons*
K.10.1   Hard fired buff ware with traces of a pale cream slip.
K.10.2   Pale grey fabric oxidised reddish buff with a white slip coating inside and out.
K.10.3   Dark grey fabric oxidised red; pale buff slip.
K.10.4   Dark grey ware, traces of exterior black slip.
K.10.5   Sandy reddish brown fabric.
          The fine flagon from Slot G.14 may also be a kiln product. The ware is similar and technically it was well within the compass of the potters.

K.11 *Small beakers*
K.11.1   Reddish brown fabric, fully oxidised, with a white exterior slip below the shoulder, giving a two-tone effect.
K.11.2   Similar two-tone colour to K.11.1, but in a light grey sandy ware.

K.12 *Miscellaneous*
K.12.1   Two handled vessel in sandy grey fabric.
K.12.2   Small complete jar in dark grey ware.
K.12.3   *Not illustrated.*
          Fragment, one of many in the kilns, of hand-made heavily gritted storage jar. These are quite common in the "military" layers (cf. *Chichester* 2, p. 125, No. 11) and could be either Roman or residual Atrebatic.

Discussion

The discovery of these two kilns, producing fine wares which were of Gallo-Belgic type and quality as well as coarse wares, raises an important point. Discovery of the wares alone, without the kilns, would have led this excavator to believe that the pottery was imported by the military at the time of, or shortly after, the invasion. Whilst the coarse wares could be accepted as being within the competence and tradition of the local Regni, the finer wares are unlikely to be so at such an early date. Moreover, outside the immediate vicinity of the kilns there are few butt beakers, rusticated jars and fine carinated bowls which can be attributed to this particular source, and it may well be that the pottery production was part of the military presence on the site for a short while after the establishment of a temporary legionary base at Chichester. Production may have continued for a while after the main body of troops had moved westwards, with the products being supplied to the forward positions. This is ultimately capable of proof if these wares are found at any of the first century marching camps west of Chichester.

It has not yet been possible to establish whether the wares from these kilns were present in the earliest levels at Fishbourne, owing to the difficulty of tracing some of the pottery from the first year or so of excavation. At the time of writing, these are missing from the research collection housed at the Roman Palace. Absence from the earliest levels at Fishbourne if this can be established, might be another pointer to a slightly later date, c. A.D. 44–45 for the functioning of the kilns, and if their operation within the context of a military depot can be accepted, then an even later date might be possible.

Fine Wares Found in the Kilns, Not Kiln Products
Fig. 10.5

Platters and cups in TN and TR

1. About half of a platter Cam. Form 14A, the variant with a marked angular offset, in hard TN. Hard fine-grained white paste with sparse dark grey grits; originally dark blue-grey surfaces, polished interior, matt exterior. A rouletted wreath defined by burnished circles on the upper surface. Part was heavily burnt after fracture, otherwise the platter is in good condition and the footring appears almost unworn. Claudio-Neronian.
2. About half of a platter Cam. Form 14B, the variant with no offset, in TN. Pale grey fine-grained paste, with sparse dark grey grog grits, blue-black surfaces – a very dense tone, highly polished interior, rather poorly finished facetted exterior. Two concentric incised circles on the upper surface. The clay had not been properly prepared before use. Claudio-Neronian.
3. *Not illustrated*
   A flange fragment from a cup Cam. Form 58, in heavily burnt TR or TN, c. A.D. 40–75.

Beakers in TR 1

4. Rim from a pedestal beaker, Cam. Form 76 in typical TR 1(A). Pale pink fine-grained soft paste; coral slip, with a highly polished finish, on the exterior only. The beaker was broken and repaired in antiquity. Tiberio-Claudian. Additionally, there are four body sherds in the same fabric.

Beakers in TR 3

5. Body sherd from a beaker, Cam. Form 84. Cream fine-grained paste; pearly grey exterior, polished finish. Decoration – incised lattice using a two-pronged comb. *Not illustrated.*

Imported beakers in TN-type fabrics

6. A large rim sherd from a carinated beaker decorated with barbotine spots, Holwerda Type 74. Black fine-grained smooth paste, brown cortex, brown and black surfaces; polished neck, roughly smoothed below the decoration. Decoration – self coloured matt barbotine spots on a matt ground. An import, not a kiln product, an almost identical beaker was found at Nijmegen stamped by the potter Titus (*Holwerda* 1941, No. 636).

Mica-coated wares

7. Rim sherd from a small jar with a lid seated rim. Orange ware with coarse sand tempering; thin mica coating through which the grits protrude. Possibly an import from the region around Rheims.

Copies of Gallo-Belgic imports

8. A small cup, Cam. Form 58 in a grey fine-grained fabric on the borderline between TN and imitation TN. Grey fine-grained sandy paste, sparse grey grog grits; the surfaces shade from blue-grey to darker blue-grey on the exterior which is poorly finished below the flange; the interior has a more constant dark-blue grey colour with a burnished finish.

210

The shade of the paste and the surface finish are not typical of true TN; however, this piece appears to have been refired or burnt. There is a burnished line on the inside of the lip where examples in true TN have a slight offset. Close copies of Cam. Form 58 are not common and their use appears to be limited to the period when the prototype was most common.

Beakers in TR 3
9. A globular jar, Cam. Form 91, in typical TR 3. Orange-red fine-grained smooth paste; grey smokey haze on the outside. Two bands of narrow coarse rouletting below the offset on the shoulder. Heavily burnt and discoloured after fracture.

Miscellaneous sherd
10. Base sherd from a small example in orange TR 3.

Samian
    Form 15 or 17. Claudian; South Gaulish.
    Ritterling 5. Claudian; South Gaulish.

Area 2, Slot G. 14 – Latrine Trench

Figs. 10.6–10.7

This latrine probably pre-dates the kilns. It cuts the timber building immediately to the west, which has kiln wares in the top of the slots, and Layer B within the latrine, which represents the top fill below the subsidence layer (Layer A), has also got kiln wares. The time scale may well be quite small (the matter of a year or perhaps two or three), and its relevance in terms of pottery development is insignificant. The finds are, however, presented in their stratigraphical order, together with a summary of the samian evidence. The description attached to the imported fine wares is that provided by Miss V. Rigby.

Layer A (subsidence into the top of the latrines)
1. Small rusticated beaker in fine red fabric, burnished on shoulder and inside rim, with a white exterior slip below the shoulder, giving the vessel an attractive "two-tone" appearance. Almost certainly made in the kilns (see Kiln Type K.31 for a larger example in reduced black and white ware).
2. High shouldered jar with slightly thickened rim and burnished shoulder, in sandy grey ware.
3. Fine grey ware, burnished on shoulder.
4. Jar in grey fabric.
5. Lid in grey ware, lower part of exterior lightly burnished.
6. Grey sandy fabric.
7. Base of a large vessel in grey ware.
8. Large vessel, probably a storage jar, in dirty light grey ware oxidised to a pinky white. The fabric is heavily gritted.
9. Base of large vessel in sandy grey ware.
10. Grey sandy fabric, exterior burnished.
11. Grey sandy fabric; burnished outside, and over lip.
12. Bead rimmed jar in sandy grey ware; traces of exterior burnish on shoulder.
13. Grey sandy fabric.
14. Grey sandy ware, burnished neck, probably kiln ware.
15. Grey fabric oxidised reddish grey; possibly kiln ware.
16. Platter in light grey sandy ware reduced black. Burnished inside and out.
17. Straight walled bowl in light grey fabric, burnished inside and out.
18. Platter in pale grey sandy ware burnished inside and out.
19. ? Lid in sandy reddish ware, probably kiln ware.
20. *Not illustrated.* Base of butt beaker, red fabric with white exterior slip. Kiln product.
21. Rim of butt beaker in pale sandy buff ware, creamy white exterior; kiln ware. *Not illustrated.*
22. Rim of butt beaker in similar fabric to 21. *Not illustrated.*
23. Three body sherds from a girth beaker; sandy fabric oxidised buff with a brown exterior slip. Probably from the kilns. *Not illustrated.*
24. Base of flagon in dark red ware with white exterior slip; from the kilns.
25. Beaker in red fabric with traces of white slip decoration on shoulder.

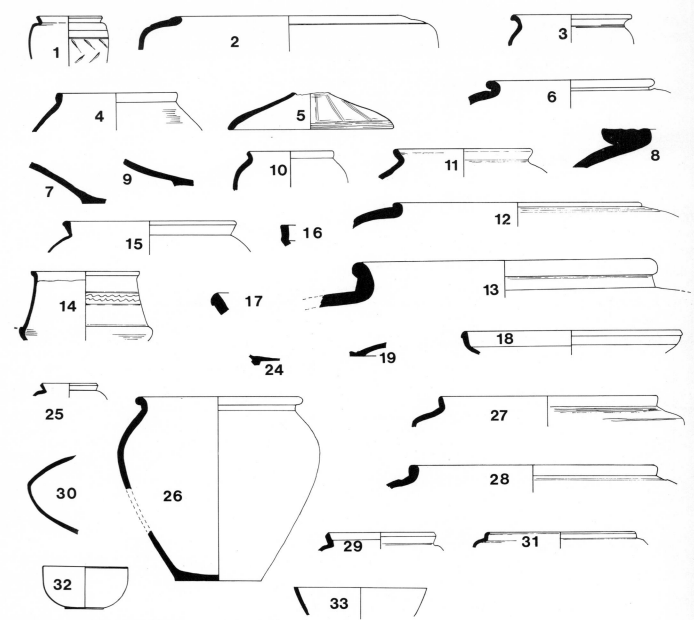

Fig. 10.6 Claudian pottery from Area 2, latrine slot G14 (¼)

Layer B (*top layer of fill below the subsidence*)

26. Sandy reddish buff fabric; similar to kiln wares and probably a kiln product.
27. Carinated jar in sandy grey fabric; burnished shoulder and rim.
28. Fine grey sandy ware.
29. Large beaker in red sandy fabric; probably kiln ware.
30. Body sherd of a flagon in fine dark grey ware oxidised red and with a pale cream exterior slip. Possibly kiln ware.
31. Beaker in a buff sandy ware; exterior metallic dark grey slip.

Layer D

32. Small bowl in slate grey fabric with a slightly roughcast exterior finish. Probably an import.
33. Small bowl in reddish fabric with an exterior red slip.

The Samian

    5 fragments of Tiberian date, Arretine or Provincial Arretine.
    1 Form 17, Tiberio-Claudian, South Gaulish.
    1 Form 15R, Claudian, South Gaulish.
    1 Ritterling 5, Claudian, South Gaulish.
    1 Form 24/25, Claudian, South Gaulish.
    1 Form 18, Claudian, South Gaulish.
    1 Form 33, Claudian, South Gaulish.

Platters and cups in TN and TR

34. A large platter, Cam. Form 2, in hard TN. Bluish-white fine-grained paste; blue-grey surfaces, highly polished interior, smoothed matt exterior.

35. A large platter, Cam. Form 2, in TN. White fine-grained sandy paste, pale blue surfaces; highly polished interior, smoothed matt exterior.

36. A large platter, Cam. Form 5 in TN. Fine-grained sandy paste, dark blue-grey core, bluish-white cortex; blue-black surfaces, highly polished upper surface, facetted lower. A rare variant of Form 5 with an additional step at the junction of the wall and the base, which has been previously identified only at Colchester, where it was found during the excavations of 1970 in a Claudio-Neronian pit group. The platter was made by the potter Medi (11us) who worked in the vicinity of Rheims (see G.B. 12, p. 194).

37. A small version of the platter, Cam. Form 13A, a variant with a low marked off-set, in TN. White fine-grained paste with sparse grey grits; dark blue-grey surfaces, polished interior and matt exterior finish. Claudian.

38. A platter, Cam. Form 14B, in TN. Pale grey fine-grained paste with sparse dark grey grits, ? grog; blue-black surfaces, highly polished interior, poorly finished facetted exterior. Identical in fabric and finish to No. 2 from Kiln G.1.

39. A platter, Cam. Form 14C, a variant with a markedly concave profile below the line of the off-set, in TN. Hard pale, blue-grey, fine-grained paste; blue-black surfaces, highly polished interior, less glossy facetted exterior finish. Claudio-Neronian.

40. *Not illustrated.* Another similar example of Cam. Form 14C.

41. *Not illustrated.* Sherds from a platter, Cam. Form 16, in badly flaked and laminated TN. Soft fine-grained paste, pale blue-grey, with dark blue-grey surfaces; traces of a polished finish.

42. Rim sherd lacking the flange, from a cup, Cam. Form 58 in TR 2. Red fine grained paste; self coloured polished surfaces.

Miscellaneous sherds not illustrated

43. Base of a large platter, possibly Cam. Form 14 in TN; badly burnt and discoloured after fracture.

44 and 45. Base from two medium sized platters in typical TN.

46. Base from a medium sized platter in poor quality TN decorated with an uneven double circle. All probably Claudio-Neronian.

Beakers in TR 3

47. Rim sherd from a globular beaker, Cam. Form 91, in typical TR 3 – orange and pink sandwich paste, smokey grey polished finish. The form is not widely found in Britain outside Camulodunum although the numbers found there suggest that it was by no means a rarity; 53 examples were found during the initial excavations, while those of 1970 produced additional examples. The continental evidence suggests that the basic form was being manufactured in the late Augustan period, for it occurs at Haltern. However, it is not represented at Hofheim, which suggests that it was scarce or entirely out of production by the Claudian period. In Britain, the dating evidence, both here and at Camulodunum favours a Claudian date for its import, for no stratified examples have been found in pre-Claudian groups, while the form is at its most common in Claudian and Claudio-Neronian groups.

48. *Not illustrated.* Body sherd from a beaker, Cam. Form 112, in TR 3 – red with a densely black external finish. Decorated with at least one broad band of rouletting.

49. *Not illustrated.* Several sherds from a large beaker, either Cam. Form 112 or 91, TR 3 – red, with smokey-grey haze to exterior. Decorated with at least one band of rouletting and one of incised cross hatching.

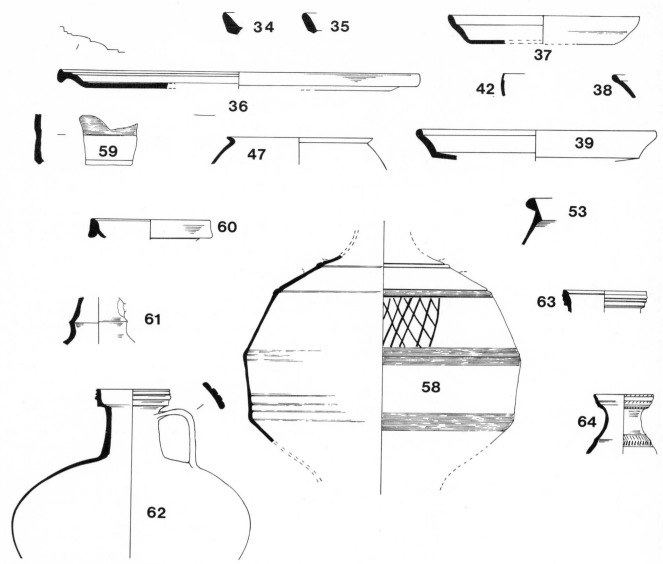

Fig. 10.7 Latrine slot G14. Imported and local fine wares ($\frac{1}{4}$)

Plain sherds from beakers in TR 3, not illustrated

50.⎫
51.⎬ Sherds from 3 beakers: Pale pink, TR 3.   Light orange, TR 3.   Red, TR 3.
52.⎭

Butt beakers in white wares – Cam. Form 113

53.   Rim sherd from a large variant of Cam. Form 113C (rim with an internal angle). The fabric is typical of examples found at Verulamium and Camulodunum; fine-grained sandy ware with a pale blue-grey core at the rim and off-white surfaces; burnished rim and neck. Pre-Flavian.

54.   *Not illustrated.* Rim sherd of a typical beaker, Cam. Form 113C. The fabric is like No. 53 above; white ware with smoke grey surfaces; highly burnished finish. Pre-Flavian.

55.   *Not illustrated.* Two rim sherds from a typical beaker, Cam. Form 113C. The fabric is like that of No. 53 above; pink core; smokey grey surfaces; highly burnished rim and neck. Pre-Flavian.

56. Base sherd; typical cream ware.
57. Rouletted body sherd from a large version in typical cream ware, possibly the same pot as No. 53 above.

Vessels with painted decoration
58. Many sherds from the body of a carinated flagon with two handles. The lower and middle carinations are undefined, the upper (third) carination is defined top and bottom by grooves which form a cordon. In addition there is a raised cordon on the shoulder with which the handles were aligned when they were applied. Fine grained sandy ware with a grey core, orange-red cortex and interior surface, the exterior is covered with a thick pinkish-cream slip. The decoration consists of red burnished bands over the carinations with at least one zone of red lattice pattern between the upper carinations. The fabric closely resembles that of the flagons, butt beakers and jars with barbotine decoration made on the site, so it is possible that this piece could be a local product. No parallels have been identified for the shape although flagons with two carinations are fairly common in 1st-century context on the Continent, and the more exotic variants from sites in Pannonia are probably the closest (*Bonis* 1942; Taf. XXVIII, 5; XXX, 12–16). The use of red painted decoration on a cream slip over a red fabric can be paralleled at the pottery at Rushden, Northamptonshire, where the range of forms includes carinated "exotics" as well as copies of Gallo-Belgic types and flagons (information from P. J. Woods).
59. Body sherd from a tall straight-sided bowl or jar, with at least one broad raised cordon. Red fine-grained micaceous ware, pinkish-cream slip on the exterior only; red burnished band on the cordon. The fabric and finish closely resemble those of the carinated flagon and they are probably from the same source.

Flagons and flasks
60. Rim sherd from a two-handled flagon, Cam. Form 161, in typical white ware. An import; pre-Flavian.
61. Neck sherd from a two-handled flagon, Hofheim, Type 59, in typical white ware. An import; pre-Flavian. *Richborough*, 111, No. 193.
62. The complete upper body of a flagon with a reeded collar and a four-ribbed handle, cf. Camulodunum Form 136. Orange fine-grained sandy ware; thick slip shading from cream to orange. It is a "second", for the body is slightly dented and distorted while the body wall is extremely thin. Although it may have been a reject, it could have been traded.

 The fabric and finish closely resemble those of both flagons and jars with barbotine decoration, Kiln Types 2.1 and 10.1, produced by potters working on the site in the Claudian period (see p. 205). In both cases the potters are copying high quality pieces originally in white ware, requiring a high degree of skill. Apparently, in the absence of supplies of white firing clay they resorted to the device frequently used by potters, of using local clay and a cream or white slip to produce the desired light surface finish. The proto-types of the jars sometimes had a mica coating or red firing slip applied to the shoulder, to produce this effect the Chichester potters had merely to confine the slip to the lower body. It is possible that this particular flagon was a reject from the same pottery which was making the barbotine jars. Pre-Flavian.
63. Two rims sherds from a flagon identical to No. 62 and from the same source.
64. Several rims and body sherds from a flask with a ribbed collar, two pairs of raised cordons on the body. Very fine-grained smooth ware, blue core, thick orange cortex and surfaces; highly polished neck and shoulder. Rouletted bands on the edges of the collar and on the broader of each pair of cordons. Flasks of this type are much less common in Britain on late Iron Age and early Roman sites than on sites of equivalent date in north-western Europe. No exact parallels have been identified, the closest is from Chichester, found in the St. Pancras cemetery, a cruder version, lacking the ribbed collar, with three notched cordons on the body (*Chichester* 1, Fig. 5.19, Group 15b). The basic form was derived from La Téne 111 vessels. It was taken up by potters working in Gaul producing high quality table wares, like TR and TN, and white ware flagons, from the Augustan period onwards.

 The group as a whole contains no obviously residual Gallo-Belgic wares, while its size and quality also suggest that it is comprised of contemporaneous material. The absence of small platters of

Discussion

Form 7 and 8 and of TR 1 and 2 suggest that the group was not deposited before A.D. 50–55, while the scarcity of platters of Form 16, and the absence of the cut Form 58 suggests that it was not deposited after A.D. 60–65. The limited range of the other Gallo-Belgic imports (beakers in TR 3), supports the date after A.D. 50, as does the presence of two flagons, one almost complete, which are without doubt products from the nearby kilns (Nos. 62 and 63).

The Roman 1st-century Wares

Figs. 10.8–10.9

The majority of stratified coarse wares groups of pre-Flavian to late 1st-century pottery came from the west side of the Chapel Street excavations (Areas 2, 4 and 5), where the earliest occupation levels had been less disturbed by later developments, being for the most part sealed by the Roman streets and gravel spread, or by later Roman buildings. The wares are subdivided into two groups, Group 1 being from layers which, by reason of their stratification are definitely or probably pre-Flavian, and Group 2, which contains Flavian samian and fine wares, and which can in most cases be seen to pre-date the late Flavian planned town.

The samian and fine wares are recorded alongside the coarse pottery even where they are seen to be residual. Samian identification is by Mr. G. B. Dannell and fine ware descriptions and dating are by Miss V. Rigby.

Group 1 – Pre-Flavian

Area 2. G.148=G.135 – Claudian
1. Grey ware.
2. Grey ware.
3. Grey sandy ware.
4. Grey sandy ware.
5. Fine red ware reduced black; exterior burnished.
6. Fine pale grey ware, probably from the kilns.
7. Reddish-buff fabric.
8. Red fabric, burnished exterior.
   Plus various butt beaker sherds from the kilns.

Fine Wares (not illustrated)
9. TN platter base, Claudian at the latest.
10. TR 2, small platter, Claudius-Nero.
11. TN small platter, probably Cam. Form 16. *c.* A.D. 40–80.

Samian
Form Ritt. 5. Tiberio/Claudian; South Gaulish.
Form 33, Tiberian; probably Arretine, South Gaulish.
Form 17, Tiberio-Claudian, South Gaulish.
? Tiberian; Arretine.

H.53=Pit H.17
12. Reddish sandy fabric; smoothed exterior.
13. Sandy grey ware.
14. Grey ware with some flint grits.

Fine Ware
15. Rim sherd from a butt beaker, Cam. Form 113; a variant with no cordon or angle on the inside of the rim. The fabric is typical of examples found at Camulodunum and Verulamium; fine grained sandy ware, blue-grey core, cream cortex, mauve, highly polished exterior. Pre-Flavian.

Samian
Form 27, Tiberio-Claudian, ? kiln.

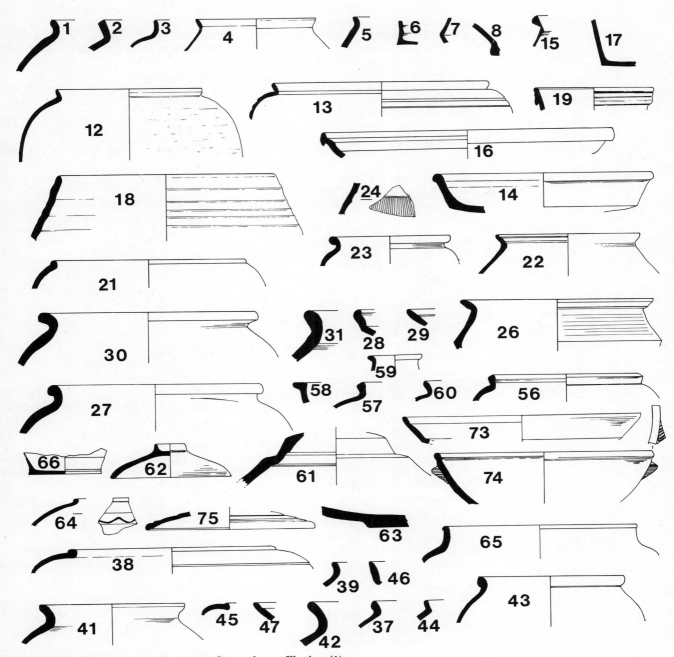

Fig. 10.8 The Roman first century wares; Group 1, pre-Flavian ($\frac{1}{4}$)

G.150 ? Claudius Nero

16. Platter, fine grey ware, burnished surface.
17. Grey fabric reduced black, burnished exterior.
18. Hard fired sandy ware with a few small grits.
19. Two rim sherds from a flagon with ribbed collar, identical in form and fabric to No. 63 from Slot G.14. A local product.
20. *Not illustrated.* Base sherd from a large platter in TR 1(C), typical in fabric and finish. Orange fine-grained sandy paste, coral red slip on the upper surface, with a polished finish. Probably pre-Claudian; Claudian at the latest.
    Plus also kiln sherds.

Samian

Plate, Tiberio-Claudian; South Gaulish.

Area 2. G.112

21. Coarse brown fabric reduced black; a few small grits, exterior burnished, may be Atrebatic.
22. Hard grey ware.
23. Hard grey ware with a few small grits.
24. Grey ware with vertical combing.
25. *Not illustrated.* Brown gritty ware reduced black, similar to No. 21 and may also be Atrebatic.

Samian

Ritt. 24/25, Claudian, South Gaulish.

E.216: Pre-Flavian, probably Claudian

26. Fine sandy ware reduced to a slate grey.
27. Similar fabric to No. 25.
28. Grey ware, burnished surface.
29. Fine sandy ware, off white, black burnished surfaces.
30. Grey ware.
31. Grey ware.
32. *Not illustrated.* Sherd from a kiln butt beaker K.1.

Gallo-Belgic imports, not illustrated

33. Rim sherd from a platter, Cam. Form 13, with a slight off-set, in TN. Pale blue-grey fine grained paste; dark blue-grey surfaces, highly polished interior, facetted less glossy exterior. Claudio-Neronian.
34. A broad handle with five ribs from a large flagon, probably Cam. Form 163 in typical fine-grained white ware. Possibly an import. Pre-Flavian.
35. Body sherds from a globular jar decorated with zones of high relief barbotine spots. White fine-grained ware; cream slip. Possibly an import and pre-Flavian.
36. Base sherd from a platter in TN, decorated with three incised concentric circles defining a matt band. Claudio-Neronian.

Samian

Form 30, *c.* A.D. 60–75 South Gaulish.
Ritt. 5 (2), Tiberio-Claudian; South Gaulish.
Loeschke 1, ? Augustan; Arretine.

J.93. Pre-Flavian

37. Grey ware.
38. Grey ware.
39. Sandy grey ware.
40. *Not illustrated.* Base in sandy pink ware reduced grey.

Samian

Loeschke 2, Tiberian; Arretine or provincial Arretine.
Loeschke 12, Tiberian; Arretine or provincial Arretine.
Loeschke 8, Tiberian; Arretine or provincial Arretine.
Form 11, Tiberian; Arretine or provincial Arretine.

E.159. Pre-Flavian
41. Sandy grey ware.
42. Hard grey ware with a few small grits.
43. Sandy grey ware.
44. Grey ware.
45. Sandy ware with exterior smoothed.
   Plus one sherd from a crucible used in enamelling (see p. 254).

Fine Wares
46. Rim and base sherds from a platter, Cam. Form 13B, a variant with an unusually thick wall, in TN. Pale blue-grey fine-grained paste; worn blue-grey surfaces. No finish survives.
47. Rim sherd from a large platter, Cam. Form 2, in TN. Hard bluish-white fine-grained paste, blue-grey surfaces, highly polished interior. Late Augustan-Claudian.
   Not illustrated.
48. A sherd from a large version of the cup, Cam. Form 58, in typical TR 2 with a highly polished finish. Claudio-Neronian.
49. Body sherd from a bowl in TN, *c.* A.D. 45–75.
50. A small body sherd from a beaker in TR 3, probably a butt beaker, Cam. Form 112. Decorated with a broad band of rouletting.
51. A body sherd from a girth beaker, possibly Cam. Form 82, in TR 3, Apricot fine-grained paste, smokey-grey polished exterior. Decoration, two pronged incised lattice.
52. A base sherd from a beaker in TR 3, Tiberio-Claudian.
53. Body sherd from a cylindrical jar or bowl identical to No. 59 from Slot G.14, and from the same source.

Local kiln products, not illustrated
54. Butt beakers, cf. Cam. 113 (K.1), rim, base and body sherds.
55. Barbotine jar, cf. Cam. 114.

Samian
   Form 27, Pre-Flavian; South Gaulish.
   Plate, Tiberio-Claudian; South Gaulish.

E.68. Pre-Flavian ?; probably Group 1
56. Fine sandy ware, burnished exterior and over rim.
57. Fine sandy grey ware.
58. Fine sandy ware, exterior black burnished.
59. Sandy grey ware, traces of exterior black burnish.
60. Sandy grey ware.

Samian
   Form 18, Pre-Flavian; South Gaulish.

Pit H.18, probably Pre-Flavian
61. ? flagon in fine sandy ware oxidised red.
62. ? lid in grey ware, possibly a kiln product.
63. Sandy ware reduced black, burnished surfaces.
64. Narrow mouthed jar in sandy grey ware.
65. Sandy fabric, burnished exterior.
66. Base in sandy fabric, traces of white slip coating.

Not illustrated.
67. Butt beaker from kilns (K.1.1).
68. Grey ware bead rimmed jar from kilns (K.7.1).
69. Jar in sandy ware reduced black (see K.8.4 for type). Fig. 10.4.
70. Jar in gritty ware (see K.8.2 for type). Fig. 10.4.
71. Small jar in grey ware (see K.8.9 for type).
72. Jar in sandy ware, with small, almost bead rim (see K.8.9).

Fine Wares

73. Rim sherd from a platter, Cam. 14B in TN. The fabric and finish are like that of No. 2 in the group from Kiln G.1. Claudio-Neronian.
74. Several sherds from a rounded bowl with at least one handle simulating twisted cord. Orange-red sandy ware; thick micaceous red slip extends over the interior to the groove below the lip on the outside, the area around the base of the handle and probably over the handle(s) also. The slip has a highly burnished finish, the self-coloured exterior has a less even and glossy burnished finish. The handle was attached to the bowl by a tang pushed through a circular hole. Burnt and discoloured in patches.
75. Several sherds from a lid with a grooved lip and at least one off-set on the outside. Probably fits the bowl, No. 74 above, since the fabric and finish are identical, and they are clearly from the same source.
   Not illustrated.
76. Rim sherd from a dish or bowl with a reeded rim. Fine-grained dark orange ware with a thin mica coating.
77. Rim sherd from a deep platter with a bead rim, in locally made sandy ware, heavily burnt and discoloured.
78. Body sherds from a small flagon in white ware.
79. Base sherd from a large platter, domed at the centre, in TN. Probably *c.* A.D. 55–65.

Group 2 – Early to mid Flavian

H.45=pit; early Flavian

80. Carinated jar in fine sandy ware, burnished zone at base.
81. Jar in fine sandy ware.
82. Light grey sandy fabric, burnished exterior.
83. Sandy grey ware.
84. Grey ware, burnished on shoulder and lip.
85. Light sandy ware, burnished exterior reduced black.
86. Sandy grey ware, smoothed exterior.
87. Sandy grey ware.
88. Sandy grey ware oxidised pale buff.
89. ? platter, sandy fabric oxidised dirty buff.
90. Platter in sandy grey ware.

Fine Wares

91. Two rim sherds from a platter with a pie-dish rim, Holwerda, Type 81(i) in TN. Buff fine-grained sandy paste; blue-black surfaces, worn, but with traces of a highly polished finish (*Holwerda* 1941, Pl. XV, 1220). A rare form in Britain which has been identified previously only at Southampton, although its similarity to Form 16 may have led to wrongful classification (*Waterman* 1957, Fig. 3, No. 1). Absent from both Haltern and Hofheim, examples have been found in Cemetery S at Nijmegen, which is dated *c.* A.D. 30–70, the Gallo-Belgic wares are of the later Claudio-Neronian and early Flavian types. Probably *c.* A.D. 50–70.
92. About two-thirds of a bowl, Cam. Form 50, in TN. Buff fine-grained paste, with grey grog grits; blue-black surfaces, highly polished finish, *c.* A.D. 45–80.
93. Two rim sherds from a bowl of the samian Form 29. Highly micaceous fine-grained sandy ware with red ? grog tempering; grey core, orange surfaces with traces of a pinkish white slip on the exterior only. The decoration in red slip is confined to a single band at the mouth. The self-coloured interior surface has a smoothed surface.
94. *Not illustrated.*
   Three matching sherds from a platter, Cam. Form 16 in TN.

Samian

   2 scraps of Tiberian date; provincial Arretine.
   Form 29, Tiberio-Claudian; South Gaulish.
   Form 24/25, Claudian; South Gaulish.
   Ritt. 8, Claudian; South Gaulish.
   Ritt. 18, Claudian; South Gaulish.
   Ritt. 27, 1st century; South Gaulish.
   Form 18, Nero-Vespasian; Lezoux.

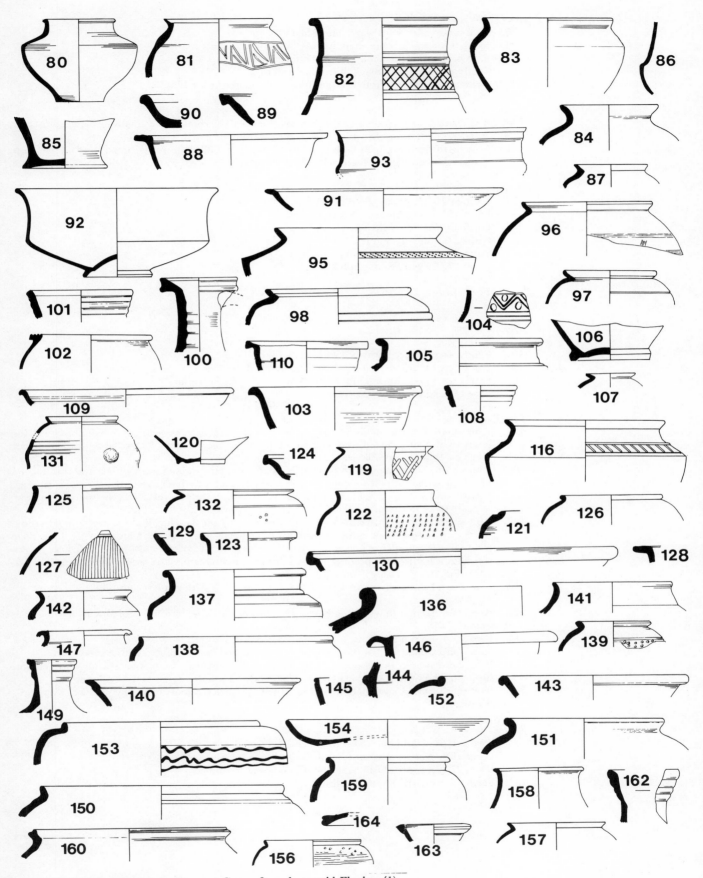

Fig. 10.9 The Roman first century wares; Group 2, early to mid-Flavian ($\frac{1}{4}$)

M.77. Flavian

95. Fine sandy micaceous ware, burnished exterior.
96. Sandy grey ware, some chalk inclusions.
97. Fine dark grey fabric, burnished shoulder and over lip.
98. Sandy ware reduced black, burnished exterior.
99. *Not illustrated.* Sherd from a large storage jar, finger printed inside.

Fine Wares

100. Rim sherd from a large flagon with a flared collar, a variant with a small simple bead lip and overhanging flange. Off-white fine-grained ware with sparse white calcite grits.
101. Rim sherd from a flagon with five low relief rings. Off-white fine-grained sandy ware with sparse red ? grog grits; matt, self-coloured surfaces.

Samian

Form 24/25, Claudian; South Gaulish.
Form 15/17, Pre-Flavian; South Gaulish.
Form 15/17R, Pre-Flavian; South Gaulish.
Form 37, Flavian; South Gaulish.
Form 29, 1st century, South Gaulish.
Form 27, Flavian, Stamp O F L I ///.
Curle 11, Flavian.
Form 18 (4), Flavian.

H.43. Flavian

102. Sandy grey ware.
103. Sandy grey fabric, burnished exterior.
104. Sandy grey fabric oxidised pale buff, burnished exterior.
105. Sandy grey grey fabric reduced black with burnished exterior.
106. Base of flagon in fine pink ware.

Fine Wares

107. Rim sherd from a small plain jar. Pink fine-grained micaceous ware with fine calcite tempering. Badly flaked and laminated surfaces, only traces of original burnished finish survives. Possibly pre-Flavian.
108. Rim sherd from a flagon with three rings. Pale pink fine-grained ware with sparse translucent brown quartz grits; pale orange slip. The fabric is similar to that used for flagons and carinated bowls found at Wigginholt, including pieces thought to be kiln products; the source therefore appears to be fairly local.
109. Rim sherd from a carinated bowl with two grooves on the rim. Pink coarse grained sandy ware with self-coloured matt surfaces. Similar bowls were found at Fishbourne (Type 86), where it was considered not to be a local product, and at Wigginholt (No. 70), where it was considered not to be a product of the kilns although cream wares were made there (*Cunliffe* 1971, Fig. 92.86; *Evans* 1974, Fig. 12.70).
110. Rim sherd from a carinated bowl. Pinkish cream ware with a micaceous pink slip. *Not illustrated.*
111. Rim sherd from a bowl with a rolled edge to the rim. Cream ware, probably from the same source as No. 110.
112. Rim sherd from a lid. Dark pink open-bodied sandy ware.
113. Rim sherd from a lid. Dark pink coarse-grained sandy ware. Burnt, with a sooty edge.
114. Rim sherd from a butt beaker, Cam. Form 113, in typical cream ware; white core, cream surfaces. The ware is similar to examples found at Camulodunum and Verulamium.
115. Base sherd from a large platter decorated with a bordered matt band. Typical TN. Claudio-Neronian.

Samian

Two scraps of Tiberian date; provincial Arretine.
Form 18R, Nero-Vespasian; South Gaulish.
Form 27 (2), probably Flavian; South Gaulish.
Form 37, Flavian; South Gaulish.

L.180 ? Flavian
116. Grey sandy ware reduced black.
     Not illustrated.
117. Carinated jar in hard grey fabric, similar form to No. 116.
118. Carinated jar in micaceous grey ware reduced black, exterior burnished. Similar form to 116 but with rouletting around the top of the carination.

Fine Wares
119. Rim sherd from a beaker decorated with crossed hairpin motifs in low relief barbotine. Dark pink dense paste; dark metallic brown slip. An import. Central Gaulish, *c.* A.D. 70–140.

H.26. Flavian
120. Sandy fabric reduced black.
121. Sandy fabric, zone of burnishing on shoulder.
122. Sandy fabric, slate grey exterior.
123. Reddish sandy ware reduced grey, burnished exterior.
124. Sandy ware.
125. Sandy reddish ware reduced black.
126. Sandy ware.
127. Reddish sandy ware.
128. Pale grey ware oxidised buff.
129. Sandy ware.

Fine Wares
130. Rim sherd from a large platter, Cam. Form 5, in TN. White fine-grained sandy paste with black flecks; pale blue surfaces; polished interior, with a smoothed and less glossy exterior. Claudian.
131. Rim and body sherd from a small jar decorated with defined raised bosses on the shoulder. Buff fine-grained ware, thin mica coating. Probably an import.
132. Rim sherd from a small jar decorated with barbotine spots. White fine-grained sand-free fabric with sparse red ? grog grits. Dark cream exterior with a burnished finish; self-coloured matt low-relief spots.
     Not illustrated.
133. Base sherd from a beaker in cream paste; dark metallic slip, grog rough casting. Possibly an import from Central Gaul.
134. Base sherd from a beaker. Orange paste, brown slip, grog rough casting. Possibly a product of the Colchester potteries.
135. Rim sherd from a butt beaker, Cam. Form 113, in typical ware. Fine-grained sandy ware, pink core; cream surfaces. Pre-Flavian.

Samian
      Form 37, Flavian; South Gaulish.
      Form 27, Pre-Flavian; South Gaulish.
      Form 27 (2), Flavian; South Gaulish.
      Form 15/17, Neronian; South Gaulish.
      Form 18, Neronian; Lezoux.
      Ritt. 12, Pre-Flavian; South Gaulish.
      Form 24/25, Claudian; South Gaulish.
      Ritt. 8, Claudian; South Gaulish.
      Form 17 (2), Tiberio-Claudian; South Gaulish.
      Ritt. 5, Tiberian; Provincial Arretine.

Pit E.90. Flavian
136. Heavily gritted storage jar.
137. Grey ware with band of burnishing above shoulder.
138. Sandy ware reduced black.
139. Fine sandy ware, applied spots *en barbotine*.
140. Sandy grey ware.
141. Sandy grey ware, burnished exterior.

142. Sandy ware reduced black, burnished exterior.
143. Sandy ware.
144. Sandy ware oxidised reddish buff.
145. Pale cream ware.
146. Pinky buff ware oxidised cream.
147. Pale cream ware.

Gallo-Belgic imports
148. *Not illustrated.* Rim sherd from a platter, Cam. Form 16, in TN. The fabric is hard with a good quality finish, highly polished interior with a less glossy facetted exterior surface.
149. Rim sherd from a flagon with three rings. Orange core, paler surfaces with a rough matt finish; flaked and slightly vesicular.

Samian
>   Form 29, Pre-Flavian; South Gaulish.
>   Form 15R, Claudian; South Gaulish.
>   Form 24/25, Claudian; South Gaulish.
>   Form 27 (2), Claudian; South Gaulish.
>   Form 27 (2), Claudius-Nero; South Gaulish.
>   Form 35, 1st century; South Gaulish.
>   Form 15/17R, 1st century, Pre-Flavian.
>   Form 18R (2), Nero-Vespasian; South Gaulish.
>   Ritt. 12 (2), Pre-Flavian; South Gaulish.

Pit L.81. Flavian
150. Gritty grey ware, black burnished over rim.
151. Sandy fabric reduced black, burnished over rim.
152. Fine grey ware, smoothed exterior.
153. Pink sandy fabric, reduced grey.

Gallo-Belgic imports
154. A number of sherds from the same platter, Cam. Form 16, in TN. Similar fabric to No. 41 from Kiln G.1, with badly flaked patchy light and dark blue-grey surfaces. *c.* A.D. 40–80.
155. *Not illustrated.* Rim sherd from a cup, Cam. Form 56C, with a slight offset at the lip, in typical TR 2; very worn surfaces, no finish survives. Late Tiberian-Claudian.
156. Rim and body sherds from a small beaker with a grooved rim, decorated with fine sand rough-casting. Soft cream powdery micaceous paste; exterior rilled before the rough casting was applied; thin patchy light brown slip. Lyons ware; Pre-Flavian. A "second", the rim and body are distorted. Sherds from beakers in Lyons ware were found in Area 2, L.136 and Pit L.102, and in Area 7, D.33.

Samian
>   Form 29, Pre-Flavian; South Gaulish.
>   Form 30, 1st century; South Gaulish.
>   Form 35/36 (2), 1st century; South Gaulish.
>   Form 17, Pre-Flavian; South Gaulish.
>   Loeschke 12, Tiberian; South Gaulish.
>   Form 18, 1st century; South Gaulish.
>   Form 29, Claudian; South Gaulish.
>   Form 17, Tiberian; South Gaulish.
>   Form 27, Flavian; South Gaulish, stamped Q U I N T I O.
>   Form 27, Pre-Flavian; South Gaulish, stamped N I T A.

J.79 ? late 1st century
157. Fine sandy ware, slightly micaceous.
158. Grey ware reduced black, smoothed exterior.
159. Grey ware.
160. Grey ware, exterior black burnished.

Fine Wares

161. *Not illustrated.* Sherd from a platter, Cam. Form 8, in TN. Pale blue-grey fine-grained paste; dark blue-grey surfaces, polished finish. Claudio-Neronian.
162. Rim and neck sherds from a flagon with four marked rings. Orange sandy ware with a self-coloured rilled finish.
163. Rim sherd from a flagon with a triangular top ring. Orange ware, probably from the same source as No. 162 above.
164. Rim sherd from a lid with a grooved edge. Off-white sandy ware with matt micaceous surfaces.

Samian

Form 37, Claudius, or Claudius-Nero; South Gaulish.
Form 37, *c.* A.D. 75–90; South Gaulish.
Form 18 (3), Flavian; South Gaulish.
Form 17 (2), Neronian; South Gaulish.
Form 29 ? Pre-Flavian; South Gaulish.
Cup, Tiberian; Provincial Arretine.
Form 27, Flavian; South Gaulish, stamped /// A P R I.

The Samian Pottery

by G. B. Dannell

(A) The Early Samian Ware from Chichester

The latest group of early Arretine forms from Chichester provides an opportunity for comparison both with the neighbouring collection from Fishbourne, and the unpublished group from Skeleton Green (forthcoming in *H.A.S.* by Clive Partridge). The Sussex material shows a considerable diversity of sources, which have been identified by Maurice Picon at the *Laboratoire de Ceramologie* of the C.N.R.S. at Lyons, and his valuable comments have begun to open a new range of possibilities for understanding the distribution and chronology of British deposits. I am deeply indebted to him for his kind interest. It is now clear that the majority of the material comes from Italian workshops, with two or three different fabrics from Arezzo, at least one from Pozzuoli, and another unidentified site. There is also a small group from La Muette (Lyons), and a few pieces from Lezoux; these latter range from the colour-coated progenitors, which have a paste close to the consistency of a digestive biscuit, to quite reasonable, levigated, hard-fired samian. The most interesting identification relates to the ATEIVS plate (*Cunliffe* 1971, p. 262.32), which has a composition more consistent with pottery from La Graufesenque than elsewhere, and is in conformity with the analysis of a f. 29 (cf. *J. P. Pappalardo, Un vase Sigillé de Montans à Balaruc-le-Vieux, Rev. Arch. de Narbonnaise*, II, 1969, pp. 123–32, and *M. Picon, A propos d'un vase faussement attribué à Montans*, ibid. VII, 1974, pp. 219–23). These results achieved from the Fishbourne group can be closely applied to Chichester, but it is clear that we must attach new standards of investigation to the material as a whole, if further refinement of the sources is to be obtained. Every piece must be broken to reveal a fresh facet, and microscopic examination is necessary for all doubtful pieces. Even so, the eye cannot easily distinguish pastes from surprisingly disparate sources, if the inclusions are scarce.

The forms and sources are given in a table below and the marked preponderance of Loeschke 2 and 8 should be noted, together with the comparative scarcity of Loeschke 1, and the presence of Loeschke 11. A useful review of the evidence of the dating of these forms, and their division into "services" is given in *W. H. Kam, De Terra Sigillata vondsten uit de tijd van Augustus*, Nijmegen, 1970. This suggests that "services" II and III are broadly contemporary with the occupation of Haltern (Loeschke 2, 8 and 11), while "service" 1 (Loeschke 1) is earlier. The dating for Haltern has recently been reassessed (see the review of the evidence in *C. M. Wells, The German Policy of Augustus*, Oxford 1972, particularly pp. 257–62, and *S. von Schnurbein, Die römische Militäranlagen bei Haltern*, 1974, Munster, so that a withdrawal in A.D. 9 is postulated, rather than

A.D. 16. Moreover, an initial survey of the stamps on Arretine wares suggests that dies and potters present at Oberaden are not generally found in Britain, while Haltern parallels are plentiful. Oberaden is considered to have closed *c.* 9 B.C., perhaps indicating that British importation in quantity commenced during the period spanned by Haltern. The evidence must necessarily be concerned with stamps, and to a lesser extent decorated wares, and both are scarce; new finds may disprove this theory, but at present it is attractive. The question must then be posed about the so-called provincial wares, which Picon has begun to place. If they were imported a little later than the Italian products it might be possible to identify and distinguish sites which yield discrete assemblages. Here, Skeleton Green is useful, with no provincial fabrics, and indications from the corroborative evidence that the earliest layers contain a rich collection of other imports. These early imports include amphorae, which are now associated with a brisk wine trade commencing shortly after the Caesarian incursions (*Dr. D. Peacock, Roman Amphorae in pre-Roman Britain, in Jesson and Hill* (eds.) 1971), and Italian containers are frequent. However, if the wine was coming straight in from Italy, why not the earlier Arretine? This problem needs resolution. It could be that the importance of the amphorae have been quantatively exaggerated, considering the years available for their importation (the number of butt beakers confirms my faith in British beer as the people's real tipple), and thus any associated Arretine and Italic wares are few and far between. On the other hand we do not know that the pottery came in directly, and it is worth reconsidering whether it is a secondary trade, dependent upon *Negotiatores*, perhaps from the Rhineland, in which case some of the dating could be later than Continental evidence. The provincial wares, all of which so far have come from Gaul, do seem to have a southern and western bias, which was continued by the pattern of 1st-century Lezoux products. It will be interesting to re-examine the Camulodunum and Silchester groups to see if these characteristics are maintained.

The context of the Chichester wares is not the same as at Fishbourne, where very little other evidence could be adduced for an Augustan deposit (cf. V. Rigby, p. 201). All of the Chichester fragments were small enough to fit small find envelopes, suggesting that it may have been residual, and in the absence of structures, even the result of muck-spreading. A recent suggestion by Rodwell (*Oppida; the beginnings of Urbanisation in Barbarian Europe, B.A.R. Supp. Ser. 11, Oxford 1976*, pp. 305–7), that the Fishbourne material came from Chichester after the Roman invasion, with the civilian reoccupation of the site, might appear attractive in the light of the comments above. However, at a critical level the argument is circular, because if the pottery survived to be brought to Fishbourne after the military withdrawal, it would have been available to the army. The theory that it was part of the legion's supplies may have to be abandoned (but what happened to those assembled for Caligula's invasion?), and it may be better to see the material as that bought from natives to supplement existing stocks. If the pottery did survive to this period, the equivalent groups at Camulodunum would then represent stocks appropriated to military use.

Finally, a word about La Graufesenque. The possibility of an ATEIVS factory is exciting, particularly in view of the latest excavations by L. Balsan and A. Vernhet (*Gallia XXIV, 1966, pp. 412–15; XXVI, 1968, pp. 517–21; XXVIII, 1970, pp. 398–402; XXX, 1972, pp. 472–6*), and vessels with similar fabrics must be pursued. *If* the Arretine and provincial centres had failed by *c.* A.D. 25 at the latest, it is inconceivable that Britain remained substantially unsupplied with samian until A.D. 43 (cf. *B. R. Hartley* in *V. G. Swann, Oare reconsidered and the origins of Savernake ware in Wiltshire, Brittania VI, 1975*, p. 59, for '. . . the general rarity of South Gaulish ware in Britain before 43 . . .'). It should be possible to establish whether the end of the Arretine exportation did occur at the suggested date, or South Gaulish ware, particularly from the earliest kilns at La Graufesenque took over, or finally that there was indeed a break in supply.

From looking at the most recent finds at Camulodunum I fancy that we shall find that South Gaulish wares of the Tiberian period are rather more plentiful than we might have previously suspected.

TABLE OF FORMS AND SOURCES FOR ARRETINE WARES

Loeschke	Total	Arezzo	Pozzuoli	La Muette	Lezoux	Provincial?
1	5	5				
2	37	29	2		1	5
3	1?	1?				
7	2	2				
8	30	26	3			1
9	3			3		
11	21	16				5
12	1	1				
15	2	2				
16	1	1				
	103	83	5	3	1	11

Notes (1) The count is on identifiable sherds. No attempt has been made, because of the size of the pieces, to restore a vessel population.

(2) The provincial column does not include any of the La Graufesenque "ATEIVS fabric", but may include other fabrics, as yet undefined from South Gaul. No Montans ware is present until the Flavian period.

(3) Other sherds in the fabrics of Pozzuoli, La Muette and Lezoux were present, but all could have come from forms covered by the occurrence table.

TABLE OF FORMS AND SOURCES FOR EARLY SOUTH GAULISH WARES WHICH CAN DEFINITELY BE ASSIGNED

Form	Total
L.2	5
L.8	8
D.17	7
D.24/25	2
D.27	2
R.8	1
R.9	2
	27

Notes (1) The criteria adopted all relate to the distinction of the wares with a light-coloured paste and slightly brown-red slip, typical of Tiberian products at La Graufesenque.

(2) No vessels in "standard" fabric with the heavily filled paste are included, since in the opinion of the writer, they belong to the Tiberio-Claudian period.

(B) The figured samian Figs. 10.10–10.12 Periods 0 to 1

1. Area 4, M.82. Form 29. Straight scroll as at Kempten, cf. *Knorr* 1919, Taf. 88g. *c.* A.D. 30–45. South Gaulish.

2. Area 2, G.181 (622), plate. Stamped ATEI XANTHI in a cross. Not attested as such, but a number of other Ateuis-group stamps are, cf. *Oxe-Comfort*[1] (a catalogue of the Signatures, Shapes and Chronology of Italian Sigillata, 1968), 145.171, 207 and 213 by Cn. Ateius; *ibid.* 160.34 and 53 by Cn. Ateius Evhodus; *ibid.* 177.147 by Xanthus himself, and 180.3 and 19 by Ateius Zoilus. Note that Mahes is not represented, although he and others shared the use of trefoil stamps. Only the Atei Zoili, 3 is from Italy.

    The paste is heavily loaded with calcareous fragments, easily visible to the naked eye. Tiberian? Provincial Arretine.

Period 2

3. Area 4, M.41. Form 29. Lower zone: straight wreath of palmate leaves above a swag design of wreathed festoons containing repeated patterns of a dog, O.1967, and a hare which is not in Oswald. Probably by BASSVS and COELVS who use the wreath, cf. *Knorr* 1919, Taf. 13.5, festoon 27, and dog, cf. *Knorr* 1952, Taf. 10G. *c.* A.D. 55–70. South Gaulish.

Fig. 10.10 The figured Samian wares Nos. 1–24 (¼)

4. Area 3, Z.68. Upper zone: opposed lyrate buds with poppy heads, bound by a fourteen-petalled rosette, which also appears in a wreathed medallion. Two sizes of roulette appear in the field.

Lower zone: large wreathed medallions containing geese alternating with a compound vegetable motif.

The upper zone is clearly connected with *Hermet* 1934, Pl. 49.9. Dr. Oswald has made a pencil note in his copy assigning the design to PETRECVS (who, Mr. B. R. Hartley informs me, is really PEREGRINVS). Similar motifs to the lower zone are shown by *Hermet*, *op. cit.*, on Pl. 49.37/9, each using the distinctive upper leaf of the present example, and the poppies. The geese are probably O.2288A and 2224 (but smaller). Certain elements occur in the work of BASSVS and COELVS; the upper leaf motif from the lower zone and the fourteen-petalled rosette appear on a f. 29 in their style from Margidunum, cf. *Oswald* 1948, 1.6; the same rosette in a wreathed medallion occurs at Strasbourg, cf. *Knorr* 1952, Taf. 10D, together with the large roulettes; bold poppy-heads come from Aislingen, *ibid.*, F; the lower leaf motif is on the Form 30 assigned to them from Aislingen, *ibid.*, G, and on a Form 29 from Vechten, cf. *Knorr* 1919, Taf. 13D. If the ascription is correct, the potter's range is extended (and cf. *Ant. J.*, XLIV, 1964, pp. 147–52, for connections with PEREGRINVS and ALBVS). It is interesting that the three lyrate buds shown by Hermet would all fit with work by BASSVS and COELVS, cf. *Knorr* 1952, Taf. 10H, for the small central binding. *c.* A.D. 55–70. South Gaulish.

5. Area 2, J.79. Form 29. A common motif, but cf. *Knorr* 1919, Taf. 58B by MODESTVS for both the wreath and well-tufted barley-ears. *c.* A.D. 55–70. South Gaulish.

6. Area 3, Z.34. Form 29. See No. 4. If this is from the same vessel (note the small roulettes again), it answers questions posed by *Hermet* 1934, Pl. 49, where three similar designs are shown, apparently on different vessels, although this is not necessarily so, since many designs were broken up in his plates. *c.* A.D. 55–70. South Gaulish.

Period 3

7. Area 4, M.53. Form 37. Double-bordered ovolo with trident tip to left, turned to the left. This bowl has clear connections with the scenes from Rottweil, cf. *Knorr* 1912, Taf. XVIII, 2/6. These are like the work of MEDDILLVS, cf. *Knorr* 1919, Taf. 54/55 on Form 29. South Gaulish.

8. Area 4, M.53. Form 37. Free style design with hare O.2055; probably by M. CRESTIO, cf. *Knorr* 1952, Taf. 19B, for similar leaf, and Oswald quotes a stamped bowl by this potter from York with the hare. *c.* A.D. 80–95. South Gaulish.

9. Area 2, L.150. Form 37. Small bowl, unfortunately the vestiges of the ovolo are unclear. The leaf is typically Flavian and very similar to one on a f. 29 at Rodez by PASSIENVS, cf. *Cunliffe* 1971, Fig. 128.20. *c.* A.D. 75–90. South Gaulish.

10. Area 4, Pit M.27. Form 78. Difficult because some of the important detail has been truncated by the rim. The rider is clearly mounted on a bullock and the style is like that of the potter who signed himself OF MO. *c.* A.D. 70–90. South Gaulish.

11. Area 2, J.77 and 79. Form 37. Double-bordered ovolo with trident tip to the right, tucked under to the left. Below a wavy line there is a scroll with a large sycamore (?) leaf and a smaller segmented leaf. The ovolo may be that of SEVERVS (*Museum of London*, unpublished), and cf. *Oswald* 1948, Pl. XI.21. The large leaf, which is rather blurred, seems to be on a Form 37 at Pompeii, cf. *J.R.S.* IV, 1914, Pl. XIII.72, and Atkinson connects this with the work of GERMANVS. *c.* A.D. 70–85. South Gaulish.

12. Area 2, E.140. Form 37. Style of IOENALIS, cf. *S. & S.*, Pl. 37.429. *c.* A.D. 100–120.

13. Area 5, O.29. Form 37. DONNAVCVS style, cf. *S. & S.*, Pl. 49.577, and also *Terrisse* 1968, Pl. XXXI.207. *c.* A.D. 100–120. Martres-de-Vere.

14. Area 2, J.49. Form 37. A small bowl in the MEDETVS – RANTO style; the columns are made from large striated rods, cf. *S. & S.*, Pl. 30.365. The figure is very blurred, but probably that restored on 375. *c.* A.D. 100–120. Martres-de-Veyre.

15. Area 4, M.38. Form 37. Fragment from a bowl by potter X-2, cf. *S. & S.*, Pl. 6.66. *c.* A.D. 100–120. Martres-de-Veyre.

16. Area 2, E.121. Form 78. Feet of small lion; *c.* A.D. 70–90. South Gaulish.

17. Area 2, E.113. Form 30. Probably by M. CRESTIO, cf. *Knorr* 1952, Taf. 19D. The ovolo appears to be a narrower version of the usual one, but it has the same four-pronged tip. *c.* A.D. 70–90. South Gaulish.

18. Area 2, L.150. Form 29. Bird, O.2247 type, in a winding scroll with the tip of a large lanceolate leaf. Very similar to a f. 29 from Mainz, cf. *Knorr* 1919, Taf. 69B, by SABINVS. *c.* A.D. 75–90. South Gaulish.

229

19. Area 7, T.68. Form 37. This looks like the OF MO ovolo, cf. *Knorr* 1919, Taf. 59A. *c.* A.D. 75–90. South Gaulish.

20. Area 6, Pit S.16A. Form 37. Work by the NATALIS group; this is a fairly clear example of the ovolo, cf. *Knorr* 1912, Taf. XXIV.4, and *Jacobs* 1912, Taf. V.30. The leaf is shown by Knorr on sherds 6 and 9. *c.* A.D. 90–120+. South Gaulish.

21. Area 6, Pit S.16A. Form 30. Perhaps by PASSIENVS, who had most of the detail. *c.* A.D. 70–85. South Gaulish.

22. Area 4, M.60. Form 37. Ovolo similar to that of the BIRAGILLVS group, but without the clipped ends to the tongue. The Hercules scene is not known to me on a stamped vessel. *c.* A.D. 90–110. South Gaulish.

23. Area 2, H.42. Form 37. The thin astragali supporting the frond are shown for MERCATOR, cf. *Knorr* 1919, Taf. 57G. I have not been able to match the leaves apart from unpublished sherds from the Museum of London (Guildhall Museum). *c.* A.D. 85–100. South Gaulish.

24. Area 2, L.106. Form 37. A fine wreathed arcade encloses a manacled (?) figure, *O*.1139A, over a panel of well-tufted barley-ears. To the right, a line of small circles. A corner tendril has a bottle-shaped bud, and the panel to the right has the remains of a small ivy (?) leaf, and a palm frond. A simple V-shaped wreath closes the design.

   Both the figure shown by Oswald, and that from La Graufesenque, cf. *Hermet* 1934, Pl. 23.259, seem to have "full" loin cloths, whilst here and at Günzburg, cf. *Knorr* 1919, Taf. 96E, the garments are tighter, with small horizontal folds. The Günzburg bowl is in the style of MERCATO. *c.* A.D. 85–100. South Gaulish.

25. Area 6, S.3. Form 37, SATTO style; the design is from Chēmery, cf. *Delort* 1953, Pl. 16.6226. The details are the wheel, "plumes" and leaf, cf. *Lutz* 1970, details G.18, 25 and V.23 respectively. *c.* A.D. 110–140. Falquemont-Chēmery.

Period 4

26. Area 2, L.88. Form 37. CINNAMVS style, his ovolo (*S. & S.*, Fig. 47.1). *c.* A.D. 150–170. Central Gaulish.

27. Area 4, M.38. Form 37. Basal wreath of potter X-2, cf. *S. & S.*, Pl. 20. Martres-de-Vere.

28. Area 6, R.28. Form 37. By the potter of the Rosette, cf. *S. & S.*, Pl. 20, 252, for the general design, and 268 for the wreath. *c.* A.D. 100–120. Martres-de-Vere.

29. Area 5, P.62. Form 37. ATTIANVS style, his leaf, cf. *S. & S.*, Pl. 85.6. *c.* A.D. 125–150. Lezoux.

30. Area 6, R.33. Form 37. The two figures on this piece, *O*.617A to the left and *O*.532, are connected with the work of the LIBERTVS/BVTRIO group. However, the design is more like that of the QVINTILLIANVS workshops. *c.* A.D. 125–145. Lezoux.

31. Area 5, O.58. Form 37. The column is Rogers, P76; unfortunately the draped figure is very indistinct, and one of its arms may be missing. *c.* A.D. 150–190. Lezoux.

32. Area 2, Slot J.56. Form 37 (burnt). Probably the ovolo of the QVINTILIANVS group, cf. *S. & S.*, Fig. 17.2. *c.* A.D. 125–150. Lezoux.

33. Area 5, Pit P3, 37B. Form 37. The ovolo has been assigned to a number of potters of Hadrianic/Antonine date, cf. *S. & S.*, p. 175, and *Rogers* B.24. The figure types are Pan, *O*.711A, which Oswald gives to mainly Antonine workers except BIRRANTVS, and the lion, *O*.1378, which is attributed to SACER and CINNAMVS. Rogers points to the use of the ovolo on bowls in the early CINNAMVS style, following Hartley in *Wacher* 1969, pp. 125–6 on Fig. 49.42 and cf. *May* 1930, Pl. XXIII.151. Hartley refers to a redness about the fabric of the Brough bowl, which is very noticeable on this one too, and takes it out of the range of Lezoux products. Vichy seems a reasonable bet. *c.* A.D. 145–160. Terre-Franche.

34. Area 5, P.48. Form 37. Rogers ovolo B.24 on a piece of Hadrianic date. The style approximates to that of SACER or ATTIANVS. *c.* A.D. 125–145. Lezoux.

35. Area 2, Pit. L.75. Form 37. BVTRIO style; his ovolo, cf. *S. & S.*, Fig. 13.3; lion, *O*.1369; stag, *O*.1805; goat, *O*.1834; sheep, *O*.1868 and horse, *O*.1894. An unidentified human figure wields a club (Hercules?) and there is a small lion to the left, which is not in Oswald. *c.* A.D. 120–140. Lezoux.

36. Area 5, O.53 and O.22. Form 37. Double-bordered ovolo with spine to central moulding. Below, two gladiators. The detail is a little indistinct, coming from a worn mould, but the ovolo looks like one shown from Lavoye (cf. *Fölzer*, Die Bilderschüsseln der Ostgallischen Sigillata-Manufakturen, Bonn, 1913, Taf. XXVIII.462) and the gladiator is similar to 342 (*ibid.*). Spirals were common at Lavoye and 424 (*ibid.*) is close. Oswald (*J.R.S.* XXXV, pp. 49–57) does not show these details from his collection emanating from M. G. Chenet, and the identification is tentative, prob. Antonine, Lavoye.

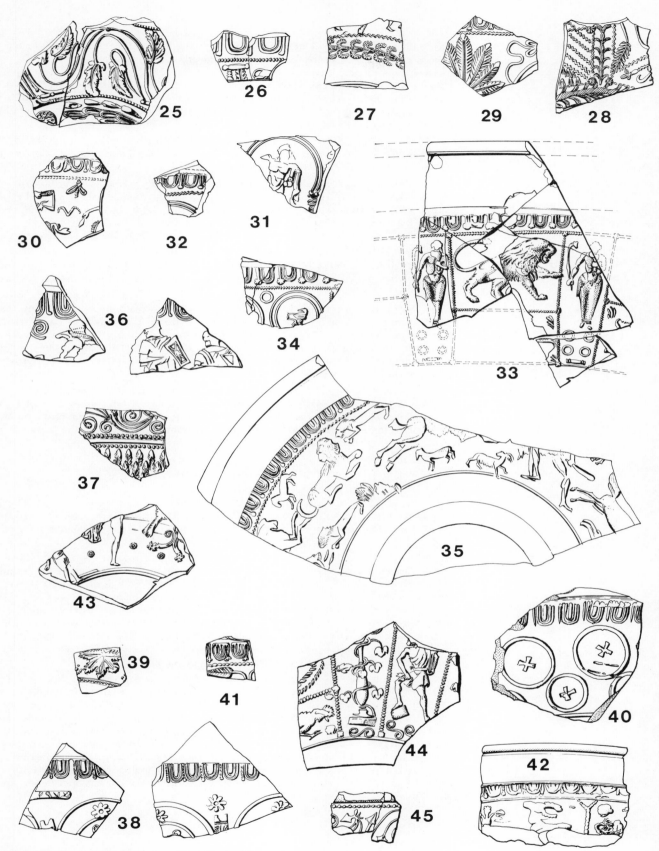

Fig. 10.11 The figured Samian wares, Nos. 25–45 ($\frac{1}{4}$)

37. Area 7, Pit E, 94. Form 29. Upper zone: winding scroll terminating in small rosettes and four-pronged motifs. Spirals spring from the bifid tendril binding.

Lower zone: pinnate leaves.

This is a smallish, thick bowl with a brown-red slip. The style is typical of MVRRANVS, cf. *Knorr* 1952, Taf. 44A and B, for the various elements of the upper zone, and C for the leaves. Very similar designs come from Colchester, cf. *Hull* 1958, Fig. 74, and the Museum of London (Guildhall), *c.* A.D. 50–65. South Gaulish.

38. Area 5, Pit. P.37 and O.58. Form 37. Style of BELSVS of Rheinzabern; his ovolo, cf. *Ricken* 1948, Taf. 262/5. The column and rosette are on a bowl from Lauriacum, cf. *Karnitsch* 1955, Taf. 46.6. *c.* A.D. 180–210. Rheinzabern.

39. Area 4, M.29. Form 37. Style of DRVSVS 1, his leaf, cf. *Rogers* H90. *c.* A.D. 100–120.

40. Area 2, G.29. Form 37. This is a very late piece from East Gaul, either by JVLIVS II or JVLIANVS I of Rheinzabern, cf. *Ricken* 1948, Taf. 262.23, for the ovolo and *Karnitsch* 1955, Taf. 98, for the general design. *c.* A.D. 200–230. Rheinzabern.

41. Area 2, L.113. Form 37. Ovolo of CRVCVRO, cf. *Knorr* 1919, Taf. 29.17; the small leaf is shown by *Hermet*, Pl. 82.1. *c.* A.D. 85–100. South Gaulish.

42. Area 7, Ditch A1–N. Form 37. Very blurred. The stag is not in Oswald, and in the absence of a decent ovolo impression the style can be noted as that connected with potters X–5 and 6. *c.* A.D. 125–145. Lezoux.

43. Area 2, Slot L.12. Form Drag 11. Small portion of straight wreath immediately below the rim. It appears to be of poppy-heads or pomegranates. The design is not shown by *Oxe* (Arretinische Reliefgefasse vom Rhein, *Materialen zur Rom-Germ. Keramik*, Heft. 5, 1933), nor in Dragendorff-Watzinger (*Arretinische Relief Keramik*, Reutlingen, 1948). In fact the use of this motif seems fairly rare on true Arretine ware, and it may be a late addition to the repertoire for wreaths. *c.* Augustan-Tiberian, Arezzo.

44. Area 7, Ditch A1–N. Form 37. Style of potter X–6 and/or the Large S potter, cf. *S. & S.*, p. 148. The large ornament, Rogers Q5, and small cockerel, *O.*2346A type, are shown on *S. & S.*, Pls. 76.33 and 74.5 respectively. The Vulcan, *O.*66 without tongs, is common to a number of Hadrianic-Antonine workers. The bead rows are more suggestive of the Large S style. *c.* A.D. 125–145. Lezoux.

45. Area 2, L.111. Form 29. Upper zone fragments, very like those of CRESTIO, cf. *Van Giffen* (Jaarverslag van de Vereeniging voor Terpenonderzoek, XXV–XXIII), Afb. 56.5. *c.* A.D. 45–60. South Gaulish.

46. Area 2, Pit L.102 and E.73. Form 37. Three sherds, probably from the same vessel. The ovolo is that of the BIRAGILLVS group, as are the birds, cf. *Knorr* 1919, Taf. 16, details 9, 10 and 16. The swag with four lobes appears on two f. 37's to be published from Winchester in the style of MERCATOR. *c.* A.D. 80–100. South Gaulish.

47. Area 4, M.60. Form 29. Lower zone: straight wreath above rows of cogged medallions containing thirteen-petalled rosettes. Upright poppy-heads on small stands separate the medallions.

BASSVS and COELVS, MEDDILLVS and SENO (SENNO ?), all used the wreath, and a similar rosette, cf. *Knorr* 1952, Taf. 58. However, although the medallion is shared between the first two workshops, the rosette used by BASSVS and COELVS consistently appears to be larger, some 18 mm to 16 mm, and as a result, on their designs there is very little clearance with the medallion. This sherd has the smaller version and is probably to be associated with either of the other workers, who both have curiously disparate styles over their working spans, cf. *Knorr* 1919, Taf. 78A and B. *c.* A.D. 50–65. South Gaulish.

48. Area 2, E.73 and Pit E.70. Form 37. Large bowl in dark-red, well-fired slip, with slightly coarse red-orange fabric. The panel decoration has a large medallion containing a boar, *O.*1664, together with a warrior. There is a large striated rod used as a candelabrum based on a fruit-basket with dolphins. The piece appears to have connections with those shown for CALETVS and SEVERVS, cf. *S. & S.*, Pl. 128.3, who themselves seem to have shared work with CASTRIVS ? IVLLINVS and SERVVS II. This should be compared with the piece described by Hartley from Mumrills (Steer, *Ant. Scot.*, Vol. XCIV, p. 101.3), where the long striated rods and a very similar fabric provide a parallel. The figure-types appear in the work of SACER, and presumably the design belongs to an early Antonine mould-maker. *c.* A.D. 140–160. Lezoux.

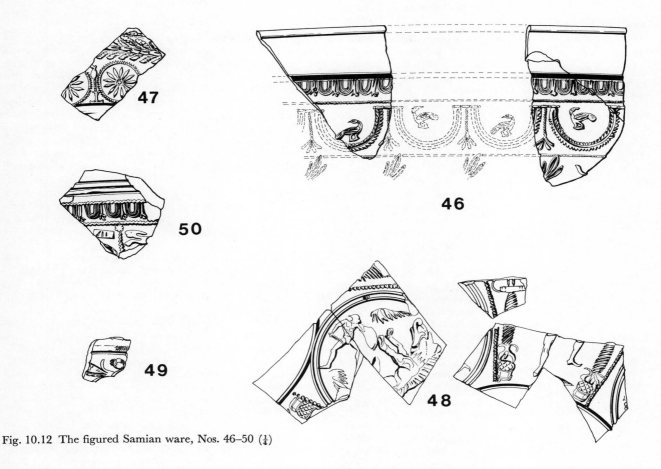

Fig. 10.12 The figured Samian ware, Nos. 46–50 (¼)

49. Area 2, G.125. Form Drag. 11. Part of the lower decorated surface of a South Gaulish crater. These vessels have not yet been published as fully as they deserve (cf. *Oxé, ante, op. cit.*). Recently, considerable quantities of fragments have been discovered in the excavations of Balsan and Vernhet at La Graufesenque, including moulds for the production of the vessels known from Bregenz (cf. *Knorr* 1919, Taf. 1–4). However, for the most part these are without animals or humans, but note the leaping lion on Taf. 3P, the claws of which are very similar to those on the present vessel. The two figures are not shown by Oswald, one appears to be playing a double-flute (the position of the legs is characteristic of the type). The fabric is standard South Gaulish. Tiberio-Claudian, South Gaulish.

50. Area 2, Pit E.84. Form 37. The ovolo is similar to the BIRAGILLVS group's trident-tipped, clipped ends type, but the tongue is curved to fit around the egg, and is not straight like theirs. A very blurred label stamp reads NIC or NIO. The fabric is red-orange and the amount of mica in the paste suggests that the piece may have been made away from La Graufesenque. *c.* A.D. 90–115 ?.

[1] My thanks are due to Prof. Howard Comfort for the comments upon which this note is based.

See Fig. 10.13 for interpretation

The Samian Stamps

by B. R. Hartley and Brenda Dickinson

1. Aisius incomplete, 1, 33, *Area 2, E.70*, (93), Lezoux.[3] This is the only known example of the stamp. Aisius was a minor Lezoux potter who produced a surprisingly wide range of forms, including 27, 31, 31R, 33, 80 and 81. Ninety-three examples of one of his stamps were in a group of samian from a shop at Bregenz, together with stamps of early- to mid-Antonine potters (*Jahresheft 26* (1930), Beib. Coll. 124). *c.* A.D. 140–175, Period 4.

2. Albinus ii, 8c, 33, *Area 3, Pit W.9*, (2134), Lezoux.[2] From one of Albinus's less common dies, this stamp has not been noted in dated contexts. However, other stamps of his are known from sites on the Antonine Wall, Halton Chesters, the Rhineland and from a group of burnt samian from Gauting of mid-Antonine date. His forms include 18/31 and 27. *c.* A.D. 150–180. Residual.

3. Amandus i, 1b, 18, *Area 2, L.131*, Montans.[2] There is only one other recorded example of the stamp, but as Amandus i is known to have made forms 16 and 17, a Tiberio-Claudian date is almost certain. Residual.

4. Amandus ii, 14a (form not noted), *Area 2, E.129*, (287), La Graufesenque.[2] This stamp was probably only used on Form 29 (with decoration belonging to the Claudio-Neronian period). Other stamps of his occur at Brecon (a survival ?), Camulodunum, in the Cirencester fort ditch, at Fishbourne (Per. 1B) and Usk and on Forms Ritt. 8, 16 and 24. *c.* A.D. 50–65. Residual.

5. Ardacus 15d Ritt. 8, *Area 7, D.45*, La Graufesenque.[2] A unique stamp, perhaps with the full reading ARDA, to judge by the spacing of the letters within the frame. Ardacus can be placed in the Claudio-Neronian period on the evidence of his decorated ware and he made many pre-Flavian forms, including Ritt. 1, Ritt. 8, Ritt. 9, 16 and 24. His stamps occur at Camulodunum and Hofheim. *c.* A.D. 45–60. Period 1.

6. Asiaticus ii, 2a, 33, *Area 2, G.40*, (359), Lezoux.[1] Although one of Asiaticus's stamps has been noted on Form 27, his main output is from the later Antonine period and includes Forms 79 and 80. His stamps are known from Catterick and South Shields. *c.* A.D. 150–180. Period 4.

7. Avitus iii, 1c, 18/31, *Area 2, Pit L.75*, Lezoux.[2] Avitus's stamps are common at sites in Antonine, Scotland, and this particular one occurs at Ardoch. His main output was Forms 18/31, 18/31R and 27, but he also produced mainly Hadrianic decorated ware. *c.* A.D. 120–150. Period 4.

8. Avitus iii, 1g, 31, *Area 2, G.29*, (414), Lezoux.[2] All the recorded examples of this stamp are either on Form 18/31 or 31, and there is one from Corbridge. *c.* A.D. 125–155. Residual.

9. Avitus iii, 7a, 18/31, *Area 2, J.57*, (678), Lezoux.[2] The stamp, always on dishes, occurs twice at Camelon, at Inveresk and three times at Newstead. *c.* A.D. 125–155. Period 4.

10. Balbus i, 2a, 18, *Area 2, G.186*, (624), La Graufesenque.[3] This stamp appears at Camulodunum and Hofheim and another one at Aislingen. To judge by his decoration on Form 29, his likely date is *c.* A.D. 45–60. Period 2.

11. Banoluccus 1e, 18/31, *Area 2, Pit L.75*, Lezoux.[2] This stamp occurs twice in a mid-Antonine pit at Alcester, as well as at Balmuildy and Newstead. Banoluccus's forms include 18/31, 18/31R, 31 and 80. *c.* A.D. 150–180. Period 4.

12. Belsa i Arve (rnicus ?) 1a, 79 ?, *Area 3, Pit Y3* (2066), Lezoux.[1] There are three examples of the stamp in the Pudding Pan Rock wreck and it has been recorded from Catterick, Halton Chesters and South Shields and on Forms 31R and 79R. *c.* A.D. 165–200. Residual.

13. Bollus 2a, 15/17 or 18, *Area 2, Slot 24A*, (930), La Graufesenque,[3] Montans.[3] Bollus may have been one of the few potters who migrated from one factory to another, but the die for this stamp was probably used only at La Graufesenque. It is known at Camulodunum and Hofheim. There is only slight evidence for his date, but the likely range is *c.* A.D. 45–65. Period 2.

14. Calendio 4a (form not noted), *Area 2, Pit L.66*, (872), Lezoux.[1] This stamp has been noted on Forms 18/31, 27 and 81 and another of his stamps comes from Balmuildy. *c.* A.D. 140–170. Residual.

15. Calvus i, 8d, 29, *Area 2, H.26*, (521), La Graufesenque.[1] The Nijmegen fortress has produced three examples of this stamp, which is likely to be one of his earlier ones. *c.* A.D. 65–85. Period 3.

16. Cantus 11d, probably 24, *Area 2, L.131*, (948), La Graufesenque.[2] A rare stamp, with only one other recorded example. Cantus worked in the Tiberio-Neronian period, making forms including Ritt. 1, 5, 8 and 9. Loeschcke 11, 17R, 24 and 29. *c.* A.D. 40–60. Residual ?.

234

17. Caratillus 2a, 18/31, *Area 4, Pit M.32*, (1181), Lezoux.[1] The stamp occurs at Birrens (in Antonine 1), Camelon and South Shields and on Forms 18/31, 27, 31, 46 and 80. His other stamps come from the Castleford Pottery Shop of A.D. 140–150 and the Pudding Pan Rock wreck, so his active life was lengthy. This one is probably to be dated *c.* A.D. 150–180. Residual.

18. A. (?) Co(sius ?) Iucundus 1a, 18R, *Area 7, B.10*, La Graufesenque.[3] This stamp has been noted from Newstead. His output seems to be entirely Flavian or later, and other stamps of his occur at Caerleon, Chester and Rottweil-Hochmauren. *c.* A.D. 80–100. Residual.

19. A. (?) Co(sius ?) Iucundus 1b, probably 27g, *Area 2, J.54*, (674), La Graufesenque.[3] A badly impressed stamp, probably from this die. It is not known from dated contexts. *c.* A.D. 80–110. Period 3.

20. Cosius Rufinus 12b, 27g, *Area 7, E.70*, La Graufesenque.[2] All the recorded examples of this stamp are on Form 27. It occurs three times in the Nijmegen fortress. Other stamps of his are known from several Flavian foundations. His decorated ware (all Form 29) is also Flavian. *c.* A.D. 70–95. Residual.

21. Crestus 1b, 27g, retr., *Area 4, Pit M.27*, (1097), La Graufesenque.[1] Most of Crestus's output is Flavian, but this stamp occurs once on Form 24. It is one of his most common stamps, and was normally used on Form 27. It has been noted from Bainbridge, Hofheim, Okarben, Risstissen and Rottweil. *c.* A.D. 65–90. Period 3.

22. Cucalus 2b, 18/31, *Area 2, Oven 1*, (896), Lezoux.[1] The stamp occurs on Forms 18/31, 18/31R, 27, 31 and 33. Other stamps are known from Newstead and Old Kilpatrick and on Forms 42, 79 and 80. One stamp is in a group of samian from Neatham, Hants, with stamps of Cintusmus i and Silvinus iii. *c.* A.D. 140–170. Residual.

23. Divicatus 3b, 33 ?, *Area 5, O.53*, Lezoux.[1] The stamp is known from Malton and on Forms 18/31, 18/31R and 27. The record for his other stamps includes Bar Hill, the Castleford Pottery Shop of A.D. 140–150, Newstead and Forms 81 and Ludowici Tg. *c.* A.D. 140–170. Residual.

24. Felix ii, 2c, 27, *Area 2, Pit L.75*, Lezoux.[3] Felix worked in the early- to mid-Antonine period, as this stamp occurs at Carzield and Newstead, as well as on Forms 18/31R, 27 and 80. One of his other stamps has been noted from the Castleford Pottery Shop. *c.* A.D. 140–170. Period 4.

25. Firmo or Firmus i, 12a, Ritt. 8, *Area 2, G.7*, (355), La Graufesenque.[2] The potter's complete name is not certain. There is no dating evidence for the stamp, which is only otherwise known on Form 27 from Vechten, but the site records for his other stamps (Camulodunum, Hofheim, Ubbergen) and his forms (Ritt. 8, Ritt. 9, 16, 17, 24 and 29) suggest a range *c.* A.D. 35–60. Residual.

26. Frontinus 14a, dish, *Area 2, Pit E.75*, (103), La Graufesenque.[1] The site record for the stamp, which was used solely on dishes, includes Brough-on-Humber, Caerleon, Corbridge, Rottweil and Watercrook. *c.* A.D. 75–95. Residual.

27. Geminus vi, 1a, 45 (stamped on the collar), *Area 5, P.28*, (2198), Lezoux.[2] This die was only used on the collars of mortaria of Form 45, which was not introduced at Lezoux before *c.* A.D. 170, *c.* A.D. 170–200. Residual.

28. Illianus 1a, 33, *Area 2, L U/S*, (1001), Lezoux.[1] The only well-attested stamp of this potter, it occurs on Forms 31, 31R, 33, 38 and probably 79, and at South Shields. *c.* A.D. 155–195 Residual.

29. Ingenuus 21e, 27g, *Area 4, M.7*, (1091), La Graufesenque.[2] The stamp, always on Form 27, has not been noted in a dated context. Ingenuus's output is basically pre-Flavian and includes Forms Ritt. 8 and 29 (with decoration typical of the Neronian period), but his latest stamp occurs also at Holt, the Nijmegen fortress and Rottweil. *c.* A.D. 59–70. Residual.

30. Iucundus ii, 5c, 27, *Area 2, H.39*, (401), La Graufesenque.[2] The record for this stamp is mainly Flavian and includes sites such as Brough-on-Humber, Camelon, Ilkley and Newstead, but is also known from one of the pre-Flavian cemeteries at Nijmegen. *c.* A.D. 65–90. Residual.

31. Ivenis 5b, 79 ?, *Area 2, G.24*, Lezoux.[2] The only dating evidence for the potter comes from the forms, which include 18/31R (stamped with 5b), 27 and 80. A date *c.* A.D. 140–180 should cover his range. Residual.

32. Iunius ii, 2a, 33, *Area 7, B.5*, (116), Lezoux.[1] A relatively minor potter of Lezoux, who made Forms 18/31, 27 and 33. At Lezoux his work was in a pit filled *c.* A.D. 135 and he presumably worked *c.* A.D. 125–150. Residual.

33. Labio 3b, 18, *Area 3, Pit W.8*, (2161), La Graufesenque.[1] All the recorded examples of this stamp, apart from the Chichester one, are on Form 29, with decoration typical of the period *c.* A.D. 50–60. Residual.

34. Labio 7a or a, 18 (with a stop in the A, below the bar), *Area 4, M.53*, (1126), La Graufesenque.[2] This stamp has been attributed to Labio, although the reading is slightly doubtful, OF.L A.BE being likely. However, as the full version occurs at Hüfingen, one of the pre-Flavian cemeteries at Nijmegen, several times at the Nijmegen fortress and at other Flavian foundations, a date *c.* A.D. 60–75 is not in doubt. Residual.

35. Lentiscus 2a, 33, *Area 7, E.22*, (610), Les Martres-de-Veyre.[1] Lentiscus seems to have only used this one stamp, on Forms 18/31, 18/31R, 27 and 33. It occurs in a group of burnt samian from the London Second Fire. *c.* A.D. 100–125. Residual.

36. Licinus 46e, dish, *Area 4, M.29*, (1107), La Graufesenque.[1] The stamp, always on dishes, occurs at Camulodunum, where his other stamps are common. He frequently made Form 29, as well as forms Ritt. 1, 8 and 9. *c.* A.D. 45–65. Residual.

37. Licinus 55a, 27g, *Area 5, O.66*, (2066), La Graufesenque.[2] The stamp was used on Form 24 and, frequently, on form Ritt. 8. *c.* A.D. 45–65. Residual.

38. Luppa (probably) 1a, cup LVP[PAF], *Area 7, Pit B.68*, Lezoux.[1] The stamp, used on Forms 18/31 and 27, has been noted several times at sites in the Rhineland, suggesting a Hadrianic-Antonine date. *c.* A.D. 130–160. Residual.

39. Maccius ii, 5a, 27, *Area 2, J.11*, (663), Lezoux.[1] The stamp was used both on plain ware (including Forms 18/31R, 27 and 31), and on moulds for decorated bowls with stylistic links with Ianuaris ii. There is one example on Form 37 in a mid-Antonine pit at Alcester. *c.* A.D. 140–170. Residual.

40. Marsus 6a, dish, *Area 4, M.38*, (1114), La Graufesenque.[2] The stamp is known from Camulodunum and on Form 16. His other forms include Ritt. 8 and 24. *c.* A.D. 50–65. Residual.

41. Mommo Uncertain 3, 27, *Area 2, J.51*, (694), La Graufesenque.[2] The stamp (from a die whose upper and lower edges have been eroded, giving the secondary version 3′) has been tentatively assigned to Mommo, but has not been noted from a dated context. Mommo's general record includes such sites as the Colchester Pottery Shop II, Corbridge, Gloucester, Kingsholme and the Saalsburg. There are several of his decorated bowls in the Pompeii Hoard. *c.* A.D. 60–90. Period 4. Phase 1 (*c.* early 2nd century and, therefore, probably just residual).

42. Marranus 21a, dish, *Area 2, L.145*, (980), La Graufesenque.[2] There is no dating evidence for this particular stamp, which is always on dishes. His output is basically Neronian, though he must have continued working in the early-Flavian period. The site-evidence includes Camulodunum, Catterick, the Cirencester fort ditch, Colchester Pottery Shop I, Malton and York. His forms include Ritt. 8, 24 and 29. *c.* A.D. 50–70. Period 3.

43. Nequres 1a″, cup ?, *Area 2, J.77*, (715), La Graufesenque.[2] Nequeres only made Forms 27 and probably only used one die, which underwent three modifications as the frame became worn or chipped. This stamp is from the second modification, which has been noted at Rottweil. The original version comes from one of the pre-Flavian cemeteries at Nijmegen and the final version (1a‴) from Chester and the Nijmegen fortress. The range *c.* A.D. 65–85 should cover all the stages, with this *c.* A.D. 70–85.

44. Nequres 1a‴, 27g, *Area 4, Slot M.3*, (1102), La Graufesenque.[2] See No. 43. *c.* A.D. 75–85. Period 3.

45. NIC.. or NIO.. , 1a, 37 NIC retr. or NIO retr., *Area 2, Pit E.84*, Montans,[1] La Graufesenque.[3] Although decorated bowls from moulds with this stamp have been noted several times at Montans, the style of the decoration is certainly that of La Graufesenque, so the potter must either have moved to Montans, sold moulds to potters there, or had two workshops. A bowl from one of his moulds was stamped inside the base, after moulding, by the Montans potter L. S- Cres (cens ?). The mould-maker's name has not been established and the stamp is far from clear, though the two suggestions above are possible, with MIO less likely. It may be from a broken die, originally giving a fuller name. The trident-tongued ovolo, which is on several of the other bowls with this stamp, was also used by Florus iv (on a mould from Montans and a bowl from Southampton, with typical La Graufesenque decoration). The hare in one panel of the Chichester bowl (O.2129 ?) is on one of the bowls from Montans, as is the rosette at the panel junction. There are so many links between Florus iv and the maker of this mould, that they must have worked together, especially as Florus's moulds also appear at Montans. *c.* A.D. 90–110. Residual.

46. Niger ii, 2b′, 27g, *Area 2, E.129*, (266), La Graufesenque.[2] The stamp is from a die made by *surmoulage* from an impression of 3b, and it underwent two subsequent modifications. Die 3b′ was used on form Ritt. 8 and has been noted from Hofheim. Later versions of the stamp occur at the Nijmegen fortress and probably at York, but the later modification of 3b′ was still being used on form Ritt. 8. *c.* A.D. 55–65. Residual.

236

47. Pass(i)enus 5a, 29 ?, *Area 7, Pit E.93(B)*, (728), La Graufesenque.[2] As all the other known examples of the stamp are on Form 29, it is almost certain that the Chichester piece is from that form. Although the record for the stamp includes Flavian foundations such as Caerleon, Carlisle, Chester and Regensburg, the decoration of most of the bowls is Neronian, rather than later. *c.* A.D. 55–75. Period 3.

48. Paterclus ii, 10a, 18/31, *Area 6, Pit R.4* 10, (2229), Les Martres-de-Veyre.[1] It is not yet possible to give separate dates for the three versions of the stamp. The final version is the most common and occurs at Malton and Nether Denton, in the London Second Fire deposit and on Forms 18/31 and 27. *c.* A.D. 100–125. Residual.

49. Paternus iii, 2a, 27, *Area 7, B.4*, (504), Lezoux.[1] A stamp of one of the earlier Lezoux Paterni, which was used on Forms 18/31, 27 and 81, and occurs at Carrawburgh and Chesterholm. Another stamp is in the Castleford Pottery Shop of A.D. 140–150. Paternus iii's decorated ware has stylistic connections with the work of Ianuaris ii. *c.* A.D. 130–160. Residual.

50. Patricius i, 4b, 18 (with a faint mark between the T and R), *Area 2*, (444), La Graufesenque.[2] The stamp occurs on Form 29 and at Caerleon, the Gloucester/colonia site, Hüfingen and the Nijmegen fortress. *c.* A.D. 70–90. Residual.

51. Patricius i, 17d (possibly), 18/31, *Area 2, G.61*, (443), La Graufesenque.[2] There are only two other examples of the stamp, neither from dated contexts, but Patricius's general record suggests an entirely Flavian date, *c.* A.D. 70–100. Period 3.

52. Paullus iii, 3c, 27, *Area 7, Pit E.94*, (730), La Graufesenque.[2] The stamp is only otherwise known on Form 27, from the Nijmegen and York fortresses. His decorated ware (Forms 30 and 37) and his other stamps on plain ware, from sites including Corbridge, the Saalburg and Wilderspool, point to a date *c.* A.D. 80–100. Period 3.

53. Plautinus 5a, 33, *Area 2, J.19*, (659), Lezoux.[2] Plautinus's general record and the associations of his decorated ware both suggest mid- to late-Antonine date. This stamp was used on Form 79, but is also recorded for Form 27, so it must be one of his earlier ones, probably used *c.* A.D. 155–170. Period 4.

54. Pontheius 1a′, 15/17 or 18, *Area 5, P.41*, (2211), La Graufesenque.[1] Stamps from the die in its complete form are known from Hofheim and Inchtuthil and occasionally on Form 29, with decoration typical of the period *c.* A.D. 70–90. Residual.

55. Primus iii, 46e, *Area 2, G.68*, (416), La Graufesenque.[2] Not one of Primus's most common dies, it has been noted on forms Ritt. 8, 24 and 27 and from Sels. *c.* A.D. 45–65. Residual.

56. Primus vi, 1a, 33, *Area 4, M.38*, (1170), Vichy Terre-Franche.[2] Primus vi apparently only made Forms 33 and 80, and the only other stamped pot known to have left the kilns is at London (also with 1a). To judge by the Terre-Franche potters who also worked at Lezoux, the date range for this factory is *c.* A.D. 150–190. Period 4.

57. Prinscinus 1a, 18/31 or 31, *Area 5, O.29*, (2035), Lezoux.[1] One of Priscinus's decorated bowls with this stamp has stylistic connections with Quintilianus i, but there is also an example of it in a group of burnt samian of the late 160's from Tác. Other stamps of his occur in the Castleford Pottery Shop and at Verulamium in Frere's Period IID (after A.D. 150). Forms noted for him include 18/31, 18/31R, 27, 42 and 80. *c.* A.D. 145–175. Residual.

58. Pupus 1f, 37, *Area 5, Pit P.37B*, Rheinzabern,[1] Lovoye,[2] Pont-des-Remes.[2] Pupus must have migrated from the Argonne to Rheinzabern, as some of his dies were used on plain ware at both centres. This stamp is from a die used only at Rheinzabern, and almost always on moulds. The ovolo (*Ricken-Fischer 1963, E.25*) is well-attested for him. In view of his forms (including 31R, 32 and 40 and Ludowici TR) and his connection with Iuvenis ii in the making of decorated ware, a date *c.* A.D. 160–200 is likely. Residual.

59. Quintio i, 2a, 27g, *Area 4, M.77*, (1169), La Graufesenque.[1] This stamp has been noted from Chester and Nijmegen (the fortress and Ulpia Noviomagus) and on Form 29 with late-Neronian or early-Flavian decoration. His other stamps occur not infrequently on forms Ritt. 8 and 24. *c.* A.D. 60–75. Period 3.

60. Reburrus ii, 4d, 33, *Area 7, Ditch 2 (D)*, (623), Lezoux.[1] The stamp is known on both Forms 18/31 and Ludowici Tx. Reburrus's general record is early to mid-Antonine and his stamps have been noted from the Worcester fire and Wroxeter forum destruction deposits, in a group of burnt samian of the 160's from Gauting and on Forms 18/31, 27 and 79. *c.* A.D. 140–170. Residual.

61. Reditus 3a, 18/31 or 31, *Area 4, M.7*, Lezoux.[3] The stamp is known from Camelon and on Forms 18/31 and 18/31R. Other stamps are on Forms 27, 31R and 79R and there are examples from the Saalburg Erdkastell and a group of burnt samian of the 160's from Tác. *c.* A.D. 130–165. Residual.

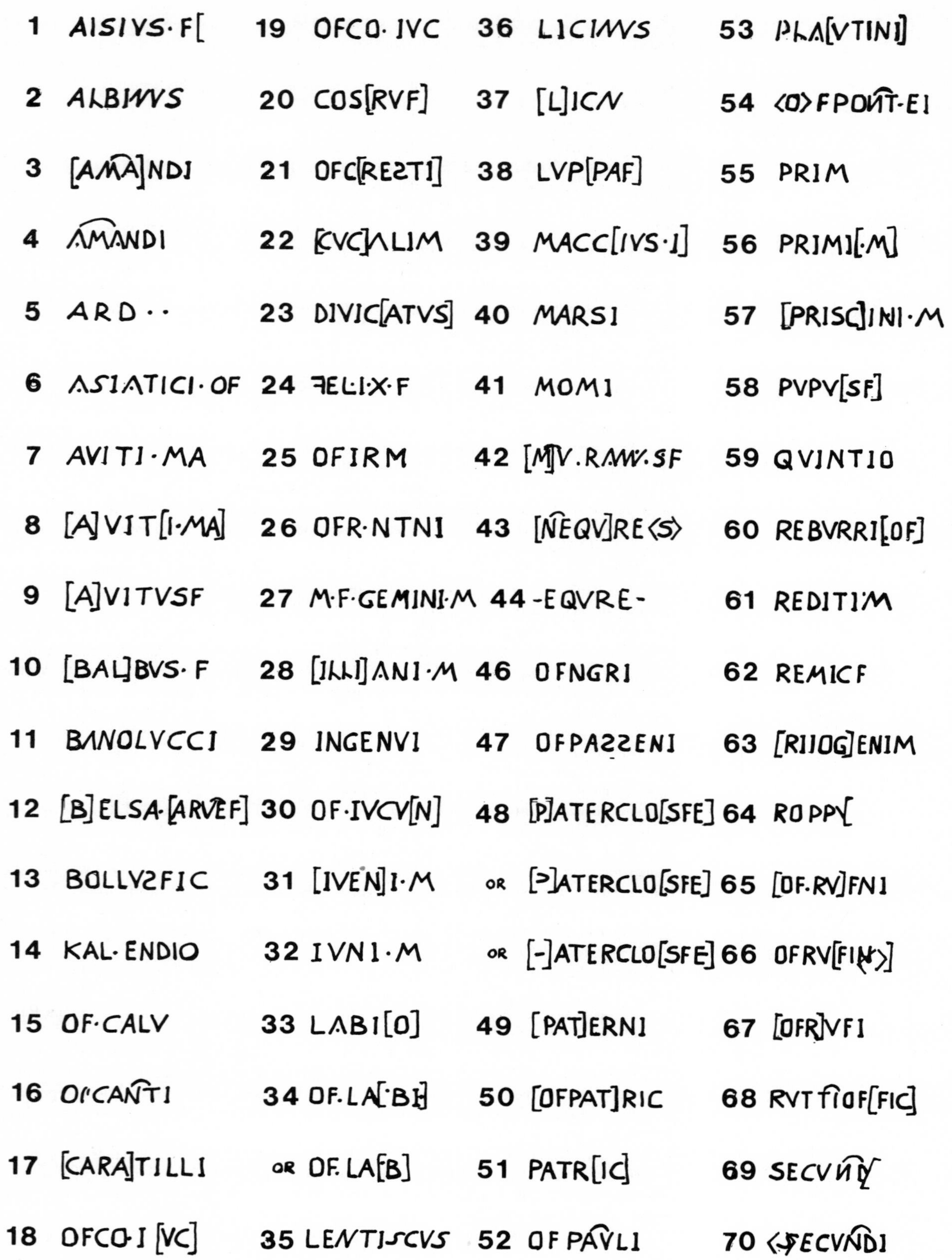

1 AISIVS·F[

2 ALBINVS

3 [AMA]NDI

4 AMANDI

5 ARD··

6 ASIATICI·OF

7 AVITI·MA

8 [A]VIT[I·MA]

9 [A]VITVSF

10 [BAL]BVS·F

11 BANOLVCCI

12 [B]ELSA·[ARVEF]

13 BOLLVSFIC

14 KAL·ENDIO

15 OF·CALV

16 OI·CANTI

17 [CARA]TILLI

18 OFCO·I[VC]

19 OFCO·IVC

20 COS[RVF]

21 OFC[RESTI]

22 [VC[ALIM

23 DIVIC[ATVS]

24 FELIX·F

25 OFIRM

26 OFR·NTNI

27 M·F·GEMINI·M

28 [ILLI]ANI·M

29 INGENVI

30 OF·IVCV[N]

31 [IVEN]I·M

32 IVNI·M

33 LABI[O]

34 OF·LA[·B]

   or OF·LA[B]

35 LENTISCVS

36 LICINVS

37 [L]ICN

38 LVP[PAF]

39 MACC[IVS·I]

40 MARSI

41 MOMI

42 [M]V·RANV·SF

43 [NEQV]RE<S>

44 -EQVRE-

46 OFNGRI

47 OFPASSENI

48 [P]ATERCLO[SFE]

   or [⊃]ATERCLO[SFE]

   or [-]ATERCLO[SFE]

49 [PAT]ERNI

50 [OFPAT]RIC

51 PATR[IC]

52 OFPAVLI

53 PLA[VTINI]

54 <O>FPONT·EI

55 PRIM

56 PRIMI[·M]

57 [PRISC]INI·M

58 PVPV[SF]

59 QVINTIO

60 REBVRRI[OF]

61 REDITIM

62 REMICF

63 [RIIOG]ENIM

64 ROPPV[

65 [OF·RV]FNI

66 OFRV[FIN>]

67 [OFR]VFI

68 RVTfIOF[FIC]

69 SECVNV

70 <SECVNDI

Fig. 10.13 Interpretation of Samian stamps, Nos. 1–70

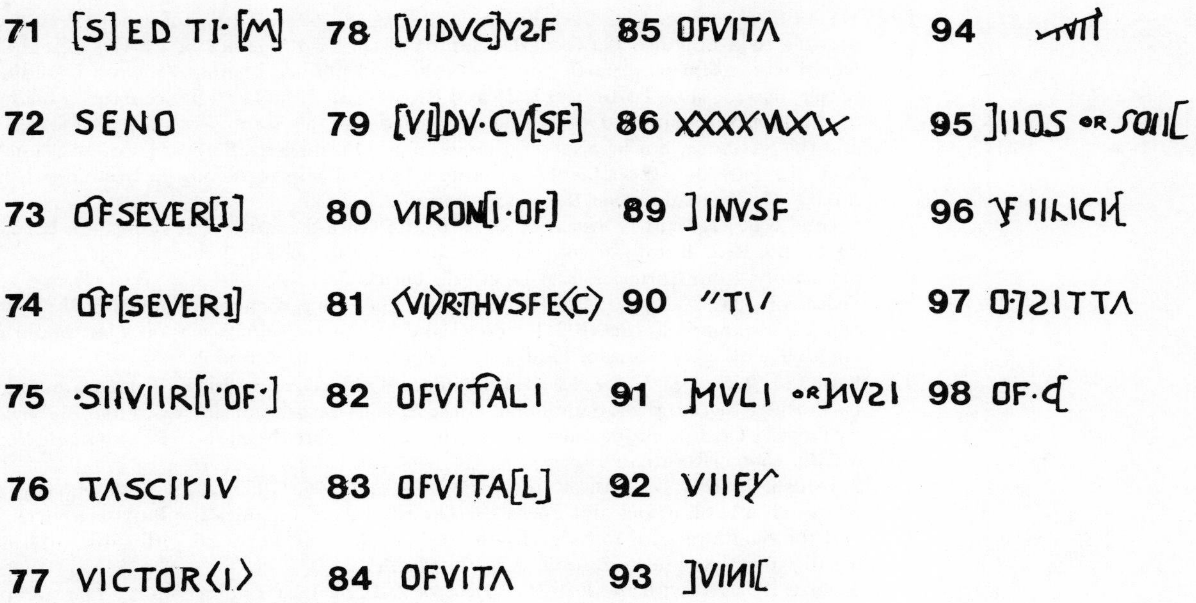

71 [S]ED TI·[M]   78 [VIDVC]V2F   85 OFVITΛ   94 ⋀Vrl

72 SENO   79 [VI]DV·CV[SF]   86 XXXXⱲXⱲ   95]IIΩS or ꟻⲀIᒋ[

73 OꟳSEVER[I]   80 VIRON[I·Oꟳ]   89]INVSF   96 ꟓ IIᒋICⱧ[

74 Oꟳ[SEVERI]   81 ⟨VⱤⱤ·THVSFE⟨C⟩   90 ″TⱯ   97 O7ꟄITTΛ

75 ·SIIVIIR[I·Oꟳ·]   82 OFVITÂLI   91]ⲘVLI or]ⲀV2I   98 Oꟳ·ꟼ

76 TΛSCIꟼIV   83 OꟳVITΛ[L]   92 VIIꟳⱯ

77 VICTOR⟨I⟩   84 OꟳVITΛ   93]VIⲚI[

Fig. 10.13 Interpretation of Samian stamps, Nos. 71–98

62. Remicus 1b, 33, *Area 2, E.55 (110)*, East Gaul[3] (La Madeleine ?). To judge from his forms (including 18/31 and 27), Remicus was one of the earlier East Gaullish potters. The die for 1b continued in use after the R was partly broken off and there are stamps from the reduced die from South Shields and Hadrian's Wall (Chesters Mus.). Probably *c.* A.D. 130–160. Residual.

63. Reogenus 1b, 33, *Area 2, H.17, (344)*, Lezoux.[1] The forms include 18/31, 27, 31 and 31R and there is one example from Catterick. Reogenus's stamps are common at sites on the Antonine Wall. One is known from the Worcester fire deposit. His name has usually been taken as Ritogenus, but there is no warrant for the reading. *c.* A.D. 140–170. Residual.

64. Roppus ii ? Incomplete 1, 18/31 ?, *Area 4, M.38, (1094)*, Les Martres-de-Veyre.[2] The only example of this stamp known, it is almost certainly to be assigned to Roppus ii, whose stamps have been noted from the Saalburg Erdkastell and the Castleford Pottery Shop. *c.* A.D. 110–145. Period 4.

65. (T.) Rufinus ii, 3a, 15/17 or 18, *Area 2, Slot L.22, (991)*, La Graufesenque.[2] Though the stamp, always on dishes, has been recorded from such Flavian foundations as Chester and Malton, Rufinus's decorated ware suggests activity in the late-Neronian period too.

  The initial T in some stamps is obscure, but perhaps a *praenomen* is in question. *c.* A.D. 65–85. Period 3.

66. (T.) Rufinus ii, 4c′ (probably), 27g, *Area 4, M.77*, La Graufesenque.[1] One of the Rufinus's most common stamps, which was reserved for Form 27, it is known mainly from Flavian foundations, such as Caerleon and the Nijmegen fortress, but there is one example from Sels. *c.* A.D. 65–85. Period 3.

67. Rufus iii, 3b, 18, *Area 2, E.73*, La Graufesenque.[2] Although Rufus began work in the late-Neronian period, the record for this stamp seems to be entirely Flavian. The sites include Baldock cemetery (in a group with a stamp of Memor), Holt and Ilkley. *c.* A.D. 70–90. Residual.

68. Ruttus 1a, 18/31R, *Area 2, Pit L.75*, Lezoux.[2] Ruttus appears to have used only one die, which when broken continued in use, giving TIOFFIC (1a′). Stamps from the original die are on Forms 18/31, 18/31R, 33 and in a mid-Antonine pit-group from Alcester. The secondary version of the stamp occurs at Benwell and Newstead. *c.* A.D. 140–165. Period 4.

69. Secundus i/ii Incomplete 6, dish, *Area 2, Pit H.19*, (621), La Graufesenque.[2] It is not always possible to distinguish between the stamps of the two Secundi of La Graufesenque, both of whom worked, at least partly, in the pre-Flavian period. Secundus i was a Claudio-Neronian potter, making such Forms as 17, 24 and Ritt. Forms 1, 5, 8 and 9. Secundus ii made Form 29s of the late-Neronian and early-Flavian period and his stamps reached Camelon, Inchtuthil and the Saalburg, but he also occasionally made Forms Ritt. 8 and 24. As far as one can judge from the lettering, the Chichester stamp is more likely to belong to Secundus i, but a date *c.* A.D. 45–75 should cover the range. Period 2.

70. Secundus ii, 22g′ cup ?, *Area 7, F.50*, (716), La Graufesenque.[2] The stamp was used frequently on Forms Ritt. 8 and 24, but an example from the original die (22g) has been identified, tentatively, from Catterick. *c.* A.D. 60–75. Period 3.

71. Sedatus iv, 2a, 33 ?, *Area 2, G.106*, Lezoux.[1] The stamp occurs on Forms 18/31, 27 and 79 (?). Sedatus also made Forms 18/31R and 31 and his cursive signature is on a jar mould at Lezoux, together with a signature of Paullus iv. *c.* A.D. 140–170. Period 4.

72. Seni 12a, 27g, *Area 6, S.4*, La Graufesenque.[2] The stamp is known from Camulodunum and on Forms Ritt. 9 and 24. Seno made Form 29 with decoration similar to that on bowls stamped by Bassus i-Coelus, but he must have started work before them, since he also made Form Ritt. 5. *c.* A.D. 45–65. Residual.

73. Severus i, 7p 18R (with the F in the O), *Area 2, L.106*, (1055), La Graufesenque.[2] The stamp was used only on dishes and Form 29. The site record includes the Butzbach vicus, Cannstatt and the Saalburg and, to judge by the style of the only Form 29 with substantial decoration, the die must have been in use *c.* A.D. 75–95. Period 3.

74. Severus i, 7s 18 (with the F in the O), *Area 7, D.28*, La Graufescenque.[2] The stamp is known from Cannstatt, Risstissen and the early cemeteries at Nijmegen. *c.* A.D. 70–95. Period 3.

75. Severus iv, 1b 31, *Area 2, E.192*, (216), Lezoux.[2] Severus iv was a mid- to late-Antonine potter whose decorated ware has stylistic links with that of Servus iv. His stamps are known on Forms 31R, 79 and 80 and from sites on Hadrian's Wall. This particular one has also been noted from Birrens and Catterick. *c.* A.D. 160–190. Period 4.

76. Tasgillus ii, 4b 27, *Area 2, Pit E.95*, (250), Les Martres-de-Veyre,[1] Lezoux.[1] Tasgillus was apparently one of the Central Gaulish potters who migrated from Les Martres to Lezoux, using this die at both factories, on Forms 18/31, 27, 33 and 42. *c.* A.D. 110–135. Residual.

77. Victor ii (?), 2a′ 33 ? VICTOR ⟨I⟩, *Area 7, C.11*, (468), Les Martres-de-Veyre.[3] There is little evidence for this potter, who made Forms 18/31, 27 and 33 (or 33a). A stamp on a burnt cup from the original die has been recorded from the London Second Fire deposit (*Ant. J. XXV* (1945), p. 76). This potter will almost certainly have worked at Les Martres, in view of the London find. There is a slight possibility that he may have moved to Lezoux, but the piece would need to be seen to assess its origin. Trajanic-Hadrianic. Residual.

78. Viducus ii, 5a 18/31, *Area 2, E.105* (114), Les Martres-de-Veyre.[1] The mark through the S is not present on other examples of the stamp. Apart from one Form 42, it is always on Form 18/31, and is known from Birrens (presumably from the Hadrianic occupation), Malton and the London Second Fire. *c.* A.D. 110–130. Residual.

79. Viducus ii, 5c 18/31, *Area 7, Pit B.14*, (508), Les Martres-de-Veyre.[1] The Forms are 18/31 and 27 and the date is presumably much the same as for the last. Residual.

80. Vironus 2a, 33, *Area 2, Pit G.14*, (318), Lezoux.[1] Vironus's forms include 27, 31, 38 and 80 and one of his stamps is known from Camelon. *c.* A.D. 145–175. Residual.

81. Virthus 3a′, 18. ⟨VI⟩ RTHVSFE ⟨C⟩, *Area 3*, (2030), La Graufesenque.[2] The original version of the stamp is at Rheingönheim and was used on Form 29. Other stamps of his are on Forms Ritt. 1R, 16 and 24 and there are examples from Valkenburg ZH (Per. I) and Verulamium (Per. IIA). *c.* A.D. 50–65.

82. Vitalis i, 2b, 24, OFVITALI], *Area 7, F.44*, La Graufesenque.[2] There is no dating evidence for this particular stamp, but the output of the earlier South Gaulish Vitalis is entirely pre-Flavian and includes Forms Ritt. 8, Ritt. 9, and 24. His stamps have been noted from the Cirencester fort ditch, Fishbourne (Per. 1B and Per. 2 construction) and the Gloucester Kingsholm site. *c.* A.D. 45–65. Residual.

83. Vitalis ii, 6d, 18, OFVITA[L], *Area 7, Pit E.51*, (701), La Graufesenque.[2] The site record seems to be entirely Flavian, and includes Catterick, Newstead, Nijmegen (the fortress and Ulpia Noviomagus) and Rottweil. *c.* A.D. 70–90. Residual.

84. Vitalis ii, 8m, 33, *Area 4, Pit M.27*, (1101), La Graufesenque.[2] Used on Forms 27 and 33, the stamp does not appear in dated contexts. *c.* A.D. 70–95. Period 3.

85. Vitalis ii, 8p, 27, *Area 2, H.17,* (345), La Graufesenque.[2] Apparently not otherwise known, this could perhaps be a careless impression from one of Vitalis's better-known dies. The lettering shows that the stamp undoubtedly belongs to Vitalis ii. *c.* A.D. 70–95. Residual.

86. Illiterate 33, *Area 5, Pit O.40c,* (2049). Illiterate stamps of this type are generally from Lezoux and Antonine. Residual.

87. Seven-petalled rosette, 79 (?), *Area 2, G.38.* Most rosettes with narrow, regularly-spaced petals were used at Lezoux in the Antonine period. *c.* A.D. 160–200. Residual.

88. Rosette with twelve segments, 32 (?), *Area 3, W.15.* Almost certainly East Gaulish, to judge by the shape of the stamp, which was current at several factories in the second half of the 2nd century. Period 4.

Unidentified stamps

89. Form 18/31 or 31, *Area 5, Pit P.37B,* (2184). The lettering suggests origin in East Gaul (probably at Rheinzabern) in the late-Antonine period or later. There is a known Rufinus of Rheinzabern and this might be his. Residual.

90. Dish, *Area 2, J.51,* (676). Probably South Gaulish and 1st century. Period 3.

91. Form 18, *Area 2, Pit L.90,* (979). Probably South Gaulish and Flavian. Period 3.

92. VIIFI (probably illiterate), 27, *Area 2, Pit L.81,* (963). Small, illiterate stamps on Form 27 are usually South Gaulish and Neronian-Flavian. Period 3.

93. Cup, *Area 4, M.75,* (1166). South Gaulish ?, just possibly a stamp of Vitalis ii. 1st century ? Period 3.

94. Form 24, *Area 2, G.64,* (520). South Gaulish and pre-Flavian. Residual.

95. Form 31, *Area 2, H.3,* (532). Probably Central Gaulish and Antonine. Residual.

96. Form 27, *Area 1, Pit A.32.* Probably a hitherto unknown stamp of Felix i and pre-Flavian. Residual.

97. Form 33, *Area 7, E.16.* Probably Central Gaulish, to judge by the lettering. 2nd century. Residual.

98. Form 18, *Area 3, W.23,* (2174). South Gaulish and 1st century. Period 3.

References

[1] Stamps from the same die are attested at the pottery or potteries in question.

[2] Stamps from other dies of the same potter are known there.

[3] Assigned to this pottery on distribution and/or fabric.

Roman Lead-glazed Wares

(For an earlier discussion of lead-glazed wares from Chichester, see Volume 1, pp. 77–9 and Plates 14–16.) The sherd from Northgate (this volume, p. 7) is discussed in that section.

Fig. 10.14

1. *Area 1. A.2.10 (residual).*
   Four sherds, two from the base and two from near the base. These last two have rouletting. The fabric is oxidised to a reddish buff and is fired harder than most of the examples from the St. Pancras Roman cemetery. The glaze is brown, quite thick and very similar to the cemetery vessels and is probably from the same production source.

2. *Area 2. E.103 (not illustrated).*
   In a mid- to late 2nd-century context. Four small sherds in a similar glaze to 1 above. Two sherds are from the same vessel and have a rippled appearance below the glaze, which is pale brown on the outside. One sherd in a similar fabric with a small patch of brown glaze adhering to the exterior surface, the remainder having flaked off. One sherd with a small splash of light brown glaze on the inside, exterior surface abraded.

3. *Area 2. E.104 (not illustrated).*
   In a mid- to late 2nd-century context. A small sherd in similar ware to those in 2 above and probably from the same vessel.

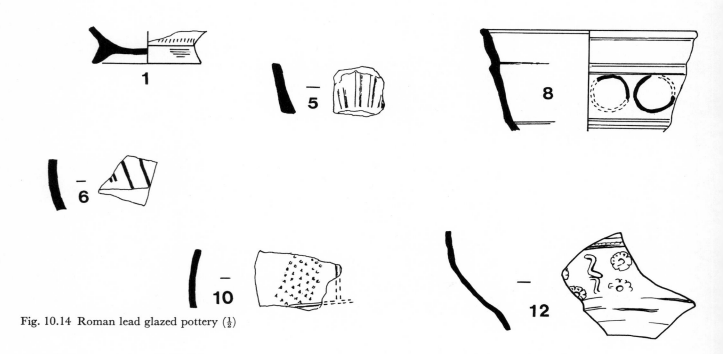

Fig. 10.14 Roman lead glazed pottery ($\frac{1}{2}$)

4. *Area 2. G.100* (*not illustrated*).
    In a mid- to late 2nd-century context. Three sherds in identical fabric to No. 2.

5. *Area 2. J.93* (from a Claudian layer).
    Sherd in a hard white fabric with an olive-green exterior glaze. Central Gaulish.

6. *Area 4. M.53* (in an early 2nd-century context).
    Sherd in a pale greyish-white fabric. It has an olive-green glaze inside and out, with a white slip decoration below the glaze on the exterior surface.

7. *Area 4. M.64* (*not illustrated*) (in an early 2nd-century context).
    Small sherd in a dark reddish fabric with a dark green glaze on both surfaces. This could easily be mistaken for a medieval piece.

8. *Area 5. P.70* (from a late Antonine layer).
    Two sherds from a vessel in a grey ware with a dark green glaze on both surfaces and with white slip decoration in the form of circles below the glaze. Similar to a vessel from Staines.[1]

9. *Area 2. H.45* (*not illustrated*) (in an early Flavian pit).
    Small body sherd from a vessel in a white fabric with a pale green exterior glaze. Central Gaulish.

10. *Area 7. Pit E.72* (residual).
    Body sherd from a small globular rough cast beaker in a similar glaze and fabric to No. 9, but glazed internally as well. Central Gaulish.

11. *Area 2. Pit E.84* (*not illustrated*) (from an Antonine pit).
    Body sherd from a vessel in similar glaze and fabric to No. 1. Exterior only glazed.

12. *Area 7. C.11* (from the Thermae robbing levels).
    Body sherd from a flagon in fine white ware with pale green external glaze. Central Gaulish, Dechelette 60.[2]

References

[1] Arthur, P., forthcoming.
[2] I am indebted to Mr. Paul Arthur for identification of this and other imported lead-glazed wares from Chichester.

The Amphorae

Fig. 10.15

I am most grateful to Dr. D. P. S. Peacock who kindly examined all the amphorae from the sites and identified the following pieces:

1. (*1032*). *Area 2, Pit L.99.* Stamped handle from a Dressel 20. These have their origin along the Guadalquivir River between Seville and Cordoba and would have held olive oil. There is a wide date range from *c.* mid 1st century to the 3rd/4th centuries for these vessels.
2. (*684*). *Area 2, J.62.* Stamped handle from a Dressel 20 (see No. 1).
3. (*512*). *Area 2, Kiln G.2.* Amphorae rim stamped AVALER from a Dressel 1B. Italian made; *c.* 10 B.C. to A.D. 10 at the latest. This should be considered in conjunction with the Arretine wares (G. Dannell, pp. 00–00).
4. (*126*), *Area 2, E.14.* Handle, stamped QCR.
5. *Area 5, P.48.* Amphora sherd in a fine pink fabric.
6. *Area 2, J.45.* Rim in sandy-reddish fabric.
7. *Area 7, Ditch A.1* (*J*). Fine reddish fabric.
8. *Area 2, H.45.* Base in a sandy-pink buff fabric.
9. *Area 2, Gulley K.1.* Rim in a very hard off-white fabric.

1

2

4

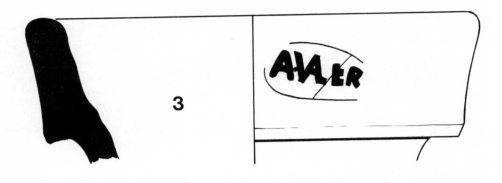

3

AVALER

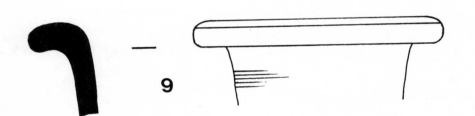

5

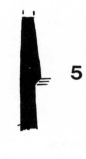

9

6

8

7

Fig. 10.15 Roman Amphorae and Stamps (½)

244

Fig. 10.16

The Roman Mortaria
by K. F. Hartley

General Comments

Out of rim-sherds from eighty-three mortaria (including two body sherds from vessels otherwise unrepresented), approximately 26.5% are 1st century, 43.4% 2nd century and 30.1% are 3rd to 4th century in date. Even allowing for possible errors this shows that, for whatever reason, more mortaria were being used in the areas investigated in the 2nd century than at other periods.

Chichester is notable for having a very high proportion of its mortarium supplies from workshops active on the Continent and/or in south-east England (excluding Colchester which does not appear to have gained a market here). There is unfortunately no conclusive evidence as yet to the precise manufacturing centres for the Claudian wall-sided mortaria, for Form *Gillam 238*, mortaria after the style of Q. Valerius Se—, Form Richborough 500, *Wroxeter 26–30* or Form *Gillam 255*, but all have in common the fact that they were almost certainly produced in Gaul or south-eastern England. The south of England might be considered as a possible source for a few of these if there were any evidence at all to show any large-scale mortarium production there in the 1st or 2nd centuries. All of the above mortarium types were sold widely in Britain though the distribution of all types is probably heavier in southern England, i.e. England south of the Thames. Form *Gillam 238* seems to have been initially dispersed by coastal traffic to judge from its distribution (*Hartley* 1973, 47, Fig. 4), and comparison of this with the distribution of mortaria from the rival contemporary pottery based in the Brockley Hill area.

The only overseas source for which we may be reasonably certain is the Soller workshop in the Rheinland (*Gillam 272*). There is evidence from excavations on the Thames waterfront (publication forthcoming by the Department of Urban Archaeology, London Museum), that mortaria from Soller were imported there. Presumably some were then taken by road to Chichester. The distribution pattern for these mortaria is noticeably similar to the distribution of *Gillam 255*, Richborough 500 and *Wroxeter 26–30* and it could perhaps be a normal distribution pattern for mortaria imported at London. In fact at least three-quarters and probably more of the 1st-century mortaria in this sample are from south-east England or/and Gaul. In the 2nd century 13.8% can be attributed to the Rheinland while another 25% could be imports making 48.8% in all. Another 25% are from kilns at or near Wiggonholt and most of the rest are from other sources in the south, south-west, with one mortarium probably from Kent. Amazingly, only 8.3% of the 2nd-century mortaria and none of the 1st-century ones are from the extensive and very important potteries south of Verulamium and including kilns at Brockley Hill, Radlett, Verulamium itself and Bricket Wood. This is in complete contrast to the picture at London and in central and northern England. The high local production at or near Wiggonholt is in keeping with most other parts of Roman Britain where there was a great deal of local production of mortaria on a small scale at this time. The large potteries seem to have made it uneconomic to continue in production.

The wall-sided mortarium made at Soller (*Gillam 272*) would certainly not have been imported before A.D. 150 and they continued to be produced in the early years of the 3rd century, possibly even up to A.D. 250. There were also small supplies from Oxford and perhaps even locally in this period but by A.D. 250 the Oxford potteries had reached their peak of production and until A.D. 400 they kept a large share of the Chichester market. In the 4th century they virtually shared this market with the New Forest potters who though not important outside the south of England were able to develop a healthy regional market extensive enough to include Chichester.

The particular interest in this sample of Chichester mortaria lies in the illustration it provides of the range of mortaria available in this part of southern England and in the contrast it provides with samples from settlements north of the Thames. It has long been known that the south is very deficient in numbers of stamped mortaria. It is possible to suggest that this could be because the area was importing mortaria to a greater extent than was the case elsewhere and that these mortaria came from workshops where the stamping of mortaria was not as rigorously practised as it was in Britain.

Stamped Mortaria

1. *Area 7*

   Pit E.76. A burnt mortarium in granular, slightly pinkish-cream fabric with a few black and white trituration grits. The two-line stamp (CAS/TVS) is from one of the six dies of Castus. Castus worked at Radlett in Hertfordshire within the period A.D. 95–140 (*Verulamium I*, 374, No. 15), but this rim-profile can confidently be attributed to A.D. 110–140.

245

2. *Area 7. Ditch A.1(N)*
Two fragments probably from the same well worn mortarium in granular, greyish cream fabric with brownish pink core and buff slip fired to orange-brown in places; some flint, red-brown and quartz trituration grit survives. The fragmentary stamp preserves part of the top border from one of the dies of Melus 1 who worked at Brockley Hill, Middx. *c.* A.D. 95–135 (*Verulamium I*, 376, No. 28). *Not illustrated.*

Unstamped Mortaria

Claudian wall-sided mortaria

This general type was ubiquitous in the Augustan-Claudian period in at least those western parts of the Empire which were dominated by the army. None of the production sites for the normal types are known but the differing fabrics used suggest that they were manufactured in several different areas. The clays used in those found in Britain suggest that the major places of manufacture would be on the Continent, probably in Gallia Belgica and even in south-eastern Britain.

Production of these early wall-sided mortaria was superseded by *c.* A.D. 50 though single examples are known to have survived in use at the Lunt and at Usk, both sites of Neronian foundation.

3. *Area 3. A.11*
A wall-sided mortarium in slightly sandy cream fabric. This is exactly paralleled by a mortarium from Richborough (*Richborough IV*, No. 489). The thick bead and undercut collar of this example probably indicates that it was certainly not made earlier than the Claudian period. *Not illustrated.*

4. *Area 5. P.35*
Two joining fragments from a worn wall-sided mortarium in fine, peachy-brown fabric with concentric scoring on the inside and on the outside of the collar. There was probably never any trituration grit. This should certainly be of earlier manufacture than No. 3.

5. *Area 2. E.103*
A wall-sided mortarium in very hard, red-brown fabric with a very thick dark grey core extending almost to the surface; the clay is so heavily laced with flint, quartz and dark grey grit, that the surface is speckled with the tempering grit. The unusual fabric, more normal in other coarse wares suggests that it may be of British manufacture and possibly made quite locally.

Flanged mortaria of pre-Flavian origin

Flanged mortaria superseded the earlier wall-sided current in Britain by about A.D. 50. The mortaria of the period A.D. 50–65 show great variety of rim-form and fabric and only one production centre, which continued into the Flavian period, because outstandingly important (see Nos. 9–11). They may have been made in many local and relatively unimportant workshops and a large proportion were almost certainly made by the army.

6. *Area 2. L.135 and 174*
(Heavily burnt after fracture.) Eight fragments from an unworn mortarium in deep orange-brown fabric with blackish core in the flange and containing tiny white flecks. Concentric scoring has been used on the inside of the vessel instead of trituration grit. The only close parallel I know is from Richborough (*Richborough IV*, No. 498, from a pre-Flavian pit). The use of concentric scoring without trituration grit was essentially a pre-Flavian practice among the potters who served the markets in Britain.

7. *Area 2. E.73*
Two joining fragments from a well-worn mortarium in fine, yellowish cream fabric with pink core. The clay has been tempered with sandy particles and there are a few tiny white, red-brown and grey trituration grits but there was probably never much. It can be most closely matched by an unpublished mortarium from Richborough, found in Pit 35 which contained material dated within the period A.D. 43–69.

8. *Area 2. E.36*

   A mortarium in fine cream fabric with pinkish core and a very few tiny white and grey trituration grits. The rim-profile is closely paralleled at Hofheim (*Hofheim* 1913, *Abb.* 78, No. 14), and at Richborough (*Richborough III*, No. 358). Although the Richborough example is from a Flavian context this type can be confidently attributed to a Neronian date.

Types used by such potters as Q. Valerius Se—, Buccus, Fronto and others, c. A.D. 55–80

The early date of these mortaria is attested by a group of over thirty identical mortaria, several stamped by Q. Valerius Se—, which were found at Colchester in a Boudiccan destruction deposit (*Dunnett* 1966, 48, Nos. 22–5). An overall date for the work of this potter and others making similar forms is *c.* A.D. 55–80. The fabric and grits indicate manufacture in Gaul (perhaps Normandy) or in south-east Britain (*Hartley* 1973, 47, Fig. 4). These mortaria usually have fine concentric scoring inside combined with abundant tiny grit and there is often similar scoring and grit on top of the flange.

9. *Area 4. M.38*

   A fragment from a quite heavily burnt mortarium in cream fabric with flint grit; there are traces of concentric scoring on the inside only. The rim-form is generally similar to one found at Fishbourne (*Cunliffe* 1971, Fig. 97, No. 135). *Not illustrated.*

10. *Area 1. Pit A.38*

    A well-worn mortarium in very fine pale yellowish brown fabric containing much very fine grit. There is concentric scoring on the inside combined with abundant small, quartz, grey and red-brown trituration grit. *Not illustrated.*

11. *Area 2. Slot L.4*

    An incomplete rim-section from a mortarium in fine pinkish cream fabric with flint, red-brown and opaque white and quartz grit on top of the flange. *Not illustrated.*

Type Gillam 238 and variants

The distribution of the stamps of potters like Q. Valerius Veranius who used this form points to dispersal by sea or coastal traffic. This, taken in conjunction with the fabric and grit points to manufacture in south-east England or Gaul, perhaps Normandy (*Hartley* 1973, 47, Fig. 4 and 41). There is ample site-dating evidence for his work from Agricolan sites in Scotland like Camelon and Cardean, from Richborough (*Richborough IV*, 92, Pit 125) and other sites to provide a basic date for manufacture of *c.* A.D. 70–100 although some variants may be slightly earlier or later. At least two or three different clays were used in making these mortaria.

12. *Area 4. Pit M.36*

    Three joining fragments from a mortarium in fine-textured yellowish cream fabric with flint and quartz grit surviving on the flange; there are traces of concentric scoring inside and on top of the flange. This mortarium was probably made in a workshop which produced form *Gillam 238* but it differs from them in being thinner in the flange and in the slightly curved flange rising above the bead. I know of no parallel for it but it seems likely to be one of their latest products. *c.* A.D. 90–110.

13. *Area 4. M.77*

    A mortarium in similar fabric and with similar grit to the above. The rim-profile is closely related to type *Gillam 238* and should be dated within the period A.D. 70–110. *Not illustrated.*

14. *Area 1. A.21*

    Two joining flange fragments from a mortarium in fine, greenish cream fabric tempered with tiny black, red-brown, grey flint and white quartz grit with scoring on top of the flange. *c.* A.D. 70–100. *Not illustrated.*

15. *Area 1. A.21*

    Three joining fragments from a mortarium in fine-textured pale brownish pink fabric fired to cream at the surfaces. There is grey flint, white quartz and red-brown trituration grit combined with concentric scoring. *c.* A.D. 70–100. *Not illustrated.*

Mortaria of form Richborough No. 500 and Wroxeter 26–30 (Wroxeter 1913, Fig. 19)
These rim-forms were very probably produced in workshops working in a single tradition. Similar clays were used and all are consistently found in deposits dated within the period A.D. 80–125. These mortaria were not stamped and none of the kilns producing them have been found. They are likely to be imports but the fabric could have been produced in southern Britain where they are fairly common.

16. *Area 6. R.28*
    A well-worn mortarium in fine-textured cream fabric with flint and possibly quartz trituration grit. This is almost identical to a mortarium from Richborough (*Richborough IV*, Pl. XCV, No. 500, dated A.D. 90–125). *Not illustrated.*

17. *Area 2. L.180*
    Two joining pieces from a very well-worn mortarium in fine, pale brown fabric with grey flint, black, chalk and possibly quartz trituration grit; traces of concentric scoring survive in the top half inch inside. A white deposit on the outside could indicate a slip but this would be unusual in one of these mortaria. It can be matched at Richborough (No. 500), and very closely at Verulamium (*Verulamium I*), No. 353. Horizon slightly in error, in a deposit dated A.D. 85–105). *Not illustrated.*

18. *Area 2. L.136*
    Two joining fragments from a mortarium in fine yellowish cream fabric with flint grit inside and on the flange. Close to Verulamium No. 353 (*ibid.*). *Not illustrated.*

19. *Area 7. C.47*
    A worn mortarium in fine, yellowish cream fabric with thick pink core and a few flint and quartz grits surviving. Generally similar in form to Richborough No. 500.

20. *Area 6. R.33*
    A mortarium in fine-textured, pale brownish buff fabric with pinkish core. This mortarium conforms almost exactly to form *Bushe-Fox 30* (*Bushe-Fox* 1913, Fig. 19), which is recorded from deposits dating A.D. 80–120. *Not illustrated.*

21. *Area 6. R.28*
    A worn mortarium in identical fabric with flint, quartz and chalk trituration grit. A rather stubby variant of Bushe-Fox type Type 26–30, and generally similar to a published mortarium from Chichester (*Chichester II*, Fig. 8.26, No. 110).

22. *Area 2. E.126*
    A mortarium of type *Wroxeter 26–30* in fine, slightly pinkish cream fabric with a few flint grits. *Not illustrated.*

Mortaria made in the extensive potteries between Verulamium and London (including Brockley Hill, Radlett, etc.)
23. *Area 6. Pit R.36*
    A worn mortarium in granular greyish cream fabric with flint and red-brown trituration grit and a buff slip. Both fabric and form point to manufacture in the extensive potteries between Verulamium and London, including kilns at Brockley Hill, Radlett and Verulamium. The rim-profile is very close to one used by Martinus I (*Evans* 1974, 50, Fig. 17, No. 173), who worked within the period A.D. 110–145/150. *Not illustrated.*

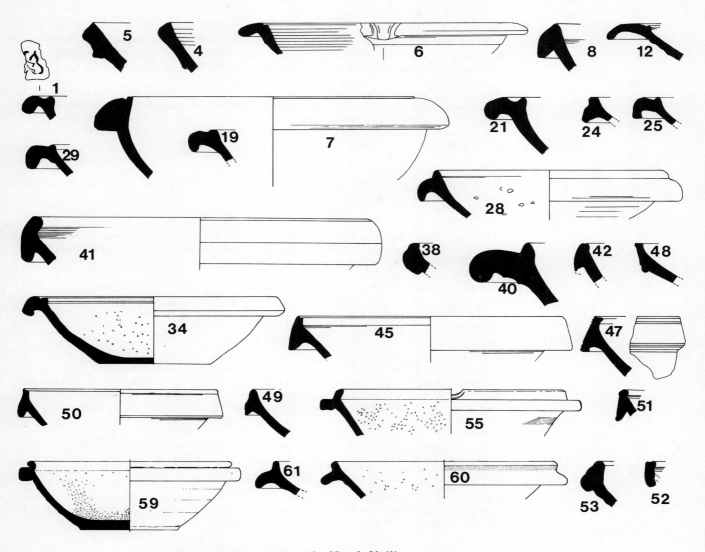

Fig. 10.16 Roman Mortaria, Nos. 1–61 ($\frac{1}{4}$)

Mortaria made in south-west England

The distribution in southern England of mortaria in rather coarse orange-brown fabric with grey core and mixed grit including quartz, shows that there were potters working in Gloucestershire, Somersetshire and possibly Dorset producing mortaria for fairly local markets. They were functioning mainly in the 2nd century, possibly continuing into the 3rd century.

24.   *Area 2. E.55*
A slightly burnt mortarium in bright brownish orange fabric with dark grey core and discoloured cream slip; the fabric is tempered with white quartz and grey grit but there is no trituration grit on the surface. It would best fit a date in the second half of the 2nd century when much experimenting took place in small workshops throughout Britain.

25. *Area 4. M.7*
A mortarium in bright orange-brown fabric tempered with tiny white grits and with cream slip; there is a little white trituration grit, probably all quartz. This was almost certainly made in the same region as No. 32 within the period A.D. 110–160.

26. *Area 7. C.11*
A mortarium in brown granular fabric with slip ranging in colour from buff-brown to grey, with grey and opaque white trituration grit. The rim-form is generally similar to those made at Littlemore, Oxon. and to those made by Melus 1 at Brockley Hill, and would best fit a date *c.* A.D. 100–135. *Not illustrated.*

27. *Area 7. Ditch A.1(B)*
A mortarium in granular orange-brown fabric with pale grey core. The profile points to a date within the period A.D. 110–150. *Not illustrated.*

28. *Area 2. Pit L.75*
A mortarium with high bead and small hooked flange in fairly fine orange-brown fabric with grey core, cream slip and flint grit. The rim-form would fit well with a date in the second half of the 2nd century.

Mortaria made in the Surrey-Sussex area perhaps at Wiggonholt
   These mortaria have a certain similarity to the 2nd-century mortaria made at Colchester in form, fabric and the type of stamps used. Production was on a small scale for local markets covering the Surrey–Sussex region.

29. *Area 6. R.17*
A worn mortarium in slightly sandy brownish cream fabric with opaque white quartz, red-brown and black trituration grit. The rim-section indicates a date *c.* A.D. 110–145 and can be closely matched in a large group of mortaria from a store or shop excavated in Castleford, Yorks., which can be dated A.D. 140–150 (information kindly supplied by P. Mayes).

30. *Area 1. A.20*
A flange fragment in very hard granular greyish fabric. 2nd century. Superficial burning after fracture. *Not illustrated.*

31. *Area 4. M.81*
A mortarium with unusually small flange in fine, pale brownish cream fabric, and a little flint trituration grit. Slightly burnt. This mortarium should probably be dated to the mid-2nd century (cf. *Evans* 1974, Fig. 17, No. 170). *Not illustrated.*

32. *Area 2. Pit G.43*
The fabric of this mortarium is quite grey with a drab cream surface. It was almost certainly made in the south in the mid-2nd century (cf. *Cunliffe* 1971, 231, Fig. 11, No. 284.1). *Not illustrated.*

33. *Area 4. M.38*
A mortarium in fine, cream fabric with flint grit. *Not illustrated.*

34. *Area 6. Pit R.20*
A worn mortarium in very hard, pinkish buff fabric with pale drab grey core. The clay has been tempered with fine sandy particles and there is abundant flint and red-brown trituration grit. The fabric is unusual but it would fit with origins in the south of England, in the mid-2nd century. A mortarium of generally similar form is published from Rapsley (*Hanworth* 1968, Fig. 20, No. 67).

35. *Area 2. E.114*
A mortarium in very hard, buff-cream fabric with pale grey core and dark brown and white trituration grit. There is a hole drilled through the body, probably for a rivet. This is very similar to No. 34 but is probably from a different vessel of similar date and origin. *Not illustrated.*

36. *Area 1. Pit A.38*

   A mortarium in fine brownish cream fabric with a little black and white grit surviving. It is probably of mid-2nd-century date and made in the Wiggonholt area (cf. *Evans* 1974, Fig. 17, Nos. 169, 170 and 177): *Hanworth* 1968, Fig. 20, No. 63). *Not illustrated.*

37. *Area 2. E.103*

   A mortarium in fine pale brownish cream fabric with pink core, probably made in the Wiggonholt area in the mid-2nd century. *Not illustrated.*

Mortaria of form Gillam 255

   These stubby flanged-mortaria were never stamped. They have a widespread but thin distribution fairly similar to that for form *Gillam 272* (the wall-sided form made at Soller, Kreis Düren) and like that form are more common in the south than elsewhere. This similarity raises the possibility that they were imported like the *Gillam 272*, but the fabric used could certainly have been produced in the south or at Colchester. Gillam dates the form A.D. 140–180, but at Fishbourne (*Cunliffe* 1971, Fig. 112, No. 296) five examples were recorded from late 2nd-century to early 3rd-century levels, and one from Rapsley (*Hanworth* 1968, 48, Fig. 21, No. 71) is from a level of similar date. A date of *c.* A.D. 160–230 would cover the possibilities.

38. *Area 4. M.7*

   A mortarium of form *Gillam 255* in brownish cream fabric with pink core and a few grey flint trituration grits.

39. *Area 2. E.97 and 103*

   Two pieces from the same mortarium in fine, cream fabric with pink core and a few small white quartz-like grits surviving. *Not illustrated.*

Mortaria manufactured at Soller, Kreis Düren in Lower Germany

40. *Area 5. P.47*

   Fragments from the same slightly burnt mortarium in fine-textured pinkish cream fabric rendered coarse by the addition of massive amounts of quartz-like and red-brown grit; no trituration grit is visible and in fact these mortaria had very little and sometimes probably none. This mortarium is identical with mortaria stamped by Verecundus and can be attributed with certainty to his workshop at Soller, Kreis Düren in Lower Germany (publication forthcoming by Frau Dkr. Dorothea Haupt, of the Rheinisches Landesmuseum, Bonn, who has kindly supplied information about the workshop). He was selling mortaria in Britain and the Rhein-land in the second half of the 2nd century. Many of his mortaria are quite huge and were presumably made for a special purpose, perhaps for use in bakehouses.

41. *Area 2. G.100*

   A wall-sided mortarium in hard, fine-textured cream fabric with cream slip. The fabric contains tiny quartz-like and red-brown grits as tempering. In form and fabric this mortarium corresponds exactly with mortaria made in the pottery workshops at Soller, Kreis Düren in Lower Germany where Verecundus worked (see No. 40 above). There is no evidence to show that Verecundus himself ever made any wall-sided mortaria but they were made on a large scale at Soller and it was a common Rheinland form, and there is no reason to doubt that large numbers of those found in Britain were imported. Rim-forms of this type (*Gillam 272*) have been recorded from Mumrills, a site of Antonine foundation (*Macdonald and Curle* 1928–9, Fig. 92, No. 34), *Rapsley* (Period II), and in a late 2nd-century deposit at *Clausentum* and production must be dated within the period A.D. 150–220/240.

42. *Area 2. L.112*

   Two fragments from the same wall-sided mortarium in hard, cream fabric with pink core and a good amount of white and transparent quartz trituration grit. It is similar in form and fabric to one found at Clausentum (*Clausentum* 1958, Fig. 31, No. 1).

43. *Area 2. H.3*

   A wall-sided mortarium in hard, creamy fabric with pink and white quartz grit. *Not illustrated.*

251

44. *Area 2. G.31*

   A weathered mortarium in hard, cream fabric with thick pink core. The fabric contains white quartz grit. *Not illustrated.*

45. *Area 2. G.60*

   A wall-sided mortarium in cream fabric with brownish pink core; the clay has been tempered with abundant quartz and a little red-brown grit. The rim-profile is close to one from Rapsley (*Hanworth* 1968, Fig. 19, No. 36).

46. *Area 5. O.58*

   A wall-sided mortarium in cream fabric with thick pink core; the clay has been tempered with quartz grit. It is generally similar to one from Richborough (*Richborough IV*, No. 510). *Not illustrated.*

   Mortaria Nos. 42–46 are almost certainly from the Rheinland and all the comments on No. 41 apply to these equally.

Wall-sided mortaria from other sources

47. *Area 2. Pit F.12*

   A very well-worn and slightly burnt mortarium in fine-textured brownish cream fabric fired to deep cream at the surface. The Colchester potters, notably *Acceptus* and *Martinus*, were the main producers of this mortarium form (*Hull* 1963, Fig. 64), but it was also made in Kent and quite possibly in the south of England as well. A.D. 170–240.

48. *Area 1. A.3*

   A worn wall-sided mortarium in pale brownish fabric with thick pale grey core; there is flint and quartz trituration grit. This is from an unknown source probably in the south of England. A.D. 150–220/240.

49. *Area 7. B.22*

   A near wall-sided mortarium in very hard greyish buff fabric with pale cream core and quartz and black trituration grit. Either imported or made in the south of England within the period A.D. 150–240.

50. *Area 2. H.26*

   A wall-sided mortarium in very pale brown fabric with a thick grey core; there is a little opaque white grit. From an unknown source, possibly in the south of England. A.D. 150–220/240.

51. *Area 5. P.62*

   A wall-sided mortarium in slightly sandy brown fabric with thick grey core; with grey flint and quartz trituration grit. This was probably made in the same workshop as No. 63. A.D. 150–220/240.

52. *Area 5. P.28*

   A wall-sided mortarium of unusual form, in sandy, drab granular fabric with pale brownish core and flint and black grit. From an unknown source probably in southern England. A.D. 150–220/240.

53. *Area 2. Pit L.75*

   (Two pieces joining.) A well-worn, wall-sided mortarium in fine-textured brownish cream fabric, with flint and possibly quartz grit. I know of no exact parallel but a generally similar mortarium is published from Rapsley (*Hanworth* 1968, Fig. 23, No. 107). A date in the first half of the 3rd century is probable for this vessel.

Mortaria made in potteries in the vicinity of Oxford

54. A mortarium in slightly sandy but fine-textured cream fabric with buff core and cream slip fired to brownish buff in parts; crystalline trituration grit. This is very closely matched by a mortarium made at Headington (*Young* 1972, Fig. 6, No. 21). A.D. 250–400. *Not illustrated.*

252

55. *Area 7. Ditch A.1(E)*
A fragment, burnt after fracture, from a mortarium in brownish pink fabric fired cream at the surface with a brownish pink slip. There is abundant crystalline pink and brown grit. This type of mortarium was made at Headington certainly later than A.D. 250 and probably in the 4th century (*Young* 1972, Fig. 6, No. 26).

56. *Area 7. Ditch A.1(B)*
A fragment burnt probably after fracture, from a mortarium in slightly sandy cream fabric with orange-brown slip with translucent brownish grit. It is very close in form to a mortarium from Headington (*Young* 1972, Fig. 6, No. 26). A.D. 250–400. *Not illustrated.*

57. *Area 7. C.11*
A battered mortarium in greyish cream fabric with the translucent grit typical of mortaria made in the Oxford potteries (cf. *Atkinson* 1941, 19, Fig. 5, Nos. 67–69). 3rd or 4th century but probably earlier than A.D. 350. *Not illustrated.*

58. *Area 6. R.26*
A wall-sided mortarium in cream fabric with creamy buff slip and crystalline pink and white grit. It is typical of mortaria made in the potteries at Oxford in the late 2nd and early 3rd centuries (cf. Rapsley (*Hanworth* 1968, Fig. 22, No. 95). *Not illustrated.*

59. *Area 4. Pit M.5*
A mortarium in fabric ranging from orange-brown to brownish ochre with slip discoloured to grey and brown, and abundant small quartz translucent grits mixed with a few black and red-brown grits. This profile with folded under flange together with the translucent grit would normally indicate manufacture at or near Oxford but both fabric and the grit, which includes none of the pink or brown shades, are out of keeping with such a source. It was, however, deliberately made in the tradition of Oxford mortaria dating to the period after A.D. 250 and is likely to be 4th century. It may, perhaps, have been made in an area adjacent to that in which the Oxford potteries were active.

Mortaria probably made in the New Forest kilns
60. *Area 5. O.48*
A mortarium in hard, buff fabric with pale grey core and pinkish buff slip with flint and red-brown trituration grit. The form points to a date certainly not earlier than the 3rd century and it would appear to be a precursor of the mortaria produced in the New Forest (cf. *Chichester* 2, Fig. 5, 10, No. 77).

61. *Area 7. C.11*
A mortarium with small, curved flange and high bead in granular, off-white fabric and cream slip; with abundant flint and a little red-brown trituration grit. Made in the New Forest potteries in the 4th century.

62. *Area 7. Ditch A.1(C)*
A well-worn mortarium in granular off-white fabric with cream slip; some flint and quartz grit surviving. An ortho-flanged mortarium of the sort produced in the New Forest potteries in the late 3rd or 4th century. *Not illustrated.*

63. *Area 5. O.48*
A mortarium with short flange and high bead in hard, off-white fabric with thick light grey core and cream slip; abundant flint, quartz and a few red-brown grits. Made in the New Forest potteries, probably in the 4th century. *Not illustrated.*

64. *Area 7. Ditch A.1(D)*
A slightly burnt, well-worn mortarium in granular greyish fabric. New Forest; probably 4th century. *Not illustrated.*

65. *Area 6. Pit R.31*
A burnt fragment from a mortarium in very granular greyish fabric with discoloured cream slip and flint grit. New Forest; 4th century, possibly later than A.D. 340. *Not illustrated.*

66. *Area 7. C.11*
A mortarium in granular greyish cream fabric with flint, red-brown and quartz grit. New Forest; 4th century. *Not illustrated.*

67. *Area 4. M.7*
A mortarium in granular brownish fabric with discoloured slip and flint grit. This mortarium was probably made in the 3rd century in the south of England. The fabric bears a notable resemblance to that produced in the later New Forest potteries and it may be that the kiln is in that area. *Not illustrated.*

68. *Area 5. Pit O.40*
A mortarium in hard, cream fabric with light grey core and flint and red-brown grit. The rim-form points to a date in the late 2nd or early 3rd century. Probably made in the south of England. *Not illustrated.*

The Roman Crucibles from Chapel Street

by Justine Bayley

A large number of "crucible" fragments from excavations of Roman levels were submitted to the laboratory for examination. The majority of these had clearly been used to melt glass as massive glassy deposits were found in them. These glassy deposits were mainly confined to the inner surfaces of the crucibles, and were often in the form of a "crust" left in a ring round the crucible just below the rim (see Fig. 10.17A). The colour of the glass was very variable, even on one sherd. It ranged from almost black through all shades of brown and opaque-red to orange. A few green and yellowish-green deposits were also noted, but only on or near the edge of the crucible. It would seem that the colour aimed at by the craftsman was an opaque "sealing-wax" red and that the other colours noted were accidental, e.g. the green seen near the rims of the crucibles is red glass which had become oxidised, changing the state – and colour – of the small amounts of copper added as colourant.

On X-ray fluorescence analysis these "red" glasses gave very strong signals for lead and weak ones for copper. One sherd (A.M. No. 697272A) was examined by H. P. Rooksby who reported that "The X-ray diffraction patterns which were obtained show that the red substance is a glass, containing some crystalline cuprous oxide, Cu_2O". In a few cases feathery crystals, typical of cuprous oxide in such glass, were seen in fractured surfaces. The range of "red" colours may be due to variation in the particle size of the cuprous oxide. Copper in the form of crystalline or even colloidal copper metal can also act as a colourant, producing a visually very similar opaque red glass. No positive identifications have so far been made of material of this type from this site.

Several crucibles had pieces of charcoal or their imprints on the surface of the glass. These would have come from the "blanket" of charcoal used to try and maintain reducing conditions while melting the glass. It appears that the crucibles were heated mainly from above as the outer surfaces show little signs of firing. Several crucibles also had small flecks, apparently of copper corrosion products in the glass, usually in bubbles or fractures. These could be due to copper added to the lead glass as a colourant, in the form of copper metal or copper oxides, and which had not completely dissolved in the glassy matrix and was hence free to corrode.

The glass containing crucibles were mostly of a shallow bowl shape (see Fig. 10.17A) with diameters typically of 10–15 cm, although many are smaller, down to 4 cm. They varied in thickness from 8 to 15 mm, the rims being the thinnest part of each individual crucible. The fabric is fairly homogeneous and fine grained and universally reduced fired.

There was one crucible fragment which contained glass that did not conform to the above description. It was a translucent deep green, and when analysed by X-ray fluorescence gave moderately strong signals for lead and copper and a weak one for iron. This sherd was of an oxidised fabric unlike those containing the "red" glass which were, understandably, of a reduced-fired fabric. The green colour was probably due mainly to the copper but likely to be somewhat modified by the presence of iron.

Included with the glass working crucibles were a number of sherds from vessels of a rather different shape. They were flat-bottomed dishes with out-turned bases of around 10 cm diameter and 3 cm deep (see Fig. 10.17B). Most of this pottery was oxidised fired. One fragment showed a distinct lip. Almost all of these sherds had a purplish stain on their inner surface which was probably due to the high temperature of the heat directed onto them from above. Some of these dishes had a sandy-looking deposit just inside the rim (see Fig. 10.17B). This varied from reddish-brown to buff. X-ray fluorescence analysis of these deposits detected only iron in small amounts; this could have come from the sandy matrix, the clay fabric of the dish or from the surrounding soil.

Fig. 10.17 Crucibles from Area 2 (⅓)

Spectographic analyses were carried out on both the clay fabric of the pot and on the sandy deposit, by John Evans of North-East London Polytechnic. He also detected iron in the sandy deposits together with significantly higher amounts of lead and alkali and alkali earth metals than in the pot fabric. On the basis of this information it is difficult to suggest a composition for the deposits which appear to be sand that may be partly fluxed and vitrified, or otherwise cemented together. It is just possible that these vessels may have had some function in the making rather than the melting of glass. One of them also had a pale greenish deposit within its thickness. This showed up particularly where the base of the pot had laminated. It is hoped that further work will lead to a better understanding of the function of these vessels without vitreous deposits.

I am grateful to Mr. Leo Biek of the Ancient Monuments Laboratory of the Department of the Environment for helpful discussions on the crucible samples.

The Later Roman Fine Wares

The problem of evaluating the later Roman fine wares from any multi-period site like Chichester is basically one of contamination. The late Roman features are all heavily disturbed by Saxon, medieval and post-medieval robbing and cesspit digging, consequently reliably sealed deposits are few and far between. The first step is essentially one of recognising the wares from the various production centres and isolating them where possible. This is attempted in the following pages.

Dr. M. G. Fulford and Mr. C. J. Young have examined all the later colour coated wares from the North-West Quadrant excavations and classified them as far as present knowledge will allow. A chart (Fig. 10.21) was prepared, showing the provenance of all types stratified in Roman layers, together with the somewhat meagre external dating evidence. Additionally, certain vessels from the main production centres have been illustrated where this has been thought necessary, and two sealed pits (pp. 262–265) have been published in full with their coarse wares.

This introductory work by Fulford and Young is important in that it points the direction into which future research on late fine wares in Chichester should go. The careful analysis of properly stratified 2nd–3rd and 3rd–4th-century deposits from future excavations should greatly enhance the value of these wares as dating criteria in the later Roman period. Much more needs to be discovered about the local colour-coated fabrics, first noted by Fulford in Volume 2, and dealt with in slightly more detail in this Volume. The proportion of these wares in the later deposits appear to be small, which may mean that the local industry had only a small share of the local market. On the other hand, discovery of the production sources might cause us to drastically revise our opinions on the origin of some of the fabrics hitherto thought to be Pevensey or New Forest.

A Discussion of the Later Roman Fine Wares

by M. G. Fulford and
Christopher J. Young

Introduction

All the colour-coated wares from 2nd century and later contexts were set aside for identification and dating, whether from residual contexts or not. A division was made between 2nd- to 3rd-century types and fabrics and later 3rd- to 4th-century forms and fabrics.

1.   Mid-2nd to 3rd century

The earlier colour-coated pottery seemed to belong to three main groups, identified as (1) Colchester, with a fine brown fabric; (2) Nene Valley with a fine white fabric; (3) Central Gaul or Rhineland with a "samian" fabric and black glossy slip. Some difficulty was met in successfully distinguishing between Colchester and the later Oxfordshire beaker and closed form fabrics. Consequently each group may be contaminated by sherds of the other. It should also be stressed that neither the brown fabric typical of much of the Colchester production in the 2nd to 3rd centuries nor the contemporary white fabric associated with the Nene Valley are unique to those two kiln centres. Both are known from sites of this date in the Rhineland and in Belgium where they are also found in forms not otherwise common in Britain.

The weights and proportions of the three early fabrics were as follows:

	gm	%
Colchester	1,100	45.6
Central Gaul/Rhineland	810	33.6
Nene Valley	500	20.7
Total	2,410	

Appropriately there was twice as much from the nearer source of Colchester as there was from the Nene Valley, although the probable British products outnumbered their continental competitors by about 2 : 1. As the colour-coated wares were studied in isolation, it was not possible to estimate the proportion of these to the rest of the ceramics of the period.

2.   Later 3rd and 4th century

Painted wares in white fabrics mostly originating from the Oxford or New Forest kilns were included in the fine wares, although the contemporary mortaria in white fabrics are reported elsewhere. Lack of stratified and securely dated groups prevented a phase by phase assessment of the interrelationships between the competing fine wares and the contemporary coarse wares. Nor was it possible to estimate the changing proportions of fine pottery to coarse overall. For the fine pottery altogether the weights and percentages were as follows:

	gm	%
New Forest	7,255	61.6
Oxford	3,785	32.2
Pevensey	290	2.5
Uncertain	395	3.4
Nene Valley	25	0.2
Argonne	22	0.2
Total	11,772	

A more detailed analysis of these figures can be provided if the fine pottery is sub-divided into three main groups consisting of (a) red-slipped bowls and mortaria; (b) beaker and closed forms; (c) bowls in white, painted fabrics.

256

(a) *Red-slipped Bowls and Mortaria:*

	gm	%
Oxford	2,700	51.0
New Forest (fabrics 1b-c)	890	35.7
Pevensey	290	5.5
Uncertain	395	7.5
Argonne	22	0.4
Total	5,297	

A small quantity (25 gm) of Nene Valley sherds was excluded from this analysis. Pottery from this source is very rare in late Roman contexts in southern Britain and it is possible that these sherds belong to the earlier Nene Valley material.

In comparison with Portchester the proportions of red-slipped wares from the various sources are very similar, particularly that of the New Forest to Oxford. The percentages compare most closely with the Portchester group dated after 345, but it should be remembered that the Chichester collection represents all late 3rd- to 4th-century material. If the Portchester figures are recalculated as if they are one group (*Fulford* 1975, Fig. 148), then, because of the greater amount of pottery from post 345 contexts, they will compare closely with Chichester. The only unusual element in the Chichester group is the amount of coarse red-slipped sherds of uncertain origin (Fig. 10.19). These were not found at Portchester and suggest that Chichester was supplied by a local kiln producing its own red-slipped pottery.

(b) *Beakers and Closed Forms:*

	gm	%
New Forest .. .. :.	4,310	73.5
? New Forest	540	9.2
Oxford	1,015	17.3
Total	5,865	

As with the red-slipped types there is close comparability between Portchester and Chichester. The comparison between the two sites is made easier because of the very small amount of variability in the proportions of this category of fine ware from the various sources at Portchester between periods (*Fulford* 1975, Fig. 146) Although there is a little less Oxfordshire material at Chichester, this might be due to some Oxford material being identified as Colchester (see above).

(c) *White Fabric, painted Bowls:*

	gm	%
New Forest, Fabric 2a	315	53.8
New Forest, Fabric 2b	200	34.2
Oxford	70	12.0
Total	585	

Although mortaria have been excluded from this category, there is nevertheless close comparability between Chichester and Portchester (*Fulford* 1975, Fig. 150). The early groups at Portchester produced several types for which no source could be recognised, but these have not so far been found at Chichester.

Summary

In the later 3rd and 4th century the fine ware assemblages at Portchester and Chichester appear closely comparable, although lack of dated groups at Chichester precludes a period by period analysis of the relationships of the fine ware sources. Comparability between the two sites is not perhaps surprising, in that Chichester is only some 15 miles due east of Portchester, even though each site may have had a different function in the 4th century.

New Forest Wares

Fig. 10.18

For type references see M. G. Fulford, "*New Forest Roman Pottery*", *B.A.R.* 17, 1975.

Closed forms: Fabric 1a
1. *Area 7, Ditch A.1(E)*. Flask, Type 1.
2. *Area 7, Ditch A.1(E)*. Plain cup, Type 53.9.
3. *Area 1, A3.1*. Base, Type 41 or 44.
4. *Area 7, C.11*. Nozzle of flagon, ? variant of Type 11.1.

Fabric 1b
5. *Area 7, Ditch A.1(D)*. Stamped bowl; Type 77.3.
6. *Area 1, A.4.1*. Bowl with white slip decoration, ? variant of Type 53.
7. *Area 2, K.U/S*. Flanged bowl with white slip decoration; Type 63.
8. *Area 2, E.21*. Stamped bowl, probably Type 77.
9. *Area 2. L.1*. Stamped bowl, probably Type 77.
10. *Area 2, Pit J.19*. Stamped bowl, probably Type 77.
11. *Area 7, Pit A.8(A)*. Stamped bowl, probably Type 77.

Fabric 2a
12. *Area 7, Pit A.45*. Mortarium, ? Type 81.1. *Not illustrated.*

Fabric 2b
13. *Area 2, E.29*. Bowl, variant of Type 89.5.

Possible New Forest types (unslipped)
14. *Area 2, G.31*. Jar; fine light grey fabric oxidised buff.
15. *Area 7, Ditch A.1(N)*. Body sherd from small ? flagon; black fabric oxidised buff.
16. *Area 5, P.37*. Jar in similar fabric to No. 14.
17. *Area 5, Pit P.37*. Base of vessel in similar fabric to No. 16, possibly from the same vessel.
18. *Area 7, C.11*. Straight-walled bowl; fine light grey fabric oxidised orange-buff.
19. *Area 2, G.31*. Bowl rim in a dark orange fabric.
20. *Area 2, Pit E.5*. Small jar in orange fabric, exterior burnished.
21. *Area 7, C.11*. Bowl in cream fabric.

Miscellaneous
22. *Area 7, Pit B.20(B)*. Bowl in cream fabric.
23. *Area 6, Pit R.31(B)*. Bowl in dirty brown fabric oxidised dark red-brown; smoothed surface inside and out.
24. *Area 2, L.2*. Body sherd from a bowl; grey fabric oxidised red-buff, white exterior slip.
25. *Area 7, C.11*. Body sherd; sandy reddish fabric, exterior reduced to grey.

Oxford Wares

Fig. 10.18

26. *Area 7, C.4*. Rosette stamped body sherd from a ? flagon; fine grey fabric with exterior dark brownish-grey slip.
27. *Area 5, O.1*. Body sherd from a flagon or beaker; reddish-brown exterior and interior slip, smoothed on the outside; pale orange fabric.
28. *Area 2, Pit E.4*. Body sherd from a folded beaker in similar fabric and slip to No. 2.

The Colchester Wares

Fig. 10.18

A number of colour-coated vessels were isolated by Fulford and Young and classified as "probably Colchester, 2nd century". A representative sample of these fabrics are reported on below, and see also those published separately in the groups from Area 5 (Pit O.40 and Pit P.37), p. 262 and Figs. 10.18 and 10.20.

29. *Area 2, G.100*. Beaker; fine reddish fabric, slip varying from reddish-brown to dark grey.
30. *Area 2, L.94*. Body sherd from folded beaker, pale grey fabric oxidised buff; metallic grey slip with white painted decoration.
31. *Area 7, C.11*. Neck of a beaker; yellowish-buff fabric, slate grey slip.
32. *Area 2, L.2*. Body sherd from beaker with a phallic motif, orange fabric, metallic grey slip.
33. *Area 7, Ditch A.1(B)*. Pale orange fabric, metallic grey slip.
34. *Area 2, E.29*. Neck of a beaker in pale cream fabric oxidised buff; metallic grey slip.
35. *Area 7, Pit A.15*. Rim of a beaker; pale orange fabric, red-brown slip.
36. *Area 5, Pit O.21*. Pale orange fabric, brownish-grey exterior slip, white painted decoration.
37. *Area 2, L.101*. Fine reddish-buff fabric; brownish-grey slip.
38. *Area 2, Pit F.12*. Fine grey fabric; metallic dark grey slip.

258

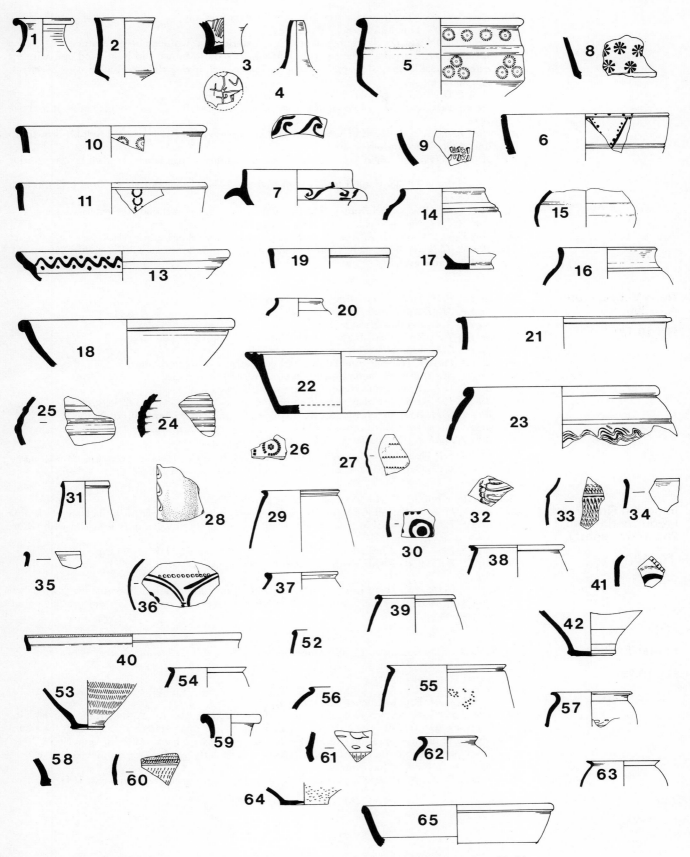

Fig. 10.18 Later Roman fine wares, Nos. 1–25, New Forest Nos. 26–28, Oxford Nos. 29–51,
Colchester Nos. 52–65, Nene Valley, all ($\frac{1}{4}$)

39. *Area 5, O.40.* Very fine pale grey fabric; matt dark grey slip.
40. *Area 5, O.29.* Fine buff fabric, red slip.
41. *Area 7, Ditch A.1(D).* Sandy buff fabric, grey exterior slip, white painted decoration.
42. *Area 7, C.11.* Base of a ? flagon; pale buff fabric, reddish-brown slip inside and out, with an exterior metallic grey slip applied over the upper part, giving the vessel a "two tone" effect. *Not illustrated.*
43. *Area 2, G.29.* Rim of beaker; orange fabric, slate grey slip.
44. *Area 3, unstratified.* Base of vessel in orange fabric with metallic grey slip terminating just above base.
45. *Area 1, A.3.4.* Body sherd of a sanded vessel in a cream fabric with internal reddish-brown slip and external greenish-grey slip.
46. *Area 2, E.116.* Body sherd from a folded beaker in a fine orange fabric; reddish-brown exterior slip.
47. *Area 3, Pit A.31.* Body sherd from a rouletted vessel in a rather soft yellowish-buff fabric with brown exterior slip.
48. *Area 6, S.4.* Body sherd from a ? beaker. Fine cream fabric, metallic grey exterior slip.
49. *Area 7, C.11.* Neck of beaker in a dark orange fabric; metallic grey slip.
50. *Area 5, O.59.* Body sherd from a sanded beaker in dark orange fabric, slate grey exterior slip.
51. *Area 2, Gulley 2.* Body sherd from a sanded beaker in dark orange fabric, slightly laminated, with metallic grey slip.

Nene Valley, *c.* pre-A.D. 250

Fig. 10.18

52. *Area 2, P.59.* Fine cream fabric; purplish-grey slip.
53. *Area 4, M.61.* Fine white fabric, dark grey slip.
54. *Area 6, R.23.* Similar fabric and slip to No. 2.
55. *Area 2, J.45.* Rough cast beaker, similar fabric and slip to No. 3.
56. *Area 2, G.29.* Fine grey fabric, brown to grey slip.
57. *Area 1, Pit A.15.* Fine creamy fabric; dark grey slip; barbotine decoration.
58. *Area 1, A.4.1.* Base of flagon in white fabric with red-brown slip.
59. *Area 7, D.19.* Rim in fine cream fabric; greenish-grey slip.
60. *Area 2, L.4.* Rouletted body sherd from flagon or beaker; fine white fabric, grey exterior slip.
61. *Area 2, G.44.* Body sherd from a carinated vessel; similar fabric and slip to No. 9.
62. *Area 7, Ditch A.1(E).* Rim in fine white fabric with red-brown slip.
63. *Area 7, Ditch A.1(E).* Beaker in pale buff fabric, dark grey slip.
64. *Area 6, S.1.* Base of heavily sanded beaker; fine white fabric, metallic grey slip. Late Roman.
65. *Area 2, E.29.* Carinated bowl in pale buff fabric; dark matt grey slip.

(See also those published with Pit O.40 and Pit P.37, p. 262).

Imported Fine Wares, Lezoux or Rhenish, ? 2nd to 3rd century

Fig. 10.19

66. *Area 7, Pit A.10(D).* Almost complete beaker in very fine dark grey fabric and glossy black slip.
67. *Area 5, Pit O.33.* Vessel in a fine reddish-buff fabric; glossy metallic dark grey slip with white painted decoration.
68. *Area 5, P.59.* Rim of beaker with barbotine decoration, similar fabric and slip to No. 2.
69. *Area 5, P.59.* Body sherds, probably from the same vessel as No. 3.
70 and 71.
72. *Area 2, G.78.* Body sherd from a barbotine beaker; fine orange fabric, metallic black slip.
73. *Area 2, Pit E.54.* Body sherd from a beaker; fine buff fabric, glossy black slip with white painted decoration.

Roman Exotica

Fig. 10.19

Dr. Fulford kindly examined the following imported wares, and his comments are below.

Argonne
74. *Area 1, A.4.1.* Rim of Chenet 328, 4th century.
75. *Area 2, E.29. Not illustrated.* Body sherd of Chenet 310, 4th century. Although the above plain forms are traditionally given the same date range as the roller stamped vessels with the same fabric and finish, there is no reason why they should not date back to the 3rd century (cf. New Forest and Oxford plain red-slipped types), particularly as they are samian forms which originate in the late 2nd century.
76. *Area 7, Pit A.10(D).* Dr. 31, East Gaulish, later 2nd to 3rd century. (Ref. *Chenet* 1941.)

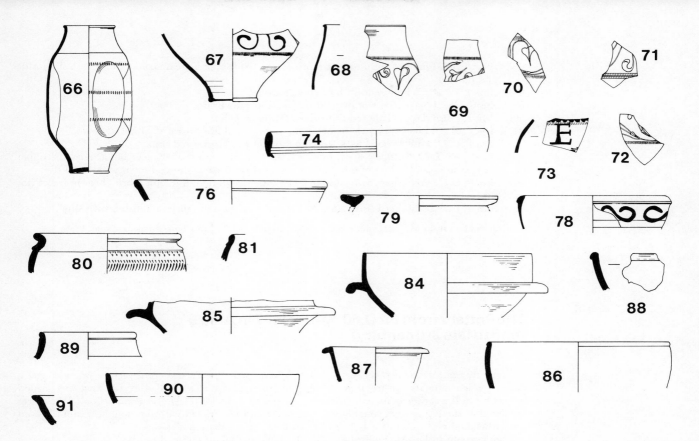

Fig. 10.19 Later Roman fine wares, Nos. 66–73, Lezoux or Rhenish Nos. 74–79, Roman Exotica
Nos. 80–83, Pevensey wares, Nos. 84–91, ? Local wares, all (¼)

"A l'eponge"

77. *Area 1, A.4.1.* Body sherd in a fine light brown fabric with red ? haematite inclusions; a glossy
marbled slip on the inside. Probably "A l'eponge", cf. M. Raimbault, *Gallia* 31 (1973), Pl. 1,
Form VI, 4th century. *Not illustrated.*

78. *Uncertain. Area 2, L.1.* Rim of a bowl in a fine, orange-brown fabric with a thick grey core; thin
white painted scrolls decorate the exterior. The fabric recalls that of the Oxfordshire red-slipped
bowls, but the overall finish is not Oxford. No known parallels, as yet.

Rhenish Coarse ware

79. *Area 7, Ditch A.1.* Rim of a lid seated jar; hard yellow sandy fabric with quartz inclusions.
This is Fabric 2 in Fulford and Bird, *Britannia* 6 (1975), 171–81, Fig. 1, 4, 3rd to 4th century.

? Pevensey Wares

Fig. 10.19

80. *Area 5, O.39.* Bowl in orange fabric, red slip.
81. *Area 7, C.11.* Bowl in similar fabric and slip to No. 1. *Not illustrated.*
82. *Area 2, Pit L.66.* Carinated bowl in orange fabric, red slip and with grid stamp decoration.
83. *Area 3, Pit A.8.* Bowl in similar fabric to No. 3; red slip, white painted decoration.

Local colour-coated wares, source unknown

Fig. 10.19

These fabrics have been isolated by Fulford and Young from the colour-coated wares found in
the North-West Quadrant. All that can be said at the moment is that they are not recognised as
being from any of the presently known production sources, e.g. Oxford, New Forest, or Pevensey
and a local source for these vessels is postulated. It is possible that some may have been made at the
other important centre at Alice Holt Forest, but current research* has not yet shown any significant
amount of colour-coated fabrics in association with known kiln sites.

84. *Area 7, C.11.* Flanged bowl; fine dark orange fabric, red slip.
85. *Area 2, K.24.* Flanged bowl, fine orange fabric, probably from same source as No. 1; red slip.
86. *Area 7, C.11.* Fine grey core oxidised orange; red slip.

261

87. *Area 1, A.5.* Fine brownish-orange fabric which oxidises to a cream colour; brownish slip inside and out.
88. *Area 1, Pit A.55.* Fine reddish-buff core; red slip.
89. *Area 3, Pit A.31(B).* Pale orange fabric; reddish-brown slip.
90. *Area 7, Ditch A1(B).* Pale reddish-brown fabric, red slip.
91. *Area 6, R.23.* Fine, very pale brown sandy fabric; reddish-brown slip. *Not illustrated.*
92. *Area 7, C.11.* Base of bowl with footring, fine orange fabric; red slip.
93. *Area 2, Pit L.10(B).* Body sherd from a beaker or jar, with a double cordon around the upper part, with a double line of tool impressions. Fabric is dark orange-brown with a red slip.
94. *Area 7, C.11.* Body sherd with stamped cresentic decoration, fine buff fabric, brownish exterior slip.
95. *Area 2, G.7.* Body sherd from a folded beaker; orange-buff fabric, reddish-brown slip.

* Information from Mr. Malcolm Lyne and Mr. Martin Millett, to whom thanks are due.

The Pottery from Pit O.40 and Pit P.37 in Area 5 (mid to late 3rd century)

These two pits are sealed by the tessellated floors of House 2, and consequently provide secure dating evidence for its construction. At the time they were dug and filled in, the area was garden belonging to the earlier house which existed on the west side of the site. A comparison of the wares suggest that these pits were roughly contemporary and were filled with the domestic rubbish from the earlier house as well as the debris from still earlier occupation levels.

I am grateful to Dr. M. Fulford and Mr. C. J. Young who examined all the colour-coated wares and classified them, including the wares from Nene Valley and Colchester and the imported material from the Rhineland and Lezoux.

Dr. Fulford in the discussion on the New Forest wares from these two pits (see below), suggests a date bracket of *c.* A.D. 260–350 at the outside, with a preferred range of 260/70–300. The New Forest wares are likely to be the latest dateable items in both deposits, as the Nene Valley and the Rhenish fall into an earlier category and, perhaps, significantly there is no Oxford ware present. The Chart (Fig. 10.21) showing the distribution of the colour-coated wares from the north-west quadrant indicates that most, if not all, the Oxford wares are present in a mid- to late 4th-century context, where it is possible to arrive at a date at all. It may well be that these two pits were just too early to receive any Oxford wares and this may perhaps narrow the gap to the end of the 3rd century.

Excavations at Chilgrove, indicate that the first quarter of the 4th century saw a big upsurge in new building, following upon a revival of business confidence and prosperity during the reign of Constantine. These events must have been paralleled in Chichester, and the construction or reconstruction of House 2 on a more grandiose scale is likely to date from the same time.

Pit O.40. The Coarse Wares

Fig. 10.20

1. Grey ware platter reduced black; burnished inside and out.
2-8. *Not illustrated.* Platters, similar in form to No. 1.
9. Dish in dark brown gritty ware, rather underfired; burnished inside and on flange and reduced black.
10. Dish with grooved rim; in sandy light grey ware with slate grey slip and burnished inside, 35 cms diameter.
11. *Not illustrated.* Flat rimmed dish, similar fabric to No. 1, burnished inside.
12. *Not illustrated.* Dish, similar in form and decoration to No. 45 (Pit P.37) but the flange is grooved for a lid.
13. Bowl in dark brown gritty ware reduced black. Burnished exterior and over rim.
14. Vessel in grey ware reduced black; burnished on shoulder and rim.
15. *Not illustrated.* Necked jar in grey ware.
16. Rim of jar in fine grey fabric.
17. Rim of jar in sandy grey ware.
18. Jar in sandy grey ware.

262

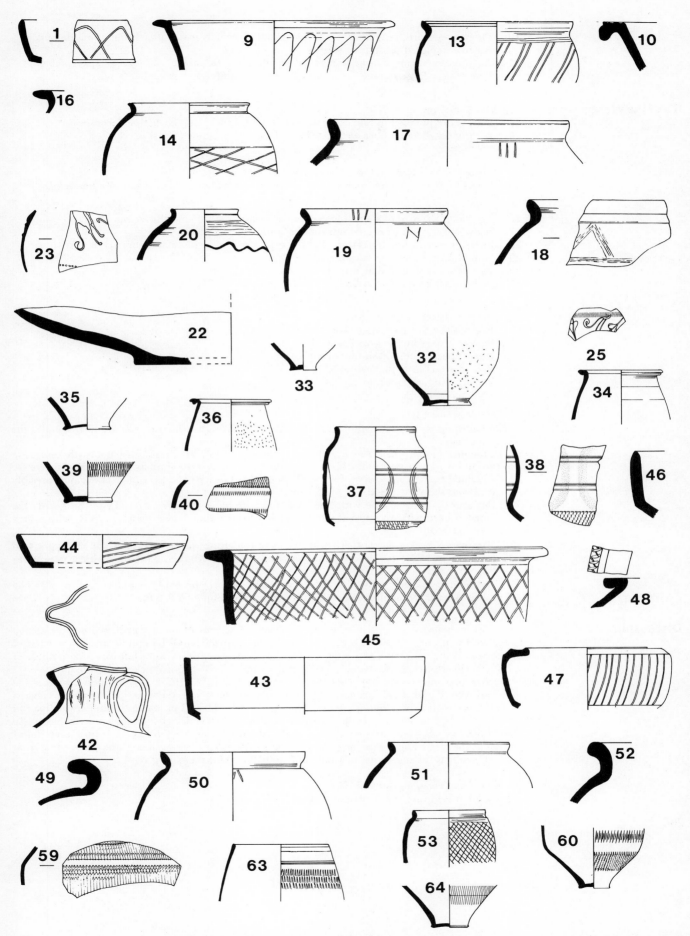

Fig. 10.20 N.W. Quadrant; Area 5; mid to late third century pottery, Nos. 1–41, Pit O.40
Nos. 42–64, Pit P.37, ($\frac{1}{4}$)

19. Jar in grey ware; tally mark on shoulder and three cuts made after firing on inside of rim.
20. Narrow-mouthed jar in grey ware.
21. *Not illustrated.* Rim of large storage jar with fingermarks inside (cf. *Chichester* 2, Fig. 5.9.58).
22. Base of very large storage vessel in sandy reddish-buff fabric, smoothed inside and out.

The Fine Wares

(a) *Nene Valley*, pre-A.D. 250.
23. Body sherd of vessel in fine cream fabric, reddish-brown slip, barbotine decoration.
24. *Not illustrated.* Rim of beaker in a white fabric with metallic grey slip.

(b) *Lezoux and Rhineland*, 2nd to 3rd century A.D.
25. Sherd from a barbotine beaker; fine buff fabric, metallic grey-black slip. *Not illustrated.*

26. *Not illustrated.* Rim of a small folded beaker; similar fabric and slip to No. 25.
27. Body sherd with fine rouletting; similar fabric and slip to No. 25.
28. Pedestal base in fine buff fabric, light grey slip with a high metallic sheen.
29. Rim of a beaker in similar ware to No. 28.
30. Base of a vessel in similar ware to No. 28.
31. Body sherd from a folded beaker; similar ware to No. 25.

(c) *Colchester Wares, c.* 2nd century
32. Bag beaker; fine hard grey fabric, metallic grey slip, exterior sanded.
33. Base of beaker in fine grey fabric, dark grey slip.
34. Rim of beaker in reddish-buff fabric, grey slip.
35. Base of vessel in similar fabric to No. 34.
36. Vessel in similar fabric to No. 34.

(d) *The New Forest Wares*
   The following notes were compiled by Dr. M. G. Fulford, to whom thanks are due; see also the discussion below:
37. Indented beaker, *New Forest*, Fabric 1a (*Fulford* 1975), as Type 27.13 but with rouletting around the lower part of the body. The fabric is hard and the slip has a dull bronze sheen.
38. Indented beaker, *New Forest,* Fabric 1a; body sherd of type and variant as above, just possibly it is from the same vessel.
39. Bag-shaped beaker; base with fine rouletting; probably *New Forest*, cf. Type 13 or 45.1; the fabric is hard with an unusual reddish quality for the New Forest (Munsell 5YR, with a grey core; Slip 5YR 4/1).
40. Bag-shaped beaker; body sherd with bands of rouletting; probably *New Forest*, cf. Types 44.6 for form and 45.1 for decoration. The fabric is hard (Munsell 5YR 6/6, with a grey core; Slip 5YR 3/2).
41. *Not illustrated.* Basal body sherd of an indented beaker; probably *New Forest*, Type 27. The fabric is hard (Munsell 2.5YR 4/2 with a grey core; Slip 2.5YR 5/6).

Discussion

   Besides an unusual reddish quality in the fabric of several of these sherds another distinctive feature of the illustrated pieces is the presence of rouletting around the middle and lower parts of the vessels. If they are all New Forest (and No. 64 is doubtful) they must fall into a date range of *c.* 260/70–350. However, 350 is the very latest date and 260/70–325 is much more probable.
   Further refinement by comparison with Portchester (*Cunliffe* 1975) may be permissible, since rouletted New Forest sherds are virtually absent there. Dr. Reece, reporting on the coins, suggests an initial occupation of *c.* 280–90, abandonment of *c.* 290–300 and probable continuous occupation until *c.* 345. The implication to be drawn from this is that in Chichester these sherds belong to 260/70–300, which would accommodate the Portchester evidence (*N.B.* There is little material of 280–90 at the fort). The consistency amongst the sherds, even allowing there is only one piece from P.37, encourages the suggestion of a date of *c.* 260/70–300 for these pit groups.

(e) *Other Fine Wares*, all residual
   Pompeian Redware, PR.1 platter, Cam. 17 – Claudius-Nero.

Samian

Fourteen samian sherds were found, of these, 1 was 1st century, 2 Hadrianic, 7 were Antonine (all Central Gaulish) and 2 were East Gaulish, late 2nd to early 3rd century.

Pit P.37. The Coarse Wares
Fig. 10.20

42. Neck of a flagon, sandy grey ware, burnished and tooled neck with traces of an exterior grey slip.
43. Shallow straight walled bowl; sandy grey ware, interior burnished.
44. Bowl in similar fabric to above, tooling on exterior.
45. Dish in brown fabric with translucent small grits, reduced black and burnished inside and out. Lattice decoration on both surfaces.
46. Bowl in hard grey ware.
47. High shouldered jar in sandy light grey ware.
48. Flat rimmed vessel in hard sandy grey fabric.
49. Large jar in sandy grey fabric.
50. Jar in hard sandy ware.
51. Small jar in grey ware.
52. Large jar in hard sandy grey ware.
53. Small beaker in sandy grey fabric; burnished and grey slipped on exterior and over rim.

The Fine Wares

(a) *Nene Valley*, pre-A.D. 250.
54. *Not illustrated.* Body sherd of a beaker with barbotine decoration; white fabric: slate-grey slip.
55. *Not illustrated.* Rouletted body sherd in similar fabric and slip as No. 54.

(b) *Lezoux and Rhineland*, 2nd to 3rd century A.D.
56. *Not illustrated.* Body sherd from a beaker in fine grey ware with slate-grey matt slip.

(c) *Colchester Wares, c.* 2nd century A.D.
57. *Not illustrated.* Rouletted body sherd from a bag beaker; reddish buff fabric; dark grey matt slip.
58. *Not illustrated.* Rouletted body sherd from a beaker. Dark orange fabric, brown/grey slip.
59. Body sherd from a large bag beaker; dirty buff fabric, metallic grey slip.
60. Base of a bag beaker; blue/grey fabric oxidised reddish-buff; grey slip.
61. *Not illustrated.* Body sherd from rouletted beaker; dirty buff fabric, metallic grey slip.
62. *Not illustrated.* Two sherds from a fine rouletted beaker, fabric as No. 61.
63. Beaker in fine reddish sandy fabric with grey slip.

(d) *New Forest Wares*
64. Bag-shaped beaker; base with rouletting; possibly Colchester or *New Forest*, cf. Type 45.1. The fabric is hard (Munsell 2.5YR 6/6; Slip 2.5YR 3/2).

(e) *Other Fine Wares* (all residual)
Samian
These may be summarised as follows:

Pre-Flavian	1
Flavian	3
Early 2nd century	5
Antonine	6
Late 2nd to early 3rd century ..	2

LAYER	EXTERNAL DATING EVIDENCE	PROVISIONAL ASSESSMENT OF DATE	NF FAB. 2A	NF FAB. 2B	NF RED SLIP FAB. 1B	NF BEAKERS & CLOSED FORMS	NF POSS. UN-SLIPPED	OX RED TYPE 30	OX RED TYPE 31	OX RED TYPE 35	OX RED TYPE 36	OX RED MORTAR	OX TYPE 42	OX PORCH TYPE 43	OX WHITE WARE	OX PARCHMENT	OX BEAKERS	OX MISC. COARSE	OX MISC. ?OXON	NENE PRE 250?	COLCHESTER?	PEVENSEY	LEZOUX & RHINELAND	LOCAL RED WARE	REMARKS
AREA 1 A3.9		late Ant. or later																			X				
PIT A55		C4 at the earliest			X																			X	
AREA 2 E6		late Roman		X																					on floor of House 1
E8		?late C3–early C4																				X			= latest floor in House 2, prob. C4
E47		?												X											occ. layer
E53		pre-dates C4																					X		earlier clay floor below House 1
E55		C2 or later																			X				
E56		late Roman		X										X											
E76		late or post Roman												X											
E116		Ant. at the earliest																		X	X				
E183		?C2–C3																		X					footings of earlier House 1
E202		late Roman			X																				
F3.26		?C4			X																		X		Roman floor base, House 1
G7	late C3 radiate	top of street prob. C4			X												X							X	
G25	C4 coin	late or sub Roman		X	X									X									X		this is the top part of G31
G29		?late C3			X	X						X					X			X	X		X		
G31		?late C3	X		X	X											X	X	X	X	X		X	X	this layer is below G7 & is rubbish dumped on earlier street surface
G60		late Ant. or later																					X		wall footing, House 2
G78		late or sub Roman																					X		late hearth cut into floor of House 1
G94		Ant. or later																			X				
H3		late C4																					X		top layer of Street 2
J21		?late Roman		X																					
J45		pre-dates house 2																			X				oven below House 2
L8		late C4			X																				
L40		late Roman																					X		
L72		?C4–C5			X																				
L94	C4 coin	late or post Roman			X																X				
L101		later than C2?			X																X				
L103		?late C3																		X	X		X		silt layer in Street 1
GULLEY G2		later than Ant.																			X				
PIT E44		?late Roman			X											X	X								
PIT E46	C4 coin	C4	X																						
PIT F12		pre C4 poss. C2 or C3																			X				
PIT J25		Ant. or later																					X		
SLOT J5		pre C4																			X				
AREA 3 Z5		late or post Roman			X																				
AREA 4 P.H M21		late or post Roman		X																					
P.H M51		?C4			X							X													robbed wall, robbing could be Roman
P.H M61		C3–C4																			X				
SLOT M6		?C2–C3																			X				wall slot of House 1
AREA 5 0.29		C2–C3																			X				Roman garden soil, sealed by later courtyard
0.39		late C3–early C4																			X				make-up for tessellated floor, House 2
0.40		?C3–C4			X																X				occ. layer;
0.53		C2 or later																			X				
0.58		?C2–C3																				X			
0.59		late Ant. at earliest																			X	X			Roman cess pit in Roman garden
0.61		?C2–C3																					X		
P3		C4			X																X				
P28		?C3 to early C4			X																X	X	X		
P33		mid C3 to early C4																			X	X			
P37		early C4 or earlier					X														X	X	X		
P44		mid C3 to early C4					X														X				
P48		Ant. or later																			X	X			courtyard of House 2
P59 (= PIT 0.40)		Roman ?C3			X																X	X			
P69		?C3–C4																					X		
PIT 0.22		?			X																X				
PIT 0.23		?late Roman			X													X			X	X		= part of PIT 0.33
PIT 0.31		?late Roman																			X				
PIT 0.33	late C3 coin	late Roman		X	X																X	X		
PIT 0.40		Roman ?C3			X																X	X		
PIT P37		?C3			X																X	X			
P.H P77		?late Roman			X																				post-dates hypocaust in House 2
P.H P26		?C3		X																					
AREA 6 R17		late Roman												X											
R23		late Roman																		X			X	
S4		could be C2																			X				
PIT R31		late Roman																X		X			X	
AREA 7 DITCH A1 A	coins late C3	late C4 or later			X															X	X			
B	coin 364-375	late C4	X	X	X	X		X					X				X			X	X	X	X	X
C		C4			X												X								
D		C4 or later	X	X	X	X				X		X				X		X			X		X		
E		C4	X	X	X	X				X				X			X	X		X		X	X	
M		C4			X																				
N		C3–C4?	X	X	X					X							X			X	X			
A17 = DITCH 2 (TOP)	coin early C4	C4																X	X					
A20 = DITCH 2 (TOP)		C4			X																				
DITCH 2	coins late C3	C3–C4				X	X										X	X			X			
B22		?			X																				
B48		?C4				X																			
B62		?late or post Roman							X																from robber trench, but robbing could be Roman
C14		?																X							
C22		?																			X				
D35		C3–C4			X																				
PIT A10 (D)	coins (3) C2	prob. C2–C3																					X		

Fig. 10.21 N.W. Quadrant; later Roman fine wares

The Roman Glass

**by Dorothy
Charlesworth**

Vessels

There is not a great quantity of vessel glass from these excavations. In date it ranges from the middle or later 1st century to the early or middle 4th century. The find numbers are cited in brackets alongside the illustrated items to facilitate museum identification.

(a) *Pillar-moulded bowls*

As these are made of rather thick metal and even small fragments are readily identified, a possibly disproportionate number of them are recorded from excavations. The finer colourless glass tends to be in small unrecognisable fragments and the number of vessels cannot be calculated. At least nine bowls were found, mostly in natural green glass. The type emerges in the 1st century B.C. but the natural green bowls generally belong to the middle and later years of the 1st century A.D. towards the end of the life of the type and the other plain colours although apparently introduced earlier than the natural greens, also occur frequently in the period 50–70. They are all made in a mould. See *Chichester* 2, 1974, p. 133.

1. (2090). *Area 5. Pit P.31 and 2096 Area 3. Y.41*
Two fragments, probably from the same vessel; green glass.

2. (*1136*). *Area 4. M.38*
Similar bowl in olive-green glass.
Not illustrated.

3. (*92*). *Area 2. E.85*
Deep blue glass.

4. (*618*). *Area 2. Pit H.19*
Amber glass.

(b) *Bottles*

The square or other angular-bodied or cylindrical bottle is another easily identified shape. Altogether a total of 26 bottles are represented, of which a selection is published below. See also *Chichester* 2, 1974, p. 134.

5. (*198*). *Area 7. Pit D.15*
Base of a square bottle with moulded base marking with part of two concentric circles.

6. (927). Base of a square bottle; moulded base marking with four circles and a central dot.
Not illustrated.

7. (181). Two pieces of poor quality glass with two concentric circles.

8. (2099). Part of a square base with a circle on it.

9. (50. B.55). Base with two concentric circles and a central cross.

10. (2074). Fragment from a cylindrical bottle.

11. (986). Part of a bottle distorted in the heat of a fire.

12. Fragment, the lower sticking part of a multi-ribbed handle, could be either from a bottle or flagon.
All these bottles are in natural green glass and blown in a mould.

(c) *Blown glass bowls*

13. (*2167*). *Area 3. W.15*
Fragment of a small bulbous bowl in light brown glass with pre-moulded ribbing (the vessel is withdrawn from the mould and further inflated), thin opaque white marvered trails added. Mid 1st century, probably made in North Italy or South Gaul (*Saalburg Jahrbuch* xvii (1958), w. von Pfeffer and T. E. Haevernick, *Zarte Rippenschale; Jahrbuch des Romisch-Germanischen Zentral museum Mainz* (1967), T. E. Haevernick, *Die Verbreitung des zarten Rippenschalen.*)

14. (1103). Ribbed, hollow – tubular rimmed bowl in blue-greenish glass with coil base ring. These bowls have an extremely long life. Examples first appear in the second half of the 1st century A.D. and they seem to be quite common throughout the 2nd century. Later examples may be survival material (*Charlesworth* 1972, p. 199).

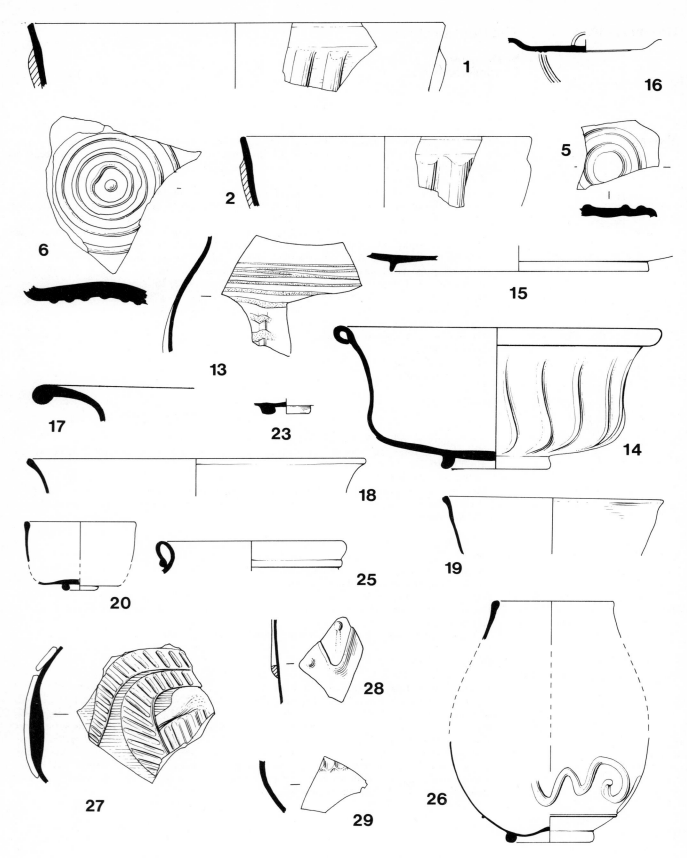

Fig. 10.22 Roman glass, No. 27, ($\frac{1}{1}$) remainder ($\frac{1}{2}$)

The following fragments seem to be from similar vessels, plain or ribbed: 561, 2246 (rim), 2124.

15. *(2103). Area 5. P.15*
Base is good quality colourless glass, polished, from a shallow bowl or plate. It is impossible to be certain of the shape from the base alone, 1st to mid 2nd century.

16. *(727). Area 7. D.41*
Flat base in good quality colourless glass from a shallow bowl, polished with single circle on the inside and two concentric circles cut on the underside of the base. 1st to early 2nd century.

17. *(2014). Area 5. O.20*
Rim in good quality colourless glass with milky weathering, outsplayed and rounded at the tip, from a shallow bowl. 1st to mid 2nd century.

18. *(2204). Area 5. Pit P.37*
Rim of a bowl in greenish glass, tip of rim rounded and slightly outsplayed.

19. *(2129 and 2153). Area 5. Pit P.37*
Similar but smaller and less well-made bowl in greenish glass. These two bowls can only be dated by their context (see p. 267).

20. *(2136). Area 5. Pit P.37*
Small cylindrical bowl in colourless glass, rim rounded and slightly thickened at the tip. This bowl has a single coil base ring, two concentric coils is perhaps more common.

21. (2042) and 22 (455); rims from similar bowls, *not illustrated.*

23. (2079). *Area 5. Pit O.40.* Base from similar bowl.

24. (2009). Base from similar bowl, *not illustrated.*
This is a common mid 2nd to mid 3rd century type plain or with decoration either cut or painted. Many come from the Cologne area and Belgic Gaul. See *Chichester* 2, 1974, p. 134, No. 15.

25. *(202). Area 2. Pit E.90*
Outfolded hollow tubular rim of a deep, probably globular bowl. This is the only piece which can certainly be attributed to this type (C. Isings, *Roman glass from dated finds*, Form 67c), but several other base and side fragments, some ribbed, could be from bowls or from flagons with bulbous bodies (typical shapes are illustrated in *Arch. Ael.* xxxvi, p. 51, Fig. 8, and Isings, Form 52a–c), 2172, 432 are such fragments. Both deep bowl and flagon types can be dated *c.* 70–150.

(d) *Beakers*

26. *(2133 and 2134). Area 5. Pit P.37*
Rim, body and base fragments of a barrel-shaped beaker in colourless glass, rim rounded at the tip, body decorated with a colourless snake-thread trail and a plain horizontal trail. The flattened snake-thread trail has the typical cross-hatching only faintly marked; coil base ring and pontil mark in centre of concave base.

27. *(412). Area 2. G.72*
Fragment in colourless glass with snake-thread decoration. The beaker was probably made in the Cologne area in the later 2nd or early 3rd century (*Fremersdorf* 1959, T.21). There are surprisingly few examples of vessels with this type of decoration in Britain, more with coloured than with colourless trails.

28. *(371). Area 2. G.44*
Fragment of a straight-sided beaker in colourless glass with a V-shaped fragment of a festooned trail or network and raised dots. 3rd–4th century. A festooned trail on conical beakers is found mainly in the 4th century, more often associated with the late olive-green metals. The addition of raised dots is not common but an example can be cited, with trails only, from Köln, etc. (*F. Fremersdorf*, No. 126) and with clusters of dots from *Lauriacum*, Grave 76 (*A. Kloiber* 1962, p. 76, 105). A fragment from Caerwent restored with a network (*Boon* 1972–73, p. 121, dated 140–230), after F. Fremersdorf, is from a convex-sided beaker.

29. *(2196). Area 5. P.28*
Fragment from the lower part of the body of a convex-sided beaker with moulded decoration, a closed diaper of oval or hexagonal depressions, colourless glass with some iridescence.

(e) *Pouring vessels (flagons, jugs, flasks)*

30. (154). Three pieces of neck, body and base of a ribbed conical bodied flagon in yellowish-green glass, *c.* 70–130 A.D.

31. *(448). Area 2. Pit G.30*
Fragment from a similar vessel, part of the ribbed conical body only.
32. (276). Three ribbed handle fragment, green glass from a flagon. *Not illustrated.*
33. *(692). Area 7. A.26*
Rim and part of the upper sticking part of a handle of a flagon, folded, "collar" type of rim, yellowish-green.
34. *(2053). Area 5. Pit O.40*
Plain blue-green handle, probably from a flagon.
35. (609). Fragment of a flat strap handle with a central rib, probably from a flagon, blue-green glass. *Not illustrated.*
36. *(666). Area 2. J.11*
Part of the infolded, flattened rim and upper sticking part with a "crest", of a flagon. From a small round mouthed flagon or spouted jug. 2nd to 3rd century.
37. *(2054). Area 5. Pit O.40*
Small handle, round in section, probably from a jug. 2nd to 3rd century.
38. *(829). Area 2. L.19*
Dolphin eyelet-handle in blue-green glass from a bath flask. 2nd to 3rd century.
39. *(4032). Area 3. A.5*
Base of a cylindrical flask, colourless glass with striations, pontil mark on base. The shape is not certain as both handled and handleless versions exist, some have outsplayed rims and some no rim (see Isings, Forms 100, 102).
40. (426). Similar base. *Not illustrated.*
41. *(36). Area 7. A.2*
Similar base.
42. *(26). Area 7. A.1*
Rim and neck of a flask; green glass; the rim is thickened with an added coil, not folded in the usual way.
43. *(143). Area 2. E.129*
Rim and neck of flask or jar, blue-green glass. 2nd century.

(f)   *Miscellaneous bases*
44. (489). *Area 7. C.11*
Colourless glass, base probably formed by pushing in a second bubble, sides of vessel expanding upwards. It could be a small flask. 3rd century.
45. *(2191). Area 5. Pit P.37*
Hollow tubular, possibly a coil, base ring with pontil mark in the centre, sides of vessel curving out from base; greenish colour. The small bowls 18 and 19 probably had a base of this type.
46. *(853). Area 2. Pit L.44*
Similar base.
47. (664). Similar base in heavier metal (see objects). *Not illustrated.*

There must be about 180 vessels represented by fragments, but the greater part are unidentifiable. There are no pieces that are necessarily earlier than A.D. 50, indeed only one piece (No. 13), which is probably so early. The majority fall into the later 1st and 2nd century, with some 3rd to early 4th (perhaps), certainly no mid- to late 4th-century glass.

Window Glass

48.   (56). *Area 7. Ditch A.1(E)*
The most interesting piece of glass from the excavations is a fragment of a crown window-pane with a folded edge and mortar adhering to it, demonstrating beyond doubt that the disc was fixed as a window-pane. It is the first example of this technique found in Roman Britain, fortunately stratified with late Roman pottery in the re-cut town sewer. This corresponds with the windows of late Roman and Byzantine date at Jerash and elsewhere in the Near East (D. B. Harden, Roman window glass from Jerash and later parallels, Iraq, vi (1939, 91) and three published examples in the museum of Aquileia attributed to the 4th century, in coloured glass (*Calvi* 1963, 174–5). There is also a fragment in the museum at Aquincum with a folded edge fixed into a groove in a mortar surround. This comes from the early excavations in the great public baths and is unstratified, but there was no medieval material on the site, so its date is certainly Roman. Another pane is known from Ravenna. These are apparently the only western examples of late Roman date. Crown glass is well known in Normandy in the 14th century and from that time both the cylinder and crown processes were used.

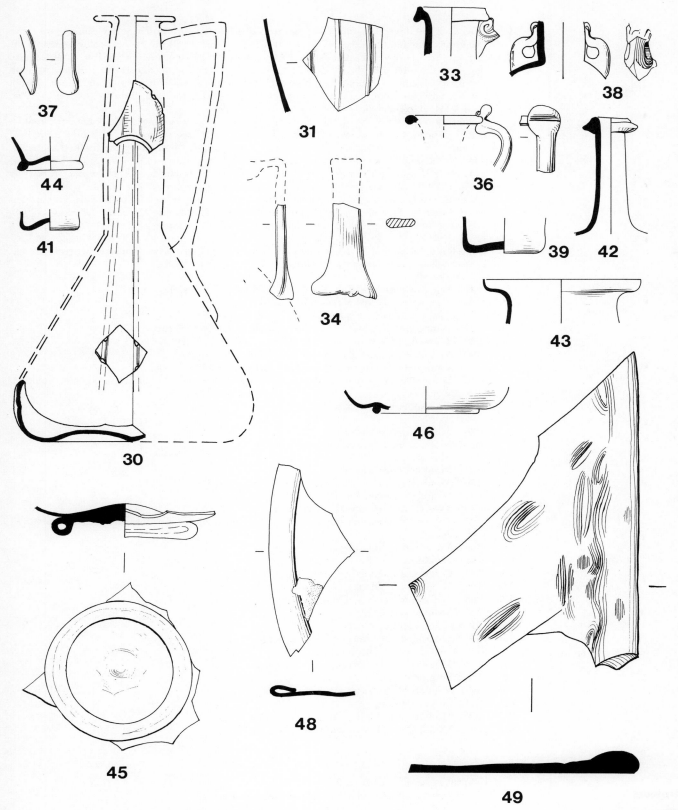

Fig. 10.23 Roman glass, Nos. 30–49 ($\frac{1}{2}$)

Roman window glass, normally natural green in colour, hitherto has divided into two categories, the moulded glass of the 1st and 2nd centuries and the cylinder-blown glass of the 3rd and 4th centuries. Except where there is an edge it is not always possible to distinguish one from the other but the moulded glass is thicker (*c.* 3–5 mm) and the side in contact with the mould is always rough. The blown glass is sometimes slightly rough on one side from contact with the floor of the annealing oven. The techniques are discussed in *Harden* 1959, Heft VIII, p. 8f, and *Boon* 1966.

Twenty-five pieces are of the moulded type, some with tooling marks where the molten glass has been pressed towards the corner of the mould (see below, No. 49). One piece is of colourless metal. Three pieces have mortar stuck to them indicating the method of fixing. The size of such panes can seldom be calculated, but a complete pane from the bath-house at Garden Hill Hartfield measured 25.5 by 23.5 cms (D. B. Harden in *Antiquaries Journal*, liv (1974), 280–1, with further references) and a larger pane from the bath-house at Red House, Corbridge, was partly reconstructed and found to measure at least 60 by 60 cms (D. Charlesworth in C. M. Daniels, "The Roman bath-house at Red House" in *Arch. Ael.* xxxvii (1959, 166). Ten pieces are probably cylinder blown.

49. (235). *Area 7. Pit B.49*
Edge fragment of moulded window glass, showing tooling marks. Thickens where glass has flowed against the edge of the mould.
Not illustrated.
50. (241). Window glass probably blown, natural green irridescent.
51. (234). Colourless window glass could be 3rd–4th century.
52. (228). Thick colourless window glass ? late Roman.
53. (224). Window glass, almost colourless, moulded 1st–2nd century.
54. (222). Thin edge fragment probably blown, 3rd–4th century.
55. (196). Moulded window glass, green iridescent, edge fragment.
56. (194). Thin greenish iridescent, has been in fire and folded over.
57. (310). Corner of window pane with tool mark where glass has been pushed into angle, moulded, blue-green.
58. (485). Greenish window glass ? blown.
59. (487). As 57.
60. (396). Moulded edge fragment.
61. Moulded glass, including edge fragments.
62. (261). Moulded, green.
63. (259). Moulded edge fragment.
64. (286). Moulded, mortar for fixing stuck to fragment.
65. (633). Moulded, mortar for fixing stuck to fragment.
66. (479). Two very sharp cut edges, greenish ? blown.
67. (399). Almost rectangular fragment of blown glass, green possibly deliberately coloured. Iridescent.
68. (398). Very thin bubbly glass, late Roman.
69. (115). Moulded.
70. (173). Colourless moulded edge fragment.
71. (160). Greenish moulded edge fragment.
72. (665). Three fragments including two edges, moulded.
73. (243). Moulded edge.
74. (2179). Moulded green edge.
75. (4019). Moulded edge, mortar on rough side.
76. (38). Moulded edge with mortar.
77. (512). Moulded corner, green.
78. (428). Fragment.
79. (380). Moulded edge fragment.
80. (234). Moulded edge.
81. (262). Moulded and blown window, including edges.
82. (101). Moulded and blown window, including edges.

i. *Gaming counters.* (All Area 2)
83. (82). Counter, circular, plano-convex in section. *Pit F.12.*

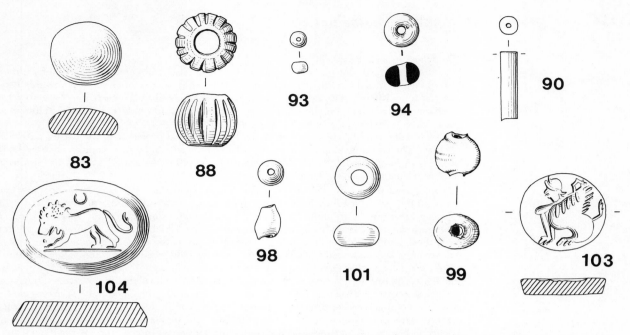

Fig. 10.24 Roman glass objects, Nos. 83–101 ($\frac{1}{1}$); Roman intaglios, Nos. 103–104, ($\frac{2}{1}$)

Not illustrated.

84. (554). Identical counters to 83 (82) above. *H.26.*
85. (683).   ,,   ,,   ,,   ,,   *H.62.*
86. (716).   ,,   ,,   ,,   ,,   *J.74.*
87. (664). Cut down base of a vessel re-used as a gaming counter. *J.11.*

ii. *Beads: All of common Roman type*

88. (111). Melon-shaped bead, turquoise paste. *Area 2. E.73.*
89. (265). About one quarter of a similar bead. *Not illustrated.*
90. (134). Bead cut from a cylindrical rod, minute central hole, iridescent blue glass. *Area 7. B.5.*
91. (260). Similar to No. 90 (134). *Not illustrated.*
92. (901). Similar to No. 90 (134). *Not illustrated.*
93. (320). Small globular bead; turquoise glass. *Area 7. B.4.*
94. (1061). Similar bead to No. 93 (320). *Area 4. M.13.*
95. (828). Similar bead to No. 93 (320). *Not illustrated.*
96. (319). Globular bead in greenish glass. *Not illustrated.*
97. (739). Half a bead in clear blue glass. *Not illustrated.*
98. (59). Irregular-shaped bulbous bead in green glass. *Area 7. Pit A.7.*
99. (2142). Irregular-shaped bead in similar glass to No. 98 (59). *Area 3. W.5.*
100. (56). Green glass bead, unstratified in Area 2. F. *Not illustrated.*
101. (410). Blue glass bead with large central hole. *Area 7. C.11.*

iii. *Miscellaneous*

102. (99). Shank of a pin in green glass, tapering to the point. *Not illustrated.*

Fig. 10.24   The Intaglios   by Martin Henig

103.   *The Sphinx from Area 3* (Z.38)

The stone is a sard, flat on both faces and almost circular, dimensions 11 by 10 by 2 mm.

It is cut, in intaglio, with the figure of a sphinx squatting on its haunches towards the left (on the actual gem). The creature wears a cap upon its head (which is presumably to be interpreted as a debased diadem), has a recurving wing and holds its tail high. Sphinxes with these features are frequently found on gems.[1]

The intaglio may be dated to the 1st century A.D. and probably to the earlier part of that century. The workmanship is schematic but vigorous and the device completely fills the field of the gem in the manner of the best Augustan intaglios. As is well known, the sphinx was used as a signet-device by Augustus.

The type of sphinx figured on his seal is known from the reverses of cistophori and aurei issued in the East *c.* 20 B.C. It has long swept-back wings, a diadem, and a short tail.[2] Such sphinxes are common in glyptic art, and a paste intaglio that reflects the Augustan seal, has been excavated at Melandra Castle, Derbyshire.[3] The Chichester stone cannot be connected with these coins, but a remarkable similarity exists between it and some of the coins of Tasciovanus and Cunobelin, which portray sphinxes with recurving wings.[4] The explanation would seem to be that these issues were derived from intaglios.[5] However, this is of merely incidental interest here in Sussex, where the native Atrebatic rulers did not strike sphinx-coins. It is, in any case, unlikely that our gem was imported until the Conquest.[6] It may have been worn by a Roman soldier or trader to whom the device would have been a potent apotropaic symbol. Although sphinxes originally symbolised destructive forces, they came to be seen as beneficient in course of time, and are frequently employed in sculpture as grave-guardians.[7]

104.   *The Lion from Area 7* (Pit B.58)

The intaglio is moulded in glass paste imitating nicolo (onyx with a blue surface on a dark ground). In shape it is an elongated oval, 15 by 10 mm above and broadening outwards and downwards to *c.* 17 by 12 mm. Both faces are flat and the gem is 3 mm thick.

It is best to view the device in impression, as intaglio gems were primarily intended for the sealing of letters, and doubtless the recipient of a communication would scrutinise the seal rather as we might a signature. In the present instance the impression shows a lion with open mouth walking purposefully to the right. Above it is a crescent moon which may imply that it represents the astrological sign *Leo*. Although a number of intaglios from British sites depict lions and a paste from Colchester shows one with a star above, this is the first portraying the beast with a crescent.[8] However, the type is probably very common and we may cite paste examples from Vechten and Aquileia.[9] The Chichester paste almost certainly dates to the 3rd century A.D.

References

[1] C. A. Niessen, *Beschreibung Romischer Altertumer, Sammlung Niessen* (Cologne 1911), No. 5439, from Cologne or Xanten.

T. de Kibaltchitch, *Gemmes de la Russie Méridionale* (Berlin 1910), No. 61, from Theodosia.

G. Sena Chiesa, *Gemme del Museo Nazionale di Aquileia* (Aquileia 1966), Nos. 1221, 1224, from Aquileia.

C. Gerra, *Acra . . . Gemmis quae compta coruscat, in Studi Calderini e Paribeni* iii (Milan 1956), 775–98, No. 1.

G. M. A. Richter, *Metropolitan Museum, New York, Catalogue of engraved gems* (Rome 1956), No. 391, have all these features. For sphinxes with diadems of normal type, and recurving wings, A. M. Napolitano, *Gemme del Museo di Udine di probabile Provenienza aquileiese Aquileia Nostra. XXI* (1950), 39, No. 33.

A. Furtwangler, *Beschreibung der geschnittenen Steine im Antiquarium* (Berlin 1896), Nos. 3323, 7974–5.

Richter, *op. cit.*, No. 390.

[2] Suetonius *Augustus* 50; Pliny *N.H.* xxxvii, 10; Dio Cassius. li, 3, 6, cf. H. U. Instinsky, *Die Siegel des Kaisers Augustas* (Baden-Baden 1962), 23–30, Pl. iii = H. B. Walters.

Catalogue of the Engraved Gems and Cameos . . . in the British Museum (London 1926), No. 3111.

For the coins, H. Mattingly and E. Sydenham, *The Roman Imperial Coinage* 1 (London 1923), Augustus Nos. 14, 43; C. H. V. Sutherland, *The Cistophori of Augustus* (Royal Numismatic Society, 1970), 90–4.

[3] R. S. Conway, *Melandra Castle* (Manchester 1906), 113 and Pl. facing 112, Fig. 2.

M. Henig, *A corpus of Roman Engraved Gemstones from British sites* (*B.A.R.* 8, 1974), Vol. 87,

No. 653, Pl. XX, now in Buxton Museum; also note Sena Chiesa, *op. cit.*, Nos. 1218–9; Walters, *op. cit.*, No. 1842.

[4] R. P. Mack, *The coinage of Ancient Britain* (second edition London 1964), No. 173 (Tasciovanus, standing sphinx with recurving wing); No. 181 (Tasciovanus, seated sphinx, recurving wing on a specimen in the Ashmolean, the creature is clearly wearing a little cap); No. 237 (Cunobelin; seated sphinx with recurving wing).

[5] M. Henig, *The origin of some Ancient British coin types, Britannia 111* (1972), 209–223, especially 215 f.

[6] For another "intaglio representing a sphinx-like figure with the name *Thermia* (OEPMIA) in Greek characters", from Colchester, cf. *Arch. Journ.* X (1853), 350.

[7] J. M. C. Toynbee, *Art in Britain under the Romans* (Oxford 1964), 112–13, and Pl. xxlx (a) The Colchester Sphinx.

[8] M. Henig, *A Corpus of Roman Engraved Gemstones from British sites* (*B.A.R.* 8, 1974), Vol. ii, 84 f., Nos. 627–35, Pl. XX, especially No. 628 (from Colchester), presumably also referring to the sign *Leo*. Like Sphinxes, lions can have an apotropaic significance (as grave guardians, etc.), Toynbee, *op. cit.* 114, and Pl. XXIX (b) The Corbridge Lion.

[9] F. Henkel, *Die römischen Fingerringe der Rheinlande* (Berlin 1913), 113, No. 1239, Pl. XLVIII = (No. 370 Pl. LXXVIII), from Vechten.
    G. Sena Chiesa, *Gemme del Museo Nazionale di Aquileia* (Aquileia 1966), 364 f., Nos. 1158, 1159, Pl. LIX.

Fig. 10.25 & Pl. 19

The Inscriptions

I am grateful to Mr. Mark Hassall, F.S.A., who kindly examined these and whose comments are reproduced below:

1. Circular lead weight, 45 mm diameter, 6 mm thick, weighing 82.59 grammes. The weight is within one gramme of a *quadrans* (81.86 grammes), a quarter of a libra. A graffito scored on the smooth upper surface of the weight reads F L A C / C I N I.[1] [2]
   From *Area 2, G.80.*

2. Sherd from the base of a black burnished ware dish. Burnished letters on the unburnished underside read ...]A V I M[... / ...]V D I T I[... / ...]R N[... (see Pl. 19).
   From *Area 5, O.20.*

3. Fragment from the edge of a slab of Purbeck marble, 0.075 by 0.1 by 0.02 m, carrying part of a letter. The back of the slab is roughly dressed. Of the letter, originally *c.* 10 cm high, only part of a flat curve terminating in a partially preserved serif survives. A blank space above (or below) the letter suggests that it formed either the top of the last letter of the first line of an inscription or the bottom of the first letter of the last line, reading either G[3] (C and S being other possibilities) or S. The size of the letter and the fact that the back of the slab is rough, make it unlikely, though not impossible, that this comes from the same inscription as the following item (see No. 4), for the letters could have been of varying heights and the inscription could have been cut on different slabs. In this case, A V]G is an obvious but not necessarily correct expansion, since, as noted above, the inscription could have continued on an adjacent slab.
   From *Area 7, F.50.*

4. Part of the left-hand side of a Purbeck marble slab, 0.12 by 0.16 by 0.22 m, found in the same context as No. 3 above. On the slab, the back of which has been worked smooth, are the remains of two lines of an inscription. The letters, which still retain traces of red colouring are, in the first line 58 mm and in the second 45 mm high. In line 1 only part of the bottom of the second letter survive. The inscription reads / F I[... / N E[... The slab, which lacks a moulding, may have been only one of several which contained a lengthy inscription. However, the vacant space between the latters and the edge of the stone shows that line 2 certainly, and line 1 probably, begin new words even if they do not begin new lines. It is, of course, possible that the inscription either lacked a moulded border altogether or that this was cut from separate pieces of stone, and that this fragment does come from the beginning left-hand edge of an inscription.

   In line 1 enough survives of the right-hand side of the bottom of the V cut to show that the letter was not an E. It is possible that it was an R but other consonants are presumably not in question. In line 2 just enough survives to show that the second letter, presumably a vowel, was an E rather than an I. The quality of the work suggests an Imperial dedication, in which case F I[L I O would be possible in the first line.
   From *Area 7, F.50.*

5. Part of a limestone inscription, 0.18 by 0.1 by 0.06 m, cut down and used upside down as a paving slab. The text reads ...]D E F . G[... ...]O I[...
   From *Area 2, E.1.*

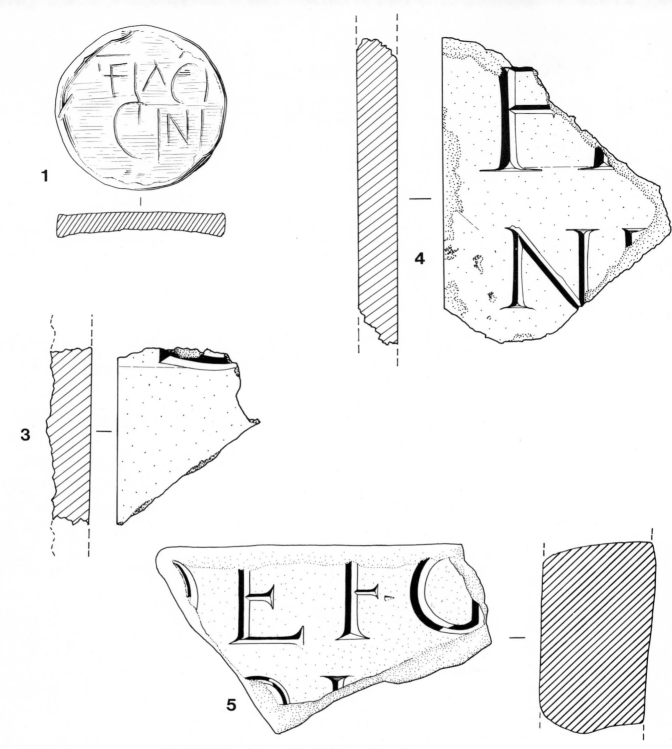

Fig. 10.25 Inscriptions, No. 1 ($\frac{1}{1}$), remainder ($\frac{1}{2}$)

[1] For Roman weights see F. Hultsch, 1882, especially table xiii.

[2] I. Kajanto, *The Latin Cognomina*, 240, points out that of the nine examples of F L A C C I N V S/A in CIL, six come from Spain. At the end of line 1, two vertical strokes have been traced between the C and the edge of the weight. They do not appear to be the symbol for a *quandrans* which, as three *unciae* was $^-$−.

[3] Reference to L. C. Evetts, "The lettering of Romano-British Inscribed stones" in *Arch. Ael.*, Fourth Series XXVI (1948), 153–71, shows that what remains of the serif is not compatible with either B or D.

276

15. Area 7, Tower Street. Base of medieval bell mould. (Photo: A. Down)

16. Adcock's Eastgate. Bread oven No. 1.

17. Adcock's, Eastgate. Bread oven No. 2. (Photos: G. Claridge RIBA)

18. Coins from the North-west Quadrant; 1-10, Early Iron Age; 11, late Saxon. Scale: approx 2 : 1

19. N.W. Quadrant. A: (*above*) Graffiti on potsherd,
B: (*right*) Inscribed lead disc, (see p. 275).

The Roman Brooches

by D. F. Mackreth

All the brooches are made from a copper alloy.

Colchesters
1. (681). Large brooch, plain bow except for two cross-cuts at the foot; marks of cold working down the back. The wings are plain and the chord of the spring is held by a very short hook which has three longitudinal mouldings. The spring has a mass of iron corrosion where the pin should have started, possibly the remains of an iron wire repair with an iron axis bar through the coils for a hinged pin. The catchplate may have been hammered out cold.
2. (704). Another large brooch, again with cold-working marks on the back. The wings are ornamented with two pairs of wide flutes separated by a very narrow one. The hook is long with a pair of cross grooves over the chord, another pair at the end and three in the middle. The catchplate shows signs of cold working.
3. (1176). Like No. 1 but smaller, with marks of cold working.
4. (2194). A small brooch with plain wings and bow which has an octagonal section whose arrises are not well marked.
5. (488). The bow is flat and plain; the wings are also plain and the hook is just long enough to curl over the chord.
6. (263). The front of the bow is flat and the back shows signs of cold working.

Individual Colchesters are difficult to place within the *floruit* of the type owing to the lack of decorative features which would normally betray change. In general, Colchesters either have decorated wings or decorated bows and most have no ornament at all. The Colchester belongs essentially to the first half of the 1st century. Although size is not a reliable criterion, early Colchesters tended to be larger than the later ones. Perhaps of greater significance is the form of the profile of the bow. In all the specimens reviewed here, the bow is curved. Nos. 4 and 6 are both much slacker than the others, which themselves do not have the marked angle at the head which those with straight profiles tend to have (*Swarling*, p. 41, Pl. XII.4 and p. 44, Pl. XIV.13). However, insufficient examples have been firmly dated to pre-Conquest times for it to be clear just how reliable such criteria are.

Attention should be drawn to the signs revealing the development of Colchester Derivatives. There can be no doubt that the evolution of such types is reflected in the decoration of the parent (cf. *Camulodunum*, p. 310, Pl. XC.27; *Stead*, forthcoming; *Griffiths*, forthcoming). Amongst present examples one may draw attention to the head and foot of the bow on No. 1, the articulation of the flutings on the wings of No. 2, as well as the ornament on the hook, the poor form of the bow as well as its profile of No. 5, and the circular piercings in the catchplate of No. 4. It would obviously be of value to know when the progeny had begun to develop, for this should provide a clue to the date of such new decorative tricks. Unfortunately, no single Colchester Derivative has been satisfactorily dated to pre-Conquest times. There is a strong possibility, however, that the type to which No. 7 below belongs had evolved then; the only Colchester Derivative to be found amongst all the brooches from Skeleton Green, Puckeridge (*Partridge*, forthcoming), was of this type. Its stratigraphical position was ambiguous, but its solitary state amongst a large collection is worthy of comment, especially when it is possible that the collection closes as early as *c.* 45 rather than A.D. 50. Hence it is possible that some of what seem to be late decorative features in the Colchester had begun to appear before the Conquest, but in most cases almost certainly belong to post-Conquest times. How long the Colchester was made after A.D. 43 is not clear, but it had probably ceased by A.D. 60 if not by A.D. 50–55, hence any Colchester in use at 60 would have been a survival. It seems clear that few survived in general use to be taken away by the army to places like Gloucester or Wroxeter, each of which places have produced an example from modern excavations, but both are clearly "late" types (*Heighway*, forthcoming). The foundation date for Gloucester seems to be in the 60's (*Ant. J.* LII, 1972, p. 38) (*Wroxeter*, p. 204, Fig. 36, H.32). The foundation date for the military sites under the later town lies in the period *c.* A.D. 55–60 (*Webster* 1973, p. 118).

277

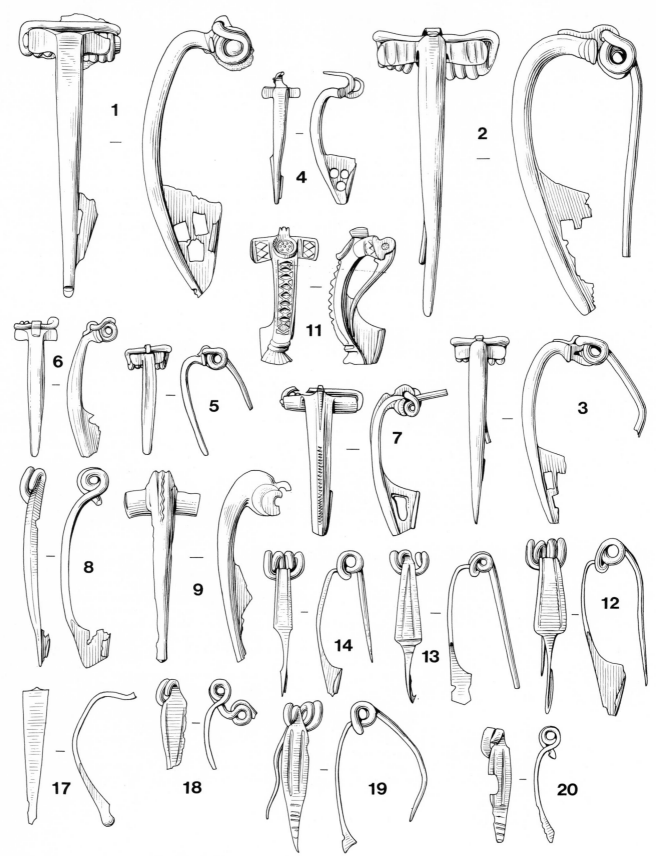

Fig. 10.26 Roman brooches, Nos. 1–20 (½)

7. (1173). The spring is held to the body of the brooch by means of a bar which runs through the coils of the spring and the lower of two holes in a projecting plate behind the head of the bow; the chord passes through the upper hole. The plate itself is carried over the head of the bow as a crest and runs down the front for a short distance before dying out. The profile of this crest is shaped to look like the hook of the Colchester (cf. Nos. 2 and 3 above). The wings are plain and curved to fit the spring behind. The bow is broad and tapers to a foot which is chamfered to either side. The distribution of this type of brooch is essentially that of the Colchester, but may be more restricted to the heartland of the Catuvellauni. As has been mentioned above, it is possible that this type had evolved by the time of the Conquest. Like the parent, the type is remarkably consistent in its details. Variations occur in the decoration of the bow; for instance, there is sometimes an incised saltire just below the crest. The rocker arm ornament is sometimes missing or placed down the concave surfaces on either side of the central flat face. The catchplate may sometimes be solid but piercings are to be expected, a common variant on the single opening being a circle above a three-sided shape.

    The dating is also fairly consistent, once the obviously late survivals or residual items are discarded; the first ten to fifteen years after the Conquest (Verulamium; *Archaeologia* 90, p. 91, Fig. 4.3, Boudiccan destruction; *Verulamium* 1936, p. 207, Fig. 44.22, up to *c.* A.D. 50–55; *Verulamium* 1972, p. 114, Fig. 29, A.D. 49–60; *Camulodunum*, p. 311, Pl. XCL.37, 43–61).

8. (1005). The spring is held as in No. 7. The plate is carried over the head as before and its profile is similarly treated, but is wider and sits on the head rather than runs down it. Down the lower part of the crest and running for a short distance down the bow is a groove. The catchplate was intended to have a clean three-sided hole in it, but the "flash" in the joint line of the mould was not cleaned out, thus obscuring the intended shape. The brooch belongs to a type which Hull describes as being very common in Kent. The dating, he adds, is probably not before Flavian times (*Arch. Cant.* LXXIII, 1959, p. 49, Fig. 9.5–8). In many ways the type is akin to that to which No. 7 belongs; it is fairly consistent and the catchplate design with the pin-groove and similar piercings as the No. 7 type may suggest that its origin is pre-Flavian.

9. (2165). The spring, now missing, was retained in the Polden Hill manner by means of an axis bar passing through the coils of the spring and through pierced plates at the ends of the wings. The chord was held by a hook behind the head of the bow. Each wing is plain except for a terminal moulding. The bow is well humped over the wings and has a sunken moulding down the upper part. This may once have been beaded. On each side of the head is a moulding which rises from the wings and is an arc when the brooch is viewed from the side. The lower part of the bow is too corroded for it to be certain whether there was a footknob.

    The writer reserves the term "Dolphin" for only this variety of Colchester Derivative. The type belongs to the West Midlands where it is widespread, but there are many outliers. It is possible that early ones of the type were without footknobs. It may be noted that the only specimen from the Roman fort at the Lunt, Bagendon, Warks., a site which seems to have come to an end as far as the early occupation is concerned by A.D. 80, is without a footknob (*T.B.A.S.* 83, 1966–67, p. 107, Fig. 19.1; *T.B.W.A.S.* 87, 1975, p. 3). Although the type is not well dated, it may be that the indications that it is of late 1st- and early 2nd-century date are accurate (*T.L.* VIII, 1966–67, p. 17, Fig. 7.7; *Verulamium* 1972, p. 114, Fig. 29.10), in that only one specimen of the type occurred at the Lunt.

10. (507). *Not illustrated.* The pin and one coil of a spring from a brooch. Normally, the coils of the spring approach the pin from the right when the brooch is viewed from the front. In this case, they approach from the left. The spring could have come from a Nauheim Derivative, but the tightness of the spiral suggests that the original brooch was a Colchester Derivative.

Headstud

11. (906). A very carefully detailed brooch. Each wing has, between a vertical groove, a rectangular panel made up of two lozenges relieved by triangles which once held enamel. On the head of the bow is a crest with mouldings along the top. Below this crest is the "stud" rising from the body of the bow. It is a little distorted but its original shape is clear; in the middle is a circular conical hole which contains a stud with a berried rosette on the top. The stud is made separately and is fastened to the body of the brooch by means of a stalk which passes through the bow. It would seem that, as the stud does not fit the hole very well, it may have been embedded in enamel which has now corroded away. The outer margin of the main "stud" is not circular but is pointed at the bottom where the lip rises to form a small peak. The rest of

the bow above the footknob arrangement has a step down each side and in the centre a sharp arris. This has been cut away by a series of V-shaped notches with triangular hollows down the sides to create the familiar lozenge and triangle pattern. The hollows would have held enamel. The foot has two cross-mouldings above a splayed out knob which has underneath another circular conical hole with a piercing running through to the catchplate. The edge of the splay has three pendant lobes on its surface. The pin is hinged and its axis bar is housed in a cylindrical case hidden behind the wings.

A well-developed specimen with, in the crest, a skeumorph hook for the now absent chord of the spring. Early Headstuds show that the spring was completely like the Colchesters in that the spring and hook was part of the body of the brooch, the stud developing from a rivet through the end of the hook and the bow (e.g. Kingsholm, Glos., *Guide to the Antiquities of Roman Britain*, London, 1958, p. 18, Fig. 9.15). The type has many variants at the beginning of its development; for instance, the hook, and therefore the stud, does not have to be present (*T.B.W.A.S.* 85, 1971–73, p. 66, Fig. 19.9; note that here the spring is separate from the body of the brooch). No less than eight brooches with the skeumorph hook come from Traprain Law where the major occupation starts in Flavian times (*Ant. Scot.* LXXXIX, 1955–56, p. 132, table 1). Developed Headstuds of any kind seem not to occur before this period and the *floruit* may be suggested as being late 1st century into the 2nd.

Nauheim Derivatives

12. (508). A complete one-piece brooch, with four coil internal chord spring.
13. (294). The same shape as No. 12, but here the decoration on the upper bow consists of three incised lines across the constriction with one down each side of the upper bow.
14. (556). Complete as the previous two, but the constriction is not so pronounced and the upper part has a border groove down each side only.
15. (442). *Not illustrated*. As the last, but the upper part of the upper bow is missing and the decoration consists of a badly placed line of rocker-arm ornament down the upper part. The constriction, in this case, is marked by four cross-cuts arranged as two pairs.
16. (722). *Not illustrated*. The upper part only of a flat bow with a slight taper. On each side is a groove. The pin is missing.
17. (278). The spring is missing from this flat bow, again with bordering grooves, which tapers to a pointed foot.
18. (2170). The design is the same as in the two previous examples. The lower bow with the catchplate is missing.
19. (1010). The bow is leaf-shaped with a pointed foot. The upper part of the bow has two grooves down each side and the lower part has six or more cross cuts-down to the point where the catchplate is now missing.
20. (622). A repeat of the last brooch.
21. (657). Similar to the previous two examples, except that each of the two broader divisions on the front of the bow has a line of rocker-arm decoration down their length.
22. (48). The bow is narrow and tapers to a pointed foot. The catchplate has three circular piercings aligned on the leading edge of the bow.
23. (2268). The bow is narrow and thick in proportion to its width, with a sharply rectangular section, and tapers to a pointed foot.
24. (17). The bow is flat and tapers to a pointed foot. Half the spring, with the pin, is missing.
25. (771). A complete brooch with a three coil spring and a flat plain bow which tapers to a pointed foot.
26. (2116). *Not illustrated*. As No. 25, but the spring is only partly present and coils out to the right instead of the left as is usual.
27. (552). *Not illustrated*. As the last, but with a narrower bow and with the spring and pin missing.
28. (2102). As the last.
29. (956). A small brooch, like the last, but with a curved front to the section of the bow.
30. (547). As the last, the bow is almost straight and may be distorted.
31. (1003). The bow has a diamond section with the arrises set to run down the front and back.

As at Fishbourne, this type of brooch is very well represented in the collection. None of them has any marked dating characteristic. Only No. 12 calls for special comment in that the decorative scheme is a little unusual and, with No. 13, 14 and 15, recalls the Aucissa-Hod Hill with its emphasis on a two-part bow design. Parallels at Fishbourne (*Cunliffe* 1971, p. 100, Fig. 36, 1–3, 5 and 6 and Verulamium (*Verulamium* 1936, p. 204, Fig. 43.3) indicate that the

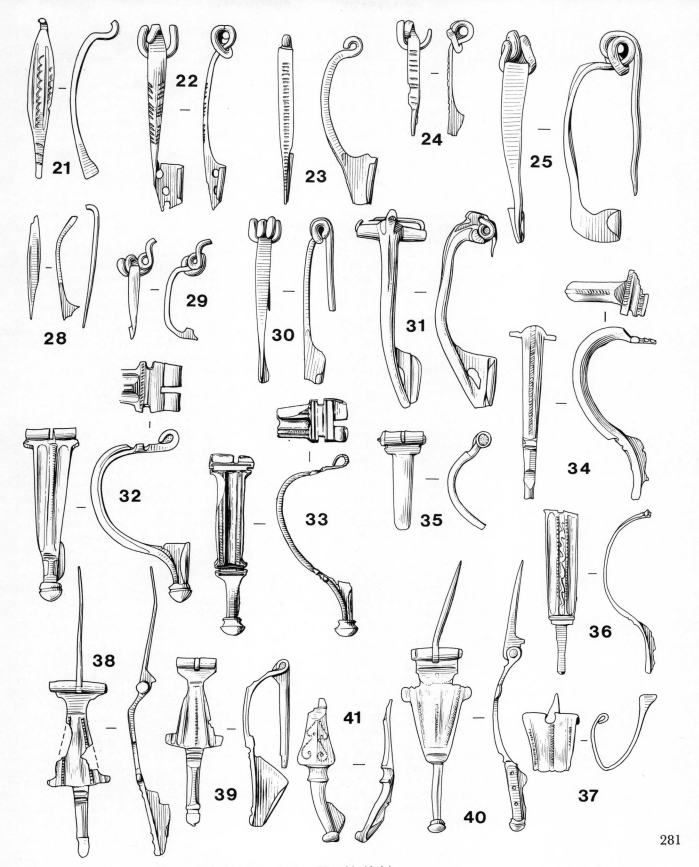

Fig. 10.27 Roman brooches, Nos. 21–41 (⅓)

281

date range is not inconsistent with this connection. The Chichester brooches are undistinguished, apart from No. 12 and do not seem to display any markedly early features. The main date range for this type is from the early 1st century into the late 1st, perhaps as late as A.D. 80. (*Newstead*, p. 318, Pl. LXXXV.1; *Chichester* 1, p. 97, Grave Group 60.J may be another with a coin of Titus), but it is hard to believe that any here is specifically a pre-Conquest type. Although simple brooches akin to No. 23 and 31 occur under the silt at Skeleton Green, Puckeridge, Herts., which would put those examples in the years immediately before the Conquest (*Partridge*, forthcoming), their very simplicity will ensure that they could occur at any point in the general *floruit* of the type.

Aucissa-Hod Hill

32. (405). An uninscribed Aucissa with, across the head, a sunken bead row on each side of a flute ending in a semi-circular cut out. The bow is well curved in profile and has, between a ridge on either side, a raised central section with a sunken row of very fine beads down the middle. The main part of the bow ends in three cross mouldings below which the bow has a wide and shallow chamfer on each side.

33. (2122). An uninscribed brooch whose head is similar to the last except that the mouldings on either side of the flute and cut outs are not beaded. The profile of the bow is slacker than that of No. 32. The design is also different in that there is a wide and deep central hollow with, on either side, a ridge with a sunken bead row which shows signs of considerable wear. At the bottom of the main part is a repeat of the cross flute on the head with the cut outs and with small projections to either side above and below. The foot is longer than in No. 32 and the chamfers less well marked, but otherwise the foot-knob and catchplate are repeats.

34. (2025). An uninscribed brooch whose head is the same as that of No. 32. The bow is different again, however, from No. 32 and 33; the section is roughly hexagonal and there is a bead-row running down the front. The lower bow is similar to No. 32's, but with only one cross moulding. The foot-knob has become detached and the head, pin and catchplate are missing.

35. (284). This specimen shows signs of the transition from the Aucissa to the Hod Hill. The ornament on the head is like that on No. 33. The bow section is flat behind and gently rounded on the front.

36. (534). Although strictly neither an Aucissa or a Hod Hill, this brooch is an imitation of a brooch belonging to the transition between them. The bow profile is very slack, much as that of a Hod Hill proper. Down each side of the bow is a wide shallow flute and the area between has a sunken ridge which has been treated with a rectangular ended punch on each side alternately to produce a very crude zigzag. At the bottom of the main bow are two cross-mouldings below which there is a sudden constriction to a very narrow plain section. The catchplate is very badly damaged and it is not clear that there had ever been a foot-knob.

37. (1167). The axis bar for the hinged pin, both of which are missing, was housed in the rolled under head of the bow, which has very slight expansions at the top. The bow tapers to the foot which, as it survives, is pointed. Down to the top of the start of the catchplate there are three bead-rows, one down each side and the third down the centre. Although the bow is now bent, there appears to have been a point of inflection in the profile at the top of the catchplate, the lower bow being more vertical. The catchplate appears to be complete in that there is no sign of a broken edge, yet there is no sign of the return and it is possible that the lower bow was once longer with a much larger catchplate.

38. (500). The axis bar for the hinged pin still retains its terminal caps. The upper part of the bow tapers upwards to a waist below the expanded head. On the waist are three cross-mouldings. Below these, the central part of the bow has a broad swelled surface with a suggestion of an arris down the middle and with a series of cross-cuts down it. To each side there is a bead-row and then a bordering ridge. Each of the lower corners of the upper bow has a wing with two vertical cross-mouldings. The lower bow is narrow and plain except for cross-mouldings at top and bottom, and ends in a foot-knob.

39. (2071). A repeat of No. 38 in general, but there is a single cross-moulding at the top, the inner bordering ridge is not beaded and there are three cross-mouldings below the upper bow.

40. (715). Similar to the last two, except that the upper bow is a triangle placed the other way up. Just below the rolled-over head is a cross-ridge. The wings at the top corners consist of a single moulding. The inner bordering ridge is beaded and there is another, sunken one, down the centre. The bottom of the triangle has four slight cross-mouldings with a wide flute between the lower two.

41. (1012). The head is missing, but part of the slot for the hinged pin survives showing that there were no mouldings above the main bow which is shaped basically to a triangle with the point uppermost. The brooch was once tinned.

42. (459). The upper part of the bow has three beaded vertical ridges separated by deep flutes. Beneath these is a strong cross-moulding and to each side at the bottom is a wing terminating in vertical mouldings.

43. (2171). This brooch is of extravagant shape. The upper bow has two central ridges and a flute down its length with a large wing to either side at the top; these end in a large knob and with two cross-mouldings on the arm. Between the upper and lower bows are two strong cross-mouldings divided by a flute and with another one to top and bottom. The lower bow has lost its foot-knob and consists of a flat plate with curved sides.

44. (2097). *Not illustrated.* Part of a tinned brooch, most probably a Hod Hill, the upper bow of which has lost its head, is flat, and has a groove down each side. The lower bow is thin, plain and tapers to a foot-knob.

45. (2172). The focus of the bow is a circular plate with peripheral mouldings and a central hole, very probably for an enamelled boss; on each side are traces of a wing. Above and below the central plate are triple cross-mouldings, the middle one of which is wide and beaded. The lower bow tapers to a foot-knob with a cross-moulding above.

46. (1059). The bow is narrow with a rounded front and tapers from a double moulding, with a wide flute at the top, to the foot-knob with a cross-moulding above.

47. (253). Very similar to the last, the upper moulding, however, lying above a right-angled band in the bow which is flat on the front face and tapers to a very narrow foot-knob like that of No. 46.

Although all the above brooches have been grouped here as part of the Aucissa-Hod Hill sequence, it is worth emphasising that the name Aucissa seems only in Britain to occur on brooches with a bow design like that of No. 32. That such brooches were not exclusively made at the same workshop is shown by the use of other names such as TARRA and ATGIVIOS (both from Wroxeter, TARRA to be published; ATGIVIOUS, *Wroxeter*, p. 199, Pl. 47, H.22). Designs such as No. 33 and 34 which are obviously related to the Aucissa should, however, be regarded as belonging to different workshops even if they are not also of essentially a different *floruit* from the better known type. It should be pointed out that No. 33 shows signs of long usage which may indicate that this type had come to the end of its *floruit* by the time of the Conquest. The design is poorly represented in Britain, but examples were obviously in use into the later 50's as one from Wroxeter indicates; this latter is a good parallel for No. 33 in that the treatment of the cross-mouldings at the bottom of the main section of the bow is virtually identical (*ibid.*, p. 201, Fig. 36, H.8).

The Aucissa and some of the related types represented at Chichester seem to belong to the period after the first decade of the 1st century. It may be noted that none occur at Dangstetten, a site which seems to have come to an end in A.D. 9 (*Dangstetten*, p. 217, Abb. 8, 2–7; *J.R.S.* LIX, 1969, pp. 145–7). Those present at Dangstetten occur sporadically in Britain and may well, where they are found, indicate pre-Conquest occupation (note those found at Skeleton Green, publication forthcoming).

The Chichester Aucissa-type brooches are clearly at the end of their manufacturing life; the numbers present are minimal and there are several brooches which show the developing Hod Hill type clearly (*Chichester* 2, p. 143, Fig. 8.15, 15; *S.N.Q.* XIV, Nov. 1955, p. 105, frontispiece, 57; 534 below) bearing in mind that they were never great in quantity compared with the Aucissa types and the succeeding Hod Hill types. None for instance, occurs in the large brooch collection from Hod Hill and the proportion there of Aucissa types as against fully developed Hod Hills is enough to ensure that it is only accident that has prevented any of the transitional types from surviving.

No. 36 above is a copy of a transitional type, if not of an Aucissa; No. 37 belongs to the same group, being apparently a copy of a Hod Hill rather than an Aucissa. In both, the foot-knobs are missing. Clearly, in No. 36 it may be because the knob has become detached, but in No. 37 the matter is in some doubt. The catchplate is so weak that it is possible that more has been lost from the bottom of the brooch than appears at first sight. While most of the copies of the Continental types in Britain seem to have been made here, there is no good guarantee that either of these specimens was. In the case of No. 36, the presence of a separately made foot-knob is most likely a feature of a Continental copy, and in the case of No. 37, the care with which the bead-rows are made is much greater than would be expected on British copies, even if the

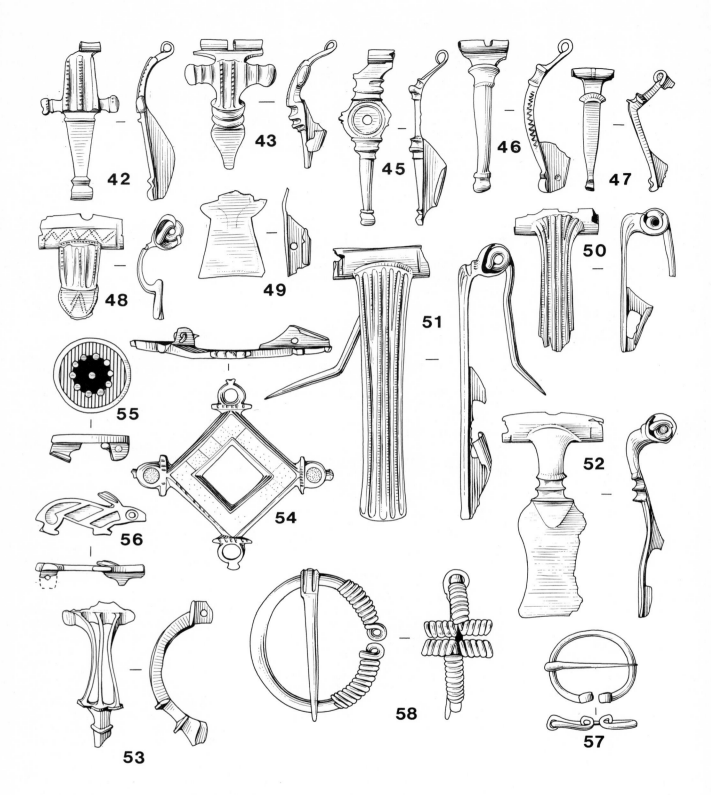

Fig. 10.28 Roman brooches, Nos. 42–58 ($\frac{1}{1}$)

attempt were to be made (*Hod Hill* i, 1962, pp. 9–10, Fig. 10, C.81). None of the Hod Hills in the collection is close to the type from which it springs, although these include the commonest of the varieties (e.g. *Ant. J.* 12, 1932, p. 64, pl. XVII.8a; *Arch. Cant.* LXXI, p. 97, Fig. 14.2; cf. *Camulodunum*, p. 322, Pl. XCVI.125 and 126). The unusual examples are No. 40 with the holes through the lower bow, No. 45 with the circular plate on the bow, and Nos. 46 and 47. Hull, in discussing the brooches from Bagendon, wished to distinguish those with iron rods through them for the mounting of knobs, from others which would normally be grouped with Hod Hills (*Bagendon* 1961, 176–82). The exercise showed that the only "group" to emerge was the secondary, imitative one. The primary group with rods which pass through the brooch was much more diffuse and revealed that the main type was, in fact, the Hod Hill, although generally esoteric in appearance. No. 40 is much more normal, but the presence of a brazed or sweated on foot-knob shows that it should be classed as an early Hod Hill. (One may note that of seven illustrated by Hull, *ibid.*, four seem to have the same form of foot-knob, Fig. 34.1–3 and Fig. 35.3. Fig. 34.4 is not included here as the projections are not applied but are part of the body of the brooch, cf. one from Ilchester, to be published.) Hull dated such brooches to Augusto-Tiberian times, but it is perhaps better to place them after 30 and before A.D. 43 One may note that the early dating once given to Bagendon now appears to have been optimistic, and the date of the major occupation 1A should be moved to begin probably at the Conquest (*Britannia*. VI, 1975, pp. 59–61). No. 45 has a parallel at Colchester (*Camulodunum*, p. 324, Pl. XCVIII.162), but the head above the disc consists of four vertical ridges. Another from Hod Hill is closer (*Hod Hill* ii, p. 113, Fig. 56.3; this may have had enamel but there is no description of the brooch in the text). The closest parallel, however, comes from Holbrooks, Old Harlow (unpublished), and may have come from the same mould. None of the parallels is dated except that any brooch from Hod Hill should have arrived there by A.D. 50 (*Hod Hill* ii, pp. 117–19). Brooches 46 and 47 both show similar characteristics but also belong to one of the smallest major groups of Hod Hill, those whose bows are essentially of one element instead of two. The Hod Hill arrives in Britain virtually completely developed and its *floruit* runs into the 60's, as examples from Gloucester and Wroxeter show, but it had largely passed from use by A.D. 70 as the paucity of specimens in the lands taken in under Petilius Cerialis demonstrates.

Rosettes

48. (229). The spring case has a rectangular panel on the front marked out by grooves. In the panel is a chevron made up of a double line of punched dots. Across the head of the bow is a beaded ridge below which is a series of vertical mouldings. These are grouped as three in the centre, separated from double ones down each side by a flute. The bow ends at the top of a roughly semi-circular plate which has two pendant triangles made up of double lines of punched dots. The fantail foot is missing, but was clearly part of the same casting.

49. (469). Part only of the upper circle and fantail foot of a plate Rosette brooch. The catchplate appears to have been worked up by hand, and the front of the plate has traces which suggest that a repousse bronze sheet once covered it.

The early versions of this type of brooch are made in several parts. The later ones are much simplified as far as manufacture is concerned but still have a complex appearance. This is well borne out by No. 48 which still has a spring case and the decorative detail to be expected on multipart brooches while being itself a single piece (cf. *Camulodunum*, p. 315, Pl. XCIII; *Chichester* 1, p. 130, Fig. 6.4, is probably of the same type as the Camulodunum brooches). The Rosette was evolving in Augustan times, but the single casting seems to come in much later and No. 48 should belong to the last few years before the Conquest (one should note that all the Rosettes at Skeleton Green, Puckeridge, Herts., were multipiece examples; to be published).

No. 49 is related, but at a remove. The general shape is the same except that the upper part of the bow has usually become subsumed into the pin fixing arrangement (*Camulodunum*, p. 316. Pl. XCIV, 82; *Dudley* 1949, Fig. 52.1), or disappears altogether once the hinge is fastened to the back of the main rosette plate (*Archaeologia* 92, 1947, p. 144, Fig. 7.6). The effect of the brooch would have been carried by the repousse plate (cf. *Ant. J.* XV, 1935, p. 250, Fig. 2; *Archaeologia* 92, 1947, p. 143, Fig. 7.5).

The dating of both these brooches matches to some extent that of the Aucissa-Hod Hill sequence. No. 48 should have lasted for a few years after the Conquest, while No. 49 should continue through the 50's. The rosette is always rarer than the Hod Hill and it is possible that it did not carry far into the 60's.

Langton Downs

50. (541). The spring is held as in No. 52 below. The front of the spring case is marked out by grooves as a rectangular panel from the centre of which rises the head of the reeded bow set off from the spring case by a moulding across the top. The catchplate is triangular and has a sub-triangular piercing.

51. (2207). As No. 50, but larger, the catchplate being damaged but retaining traces of two piercings separated by a bar.

The Langton Down is not a brooch which shows much typological change. It was once thought that early specimens could be distinguished from late ones by means of their size and an inflected bow (*Camulodunum*, p. 317), but it seems that the picture is much more complex; the range of designs on the Langton Down suggests various workshops and the size may have been dictated by price as much as by any other criterion. Thus, there is nothing in either No. 50 or 51 to say which is the earlier and they could well be contemporary. The reeded bow of both is the common design and it is possible that it is slightly later in introduction than the flat, straight-sided type which has decoration in the form of ridges and, often, bead-rows, but the evidence is weak (the normal reeded bow only comes in at Skeleton Green in the last phases of that site, but the numbers are not great and it may be chance alone which has dictated which decorative types survived in which phase). It is coming into the country near the beginning of the 1st century A.D. and continues until the Conquest. Thereafter it was waning and it is unlikely that the type was still being made as late as A.D. 50.

Unclassified

52. (447). The spring is held in a sheet bronze tube which forms a cylinder across the head of the brooch. The tube is formed by means of two flaps of metal which are closed round the spring and which have a slit behind for the pin. The head is too corroded to reveal if there was any decoration on top of the tube, but such ornament is to be expected. Normally, a panel is defined by incised lines and the space filled with incised or punched dot decoration. The head of the bow is shaped like a trumpet and is set off from the spring-case by a moulding which is very often beaded, but is here too corroded for beading to show. At the bottom of the trumpet head are three cross-mouldings separated one from another by deep flutes. The lower part of the bow is a flat plate with ogee sides and the bottom is squared off. Beneath the lowest cross-moulding at the top is a raised triangular area. The catchplate is damaged but had one large piercing. Such brooches are not common in Britain and like the Langton Down type, probably had a *floruit* roughly parallel with those Rosettes whose spring is held in the same fashion, roughly the first half of the 1st century A.D., but possibly not becoming relatively common until the second decade. Elaborate examples are rare (cf. *Camulodunum*, p. 319, Pl. XCV.113; parallels for the present specimen come from Colchester, *Ant. J.* XXII, p. 61, Fig. 1.7) where they were associated with Claudian pottery. A less splendid version is also to be found in Britain where its associations suggest that it was coming in with the army of conquest and its followers (*Britannia* V, 1974, p. 44, Fig. 23.6; *Hod Hill* i, p. 8, Fig. 8.C43).

53. (2061). The spring, now missing was held to the body of the brooch by means of an axis bar through the coils of the spring and through a pierced plate behind the head of the bow. The main part of the surviving fragment consists of three thin ribs, each with a groove down it, joined at top and bottom by narrow plates. That at the top has rounded ends and traces of the triangular plate which once rose above the head. The bottom plate is shaped to three triangular peaks each of which occurs in front of one of the ribs. Beneath this plate the bow section is triangular and there is a cross-moulding just above the break which is at the top of the catchplate.

The full form of this brooch can be seen in an example from Richborough (*Richborough* II, p. 43, Pl. XVII.13), and in another one from Corbridge (*Corstopitum* 1911, p. 42, Fig. 22). The date range appears to be the latter part of the 2nd century and far into the 3rd. Examples from Dura-Europos fit in well with this as the site was only occupied by the Romans in the relevant period from 165 to A.D. 256 (*Dura-Europos* IV, p. 58, Pl. XIV.98, and *ibid.*, p. 59, Pl. XIV.110). The number of examples of this and related types from Saalburg and Zugmantel, sites which ceased to be occupied *c.* A.D. 260 (*Saalburg* 1972, on date; pp. 9–10 and pp. 25–6 under Type 27, Nos. 655–97, Taf. 15–16) suggests that the date range is reasonably secure, and another brooch from Carpow, Perth., sits neatly in the middle (*Ant. Scot.* XCVI, p. 206, Fig. 11.4).

54. (903). The main part of the brooch is an open square set in diamond fashion. Sunk into the body of the square is a continuous strip of glass/enamel panels which are now heavily corroded but may once have been of *millefiore* glass. Mounted on each point of the diamond is a beaded cross-bar which supports a circular plate with a knob at the opposite side from the diamond. The circular plates to each side are voided, while those to top and bottom, the latter of which hides the catchplate, have rounded enamel inserts, now stained green.

This is almost certainly a continental import and presumably belongs to the main run of imported enamelled plate or pseudo-bow brooches. They occur fairly frequently in this country, but seldom in a dated context. One from Chichester comes from a grave dated towards the end of the 2nd century (*Chichester* 1, p. 113, Grave 228K), while another from Chichester comes from a grave in Northgate containing a ring set with a coin of Caracalla (this volume p. 7 and Fig. 10.48). One from Camerton dates from before A.D. 180 (*Wedlake* 1958, p. 230, Fig. 53.48). The date can be taken further back at Verulamium where one comes from a context of about A.D. 155–160 (*Verulamium* 1972, p. 118, Fig. 31.23). That such brooches are likely to be common in the 3rd century is shown by their occurrence in numbers at Dura-Europos, Saalburg and Zugmantel (*Dura-Europos* IV, part IV, Fascicule 1, pp. 40–1, Pls. viii–ix, 17–29; *Saalburg* 1972, Type 41, pp. 36–3, Taf. 24–6).

55. (2121). A circular plate with a recessed field from which rises, in the centre, a small circular stud, between this and the border lie ten enamel dots arranged in circle around the centre. The field is filled with enamel coloured blue between the middle and the encircling dots, and green in the rest. It is probable that the green enamel was a fugitive colour now stained by corrosion products. The pin was sprung with three coils and an internal chord caught between two projecting plates.

It is possible that this is a British brooch rather than a Continental import. The parallels seem to be here although there is little to provide a date; probably 2nd century.

Zoomorphic

56. (299). A plate cast to the shape of a hare with two legs showing and its ears laid back. On the body there are three cells for enamel and the eye is a sunken ring, presumably for more enamel. No enamel survives. The pin was sprung but is now missing. Animal brooches are not particularly common in Britain and the most popular subjects are birds and hares. In general, rarity usually means that there is a paucity of dating evidence. Hares are shown running or crouched. The latter type having two enamelled leverets set into the body of the mother (*Richborough* IV, p. 116, Pl. XXIX.44). One from Winchester comes from a context of about A.D. 60. However, in the present case the date, like that of so many enamelled plate brooches, is probably 2nd century.

Penannulae

57. (648). The ring is small, thin and has a circular section. The terminals are turned back at right angles to the plane of the ring and show a slight tendency towards a spiral.

This brooch belongs to Fowler's Type C (*P.P.S.* XXVI, 1960, p. 152). The distribution of the type belongs to the Lowland areas of Britain with an emphasis on the Belgic areas of south-east and central southern England (*ibid.*, Fig. 9), although there seems to be a general lack in Atrebatic territory (*ibid.*, p. 166). The type is well established by the earliest years of the Conquest and should be pre-Conquest in origin and development.

58. (1160). A very impressive brooch, the ring is sturdy and has a circular section tapering out from the thickest part opposite the opening. The terminals are, in fact, the hammered out ends of the ring which are then coiled elaborately in the manner of a Colchester spring; out to the left for five coils then a chord passes to the extreme right-hand end and returns to the centre in five coils; there, the wire is then wound round the ring for eleven or twelve turns, the very end tapering out neatly. The pin flattens out at the ring end, has a groove across the beginning of the wrap round which has two circumferential grooves stopped at the far end by another cross-groove.

This splendid specimen is an exaggerated example of Fowler's Type C.1 (*ibid.*, p. 152). Its date should be 1st century and to the period before the demise of the Colchester whose spring system is imitated.

Of the two brooches reported on below by Miss S. A. Butcher, F.S.A., one comes from a grave group in Northgate and was discovered during road works (see below, p. 288) and the other was found during trial excavations at County Hall in 1960, which were supervised by the writer under the direction of Mr. John Holmes. The brooch was found many years later in the local museum, where it had been labelled as "medieval". In view of its comparative rarity it has been thought useful to publish it. No other brooch of this type has been found in the city.

A Note on Two Roman Brooches from Chichester

by S. A. Butcher, F.S.A.

Northgate Cemetery

Fig. 10.48

Enamelled disc-brooch. Diameter 32 mm (without lugs). Disc-brooch with raised centre bearing two zones of enamel and millefiori decoration and a border of plain metal with beaded rim, on which there are eight small plain lugs. The pin is hinged between two stout lugs; these and the catchplate are attached to the flat rim at the back of the brooch. There is a recess in the back corresponding to the raised disc on the front, but in the centre there is an opening through which the back of the enamel decoration can be seen, and this is surrounded by a metal flange forming a cup which has no apparent function; one can only speculate that it may have been a device for holding the brooch for polishing (concentric striations are visible), or that castings were made which could either take a central stud or opening (cf. examples from Hungary quoted below) or a uniform field as in the present case. The circular central field contains blue and white square chequers (of nine canes, with white in the outer corners) set irregularly in a field of red enamel. In some areas this is missing and the base of the chequers can be seen attached to the metal. The surrounding ring contains a circle of twenty-one spots formed of slices of a rod of opaque white wrapped in translucent greenish brown glass.[1] These were presumably set in a field of enamel but none of this remains. Four of the spots have some white glass on their outer surfaces; if not an overflow from the centre this may indicate the colour of the field.

The metal plate (which is bronze; milliprobe analysis established the presence of copper and tin), is finely moulded and the design accurately laid out. There are ridges of metal separating the main rings of the design; that bordering the raised central area has what appears to be a punched decoration of irregularly-spaced triangles, their apexes pointing outwards. The outer rim is decorated with fine diagonal lines, producing a beaded effect. These two types of decoration could only be applied to a positive and therefore could not have been cut in the mould. It seems unlikely that they were applied to the pattern from which the mould was made but certainty on this point is impossible without sectioning the brooch. Both the form and decoration of this brooch can be paralleled, but seldom on the same example. In Britain two brooches from Nornour (*Archeol. Journ.*, 124, 1968, Fig. 22, Nos. 202 and 203) have the form and the two types of millefiori, but each has only one enamelled zone and they lack the fine detailing of the metal. There is little doubt that the type is Continental and the closest parallels appear to be two brooches from Hungary published by Sellye (*Sellye* 1939, Ser. 2, fasc. 8). These, and one from Biesme (*Annales de la Soc. Archeologique de Namur*, 55, 1969, Fig. 47.18, seem, from the published illustrations, to have a central opening or possibly a stud as part of the design. Exner (*Exner* 1939, Taf. 17.2, p. 114), gives an example from Trier with only a single enamelled field (containing chequers) but which does have the beaded rim. None of the examples quoted is well-dated, but this type should belong to the general class of profiled disc brooches with enamel decoration in concentric rings, which Exner (*op. cit.*) dates to the second half of the 2nd century A.D.

Brooch from County Hall Site, 1960

Bronze brooch. L. 44 mm. It consists of a flat, keyhole-shaped plate which bears two applied bosses on the circular part and traces of a third on the triangular foot. There are no rivets and the bosses must have been fixed by solder or some form of adhesive. They are badly corroded but show signs of concentric rings of embossed mouldings, the outer one beaded. The pin is hinged between two lugs behind the disc and the catchplate is behind the centre of the foot.

A few generally similar brooches are known from Britain; e.g. Bushe Fox, *Richborough* IV, XXV.5, although this had a rivet to attach a (missing) decorative plate. Cunliffe, *Richborough* V, Pl. XXIX.41, is another. The closest parallel is Hawkes and Hull, *Camulodunum*, Pl. XCVIII.166, p. 325. This has traces of two beaded bosses on the circular plate similar to those on the Chichester brooch. It came from a pit dated to A.D. 50–60 and a date in the mid-1st century seems suitable for the other examples on typological considerations.

Footnote

[1] I am grateful to Leo Biek and Justine Bayley of the Ancient Monuments Laboratory for examining the brooch. The remarks on the techniques of decoration are theirs.

The Pipeclay Figurine

by Frank Jenkins, F.S.A.

Fig. 10.47

The head of a female personage made of white pipe-clay found at Chichester certainly belonged to a so-called "portrait bust", which when complete would have been *c.* 13.2 cms high, including the basal plinth. These busts were made in two-piece moulds in the *officinae* of Central Gaul, in fact an incomplete example was found in the remains of a potters habitation associated with a kiln at Banassac (Lozère).

The moulding of the face is rather flat, the chin is pointed and the forehead is receding. The nose is long and straight, the eyes are rather large and set close together and the neck is slender. A globular object on each ear lobe is probably ornamental. The hair is elaborately arranged in a high semi-circular diadem-like style, concave at the front and composed of three tiers of stylised curls. The hair at the back is indicated by short incised vertical lines, and other lines show that it was combed straight back close to the head and coiled up anti-clockwise into a small chignon placed midway between the nape of the neck and the crown of the head. A few closely similar or exact parallels are known and are listed below. None of these is dated by associated archaeological material, but the distinctive hair style may provide a clue. Elaborate coiffures of this kind were affected by the ladies of the Flavian court[1] and remained in vogue throughout the reign of Trajan.[2] Under Hadrian there was a return to the more simple classical Greek and Hellenistic models.[3] The art displayed by these busts is of such a low order that it is impossible to identify the subject as one particular female member of the Imperial Court. There is, however, a possibility that there was a demand for cheap mass-produced inferior copies in clay of an expensive fine art portrait bust of one of these ladies, for purchase by members of the lower classes of provincial society to serve as expressions of their loyalty, to be placed in the home or to be presented at temples on some national festival occasion. The inference to be drawn from the hair style is that this type of bust was manufactured at some time between A.D. 80–120, certainly in the Central Gaulish clay statuette factories.

List of clay busts of the Chichester type:
1. Vichy (allier) probably, but now without provenance. Complete. St. Germain-en-Laye Museum, Inv. No. 25484.[4]
2. Banassac (Lozère), incomplete. St. Germain-en-Laye Museum, Inv. No. 19612.[5]
3. Clermount-Ferrand (Puy de Dôme), incomplete. St. Germain-en-Laye Museum, Inv. No. 28118.
4. Tannkirch near Ribeauville (Haut Rhin), fragment of face. St. Germain-en-Laye Museum, Inv. No. 6880.[4]
5. Silchester (Hants.), fragment of face as No. 4 above. Reading Museum.[5]

289

[1] For example, Julia the daughter of Titus: Domitia the wife of Domitian.

[2] For the Trajanic examples on the coinage cf. Mattingly and Sydenham, *The Roman Imperial Coinage*, Plotina, Pl. IX.160; Pl. XII.215; Vibia Matidia, Pl. IX.160; Marciana, Pl. XII.216; Vivia Sabina, Pl. IX.335.

The same coiffure is affected by a female personage, possibly Vibia Matidia, the subject of a portrait bust in marble, cf. Rannuchio Bianchi, *Rome, the Centre of Power* (Thames and Hudson).

[3] J. M. C. Toynbee, *The Art of the Romans* (Thames and Hudson, 1965), p. 36.

[4] M. Rouvier-Jeanlin, *Les figurines gallo-romaines en terre cuite au Musée des Antiquités Nationales, XXIVe supplément à "Gallia"* (Paris 1972), Nos. 772, 773, 774 and 793 for the Gaulish examples.

[5] T. May, *The Roman pottery found at Silchester* (Reading 1916), p. 103, Pl. XXXIX B, No. 8.

The Military Finds

Figs. 10.29–10.36

Over one hundred items of military equipment, or pieces which were probably associated with a military presence in Chichester, were found during the excavations. The majority of the finds came from the lower levels beneath the school playground in Area 2 in Chapel Street, in an indisputably mid 1st century context. They must belong either to the earliest military presence on the site, that of the Second Legion, *c.* A.D. 43–44 or possibly to a small Depot which may have been established for a few years after the invasion. I am most grateful, first to Dr. Graham Webster, F.S.A., who kindly examined a number of the earlier finds and reported on them, and secondly to Mr. H. Russell Robinson, F.S.A., who looked at the material from the later excavations and identified those which were from military equipment. Dr. Webster's comments are reproduced in full where possible, with his initials against each note.

(a) *Objects of iron*
1. Ballistae bolt head, tapered form, cf. *Longthorpe* 1974, 77, Fig. 41.9. *Area 3. A.8.*
2. Pilum head and part of shank of square section; total remaining length *c.* 52 cms. *Area 2. G.176.*
3. Spear head with flat leaf-shaped blade, broken at the tip, *op. cit.* 75, Fig. 40. Nos. 4–6. *Area 2. G.86.*
4. Ballistae bolt head; see No. 1. *Area 5. P.70.*
5. Ballistae bolt head; *Area 2. Pit L.81(D). Not illustrated.*
6. Fragment of flat iron sheet, found with belt buckle and plate No. 10 below. One edge is overlapped and beaten flat and there are faint traces of bronze corrosion products in the surface which may be from a bronze lobate hinge. Probably from the *lorica segmentata*. *Area 2. J.93.*
7. Part of a bow saw, teeth set 7 to the inch; *op. cit.* 79, Fig. 42, Nos. 27 and 28. *Area 2. E.150.*
8. Socketed iron chisel, cf. *Newstead* Pl. LIX.8. *Area 2. E.148.*
9. Pickaxe blade. *Area 2. E.125.*

(b) *Objects of bronze*
10. Belt buckle with attached belt plate, the latter being tinned. Found with No. 6 above. *Area 2. J.93.*
11. Belt plate with traces of the iron hinge pins on each side. *Area 2. G.118.*
12. Belt plate with a hinge at one end and a central boss and ring in relief, and decorated with tool marks. Similar to those found on a complete belt at Risstissen (Taf. 32, No. 5, cf. also Rheingönheim, Taf. 27, No. 3). G.W. *Area 3. Z.48.*
13. Flat belt plate decorated with a circular pattern of five dogs chasing a boar, formed by light punch marks and scored lines. There are copper rivets at each corner to fasten it to the belt. Plates of this type are unusual, but it can be matched by one from Hofheim (Taf. XII, No. 15). G.W. *Area 2. E.115.*
14. Scale, one of two found, from the *lorica squamata*, cf. *Longthorpe* 1974, Fig. 27, No. 35. *Area 2. G.31.*
15. Tongue from buckle, fleur-de-lis type, used with buckle type shown in 10 above; traces of tinning on upper surface. *Area 4. M.67.*

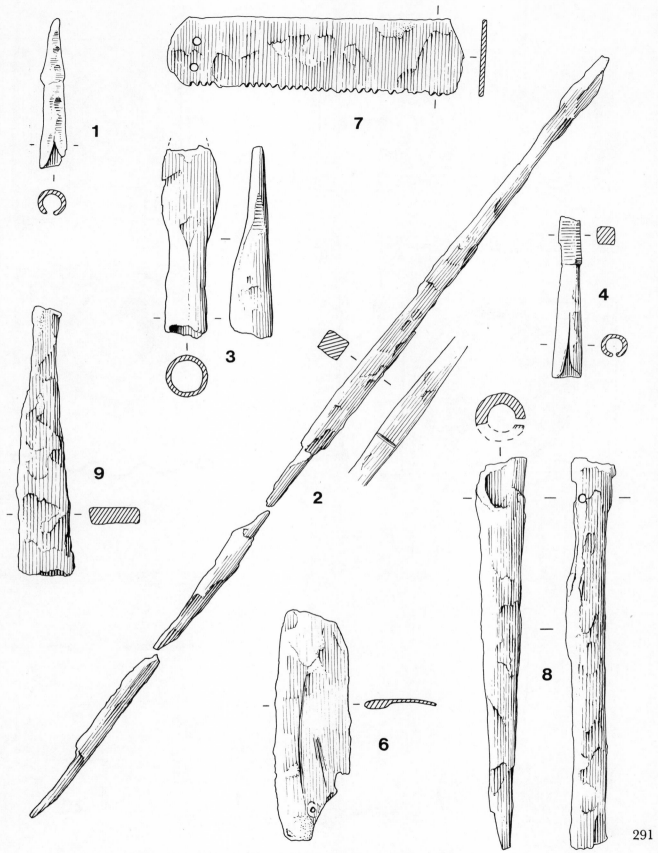

Fig. 10.29 Roman military finds, of iron, Nos. 1–9 (¼)

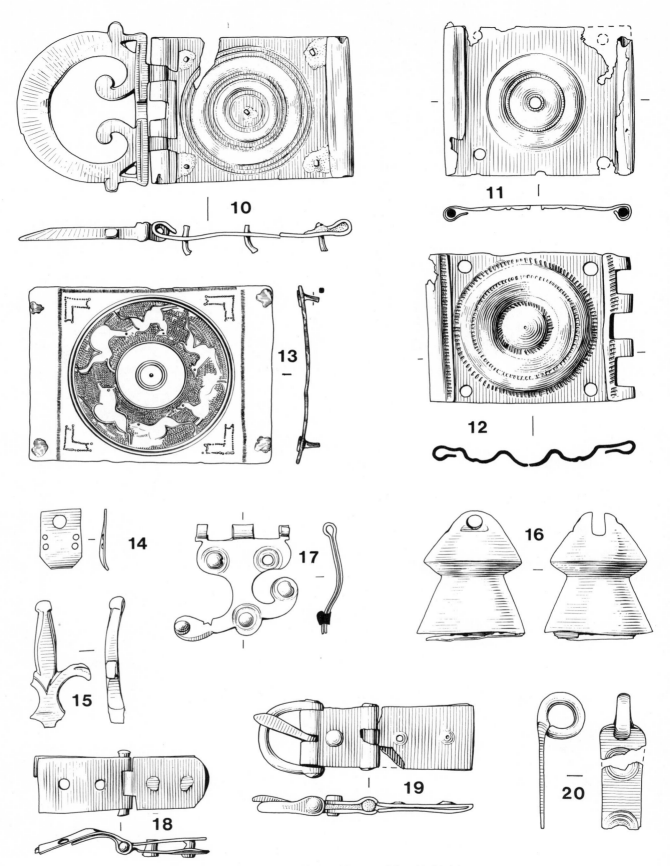

Fig. 10.30 Roman military finds, of bronze, Nos. 10–20 (½)

16. Crest knob from the top of a legionary helmet of Coolus type, with a slot 4 mm wide in the top to take the base of the plume or crest. This was fastened by a pin passed through two holes on either side of the slot. It is made from a solid bronze casting, and although the method by which it was fixed to the top of the helmet is not quite certain, it is likely that it was secured by means of a rivet, cast integrally with the knob, which was passed through a fixing hole at the top of the helmet and then hammered over. There are traces of cloth impression in the corrosion products on the flattened surface which would have been inside the helmet, and this may be from the helmet lining. See *Robinson* 1975, pp. 38–9, for typical examples. *Area 3. Pit Z.34.*

17. Bronze lobated hinge from the *lorica segmentata*, cf. *Longthorpe* 1974, 46, and Fig. 25. See also *Robinson* 1975, 176–8, for reconstructions of the *lorica segmentata*. *Area 2. E.104.*

18. Cuirass hinge plate, cf. *Hod Hill* 1, Fig. 3, A.64. *Area 2. Pit E.90.*

19. Cuirass buckle from *lorica segmentata*, cf. *Longthorpe* 1974, Fig. 25, and *Hod Hill* 1, Fig. 3, A.54. *Area 3. Z.31.*

20. Cuirass hook, cf. *Longthorpe* 1974, 50, (31), and Fig. 26. *Area 3. Pit Z.34.*

21. Strip of bronze, *c.* 15 cms long by 2.5 cms wide. An attempt has been made to roll it into an overlapping tube, but this has apparently been abandoned and the strip discarded. There are three small holes present in the flat section, with what may be another one at the other end. This may possibly be an unsuccessful attempt to repair the binding on a shield. *Area 2. G.64.*

22. Embossed mount from the scabbard of a Mainz type sword, with traces of tinning or silvering remaining, cf. *Mainzer Zeitscrift* XII/XIII (1917–18), p. 175, Abb. 6. See also *Hod Hill* i, Fig. 1, A.7, for similar relief pattern. *Area 2. E.103.*

23. Part of a loop from a similar scabbard mount to 21. *Area 3. Z.31.*

24. Boss, probably from an Imperial/Gallic helmet, cf. *Robinson* 1975, 52, No. 111. *Area 2. E.73.*

25. Cuirass hinge plate, similar to No. 17, with iron hinge remaining. *Area 2. Slot 14(b).*

26. Hinged plate with two rivet holes, with the upper surface chip carved to give a serrated surface. Possibly from the *lorica*. *Area 7. D.5.*

27. Plume tube from the legionary helmet. *Area 6. R.12.*

28. Strip of tinned bronze with the remains of rivets on the face side; probably from a hinge plate. *Area 2. E.156.*

29. Scabbard ring for attachment of the scabbard mount (see No. 21) to the baldric; cf. *Robinson* 1975, Pl. 1. *Area 5. P.71.*

30. Scabbard ring (see No. 28). *Area 2. L.145.*

31. Scabbard ring (see above). *Area 2. Posthole E.123.*

32. Well formed ring recessed for a collar attachment, function uncertain. From an early Roman layer. *Area 2. E.164.*

33. Part of the sheath for an axe, normally carried by legionaries, cf. *Newstead* 279, *Hod Hill* 1, Fig. 5, A.137. *Area 3. Pit Z.39.*

34. Helmet carrying handle, cf. *Robinson* 1975, p. 59, No. 138, see also Fig. 76 for nearest example. The handle was retained on the helmet by two rivetted strips, one of which survived with the handle.

35. Large square buckle with a pair of plates with four copper rivets for attachment to a strap 52 mm wide. Large buckles of this type were normally used for harness straps like a girth band, or possibly as a pack strip on a mule, cf. *Hofheim*, Taf. XIV, No. 23; *Aislingen*, Taf. 18, No. 26; *Risstissen*, Taf. 61, No. 26. *From Area 2. G.125.*

36. Pin from a large buckle, probably a girth buckle similar to 35. *Area 5. J.84.*

37. Cast bronze fitting with fixing holes at each end. Both ends have been cut away presumably to allow the head of the stud or whatever fixing was used, to lie flush with the surface. This might be one of a pair of harness fittings for a horse. *Area 3. Pit Y.16.*

38. Fitting, possibly part of a curb bit. *Area 2. L.115.*

39. Fragment of scabbard edging, tinned or silvered, heavily corroded. *Area 2. Pit E.89.*

40. ? Bridle ring. *Area 2. E.162.*

41. Ring, possibly from a harness. *Area 5. Pit O.29.*

42. Swan's head harness pendant, cf. *Longthorpe* 1975, Fig. 30.62 and *Hod Hill* 1, Fig. 3, A.40. *Area 2. Pit J.8.*

43. Similar pendant to 42 but lacking the suspension loop. *Area 5. Pit P.37(b).*

44. Bronze convex disc with a flattened rim and slightly sunken central area. It is decorated on the raised part with niello leaves and dots. There are four rivet holes placed symmetrically

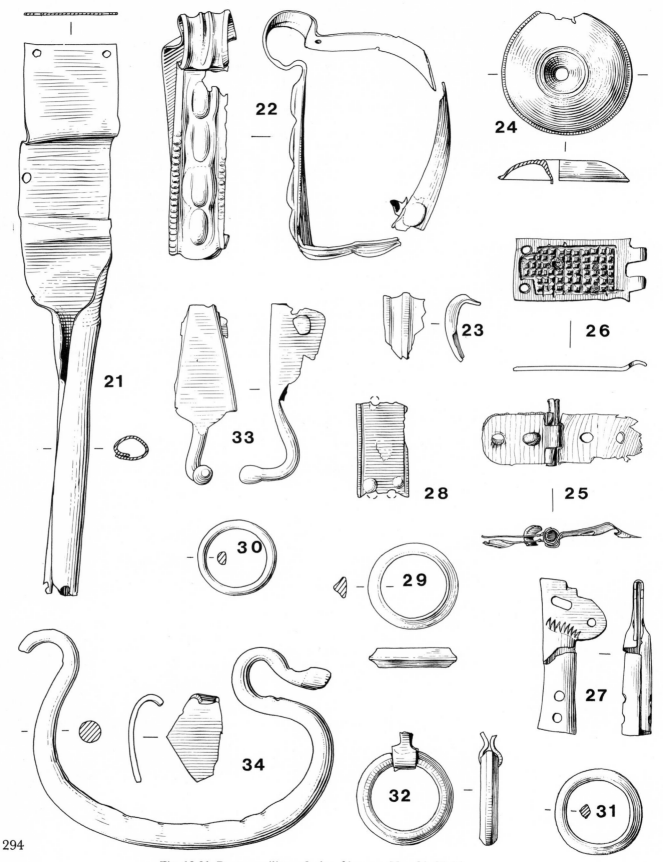

294

Fig. 10.31 Roman military finds, of bronze, Nos. 21–34 ($\frac{1}{2}$)

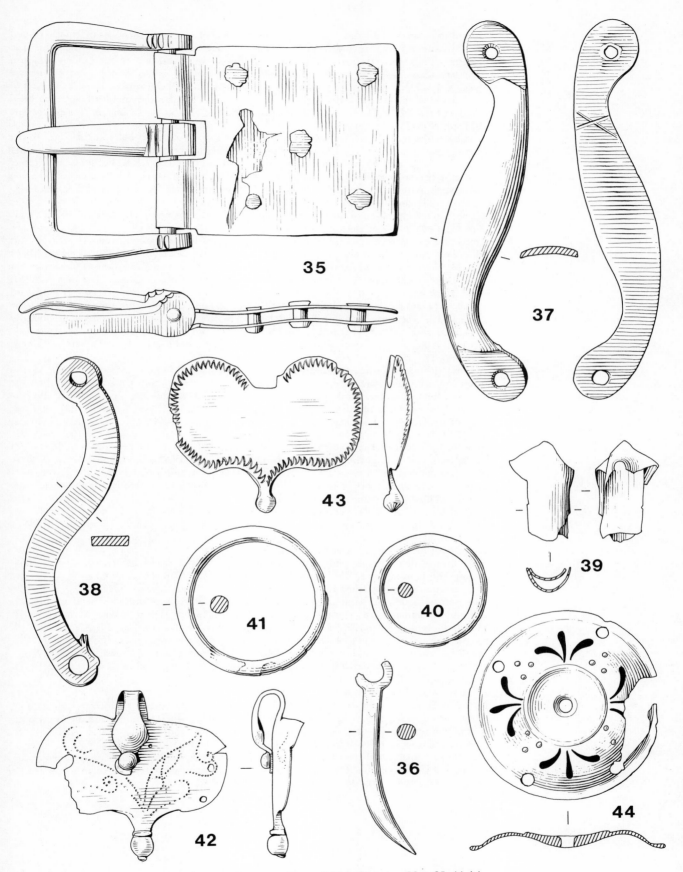

Fig. 10.32 Roman military finds, of bronze, Nos. 35–44 ($\frac{1}{1}$)

around the edge and a countersunk stud hole in the centre. The surface was originally tinned but this was lost in conservation. The classic publication of equipment to which this disc belongs is the Doorweth hoard found in the Rhine in 1895 and now in the Leiden Museum (*Oudheidkundige Mededeelingen uit 'sRijksmuseum van Oudheden te Leiden*. Supplement bij nieuwe reeks, XII, 1931, 1–26). A study of this hoard showed how all the various items were part of the harness of horsemen of the early Flavian period. A similar but smaller hoard has been found at Fremington Hagg, near Richmond, Yorkshire (*Soldier and Civilian in Roman Yorkshire* 1971, pp. 107–25).

The peculiarity of this Chichester disc is the presence of four rivet holes at the edge. In the cavalry examples it is normal to find loops and hinges at the back for attachment to leather straps. It is unusual, but very similar to a Newstead example (Pl. LXXIV, No. 9) and it may be that they were attached to bronze plates rather larger than usual, or for harness decorating straps such as those reconstructed from the Doorwerth pieces (Afb. 8), or rather less likely for the saddle cloth (*ibid.*, Afb. 7). (G.W.). *Area 2. E.157.*

45. Three bronze studs found together; probably from the sporran; cf. *Robinson* 1975, Pl. 1. *Area 4. M.38.*
46. Bronze ink pot with hinged lid. It had several lumps of iron corrosion products sticking to it when excavated and this may indicate that it was housed in an iron stand. See *Longthorpe* 1974 Fig. 33, No. 85, for a lid from a similar vessel. There was an accumulation of black powder in the bottom of the pot which must have been the dried residues of the ink. *From Area 2. E.191.*
47. A heavy bronze terminal in the form of an eagle's head. An iron tang is attached with lead which has been run into the hollow casting. The upward curved projection normally at the front and in the form of a bird's head has been broken away. These objects are usually associated with military cart fittings and a brief discussion of them exists elsewhere (*Arch. J.* CXV (1960), pp. 74–5, see also one from Genisheim–Böbingen 1969, Taf. 11). (G.W.). *Area 2. G.32.*
48. A heavy decorated bronze head attached to an iron shank 13 mm square. There is a 14 mm square projection on one face with a hole for a pin or rivet which penetrates only half the width of the metal. This could presumably be a linch pin, for holding together the timbers of a cart. Newstead has produced similar objects (Pl. LXXXIV, Nos. 2 and 3) and the same type of decoration on an iron object of unknown use (Pl. LXIV, No. 6). (G.W.). *Area 2. Slot G.34.*
49. A bronze pendant of lunate form with a phallus and tests below. The casting is hollowed out at the back and around the edge are four small projecting rings. Still attached to one of these is the copper head of a rivet. The shank of another rivet is still attached to the lower inner edge; there are two more rings at the horns of the crescent and there is a hole beneath the phallus. Thus the pendant did not hang freely, but was fastened to a leather strap. This general form of amulet is common and the normal types have been discussed (*T.B.A.S.* 83 (1969), 126–9, but a precise parallel for this particular form cannot be offered. (G.W.). *Area 2. E.129.*
50. Heavy cast bronze plumb weight. *Area 2. G.64.*
51. Thin bronze pelta-shaped plate with rivet holes, possibly a shield decoration. *Area 2. G.64.*
52. Button and loop fastener, Wild Type VIIIb (*Britannia* i, 1970). *Area 2. H.45.*
53. Bronze wing, probably from an eagle, or less likely, a Victory. *Area 2. L.127.*
54. The curved handle of what may be a clasp knife or razor; the animal's head terminal is probably intended to represent a lion. There is a similar object with a knife attached in the British Museum (*B.M.* 1929, Fig. 157d). See also Pitt Rivers, *Woodcuts*, Pl. XVIII, No. 10, for the more common type of straight knife with the dog chasing a hare. (G.W.).
55. Small leaf shaped pendant, one of three found, in the form of a tragic mask. *Area 2. G.105.*
56. Small pendant, or alternatively a hook, with the two holes being used to secure it to leather or cloth. *Area 7. F.27.*
57. Pendant, probably from a horse's harness. *Area 3. Z.*
58. Cast bronze fitting with an iron shank 9 mm diameter and with a slight taper on it. The shank has had a few flats roughly filed to prevent it turning when hammered home into wood. Probably a furniture fitting, possibly belonging to a camp stool. *Area 2. G.41.*
59. Apron mount with niello decoration, cf. *Longthorpe* 1974, Fig. 28, 45. *Area 2. J.77.*
60. Cast bronze object, half round in section and broken at the top. It is difficult to envisage the function of this piece, but it might be part of the decorative inlay for a box. *Area 2. E.115.*
61. Small pendant with ring dot decoration. *Area 7. Pit E.50.*

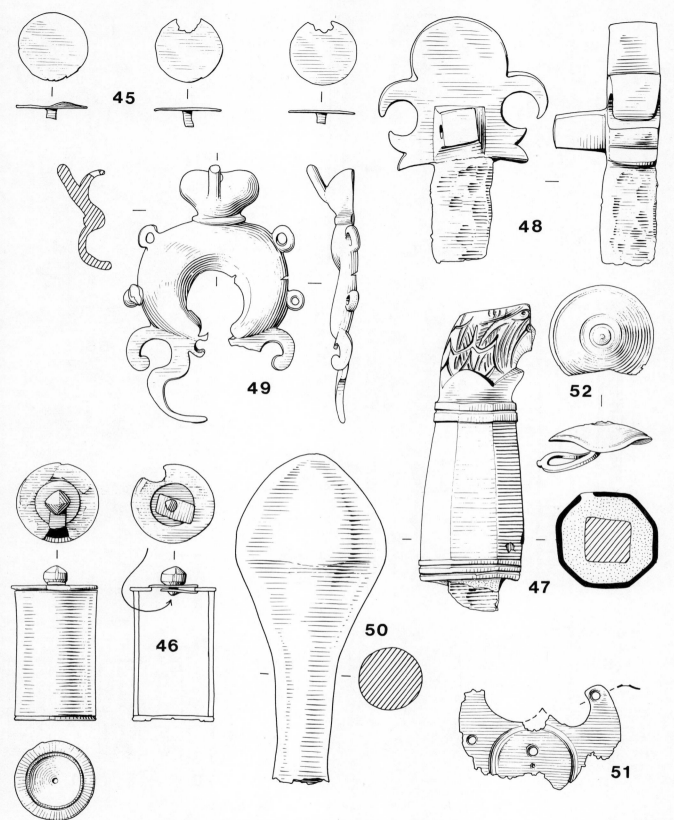

Fig. 10.33 Roman military finds, of bronze, Nos. 45–52 (⅓)

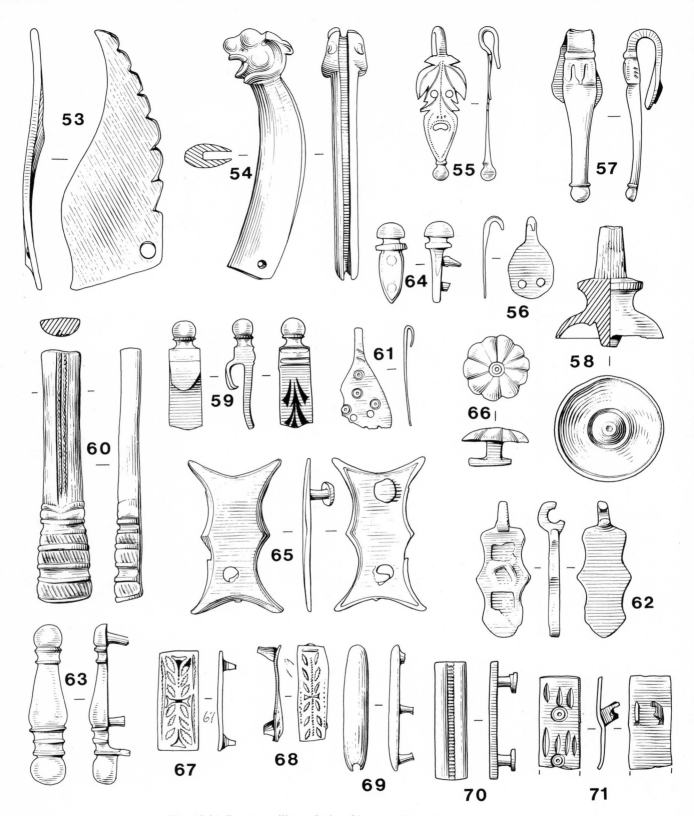

Fig. 10.34 Roman military finds, of bronze, Nos. 53–71 (⅓)

62. Cast bronze pendant with traces of enamel inlay. *Area 2. J.19.*
63. Hollow cast strap end, possibly from a horse's harness. *Area 2. P.70.*
64. Strap terminal, originally tinned. *Area 5. O.64.*
65. Bronze fitting for leather, possibly a belt stiffener. *Area 2. Pit G.36.*
66. Stud with a hollow convex head and square sectioned key fitting; function uncertain. *Area 6. Slot R.2.*
67. Belt stiffener with traces of niello decoration. *Area 6. Pit S.3.*
68. Belt stiffener. *Area 3. Z.59.*
69. Belt stiffener. *Area 2. G.106.*
70. Belt stiffener. *Area 2. L.72.*
71. Part of a bronze attachment for leather. *Area 2. Pit L.8(B).*
72. Zoomorphic cast bronze loop fastener with traces of red enamel inlay in the eyes. Variant of Wild Type 2, *Britannia* 1, Fig. L. *Area 2. Slot L.4(B).*
73. Cast bronze stud with lugs cast into the underside of the head to prevent it from turning. *Area 2. G.106.*
74. Bronze stud, possibly furniture fitting. *Area 2. J.93.*
75. Stud with flat head, similar to 73. *Area 2. H.42.*
76, 77, 78. Domed headed bronze studs, probably furniture fittings. *Area 2. G.29* and *Area 3. Z.38.*
79. Part of a thin circular plate of bronze with a central square hole punched into it. See *Longthorpe* 1974, Fig. 34, 102, for a plate of identical size. *Area 2. G.155.*
80. Part of a hinged buckle plate from a 1st-century *lorica segmentata*. *Area 7. Pit F.34.*
81. Tie ring from either the front or back of a girdle hoop of a *lorica segmentata*. This type were rivetted through a slot in the iron plate by the projecting tongue. They have been found at Carnuntum and Caerlyon; cf. *Robinson* 1975, p. 181, No. 184. *Area 5. P.114.*
82. Pendant, probably from a harness strap, originally one of a set of six or more, from breast and crupper straps or from a bridle. It may have been wrapped with a decorated silver plate. *Area 2. L.113.*
83, 84. These are both probably loops used for horse harness connections. *Area 7. B.60* and *Area 7. Posthole D.145..*
85. Fragment of tinned bronze, function unknown. It came from the earliest level in Area 7 and may be military. *Area 7. D.41.*
85B. *Objects of iron and bronze possibly or certainly military.*
The following fragments of sheet iron are all from Area 2; they were identified as military or possibly so in most cases only after X-ray photography had shown that there were the remains of bronze rivets and hinges below the iron corrosion products.
(i) *Pit L.101.* Fragment from a shoulder plate of the *lorica segmentata* with a bronze lobate hinge still attached and folded back.
(ii) *G.59.* Five fragments of armour plate with part of a bronze lobate hinge. Possibly from the front shoulder plate of a Corbridge Type B harness (*Robinson* 1975, p. 178).
(iii) *Kiln G.1.* Small fragment of iron sheet with traces of a bronze rivet attached.
(iv) *Slot E.4.* Fragment of ? armour plate showing four ornamental rivets, two with octagonal washers behind them.
(v) *E.144.* Fragment with a returned edge; possibly from the girdle of the lorica, with traces of two bronze rivets.
(vi) *Pit H.19.* Fragment with traces of a bronze rivetted strap and one decorative rivet head.
(vii) Large fragment, function uncertain, but could be armour, with seven holes punched through and traces of two bronze rivet heads. A large jagged hole has been punched through it.
(viii) *G.169.* Curved fragment of iron sheet with one bronze rivet.

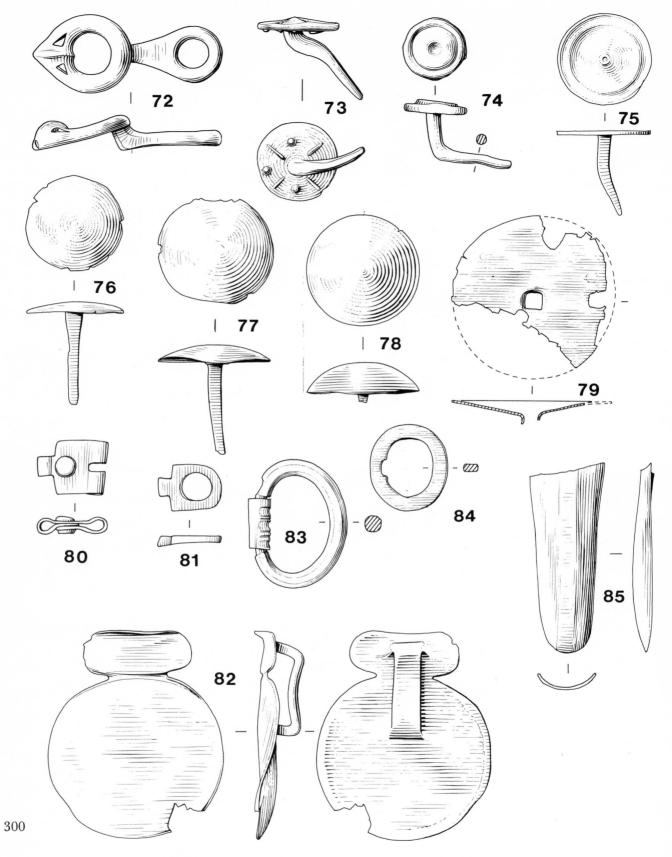

72

73

74

75

76

77

78

79

80

81

82

83

84

85

Fig. 10.35 Roman military finds, of bronze, Nos. 72–85 (¼)

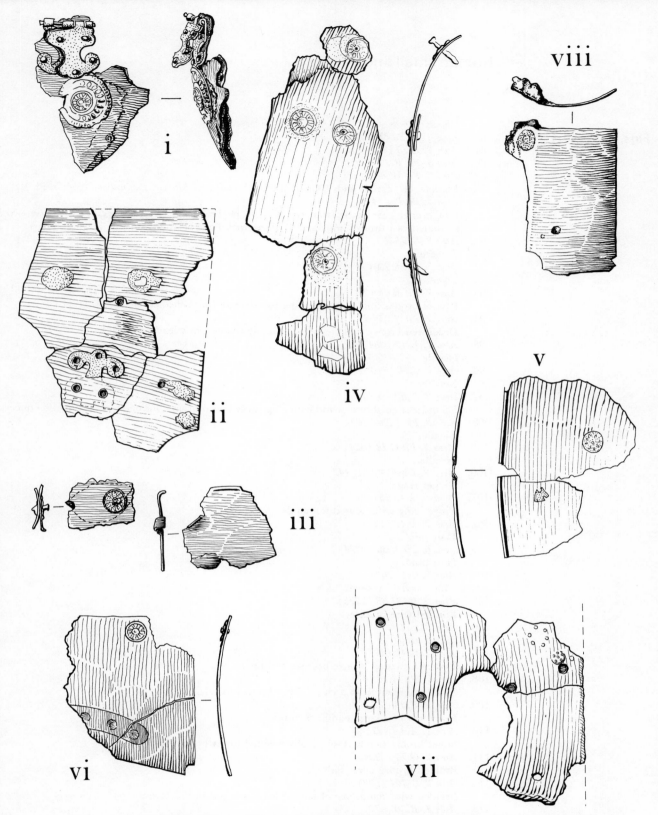

Fig. 10.36 Objects of iron and bronze, military or probably so, No. 85B, i to viii. All ($\frac{1}{1}$)

Roman small finds

Figs. 10.37–10.41

Objects of bronze

86. *Area 2. M.38 (1095)*
87. *Area 2. E.28 (96)*
88. *Area 6. Pit R.29 (2263)*
89. *Area 6. Pit W.8 (2152)*
Ligulae, cf. "Small finds from Walbrook", *Guildhall Museum Publication*, 1954–5, Pl. V.
90. *Area 7. Pit F.4 (490)*
Flat bronze case made from two thin sheets originally rivetted together to house two flat-sectioned cast bronze implements. These may have been for toilet or surgical use.
91. *Area 2. G.51 (372)*
Tweezers.
92. *Area 7. Ditch 1A (31)*
Tweezers.
93. *Area 7. Pit B.68 (703)*
Part of bronze toilet set, including tweezers and nail cleaner, *op. cit.* Pl. II.3.
94. *Area 2. Pit J.23 (658)*
Decorated bronze nail cleaner, originally rivetted to a leather strap.
95. *Area 2. H.17 (384)*
Needle.
96. *Area 7. F.50 (713)*
Needle.
97. *Area 3. Z.50 (2036)*
Round sectioned bronze rod with chip carved decoration. One end is split. Function uncertain.
98. *Area 2. Pit E.90 (209)*
Needle.
99. *Area 2. Pit G.14 (324)*
Needle.
100. *Area 7. Ditch A.1(A) (43)*
Finger ring.
101. *Area 1. A.1 (35)*
Finger ring with incised numerals.
102. *Area 7. B.12 (186)*
Hair pin.
103. *Area 6. Pit R.36 (2274)*
Hair pin.
104. *Area 7. C.1 (360)*
Chip carved bracelet.
105. *Area 5. Pit O.33 (2025)*
Braided wire bracelet.
106. *Area 3. u.s.*
Finger ring.
107. *Area 2. G.40 (471)*
Part of a twisted bronze bracelet terminal.
108. *Area 7. Pit A.10 (47)*
Small fragment from a chip carved bronze bangle.
109. *Area 2. E.23 (99)*
Fragment of a large bangle or torc.
110. *Area 1. A.3.4 (27)*
Small bronze pendant, originally rivetted to leather or cloth.
111. *Area 2. G.74 (599)*
Braided bronze wire chain.
112. *Area 2. G.124 (503)*
Braided wire chain, one of several lengths found in this layer.
113. *Area 7. B.58 (670)*
Braided bronze chain with terminal plate attached, possibly a cloak fastening.

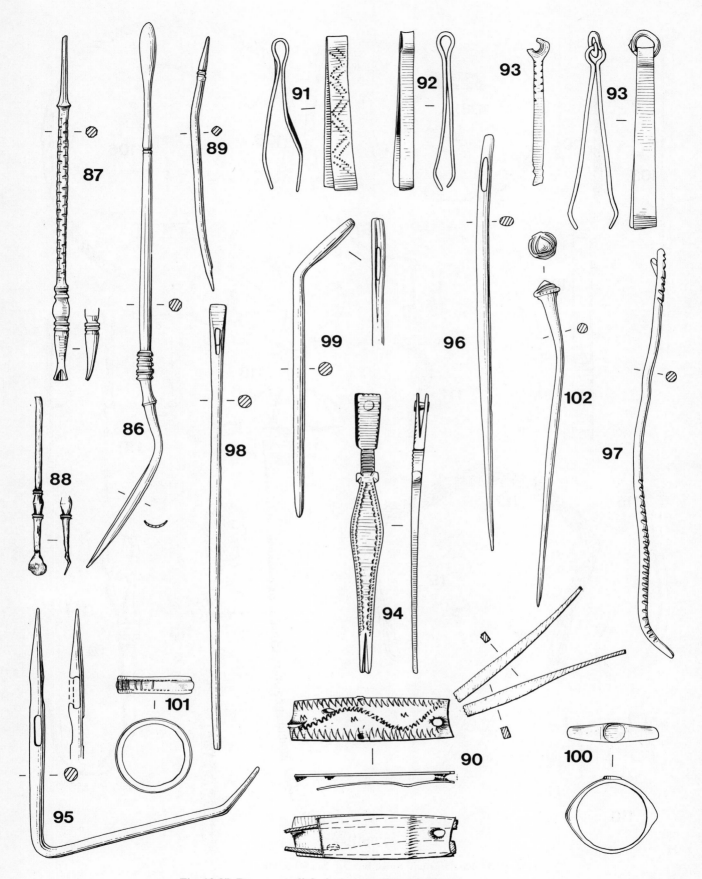

Fig. 10.37 Roman small finds, bronze, Nos. 86–102 (⅓)

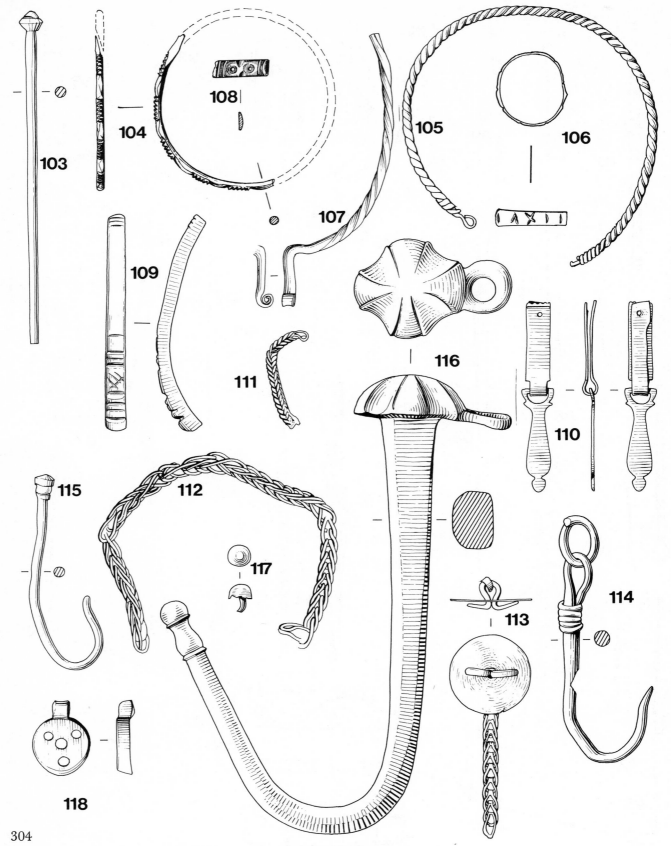

Fig. 10.38 Roman small finds, bronze, Nos. 103–118 ($\frac{1}{1}$)

114. *Area 2. L.113 (908)*
Hook with one link of a chain attached, probably from a steelyard weight.

115. *Area 2. L.119 (919)*
Hook similar to No. 28, but with no means of attachment.

116. *Area 2. L.113 (928)*
Large cast bronze hook with embossed head which incorporates a loop for fixing. Possibly a lamp suspension hook.

117. *Area 2. J.82 (711)*
Small dome headed stud from a narrow leather belt. Forty-five identical examples survived of which only one is illustrated here. The studs were set close together in rows, the leather having completely disintegrated.

118. *Area 5. Pit O.40 (2045)*
Half of a seal box.

119. *Area 2. G.31 (542)*
Bronze boss with lead reinforcement piece behind.

120. *Area 6. R.6 (2254)*
Small decorative boss with traces of a lead reinforcement on the inside face.

121. *Area 2. Pit E.86 (184)*
Rectangular bronze tube; the edges may have been soldered at one time. Function unknown, but possibly some form of blowpipe for use in fine metal working.

122. *Area 2. E.180*
Fragment of bronze sheet, possibly the remains of a stylus case.

123 and 124. *Area 2. E.103 (116 and 257)*
Two rings, use uncertain, but possibly from a harness.

125. *Area 7. Pit B.36 (190)*
Bronze ring, recessed to take a loop attachment for fixing to wood or leather.

126. *Area 4. M.38 (1127)*
Fragment of lathe turned, cast bronze tube. This is not faced off on either end and must be part of a longer object. Function uncertain.

127. *Area 7. Ditch A1(M) (125)*
Bronze ring, use uncertain.

128. *Area 6. R.16 (2255)* (bottom of medieval plough soil)
Ring fastening, probably Roman.

129. *Area 2. J.77 (720)*
Bronze ring.

130. *Area 2. G.145 (569)*
Part of a small buckle.

131. *Area 4. M.38 (1151)*
Bronze fitting in the form of a cloven hoof, cast integrally with a tang which is filed flat on the top and which has a dowel pin protruding upwards from it. This is one of four feet, part of a decorative base assembly, possibly for a casket.

132. *Area 2. Pit G.30 (446)*
Bronze terminal belonging to a bronze or bone pin, in the form of a right hand holding a round object (cf. *Richborough* III, 23; *Wroxeter* 1913, Fig. 5, 10 and 11; a silver pin from the Walbrook, London, now in the British Museum (*B.M.* 1951, Fig. 14, No. 12).

133. *Area 7. B.55 (592)*
Bronze stud, head recessed for enamel inlay.

134. *Area 7. F.20 (714)*
Small rectangular cast plate 2 mm thick with the edges slightly undercut, suggesting perhaps that the plate is an inlay. There is a small protuberance near the bottom left side as viewed; this seems to have been left deliberately when the panel was being filed, and it does not appear to have been caused by a hammer blow. A diagonal groove has been filed in it which may have been for enamel inlay.

135. *Area 5. P.95 (2208)*
Small bronze pendant or possibly a decorative fitting for leather.

136. *Area 7. A.21 (189)*
Bronze object, cut and formed from bronze sheet with a double punch-dot pattern running down its length. This pattern is carried round the bend and up the reverse side (not shown on the drawing). The top is broken off. The whole object was tinned at one time and this

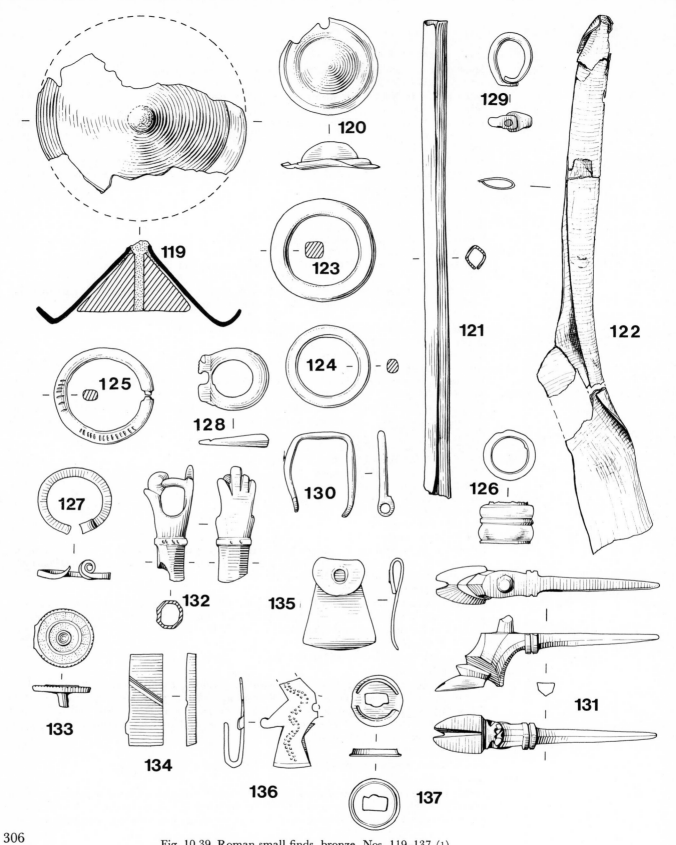

Fig. 10.39 Roman small finds, bronze, Nos. 119–137 (¼)

remains on the reverse face. It appears to have been formed around a leather or metal strap and secured to it by rivets, of which part of one fixing hole remains. Possibly some form of belt stiffener.

137. *Area 5. P.42 (2115)*
Bronze stud head, recessed for enamel inlay.

138. *Area 5. O.62 (2059)*
Cast bronze corner fitting, probably for a wooden chest.

139. *Area 2. L.1 (748)*
Leather fitting with ring dot decoration.

140. *Area 4. M.36 (1113)*
Fragment of hinged strap.

141. *Area 7. Pit D.27 (350)*
Fragment of plate with holes punched through.

142. *Area 2. G.31 (547)*
Bronze hook.

143. *Area 2. Pit K.5 (603)*
Bronze pin.

144. *Area 2. Slot L.4 (1008)*
Bronze nail.

145. *Area 4. M.20 (1072)*
Bronze nail.

146. *Area 2. G.32 (387)*
Bronze tube, possibly a spacer.

147. *Area 6. R.16 (2266)*
Small bronze domed piece with 8 small holes drilled in it. This may be Roman; it comes from the bottom of the medieval plough soil and was probably ploughed out from the Roman layers.

148. *Area 5. O.29 (2068)*
Cast bronze object with a rectangular tapered tang. This may be part of a similar base fitting to No. 45.

149. *Area 3. Y.36 (2093)*
Handle.

150. *Area 2. G (600)*
Lock plate made of thin bronze sheet. One dome headed fixing stud survives with it.

151. *Area 2. Pit E.92 (215)*
Bronze strap with chisel cut decoration.

152. *Area 7. C.11 (460)*
Small bronze decorative casting with traces of gilding. From the Thermae destruction levels.

153. *Area 7. D.36 (685)*
Cast bronze jug handle.

154. *Area 7. C.11 (400)*
Part of a square-headed bronze pin.

155. *Area 7. F.50 (717)*
Lathe turned bronze tube, function uncertain.

156. *Area 2. L.119 (917)*
Cast bronze object.

157. *Area 5. P.36 (2096)*
Fragment of rivetted bronze strip.

158. *Area 2. L.169 (1025)*
Small bronze strip with three rivet holes.

159. *Area 7. D.8 (176)*
Bronze object with two fixing holes, use uncertain.

160. *Area 2. Pit H.18 (615)*
Bronze strapping.

161. *Area 7. Pit A.9 (38)*
Fragment of bronze strapping.

162. *Area 3. W.23 (2181)*
Cast bronze object, use uncertain.

163. *Area 7. Pit E.76 (600)*
Shank of a cast bronze object, heavily corroded, use uncertain.

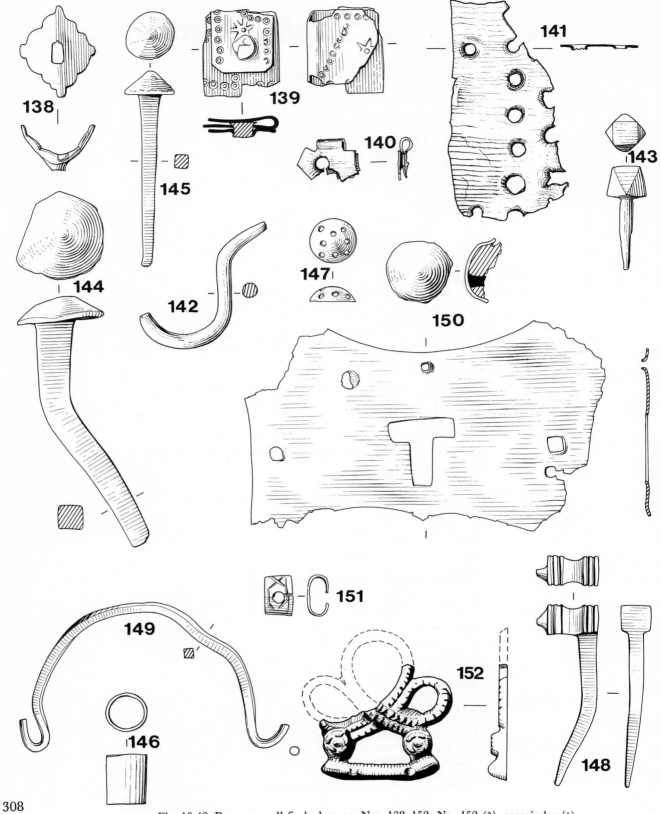

Fig. 10.40 Roman small finds, bronze, Nos. 138–152. No. 152 ($\frac{2}{1}$), remainder ($\frac{1}{1}$)

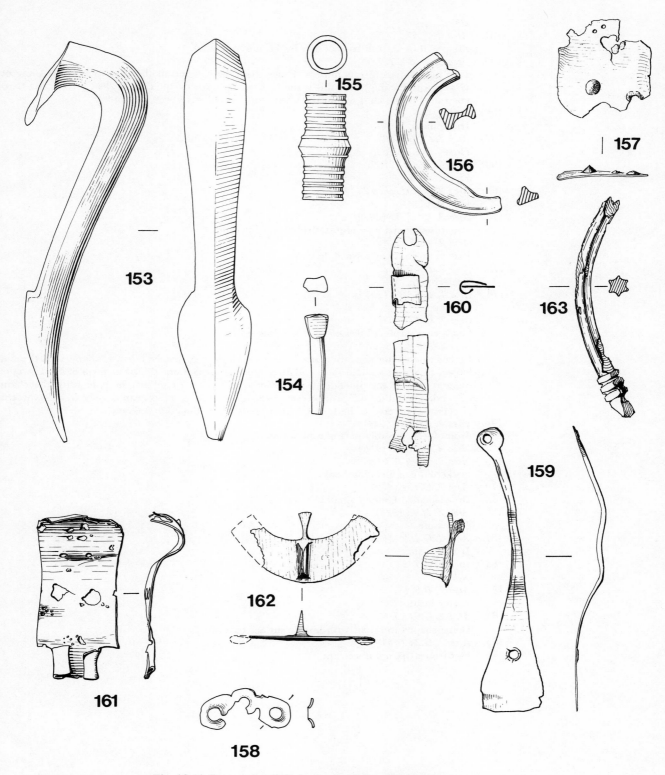

Fig. 10.41 Roman small finds, bronze, Nos. 153–163 (¼)

Objects of iron

164. *Area 3. Z.57 (2047)*
Fragment of an iron bar, 22 mm by 11 mm in section.

165. *Area 3. W.8 (2157)*
Iron ploughshare tip. Numbers of these have been found at the Roman villas at Chilgrove (*Down*, forthcoming), but this is the first example within the City Walls – a reminder that a good deal of the land within the town limits would have been cultivated.

166. *Area 2. G.31 (391)*
Iron punch.

167. *Area 7. C.58 (680)*
Heavy iron spike.

168. *Area 3. W.20 (2169)*
Flat iron ring.

169. *Area 2. Slot II, ph. 128 (165)*
Iron staple.

170. *Area 3. Pit Z.39 (2049)*
Square-sectioned iron object, probably a linch pin.

171. *Area 2. L.18 (818)*
Part of an iron key for a slide lock.

172. *Area 2. E.120 (175)*
Eyelet spike.

173. *Area 1. Pit A.42 (19)*
Iron hook.

174. *Area 2. G.47 (562)*
Small ring staple, cf. *Longthorpe* 1975, Fig. 44.45.

175. *Area 2. Pit E.103 (283)*
Linked assemblage consisting of a U-sectioned iron strap formed into a U-shape, with the ends looped to accept a chain link. Only one link survives on one side. The form of the U-section suggests that it was intended to fit over a horizontal round bar or pole, with the chains suspended on either side. Any tension exerted on the chain links can only be in a downwards direction as otherwise the U piece would pull apart. Function unknown.

176. *Area 2. Pit H.4 (314)*
Iron object, possibly part of a horseshoe.

177 & *Area 2. Pit E.84 (156)*
178. *Area 7. Ditch A.1 (B)*
Socketed iron pruning hooks.

179. *Area 2. G.134 (479)*
Broad-bladed knife or small cleaver.

180. *Area 2. H.43 (523)*
Iron knife.

181. *Area 2. G.169 (586)*
Iron handle.

182. *Area 1. A.7*
Needle.

183. *Area 7. B.3(1)*
Arrow head.

184. *Area 2. G.61 (576)*
Dome-shaped iron nail with bronze surface covering.

185. *Area 2. G.31 (543)*
Flat iron strip, use uncertain.

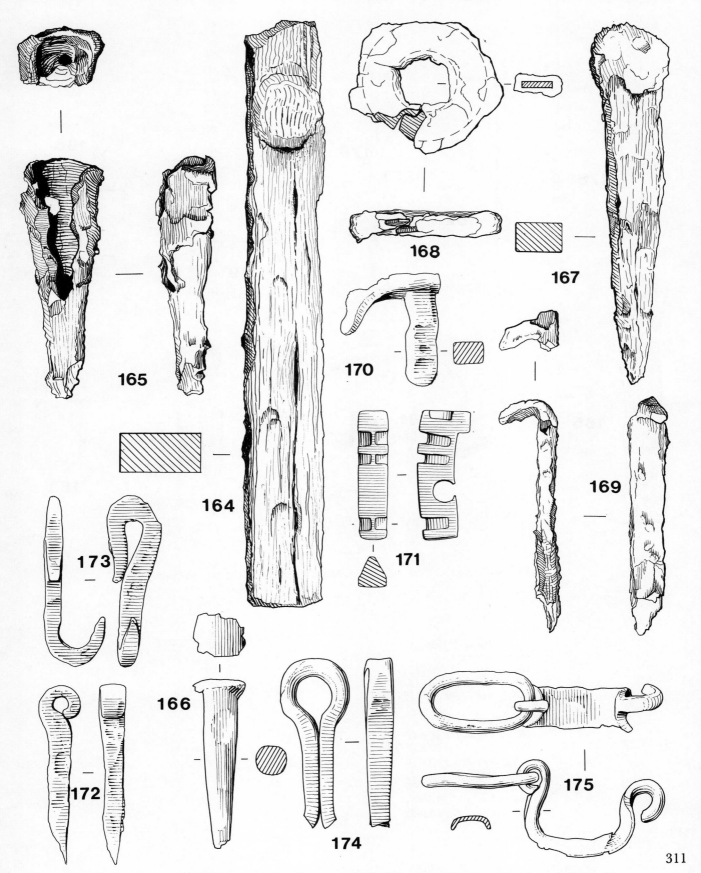

165   164   168   167   170   169   171   173   172   166   174   175

311

Fig. 10.42 Roman small finds, iron, Nos. 164–175. Nos. 171 & 174 ($\frac{1}{4}$), remainder ($\frac{1}{2}$)

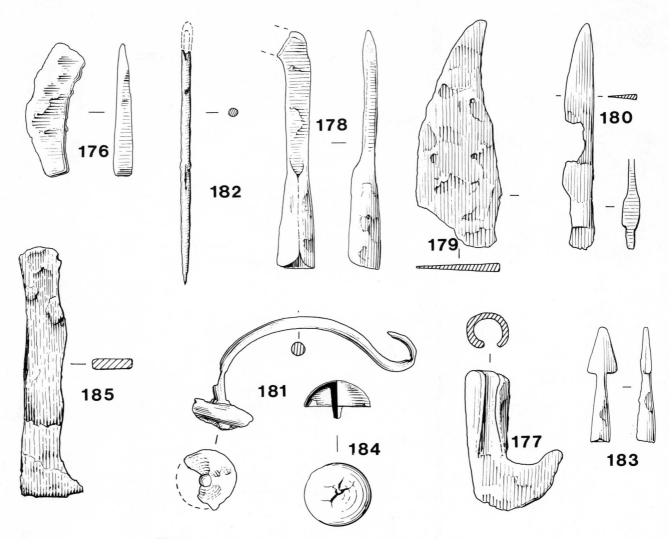

Fig. 10.43 Roman small finds, iron, Nos. 176–185. No. 182 ($\frac{1}{1}$), remainder ($\frac{1}{2}$)

Objects of bone

(a)   NEEDLES
186.   *Area 2. E.120 (155)*
187.   *Area 2. E.118 (151)*
188.   *Area 7. Pit A.32 (79)*

(b)   PINS
189.   *Area 3. Pit W.8 (2149)*
190.   *Area 3. Pit W.8 (2148)*
191.   *Area 2. G.u/s (363)*
192.   *Area 7. E.65 (617)*
193.   *Area 5. O.29 (2057)*
194.   *Area 2. G.29 (366)*
195.   *Area 2. G.31 (392)*

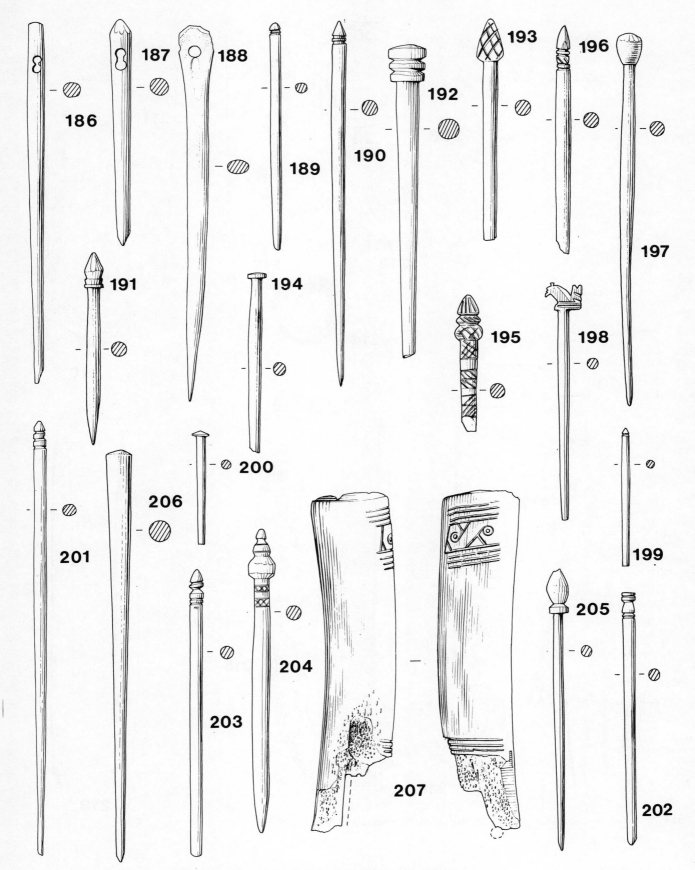

Fig. 10.44 Roman small finds, bone, Nos. 186–207 (⅓)

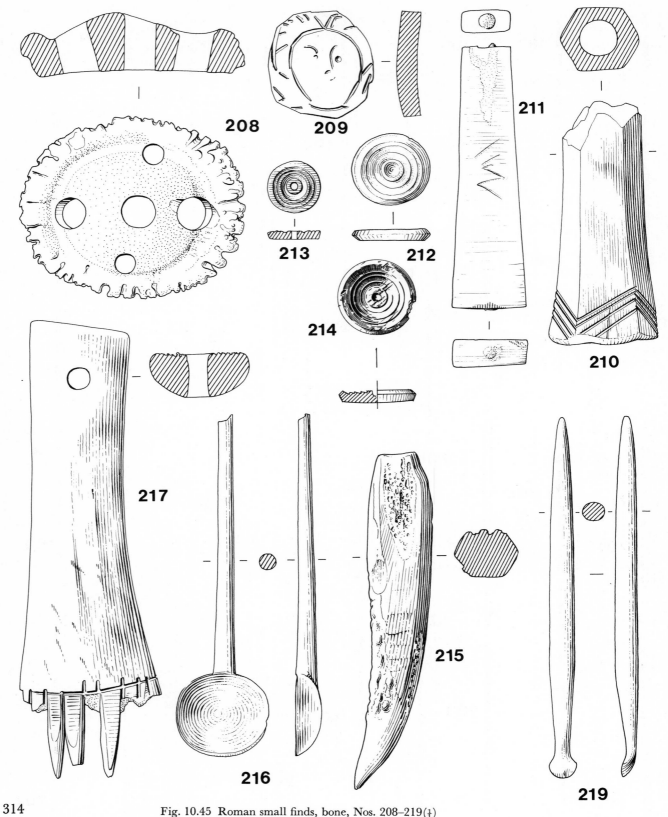

Fig. 10.45 Roman small finds, bone, Nos. 208–219(¼)

196. *Area 2. Slot H.7 (377)*
197. *Area 2. G.30 (354)*
198. *Area 3. Pit A.1 (4007)*
199. *Area 2. Slot E.7 (375)*
200. *Area 7. B.61 (687)*
201. *Area 7. E.65 (619)*
202. *Area 3. Pit W.8 (2158)*
203. *Area 2. Pit E.34 (54)*
204. *Area 5. Slot P.3 (2093)*
205. *Area 3. u/s (4013)*
206. *Area 2. L.107 (978)*

(c) MISCELLANEOUS
207. *Area 7. Pit B.59 (290)*
   Handle with anthropomorphic decoration; probably from a knife.
208. *Area 7. D.31 (729)*
   Flat disc, probably an amulet, sawn from the base of a deer antler, with five holes drilled in it. See *Longthorpe 1975*, p. 69, No. 122 and Fig. 37 for a similar example. Like the Longthorpe disc, the Chichester amulet does not carry a phallus, but the central hole may have been intended to house one as a separate attachment. See also *Rheingonheim*, Taf. 45.1, 2 and Taf. 60.3, 4; *Hofheim* (1913), Taf. xxxv, 3; *Newstead*, p. 314f., Pl. LXXXIV, 14; *Antiq. Journ.* XXVIII (1948), 176 and Pl. XXVI.A.
209. *Area 5. Pit O.33 (2026)*
   Carved trial piece, probably intended to represent Medusa.
210. *Area 7. Pit B.27 (146)*
   Knife handle.
211. *Area 5*, from clay wall of 2nd-century house *(2111)*.
   Flat bone object, possibly the handle of a specialised piece in a toilet set. It has been drilled lengthways through the centre and an iron pin inserted, probably the tang of the toilet instrument.
212. *Area 2. H.17 (386)*
   Gaming counter.
213. *Area 2. L.4 (772)*
   Gaming counter.
214. *Area 7. B.61 (690)*
   Gaming counter.
215. *Pit E.29 (51)*
   Worked antler tine, probably used as an awl.
216. *Area 2. G.134 (495)*
   Spoon

217. *Area 2. Slot G.14 (latrine) (479)*
   Bone teasing comb.
218. *Area 2. Slot G.13. Not illustrated (480)*
   Part of an ox rib bone notched at one end for use as a teasing comb.
219. *Area 2. E.129 (261)*
   Small toilet instrument.

   Objects of lead
220. *(598). Area 7. Pit E.67*
   Strip of twisted lead formed into a rough hook.
221. *(17). Area 7. Pit B.5*
   Strip of lead binding with hole for nail punched through.
222. *(298). Area 7. Pit B.58*
   Strip of lead, 30 mm by 2 mm thick by 78 mm long, with iron nail punched through one end. *Not illustrated.*

315

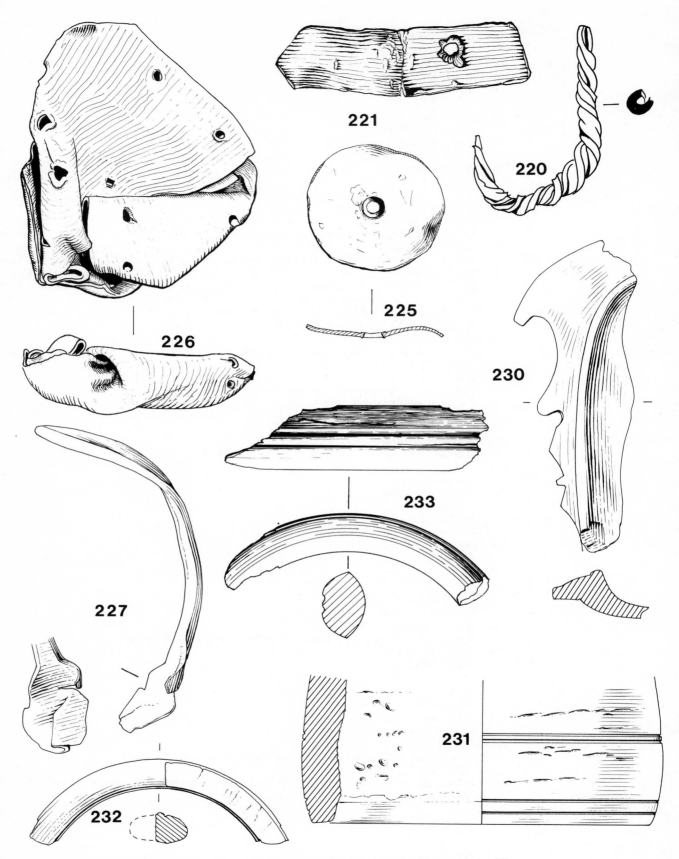

Fig. 10.46 Roman small finds, lead, Nos. 220–229. Shale, Nos. 230–233. No. 221 ($\frac{1}{2}$), remainder ($\frac{1}{1}$)

223 and 224.   *Area 7. B.33 (246) and Area 7. B.2 (28)*
Similar strips of lead to No. 2 above, each with an iron nail punched through. *Not illustrated.*

225.   *(375). Area 2. G.31*
Circular lead disc with countersunk central hole.

226.   *(706). Area 2. J.68*
Lead sheet with a number of holes punched through it, some square, some round. It has been rolled and flattened, but probably functioned as some kind of strainer.

227.   *(506). Area 2. Pit G.30*
Strip of lead shaped in the form of a rough spoon.

228.   *(330). Area 2. Pit H.7*
Fragment of lead sheet, 130 by 110 mm by approximately 8 mm thick. Weight 600 gms. *Not illustrated.*

229.   *(696). Area 2. J.51*
Irregular shaped lead off-cut, weight 225 gms, approximately 4 mm thick. *Not illustrated.*

Fig. 10.46

Objects of shale

230.   *(960). Area 2. L.136*
Rim of a dish with a scalloped edge.

231.   *(882). Area 2. Pit L.37*
Part of a circular band of shale. The full width of this object cannot be determined but the exterior is finished on the lathe, as is small section of the inside rim; cf. *Porchester* 1, 1975, Fig. 149, p. 230.

232.   *(936). Area 2. L.118*
Part of a shale bangle.

233.   *(720). Area 7. Pit B.73*
Part of a shale bangle approximately 88 mm inside diameter.

Fig. 10.47

Objects of pottery and slate

234.   *(695). Area 2. J.75*
Head of a pipeclay figurine; see note by Mr. Frank Jenkins, p. 289.

235.   *(162). Area 7. D.4*
Base and lower part of a pipeclay figurine, showing the feet and lower part of the legs of a ? draped figure.

236.   *(478). Area 2. Slot G.14 (latrine)*
Curved hollow tube of fired clay, possibly part of a puzzle jug.

237.   *(138). Area 2. E.55*
Corner of a chamfered slate palette. For a complete example see *Chichester* 1, Fig. 5, 17, 213 L.

238.   *(568). Area 2. H.47*
Strip of slate, 20 mm wide by 85 mm long by 6 mm thick, possibly an inlay.

239.   *(2217). Area 5. P.102*
Small fragment of slate from a panel. It has broken at one of the fixing holes so that only a short piece 16 mm long survives. This has been neatly finished around the edges, the left-hand edge, as viewed, being chamfered. Possibly a small inlay piece, or a nameplate with fixing holes at each end.

Fig. 10.48

Miscellaneous small finds

240.   *Area 7. Pit D.27(B)*
Neolithic polished flint axe with squared sides; traces of ancient damage along cutting edge; heavy ochreous patina. (Identification by Mr. A. Woodcock, Chichester District Museum, to whom thanks are due.)

241.   *Area 7. C.11*
Candlestick, lathe turned from hard chalk; probably Roman. From the Thermae destruction levels.

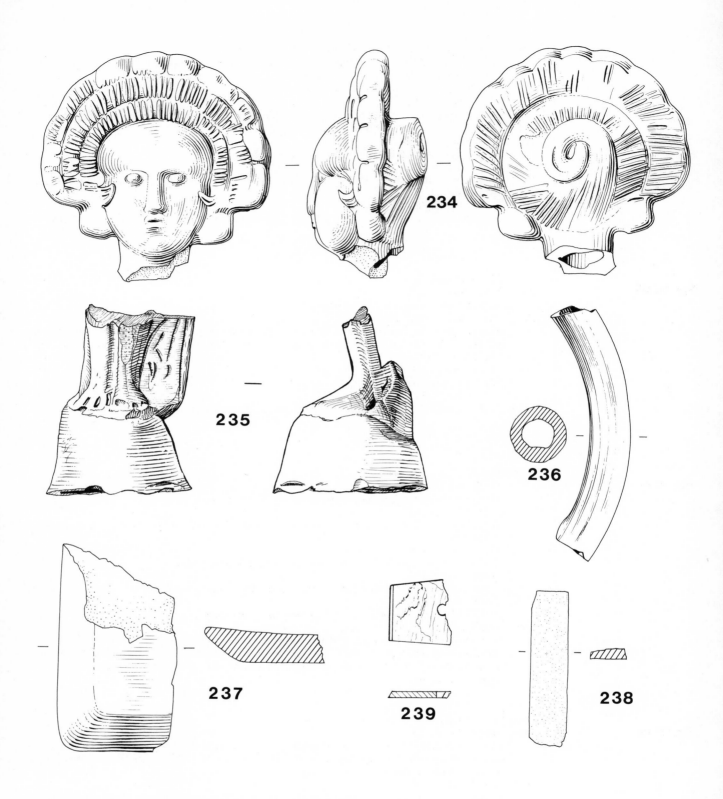

Fig. 10.47 Roman small finds, pottery and slate, Nos. 234–239 ($\frac{1}{1}$)

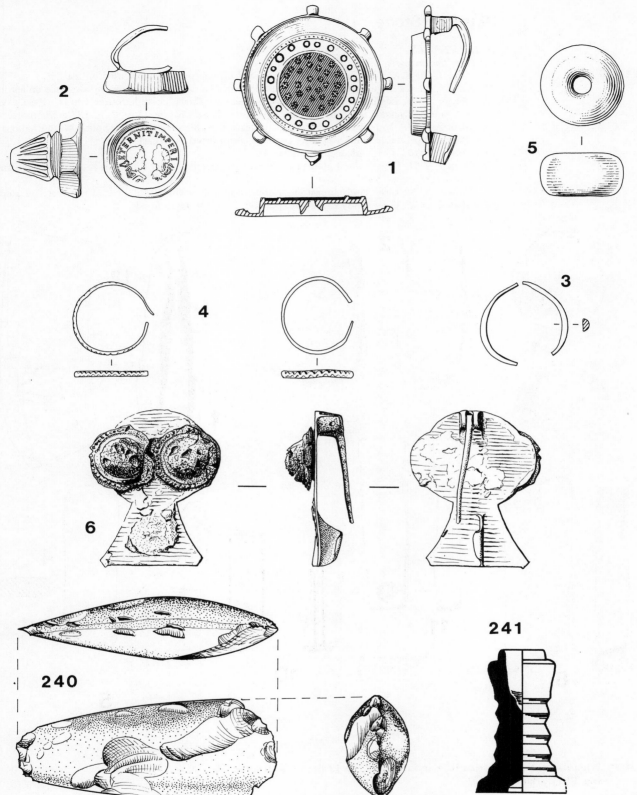

Fig. 10.48 Nos. 1–5; Grave goods from Northgate   No. 6; The Roman Brooch from County Hall

Nos. 240–241; Miscellaneous small finds. (All ¼)

319

Objects of Stone

Fig. 10.49

WHETSTONES
(a) *From Roman layers*
1. *Area 1. Pit A.42.* Flint beach pebble, polished on one side, possibly used on leather.
2. *Area 1. Pit A.42.* Quartzite sandstone pebble, polished on two faces, possibly also used on leather.
3. *Area 2. H.43.* Glauconitic sandstone from greensand beds, possible source Church Rock, West Wittering, Sussex, seven miles from Chichester. Cf. *Fishbourne*, Vol. 2, p. 1. *Not illustrated.*
4. *Area 2. E.218.* Indurated greywacke sandstone, possible origin Wales, South-West England or Brittany, probably from a pebble, perhaps transported as ballast.
5. *Area 2. E.105.* Grey micaceous sandstone.
6. *Area 2. J.51.* Fine-grained glauconitic sandstone, architectural fragment re-used as whetstone; burnt. *Not illustrated.*
7. *Area 4. M.38.* Grey sandy limestone similar to that from the Hythe beds of Kent. *Not illustrated.*
8. *Area 7. D.32.* Grey sandy limestone, possibly from the Hythe beds.

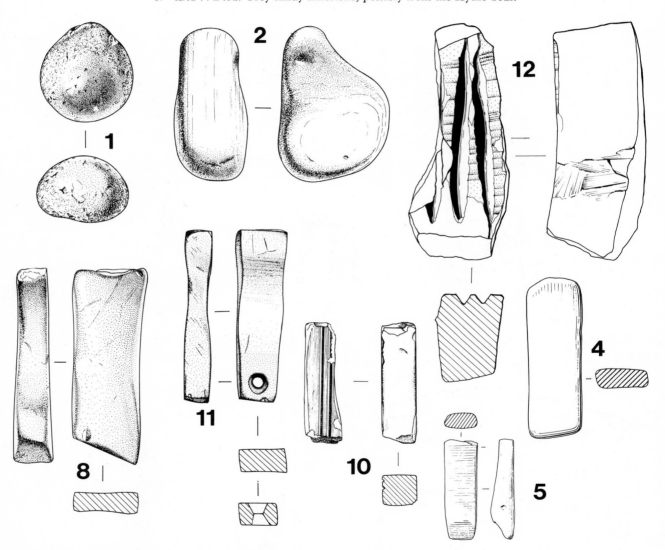

Fig. 10.49 Whetstones, Nos. 1–8 from Roman layers Nos. 10–12 from post-Roman layers Nos. 1, 2, and 12 ($\frac{1}{3}$), remainder ($\frac{2}{3}$)

320

(b) *From post-Roman layers*

9. *Area 2. G.10.* Grey micaceous sandstone. *Not illustrated.*
10. *Area 3. Pit Z.8.* Grey sandy limestone, similar to that from the Hythe beds of Kent. Burnt; architectural fragment re-used as a hone.
11. *Area 7. Pit E.86.* Imported fine-grained indurated sandstone, cf. Bagendon, *Transactions of the Birmingham Arch. Soc.*, No. 83 (1969).
12. *Area 7. C.11.* Fine-grained glauconitic sandstone probably Wealden. This has been used for both knife and possibly narrow chisel honing.
13. *Area 7. Pit B.35.* Grey sandy limestone probably from the Hythe beds, cf. *Fishbourne. Not illustrated.*

Inlay and flooring

Fig. 10.50

1. *Area 2. Pit L.4(D).* Fragment of inlay in imported buff mottled marble.
2. *(692). Area 2. J.51.* Fragment of ? wall panel in white coarse crystalline marble of Mediterranean origin.
3. *(2055). Area 5. O.54.* Fragment of wall veneer petrologically similar to No. 2.
4. *(433). Area 2. H.26.* Fragment of paving ?, in Purbeckian marble.
5. *(669). Area 7. F.37.* Fragment of coarse white, grey veined crystalline marble, possibly flooring, from the Mediterranean region.

Frame mouldings

Figs. 10.50–10.51

6. *(552). Area 7. D.5.* Frame moulding fragment in Purbeck or Sussex marble.
7. *(436). Area 2. G.104.* As No. 6.
8. *(668). Area 7. F.14.* As No. 6, but re-used.
9. *(913). Area 2. L.91.* Corner fragment of frame moulding in Purbeck or Sussex marble.
10. *(608). Area 7. E.60.* As No. 6. Similar profile to No. 8. *Not illustrated.*
Not illustrated.
11. *(41). Area 7. A.2.* As No. 6.
12. *(514). Unstratified.* As No. 6.
13. *(586). Area 7. B.24.* As No. 6.
14. *(4034). Area 3. A.8.* As No. 6.
15. *(501). Area 7. F.8.* Architectural moulding in sandstone, probably post-Roman and possibly medieval.
16. *(117). Area 7. Pit B.16(c).* Fragment from a marble framing in coarse white crystalline marble, similar to No. 2.
17. *(708). Area 7. F.50.* Fragment of frame panel in Purbeck marble, dressed on three faces and with a dowel hole at the back.
18. *(432). Area 7. Pit E.53.* Fragment of roughly carved hard chalk, post Roman and could be late Saxon.

Architectural fragments

Figs. 10.51–10.52

19. *(81). Area 2. E.4.* Fragment of ? moulding in coarse-grained sandstone.
20. *(531). Area 7. C.20.* Fragment of small column in Purbeck/Sussex marble, perhaps a medial shaft from a cluster.
21. *(630). Area 7. E.72.* Fragment of lower torus moulding from a Roman column in Jurassic medium-grained sandy limestone (burnt).
22. *(564). Area 7. Pit F.7.* Section, probably of door framing, in fine-grained sandy limestone. Not Roman, probably medieval or later.
23. *(254). Area 7. Posthole A.18.* Fragment of carved greensand, probably Roman.
24. *(65). Area 2. Pit E.43.* Fragment of greensand, possibly from a large inscription, keyed on the back face.

MORTARS AND BASINS

Fig. 10.52

1. *(2242). Area 6. R. unstratified.*
   Fragment of a mortar made from a fine-grained sandstone.
2. *(2088). Area 3. Y.19*
   Base of a mortar in Purbeck/Sussex marble. *Not illustrated.*
3. *(2067). Area 3. Pit Y.3*
   Rim of a mortar or cresset in shelly Purbeck limestone.

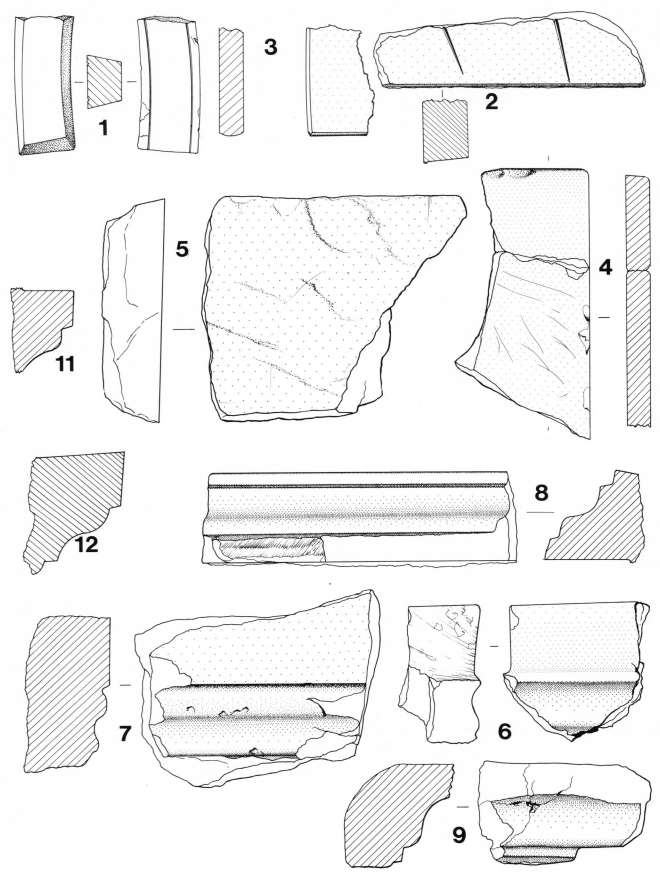

Fig. 10.50 Objects of stone, Nos. 1–5 inlay and flooring Nos. 6–12 frame mouldings. No. 1 ($\frac{2}{3}$), remainder ($\frac{1}{3}$)

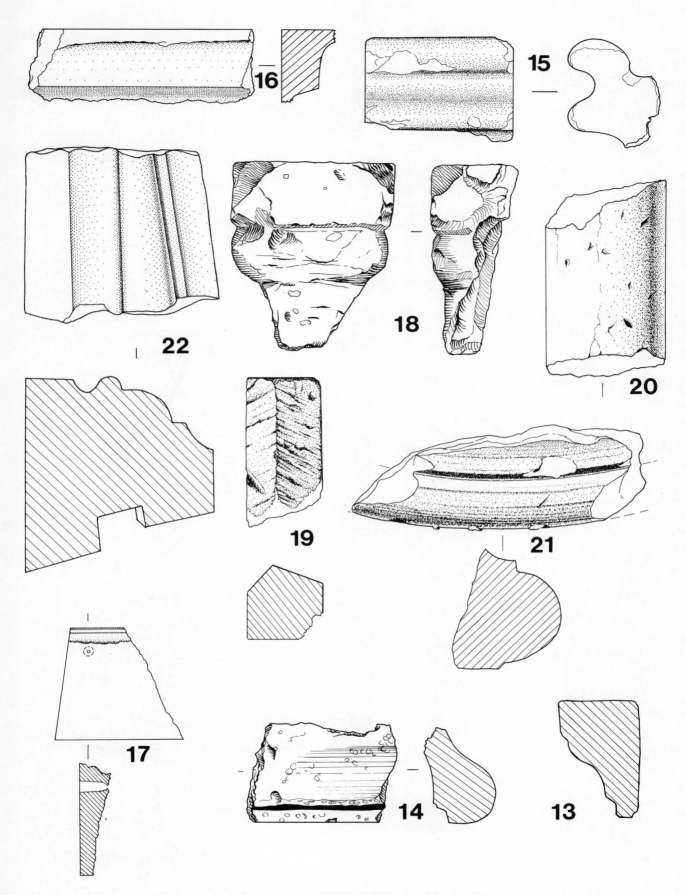

Fig. 10.51 Objects of stone, Nos. 13–17 Roman frame mouldings Nos. 18–22 miscellaneous architectural fragments, Roman and post-Roman. No. 16 ($\frac{2}{3}$), remainder ($\frac{1}{3}$)

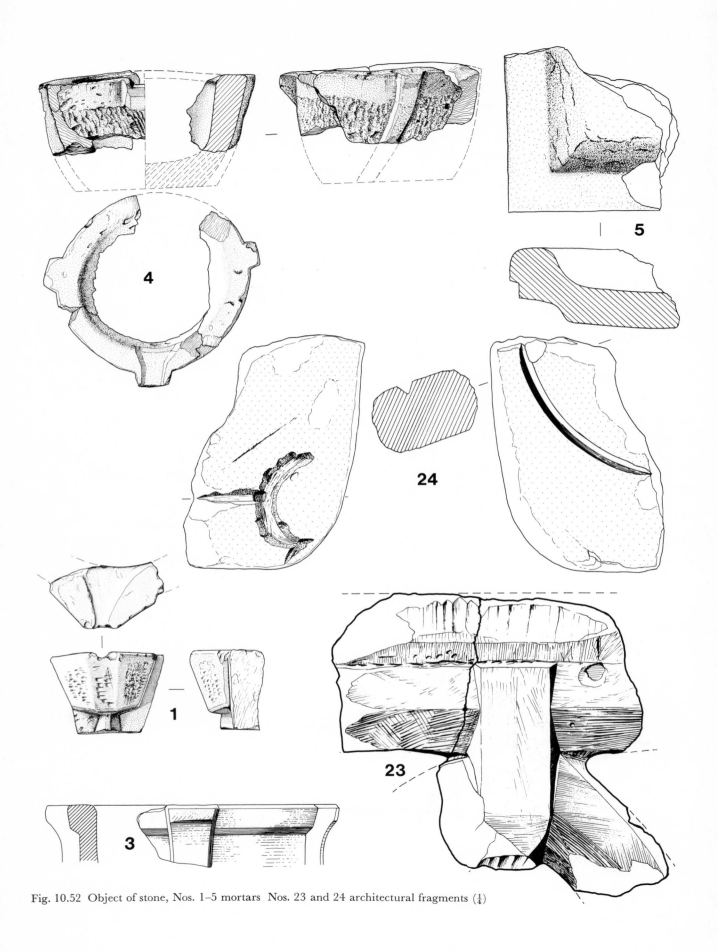

Fig. 10.52 Object of stone, Nos. 1–5 mortars Nos. 23 and 24 architectural fragments ($\frac{1}{4}$)

4. *(721). Area 2. K.1*
   Mortar in shelly Purbeck limestone.
5. *(105). Area 2. Robber Trench*
   Fragment of basin in Purbeck/Sussex marble.

Small Finds, Post-Roman or uncertain

Figs. 10.53–10.56

(a) *Pottery*
1. *Area 6. R.7.* Baked clay plumb bob with groove for string. From the upper cultivation levels, probably late or post-medieval.
2. *Area 7. Pit D.39(B).* Base of pottery candlestick, probably medieval.
3. *Area 2. Pit L.8.* Baked clay loom weight, one of five found. From a late Saxon pit, cf. *Chichester 2*, Fig. 8.20, 70.

(b) *Bone*
4. *Area 3. Pit W.14* (Saxo-Norman to early medieval pit). Large bone needle.
5. *Area 2. Pit H.4* (late Saxon pit). Rivetted bone strip, probably from a handle.
6. *Area 2. Pit L.8* (late Saxon pit). Knife handle.

(c) *Iron*
7. *Area 1. A1.8.* Part of a knife with bone handle; post medieval.
8. *Area 7. C.16.* Knife; from the Thermae robbing levels, could be either Roman or late Saxon.
9. *Area 2. Pit H.4* (late Saxon pit). Knife.
10. *Area 7. Pit C.10(A).* Knife.
11. *Area 1. A1.2.* Medieval rowel spur.
12. *Area 7. Pit E.34(B).* Iron shears.
13. *Area 7. Pit A.15.* Iron spike.

(d) *Bronze*
14. *Area 2. Pit F.1.* Candle snuffer, *c.* 18th–19th century.
15. *Area 2. L.1.* Gilded belt buckle, post-medieval.
16. *Area 2. Unstratified.* Tinned spoon handle.
17. *Area 2. L.1.* Bronze spoon, stamped HG.
18. *Area 7. Pit D.27(B)* (medieval, ? 14th century). Escutcheon plate for a lock.
19. *Area 6. R.7.* Cast bronze handle. The remains of an iron insert protrude from the base.
20 and 21. *Area 6. R.16 and R.9.* Two bronze buckles and rivetted plates for attachment to leather strap. These are from the upper and lower levels of the ploughsoil and are likely to be late-post medieval.
22. *Area 2. Pit L.11.* Part of the handle of a small shovel, possibly for charcoal. It consists of rolled bronze sheet formed into a cylinder and flattened at one end where it was rivetted to the shovel. The other end would have housed a small wooden handle to which it was secured by a small nail. Probably post-Roman.
23. *Area 7. F.25.* Rivetted bronze strip, function uncertain.
24. *Area 7. E.13.* Part of a small handle in cast bronze.
25. *Area 7. B.34.* Rolled bronze tube; the reinforcing bands have loops for attachment, and the right-hand end as viewed is expanded to fit into another tubular section. Function unknown. The object is from a medieval context, but could be Roman.
26. *Area 2. Pit E.29.* Fragment of bronze strapping.
27. *Area 2. Pit E.29.* Bronze nail.
28. *Area 2. E.1.* Bronze nail.
29. *Area 4. M.10.* Bronze pin, probably a Chichester pin; late or post-medieval.
30, 31 and 32. *Area 7. Pit D.27(B).* Bronze needles, mid to late medieval.
33. *Area 7. Pit A.25.* Bronze belt buckle.
34. *Area 6. R.16.* Small bronze buckle, from the bottom of the medieval ploughsoil.
35. *Area 5. Pit O.43.* Brass buckle.
36. *Area 7. Pit E.5.* Small bronze belt buckle, probably late Saxon or medieval.

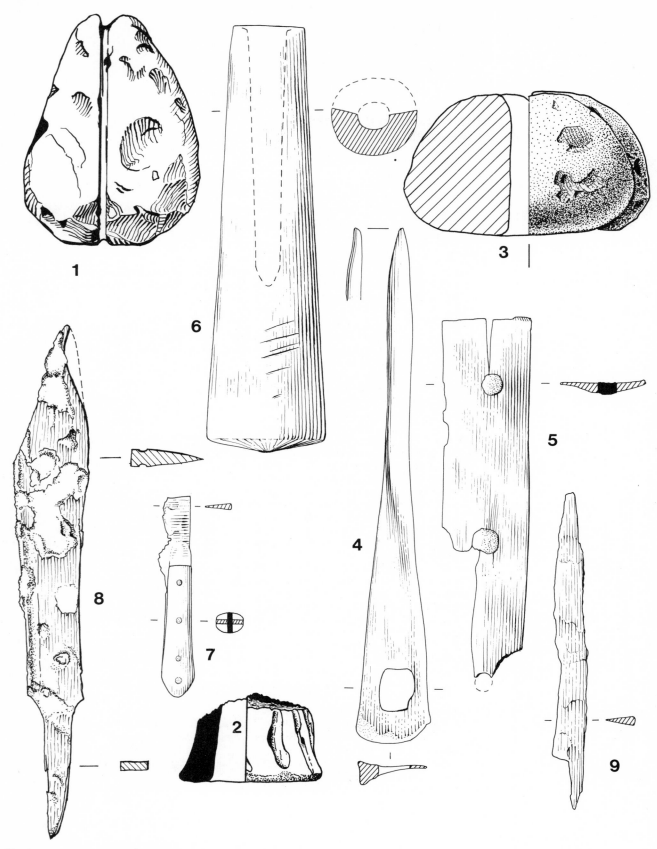

Fig. 10.53 Post Roman-small finds, Nos. 1–9 (¼)

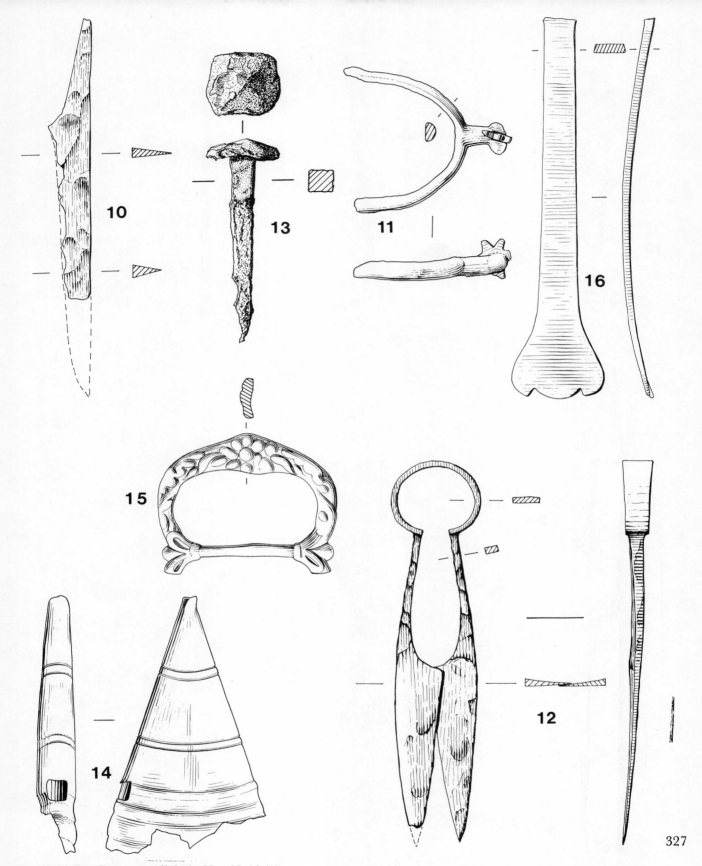

Fig. 10.54 Post-Roman small finds, Nos. 10–16 ($\frac{1}{1}$)

327

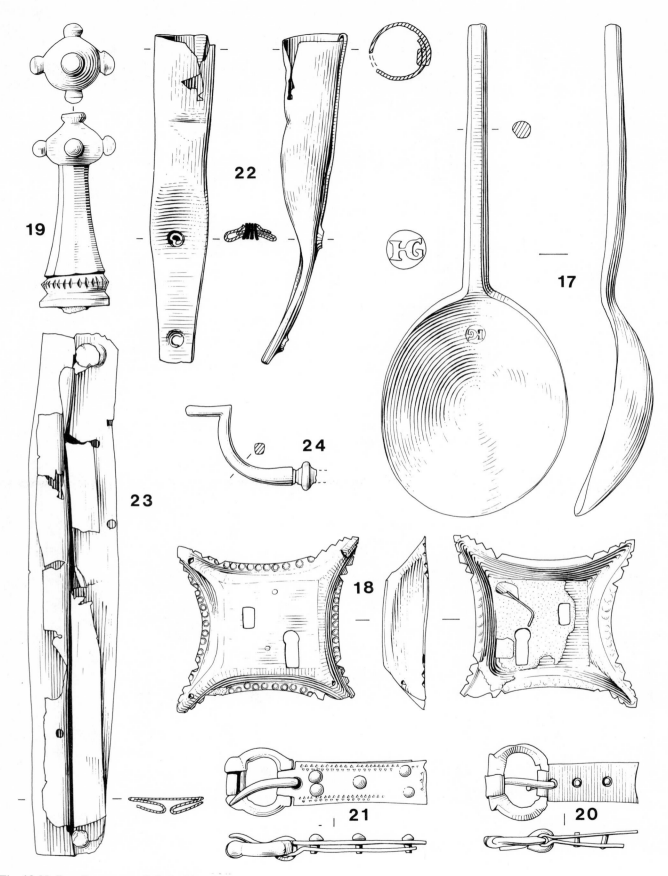

Fig. 10.55 Post-Roman small finds, Nos. 17–24 (⅓)

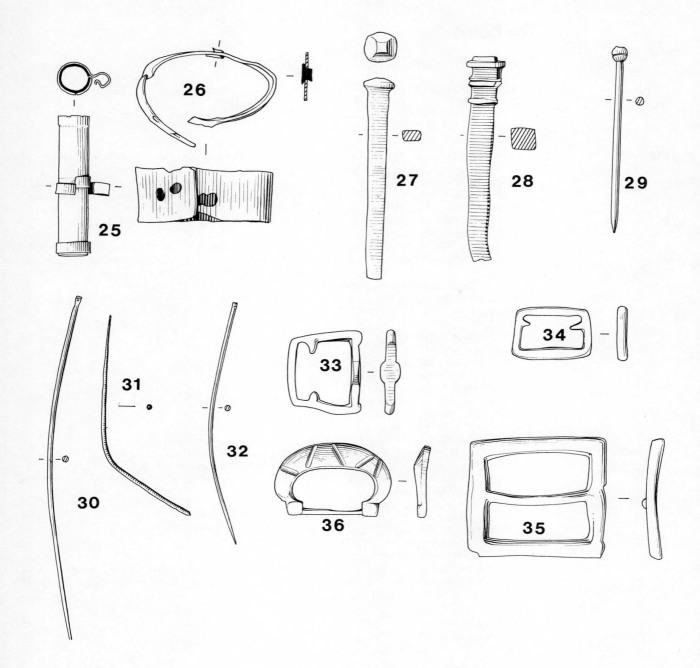

Fig. 10.56 Post-Roman small finds, Nos. 25–36 (¼)

The Coins

The Early British Coins

by R. A. G. Carson

Plate 18

It is noteworthy that of the twelve British coins found, no less than five are of the Catuvellauni, and other areas of the town have also yielded Catuvellaunian coins. Since all the coins discussed here come from post-Roman invasion levels, they may constitute evidence, not for an extension of Catuvellaunian influence into Atrebatic territory, but for the continuation of British issues alongside Roman in circulation. The Catuvellaunian coins may well have reached Chichester in the hands of Roman troops after the taking of Colchester or, alternatively, have been circulating locally at the time of the invasion.

Although the coin finds were comparatively few in number, many of them are of considerable importance as objects in their own right. They included nine silver coins, mainly minims, almost all of which were either extremely rare or quite new. All these have either been presented to the British Museum or deposited there on permanent loan.

For ease of identification, the excavation small finds number has been placed in brackets against the catalogue number.

ATREBATES AND REGNI
Tincommius (*c.* 20 B.C.–A.D. 5)
1. Find No. 642. AR, wt. 1.14 gm. *Area 2. G.190*
   Obv. Letters TINC disposed in a circle.
   Rev. Lion to l.: around, COMF.
   New type, but for lion reverse in this series, cf. coin No. 2 below of Verica.
Verica (*c.* A.D. 10–40).
2. Find No. 2154. AR, wt. 0.30 gm. *Area 3. W.3*
   Obv. Small circle with central dot, all surrounded by four groups of three dots.
   Rev. Lion to r.: above, VIR: below, trefoil between two annulets.
   Second example of coin found at Owlesbury near Winchester (*B.N.J.* XXXVI, Pl. 14.14).
3. Find No. 211. AR, wt. 0.34 gm. *Area 2. E.115*
   Obv. VIR/VAR in two lines on tablet.
   Rev. Pegasus to r.: below, C O.
   New type.
4. Find No. 502. AR, wt. 0.29 gm. *Area 2. G.134*
   Obv. Bucranium; around, VERICA.
   Rev. Tomb or monumental altar; to l., C: to r., F.
   New type. The domed roof of the building suggests that it might be a tomb, but the other details are reminiscent of the monumental altar on the *Divus Augustus Pater* copper asses of Tiberius (cf. *R.I.C.* I, p. 95, No. 6).

CATUVELLAUNI
Cunobelin (A.D. 10–40)
5. Find No. 2190. Æ, wt. 2.32 gm. *Area 5. P.89*
   Obv. CVNOB. Head of Jupiter Ammon to r.
   Rev. Lion crouching r. beneath tree; below, on tablet, CAM. cf. Mack 253.
6. (444). Æ, wt. 1.84 gm. *Area 7. Pit A.19(B)*
   Obv. Sphinx to r.: below, CVNO.
   Rev. Male figure standing to l., holding human head in r. hand, and staff in l. In field CAM. cf. Mack 260.

Epaticcus (A.D. 25–35)
7. (1164). AR, wt. 1.03 gm. *Area 4. M.71*
   Obv. Head of Hercules to r.: in front, EPATI.
   Rev. Eagle facing, head to l. and wings spread, standing on serpent. cf. Mack 263.

8. (2182). AR, wt. 1.13 gm. *Area 3. W.27. Slot W.4*
   Obv. Victory seated to r., holding wreath. TASCIOV.
   Rev. Boar to r.; below, EPAT, cf. Mack 263A.
   Second example of coin found in the Bagendon excavations (cf. Clifford, *Bagendon: a Belgic Oppidum*, p. 114, No. 31).
9. (1179). AR, wt. 0.31 gm. *Area 4. M.83*
   Obv. EPATI. Above and below, an annulet enclosing a pellet.
   Rev. Boar's head to r.; below, TA. cf. Mack 264.
   Previously known only from an electrotype copy of a coin of unknown provenance in the British Museum.

CANTI;
Aminus (*c.* A.D. 15)
10. (528). AR, wt. 0.39 gm. *Area 2. G.153*
    Obv. Letter A in centre of two interlaced squares with curved sides.
    Rev. Bird to r., cf. Mack 316.
    cf. also *Chichester Excavations* 2, p. 55, for an identical coin found at Tower Street.

DUROTRIGES
11. (63). Æ, wt. 3.17 gm. *Area 7. D.4*
    Obv. Trident shape; on either side, crescent and five pellets.
    Rev. Circle of pellets enclosing a wreath; below, five pellets. cf. Mack 331.
    Badly corroded and *not illustrated*.

See Table I and Fig. 10.57

The Roman and Post-Roman Coins

by Roger Lintott

(a) *Roman*
   These are presented in order of date, and the small finds number and location is included to facilitate identification. With the exception of a hitherto unpublished coin of Carausius, all the coins have been deposited in the Chichester District Museum. The exception has been donated to the British Museum by the Chichester City Council.
   The latest fully identified coin in the list is of Gratian (A.D. 367–383), finds No. 305, Area 2, mint of Arelate, dated to 375–378, *R.I.C. 1813*. A close examination of the coins of Valentinian, Valens and Gratian indicates that with one exception, the uncorroded ones show very little signs of wear.
   No attempt is made in this volume to discuss the implications of the Roman coin series; this would be premature, partly because the sample is from one area of the town only and partly because the current heavy excavation programme being carried out both inside and outside the city walls might conceivably alter the final picture. A histogram is published with this list which shows a sharp break-point in the last quarter of the 4th century, the series ending with Gratian. This is briefly discussed by the author (p. 83) but more work has to be done on the material from earlier excavations as well as those currently in progress before any valid conclusions can be drawn, and further discussion is postponed to a later volume.

List of Abbreviations

Æ – Copper, bronze or orichalcum
Æ 1 – coin diameter from 25 mm
Æ 2 – coin diameter from 21 mm
Æ 3 – coin diameter from 17 mm
Æ 4 – coin diameter under 17 mm
ANT – Antoninianus
AR – Silver
BR – Barbarous radiate
C – Centenionalis
DEN – Denarius
DUP – Dupondius

FOL – Follis
GNS – Gloria Novi Saeculi
GR – Gloria Romanorum
LRBC – *Late Roman Bronze Coinage*, Carson, Hill and Kent
OBV – Obverse
Px or REV – Reverse
Q – Quadrans
QUI – Quinarius
RIC – *Roman Imperial Coinage*, Mattingley, Sydenham, Sutherland and Carson
1 STD – One standard on Gloria Exercitus
2 STD – Two standards on Gloria Exercitus
SES – Sestertius
SIL – Siliqua
SR – Securitas Republicae
SYD – Sydenham

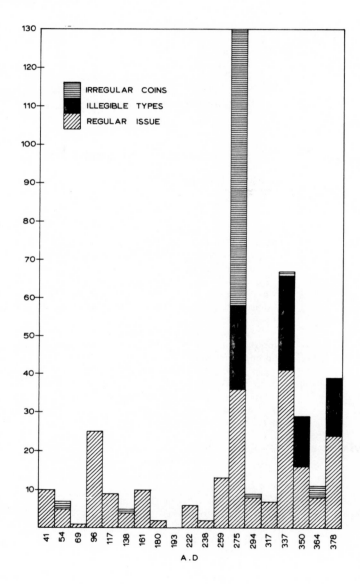

Fig. 10.57 Histogram of Roman coin types

TABLE I – THE COINS

Area	Find No.	Denomination	Emperor and Date	Reverse Type	Mint	Date of Coin	Ref. No.	Notes
6	2225	Æ AS*	Head of Janus	Prow		187–155 B.C.	SYD 299	SYD Republican; not included in histogram.
5	2027	Æ DEN*	Mark Anthony 83–30 B.C.	Leg XII		83–30 B.C.	SYD 1231	" " " Plated
2	197	Æ AS	Agrippa	Neptune		23–32	RIC(Tib)32	RIC Struck under Tiberius 14–37.
2	616	Æ AS	"	"		"	"	" " "
7	279	Æ AS						
2	995	Æ AS	Caligula 37–41	Vesta		37–41	RIC 30	
	2000	Æ Q	"	Cap of Liberty		"	RIC 38	
7	662	Æ AS	Germanicus	Vesta		"	RIC 30	Struck under Caligula 37–41.
7	725	Æ AS	"	SC		39	RIC 44	" " "
2	1016	Æ DUP	Nero and Drusus Caesars	Germanicus		37–41	RIC Vol. 1, p. 19	" " "
2	525	Æ DUP	"	Nero and Drusus		"	RIC 43	" " "
2	1058	Æ DUP	"	"		"	"	" " "
2	1056	Æ AS	Claudius 41–54	Minerva		41–54	RIC 66	Barbarous contemporary copy. Good style.
2	522	Æ AS	"	"		"	"	" " " Poor style.
4	1128	Æ AS	"	"		"	RIC 68(E)	
4	2044	Æ AS	"	Constantia STG		"	RIC 315	OBV legend ending PP.
4	327	Æ AS	Nero 50–68	Altar		54	RIC 319	
7	218	Æ AS	"	"		"	RIC 364	
7	707	Æ AS	"	Victory		"		
7	924	Æ AS	"	Nero ?		63–64		
7	678	Æ DUP	Vespasian 69–79	Security Seated		71	RIC 479	
7	2108	Æ DUP	"	Fides STG		"	RIC 486	
7	923	Æ AS	"	Fortune STG		"	RIC 487	
7	644	Æ AS	"	Victory		72–3	RIC 502	
7	259	Æ AS	"	Eagle on Globe	Lugdunum	"	RIC 528A	
	2216	Æ AS	"	"		76?	RIC 747	
7	300	Æ SES	"	Wreath		77–78	RIC 458	But VII at end of Obv. legend
7	634	Æ DUP	"	Fides STG		"	RIC 753	
7	621	Æ AS	"	Eagle on Globe			RIC 764A	
7	132	Æ SES	"	Judea Capta				Corroded.
7	306	Æ SES	"	Roma				Worn.
7	128	Æ DUP	"	"				Worn.
2	988	Æ AS	"	"				Corroded.
7	260	Æ AS	Domitian 81–96	SPES		77–78	RIC 791A or B	Struck under Vespasian.
5	611	Æ DEN	"	Clasped Hands		79	RIC 246	" "
7	2070	Æ AS	"	Jupiter		85–86	RIC 269	
2	181	Æ AS	"	Virtus		85–86	RIC 305A	
2	976	Æ SES	"	Jovi Victori		86	RIC 313	Mint condition.
6	2156	Æ DUP	"	Fig. holding Cornucopiae		86	RIC pp195	Rev. corroded.
7	2240	Æ DUP	"	Fortuna		86	RIC 326A	
2	607	Æ DUP	"	Moneta		86	RIC 327	
2	307	Æ AS	"	"			RIC 335	
2	130	Æ DUP	"	"		81–96		Rev. corroded.

Table I – The Coins – *cont.*

Area	Find No.	Denomination	Emperor and Date	Reverse Type	Mint	Date of Coin	Ref. No.	Notes
7	275	Æ SES	Domitia 81–96			81–96		Wife of Domitian/worn and corroded.
3	2175	Æ DUP or AS	„ „			81–96		„
2	2032	Æ AS	Trajan 98–117	Pietas		98–99	RIC 393	From lowest street metalling G.32.
3	510	Æ DUP	„ „	Abundantia		99–100	RIC 411	„
3	2163	AR DEN	„ „	Aequitas		103–111	RIC 119	
2	50	Æ SES	„ „	Roma		103–111	RIC 485	Worn and corroded.
3	2153	Æ SES	„ „	Aequitas				„
7	267	Æ SES	„ „					„
5	2034	Æ SES	„ „					„
2	637	Æ DUP	„ „					„
2	530	Æ DUP	„ „					„
2	880	Æ SES	Hadrian 117–138	Jupiter		119	RIC 561B	
2	170	Æ SES	„ „					Worn smooth.
7	653	Æ SES	„ „					Worn and corroded.
2	672	Æ AS*	„ „			119*	of RIC 577A	Contemporary cast imitation.
2	934	Æ AS or DUP	„ „			119		Worn and corroded.
7	274	Æ SES	Antoninus Pius 138–161			c. 138–139		
6	2286	Æ DUP	„ „	Britannia	Rome	154–155	RIC 930 or 934	
5	2024	Æ DUP	„ „	„	„	„	RIC 934	
2	419	AR DEN	Faustina II under A/Pius	Pieta	„	160–161	RIC 313C	
2	604	Æ AS	„ „	Juno	„	145–146	RIC 1398 ?	
3	418	Æ SES	„ „			138–161		Worn and corroded.
3	2151	Æ AS or DUP	„ „			138–161		Corroded.
7	2133	AR DEN	„ „					
3	273	Æ DUP	„ „					Worn and corroded.
2	193	Æ SES	Lucilla 161–169	Laetita	Rome		RIC 506A	
3	4039	Æ SES	Marcus Aurelius 161–180	Venus				
2	889	Æ SES	„	Liberalitia		c. 161	RIC 1771	Worn smooth.
7	164	AR DEN	Septimus Severus 193–211	Fortuna		196–197	RIC 77 or 78A	„
2	545	AR DEN	Julia Domna wife of S.S.					
5	905	Æ DUP	„					Corroded.
	2102–377–2171	„						Illegible 2nd century.
	632–483							„
7	983	AR DEN	Geta 209–212	Castor	Rome	200–202	RIC 6	„
7	509	AR DEN	Severus Alexander 212–235	Annona		233–235	RIC 133	BASE Denarius.
3	2016	Æ AS	Julia Mamaea	Felicitas		226–235	RIC 677	Struck under Severus Alexander.
7	388	Æ AS	Gordian III 238–244	Virtvs	Rome	240	RIC 293B	
7	c38	AR ANT	„ „	Liberalitia	„	240	RIC 67	Corroded.
1	5	AR ANT	„ „	Providentia				
2	824	Æ ANT	Gallienus 253–268	Captives and Trophy	Lugdunum		RIC 17	But PF in legend.
7	405	Æ ANT	„ „	SPES	Rome ?		RIC 203	Mint mark IG.
1	22	Æ ANT	„ „	Aeternitas	Rome		RIC 160	

Table I – The Coins – *cont.*

Area	Find No.	Denomination	Emperor and Date	Reverse Type	Mint	Date of Coin	Ref. No.	Notes
2	775	Æ ANT	Gallienus 253–268—*cont.*	Dianae	Rome		RIC 178	Reverse illegible.
7	886	Æ ANT	"	"				
7	177	Æ ANT	"	Dianae	Rome		RIC 176	
1	28	Æ ANT	"	Sol	Rome		RIC 160	
2	994	Æ ANT	"					Heavily corroded but little wear.
3	4014	Æ ANT	"					Heavily corroded.
7	419	AR ANT	Salonina. w of Gallienus					
3	4009	Æ ANT	Postumus 259–268	Hercules	Lugdunum		RIC 64	
5	2210	Æ ANT	"	Pax	Cologne		RIC 318	
7	477	Æ ANT	Claudius II 268–270	Annona	Rome		RIC 18	
4	1121	Æ ANT	"	Fides	Rome		RIC 37	
7	402	Æ ANT	"	Virtus				Obv. illegible.
4	1104	Æ ANT	"					
2	661	Æ ANT	" *	Eagle	Cyzicus	270	RIC 266	*Struck by Quintillus A.D. 270.
2	756	Æ ANT	" *	"	"	"	"	* " "
6	2244	Æ ANT	" * BR	Large Altar				* " "
7	272	Æ ANT	"	"				BR.
7	484	Æ ANT	"	"				"
7	574	Æ ANT	"	"				"
7	450	Æ ANT	"	"				"
7	698	Æ ANT	"	"				"
7	191	Æ ANT	"	Small Altar				" 6 mm Minim.
2	317	Æ ANT	"	"				BR.
4	1087	Æ ANT	Victorinus 268–270	Virtus	Southern		RIC 78	
7	180	Æ ANT	"	Sol	Cologne		RIC 114	
7	135	Æ ANT	"	"	"		RIC 112	
7	612	Æ ANT	"	Salus	"		RIC 122	
7	473	Æ ANT	"	Providence	Southern		RIC 61	Heavily corroded.
3	0	Æ ANT	"	Sol				
2	295	Æ ANT	" or Tetricus I	Hilaritas				
2	893	Æ ANT	Tetricus I 270–273	Sol				
3	2009	Æ ANT	"	"				
4	1086	Æ ANT	"	Laetitia			RIC 82	
5	2017	Æ ANT	"	"			RIC 90	
7	433	Æ ANT	"	Providentia			RIC 86	
1	8	Æ ANT	"	Pax				
7	165	Æ ANT	"	"				
3	4012	Æ ANT	"	"				
2	28	Æ ANT	"	Salus				
3	4024	Æ ANT	"	"			RIC 126	
7	2018	Æ ANT	"	Spes			RIC 135	
7	457	Æ ANT	"	"				
3	4015	Æ ANT	"	Virtus			RIC 148	

Table I – The Coins – *cont.*

Area	Find No.	Denomination	Emperor and Date	Reverse Type	Mint	Date of Coin	Ref. No.	Notes
7	182	Æ ANT	Tetricus I 270–273—cont.					
2	881	Æ ANT	"					
6	1100	Æ ANT	" BR	Pax type				
3	4002	Æ ANT	"	"				
5	2089	Æ ANT	"	"				
7	677	Æ ANT	"	"				
2	340	Æ ANT	"	"				
2	316	Æ ANT	"	Fides type				
2	847	Æ ANT	"	Spes type				
2	846	Æ ANT	" "					
2	864	Æ ANT	Tetricus I 270–273 BR					
3	2004	Æ ANT	" "					
6	2262	Æ ANT	" "					
3	2071	Æ ANT	" "					
2	71	Æ ANT	" "					
3	2010	Æ ANT*	" " I and II					*Hoard of 10 B.R. coins
2	746	Æ ANT	" " " "					
2	565	Æ ANT	Tetricus II 270–273	Pax			RIC 248	Illegible coins of late 3rd century – 38.
3	4010	Æ ANT	" "	Virtus			RIC 280	Illegible 3rd century ANTS – 22.
7	13	Æ ANT	" "					
2	80	Æ ANT	" "					
1	30	Æ ANT	" " BR	Pax				
3	573	Æ ANT	" "	Tetricus			as RIC 260	
3	4005	Æ ANT	" "					
2	744	Æ ANT	" "					
2	750	Æ ANT	" " "					
7	438	Æ DEN	Severina w of Aurelian 270–5	Venus Felix	Rome		RIC 6	
2	770	Æ ANT	Carausius 287–293	Pax	London	290–292	RIC 100	
2	830	Æ ANT	" "	"	Camulodunum	"		
7	499	Æ ANT	" "	"	Camulodunum	290	RIC 322	Mint mark off flan.
7	192	Æ ANT	" "	"				Reverse corroded.
3	4006	Æ ANT	" "	"	Camulodunum		as RIC 32	
3	2140	Æ ANT	" "	Fides				Heavily corroded.
3	418	Æ ANT	" "	Pax				Brass.
2	319	Æ ANT	" " BR	Fides EQVIT				New type.
1	3	Æ ANT	Allectus 293–296	Pax	London	293	RIC 28	
3	472	Æ ANT	" "	Providence	Camulodunum		RIC 103 ?	Heavily corroded.
3	2072	Æ ANT	" "	"	"		RIC 111	
1	36	Æ QUI	" "	Laetitia	"		RIC 124	
7	497	Æ FOL	Constantius I 293–306	"	Treveri	303–1/5/305	RIC 594A	
7	381	Æ FOL	Licinius I 308–324	Genius	London	310–312	RIC 210	
7	624	Æ FOL		"				

5

Table I – The Coins – *cont.*

Area	Find No.	Denomination	Emperor and Date	Reverse Type	Mint	Date of Coin	Ref. No.	Notes
2	52	Æ FOL	Constantine I 306–337	Sol	London	310	RIC 121A	
2	350	Æ FOL	"	"	Trier	310–313	RIC 869	Fragment.
2	13	Æ FOL	"	"	London ?	c. 318		
3	4023	Æ 3	"	Globe on Altar	Trier	321	RIC 318	
4	1083	Æ 3	"	Victory	Lyons	323	RIC 198	
2	33	Æ 3	"	"	Trier	323–324	RIC 435	
2	648	Æ 3	"	Camp Gate	"	324–325	RIC 449	
2	488	Æ 3	"	Victory		c. 323		
2	890	Æ 3	"	2 STD	Rome	333–335	RIC 350	
3	4008	Æ 4	"	"		c. 335		
7	27	Æ 4	"	1 STD		335–337		
2	347	Æ 4	" I or II	"	Trier	"	LRBC 92/93	
2	147	Æ 4	" I	Quadiga	Lugdunum	337–341	LRBC 245	
2	128	Æ 3	Crispus 317–326	Vot X	Rome ?	321 ?		Corroded.
5	2116	Æ 3	Constantine II 337–340	2 Captives 1 STD	London	320–321	RIC 197	
3	2125	Æ 3	"	"	"	"	RIC 198	
7	4	Æ 3	"	Vot X	Arles	322–323	RIC 255	Mint condition.
2	12	Æ 4	"	2 STD	Lyons	330–331	RIC 236	Mint condition.
2	36	Æ 4	"	"	Trier	330–335	LRBC 68	Worn.
4	1066	Æ 4	"	"				
7	113	Æ 3	"	"				
3	2213	Æ 4	"	1 STD	Lyons			
7	4033	Æ 4	"	"				Worn.
7	19	Æ 4	Constans 337–350	Victory		337–346	LRBC 785	
7	335	Æ 4	"	2 Victories	Trier	341–346	LRBC 162/164	
3	2144	Æ 4	"	"	"	"		
1	14	Æ 4	" BR	1 STD	As/Trier	330–335	LRBC 50	Good style Barb. Rev. axis ↑.
2	973	Æ 4	Constantius II 324–361	2 STD	Trier	330–335	"	
2	79	Æ 4	"	"	"	"	LRBC 68	
2	11	Æ 4	"	"	"	"	LRBC 57	
2	44	Æ 4	"	"	"	"	LRBC 354	
7	133	Æ 3	"	1 STD	Arelate	335–337	LRBC 89	
7	61	Æ 3	"	"	Trier	"	"	Mint condition.
2	325	Æ 4	"	"	"	"	"	
7	102	Æ 4	"	2 Victories	"	341–346	LRBC 139	
2	12	Æ 4	"	"	"	"	LRBC 147	
7	26	Æ 4	"	"	"	"	LRBC 269	
7	32	Æ 4	"	"	Lugdunum	"	LRBC 452	
7	19	Æ 4	"	"	Arelate	"	"	
2	967	Æ 4	"	"	"	"		
2	803	Æ 4	"		Trier ?	346–350	LRBC 32 ?	
6	2277	Æ 4C	Constans or Constantius II	Pheonix on Globe		346–350		
7	635	Æ 4	"	2 STD		330–335		

Table I – The Coins – *cont.*

Area	Find No.	Denomination	Emperor and Date	Reverse Type	Mint	Date of Coin	Ref. No.	Notes
7	40		Constans or Constantius II	2 Victorys		c. 343–349		
2	58		"	"		"		
2	636		"	"		"		
2	649		"	"		"		
2	669		"	"		"		
2	857		"	"		"		
6	2002		"	"		"		
7	159		Illegible	"		"		
2	87		"	"		"		
2	653		"	"		"		
2	797		"	"		"		
6	2252		"	"		"		
7	322		House of Constantine					
2	90		"					
6	2243		"					
2	83		"					
2	107		"					
2	362		"					
2	795		"					
2	838		"					
2	854		"					
3	2114		"					
4	1082		"					
5	2084		"					Illegible 4th century, 6 no.
2	35	Æ 4	Urbs Roma 330–346	Wolf and Twins	Lyons	330–331	RIC 242	
2	34	Æ 4	"	"	Trier	"	RIC 529	As 242 but extra dot in M.M.
2	352	Æ 4	"	"	"	332–333	RIC 547	
3	2212	Æ 4	"	"	Lyons	333–334	RIC 267	
6	2283	Æ 4	"	"	Trier	"		
3	4036	Æ 4	"	"	"	"	RIC 553	
7	244	Æ 4	"	"	Lyons ?	330–335		
7	77	Æ 4	Constantinopolis 330–346	Victory on Prow	Lyons	330–331	RIC 241	
2	78	Æ 4	"	"	Trier	"	RIC 523	
2	357	Æ 4	"	"	"	333–334	RIC 563	
1–7	1–29 1–31	2–300 7–540	?2–959 6–2220 all Constantinopolis with illegible mint marks.					
7	223	Æ 3	Helena w. of Constantius	Helena	Trier	324–325	RIC 458	
2	780	Æ 4	"	Pax	"	337–341	LRBC 128	
2	863	Æ 4	"	"	"	"	LRBC 112	
2	2015	Æ 4	"	"	"	"		
7	463	Æ 4	Theodora 2nd w. Constantius	Pietas	"	337–340	LRBC 120	
2	821	Æ 4	"	"	"	"		
7	330	Æ C	Magnentius 350–353	2 Victorys	Amiens		LRBC 9	
7	337	Æ C	"	"	"		LRBC 10	

Table I – The Coins – *cont.*

Area	Find No.	Denomination	Emperor and Date	Reverse Type	Mint	Date of Coin	Ref. No.	Notes
7	331	Æ C	Magnentius 350–353	,,	Trier	351–353	LRBC 58/61	
2	329*	Æ C	,,	,,	2 Victorys	,,	LRBC 58 or 907	
2	329*	Æ C	,,	,,				
7	90	Æ ¼C 12 mm	,, Barb.	,,				Barb.
1	26	Æ 1¼C 15 mm	,, ,,	,,				Barb.
7	333	Æ ¼C	Decentius 351–353	2 Victorys	Arles ?			No evidence of clipping or heavy wear but only 1.60 gm weight, norm. *c.* 2.25 gm. Struck counterfeit ?
7	595	AR SIL	Julian II 355–363	Votis/V/Mvltis/X				
2	298	Æ 10 mm	Barbarous Minim	Falling Horseman				Good style.
5	2005	Æ 9 mm	,,	,,				
7	68	Æ 3	Valentinian I 364–375	Victory Advancing SR	Cyzicus	367–375	RIC 13B	SR Securitas Repvblicae.
7	699	Æ 3	,,	,, SR				
7	67	Æ 3	,,	,, SR				
7	221	Æ 3	,,	,, SR				
2	296	Æ 3	,,	,, GR				GR Gloria Romanorvm.
7	81	Æ 3	,, ,,	,, GR	Lugdunum	367–375	RIC 10A	
2	37	Æ 3	Valens 364–378	,, SR	Arelate		RIC 9B	
2	656	Æ 3	,,	,, SR	Aquileia		RIC 9B	
2	972	Æ 3	,,	,, SR	,,		RIC 17A	
2	820	Æ 3	,,	,, GR	Arelate	367–375	RIC 16A	
5	2011	Æ 3	,,	,, SR	Lugdunum			
5	850	Æ 3	,,	,, SR				
7	44	Æ 3	,,	,, SR				
7	3	Æ 3	,,	,, SR				
1	849	Æ 3	,,	,, SR				
5	645	Æ 3	,, or Valentinian I	,, SR	Arelate		RIC 17A or B	
2	304	Æ 3	Gratian 367–383	Gloria Novi Saecvli GR	Arelate	367–375	RIC 15	
2	305	Æ 3	,,	Gratian and Captive GR	,,			
2	1052	Æ 3	,,	,,	Lugdunum	,,	RIC 20C	
2	902	Æ 3	,,	,,	Arelate	375–378	RIC 18B	
2	27	Æ 3	,,	GNS	,,			
2	424	Æ 3	,,	Gratian and Captive GR				
2	687	Æ 3	,,	,, GR				
2	64	Æ 3	,,	GNS				

7-397 2-888 5-2007 Valens or Valentinian I Victory type.

2-301 2-644 2-869

2-95

2-88 2-360 2-785 Gloria Romanorum types.

2-6 2-10 2-17 2-18 2-312 Securitas Republicae types.

(b) *Post-Roman coins*
(The numbers run on from the Early Iron Age series.)
SAXON
11. (865). AR, wt. 0.33 gm (5.1 gr). Edgar (A.D. 957–975), see Pl. 00.
   Obv. + EADGAR R·EX. Small cross patée; extra cross in field.
   Rev. + CISE CIFITAS. Small cross patée with an extra pellet at the extremity of each arm.
   Halfpenny, cf. B.M.C. Type III (variety). Mint of Chichester.
12. (819). AR, Aethelred II (A.D. 978–1016), silver penny.
13. (370). AR, Aethelred II (A.D. 978–1016, coin date A.D. 985–991), silver penny.
14. (315). AR, Edward the Confessor (A.D. 1042–1066), silver penny.

NORMAN
15. (469). AR, William I (A.D. 1066–1087), penny, mounted and gilded as a brooch.

MEDIEVAL AND LATER
16. (971). Edward I or Edward II (A.D. 1272–1327).
17. (324). Clipped medieval longcross penny (from 1247).
18. (25). Charles I or James I (A.D. 1603–1649), silver shilling.
19. (373). Charles I (A.D. 1625–1649), Rose farthing, Type 2.
20. (1075). William III (A.D. 1694–1702), farthing, worn.
21. (580). William III (A.D. 1694–1702), halfpenny, worn.
22. (379). Joseph Whitehead, I.O.W. bronze token, A.D. 1664.
23. (6). Bronze 17th-century token.
24. (32). John Eede, Petworth. Bronze token A.D. 1670.
25. (2). Nuremburg jeton.
26. (318). Nuremburg jeton.
27. (661). Nuremburg jeton.
28. (2003). Nuremburg jeton.
29. (2007). Nuremburg jeton.
30. (2101). Nuremburg jeton.
31. (2221). Nuremburg jeton.
32. (467). George I, A.D. 1720, halfpenny.
33. (722). George II, A.D. 1733, halfpenny.
34. (2000). George II, A.D. 1738, halfpenny.
35. (255). George II, halfpenny.
36. (20). George III, A.D. 1797, cartwheel penny.
37. (118). George III, A.D. 1797, cartwheel penny.
38. (721). George III, A.D. 1797, cartwheel penny.
39. (84). George III, A.D. 1806, penny.
40. (87). George III, A.D. 1806, penny.
41. (851). George III, halfpenny.
42. (351). George III, halfpenny.
43. (700). George III, Irish halfpenny, 1775 to 1783, Type 3.
44. (524). French, 12 denier piece, A.D. 1792.
45. (805). Bronze coin, foreign, A.D. 1777.

11

The Post-Roman Pottery

The Middle to Late Saxon and Saxo-Norman Wares

The large amount of Saxon material recovered from excavations in the North-West Quadrant of the City in the last seven years makes it possible to take a stage further the work of classifying these wares which began in Volume 2 (*Chichester* 2, pp. 85–9, Figs. 7.8 to 7.10).

Most of the pottery is from pits of the late Saxon and Saxo-Norman period (and here the term "Saxo-Norman" is applied to wares adjudged to have been produced between the first quarter of the 11th century up to the mid 12th), and some is residual from later deposits. One vessel, No. 81, Fig. 11.5, is from a village outside the City, but is included because it is the only complete example of the type known to us. The classification is highly tentative and is based partly on fabric and form and partly on the contents of a few closed pit groups. Some cross referencing with material excavated at Porchester has been possible by courtesy of Professor B. W. Cunliffe, who kindly made the proofs of his second Porchester Report available to me in advance of publication. In addition to the typological sequence discussed below it has been thought useful to publish a description of certain pit groups in full where these are fairly representative.

The problem of selecting these groups from the vast mass of excavated material was formidable, especially for Group 3, and some arbitrary decisions had to be taken.

The separate pit groups are available to students at the Chichester District Museum, and a schedule of all excavated material, stratigraphically arranged, can be had from the Curator.

No firm dating evidence can be offered; only a rough chronological sequence which will need to be constantly revised in the light of evidence from future excavations. In Group 3 (Saxo-Norman), only those pits which are free of glazed wares are considered. Nothing is yet known of late Saxon glazed wares in Chichester: "Winchester type" (*Cunliffe* 1970, pp. 67–85) wares have not been identified. This is not to say that they are not present, but they have not yet been isolated if they are, and it is felt by this writer to be safer, in the context of highly disturbed urban sites, to proceed on the basis that what glazed wares we have associated with groups which are otherwise Saxo-Norman in content, probably indicate that the pit is slightly later than early 12th century, and that the Saxo-Norman wares are residual.

In the initial attempt at classification the wares were broken down into six groups ranging from *c.* 8th/9th century through to the early-mid 12th, but too much sub-division was felt to be unrealistic as the problems of overlapping styles and techniques, plus rubbish survivals make a close definition impossible. Finally, three main groups were worked out, with further sub-divisions in Groups 1 and 2 in an attempt to produce a valid chronological sequence.

Group 1: *c.*8th to early 10th century

Fig. 11.1

Hand-made wares, fabrics usually soft and gritty and almost always reduced to black or dark grey. Some organic tempering media (grass or chaff) used occasionally. Exterior lumpy and hand smoothed or knife trimmed. So far it has not been possible to isolate with any confidence, closed groups of Group 1A wares; they have always been found to occur with fabrics and forms which are adjudged on present knowledge to be slightly later. This kind of problem is bound to occur when the ceramics of a primitive society making pots by hand over a long period, is studied. It is impossible to know which is residual and which represents a continuation of existing traditions in the face of local innovations.

The total number of Group 1A and B pots is low. This may well be because the population of Chichester during the period was small, but it must not be forgotten that the soft fabrics can easily disintegrate and become unrecognisable in a frequently disturbed urban environment.

Group 1(A): *c.*8th to 9th century

For the middle date of these types, some could go back into the late 7th century.

Area 2. Pit L.20 (residual in a medieval pit)
1. Handmade; soft with some shell tempering; reduced dark grey.

Area 6. Pit R.9 (residual in 10th century pit)
2. Handmade, and finished on a slow wheel; gritty, reduced dark grey.

341

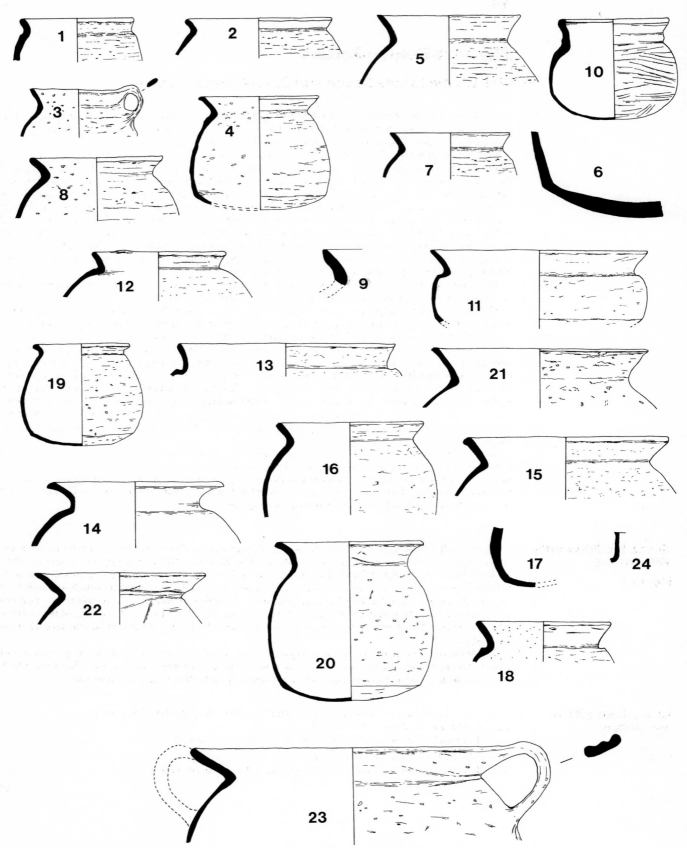

Fig. 11.1 Mid to late Saxon pottery, Group 1a, b and c, *c* 8th to early 10th century (¼)

3. Handmade, soft fabric heavily flint gritted; reduced dark grey.
4. Handmade, similar fabric to No. 3.
5. Similar fabric to No. 2; rim form suggests that it might possibly be 10th century.
6. Base of a large storage vessel, soft brown fabric heavily gritted with small sharp angled flints; some chalk tempering.

Area 2. Pit L.28 (residual in a Saxo-Norman pit)
7. Handmade; similar fabric to No. 2.

Area 2. Pit L.70
8. Handmade; similar fabric to No. 2.

Area 2. E.172 (residual in a Saxo-Norman cellar)
9. Handmade; brown gritty fabric reduced dark grey.

G.P.O. Service trench, Chapel Street, 1960 (unstratified)
10. Hard gritty fabric, handmade and knife trimmed on a slow wheel; partially oxidised.

Group 1(B): c.9th to early 10th century

Area 5. Pit O.34
This pit is possibly late Saxon (Group 2) in date and Nos. 11–13 could be residual. No. 14 is uncertain and may indicate a slightly later date for the pit, as could the other vessels (see below).
A total of seven vessels were identified; all cooking pots.
11. Soft gritty fabric, reduced black.
12. Soft gritty fabric reduced black on exterior, roughly flattened rim.
13. Brown gritty fabric finished on a slow wheel.
14. Grey fabric, flint and chalk tempered, partially oxidised, ? finished on a slow wheel.

Not illustrated
Elements from cooking pots in hard grey, chalk and grit tempered fabric 3

Area 6. Pit R.23 (only 3 vessels represented in this pit)
15. Soft brown gritty fabric reduced black outside.
16. Handmade; soft black ware heavily grogged with small flint grits.
17. Handmade; base of vessel in soft brown gritty fabric reduced dark grey.

Area 7. Pit E.35(b) (residual in late Saxon to Saxo-Norman pit)
18. Handmade; soft dark grey ware oxidised brown; heavily loaded with small flint grits.

Group 1(C): c.early 10th century

Area 2. Pit E.49 (residual in a Saxo-Norman pit)
19. Handmade; gritty ware, soft and oxidised reddish buff.

Area 7. Pit D.38
This appears to be a closed group; it may in fact be slightly later than early 10th century on the basis of Nos. 23 and 24, but the rest of the material seems to indicate an earlier date.
20. Handmade; grey gritty fabric oxidised red.
21. Handmade; dark grey gritty fabric oxidised red.
22. Soft brown gritty fabric reduced dark greyish brown. Finished on a slow wheel.
23. Grey gritty fabric oxidised reddish buff, slightly harder fired than the other examples from this pit.
24. Grey gritty fabric, very soft; oxidised reddish buff, wheel finished. Looks almost medieval.
A total of 20 cooking pots with everted or up-standing rims were identified. All were in similar fabric to those illustrated; some showed patchy oxidisation and most were wheel finished. Only one rim, No. 24, is flattened.

Group 2: c.mid to late 10th to early 11th century

Some handmade wares, but most finished on a slow wheel. Fabrics are soft and gritty with some organic tempering, and some chalk or shell. Firing is usually harder than Group 1 wares and more products are oxidised. Some rilling on cooking pots (Porchester type wares, *Cunliffe* 1974, pp. 125–35), and some stamp and "stick end" decoration.

Group 2(A): mid to late 10th century Fig. 11.2

Area 2. Pit L.24
The top fill of this pit (Layer A) contained early Saxo-Norman wares, whereas the two layers below (Layers B and C) had earlier fabrics. No. 25 *could* be residual in this pit.

343

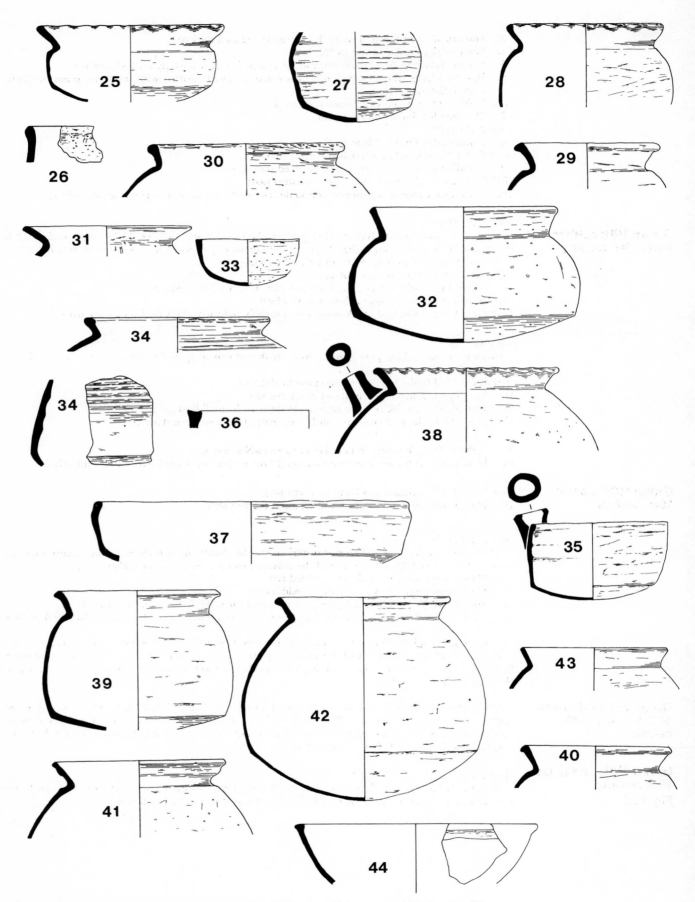

Fig. 11.2 Late Saxon pottery, Group 2a and b, c mid to late 10th to early 11th century ($\frac{1}{4}$)

25. Soft black gritty ware, heavily burnt, slightly crinkled rim, ? wheel turned. *Not illustrated.*
   Layer A. A dish with finger impressed rim, hard fired and reduced
   (see No. 68 for type) 1
   Dishes with plain rim (Type 45) 1
   Cooking pots with frilled rim (Type 50) 2
   Cooking pots with up-standing rims (Type 32) 2

Area 2. Pit L.66 (residual in Saxo-Norman pit)
26. Soft brown gritty fabric with chalk and some organic tempering material (probably chaff), oxidised to pale reddish buff.
27. Black gritty fabric, rilled body (Porchester type), wheel turned.

Area 7. Pit E.82 (probably residual in a late Saxon to Saxo-Norman pit)
28. Soft black gritty fabric with some organic tempering material that has burnt out. Knife trimmed off a slow wheel.
29. Soft black gritty ware, reduced black outside.
30. Grey gritty ware with some shell tempering, reduced to a dirty grey outside. ? finished on a slow wheel. Fired slightly harder than 28.

Area 2. E.172 (probably residual in a late Saxon to Saxo-Norman cellar)
31. Soft dark gritty ware oxidised red-brown with some terminal reduction to black outside. Rim is flattened; wheel turned.

Group 2(B): *c.*10th to 11th century

Figs. 11.2–11.3

Area 1. Pit A.12 (all the wares from this pit appear to be contemporary)
32. Complete vessel, gritty grey fabric partially oxidised reddish buff.
33. Grey gritty fabric; chalk tempered; reduced.
34. (Sherds A and B, probably from the same pot), grey gritty fabric partially oxidised a reddish colour. Some chalk tempering, rilled body, Porchester type.
35. Spouted bowl in grey gritty ware.
36. Rim of a ? dish; hard greyish gritty ware, some chalk, oxidised reddish buff.
37. Black gritty fabric with a few chalk flecks; patchy oxidisation.
   Not illustrated
   Elements from cooking pots with plain rims (Type 32) 22
   Dishes with heavily impressed rims (Type 68) 5
   Spouted pitchers (Type 38) 1
   All in grey gritty fabric, some oxidised; some with a patchy reduction. The variable results attained indicate firing in fairly uncontrolled conditions such as a clamp.

Area 2. Pit L.44 (late Saxon to Saxo-Norman)
38. Spouted pitcher, dark grey gritty fabric oxidised red.
39. Dark grey gritty ware oxidised buff.
40. Grey fabric, few grits, oxidised dirty reddish brown.
41. Soft brownish gritty ware reduced to a dirty grey.
42. Grey fabric with a few small grits.
43. Softish gritty fabric reduced black, wheel turned.
   Not illustrated
   Cooking pots with flattened rims 16
   Cooking pots with lightly frilled rims 3
   The majority are oxidised.

H.5 (*residual in a Saxo-Norman robber trench*)
44. ? Dish in a soft dark brown gritty fabric oxidised reddish buff.

Area 1. Pit A.29
45. Dark grey fabric; some chalk tempering; oxidised reddish buff.
46. Light grey fabric with small flints, well fired. Oxidised reddish buff outside.

345

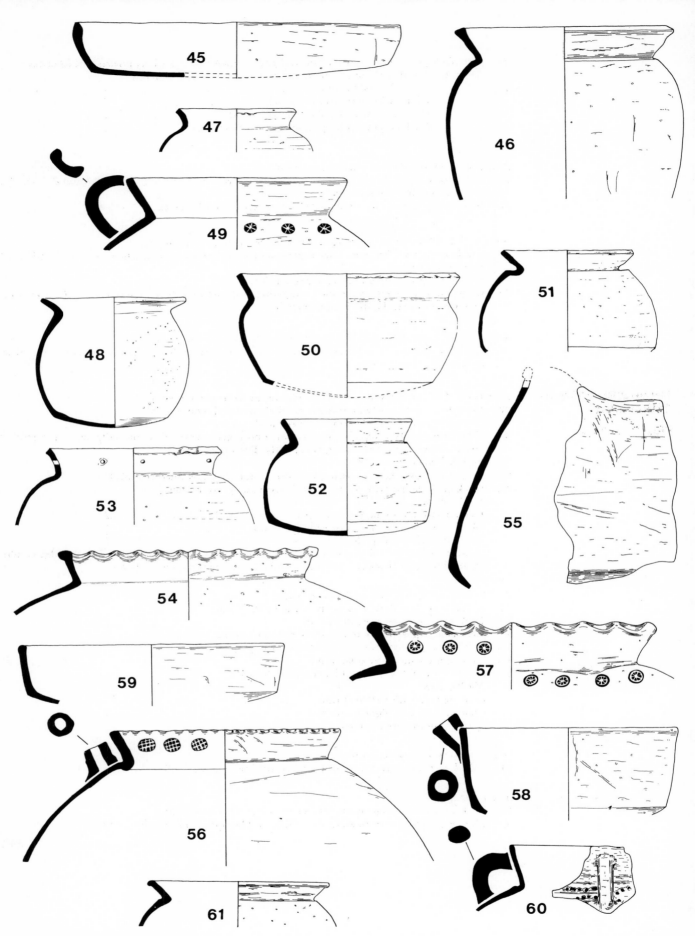

Fig. 11.3 Late Saxon pottery Group 2b, Nos. 45–51 Group 3, Nos. 52–61, *c* 11th to early 12th century ($\frac{1}{4}$)

47. Grey fabric oxidised to a dirty brown; chalk and flint tempered, probably handmade and finished on a slow wheel.
Not illustrated
Spouted pitchers (Type 38) 1
Cooking pots with flattened rims 14
Cooking pots with frilled rims 1
Dishes with plain rims (Type 45) 2
Cresset lamp (Type 82) 1

Area 7. Pit E.92
48. Complete vessel, dark grey gritty fabric fired medium hard and finished on a slow wheel.

Area 7. Pit E.35 (late Saxon to Saxo-Norman)
49. Hard grey fabric with angular flint grits, partially oxidised to a reddish brown.
Not illustrated
Cooking pots with everted rims in similar fabric to 48 3
 Rim of a waster in soft vesicular fabric.

Area 2. Pit L.25 (residual in Saxo-Norman pit)
50. Soft black gritty ware oxidised brown inside; slightly frilled rim; slow wheel finished.

Area 2. Pit H.4 (residual in Saxo-Norman pit)
51. Grey fabric with a few small flints; lumpy finish.

Group 3: *c.*11th to early 12th century (Saxo-Norman) Figs. 11.3–11.5

   This is by far the largest group and merges imperceptibly into the domestic wares of the early medieval period. Vessels are mostly wheel turned and harder fired, often heavily gritted and sometimes chalk tempered as well. A minority of the wares are sand tempered. Stamp decoration and applied strips, heavily thumbed, are common as is the "frilling" of cooking pot and bowl rims. Wares tend to have a greater degree of oxidisation and it is generally more even, suggesting perhaps that it was part of a deliberate policy of production. This may represent the beginnings of commercial production of these domestic wares. Certainly by the 13th century, as Barton has shown (*Chichester* 1, pp. 153–64), oxidisation of the kiln produced wares in Chichester was the norm.

Area 7. Pit E.89
52. Complete vessel; dark grey gritty fabric reduced black outside. Finished on a slow wheel.
53. Grey gritty fabric oxidised light brown/buff outside. Has a series of holes drilled in the rim after firing.
54. Grey fabric partially oxidised to a reddish brown; a few small grits but mainly chalk tempered.
55. Steep walled vessel; grey fabric, chalk tempered. Hard fired and oxidised to a patchy reddish buff outside.
Not illustrated
Cooking pots with plain rims 11
Cooking pots with frilled rims 1
Dishes with plain rims (Type 59) 1

Area 2. Pit H.4
56. Spouted pitcher, dark grey fabric with angular grits. Exterior oxidised to a lighter grey-brown. Grid stamps inside frilled rim.
57. Large storage jar flint and chalk tempered, oxidised reddish buff on outside. Wheel stamps inside rim and on shoulder.
58. Grey fabric; flint grogged, evenly oxidised inside and out.
59. Soft dark grey fabric oxidised to a light reddish grey.

Not illustrated

Spouted bowls with plain rims (Type 58)　..　　..　　..　　..	4
Bowls with plain rims (uncertain if spouts) (Type 59)　..　　..	11
Dishes with frilled rims (Type 68)　..　　..　　..　　..　　..	10
Stamped jars with frilled rims (Type 56)　..　　..　　..　　..	3
Cooking pots with rounded rim tips　..　　..　　..　　..　　..	37
Cooking pots with flattened rims　..　　..　　..　　..　　..	16
Body sherds with applied strips..　　..　　..　　..　　..　　..	3
Porchester type rilled wares (residual)..　　..　　..　　..　　..	2 body sherds

Area 2. L.39

60.　Dark grey fabric; a few flint grits; evenly oxidised reddish buff.

Area 2. Pit L.37

61.　Dark grey fabric, flint and chalk tempered; uniformly oxidised exterior.

62.　Dark grey fabric; flint grogged with a little chalk and some sand; wheel turned, hard fired; grid stamps inside rim and on shoulder.

Not illustrated

Cooking pots with flattened rims　　..　　..　　..　　..　　..	13
Spouted bowl　..　　..　　..　　..　　..　　..　　..　　..	1
Bowl with frilled rim and suspension holes (Type 71)　..　　..	1
Plain rimmed bowls (Type 45)..　　..　　..　　..　　..　　..	2

Area 7. Pit E.54 (residual in medieval pit)

63.　Grey fabric; flint grogged and chalk tempered, oxidised reddish buff.

Area 7. Pit F.9

64.　Grey fabric, oxidised exterior; flint and chalk tempered with heavily thumbed rim. Alternate bands of stamps and applied strips on shoulder.

Not illustrated

Cooking pots with rounded rim tips　..　　..　　..　　..　　..	1
Cooking pots with flattened rims　　..　　..　　..　　..　　..	2

Area 5. Pit O.8

65.　Grey fabric, flint and chalk tempered; oxidised.

66.　Dark grey fabric, flint and chalk tempered, evenly oxidised inside and out. Heavily pitted on inside surface where chalk has slaked out.

Not illustrated

Spouted pitchers with applied strips (Type 38)　..　　..　　..	2
Handle from a cooking pot.	
Cooking pots with lightly frilled rims　..　　..　　..　　..　　..	1
Cooking pots with flattened rims　　..　　..　　..　　..　　..	8
Plain bowls　..　　..　　..　　..　　..　　..　　..　　..	1
Spouted bowls (Type 69)　..　　..　　..　　..　　..　　..	1
Dishes with frilled rims (Type 68)　..　　..　　..　　..　　..	3

Area 7. Pit E.38

67.　Reduced black fabric, hardly any flints but a good deal of organic material incorporated. Stamped and ribbed on shoulder. May be earlier in view of the fabric.

Not illustrated

Cooking pots with plain rims　..　　..　　..　　..　　..　　..	6

(All in a black reduced fabric.)

　　Two types of ware were noted in the large amount of body sherds in the pit:
　　　　Fabric A – as No. 67.
　　　　Fabric B – oxidised grey, with selected small flints and harder fired than A.

Area 2. Pit L.42

68.　Dark grey fabric, flint grogged with some chalk tempering; partially oxidised.

348

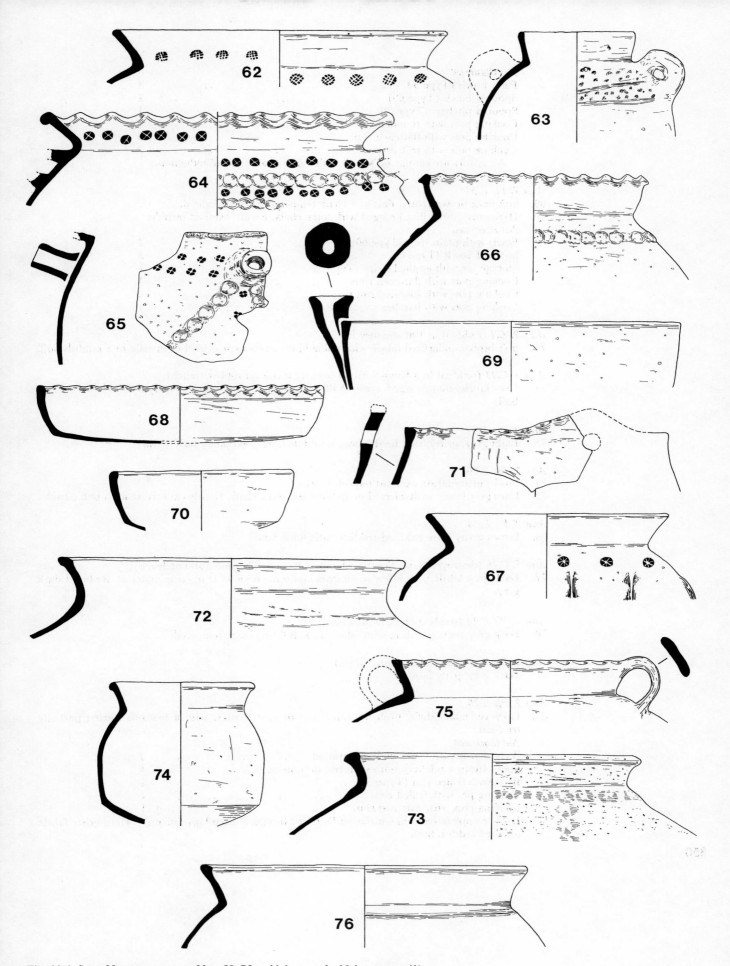

Fig. 11.4 Saxo-Norman pottery, Nos. 62–76, *c* 11th to early 12th century (¼)

Not illustrated

Plain bowls (Type 59)	3
Spouted bowls (Type 69)	2
Spouted pitchers (Type 38)	1
Cooking pots with rounded rim tips	9
Cooking pots with flattened rims	6
Cooking pots with frilled rims	2

All fabrics are similar to No. 68 with variable amounts of reduction.

Area 7. Pit E.51

69. Soft dark brown fabric, flint and chalk tempered, evenly oxidised.
70. Dark grey fabric, flint grogged with some chalk, evenly oxidised outside.

Not illustrated

Bowls with plain rims (Type 59)	2
Spouted bowls (Type 69)	3
Storage jar with applied strips (Type 82)	1
Cooking pots with flattened rims	14
Cooking pots with rounded rim tips	4
Cooking pots with handles	1

Area 2. L.1 (residual in 19th-century layer)

71. Soft brown underfired fabric with a few flint inclusions; oxidised externally to a reddish buff.

Area 7. C.11 (residual in a Saxo-Norman to early medieval robber trench)

72. Grey fabric, flint grogged, some chalk tempering, slightly sandy; evenly oxidised to a reddish buff.

Area 3. Pit Z.28

73. Light grey, gritty hard fired fabric, sand filled, oxidised pinky buff outside.

Area 7. Pit B.66

74. Brown gritty fabric oxidised reddish brown.
75. Dark grey fabric with selected small flints and some chalk. Evenly oxidised reddish buff outside.

Area 2. Pit L.28

76. Brown gritty ware oxidised reddish buff; some sand.

Area 7. C.16 (destroyed Saxo-Norman clamp in Roman Thermae robbing levels)

77. Dark grey fabric with a few small grits and some organic tempering material. Reduced dark grey.

Area 7. Pit E.44 (residual in early medieval pit)

78. Dark grey reduced fabric with selected small flints; chalk tempered.

Area 3. Pit W.6 (residual in medieval pit)

79. Dark grey gritty fabric.

Area 2. Pit L.25

80. Grey vesicular fabric, probably burnt out organic matter, with a few small grits; partially oxidised.

Not illustrated

Body sherds with "stick end" decoration	3
Spout (from a pitcher), with stick end decoration	1
Bowl with frilled rim (Type 68)	1
Cooking pot with frilled rim	1
Cooking pots with flattened rims	11

81. Large complete vessel in Chichester District Museum ("from Upwaltham"). Hard gritty fabric oxidised reddish buff.

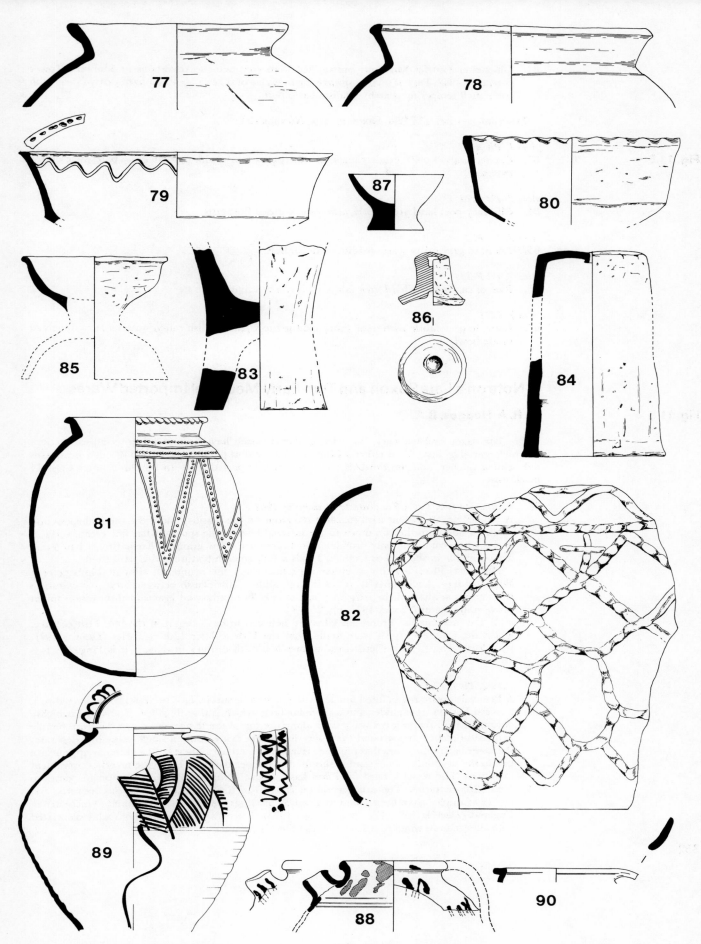

Fig. 11.5 Saxo-Norman pottery, *c* 11th to early 12th century, Nos. 81–82 (⅛). Remainder (¼).
Imported wares, late Saxon to early medieval, Nos. 88–90 (¼)

Fig. 11.5

82. Chichester District Museum; unstratified from contractor's excavations in Morants, Tower Street, in 1962. Part of a large storage jar in excess of 0.74 m high in a hard gritty fabric with some shell tempering. Patchy oxidisation to buff.

Miscellaneous items of Late Saxon to Saxo-Norman date.

Area 1. Pit A.29
83. Cresset lamp (1 of 2), crudely made in a dirty grey fabric with random grits; partially oxidised exterior.

Area 2. Pit L.25
84. Chimney pot; hard grey fabric with some crushed flint grits.

Area 2. Pit H.4
85. Lamp in grey gritty ware, oxidised reddish buff.

Area 7. Pit F.33
86. Base of candlestick; hard grey fabric with crushed flint grits.

Area 7. C.11
87. Lamp in grey fabric with small flints, oxidised to a pale reddish colour outside. Heavily sooted inside bowl.

A Note on a Late Saxon and Two Early Medieval Imported Wares

by R. A. Hodges, B.A.

One late Saxon and two early imported medieval vessels have been found in recent excavations in Chichester. The first (88) is either a Limburg or Pingsdorf pitcher, the second (89) is a Beauvaisis red-painted pitcher, and the third (90) is a Hamwih imported type, an 8th/9th-century Class 14 black ware.

88. *Unstratified from Post Office contractors trenches in 1962*
A pitcher rim and spout with splashed red paint on the outside, under the rim and spout and on the inside from the rim down to the internal level of the spout. It has fine cream surfaces and a white core. The only prominent inclusions are a few grains of haematite, *c.* 1 to 4 mm across, visible in the broken sections. It has a very smooth texture and is hard fired.

Hurst has identified this as either a product from the Brunnsum kilns in Limberg or a Pingsdorf type. Unfortunately, it is still impossible to distinguish between these two wares; to this end an analysis of the frequency against size of quartz-sand grains in thin section might prove to be useful (*Peacock* 1971, pp. 257–9).

At the moment the Brunnsum kilns are believed to have begun in the late 11th century, whilst the Pingsdorf types were made from the 10th to later 12th centuries (*Dunning* 1971, pp. 55–6). Thus, if this sherd is the former it is 12th century in date, if it is Pingsdorf it is 10th to 12th.

89. *Area 2. Pit L.17*
A Beauvaisis ware red painted pitcher with one handle surviving. The vessel has a flanged rim, a raised line on its shoulder and a globular body which is slightly rilled. The vessel is highly decorated with red painted wavy lines along the top of the flange and down the strap handle and with hatched arcs around the upper half of the body. Only a single wavy line decorates the lower half of the vessel that remains. It has cream surfaces; these have a granular appearance due to the prominent large sand grains used to temper the clay. There are no other prominent inclusions. The vessel is hard fired and has a coarse texture. This Beauvaisis pitcher dates to 10th–12th centuries. The arc decoration is a distinctive characteristic of this industry and earlier examples have been found at Beauvais itself, as well as at Ipswich and Winchester in England (*Dunning* 1959, Fig. 29.5; *Hodges* 1977). Beauvaisis vessels were probably associated with the trade in wine from Rouen to Southern England.

Fig. 11.5

90. *Area 2. Pit L.8(C)*

A pitcher rim and handle of a Class 14 black ware (*Hodges* 1977). It has black surfaces and a dark grey core. There are traces of burnishing across the strap handle. It has large sand grain inclusions and a granular texture. In thin-section it has an optically anisotropic light brown clay matrix with a scatter of sub-angular quartz-sand averaging about 0.4 mm across, and a grain of flint of the same size which were probably added. There are also grains of angular quartz-sand averaging 0.03 mm, which were probably in the clay.

This is an unusual example of the Class 14 which is a tradition of potting believed to have been made in several centres across northern France and in south-eastern Belgium. Most of the Class 14 vessels from the excavations at Hamwih, Saxon Southampton, have finer sand-grain inclusions, and finer surface finishing. The thin-section shows this vessel to belong to the Class 14, petrological Group 3 defined as a result of analyses of the Hamwih wares as well as other examples. However, the fabric to the eye and in thin-section is similar to another of the imported classes at Hamwih, the Class 25. This class was made in the environs of Paris, and has been found there.

The tradition of blackening the surfaces of pots began again in the Merovingian period, and, as shown by the analyses of the Hamwih wares, was maintained in many northern French and Belgian potting centres until the early 10th century. It is possible that this is evidence of the technique being occasionally employed by the "Class 25" potters who normally produced oxidised vessels. Yet their use of the technique of blackening should not be surprising since these potters were among the first to adapt to the revived fashion of red-painting their wares, in the later 8th or early 9th centuries.

Medieval Pottery

The pottery published in this section takes a stage further the task of producing a representative selection of medieval wares found in the City, which was started in Volume 1 and continued in Volume 2.

All the material illustrated was recovered from the North-West Quadrant excavations, most of it being well stratified. It is noteworthy that the majority of the fine glazed wares come from pits associated with the medieval houses fronting on to the east side of Tower Street, possibly an indication that during the 13th to 15th centuries the holdings along Chapel Street did not support many tenements.

It is now possible to identify some of the wares as being from the pottery kilns which functioned outside the City Wall in the late 13th century, but the production centres for the majority of the 14th-century glazed wares have still to be located. A few are probably from the Binsted kilns[1] and others may have been made at Graffham,[2] but it is likely that the bulk of the wares were produced near to the City, where the demand would be greatest and where suitable clay could be had.

Jugs and Pitchers

Figs. 11.6–11.7

1. *Area 7. F.18 (13th/14th-century layer)*
   Neck of jug in sandy ware oxidised reddish buff, external patchy green glaze. ? Early West Sussex ware, possibly of Orchard Street type, ? 13th century.
2. *Area 7. C.26*
   Jug handle; dark grey sandy fabric. Top surface has a patchy brown/green glaze, ? 13th century.
3. *Area 7. E.10 (13th-century layer)*
   Strap handle in a fine grey sandy ware: light green glaze.
4. *Area 7. Pit D.39(A) (medieval well)*
   Strap handle; sandy oxidised ware, green/brown glaze. Orchard Street type, *c.* late 13th century.
5. *Area 7. Pit D.26 (13th-century pit)*
   Jug or tripod pitcher in sandy pale fabric, patchy green glaze. Orchard Street or Southgate type, *c.* late 13th century.
6. *Area 7. D.22 (early medieval layer)*
   Base of a jug in sandy grey ware with a pale green glaze, ? 13th century.
7. *Area 7. Pit D.55*
   Rim of an unglazed jug or pitcher in a dark grey gritty ware oxidised outside to a reddish buff, ? 12th–13th century.

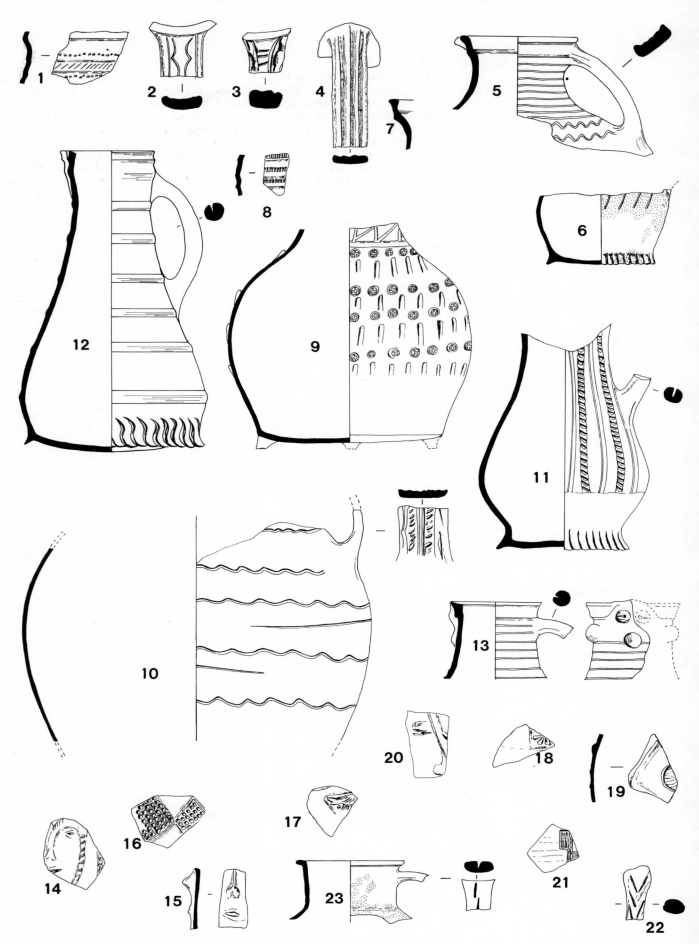

Fig. 11.6 Medieval pottery from the N.W. Quadrant, Nos. 1–23 ($\frac{1}{4}$)

8. *Area 7. Pit E.55(B) (early medieval)*
Body sherd in a sandy grey ware oxidised buff, external green glaze over rouletting.
    This vessel could be 12th century, being similar to wares of that date from Winchester.[3] The lower levels of the pit contained only Saxo-Norman coarse wares plus two glazed sherds of "medieval" date, while the top fill, which could be much later, had one glazed medieval sherd, probably late medieval, with the remainder of the pottery being coarse Saxo-Norman fabrics. The sherd discussed here came below the top fill and is only the second of its type noted from Chichester by the writer.

9. *Area 7. Pit B.6(C) (13th century)*
Part of a tripod pitcher in a fine oxidised buff fabric, patchy dark green/brown glaze. Unusual body decoration in the form of heavily impressed stamped crosses between rows of applied strips. From a pit classified as 13th century on the basis of the rest of the wares, but this piece might be earlier in view of the decoration.

10. *Area 7. E.10 (13th-century layer)*
Jug or pitcher in fine sandy grey fabric oxidised reddish buff and with a patchy brown green glaze. Possibly 13th century in view of the decoration and handle.

11. *Area 7. Pit F.25 (bellfounding pit)*
Hard grey sandy fabric, neck and rim uncertain but probably as No. 12. Completely green glazed exterior; possibly Horsham type West Sussex ware, 14th century.

12. *Area 7. Pit E.66 (bellfounding pit)*
Almost complete jug in a fine sandy dark grey ware oxidised buff. White painted band inside rim; complete external green glaze. Early West Sussex ware, Horsham type, 14th century.

13. *Area 7. Pit F.26 (14th/15th-century well)*
Neck of jug in hard grey fabric with some sand. Olive-green glaze with applied "face" and shallow grooving on neck. Early West Sussex Ware, Binsted type, ? *c.* 14th century.

14. *Area 7. C.29 (14th-century layer)*
Body sherd from a face jug. Sandy off-white ware with a good green glaze, ? late 14th century.

15. *Area 7. E.11 (14th-century layer)*
Body sherd from a moulded face jug in a sandy light grey ware, very fine. Dark green glaze, 14th century.

16. *Area 7. Pit A.35 (14th-century layer)*
Body sherd from a jug; similar ware to No. 15, and with olive-green glaze.

17. *Area 7. Pit E.76 (residual in 17th-century well pit)*
Body sherd in a similar ware to No. 15. Dark green glaze with moulded decoration in the form of a hen laying an egg.

18. *Area 7. Pit E.22*
Body sherd from a jug in similar ware to No. 15; speckled green glaze, stamped rosette decoration.

19. *Area 2. Pit L.2 (late medieval)*
Body sherd from a jug in a fine grey ware with applied decoration. Speckled green glaze, with the applied rosette being a darker green; Binsted type.

20. *Area 3. Pit Y.3 (14th century)*
Body sherd from a face jug; hard sandy greyish ware, dark olive-green glaze.

21. *Area 7. Posthole C.3*
Sherd in a dark grey sandy fabric. Yellow external glaze with recessed decoration glazed brown.

22. *Area 7. Pit A.72*
Jug handle with shallow chevron slashing, in a hard grey sandy ware.

23. *Area 2. Pit L.2*
Rim of a jug in a sandy light grey fabric with a patchy green glaze and slashed strap handle. Possible late West Sussex ware, *c.* 14th to 15th century.

24. *Area 7. Pit C.12 (late medieval)*
Jug in a similar fabric to No. 23; patchy green glaze over white slip decoration. The handle is pricked, with applied blobs on the underside to facilitate gripping. Late West Sussex ware.[1]

25. *Area 7. D.20 (residual in a 17th-century layer)*
Base of a jug in sandy ware oxidised buff, with patchy green glaze inside. Possibly 15th century.

26. *Area 7. Pit C.10(A) (15th-century garderobe)*
Handle in an off-white sandy fabric with a pale green glaze. From the top fill of the garderobe.

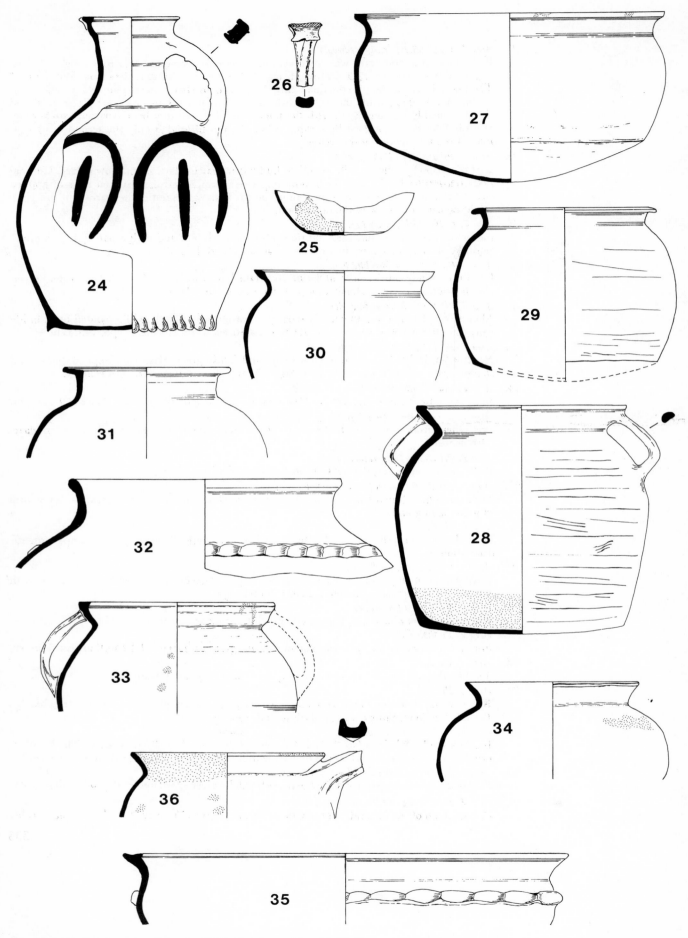

Fig. 11.7 Medieval pottery from the N.W. Quadrant, Nos. 24–36 ($\frac{1}{4}$)

Cooking Pots and Storage Jars

(Figs. 11.7–11.8)

27. *Area 7. Pit F.23 (13th century)*
Oval vessel in a grey fabric with selected small grits and patchy internal green glaze.
28. *Area 7. Pit E.34(B) (late medieval)*
Two-handled pot in a hard grey sandy ware. Knife trimmed on base.
29. *Area 7. Pit A.23(A) (medieval)*
Sandy grey ware with a few small grits, oxidised buff.
30. *Area 7. Pit B.53 (13th century)*
Sandy ware oxidised buff.
31. *Area 6. Pit S.22 (14th century)*
Pale sandy grey ware oxidised buff.
32. *Area 7. Pit C.35 (13th century)*
Storage vessel, flint grogged grey ware oxidised dirty buff.
33. *Area 7. Pit F.19 (late medieval)*
? Two-handled pot in a sandy fabric with splashes of glaze inside.
34. *Area 6. Pit S.22 (14th century)*
Oxidised ware, some sand and small grits. Splashes of glaze on body.
35. *Area 7. Pit C.10(A) (15th century)*
Dark grey sandy ware oxidised buff.
36. *Area 7. C.12 (14th century)*
Vessel, possibly with two handles, sandy buff fabric with a patchy yellow brown glaze on the inside of the rim.
37. *Area 7. Pit A.18 (medieval)*
Sandy dark grey ware oxidised reddish buff, knife trimmed base. Splashes of green glaze on shoulder.
38. *Area 7. F.27 (residual in a late medieval pit)*
Dark grey gritty fabric oxidised reddish buff, possibly Saxo-Norman.
39. *Area 3. Pit Y.3 (14th century)*
Cooking pot in a hard light grey sandy fabric, oxidised outside.
40. *Area 3. Pit Y.3 (14th century)*
Cooking pot in a fine grey ware, oxidised reddish buff, probably Orchard Street ware.

Bowls and Dishes

(Fig. 11.8)

41. *Area 3. Pit W.14 (late medieval)*
Sandy grey fabric oxidised buff. Knife trimmed on sides, dark green interior glaze.
42. *Area 6. Pit S.22 (14th century)*
Sandy ware reduced to a dirty grey brown, traces of brown glaze inside base.
43. *Area 3. Pit Y.3 (14th century)*
Dish in a fine grey fabric oxidised reddish buff.
44. Dish (or possibly a curfew) in a grey fabric heavily grogged with flint and shell, oxidised reddish buff.

Pans (Fig. 11.8)

45. *Area 7. E.16 (14th century)*
Sandy pinky buff fabric with large flint grits and internal patchy green glaze.
46. *Area 6. Pit O.1*
Pan in gritty greyish ware with patchy internal brown/green glaze.

Jars Fig. 11.8

47. *Area 3. Pit Y.3 (14th century)*
Sandy greyish ware, dark green glaze inside and over rim.

Lids Fig. 11.8

48. *Area 3. W.5 (late-post medieval)*
Part of a lid in a heavily gritted fabric with some chalk tempering.
49. *Area 7. Posthole D.29 (medieval)*
Possible lid in a gritty grey ware oxidised buff.

Lamps Fig. 11.8

50. *Area 7. Pit B.58 (medieval)*
Base of a lamp in gritty grey ware.
51. *Area 7. C.1 (residual)*
Lamp in a grey gritty fabric, heavily sooted inside bowl.
52. *Area 7. Pit D.23(c) (13th century)*
Lamp in a hard grey sandy ware, green glazed inside bowl and around stem.

357

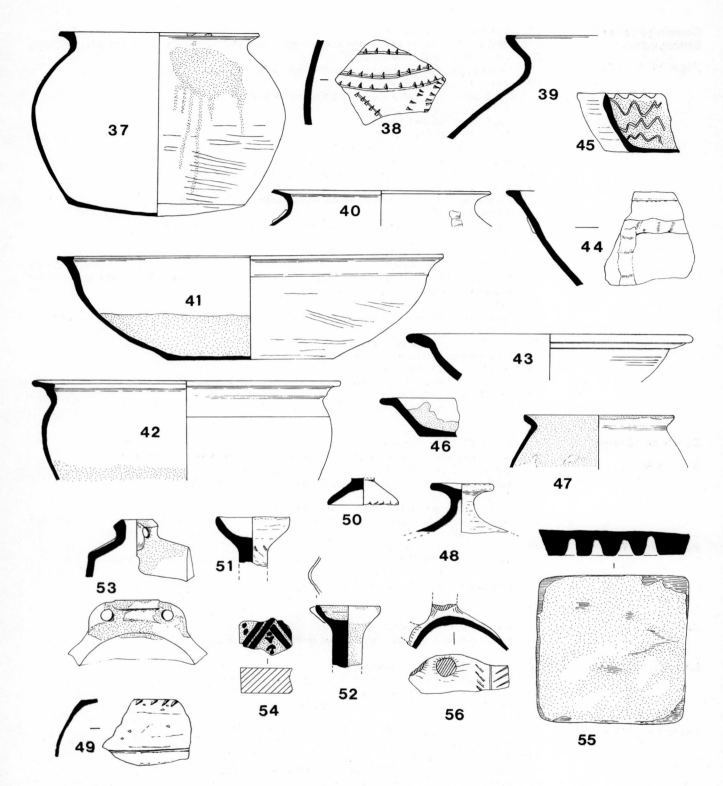

Fig. 11.8 Medieval pottery from the N.W. Quadrant, Nos. 37–56 ($\frac{1}{4}$)

53. *Area 7. F.27 (post-medieval layer)*
    Costrel in fine grey ware oxidised buff, patchy dark green glaze.
54. *Area 7. B.7 (bell founding pit)*
    Fragment of glazed tile; dark green glaze with white slip decoration.
55. *Area 7. F.23 (re-used in late medieval bread oven)*
    Green glazed floor tile (one of a large number found), from the 15th-century house in Tower Street.
56. *Area 3. Y.15*
    Sherd, probably from an acquamanile, in a grey fabric oxidised buff, and with a dark green exterior glaze.[1]

Footnotes

[1] I am indebted to Mr. C. Ainsworth, the excavator of the Binsted kilns, who kindly examined the material and identified some of the products.

[2] Recent work in the Graffham area, following upon earlier investigations by Miss P. A. M. Keef and C. J. Ainsworth indicate that a considerable pottery industry functioned there from *c.* 13th century up to the 19th (see the section on Painted wares from the City, this volume, p. 363). The Graffham pottery industry is now the subject of a research project sponsored by the Chichester Excavations Committee.

[3] Information from Miss K. Barclay of the Winchester Research Unit.

[4] For a discussion of West Sussex wares, see Barry Cunliffe, "Manor Farm, Chalton, Hants" in *Post Med. Arch.*, Vol. 7, 1973.

[5] Information from Mr. J. G. Hurst, to whom thanks are due.

Medieval Roof Fittings

Figs. 11.9 & 11.10

Roof slates

Few roofing slates from the medieval period survive in large enough fragments in medieval contexts to enable a reasonable assessment of size and date. The following examples are complete or nearly so, and are well stratified. The problems of the dating of these slates remains however, as they would have had a long life and, in some instances, would be re-used.

Area 7. E.41 (from the destruction levels of a 14th-century house)
1. 119 × 167 mm, 4 to 7 mm thick.
2. 96 × 167 × 9 mm thick.

Pit E.68 (14th century or perhaps slightly later)
3. 91 × 232 mm, 3 to 7 mm thick.

Pit B.35(B) (*13th century*)
4. 100 × 165 mm, 3 to 6 mm thick.

Pit D.27(C) (*14th–15th century*)
5. 120 × 225 × 5 mm thick.
6. 126 × 222 mm × 3 to 8 mm thick.
    Nos. 2 and 5 had been bedded in a cream-coloured mortar and traces of this remained on the reverse face.
    For an earlier discussion of medieval roofing slates see *Holden* 1963, pp. 157–8. The source for these slates is almost certainly Devon or Cornwall.

Roofing tiles (see also this volume, p. 13)

A number of baked clay roofing tiles were recovered from medieval and post-medieval layers and it has been thought useful to offer a selection of these for discussion. All the tiles illustrated are well stratified but as with the case of the slates, the tile is seen where it has been finally deposited having come off the roof it was laid on. In general it can perhaps be assumed that complete or near complete tiles indicate, not a re-cladding of the roof of a house, but the destruction, or re-planning of part or

359

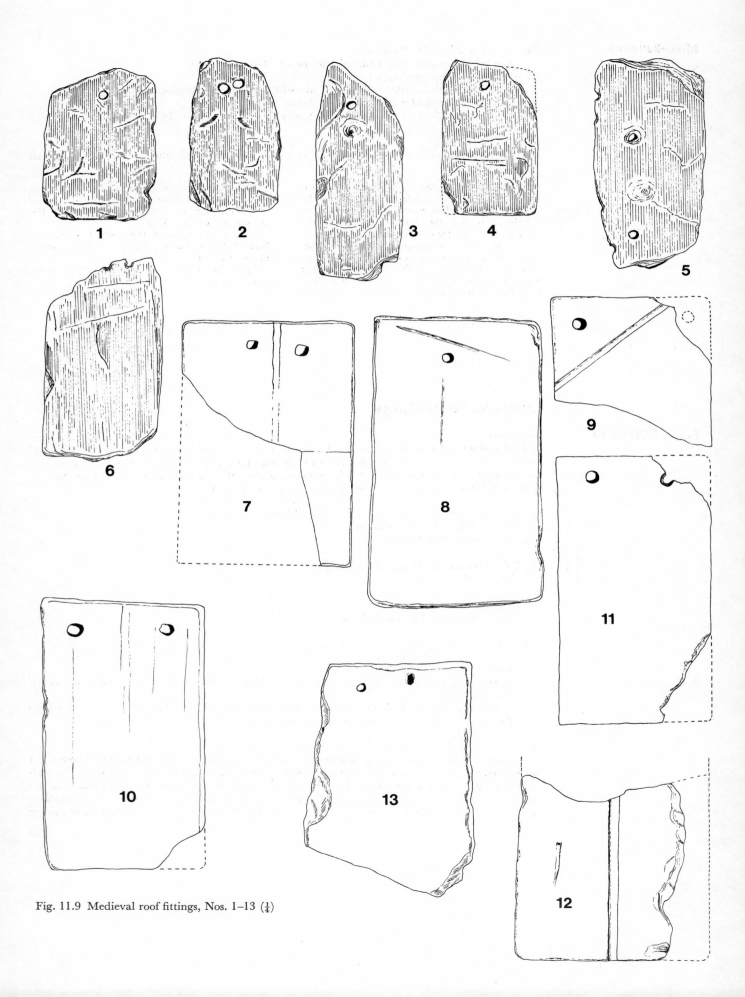

Fig. 11.9 Medieval roof fittings, Nos. 1–13 ($\frac{1}{4}$)

all of it. Most of the tiles finally came to rest in a cesspit, and like the pottery, would have been around as surface rubbish when the pit came to be back-filled. In the medieval period, as now, clay peg tiles would have had a long life provided that they were well fired and not too absorbent. The glazing of the lower half of the tile, which was the area exposed most to the elements (see p. 15) would be an important factor in prolonging its life.

None of the tiles illustrated in this section are glazed.

Pit D.27(c) (14th–15th century)
7. The illustration is built up from fragments of three tiles in the same fabric, which is a pale buff colour with some sand but no flint. One of the three fragments has a central fillet on the facing side, with square peg holes, 266 × 180 × 12 mm thick.

Pit B.6(c) (13th century)
8. Complete roof tile in grey sandy fabric, oxidised dirty buff, 308 × 126 × 10 mm thick.

Pit C.10(A) (top layer of garderobe pit belonging to the 15th-century house in Area 7)
9. Tile of unknown length in an oxidised buff fabric with selected flint grits, 165 mm wide × 10 mm thick.

F.23 (from the bread oven in House M.6, Area 7)
10. Tile in similar fabric to No. 9 and almost certainly from the same kiln, 288 × 170 × 12 mm thick.

Pit B.32 (medieval)
11. Sandy reddish fabric with a few small grits, 295 × 162 × 12 mm thick.

F.12 (post medieval cesspot)
12. Similar fabric and appearance to No. 7, but wider; assuming the fillet to be central as in the case of No. 7, it would be *c.* 200 mm wide by 11 mm thick.

Area 6. R.5 (? residual in 17th-century layer)
13. Similar fabric to No. 12, 155 mm wide at top × 12 mm thick and tapers outwards to at least 180 mm. Not curved like a hip tile; one hole not fully pierced.

Hip Tiles
Area 7. Pit B.33 (late to post medieval)
14. Pale buff fabric, 12 mm thick.

Pit E.48 (? 14th century)
15. Heavily gritted reddish fabric, 11 mm thick.

Ridge Tiles
Area 3, Pit Z.16 (1 of 2); ? residual in a post-medieval pit.
16. Pale buff fabric, some sand, no flints. Green glazed along crest. The conjectural restoration gives a length of 360 mm.

Chimney vents (see also p. 16)
Both examples illustrated are unstratified but are included because these types have not been illustrated before from Chichester.

North-West Quadrant. Area 3
17. Pale greyish buff gritty fabric.

Adcocks, Eastgate
18. Grey gritty reduced fabric.

Miscellaneous. North-West Quadrant. Area 7. F.25
19. Fragment of tile, possibly roofing tile, 13 mm thick; hard fired fabric with a few selected grits. It has stamped decoration in the form of crosses on the upper face, which also has a patchy green glaze.

Area 7. Pit E.76 (residual in 17th-century well pit)

20. Part of the flange on the right side of an aperture on a louver. The aperture would have been triangular (see suggested reconstruction). In a fine grey fabric with external green glaze and with a white slip coating on the inside of the louver.[1]

Reference

[1] Similar apertures are on louvers from Great Easton, Essex, and the Manor of the More, Rickmansworth (*Medieval Archaeology*. X (1966), 74, Figs. 26 and 28). I am greatly indebted to Dr. G. C. Dunning for identification of this piece.

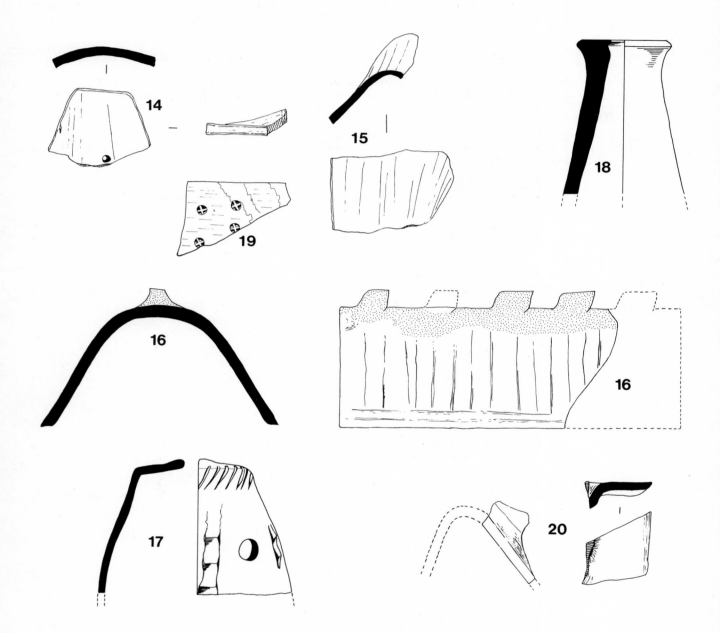

Fig. 11.10 Medieval roof fittings, Nos. 14–20 (¼)

The majority of the painted ware vessels found in Chichester are in a fine grey fabric with a little sand tempering. They are usually oxidised buff and are sometimes given a terminal reduction to black on the outside, presumably to enhance the white slip decoration. The dishes are usually glazed inside and the larger cooking pots are sometimes glazed inside the rim, and occasionally a band of glaze is applied externally around the neck. Many vessels show accidental splashes of glaze, indicating that they were fired in a batch with glazed wares. These wares are discussed in *Cunliffe* 1973, pp. 45–56, where a tentative chronology is offered; see also *Chichester* 2, Fig. 7.11, Nos. 36–42, for an illustration of other forms found in Chichester.

Recent information from the Graffham area indicates that there was a pottery industry operating there from the 13th century onwards. Large amounts of painted wares have been found, some in the bed of a stream, and some of these are wasters. These wares will be published in full as part of a research programme currently being pursued by the Excavations Committee, but in the meantime it can be said that the fabrics are very similar to those found within the City and it is more than likely that Chichester was the main market for the Graffham products. The painted wares from Chalton,[1] whilst similar in form and decoration, are not in the same fabric, having a higher proportion of sand filling, and it seems that there is another production centre, nearer to Chalton, supplying these wares in the 15th–16th century.

Area 3. Z.1
1. Large jar in fine grey ware oxidised buff, white slip on rim.
2. Rim of a large jar, similar fabric and colour to No. 1.
3. Large dish, 40 cms diameter, similar fabric to No. 1, green glaze inside.

Area 3. Z.9
4. Dish in dark grey fabric oxidised buff, green glaze inside, white slip on rim.
5. Large jar, similar fabric to No. 4, reduced black on exterior.

Area 3. W.12
6. Rim of dish in typical painted ware fabric but without the white slip decoration and with a patch of glaze on the rim.

Area 6. R.5
7. Jar in similar fabric to No. 5 with a band of green glaze inside rim.

Area 7. Pit F.10
8. Slashed handle in painted ware fabric with applied white slip decoration.
9. Narrow-necked vessel, similar fabric to No. 8, reduced black outside.

Area 7. Pit C.14
10. Similar fabric to No. 7.

Footnote

[1] I am grateful to Mr. John Budden, the owner of Manor Farm, Chalton, for the opportunity of examining the wares from Chalton.

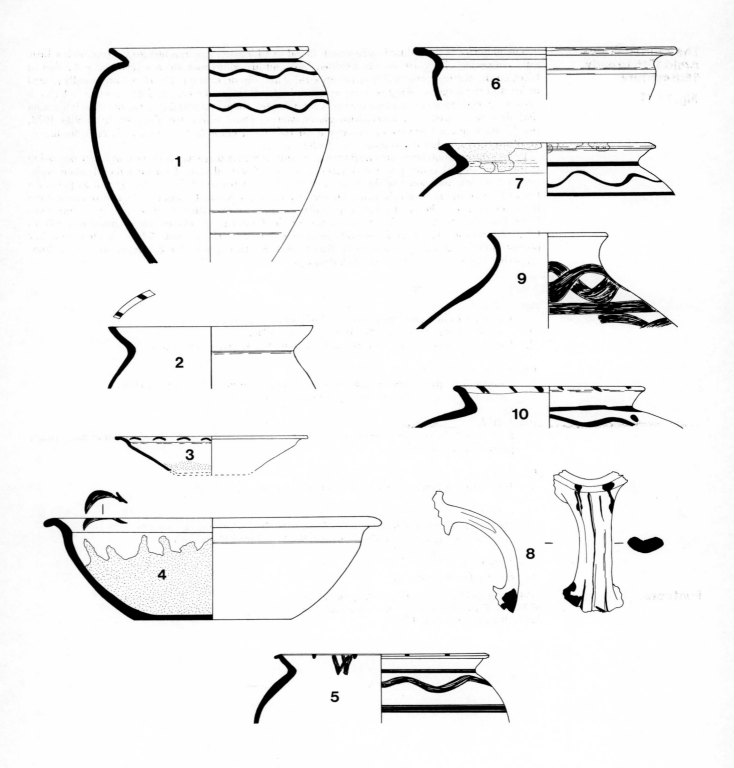

Fig. 11.11 Painted wares, mid 15th to early 16th century; No. 3 ($\frac{1}{8}$), remainder ($\frac{1}{4}$)

Large amounts of post-medieval wares were recovered from the sites; some being well stratified in pit groups. In an attempt to close some of the gaps in our knowledge of the post-medieval ceramics of the Chichester region (including wares imported from elsewhere), as much hitherto unpublished material as possible is recorded in this volume, thus taking a stage further the work started in *Chichester* 2. The emphasis is placed on pit groups for which a reasonably close dating is possible.

I am grateful to Mr. John Hurst who kindly commented on a cross section of the wares submitted to him, and to Mr. Felix Holling, the Curator of the Guildford Museum, for much information on the Surrey wares. I am also indebted to David Rudkin and Russell Fox of the Portsmouth City Museums for discussions on the problems of the local "Fareham" type wares. The urgent need is now to identify and excavate the kilns from the Fareham-Portsmouth region that produced some of these wares in the 16th and 17th centuries and dominated the local markets. Since work on this report commenced, a large amount of unstratified pottery has come into the Chichester District Museum from the Graffham area, most of the pots being wasters. The date range for the industry would appear to be from *c.* late 13th to 18th centuries and there is little doubt that some of these wares found a market in Chichester.

The research project recently initiated by the Excavations Committee should eventually enable us to distinguish between the products of these kilns and the Portsmouth-Fareham group. In the meantime, publication of the wares in a dateable context will help to date the kilns.

The group of pottery published below is available for consultation in the Chichester District Museum. See also the groups from All Saints, published in *Chichester* 2, pp. 85–98.

Area 7. Pit F.4; c. late 17th to early 18th century
1. Shallow dish, one of two, in a fine reddish fabric; some sand tempering. Internal brown glaze worn thin on the bottom. Patches of brown glaze on the outside. Probably local; *c.* 16th–17th century.
2. Complete small plate in fine buff fabric. Internal yellow glaze with dark brown combed slip, *c.* late 17th to mid-18th century.
3. Almost complete jug; green glazed inside neck and over neck and shoulders. The fabric is sandy and greyish white with a slight pinky tinge. It is similar to local fabrics from the Portsmouth area and is almost certainly a local product. Date is *c.* mid to late 17th century at the latest.
4. Slipware dish, 38 cms diameter in a fine pale grey fabric oxidised to a very pale buff. Some sand tempering; internal yellow glaze spreading partly over rim; brown slip decoration, *c.* 17th–18th century.
5. Large dish, 37 cms diameter, in a reddish buff fabric with internal orange-brown glaze. This is a common local ware, well attested at Chichester from late 17th to possibly early 19th century. Source not yet identified.
6. Sack bottle with seal. A drawing was submitted to Dr. Francis Steer, F.S.A., Maltravers Herald Extraordinary, who identified it as being the crest of Charles Seymour (*Steer* 1965/66, pp. 270–72), sixth Duke of Somerset who lived at Petworth House, 15 miles from Chichester. He was born in 1662, installed as a Knight of the Garter in 1684, and died in 1748. The bottle could not have been made until after 1684 as it carries the Garter motto, and therefore the pit cannot have gone out of use until the late 17th century at the earliest.
7. Sack bottle, complete.
8. Sack bottle, complete.
9. Staffordshire type slipware two-handled posset pot (one handle missing). Buff body covered with cream slip and circular dark brown spots on the outside. Yellow glaze inside and out; foot unglazed, *c.* A.D. 1700.
10. Cup, slightly waisted, in similar ware to 9. Similar to one illustrated in Stoke-on-Trent Museum, *Archealogical Report* No. 4, 1973, No. 235, from the post-medieval pottery site, Albion Square, Hanley (identification by Mrs. Sheila Morgan).
11. (Sherds 48 and 49). Chamber pot in buff fabric with internal brown glaze. Local ware, *c.* ? 16th–17th century.

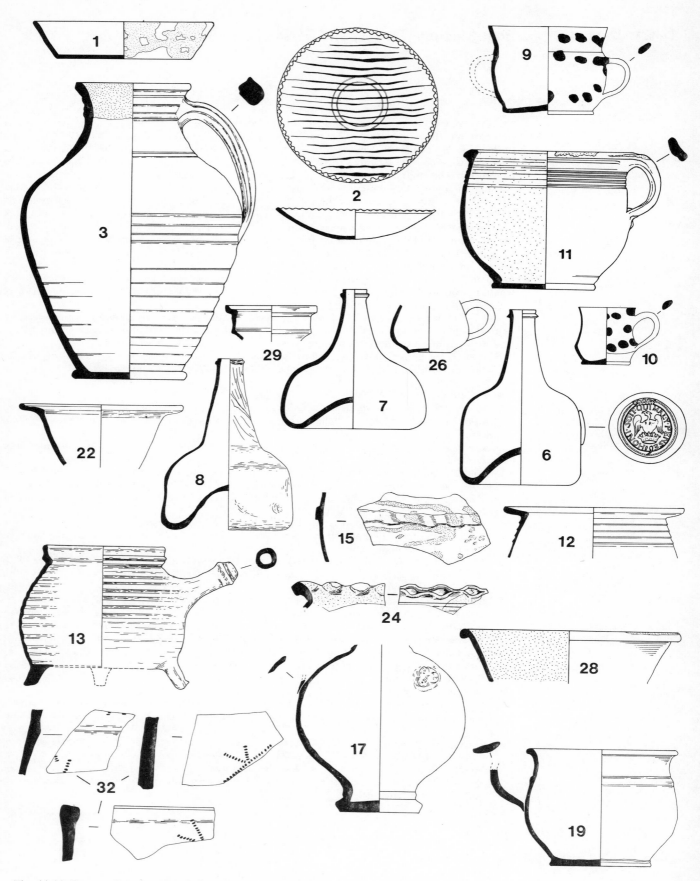

Fig. 11.12 Post-medieval pottery and glass, late 16th to 19th century, Nos. 1–3, 6–26, 28 and 32.
No. 32 ($\frac{1}{2}$), remainder ($\frac{1}{4}$)

Area 2. L.1

12. Chamber pot in similar fabric to 11 and probably from the same source.

Area 3. W.1

13. Pipkin in a white fabric with internal green glaze; probably Surrey ware, just before 1650 (*Holling* 1971, Fig. 3, E.1B).
14. *Not illustrated*. Base of a pipkin in a white fabric with a patchy yellow internal glaze. Probably Surrey ware and second half of 17th century (*op. cit.*, p. 76).
15. Sherd from a vessel in a grey fabric oxidised red with patches of green and brown glaze on the exterior. Local ware, possibly 17th century or later.
16. *Not illustrated*. Sherd from a plain Frechen stoneware jug; second half of 16th century.

Area 2. Pit L.10

17. ? Jug in a dark grey fabric oxidised red and with a thick dark brown exterior glaze on a patchy glaze inside. Probably a local ware, date uncertain but likely to be 19th century.
18. *Not illustrated*. Body sherd from a stoneware jug; ? English, *c*. early 18th century.
19. Vessel in a fine buff fabric with a patchy apple-green glaze inside and out; *c*. late 17th to early 18th century.
20. *Not illustrated*. Rim of a Delft plate, early 18th century.
21. *Not illustrated*. Base of a China dish: Chinese, Kang Hi, ? late 17th century.

Area 3. Pit Z.3

22. Rim sherd from a vessel with internal green glaze; sandy off-white fabric; ? Fareham, possibly 17th century.
23. *Not illustrated*. Body sherd of a vessel with internal brownish glaze with iron flecks, pale pinky white fabric; probably a local ware, ? 17th century.

Area 3. Pit Y.12

24. Scalloped rim of a vessel with brown interior glaze partially over rim; ? Fareham, *c*. 17th century.
25. *Not illustrated*. Body sherd of a vessel with internal brown glaze, dark grey fabric oxidised red. Local ware, *c*. 18th century.

Area 4. Pit M.7

26. Cup in a reddish buff fabric with brown glaze inside and out. Local ware, *c*. 17th century?
27. Rim of dish with internal green glaze and off white fabric, probably Fareham type, *c*. 17th century.

Area 4. Pit M.6

28. Vessel in a white fabric with dark green internal glaze, possibly Fareham ware, ? 16th century.
29. Tudor green cup, *c*. 16th century.

Area 3. L.22

30. Not illustrated. Body sherd from a Bellarmine stoneware jug, 17th century.

Area 3. Pit W.9

31. *Not illustrated*. Unusually thin handle from a 17th-century Bellarmine jug.

Area 7. B.2

32. Three sherds from a plate in a fine off-white fabric with a green glaze on the inside. All three sherds have a stamp on the interior face. Although similar in fabric and glaze to the local wares this type of decoration cannot yet be paralleled either at Chichester or Portsmouth.
33. Sherd of a 17th-century Delft plate with blue and red decoration. *Not illustrated*.
34. Base of a tyg, stacking marks on underside. Reddish fabric and dark brown glaze similar to No. 26 and probably from the same source. Local, second half of 17th century.

Area 7. C.1

35. Rim of vessel with internal pale glaze. Fabric is off-white, similar to vessels from Oyster Street, Portsmouth, and probably local, ? mid to late 17th century.

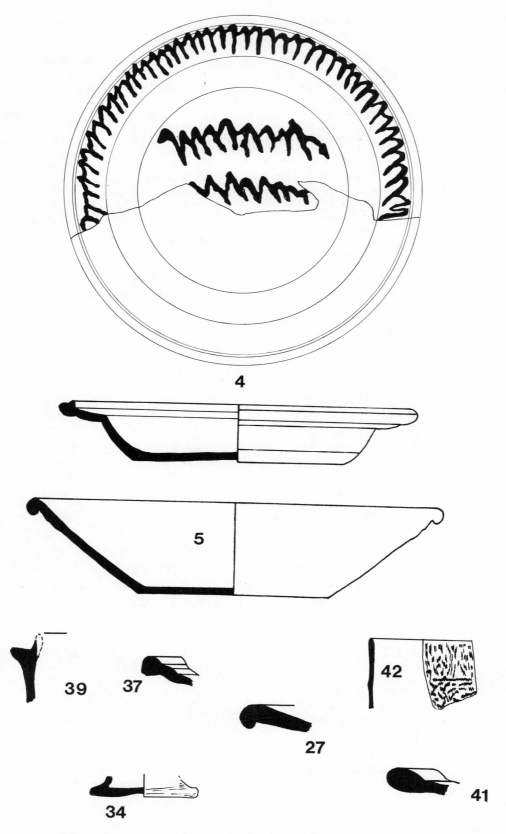

Fig. 11.13 Post-medieval pottery, late 16th to 19th century, Nos. 4 and 5, 27, 34, 37, 39, 41 and 42.
Nos. 4 and 5 ($\frac{1}{4}$), remainder ($\frac{1}{2}$)

36. Rim in dark grey fabric with dark green internal glaze extending over the rim and shoulder. Local ware, *c.* 17th century.
37. Rim of a plate in off-white fabric with internal green glaze, ? Fareham, 17th century.
38. Dish in similar fabric to No. 37 with yellow-green glaze inside, ? Fareham, 17th century.
39. Rim of vessel in a dirty off-white fabric with internal yellow glaze, ? Fareham ware.

Area 7. Pit E.24
40. *Not illustrated.* Sherd from a Delft plate, *c.* mid-17th century.
41. Rim of shallow plate, hard off-white fabric with a mottled brown glaze. Possibly Beauvais, 17th century or earlier; diameter 35.5 cms.
42. Rim of China cup with mottled manganese glaze. Southwark Delft, second half of 17th century.
43. Rim of vessel in a fine reddish fabric with internal pale brown glaze, *c.* 17th century.
44. Rim of vessel in a hard off-white fabric with internal green glaze, Fareham type, *c.* 17th century.
45. *Not illustrated.* Body sherd in a dirty off-white fabric with a light yellow internal glaze. Possibly from a pipkin, ? Fareham type, 17th century.
46. Vessel in a fine grey fabric oxidised to a reddish buff with splashes of yellowish glaze on the outside. Local ware, *c.* 17th century or earlier.
47. Cup in an off-white fabric with internal yellow glaze. Surrey ware, 17th century. (*Holling* 1971, Fig. 2, B, 2b and p. 74.)
48. Complete vessel in a fine grey fabric oxidised to a reddish buff, partially reduced outside. There are dribbles of glaze on it from other pots fired at the same time. Painted ware type, *c.* mid to late 15th century.
49. Vessel in a dark grey fabric oxidised to a reddish buff, dark green internal glaze. Probably a local ware, *c.* 16th century.

Area 7. Pit E.76
50. *Not illustrated.* Base of a Raeren stoneware jug; first half of 16th century.

Area 7. F.7
51. Base of a Raeren stoneware jug, first half of 16th century (*Chichester* 2, Fig. 7.14, No. 42). *Not illustrated.*
52. *Not illustrated.* Body sherd from a Raeren jug, similar to No. 49.

Area 7. F.25
53. Raeren stoneware jug, first half of 16th century.
54 and 55. *Not illustrated.* Body sherds from Raeren stoneware jugs.
56. *Not illustrated.* Sherd from a vessel, probably a cup, in a hard white fabric, with light brown external glaze, *c.* 17th to early 18th century.

57. *Not illustrated.* Body sherd from a chafing dish in a grey fabric oxidised red and with a discontinuous green-brown glaze inside and out. Local ware, *c.* first half of 16th century.

Area 7. C.20
58. Two sherds from the body of a jug; hard white fabric with external ? tin glaze. Probably from a French polychrome vessel, *c.* 16th century.
59. *Not illustrated.* Rim sherd in a white fabric with internal Tudor plain green glaze. *c.* 16th century.

Area 2. E.1
60. Vessel in a hard dirty off-white fabric, dark green glaze inside and out; *c.* 17th–18th century, local ware.

Area 2. L.1
61. Chafing dish in a buff fabric with internal green-brown glaze.
62. Shallow dish in a hard white fabric with internal yellow glaze, possibly Surrey ware.
63. Rim of a vessel in a dirty off-white fabric with internal green glaze with brown flecks in it. Probably Fareham ware.
64. Base of a candlestick in a dirty off-white fabric, oxidised buff, *c.* late 16th century.

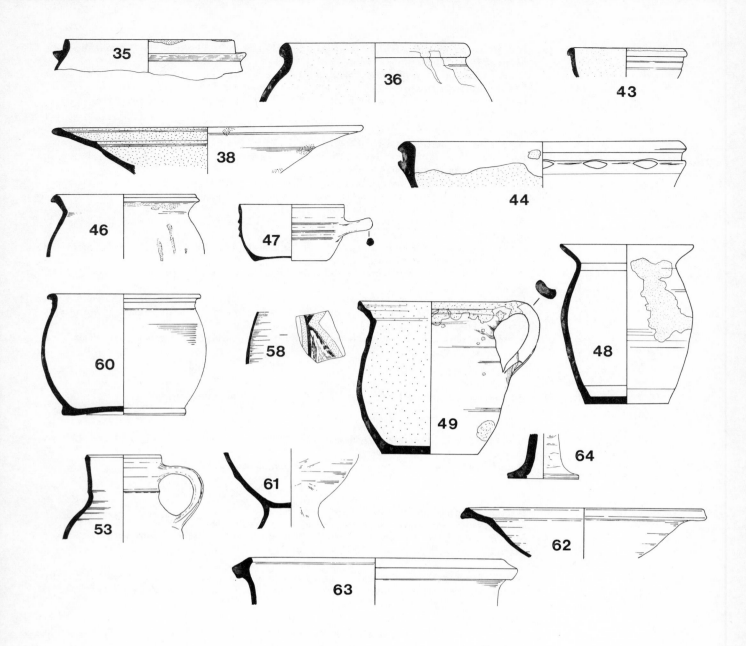

Fig. 11.14 Post-medieval pottery, late 16th to 19th century, Nos. 35 and 36, 38; 43–63 (¼)

Two Groups of 18th- and 19th-century Wares from Chichester

by Sheila Morgan

The 19th-century pottery from Area 2, Central Girls School, Chapel Street

The pottery discussed below came from a cesspit beneath the Girls' School. The Documentary Research Group reports that in 1625 a lease refers to a "tenement and garden plot" on the site. The Gardner map of 1769 shows five houses on the site and this is confirmed by the Land Tax records of 1786. Presumably these were the houses demolished when the School was built *c.* 1882. They were terrace built with frontages varying from 18 to 31 feet. Examination of trade directories has not revealed any shopkeepers or traders using the buildings, nor are any "Gentry" listed. It seems reasonable to assume, therefore, that the later occupants were working class townspeople.

The pottery from the pit consists of a large quantity of blue and white transfer printed earthenware, with backstamps which suggest a date range of 1820–70. Specifically the items were tea and dinner ware, together with a number of teapots and chamber pots. A large quantity of mocha ware, the kitchen pottery of this period, consisting of bowls, basins, jugs, etc., was also found, one mug having an imperial measure mark on it. A quantity of brown stoneware dishes, storage jars, etc., complete the domestic picture. By comparison, the pottery from the garden of No. 41 Southgate (*Chichester* 2, pp. 27–31) although of an earlier date, included items of a higher original value, e.g. porcelain and bone china, which is barely represented in Chapel Street, and which suggests that the occupants of these houses were less affluent than the Southgate residents. The quantity and range of pottery sherds also illustrates the large increase in the supply of cheap domestic pottery available in Chichester in the 1820's with the opening of the Chichester Canal, and which was superseded by the coming of the railway in the 1840's.

The Staffordshire Potter could now supply everyone with his wares and Chapel Street residents joined the rest of the country and ate their meals from Willow Pattern plates.

None of the wares listed below are illustrated; they are stored in the Chichester District Museum.

The Wares

1. Part of a blue and white printed oval-shaped teapot. Hardly any pattern left – rural scene possibly. Brown painted edges to handle and round the rim. Floral border.
2. Cup printed with crude loop pattern round the top. Base impressed: J. G. MEAKIN 12. (Eagle Pottery, Hanley, 1851.)
3. Blue and white printed teaplate, floral border, man, woman and child in foreground. No mark.
4. Part of a pale blue and white printed saucer, willow pattern, two men on bridge, scalloped edge. No mark. (Similar ware found at Southgate.)
5. Cup, blue and white printed, London shape. Figure "3" printed on base. Design inside cup of man on horseback carrying a standard, another man holding a rifle, mountain in the background. Elephants incorporated in design round the outside of the cup.
6. Part of blue and white printed cup, remains of printed numerals "53" on base. Outside of cup decorated with ornate circular symbol with leaves and flowers. Inside border design of long-tailed birds in a cage.
7. Part of blue and white printed plate. Design: two men and bridge over water. Back mark: lion in garter. S. B. & S. underneath. (Don pottery, 1851 onwards.)
8. Part of a white saucer with dark blue lines radiating from central blue circle. Back stamp: impressed rosette.
9. Part of a dinner plate with scalloped rim. Dark blue printing on thick heavy earthenware, possibly ironstone. Design similar to Plate 43 in *English and Scottish Earthenware*, by C. Bernard Hughes, 1961, and attributed to Hilditch & Son, Lane End, Staffs., 1822–50.
10. Traditional Willow Pattern printed plate. No mark.
11. Part of a meat dish printed with Willow Pattern. Back mark.
12. Willow Pattern printed plate. Part of back mark; Cartouche around the words "Iron Stone China".
13. Five other pieces of Willow Pattern plates, all slightly different printings. No back marks.
14. Plate printed in misty blue Willow Pattern. Similar to one from Southgate. No back mark.
15. Blue and white plate, with scalloped rim and gadroon moulding. The printed design is the same as the one called Chinese Marine in Bulletin No. 5 of the Kingston upon Hull Museum's *Hull Pottery* (Belle Vue), 1826–41. Impressed CROWN POTTERY.

371

16. Part of a blue and white printed dinner plate. Similar design illustrated in *Blue and White Transfer Ware*, by A. W. Coysh, Plate 29, and attributed to Davenport, 1815–25, Bamboo and Peony pattern.

17. Bowl printed in blue and white. Pattern of two birds and eggs in nest. Deep border of large flowers, trellis and sawtooth band on inside of bowl.

18. Part of blue and white printed plate, similar design illustrated in *Spode*, by Leonard Whiter, No. 47, "Filigree" pattern.

19. Part of a deep oval blue and white printed dish. Similar design illustrated in Leonard Whiter's book (see above), Plate 5, "Parasol Figure" design. First quarter of the 19th century.

20. Base of deep blue and white printed dish. Design of fir tree sprays and cone border. Three men in Arab dhow, gothic buildings in the background. No mark.

21. Saucer printed in blue and white with all over design of sprays of fern leaves. Back stamp – impressed rosette (see No. 8).

22. Part of a very dark flown blue saucer with scalloped edge. Flower and scroll border, vase of flowers in centre of design. Back mark; "ASKET" within three sides of an oblong.

23. Base of cup, similar design to the above.

24. Saucer printed with a dark grey transfer. Flowers around the edge and centre, divided by narrow border of stylised flower heads and trellis, etc. Back mark; Cartouche of leaves and ribbon above initials CM. & S. (Cha-rles Meigh & Son), 1851–61.

25. Part of a blue and white Willow Pattern perforated dish.

26. Part of another blue and white perforated dish with design similar to one illustrated in Coysh (*ibid.*), Plate 47, and attributed to Robert Hamilton, Stoke, 1811–26, Ruined Castle pattern.

27. Part of a Willow Pattern plate. Back mark; Coat of Arms above initials L. & A. (Lockhart & Arthur, Pollokshaws, Glasgow, 1855–64).

28. Part of another Willow Pattern plate. Back mark; STAFFORDSHIRE above part of a Crown.

29. Part of a large bowl printed in blue with a picture of a man with a stick in his right hand, pointing with his left hand, a child standing beside him and a farmhouse and horse in the background. Inside border of large flowers and leaves.

30. Part of a blue and white printed saucer. Decorated with a design of a girl with straw hat in her right hand. Border of alternating vertical lines of flowers and circles. Back stamp; UIT GIRL within feathery-lined oval.

31. Part of a saucer rim decorated with blue and white design of trellis, flower heads, lines, dots and circles, very crudely drawn.

32. Part of a plate, blue feather edged.

33. Part of a mug with printed design of Chinese man and two vases, tents in background. (T. Godwin, 1834–54.)

34. Saucer rim printed in flown blue with stylised flowers and interlacing lines.

35. Part of dinner plate with grey transfer print of flowers and leaves. Back mark; Copeland, Late Spode (1847–67).

36. Saucer, fine white china, slightly ribbed just below the rim. Blue flower cluster motifs sprigged on.

37. Pale blue dipped earthenware vase. White flower sprigging and white dots around bottom and top. Remains of base of handle.

38. Part of rim of plate, printed with a blurred grey transfer print. Back mark under rim: Cartouche around "Asiatic Pheasants", S.B. & S. (Don Pottery, 1851 onwards).

39. Plate, part of base, with pale blue print. Back mark; K.E. & Co. within diamond-shaped motif. (Knight Elkin & Co., Foley Potteries, Fenton, 1826–46.)

40. Part of plate rim, Willow Pattern border. Back mark; Crown over ribbons and leaves and "R". Marked "Iron Stone China".

A Group of Stoneware Tankards from Tower Street

Fig. 11.15

Area 7. Pit E.13/17

The tankards in this group bear a very close resemblance to stonewares found at Vauxhall Cross, London, in 1969–70.[1] All have an incised line round the rim, three lines of reeding just above a slightly spreading base and grooved strap handle with the lower terminal turned upwards on itself where it is attached to the body of the tankard. The pint-size tankard has only two lines of reeding and the spreading base is more pronounced. It is reasonable to assume that the tankards were made in London and officials at the Victoria and Albert Museum date them to *c.* 1720–30, which ties in with the GR Excise Mark on the drab stoneware tankard.

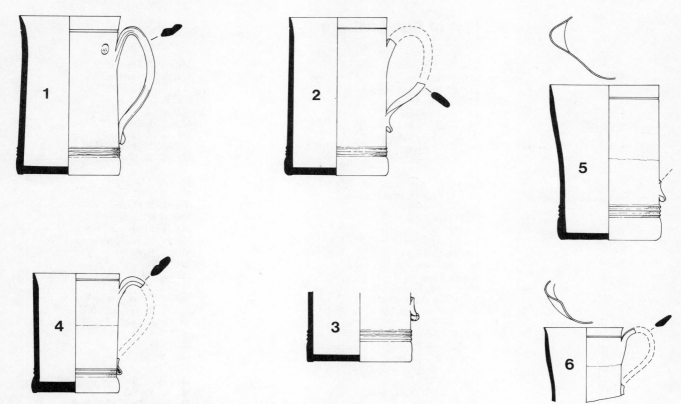

Fig. 11.15 A group of early 18th century tankards from Area 7 ($\frac{1}{4}$)

The pit containing the group was at the rear of an area at one time covered by the backyard of the Fighting Cocks public house. The first reference to this tavern is in 1808, but in 1766 the property was owned by Wm. Humphrey, brewer, and occupied by George Gray, publican, so presumably it was an alehouse at that date. Whether it was known as the Fighting Cocks then is uncertain. In 1752 the premises were used as the Poorhouse for the Parish of St. Peter the Great. Previous to this it was shown as a tenement in private occupation, from 1708 and again in 1724, John Clarke is shown as the occupier, while in 1738, James Ingram, gardener, lived there.

In view of the date ascribed to the tankards, it must be doubtful if they were ever used by customers at the Fighting Cocks. It must also be unlikely that the inhabitants of the poorhouse owned or used these vessels, and they are most likely to have been the property of John Clarke or James Ingram.

1. Quart-size tankard in drab colour stoneware, impressed with "GR" and crown Excise Mark. Remains of brown colouring along incised line round rim and underneath the top curve of the handle. Three lines of reeding round the base.
2. Part of grey stoneware tankard, upper half covered with brown mottling. Three lines of reeding round the base.
3. Lower half of grey stoneware tankard. Decorated as 2 above. Pinky-brown interior.
4. Part of pint-size tankard. Grey body. Lower half exterior drab colour, upper half dark brown continuing over to inside of rim. Light brown interior. Two lines of reeding round the base.
5. Quart-size tankard with rim pulled out to form a pouring lip. Lower half drab colour, upper half russet brown continuing over inside the rim. Pinky-brown interior. Three bands of reeding round the base.
6. Fragment of upper half of half-pint tankard with lip similar to 5 above. Lower portion drab colour, upper portion and inside rim dark brown.

Reference

[1] See *English Ceramic Circle Transactions*, Vol. 9, Pt. 2, p. 240 and illustrations, Pl. 139(c) and (d) and Pl. 140(d).

List of Subscribers

Mrs. A. Adams
Mr. P. Adorian
Mr. C. Ainsworth
Major J. F. Ainsworth
Mr. S. J. Aldred
Mr. F. G. Aldsworth
Avon County Library
Mr. J. G. Ayling
Mr. J. E. Ayto

Dr. H. M. Barnes
Mr. A. Barr-Hamilton
Mr. T. Beaumont
Mr. O. Bedwin
Mr. M. Bell
Miss J. A. Bestow
Mr. D. G. Bird
Mrs. A. Booker
British Museum
Miss A. M. Burnet
Mr. C. G. Busbridge
Dr. N. F. H. Butcher

Mr. P. B. Cartwright
Chelmsford Excavation Committee
Mrs. E. M. Clarke
Miss G. Clegg
Mr. M. Coker
Mr. A. H. Collins, M.A., F.S.A.
Mr. T. J. Cox
Mr. E. Crossland, I.S.O.
Mr. R. Curry

Mr. P. G. Day
Mr. J. C. Dove
Mr. P. J. Drury

Mr. J. E. Eschbaecher
Miss S. C. Eeles

Mr. J. H. Farrant
Mr. F. E. Ford, A.R.I.B.A.
Mr. D. Freke

Mr. R. E. Graebe
Mr. K. W. E. Gravett
Mr. T. K. Green
Mr. F. W. Greenaway
Mr. I. W. Griffiths
Guildford Museum

Mr. R. C. Hammond, B.Sc., D.Phil.
C. & S. Haselgrove
Mrs. S. Hattersley
Mr. E. W. Holden, F.S.A.
Mr. D. Howell-Thomas

Mr. R. F. Hunnisett
Mr. J. P. Hurd

Mr. B. Isaacs

Mrs. P. Laing
Mr. J. W. Lee
London University
Mr. H. H. Ludlow

Miss A. Macaulay
Mrs. A. McCann
Mr. R. J. Maskelyne
Mason & Hodges Ltd.
Mr. R. Merrifield, F.S.A.
Mr. A. G. E. Millington
Mrs. J. R. Mills
Mr. J. Munby
Miss K. M. E. Murray, F.S.A.

National Museum of Wales
Mr. K. J. Neale, O.B.E., F.S.A.
New England College Library

Mr. J. O'Hea
Mrs. M. Oliver

Mrs. R. N. Palmer
Mr. K. Parfitt
The Rev. Dr. T. M. Parker
Mr. J. G. Penford
Mr. I. S. Pettman
Miss J. G. Pilmer
Mr. J. L. Piper
Mr. M. W. Pitts
Portsmouth City Museum and Art
   Gallery
Mr. J. Pratt

Dr. C. W. W. Read
Mr. R. Reece
Reflex 1946
Mrs. R. Reilly
Dr. W. J. Rodwell
Romisch-Germanische Kommission
Ms. J. Russell

Mr. A. G. Scott
Mrs. C. Scott
Mr. D. J. Screen
Mr. C. G. Searle
Mr. W. Shannon
Mr. M. Shepherd
Mr. J. L. Shields
Mr. H. C. P. Smail
Mr. L. Smith

Mr. M. J. Smith
Miss V. Smith
Mr. G. Soffe
Miss K. M. Stanford
Dr. F. W. Steer, F.S.A.
Mrs. V. G. Swann

Mr. T. W. T. Tatton-Brown
Mr. H. L. Tewkesbury
Mr. M. Todd, F.S.A.

Mr. & Mrs. R. H. C. Upton

Miss Mollie Vernon
Victoria and Albert Museum

Mr. C. V. Walthew
Mr. P. V. Webster
Mr. B. T. Wedmore
Mr. M. G. Welch
West Sussex County Council
Mr. P. M. Wilkinson
Mrs. J. Williams
Mr. N. A. Wilson
Mrs. J. Wyatt